Fodor's 2012
ALASKA

Fodor's Travel Publications   New York, Toronto, London, Sydney, Auckland
www.fodors.com

FODOR'S ALASKA 2012

Editors: Kelly Kealy; Laura Kidder

Writers: Teeka Ballas, Jessica Bowman, Lisa Hupp, E. Readicker-Henderson, Jenna Schnuer

Production Editor: Carrie Parker
Maps & Illustrations: Mark Stroud and David Lindroth, *cartographers*; Bob Blake, Rebecca Baer, *map editors*; William Wu, *information graphics*
Design: Fabrizio La Rocca, *creative director*; Guido Caroti, *art director*; Tina Malaney, Nora Rosansky, Chie Ushio, Jessica Walsh, *designers*; Melanie Marin, *associate director of photography*
Cover Photo: (Brown bear fishing for spawning salmon at Geographic Harbor): Paul Souders/Corbis
Production Manager: Angela L. McLean

ISBN 978–0–679–00955–9

ISSN 0271–2776

SPECIAL SALES

This book is available at special discounts for bulk purchases for sales promotions or premiums. Special editions, including personalized covers, excerpts of existing books, and corporate imprints, can be created in large quantities for special needs. For more information, write to Special Markets/Premium Sales, 1745 Broadway, MD 3-2, New York, NY 10019, or e-mail specialmarkets@randomhouse.com.

AN IMPORTANT TIP & AN INVITATION

Although all prices, opening times, and other details in this book are based on information supplied to us at press time, changes occur all the time in the travel world, and Fodor's cannot accept responsibility for facts that become outdated or for inadvertent errors or omissions. So **always confirm information when it matters**, especially if you're making a detour to visit a specific place. Your experiences—positive and negative—matter to us. If we have missed or misstated something, **please write to us.** Share your opinion instantly through our online feedback center at fodors.com/contact-us.

PRINTED IN COLOMBIA

10 9 8 7 6 5 4 3 2 1

CONTENTS

MAPS

ABOUT THIS BOOK

Our Ratings

At Fodor's, we spend considerable time choosing the best places in a destination so you don't have to. By default, anything we recommend in this book is worth visiting. But some sights, properties, and experiences are so great that we've recognized them with additional accolades. Orange **Fodor's Choice** stars indicate our top recommendations; black stars highlight places we deem **Highly Recommended**; and **Best Bets** call attention to top properties in various categories. Disagree with any of our choices? Care to nominate a new place? Visit our feedback center at www.fodors.com/feedback.

TripAdvisor ⊙⊙

Fodor's partnership with TripAdvisor helps to ensure that our hotel selections are timely and relevant, taking into account the latest customer feedback about each property. Our team of expert writers selects what we believe will be the top choices for lodging in a destination. Then, those choices are reinforced by TripAdvisor reviews, so only the best properties make the cut.

> For expanded hotel reviews, visit **Fodors.com**

Hotels

Hotels have private bath, phone, TV, and air-conditioning, and do not offer meals unless we specify that in the review. We always list facilities but not whether you'll be charged an extra fee to use them.

Restaurants

Unless we state otherwise, restaurants are open for lunch and dinner daily. We mention dress only when there's a specific requirement and reservations only when they're essential or not accepted—it's always best to book ahead.

Credit Cards

We assume that restaurants and hotels accept credit cards. If not, we'll note it in the review.

Budget Well

Hotel and restaurant price categories from ¢ to $$$$ are defined in the opening pages of the respective chapters. For attractions, we always give standard adult admission fees; reductions are usually available for children, students, and senior citizens.

Listings			Hotels & Restaurants	Outdoors	
★	Fodor's Choice	✉ E-mail	☒ Hotel	✗	Golf
★	Highly recommended	▦ Admission fee	⇴ Number of rooms	⚠	Camping
⊠	Physical address	◷ Open/closed times	⌂ Facilities	**Other**	
⊕	Directions or Map coordinates	Ⓜ Metro stations	⍾ Meal plans	◔	Family-friendly
⌑	Mailing address	▭ No credit cards	✗ Restaurant	⇨	See also
☎	Telephone		⌎ Reservations	⊠	Branch address
⊞	Fax		⋔ Dress code	☞	Take note
⊕	On the Web		↘ Smoking		

Experience
Alaska

WHAT'S WHERE

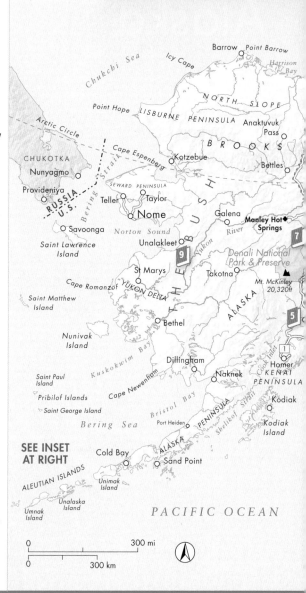

Numbers refer to chapter numbers.

4 Southeast Alaska.
Southeast Alaska (or "the Panhandle") includes the Inside Passage. Here you'll find Juneau, the state capital, and Sitka, the former Russian hub. Only Haines and Skagway have roads to "the Outside." A boat trip through the Alaska Chilkat Eagle Preserve will take you into protected wilderness that draws about 4,000 eagles to the Haines area. Along this passage, long fjords snake between the mountains, timbered slopes plunge to the rocky shores, and marine life abounds.

5 Anchorage. With nearly half the state's population, Anchorage is Alaska's biggest city and a good jumping-off point for visitors. The restaurants, art and history museums, copious espresso stands, and performing arts have earned the city the sobriquet "Seattle of the North." Alaskans often deride the place as "Los Anchorage," but the occasional moose ambling down a street hints at the nearby wilderness.

6 South Central Alaska.
South Central offers great fishing, hiking, rafting, and wildlife viewing. Seek out the towns of Seward and Homer on the Kenai Peninsula. Kodiak, in the

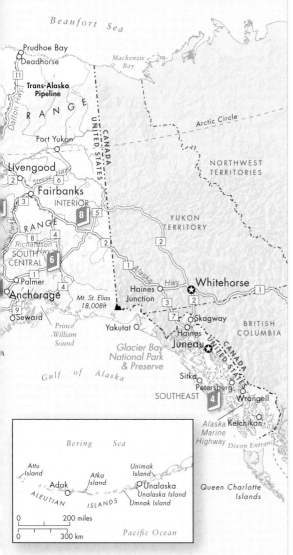

Gulf of Alaska, is known for its green-carpeted mountains and Kodiak brown bears. Charter outfits take you to remote wilderness spots. Although the summer crowds can be daunting, a little research will take you to areas of true wilderness.

7 Denali National Park. Home to Mt. McKinley—the highest peak in North America—Denali National Park and Preserve comprises 6 million acres of Alaska's best wildlife, scenery, and adventures.

8 The Interior. Bound by the Brooks Range to the north and the Alaska Range to the south, the Interior is home to Denali National Park and Preserve. The region's major city is Fairbanks (gateway to the towns of the Arctic), the Bering Coast, and Canada's Yukon Territory.

9 The Bush. Many call the Bush the "real" Alaska. Inupiaq people share the tundra with the Prudhoe Bay oil fields. Brown bears roam Katmai National Park. Volcanoes shake the Alaska Peninsula. Prospectors still pan for gold on the beach in Nome. Except for the Dalton Highway and a handful of short roads near Nome, the region is essentially roadless. Traveling here requires planning; the reward is true adventure.

ALASKA TODAY

Politics

Alaska's politics and policies seem as wild as its hundreds of thousands of untamed acres. This is partly due to the fact that the largest state in the nation comes with a seemingly limitless supply of natural resources, and with them come conflict and controversy. Alaska's politics are thus saddled with a vast array of fiscal and environmental responsibilities, none of which are easily met. As a state that is often overlooked in the political media sector, it caught the public eye in 2008 when former Governor Sarah Palin was nominated for vice president. Since then, Alaska has managed to continue to stay in the limelight.

Gas and mining corporations have enormous influence on public policy in Alaska, but not without rivalry from environmentalists and subsistence advocates. There are ongoing and highly publicized battles over the proposed Pebble Mine project and the Donlin Creek Mine project. If built, they could potentially be the largest copper and gold mines in the world. Supporters of the mines claim they will bring much-needed jobs to local Native populations. Opponents say they will irrevocably pollute the lakes, rivers, and surrounding terrain (not to mention, near Pebble Mine project, vast swaths of Bristol Bay), destroying the large fishing industry and other subsistence ways of life on which local populations rely.

Gaining an increasing amount of national attention is the Arctic National Wildlife Refuge (ANWR), 19.2 million remote roadless acres supporting 45 species of land and marine mammals, 36 species of fish, and 180 species of birds. ANWR is in the northeast corner of the state and has been dubbed the Last Great Wilderness.

The only way to get there is by small bush plane. Area 1002, 1.5 million acres along the refuge's coastal plain, has long been a subject of controversy, as it is thought to contain a large supply of oil.

From the Iditarod to cabin building, everything in Alaska is steeped in politics. This is inevitable, as there are more politicians per capita than police officers.

Economics

More than 75% of Alaska's revenue is derived from oil extraction. The state is also the nation's leader in commercial fishing, but ranks dead last in number of farms and farm products. There is very little manufacturing in the state. Thus the cost of manufactured goods, produce, and other foodstuffs is considerably higher than in other states.

Because Alaska is predominantly comprised of rural villages, thousands of miles from any distribution center, the cost of living is relatively high. In Barrow, for instance, one can expect to pay $10 for a gallon of milk.

The Permanent Fund Dividend (PFD) is a sacred check that Alaskans receive once a year, and for many in the Bush it is quite literally a lifesaver. In 1977 the fund was created to receive 25% of Alaska's oil royalty income. It was designed to maintain a state income even after the reserves had been tapped out. Residents receive a check every October in amounts that vary from year to year, but are in the ballpark of $1,200. For many who live in the Bush, this annual check helps heat their homes in the winter. And every bit helps; in recent winters, rural and remote Alaska has seen heating fuel go as high as $10 per gallon.

Global Warming

In Alaska few people disagree that the glaciers and permafrost are melting; it's just a fact. It is what to do about it that has politicians and constituents bickering.

Regardless of anyone's political persuasion, however, things are undeniably changing in Alaska. Icebergs are melting, and unfortunately for polar bears, that's where they live. In 2008 the Interior Department put polar bears on the protected species list, but some environmentalists believe that without addressing the causes of global warming the designation will do little to help.

As ocean temperatures rise, new migrations are starting to take effect. One unfortunate one, however, is the steady northward migration of the Humboldt giant squid. It is a voracious predator that travels in packs and is starting to be found as far north as Sitka. This could pose a serious threat to the salmon population and the fishing industry in general.

Warmer temperatures also mean new economic opportunities. As the Arctic ice melts, the region is becoming more accessible, which means there is greater possibility for more oil and gas exploration.

Many of the indigenous tribes in the Arctic region have already begun to adapt to the changes. Their hunting patterns have adjusted to the new migration times and routes of their game. Unfortunately permafrost, the frozen ground they live upon, is also melting. Centuries-old towns and villages are sinking, and the cost of possible relocation is rising into the billions of dollars. Permafrost that once held the coastline together is disappearing, and groups like the Army Corps of Engineers are scrambling to save villages from falling off into the ocean.

The Arts

Visitors are often surprised to find that Alaska is filled with talented contemporary artists. Not only do some of the world's foremost artists, writers, and photographers reside in Alaska, there is equal talent found among those whose work never sees the Outside. For many Alaskans the long, dark winter is a great time to hunker down, season their craft, and prepare to sell their wares in the summer at galleries, museums, and theaters all over the state. In summer, weekend outdoor markets are also a great place to find local and Native talent. Look for the Made in Alaska sticker for authenticity.

Sports

In a state of renegades, thrill seekers, and aficionados of extreme forms of entertainment, it is no wonder that the biggest sporting event of the year occasionally requires a racer to permanently relinquish feeling in a finger or a foot. The Iditarod Trail Sled Dog Race, a 1,150-mi-long trek, is by far the most popular sporting event in Alaska. It began in 1973 in homage to the brave souls who ventured to Nome in 1925 to take medicine to villagers struck with one of the worst outbreaks of diphtheria ever recorded. Now more than 100 racers and their packs of canines converge on the ice and snow every year on the first Saturday in March to race from Anchorage to Nome. The sport is not without controversy though; mushers have come under scrutiny, since several groups have made allegations of animal cruelty.

Although Alaskans from all over the state are passionate about their dog mushers, the most popular team sport is hockey. College hockey is big news, as are the Alaska Aces, the state minor-league team that feeds into the NHL's St. Louis Blues.

ALASKA
TOP ATTRACTIONS

Katmai National Park

(A) When people come to Alaska they want to see bears. Yet most visitors never get a glimpse (bears prefer their privacy). However, at Katmai National Park, which boasts the world's largest brown bear population, you're guaranteed a photograph of bears doing bear things. Just remember, their teeth and claws are mighty sharp.

Alaska Native Heritage Center

(B) There are more than 200 Native tribal entities in Alaska. At the Heritage Center, experience the lifestyles and traditions of these Native cultures through art and artifact displays and activities like blanket tossing, parka sewing, and drumming.

Mt. McKinley

(C) There are a dozen places between Anchorage and Fairbanks that boast the best viewing of Mt. McKinley (which most Alaskans refer to by its original name, Denali). At 20,320 feet, McKinley

is the highest peak in North America, and most places within 100 mi can be good viewing areas. It is so large it creates its own weather patterns, and when the skies are otherwise clear, the mountain may be completely obscured. Try not to get too disappointed if you don't see it; just know you've been in the company of greatness.

Denali National Park

(D) Denali National Park is one of the most popular destinations in the state. It is a spectacular region that can be experienced by saddle safari, bus trip, hike, raft, or flightseeing tour. The first 15 mi of the park road are paved, but after that visitors must ride on a bus or get off and see Denali on foot. No matter which adventure you choose, Denali is truly a wonderful experience.

The Aurora Borealis

(E) The most popular attraction in the wintertime doesn't charge admission or have set viewing times. The northern lights

1

seem to appear without rhyme or reason. There is a science to it, but explanations are still hotly debated by meteorologists, astronomers, and pretty-color enthusiasts. Seeing the northern lights requires that there be no nearby city light, very little moonlight, the cold fall and winter months, and a lot of luck. Hot springs outside Fairbanks keep the hopeful warm while they watch the skies.

Mendenhall Glacier

(F) Alaska's capital, Juneau, is surrounded by ice and water and can be reached only by boat or plane. The best way to understand this is to fly over the ice fields just outside the city and visit the Mendenhall Glacier. Only 13 mi from downtown Juneau, this gargantuan glacier is right outside the city in plain view. It's 12 mi long—nearly the same distance as between it and downtown Juneau.

The Inside Passage

(G) If you don't arrive in Alaska by cruise ship, make a point of taking a ferry trip along the longest, deepest fjord in North America. Depending on which ferry you take, the trip from Juneau to Skagway can be two or six hours long. In summer the tall peaks surrounding the boats release hundreds of waterfalls from snow and glacial melt. You might see pods of orcas, humpbacks, and dolphins.

Mt. Marathon Race

(H) On July 4 the scenic small town of Seward hosts the Mt. Marathon Race. This race is 1½ mi straight up and 1½ mi straight down the mountain. It began with a bet between two sourdoughs in 1915, and now the celebration turns a town of 2,000 into a city of 40,000 overnight. It's a great way to participate in Alaskan life, and you don't even have to race.

TOP EXPERIENCES

Drive the Alcan

When driving the Alaska Highway, or Alcan, you quickly realize that "rural" means something entirely different in Alaska. (While we're on the subject, so does "remote"; here the word refers to areas with no road access.) You will drive through regions, villages, and towns that are nearly 1,000 mi from the nearest city. Inhabitants have never seen anything that even slightly resembles a shopping mall or fast-food stand. Gas stations can be 75 to 150 mi apart, and mechanics rarer than a wolverine sighting. The Alcan is the true Alaskan experience. Driving 1,000 mi on a long, potholed stretch of highway can put things into perspective. It is also a great way to be guaranteed wildlife sightings.

Sleep on a Deserted Island

Gustavus is the gateway to Glacier Bay, the place that the father of the national parks system, John Muir, called "unspeakably pure and sublime" in 1879. It is considered by many to be 70 mi of the finest sea kayaking in the world. The first 24 square mi comprise the Beardslee Islands, a complex system for kayakers who glide atop flat water between tides, enveloped in silence except for the sound of water slapping paddles, the soft spray from a nearby porpoise, and the howl of a wolf in the distance. And you'll likely be enjoying these sights with no other travelers nearby. Still, kayaking in this region presents challenges. There is a lively population of moose and bears on the islands, so it is imperative to choose wisely when setting up camp. Most visitors kayak only to the top of the Beardslees, which can take three to five days round-trip.

Safari through the Last Great Wilderness

The Arctic National Wildlife Refuge (ANWR) is 19.2 million acres of untamed land in the northeastern corner of Alaska. This is where there is still a sense of the unknown, where mountain peaks are unnamed and valleys are yet to be explored. There are no shops and no roads. The only way to get to ANWR is by small bush plane. You can be dropped off by air taxi, or you can arrange a guided group tour. The refuge is a great place to hunt, hike, camp, paddle, or climb in solitude. Fewer than 1,000 people visit this region every year, but tours must be booked months if not a year in advance. Even Alaskans dream of getting to this place someday.

Bed, Breakfast, and Snowmachine

Everywhere there is snow there seems to be a bitter rivalry between snowmachiners (aka snowmobilers) and skiers. If you're looking to have the perfect snowmachine experience without enmity or opposition, the best way to do it is to find one of the many rural wilderness lodges around Alaska that offer snowmachine rentals and tours. Yentna Station Roadhouse and Alaska Snow Safaris are just two of the many stellar rural establishments that are a day's drive or a short bush flight away. It's a great adrenaline rush to speed over frozen lakes and untouched powder with a motorized sled beneath you and wind in your face.

Ski under the Stars

There is something about the incongruous number of hours of sunlight and darkness Alaska gets that makes Alaskans yearn to break the rules of time. When you arrive in Alaska you may feel inclined to do the same. In many parts of the state bars still

stay open all night long, fishermen can be sitting on the ice all hours of the night, and some people ski best when the witching hour strikes. At Alyeska Ski Resort in Girdwood, skiers can take the lift and bite the powder under the stars. On weekends this popular ski resort offers night skiing, and afterward, in the bar, rewards its visitors with live, high-energy, danceable music. This provides a good look at local Alaskan culture, as it caters to tourists and residents alike.

The Longest Museum in the World

In the 1890s, during the gold rush, more than 20,000 stampeders disembarked from their steamships in Skagway, Alaska, and hiked the 35 mi of the Chilkoot Trail, just to get back into a boat and travel the remaining 600 mi to Dawson City (where the gold was). It took approximately three months to hike the trail back then. Their packs were heavy, their shoes were hard, and they had to hike the trail several times in order to get all of their possessions over the pass. These days, hiking history buffs can retrace the stampeders' steps in three to five days, with the help of lighter gear and equipment.

Drink Like an Alaskan

Every state in the nation has a list of attributed symbols: the state bird, flag, flower, song—and in Alaska there is the state drink. It's called the Duck Fart. It is quintessentially Alaskan, as it manages to weed out the meek and shy just by its name alone. It is comprised of Kahlúa, Bailey's Irish Cream, and Crown Royal. No need to be timid when it comes to ordering this drink; locals drink it, too. Once you've had a Duck Fart, you can honestly say you've experienced Alaska like an Alaskan.

Ski Like It's Halloween

Many Alaskans like to embrace their eccentricities, and a popular way to do it is to get dressed up in costume and ski. One such event is called the Ski Train. Every year in March, since 1972, approximately 1,000 people from all over the country come to Anchorage to get on a train. They come dressed up in a mad array of homemade costumes and bring libations, food, and skis. It's a hilarious event that entails a long, scenic train ride that eventually dumps you off in the middle of nowhere to cross-country ski for an afternoon. After a couple of hours, it's back on board to dance in the back cabin where a live polka band plays in rhythm with the sway of the train.

Halibut Cove

Sometimes the best thing to do is nothing at all. Halibut Cove is a gorgeous little piece of euphoria-inducing land tucked into a corner of Kachemak Bay State Park, Alaska's first state park. It is a town of only 22 year-round residents, but there are two fantastic lodges and several across the bay that offer the same thing: a peaceful look at the gorgeous scenery. Halibut Cove has no stores, but does offer a handful of art galleries, a post office (only open on mail-boat days), a high-end restaurant, and a floating espresso bar. There are plenty of outdoor activities, but there's not much else to do there, which is a good thing.

QUINTESSENTIAL ALASKA

Seafood and Sourdough

Alaska's primary claim to gastronomic fame is seafood. The rich coastal waters produce prodigious quantities of halibut, salmon, crab, and shrimp, along with such specialties as abalone, sea urchin, herring roe, and sea cucumbers. If you haven't yet tasted fresh Alaska salmon, do so here—there's nothing quite like a grilled Copper River king salmon.

Sourdough bread, pastries, and pancakes are a local tradition, dating back to the gold-rush days. Prospectors and pioneers carried a stash of sourdough starter so that they could always whip up a batch of dough in short order. The old-timers became known as sourdoughs, a title that latter-day Alaskans earn by living here for 20 years. Newcomers and those still working to earn the title are referred to as Cheechakos.

After you return from your outdoor adventure, indulge your cravings with the best of Alaskan culinary delights. Start with sourdough pancakes for breakfast; for lunch, go for smoked salmon spread on sourdough bread; top it off with a dinner of fresh halibut and wild-berry cobbler. Then you can consider yourself an honorary Alaskan sourdough.

Kayaking

Sea kayaking is big among Alaskans. It was the Aleuts who invented the kayak (or *bidarka*) for fishing and hunting marine mammals. When early explorers encountered the Aleuts, they compared them to sea creatures, so at home did they appear on their small ocean craft. Kayaks have the great advantage of portability. More stable than canoes, they also give you a feel for the water and a view from water level. Oceangoing kayakers will find plenty of offshore Alaska adventures, especially in the protected waters of the Southeast, Prince William Sound, and Kenai Fjords National Park.

The variety of Alaska marine life that you can view from a sea kayak is astonishing. It's possible to see whales, seals, sea lions, and sea otters, as well as bird species too numerous to list. Although caution is required when dealing with large stretches of open water, the truly Alaskan experience of self-propelled boating in a pristine ocean environment can be a life-changing thrill.

Native Crafts

Alaska's rich Native culture is reflected in its abundance of craft traditions, from totem poles to intricate baskets and detailed carvings. Many of the Native crafts you'll see across the state are result of generations of traditions passed down among tribes; the craft process is usually labor-intensive, using local resources such as rye grasses or fragrant cedar trees.

Each of Alaska's Native groups is noted for particular skills. Inuit art includes ivory carvings, spirit masks, dance fans, baleen baskets, and jewelry. Also be on the lookout for mukluks (seal- or reindeer-skin boots). The Tlingit peoples of Southeast Alaska are known for their totem poles, as well as for baskets and hats woven from spruce root and cedar bark. Tsimshian Indians also work with spruce root and cedar bark, and Haida Indians are noted basket makers and carvers. Athabascans specialize in birch-bark creations, decorated fur garments, and beadwork. The Aleut, a maritime people dwelling in the southwest reaches of the state, make grass basketry that is considered among the best in the world. ⇨ *For tips about buying an authentic item, check out Made in Alaska at the end of this chapter.*

ALASKA'S HISTORY

The First People

No one knows when humans first began living in the northwest corner of the North American continent, and it is still a subject of great controversy and debate. One popular theory is that 12,000 years ago humans followed the eastern migration of Ice Age mammals over the Bering Land Bridge, a 600-mi-wide stretch of land that connected present-day Alaska to Siberia. To date, the oldest human remains found in Alaska are 11,500 years old, the second-oldest Ice Age remains to be found in the world. Found in Central Alaska near the Tanana River, the remains of the three-year-old girl are thought to possibly be that of an Athabascan ancestor.

No matter when humans first arrived, by 1750 there were 57,300 Native peoples living in Russian Alaska, including Aleuts, Alutiiqs, Yup'iks, Inupiats, Athabascan, Tlingit, and Haida. Today there are more than 100,000 American Indians and Alaska Natives living in Alaska.

Russians in Alaska

Alaska was a late bloomer on the world scene. It wasn't until 1741 that Danish navigator Vitus Bering, under Russian rule, made the Alaska region known to the world. Bering died before he could ever explore the continent or return to Russia.

Politically speaking, Russia imposed itself on Alaska in varying degrees. It was the arrival of the *promyshlenniki*, or fur hunters, that had the biggest impact on the Native cultures. By most accounts, the hunters were illiterate, quarrelsome, hard-drinking, and virtually out of control. They penetrated the Aleutian Chain and made themselves masters of the islands and their inhabitants, the Aleuts. Several times the Natives revolted; their attempts were squelched, and they were brutalized.

By 1790 the small fur traders were replaced by large Russian companies. Siberian fur trader Aleksandr Andreyevich Baranov became manager of a fur-trading company and director of a settlement on Kodiak Island in 1791. He essentially governed all Russian activities in North America until 1818, when he was ordered back to Russia. Word was spreading to the Russian government that foreigners, particularly Americans, were gaining a disproportionate share of the Alaskan market. The Russian Navy was ordered to assume control of Alaska, and by 1821 it had barred all foreign ships from entering Alaskan waters. Russia created new policies forbidding any trade with non-Russians and requiring that the colonies be supplied solely by Russian ships.

The 1853 Crimean War between Imperial Russia and Britain and France put a great financial burden on Russia. It fiscally behooved the country to sell Russian Alaska. In 1867, under a treaty signed by U.S. Secretary of State William H. Seward, Alaska was sold to the United States for $7.2 million. On October 18, 1867, the territory officially changed hands. Newspapers around the nation hailed the purchase of Alaska as "Seward's Folly." Within 30 years, however, one of the biggest gold strikes in the world would bring hundreds of thousands of people to this U.S. territory.

The Gold Rush

The great Klondike gold discoveries of 1896 gained national (and worldwide) attention. Due to the depression of 1893, the need for food, money, and hope sparked a gold fever unmatched in history. Men and women alike clamored for

information about Alaska, not realizing that the Klondike was in the Yukon Territory of Canada. Perhaps if they'd known their geography Alaska would never have become the state that it is now.

The most popular route for the gold stampeders was to go entirely by water. It wasn't cheaper, but it was far easier than taking the inland route. They would start in either San Francisco or Seattle, buy passage on a steamship, and disembark more than 1,000 nautical mi later in Skagway, Alaska. No gold was in Skagway, but overnight it became a city of 20,000 miners. Gold-seekers used it as a place to negotiate and get ready for the only part of their journey that would be traversed on foot. The Chilkoot Trail was 35 challenging miles that were too rugged for pack horses. The hardest part of the journey was the climb to the summit, Chilkoot Pass. This climb was known as the Golden Staircase, a 45-degree-angle hike of nearly .75 mi. Chilkoot Pass was the gateway to Canada and the point at which the Canadian government required each person entering the territory to have at least a year's supply (approximately one ton) of food. This is partially why it took most stampeders one to three months to complete this 35-mi stretch. At the base of the Golden Staircase was where stampeders had to have everything they were taking over the pass weighed, and were charged $1 per pound. Once into Canada, they built boats and floated the remaining 600 mi to Dawson City, where the gold rush was taking place. By 1899 the Yukon Gold Rush was over, however, and the population of Skagway shrank dramatically.

Alaska experienced its own gold strike in Nome, on the Seward Peninsula, in 1898.

The fever didn't actually hit until 1900, but because it did, gold mining all over Alaska began to get national attention.

World War II

In 1942, after the United States entered the war, the War Production Board deemed gold mining nonessential to the war effort, and forced gold mining all over the country to come to a halt. Despite the closing of mines, World War II was financially beneficial to parts of Alaska. Numerous bases and ports were strategically built around the state, and the Alaska Highway was created to help deliver supplies to them.

The only time Alaska had any direct involvement with the war was in June 1942, when the Japanese attacked Attu and Kiska islands in the Aleutian Chain. The attack has been recorded in history as an "incident," but it had a great impact on many lives; a few hundred casualties occurred due to friendly fire. Nearly a thousand inhabitants were relocated and many died in the process.

Statehood

On January 3, 1959, "Seward's Folly" became the 49th state in the nation—more than 100 years after Seward first visited. Soon, a mass of investors, bold entrepreneurs, tourists, and land grabbers began to arrive. It is still a new state, far from direct scrutiny by the rest of the nation. With a constantly growing, competitive industry of oil and other natural resources, Alaska has made an identity for itself that resembles that of no other state in the nation. It boasts the second-highest production of gas and oil in the country, is twice the size of the second-largest state, and has millions of lakes, minimal pollution, and endless possibilities.

IF YOU LIKE

Mountains and Glaciers

Alaska has roughly 100,000 glaciers and ice fields covering more than 29,000 square mi, and 17 of the 20 highest mountains in the United States. Most of these awe-inspiring sights are in remote and inaccessible regions. However, with time, effort and, on occasion, a few bucks, these scenic wonders can be yours.

Mendenhall Glacier, Juneau. This drive-up glacier comes complete with visitor center, educational exhibits, nature trails, and, when the cruise ships are in town, lots of bused-in tourists. Don't let the crush of visitors dissuade you from stopping by, though—it's a great resource for learning about glacier dynamics and the natural forces that have shaped Alaska.

Mt. Roberts, Juneau. The tram takes you up the mountain and, if the weather cooperates, offers great views of the area. It's another cruise-ship favorite, but at least you can have a quick beer as you soak in the scenery.

Glacier Bay National Park, Gustavus. Whether you view this natural wonder by air, boat, or on foot, Glacier Bay is well worth the effort and expense it takes to get there.

Portage Glacier, Anchorage. This glacier has been receding rapidly, but you can ride the tour boat *Ptarmigan* across the lake to view its face. Keep an eye out for office building–size chunks of ice falling into the water.

Exit Glacier, Seward. You can take a short, easy walk to view this glacier, or if you're in the mood for a challenge, hike the steep trail onto the enormous Harding Icefield. Scan the nearby cliffs for mountain goats and watch for bears.

Flattop Mountain, Anchorage. Drive to the Glen Alps parking lot in Chugach State Park, pay the $5 parking fee, and take the short walk west to a scenic overlook—on a clear day the view sweeps from Denali south along the Alaska Range past several active volcanoes on the other side of Cook Inlet. Or follow the hikers to the top of the mountain for even more stunning scenery.

Mt. McKinley, Talkeetna. For the ultimate mountain sightseeing adventure, take a flight from Talkeetna and land on a glacier—if you're early enough in the summer, you can fly onto the Kahiltna Glacier, where teams attempting to summit the mountain gather.

Bicycling

The paved-road system is straightforward, and traffic is usually light. However, the road shoulders can be narrow, and people drive fast in rural areas. Unpaved highways are bikeable but tougher going.

Anchorage. Anchorage has an excellent bike-trail system. Biking this city is a good way to appreciate its setting as a metropolis perched on the edge of vast wilderness—but beware the occasional furry creature sharing the bike trail with you!

Denali National Park and Preserve. Take your mountain bike on the Alaska Railroad and bike Denali. Although the park road is largely unpaved, it has a good dirt surface and only light traffic.

The Interior. Fairbanks has miles of scenic bike paths along the Chena River. Most roads have wide shoulders and those incredible Alaska views. Trails used in winter by mushers, snowmachiners, and cross-country skiers are taken over by bikers when the snow melts.

Southeast Alaska and the Ferry System. You can bring your bike on Alaska's ferry system at an extra charge. Use it to explore Southeast's charming communities and surrounding forests, but come prepared for heavy rain.

Creature Comforts

Alaska isn't only tundra hiking, grizzly-bear watching, and salmon fishing. It's possible to spend your vacation pampering yourself, enjoying a nice glass of wine and excellent food, and still experience outdoor adventures.

Lodging properties can be divided into those on the road system and those that require a boat or air journey. In Southeast Alaska many lodges can be reached by boat from a nearby town or village, while properties elsewhere in the state usually require a flight in a small plane.

Alaska's Capital Inn, Juneau (✉ *113 W. 5th Ave.* ☎ *907/586–6507* ⊕ *www. alaskacapitalinn.com*). Luxury meets history in this gracious hilltop bed-and-breakfast with upscale services, delicious breakfasts, and period furnishings from the early 1900s.

Hotel Alyeska, Girdwood (✉ *1000 Arlberg Ave.* ☎ *907/754–1111* ⊕ *www. alyeskaresort.com*). An hour south of Anchorage, this luxurious hotel offers plenty of opportunities for spoiling yourself silly. The crown jewel of the resort is the Seven Glaciers Restaurant, a seven-minute tram ride up Mt. Alyeska. There you can enjoy the stunning view of the valley and the namesake glaciers; knowledgeable diners consider the restaurant to be Alaska's finest.

Chena Hot Springs Resort, Chena Hot Springs (☎ *907/451–8104* ⊕ *www.chenahotsprings. com*). If you are in or near Fairbanks, some thermal soaking is a must. Here you can spend the day enjoying a wide range of outdoor activities, followed by a long soak in the hot springs–warmed hot tubs topped off by an exceptional dinner.

Kachemak Bay Wilderness Lodge, Homer (☎ *907/ 235–8910* ⊕ *www.alaskawildernesslodge. com*). Across Kachemak Bay from Homer, and accessible by boat or floatplane, you can fill your days hiking, fishing, boating, and sightseeing, followed by delicious seafood dinners. The owners are longtime Alaskans who cater to nature lovers.

Kenai Princess Wilderness Lodge, Cooper Landing (☎ *800/426–0500* ⊕ *www. princesslodges.com*). Charming bungalows with fireplaces and vaulted ceilings of natural-finish wood make up this sprawling complex on a bluff overlooking the Kenai River. Try flightseeing, fishing, and hiking, or just read a good book and enjoy the view.

Pearson's Pond Luxury Inn and Adventure Spa, Juneau (✉ *4541 Sawa Circle* ☎ *907/789–3772* ⊕ *www.pearsonspond.com*). Yoga in the morning; wine and cheese in the evening; whirlpool tubs with rain showers; private balconies; and a well-stocked breakfast nook—luxurious amenities define this B&B on a small pond near Mendenhall Glacier.

Seven Seas Mariner, Seven Seas Cruises (☎ *877/ 505–5370* ⊕ *www.rssc.com*). Cordon Bleu cuisine, a luxurious spa, and impeccable service make this all-suites, all-balcony ship a top choice for high-end relaxing while cruising amid dramatic Alaska scenery.

Small Town Life

Alaska's entire population is barely more than 700,000 people, and almost half of that population calls Anchorage home. Scrolling down the list of Alaska cities, by the time you get to Sitka, the third largest town, you're looking at a population of fewer than 9,000 souls. Nearly 60 percent of Alaskans reside in small towns.

There's a considerable variety of small town experiences available in Alaska, such as **Kotzebue,** the regional hub for Northwest Alaska and Alaska's largest Eskimo community. Perched on the shore of Kotzebue Sound, the town strikes a fine mix of Native and contemporary American cultures. Be forewarned: landing at the one-runway airport is . . . interesting.

At the towns of **Kenai and Soldotna,** about 150 mi southwest of Anchorage, commercial fishing boats fill the harbor at the mouth of the Kenai River and Kenai's onion-dome Russian Orthodox Church accent's the old town's skyline. During the salmon dip-netting season in July, you can watch Alaskans stocking up for the coming winter.

The towns of **Haines and Skagway** in Southeast Alaska present an interesting set of contrasts when looking at attitudes about the effects of tourism on small town life. Both of these coastal communities are connected to the road system; although they're a mere 17 mi apart as the eagle flies, they're light years apart in their ambience. Haines has chosen to limit cruise-ship visitation to a mere fraction of what Skagway sees. The result is a laidback, small-town feeling in Haines, where you can enjoy fantastic views of Portage Cove, fishing, and a yearly migration of eagles visiting the late run of succulent chum salmon. Just miles away is another reality: Skagway has embraced its Gold-Rush history, with plenty of restored false-front stores and historic memorabilia; most of its downtown district makes up part of the Klondike Gold Rush National Historic Park.

MADE IN ALASKA

Intricate Aleut baskets, Athabascan birch-bark wonders, Inupiaq ivory carvings, and towering Tlingit totems are just some of the eye-opening crafts you'll encounter as you explore the 49th state. Alaska's native peoples—who live across 570,000 square miles of tundra, boreal forest, arctic plains, and coastal rain forest—are undeniably hardy, and their unique artistic traditions are just as resilient and enduring.

TIPS ON FINDING AN AUTHENTIC ITEM

1 The Federal Trade Commission has enacted strict regulations to combat the sale of falsely marketed goods; it's illegal for anything made by non-native Alaskans to be labeled as "Indian," "Native American," or "Alaska Native."

2 Some authentic goods are marked by a silver hand symbol or are labeled as an "Authentic Native Handicraft from Alaska."

3 The Alaska State Council on the Arts, in Anchorage, is a great resource if you have additional questions or want to confirm a permit number. Call 907/269–6610 or 888/278–7424 in Alaska.

4 The "Made in Alaska" label, often accompanied by an image of a polar bear with cub, simply denotes that the handicraft was made in the state.

5 Be sure to ask for written proof of authenticity with your purchase, as well as the artist's name. You can also request the artist's permit number, which may be available.

6 Materials should be legal. For example, only some feathers, such as ptarmigan and pheasant feathers, comply with the Migratory Bird Act. Only native artisans are permitted to carve new walrus ivory. The seller should be able to answer your questions about material and technique.

THE NATIVE PEOPLE OF ALASKA

There are many opportunities to see the making of traditional crafts in native environments, including the Southeast Alaska Indian Cultural Center in Sitka and Anchorage's Alaska Native Heritage Center.

After chatting with the artisans, pop into the gift shops to peruse the handmade items. Also check out prominent galleries and museum shops.

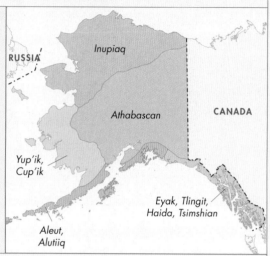

RUSSIA

Inupiaq

Athabascan

CANADA

Yup'ik, Cup'ik

Eyak, Tlingit, Haida, Tsimshian

Aleut, Alutiiq

NORTHWEST COAST INDIANS: TLINGIT, HAIDA & TSIMSHIAN

Scattered throughout Southeast Alaska's rain forests, these highly social tribes traditionally benefited from the region's mild climate and abundant salmon, which afforded them a rare luxury: leisure time. They put this time to good use by cultivating highly detailed crafts, including ceremonial masks, elaborate woven robes, and, most famously, totem poles.

TOWERING TOTEM POLES

Throughout the Inside Passage's braided channels and forested islands, Native peoples use the wood of the abundant cedar trees to carve totem poles, which illustrate history, pay reverence, commemorate

a potlatch, or cast shame on a misbehaving person.

Every totem pole tells a story with a series of animal and human figures arranged vertically. Traditionally the totem poles of this area feature ravens, eagles, killer whales, wolves, bears, frogs, the mythic thunderbird, and the likenesses of ancestors.

(left) A wagging tongue at the Juneau-Douglas City Museum
(right) A Tlingit totem reaches for the skies in Ketchikan

K'alyaan Totem Pole

Carved in 1999, the K'alyaan totem pole is a tribute to the Tlingits who lost their lives in the 1804 Battle of Sitka between invading Russians and Tlingit warriors. Tommy Joseph, a venerated Tlingit artist from Sitka, and an apprentice spent three months carving the pole from a 35-ft western red cedar. It now stands at the very site of the skirmish, in Sitka National ßHistorical Park.

Raven: Atop the pole sits the striking raven, the emblem of one of the two moieties (large multi-clan groups) of Tlingit culture.

Sockeye Salmon (above) and Dog/Chum Salmon (below): These two symbols signify the contributions of the Sockeye and Dog Salmon Clans to the 1804 battle. They also illustrate the symbolic connection to the tribe's traditional food sources.

Woodworm: The woodworm—a Tlingit clan symbol—is a wood-boring beetle that leaves a distinctive mark on timber.

Beaver: Sporting a fearsome pair of front teeth, this beaver symbol cradles a child in its arms, signifying the strength of Tlingit family bonds.

Frog: This animal represents the Kik.sádi Clan, which was very instrumental in organizing the Tlingit's revolt against the Russian trespassers. Here, the frog holds a raven helmet—a tribute to the Kik.sádi warrior who wore a similar headpiece into battle.

Tools and Materials

As do most modern carvers, Joseph used a steel adz to carve the cedar. Prior to European contact—and the accompanying introduction of metal tools—Tlingit artists carved with jade adzes. Totem poles are traditionally decorated with paint made from salmon-liver oil, charcoal, and iron and copper oxides.

ALEUT & ALUTIIQ

The Aleut inhabit the Alaska Peninsula and the windswept Aleutian Islands. Historically they lived and died by the sea, surviving on a diet of seals, sea lions, whales, and walruses, which they hunted in the tumultuous waters of the Gulf of Alaska and the Bering Sea. Hunters pursued their prey in *Sugpiaq*, kayaklike boats made of seal skin stretched over a driftwood frame.

WATERPROOF *KAMLEIKAS*
The Aleut prize seal intestine for its remarkable waterproof properties; they use it to create sturdy cloaks, shelter walls, and boat hulls. To make their famous cloaks, called *kamleikas*, intestine is washed, soaked in salt water, and arduously scraped clean. It is then stretched and dried before being stitched into hooded, waterproof pullovers.

FINE BASKETRY
Owing to the region's profusion of wild rye grass, Aleutian women are some of the planet's most skilled weavers, capable of creating baskets with more than 2,500 fibers per square inch. They also create hats, socks, mittens, and multipurpose mats. A long, sharpened thumbnail is their only tool.

ATHABASCANS

Inhabiting Alaska's rugged interior for 8,000 to 20,000 years, Athabascans followed a seasonally nomadic hunter-gatherer lifestyle, subsisting off of caribou, moose, bear, and snowshoe hare. They populate areas from the Brooks Range to Cook Inlet, a vast expanse that encompasses five significant rivers: the Tanana, the Kuskwin, the Copper, the Susitna, and the Yukon.

BIRCH BARK: WATERPROOF WONDER
Aside from annual salmon runs, the Athabascans had no access to marine mammals—or to the intestines that made for such effective boat hulls and garments. They turned to the region's birch, the bark of which was used to create canoes. Also common were birch-bark baskets and baby carriers.

FUNCTIONAL & ORNAMENTED PIECES
Much like that of the neighboring Eskimos, Athabascan craftwork traditionally served functional purposes. But tools, weapons, and clothing were often highly decorated with colorful embroidery and shells. Athabascans are especially well known for ornamenting their caribou-skin clothing with porcupine quills and animal hair—both of which were later replaced by imported western beads.

INUPIAQ, YUP'IK & CUP'IK

Residing in Alaska's remote northern and northwestern regions, these groups are often collectively known as Eskimos or Inupiaq. They winter in coastal villages, relying on migrating marine mammals for sustenance, and spend summers at inland fish amps. Ongoing artistic traditions include ceremonial mask carving, ivory carving (not to be confused with scrimshaw), sewn skin garments, basket weaving, and soapstone carvings.

Thanks to the sheer volume of ivory art in Alaska's marketplace, you're bound to find a piece of ivory that fits your fancy—regardless of whether you prefer traditional ivory carvings, scrimshaw, or a piece that blends both artistic traditions.

IVORY CARVING

While in Alaska, you'll likely see carved ivory pieces, scrimshaw, and some fake ivory carvings (generally plastic). Ivory carving has been an Eskimo art form for thousands of years. After harvesting ivory from migrating walrus herds in the Bering Sea, artisans age tusks for up to one year before shaping it with adzes and bow drills.

KEEP IN MIND

The Marine Mammal Protection Act states that only native peoples are allowed to harvest fresh walrus ivory, which is legal to buy after it's been carved by a native person. How can you tell if a piece is real and made by a native artisan? Real ivory is likely to be pricey; be suspect of anything too cheaply priced. It should also be hard (plastic will be softer) and cool to the touch. Keep an eye out for mastery of carving technique, and be sure to ask questions when you've found a piece you're interested in buying.

WHAT IS SCRIMSHAW?

The invention of scrimshaw is attributed to 18th-century American whalers who etched the surfaces of whale bone and scrap ivory. The etchings were filled with ink, bringing the designs into stark relief.

More recently the line between traditional Eskimo ivory carving and scrimshaw has become somewhat blurred, with many native artisans incorporating both techniques.

TIPS

Ivory carving is a highly specialized native craft that is closely regulated. As it is a by-product of subsistence hunting, all meat and skin from a walrus hunt is used.

Ivory from extinct mammoths and mastodons (usually found buried underground or washed up on beaches) is also legal to buy in Alaska; many native groups keep large stores of it, as well as antique walrus tusk, for craft purposes. Many of the older pieces have a caramelized color.

The Alaska Wilderness

BIODIVERSITY AND OUTDOOR ADVENTURE IN THE LAST GREAT PLACE

WORD OF MOUTH

"Last week of Aug. is peak week for tundra changing colors on your trip to Denali."

—Bill_H

If Alaska were a country, it would be the seventh largest, just behind Australia but way ahead of India. And the state is as diverse as it is vast, with more than 5,000-miles of coast, myriad mountain ranges, alpine valleys, salmon-rich rivers, clear lakes, blue glaciers, temperate rainforests, and sweeping tundra. The Alaska wilderness is clearly *the* place for unforgettable outdoor adventures.

While Minnesota is busy bragging about 10,000 lakes, Alaska stopped counting after 2 million. Four great mountain ranges—the St. Elias, Alaska, Brooks, and Chugach—and more than 30 lesser chains sweep through the state. The St. Elias Mountains form the world's highest coastal range. The Alaska Range contains North America's highest peak: Mt. McKinley—or Denali, as Alaskans call it—at 20,320 feet. The Brooks Range roughly follows the Arctic Circle, and the Chugach arcs through the state's most populous region along the South Central coast.

Alaska flora and fauna is just as varied. Along the northern coast polar bears take to the ice to hunt seals. Whales with 90-foot fins swim slowly past the grassy islands of the Aleutians. Voles weighing not much more than a postcard hide in the thick Southeastern rainforest. The sky is filled with nearly 500 species of birds, including the largest population of bald eagles anywhere. Between all those mountains lie North America's two largest national forests with more than 30 kinds of berries for the grizzly bears, which can grow to 11 feet tall and weigh more than a thousand pounds.

Indeed, this state has more parks, wilderness areas, and wildlife refuges than all the others combined, and few animals care about park boundaries, so it's all their home. You can travel here for a lifetime and still find surprises, so the first step in planning any visit is determining which Alaska flora and fauna interest you most. Understanding the various eco-zones; learning about the wildlife-viewing opportunities they hold; and finding the best activities, tours, and guides in each will go a long way toward creating a memorable Alaska outdoor adventure. Pick as much territory as time allows, and get ready for the last great place.

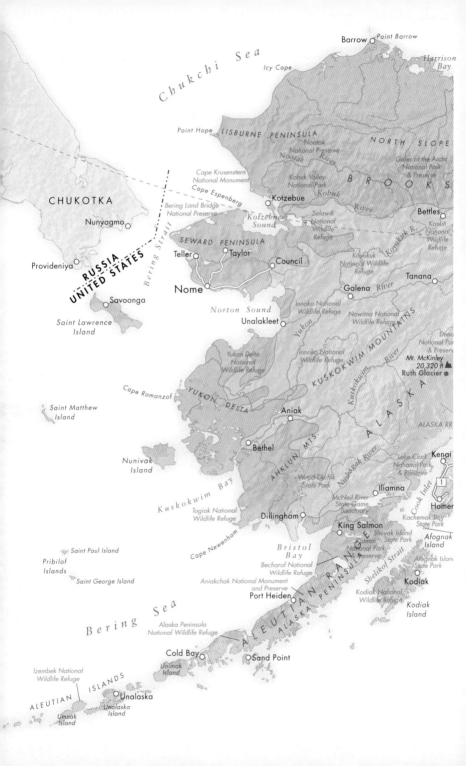

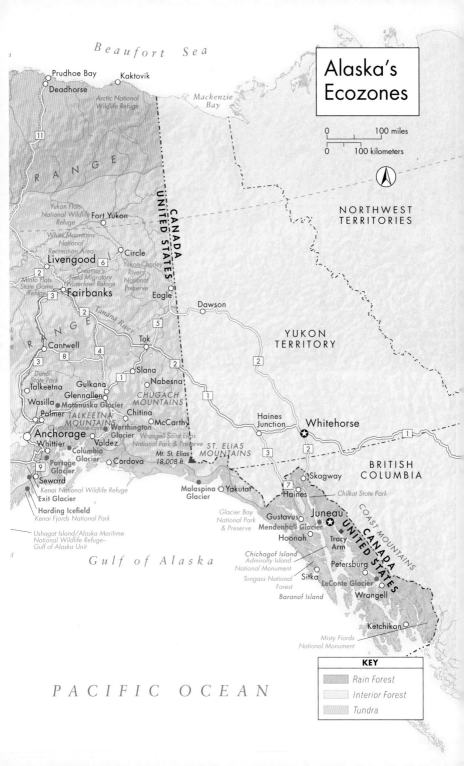

Alaska's Ecozones

Beaufort Sea

Prudhoe Bay
Deadhorse
Kaktovik

Mackenzie
Bay

Arctic National
Wildlife Refuge

0   100 miles
0   100 kilometers

RANGE

NORTHWEST
TERRITORIES

Yukon Flats
National Wildlife
Refuge   Fort Yukon

White Mountains
National
Recreation Area   Circle

Livengood   6

Creamer's
Field Migratory
Waterfowl Refuge

Minto Flats
State Game
Refuge   Fairbanks   Eagle

3

Tanana River

Dawson

YUKON
TERRITORY

RANGE   5

Cantwell   8   Tok

3   4

Denali
State Park
Talkeetna   Slana
Gulkana   Nabesna
Glennallen

Wasilla   Matanuska Glacier   Chitina   CHUGACH
MOUNTAINS

Palmer   TALKEETNA   McCarthy
MOUNTAINS   Worthington

Chugach State Park   Glacier   Wrangell-Saint Elias
Anchorage   Valdez   National Park & Preserve   ST. ELIAS
Whittier   Columbia   Mt. St. Elias   MOUNTAINS
Glacier   18,008 ft
Portage   Cordova

Haines
Junction   Whitehorse

BRITISH
COLUMBIA

9   Glacier
Seward   Chilkat State Park
Exit Glacier   Malaspina   Yakutat   Skagway   1
Harding Icefield   Glacier   7
Kenai National Wildlife Refuge   Haines
Kenai Fjords National Park

Ushagat Island/Alaska Maritime
National Wildlife Refuge–
Gulf of Alaska Unit   Gulf of Alaska

Glacier Bay   Gustavus   Juneau
National Park   Mendenhall Glacier
& Preserve   Hoonah   Tracy
Arm

COAST MOUNTAINS

UNITED STATES
CANADA

Chichagof Island
Admiralty Island
National Monument   Sitka   Petersburg
Tongass National
Forest   LeConte Glacier
Baranof Island   Wrangell

PACIFIC   OCEAN   Ketchikan

Misty Fiords
National Monument

KEY	
	Rain Forest
	Interior Forest
	Tundra

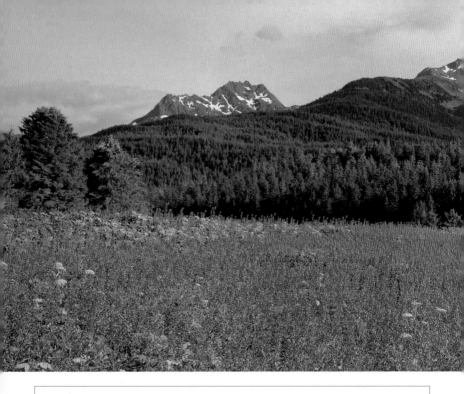

RAIN FOREST

The largest chunk of intact rain forest in North America lies in Alaska, scattered across hundreds of islands of the Southeast panhandle. This area—stretching from south of Ketchikan up to Skagway and mostly set aside as the Tongass National Forest—is a rich, dripping landscape of forested mountains coming straight out of the sea.

The spaces between the trees are filled with devil's club, shelf fungus, dozens of kinds of ferns and moss and lichens, and enough berries—salmonberries, blueberries, huckleberries, raspberries, crowberries, and more than a dozen other kinds—to explain the common sight of the deep impression of a bear's footprint in the ground.

But it's water that truly defines the region: the 100 inches or more of rain that fall on most parts of it, feeding streams that lace through the forest canopy, bringing salmon and everything that hunts salmon, from seals

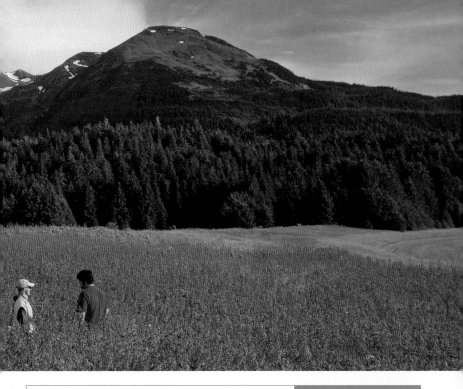

to bald eagles. Even the trees along streambeds get a large percentage of their nutrients from bits of salmon left after everyone is done eating, water dripping from branches and needles and leaves speeding the decay.

Throughout the forest, decay is vital, because there is almost no soil in the Tongass—a couple of inches at best. New life sprouts on fallen trees, called "nursery logs," and often a couple of dozen species of plant grow on a spruce knocked down by spring storms; adult trees grow oddly shaped near their base, evidence of the nursery tree they once grew on.

And the Tongass isn't the only rain forest in Alaska; much of the Chugach National Forest, as well as most of the coastline from Valdez to Seward and beyond, is also rain forest.

Under the canopy, ravens yell, bears amble from berry bush to berry bush, Sitka black-tailed deer flit through the thick underbrush like ghosts. The rain forest is a riot of life, the best of what water, time, and photosynthesis can build.

SAFETY TIP

Although Devil's Club, or Pushki, is commonly used for medicinal tea by Southeast Natives, it's also the region's only dangerous plant: the spines covering the plant's branches and undersides of the leaves can break off and dig into the skin of passing animals and hikers, where they can fester and infect.

Look out for tall plants with five-lobed leaves 6 inches across. It grows in large patches or solitarily in well-drained areas.

FLORA

Southeast's rain forest is one of the most diverse territories in the world: from towering old-growth to dozens of species of moss, all glistening with rainfall.

SALMONBERRY *(RUBUS SPECTABILIS)*

The salmonberry canes, on which the leaves and fruits grow, may reach 7 feet tall; they grow in dense thickets. The juicy raspberry-like fruits may be either orange or red at maturity; the time of ripening is late June through August. The favorite fruit of Alaska's bears.

SITKA SPRUCE *(PICEA SITCHENSIS)*

Alaska's state tree, grows 150–225 feet high, up to 8 feet in diameter, and lives 500–700 years, although few make it that long. A combination of storms and very shallow soil tend to knock down most spruce within a couple of hundred years. The leaves are dark green needles, about an inch long, pointing up, and they cover all the branches. At the top of the tree, light orange-brown cones develop. Spruce buds were used by early mariners for making beer, and Sitka spruce wood, now mostly used for making guitars, has always been one of the great treasures of the forest: the Russians used it for the beams and decks of ships that they built in their Sitka boatworks and for housebuilding. During World War II, it was used for airplanes—the British made two of their fighters from Sitka spruce, and of course that's what went into Howard Hughes's Spruce Goose.

WESTERN HEMLOCK *(TSUGA HETEROPHYLLA)*

Western hemlock grow to a maximum of about 150 feet, and they're thin, with a large tree only about 4 feet in diameter. Maximum lifespan is about 500 years, but few make it that long. The leaves are wider and lighter green than spruce leaves, pointing down, and the cones are a darker brown. Bark is a gray-brown. Western hemlock loves to come back in clear-cut areas, a fact that has changed the natural balance in some logged parts of Southeast Alaska.

WESTERN RED CEDAR *(THUJA PLICATA)*

Western red cedar covers a wider range, from sea level to about 3,000 feet in elevation. The leaves are much like those of the yellow cedar, but more yellow-green in color. The cones are oval, as opposed to the round yellow cedar cones. Red cedar was the treasure species for Southeast Natives, who used it for everything from house building to making clothes.

Sitka Spruce

Western Hemlock

Western Red Cedar

Salmonberry

FAUNA

Making their home in the spaces between the trees of the rainforest are bears, moose, wolves, and deer. Watch estuaries for seals, streams for salmon, and keep an eye on the sky for eagles, ravens, crows, and herons.

BALD EAGLE *(HALIAEETUS LEUCOCEPHALUS)*

With a wingspan of 6 to 8 feet, and weighing as much as 20 pounds, these grand Alaska residents are primarily fish eaters, but they will also eat birds or small mammals. As young birds, they're all brown, with the characteristic white head developing in adulthood. The world's largest gathering of bald eagles occurs in Southeast Alaska each winter, along the Chilkat River near Haines. Bald eagles build the biggest bird nests in the world, weighing up to 1,000 pounds.

Black Bear

BLACK BEAR *(URSUS AMERICANUS)*

Black bears are found on nearly every large island in the Southeast, throughout South Central Alaska, and in coastal mainland areas. They average five feet in length and weigh from 150 to 400 pounds. A good-size black bear is often mistaken for a brown bear because black bears are not necessarily black: they range from black to very light brown. Black bears have a life expectancy in the wild of about 25 years.

Brown Bear

BROWN BEAR *(URSUS ARCTOS)*

Brown bears, or grizzlies, are rarer and considerably larger than their black cousins. In Southeast's rain forest, browns are most often seen on Admiralty Island, where they outnumber the human population; near Wrangell; and on Baranof, Chichagof, and Kruzof Islands. Brown bears run 7 to 9 feet, with males ranging from 400 to 1,100 pounds; if they live in a place with a rich fish run, they can grow to 1,500 pounds. Brown bears range in color from a dark brown to blonde. The easiest way to distinguish them is by the hump on their back, just behind the head. They have a life expectancy of about 20 years in the wild.

Sitka Blacktailed Deer

SITKA BLACKTAILED DEER *(ODOCOILEUS HEMIONUS SITKENSIS)*

The Panhandle's rain forest is the primary home of this deer, though it has been transplanted to Prince William Sound and Kodiak. Dark gray in winter and reddish brown in summer, it's smaller but stockier than the whitetails found in the Lower 48. The deer stay at lower elevations during the winter, then move up to alpine meadows in summer.

Bald Eagle

EXPERIENCING A RAIN FOREST

Sitka Blacktailed Deer are common throughout Alaska's rain forests.

Any trip into Southeast Alaska puts you in the rain forest. Even in a landscape this beautiful there are some highlights.

ANIMAL WATCHING

At **Pack Creek** on Admiralty Island, brown bears fish for spawning salmon. To get here, you can fly by air charter or take a boat from Juneau. Another option is near Wrangell; **Anan Bear Reserve** is at one of the few streams in the world where black and brown bears share the waters, fishing at the same time.

BY SEA

The Alaska Marine Highway runs ships to every major town—and many of the smaller ones—in Southeast Alaska. The local equivalent of a bus service, AMH ships go into small channels, offering views of rain-forest slopes, forays into quiet bays and inlets, and perhaps the best look at how the landscape was carved by glaciers.

FLIGHTSEEING

Misty Fiords National Monument, south of Ketchikan, is one of the most beautiful areas of drowned fjords and pristine rain-forest habitat in the Southeast. Covering more than 3,500 square mi, Misty Fiords is the Southeast's most popular flightseeing destination (though the monument is also laced with hiking trails and is perfect for kayaks).

HIKING

The Tongass has hundreds of miles of hiking trails, from short loops to ambitious multiday expeditions. Rain gear and a proper understanding of bear safety are essential. Hiking give you a chance to have the forest to yourself, and lets you appreciate the intricacies of the forest, from tiny lichen to the towering canopy. This might just be the best way to understand the rain forest.

TOP GUIDES

BEAR-VIEWING

Essentially all of the Anan Wildlife Observatory-authorized guide companies we recommend *(⇨ see Ch. 4, Southeast)* are excellent, but a top stand-out is **Alaska Vistas** (☎ *907/874–3006 or 888/874–3006* ⊕ *www.alaskavistas. com)*. Based out of Wrangell, Alaska Vistas offers a highly accommodating level of trip-planning service, and their enthusiasm and respect for the bear experience they're sharing with their guests makes a trip with them unforgettable in the best way possible. They also offer jet boat tours up the Stikine, kayaking and canoe trips, and guided hikes, all of which come with that same special Alaska Vistas touch.

NATURAL HISTORY

An excellent guide to the rain forest of the southeast can be found quite easily and with minimal expense (once you get yourself to Juneau, that is): the docents at **Glacier Gardens** (✉ *7600 Glacier Hwy.* ☎ *907/790–3377* ⊕ *www.glaciergardens. com)* are Native Alaskans and will teach you more about the local forest than you're going to learn anywhere else.

HIKING

If you have any inclination to go hiking, make sure you consider fitting it in out of Skagway with **Packer Expeditions**

A brown bear and cubs

(☎ *907/983–3005* ⊕ *www.packerexpeditions.com)*. They offer trips on the famous Chilkoot Trail but also along local trails more popular with the area's residents both human and ursine. Packer Expeditions also offers lots of ways to combine straight-up rain forest hiking with other modes of locomotion such as a helicopter ride or a ride of the White Pass Railroad (either one-way or, for accessing more-remote trailheads, return). They are a good choice if you're eager to combine rain forest and glacier ecozone experiences; one hiking trip offers a hike up to the Laughton Glacier, and a different itinerary will bring you there partially by train and leave time for hiking on the glacier itself.

If you have sufficient bear safety experience and wilderness knowledge, the **Alaska Travel Industry Association** (⊕ *www.alaskatia.org)*, or ATIA, provides fantastic guidance on exploring the rainforests of Southeast.

Bald eagle

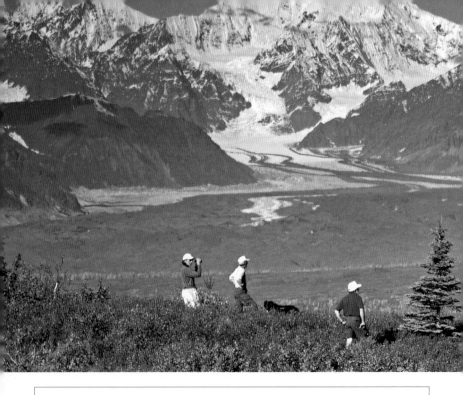

INTERIOR FORESTS

Rain forests dominate the southern coast of Alaska; but move inland, and a different kind of forest appears. Much of the interior is covered by thick spruce and birch forests, trees that can grow in harsher conditions—temperatures in the middle of the state can hit 100 degrees in summer and minus 50 in the winter—than their coastal counterparts.

The soil is usually deeper here, but as much as 75% of the region that this taiga or boreal forest covers may have patches of permafrost—soil that never thaws. The plants also have to cope with a very short growing season; in most areas, the entire season from beginning to end spans no more than four months.

The interior forest is dominated by conifers—spruce, pine, fir—but also has plenty of broadleaf trees, such as birch and aspen. Fires are a regular occurrence throughout the region, usually caused by lightning strikes, and they can quickly burn out thousands of acres. Although

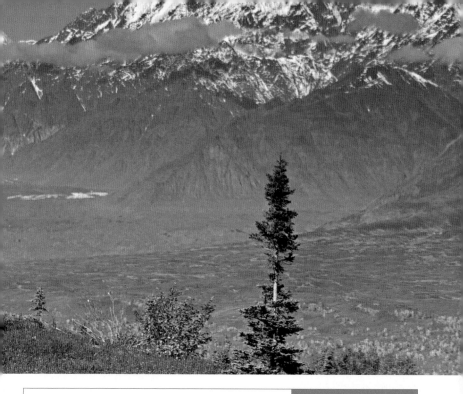

this may seem alarming (and no doubt is to anyone whose home is near a burning forest), these fires are actually beneficial to the long-term health of the forest. They serve to clear out dead trees and underbrush, and also open up the canopy to allow for new growth.

Taking advantage of the resources within these forests is a wide variety of animals, from bears and moose all the way down to the tiny vole. Like the trees, these animals have to know how to survive in dramatic temperature changes; come winter, many hibernate, but others find ways to scrape for food beneath the snow and ice. Still others rely on migration to stay warm; perhaps as many as 300 bird species spend part of the year in the forests, but only a couple dozen have found ways to winter there.

Covering the vast, broad center of Alaska, the interior forests cover as much as 80,000,000 acres; include the parts of the state where the forests are patchier, and you get up to 220,000,000 acres of interior forest—an area bigger than Texas and Oklahoma combined. These forests are the heart of Alaska.

SAFETY TIP

So much of Alaska's interior forests are roadless wilderness that rivers often serve as the best avenues for exploring them. However, rivers can be dangerous. River difficulty is ranked Class I through Class IV; only very experienced river runners should attempt anything above Class II on their own. If you're traveling with a guide, research their safety record before you sign up.

FLORA

Alaska's interior forests aren't as biologically rich as some areas of the state, but what they lack in diversity, they more than make up for in beauty and sheer vastness of the land they occupy.

ALASKAN PAPER BIRCH *(BETULA NEOALASKANA)*

A near relative of the more common paper birch (*Betula papyrifera*) and once commonly used by Natives for making birch-bark canoes, the Alaska subspecies grows up to 45 feet tall. It's noted for having a narrow trunk and leaves about three inches long. The bark is dark red-brown when the tree is young, and turns a delicate white or pinkish as the tree ages; like that of its relative, the bark peels off in layers, although not quite as well as does *Betula papyrifera* (the Latin name for the more-common paper birch). In Alaska the Alaskan paper birch grows in bogs and on poorly drained soils, and is commonly mixed in with black spruce trees. It's one of the iconic features of the landscape of the Interior, often the subject of art from the region.

Alaskan Paper Birch

ALDER *(ALNUS)*

Common throughout central Alaska, alders range from trees (such as the Sitka alder, one of the first species to come back in a disturbed area, such as after a fire or intensive logging) to bushes (like the mountain alder, which grows along streams and in other areas with wet soil). Mountain alder, despite being classified as generally shrublike, can actually grow up to 30 feet high, with thin trunks of about 6 inches in diameter. Sitka alder can grow to about the same height, but with a slightly thicker trunk. Both types have saw-toothed leaves with parallel veins and smooth gray bark. It's difficult to tell them apart when they're young.

Tall fireweed

TALL FIREWEED *(EPILOBIUM ANGUSTIFOLIUM)*

The fireweed is among the first plants to reinhabit areas that have been burned out by wildfire, and in the proper conditions it grows well. Found throughout much of Alaska, it's a beautiful plant, with fuchsia flowers that bloom from the bottom to the top of stalks; it's said that the final opening of flowers is a sign that winter is only weeks away. Spring fireweed shoots can be eaten raw or steamed, and its blossoms can be added to salads. A related species is dwarf fireweed (*Epilobium latifolium*), which is also known as "river beauty" and tends to be shorter and bushier.

Alder

FAUNA

With all that space, there's plenty of space for animals. From the rarely seen wolverine to the very common moose, the heart of the state has room for everything.

COMMON RAVEN *(CORVUS CORAX)*

A popular character in Alaska Native stories, the raven is both creator and trickster. Entirely black, with a wedge-shape tail and a heavy bill that helps distinguish it from crows, the raven is Alaska's most widespread avian resident. Ravens are also the smartest bird in the sky; scientists have shown that they are perfectly capable of abstract reasoning and teaching other ravens their tricks. They're among the most articulate of birds, with more than 50 calls of their own, plus the ability to mimic almost any sound they hear.

LYNX *(LYNX CANADENSIS)*

The lynx is the only wild cat to inhabit Alaska. It's a secretive animal that depends on stealth and quickness. It may kill birds, squirrels, and mice, but the cat's primary prey is the snowshoe hare (*Lepus americanus*), particularly in winter; its population numbers closely follow those of the hare's boom-bust cycles.

MOOSE *(ALCES ALCES GIGAS)*

The moose is the largest member of the deer family; the largest bulls stand 7 feet tall at the shoulders and weigh up to 1,600 pounds. Bulls enter the rut in September, the most dominant engaging in brutal fights. Females give birth to calves in late May and early June. Though most commonly residents of woodlands, some moose live in or just outside Alaska's cities.

WOLF *(CANIS LUPUS)*

The largest and most majestic of the Far North's wild canines, wolves roam throughout Alaska. They form close-knit family packs, which may range from a few animals to more than 30. Packs hunt small mammals, birds, caribou, moose, and Dall sheep. They communicate through body language, barks, and howls.

WOLVERINE *(GULO GULO)*

Consider yourself lucky if you see a wolverine, because they are among the most secretive animals of the North. They are also fierce predators, with enormous strength and endurance. Denali biologists once reported seeing a wolverine drag a Dall sheep carcass more than 2 mi; they can run 40 mph through snow. Though they look like very small bears, wolverines are in fact the largest members of the weasel family.

Lynx

Wolverine

Moose

Wolf

EXPERIENCING INTERIOR FORESTS

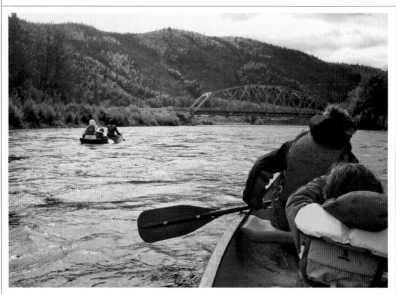

By river or by train, it's hard to find an unimpressive vista in Alaska's interior forests.

The interior forests are big enough you could spend years exploring and never see the same area twice. Or you could just go for a nice day-hike. Whatever adventure you're after, you'll find it here.

CANOEING AND KAYAKING
It can be a lot easier to see the forest from a river than from the inside. Alaska's premier long canoe trip is along the Yukon River, starting across the Canadian border in Dawson City and taking out at Eagle. A wilder option is whitewater kayaking the Fortymile, from Chicken, though this is definitely not for the faint of heart. Another popular float trip is one that takes you down the Nenana, through Fairbanks. Guides are available on all these rivers and more; no one unfamiliar with Alaskan conditions should try these trips alone under any circumstances.

DOG SLED
For those hardy enough to come to Alaska in winter, dog-sled tours offer the most classic way to see the state: behind a pack of howling dogs who are having the time of their lives, running as fast as they can. Trips range from short runs through forest loop trails to multiday adventures, and all you need are warm clothes and the ability to hang on tight.

HIKING
Nearly every town in the central forests has hiking trails lacing the woods around it. Especially popular are Angel Rock, Granite Tors, and Ester Dome hikes, all near Fairbanks. For something longer, try the Kesugi Ridge Trail, near Talkeetna; it's a two- to four-day alpine traverse along a beautiful ridgeline with possible views of Denali if the weather's right.

TOP GUIDES

HIKING

For a backcountry hiking experience in Wrangell-St. Elias National Park, contact **St. Elias Alpine Guides** (☎ *907/ 345–9048 or 888/933–5427 ⊕ www. steliasguides.com*), based in McCarthy. The guides here will facilitate anything from a few hours in the woods to a month-long foray into the wilderness. This is the only company contracted by the Park Service to run tours of historic Kennicott buildings *(⇨ see Kennicott in Ch 5, South Central)*; if you have any interest in Alaska's History it's a very compelling way to get out into the country.

RIVER SPORTS

St. Elias Alpine Guides also leads rafting trips through its river-travel-focused division, **Copper Oar** (⊕ *www.copperoar. com*). Also based in McCarthy, they will outfit and guide you along pristine waters into the heart of the wilderness.

Fishing trips are a great way to get out on the water, too. The Kenai Peninsula might be the best spot to combine fishing with boreal forest scenery. **Hi-Lo Charters** (⊕ *www.hilofishing.com*), in the town of Kenai, run fishing trips from its home base on the Russian River; this fishing lodge scores high in all the important ways—excellent service, knowledgeable

Moose enjoy a view from the water, too.

guides, comfortable quarters—but the custom-built sheltered outdoor grilling area is a great additional perk.

Out of Fairbanks, a simple but highly educational and entertaining way to experience the surrounding landscape is to simply take a ride on the *Riverboat Discovery*. Onboard naturalists are enthusiastic and highly knowledgeable. If you prefer to go it alone, **Alaska Outdoor Rentals and Guides** (✉ *Pioneer Park Boat Dock, along Chena River next to Peger Rd.* ☎ *907/457–2453 ⊕ www.2paddle1.com*) can rent you gear and facilitate drop-offs and pickups along the lower Chena River in Fairbanks or other local waterways.

DOG SLED TOURS

Sun Dog Express Dog Sled Tours (☎ *907/479–6983 ⊕ www.mosquitonet. com/~sleddog*), out of Fairbanks, runs winter and summer tours (weather permitting), and can accommodate whatever level of involvement you're looking for—from simple demonstrations to a full-tilt three-day mushing camp. Another great winter option in the Fairbanks area is **Chena Dog Sled Tours** (☎ *907/488–5845 ⊕ www. ptialaska.net/~sleddogs*), out of Two Rivers (near Chena Hot Springs).

Racing sled dogs

TUNDRA

At first glance the tundra might not look like very much: a low car-pet plants, few more than shoelace high. But take a closer look and you'll realize you're encountering an ecozone every bit as fascinat-ing and diverse as the showier forests, glaciers, and intertidal zones elsewhere in the state.

Tundra stretches throughout the Bush in Alaska, with patches as far south as Denali National Park. Charac-terized by dwarf shrubs, sedges, grasses, mosses, and lichen, tundra occurs in places where the temperatures are low (so it makes sense for plants to hug the ground) and the growing season is short—some prime tundra spots might not get more than a few weeks of summer.

Arctic tundra has roughly 1,700 species of plants grow-ing in it; a single square foot of tundra might contain several dozen species, from saxifrage to bear berry to arctic rose. It does make for a hard place for most

animals to build homes; mammals that depend on the tundra tend to cover a fair chunk of territory in their search for food, be they musk ox, lemmings, or caribou.

Throughout most of the tundra zone in Alaska the ground beneath is permafrost—permanently frozen soil—and too hard for many plants to put down deep roots. Permafrost happens when the average temperature of an area is below freezing, and it comes in both continuous—an entire region's soil encased in ice at a more or less uniform depth—and discontinuous—where some places get warm enough to thaw (see black spruce, in the interior forest section).

Tundra is extremely fragile; the short growing season means even the slightest damage can take years to recover. Footprints across tundra might not fade for decades. But at the same time, tundra is extremely resilient, able to thrive in the most extreme conditions, regrow after a herd of a hundred thousand caribou have crossed over it, nibbling, and ready again to help feed the millions of birds who depend on tundra areas as part of their migration route. The closer you look, the more you'll find in the tundra.

SAFETY TIP

Alaska has at least 27 species of mosquito, and in summer the biomass of the mosquitoes can actually outweigh that of the caribou. The bite of a mosquito from up this way can be enough to raise welts on a moose. While the mosquitoes provide a huge base of the food chain for tundra birds, small mammals, and fish, they can cause serious discomfort for travelers. Apply DEET, wear long sleeves, and consider traveling with a head net if you're hiking.

FLORA

The tundra is a close-up territory: the longer and closer you look, the more you'll see. Take it on its own terms and you'll find a whole world to discover.

BLUEBERRY *(VACCINIUM)*

A favorite of berry pickers, blueberries are found throughout Alaska, except for the farthest northern reaches of the Arctic. They come in a variety of forms, including head-high forest bushes and sprawling tundra mats. Pink, bell-shape flowers bloom in spring, and dark blue to almost black fruits begin to ripen in July or August, depending on the locale. But the tastiest are the tundra blueberries, which almost carpet the ground in some places; this is the true flavor of the midnight sun, and you'll want to factor in time on any hikes for plenty of berry-eating breaks.

REINDEER LICHEN *(CLADONIA RANGIFERINA)*

A slow-growing white lichen that grows in shapes somewhat reminiscent of reindeer antlers, or a small sea coral, reindeer lichen come up in a tangle of branches. Another reason for its name: it is a favored food of both reindeer and caribou (it's sometimes called caribou moss). It's also used traditionally in medicinal teas and in poultices for arthritis; nutritionally there's not much to be gained from eating it, but if you did it would feel sort of like chewing soft toothpicks.

SAXIFRAGE *(SAXIFRAGA RAZSHIVINII)*

One of the most characteristic plants of the tundra, able to grow in even the thinnest soil (the name translates to "stone breaker"), saxifrage is close to the ground, tends to grow in a kind of rosette shape, and sends up small, five-petaled flowers, which are usually white, but may also be red or yellow. Saxifrage is one of the first bits of color that show up on the tundra in spring, making it a particular favorite of many who live up here during the (very long, very cold) winters.

WILLOW *(SALIX)*

An estimated three-dozen species of willow grow in Alaska. Some, like the felt-leaf willow (*Salix alaxensis*), may reach tree size; others form thickets. In the tundra, what you'll find are others, like the Arctic willow (*Salix arctica*), that hug the ground; a plant an inch tall might be a hundred years old. Whatever the size, willows produce soft "catkins" (pussy willows), which are actually columns of densely packed flowers without petals.

Willow

Blueberry

Saxifrage

Reindeer lichen

FAUNA

The tundra is perfect for animal spotting.

ARCTIC GROUND SQUIRREL (*SPERMOPHILUS PARRYII*)

These yellowish-brown, gray-flecked rodents are among Alaska's most common and widespread mammals. Ground squirrels are known for their loud, persistent chatter. They are easiest to spot standing above their tundra den sites, watching for grizzlies, golden eagles, weasels, and anything else after the average 2,000 calories an arctic ground squirrel provides.

CARIBOU (*RANGIFER TARANDUS*)

Sometimes called the "nomads of the north," caribou are long-distance wandering mammals. The Western Arctic Caribou Herd numbers nearly 500,000, while the Porcupine Caribou Herd has ranged between 70,000 and 180,000 over the past decades. They are the only members of the deer family in which both sexes grow antlers. Caribou might migrate over hundreds of miles between summer and winter grounds, a feat eased by the tendon in their ankle that snaps the foot back into place with each step with an audible click.

MUSK OX (*OVIBOS MOSCHATUS*)

The musk ox is an Ice Age relic that survived partly because of a defensive tactic: they stand side by side and form rings to fend off predators such as grizzlies and wolves. Unfortunately that tactic didn't work very well against humans armed with guns. Alaska's last native musk oxen were killed in 1865. Musk oxen from Greenland were reintroduced here in 1930; they now reside on Nunivak Island, the North Slope of the Brooks Range, and in the Interior. The animal's most notable feature is its long guard hairs, which form "skirts" that nearly reach the ground. Inupiats called the musk ox *oomingmak*, meaning "bearded one." Beneath those coarser hairs is fine underfur called *qiviut*, which can be woven into incredibly soft, warm clothing.

SANDHILL CRANE (*GRUS CANADENSIS*)

The sandhill's call has been described as "something between a French horn and a squeaky barn door." Though some dispute that description, most agree that the crane's calls have a prehistoric sound. Scientists say the species has changed little in the 9 million years since its earliest recorded fossils. Sandhills are the tallest birds in Alaska; their wingspan reaches up to 7 feet. The gray plumage of adults is set off by a bright red crown.

Musk Ox

Sandhill crane

Arctic Ground Squirrel

Caribou

EXPERIENCING ALASKA'S TUNDRA

If you keep your eyes open, you might spot musk oxen grazing on the tundra.

Get out and spend some time in this landscape and discover just how big the world of the tundra really is.

DRIVE (OR BE DRIVEN)

With a road system that leads into nearly uninhabited parts of Alaska, Nome offers the perfect jumping-off point for tundra fans. It's also the only town in Alaska where you are likely to spot musk oxen within a few miles of buildings. You can do this on your own, but many people prefer the extra knowledge gained by doing this with a guide. Hiring a guide also supports the local economy and helps promote preservation of Native knowledge.

HIKE

The easiest place to go for a tundra hike is in Denali National Park: away from the mountains, the park contains huge swatches of tundra, where you might also see bears, moose, and caribou.

The best time is in early autumn, when the colors start to change; that's when "the ground looks like a giant bowl of Captain Crunch." However, so long as you're properly equipped against mosquitoes, summer (when visitors are most likely to be here) is also a fine time to explore the tundra on foot.

RAFT

Several of Alaska's great arctic rivers cut through tundra: the Hulahula heads north through the Alaska National Wildlife Refuge, the largest patch of undisturbed land left in the United States. Another good option is the Kongakut, which rises in the Brooks Range and then flows towards the Arctic plain where the caribou calve. Either river offers a week or more of the ultimate wilderness experience.

TOP GUIDES

DRIVE OR HIKE

A trip with **Nome Discovery Tours** (☎ *907/443–2814*) is maybe one of the most memorable experiences you could have in Alaska's tundra. Touted as Alaska's best tour guide by many who have had the pleasure of being shown around the tundra by him, former Broadway showman Richard Beneville has lived in the Far North for over 20 years and has developed an intimate knowledge of the land and its history. One tour includes Safety Sound, a tidal wetland about 30 miles out of Nome that has some fantastic birding. Another includes a tundra walk on which Richard serves as tundra-savvy interpreter.

The best guide companies to the remotest places in Alaska tend to be owned and operated by those who have lived here for a while, and **Kuskokwim Wilderness Adventures** (☎ *907/543–3900* ⊕ *www.kuskofish.com*) is no exception. Local expert Jim McDonald does much of the guiding for this family-owned operation. Several birding and fishing tours are available. Spending a weekend fishing at their Kisaralik Camp 80 miles north of town by river boat is a great way to spend several days in one place on some of the remotest tundra in the world without forgoing modern conveniences like a shower.

Spring is the best time to see baby animals.

Autumn on the tundra is a riot of color.

TOUR BUS

Not everyone will have the time to get out to the far Northwest; luckily, there's tundra to be found much closer to one of the main attractions in Alaska: Denali National Park. Take any of the guided bus tours in Denali (except for the shortest which doesn't get out of the forest). Since you're on a bus, you don't get the full benefit of seeing it up close and personal except for photo stops, but it's still a lot of reward for very little effort.

RAFT

Like the forests of the interior of the state, the tundra is a great place for a rafting trip. **Arctic Treks** (☎ *907/455–6522* ⊕ *www.arctictreksadventures.com*) runs top-notch rafting trips (and also hiking, bird-watching, and photography tours) to the Brooks Range, Arctic National Wildlife Refuge, and Gates of the Arctic National Park, among other locations. They've been in operation for over 30 years, and guides have deep knowledge of the tundra and its wildlife.

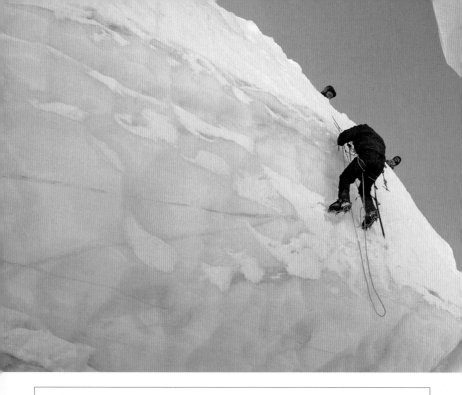

ICE

Ice is its own ecosystem in Alaska, and a vital one, as well as being the part of the state's environment that is at the most risk. Ice covers roughly 5 percent of Alaska—from the southernmost tidewater glacier at LeConte, through the Juneau Icefields, past Glacier Bay, and up to the Malaspina Glacier, the largest nonpolar glacier in the world.

Glaciers form when more snow falls than melts. If this keeps up year after year, the new snow presses down on the old snow, compacting it, turning it to ice. And after a time it all grows heavy enough to start moving, flowing with the landscape and the call of gravity.

Historically, nothing has shaped Alaska more than ice. A quick look at the mountains in Southeast Alaska offers ready proof: mountains under about 3,500 feet are rounded; those above, sharp and jagged. Why? Because during the last ice age that's the height the glaciers came through, smoothing everything.

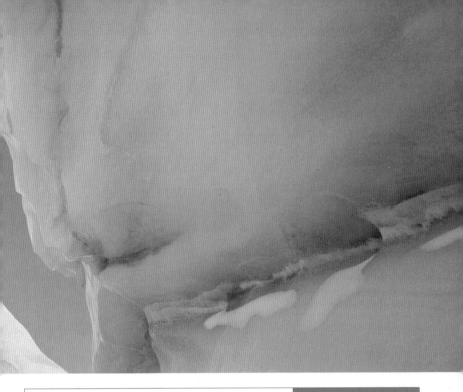

But it's not just that glaciers carve the landscape. They also rejuvenate it; a walk toward a glacial face is like walking backward in time. Glaciers leave behind them the ultimate clean slate, a chance for nature to move back in and regrow from scratch.

Glacial winds, known as katabatic winds, carry seeds for hundreds of miles, allowing plant species to spread; the fresh water held in Alaska's ice feeds countless rivers, streams, and lakes, supporting everything from the incredibly delicate freshwater snails of the Brooks Range to the spawning grounds of the biggest king salmon.

And it's all under threat. Over the past decades nearly every glacier in Alaska has gotten smaller. Glaciers that used to be easily visible—Worthington, Exit, Portage—have almost disappeared from sight. Estimates are that Alaska has nearly 100,000 glaciers, but that number will likely change in the future.

SAFETY TIP

Glacier terrain includes a mix of ice, rock debris, and often-deep surface snow; sometimes frigid pools of meltwater collect on the surface. Watch out for glacier crevasses; sometimes hidden by snow, these cracks in the ice may present life-threatening traps. Glacier travel should be attempted only after you've been properly trained. If you haven't been taught proper glacial travel and crevasse-rescue techniques, hire a backcountry guide to provide the necessary gear and expertise.

FLORA

As a general rule, plants don't grow on ice, but Ruth Glacier, has a fully mature forest growing on it. Still, for the most part, about the only life found on the ice might be some bacteria and algae, and a few lichen growing on rocks the ice is carrying along. The interest lies at the face of the glacier, and in the progression of plants leading away from it.

Lichen

ALGAE

At least seven species of algae have been found on Alaska's glaciers. The most common include *Chlamydomonas nivalis*, technically classified as a green algae, which stains snow atop glaciers red when they bloom; and *Ancylonema nordenskioldii*, which is another green algae, and is perhaps the most common algae found on ice. Again, like the bacteria and the fungus, unless you know what you're looking for, you won't see much.

BACTERIA

A close look on Alaska's glaciers might uncover some *Rhodobacteracae*, some *Polaronomas*, and *Variovorax*, and a few dozen more species of bacteria. For most people, all of these are going to either be invisible, or look like small smudges on the ice.

LICHEN

A bit more showy than the bacteria, lichen tend to grow near glacial faces; in fact, tracking lichen in moraines is a way scientists date glacial movement. A combination of a fungus and a bacteria, lichen are among the first things to grow near a glacier. Lichen get their nutrition from air and water, digging rootlike structures called rhizomes into the rocks where they grow, eventually breaking them down and turning them into soil. Favored among glacier scientists are *Rhizocarpon geographicum* (green and blotchy); but you'll also spot some that look like burned ash, some that look like branches, and, if the air is really clear, some that are orange. In all, Alaska has more than a thousand species of lichen, and hundreds can show up around glaciers.

Algae

SPRUCE FOREST (THE RUTH GLACIER EXCEPTION)

Although most of what grows on glaciers is nearly invisible, there is one exception. At the end of Ruth Glacier, which flows off Mt. Mckinley, is a forest, growing atop the ice. Not the best place to be a tree: as the glacier moves (at a rate of about 3 feet a day), the trees at the edge get pitched into the river below.

Spruce Forest

FAUNA

Most animals can't live on the ice—nothing to eat. But living near the ice has some distinct advantages.

HARBOR SEAL (*PHOCA VITULINA*)

Ice broken off the face of tidewater glaciers is a favorite place for seals to pup, to sunbathe, and most of all, to stay safe from orcas on the prowl. All those berg shapes confuse the orca's sonar, making it a perfect place to be a seal. In Southeast Alaska, the easiest place to see them, they will be harbor seals, which grow to about 180 pounds. They're covered with short hair, and are usually colored either with a dark background and light rings, or light sides and a belly with dark splotches. They can dive to 600 feet and stay down for more than 20 minutes, their heart rate slowing to 15–20 beats per minute, about a fourth of their heart rate when at the surface. The easiest way to tell a seal from a sea lion is by the ears: seals have no external ear structure.

ICE WORM (*MESENCHYTRAEUS*)

Robert Service described this animal in his poem "Ballad of the Ice Worm Cocktail," where he wrote that they are "indigo of snout./And as no nourishment they find, to keep themselves alive/They masticate each other's tails, till just the Tough survive./Yet on this stern and Spartan fare so rapidly they grow,/That some attain six inches by the melting of the snow." He was very wrong. Pin-size, usually blue, black, or brown, and hard for even scientists to find, ice worms come to glacial surfaces only in morning and evening; they can actually melt at temperatures just a few degrees above freezing.

ORCA (*ORCINUS ORCA*)

Maybe the harbor seals are hiding from the orca, but that doesn't mean the orca don't view the ice edge as an open fridge door. Orca, or killer whales—a term that has fallen out of favor with the politically (and taxonomically, as the scientific name translates out to "one from the realms of the dead) correct, as they are neither killers *per se* nor, since they're really the largest member of the porpoise family, whales. Orca can be more than 30 feet long, and the dorsal fin on a male can be as much as 6 feet high. At birth, orca weigh roughly 400 pounds. A full-grown orca can weigh as much as 9 tons, and can swim 34 mi per hour; they can live as long as 80 years. Watch for the tall fin, the distinctive black and white markings, and size—Dall's porpoise are also black and white, but are smaller than a newborn orca.

Ice worm

Harbor Seal

Orca

EXPERIENCING ALASKA'S ICE

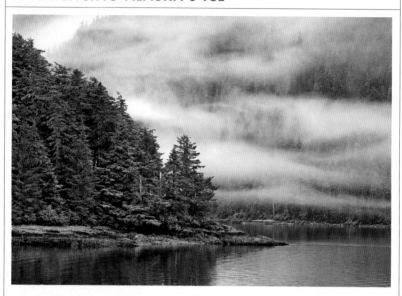

In Chatham Straight, be sure to view the landscape to your west—Baranof Island's misty rainforest appearance belies the fact that it's home to more glaciers than any other island in the world.

What most people want to see in Alaska is a glacier. Luckily there are plenty of them, to explore.

FLIGHTSEEING
In the Southeast, helicopter tours to **Mendenhall Glacier**, an 85-mi-long, 45-mi-wide sheet of ice, just the tiniest finger of the 1,500-square-mi Juneau Icefields, provide fantastic views; most tours land on the ice for an up-close look. In South Central, trips over Ruth Glacier toward Mt. McKinley offer the best ice views.

HIKING
The **Matanuska Glacier**, at Mile 103 off the Glenn Highway (about a 90-minute drive northeast of Anchorage) is not only Alaska's biggest nonpolar glacier, but also one of the easiest to get to, with readily accessible ice; however, the inexperienced should not consider going far without professional guides.

KAYAKING
Some outfitters offer kayaking near glaciers and icebergs. The experience can be transformative. It can also be extremely dangerous; bergs can roll over and glaciers can calve at any moment. Be sure to go with an experienced guide and do exactly as he or she instructs.

SAILING
Glacier Bay is where most people get on boats to see calving glaciers (when big chunks of ice fall into the sea). Other options include Tracy Arm, near Juneau (smaller, but more dramatic); LeConte Glacier, between Wrangell and Skagway; or glacier cruises from Valdez and Seward. You're hard-pressed to find a cruise in the southeast that doesn't put you within sight of a glacier. It can be dangerous to get too close to a glacier when cruising; you never know when it will calve and create a nasty wave before you can sail to safety.

TOP GUIDES

GLACIER CRUISES

Glacier-viewing cruises are sextremely popular in Alaska, particularly in Prince William Sound. Of the plethora of operators these stand out for their commitment to good environmental stewardship, charismatic guides, and customer service.

Major Marine Tours (☎ *907/274–7300 or 800/764–7300* ⊕ *www.majormarine. com*), out of Whittier, runs excellent glacier-viewing tours into Prince William Sound. They visit at least two tidewater glaciers on each sailing, have an itinerary that is kind to those who are nervous about seasickness.

Kenai Fjords Tours provide a comfortable boat, a whole lot of glaciers, and excellent wildlife-watching along the way. You can see rainforest, mountains, glaciers, and the sea all at once. The route out for all trips to Kenai Fjords, covers some open ocean that can be very rough at times; take the necessary seasickness precautions beforehand regardless of the weather. Do tough it out; Kenai Fjords Tours are excellent and worth any temporary discomfort.

The most exclusive guest list in Prince William Sound is with retired biologist Gerry Sanger of **Sound Eco Adventures** (☎ *888/471–2312* ⊕ *www.soundecoadventure.com*); he takes groups of no more

Sitting Pretty on Ruth Glacier

than three people for an all-day cruise on his 30-ft boat. The tour has a photography focus.

If you have limited time **26 Glacier Cruise** (☎ *907/276–8023 or 800/544–0529* ⊕ *www.26glaciers.com*) travels 135 mi in under 5 hours. You'll head out of Whittier and see 26 glaciers from a comfortable reserved-seating catamaran. This is another smooth-ride standout; even those who are always seasick will be pleasantly surprised.

FLIGHTSEEING

Air Excursions (☎ *800/354–2479* ⊕ *www.airexcursions.com*) and **Wings of Alaska** (☎ *907/789–0790* ⊕ *www. wingsofalaska.com*) are top choices for glacier flights. Both have offices throughout the Southeast and can create custom flights. **ERA Aviation of Era Alaska** (⊕ *www. eraalaska.com*) can fly you via helicopter from Juneau or Skagway to various places, the cheapest and quickest (but no less dazzling) of which is the trip to Mendenhall Glacier.

KAYAKING

Tongass Kayak Adventures (⊕ *www. tongasskayak.com*), out of Petersburg, leads kayaking trips to the icebergs of nearby LeConte Glacier, among many other worthwhile adventures.

Cruise ship in Seward harbor, Alaska

THE MOUNTAINS

An awful lot of Alaska lies a considerable way above sea level. The state is covered with mountains, from the relatively small peaks of Southeast Alaska—only a few much above 4,000 feet—to the highest point in North America, Mt. McKinley, at 20,320 feet above sea level.

The state's mainland is divided by mountains: the Chugach range along the South Central coastline; the Alaska Range, which includes Mt. McKinley, close to the center of the state; and the Brooks Range, which divides the interior from the arctic coast. On the eastern edge of the state lies the Wrangell Range, which, with the St. Elias mountains north of Glacier Bay and stretching into Canada, offers more unexplored high peaks than any other area in the hemisphere. Lesser ranges include the Ogilvie, Kuskokwim, and Talkeetna mountains, as well as the Aleutian Range, which never

gets very high, but offers dramatic views from the storm-tossed sea.

The higher the peak, the less that grows on it, but along the way to the top mountains provide rich biodiversity, from the trees on their lower slopes to the alpine meadows along the way to the peak. The mountains also influence everything around them, creating weather patterns that spread out across the state; the main reason why so few people ever see the peak of Mt. McKinley is because the mountain makes weather, and the weather that mountains like most is clouds.

In the Southeast, the Coast Mountains, the effect of altitude on weather is particularly dramatic: the east sides of the mountains are relatively dry (for a rain forest), getting only a hundred or so inches of rain a year; some spots on the west sides of the mountains get as much as 300 inches of rain.

Once above the alpine meadow level, not a whole lot grows or lives in the mountains, but mountains have shaped everything in Alaska, from Native culture to wildlife migrations. They're the birthplace of glaciers and the last truly unexplored edge of the state.

FLORA

Each mountain is its own complete ecosystem; what you'll find depends on altitude, on exposure, on what other mountains are nearby.

ALPINE FIR *(ABIES LASIOCARPA)*

The alpine fir is a fairly large tree growing up to 150 feet tall, although more commonly around 60 feet, with a trunk around three feet in diameter. Branches are covered with needles about an inch long. Like ideal Christmas trees, the crown is very narrow, often only a single spike. Bark on young trees is smooth and gray, but roughens as the tree ages.

Avens

AVENS *(DRYAS)*

The Avens is a low evergreen flowering plant (technically a subshrub) common in high alpine meadows, most frequently found in areas that were once glaciated. Usually growing in patches, avens have small leaves, and produce eight-lobed flowers with a yellow center. Avens is considered to be a member of the rose family.

Alpine fir

CHOCOLATE LILY *(FRITILLARIA LANCEOLATA)*

A high-alpine meadow plant, the chocolate lily grows up to four feet high, with one to five rich, brown flowers coming off the central stalk. Leaves are broad and flat, shaped like spearheads. The chocolate lily usually blooms from mid-June to mid-July, and is characterized by a smell that is very distinctive; nicknames for the chocolate lily include outhouse lily, skunk lily, and dirty diaper.

VALERIAN *(VALERIANA SITCHENSIS)*

One of the most common alpine flowers in Alaska, valerian, grows on stems that range from about a foot to 4 feet long. Leaves grow in pairs, leading up to beautiful flower clusters, of white, five-lobed flowers with long stamens shooting above the petals. Valerian has a sweet smell to it, and can be used for helping ease insomnia. While not native to Alaska, it's become an important part of the Alaskan plantscape.

Chocolate lily

Valerian

FAUNA

For many animals, up is the way to go to be safe from most predators. Changing altitude is also like changing seasons—up leads to cooler weather.

DALL SHEEP *(OVIS DALLI DALLI)*

One of four wild sheep to inhabit North America, the white Dall is the only one to reside within Alaska. Residents of high alpine areas, the sheep live in mountain chains from the St. Elias Range to the Brooks Range. Though both sexes grow horns, those of females are short spikes, while males grow grand curls that are "status symbols" displayed during mating season.

Dall Sheep

GOLDEN EAGLE *(AQUILA CHRYSAETOS)*

The bald eagle is mostly a coastal species in Alaska; golden eagles prefer the interior, especially around Denali and the Brooks Range. Characterized by the golden feathers on their head and neck, golden eagles have wingspans of 6 to 7 feet, and can weigh up to 12 pounds, with females much larger than males. They feed on squirrels, hares, and small birds, but they've also been known to occasionally attack larger animals, such as Dall sheep lambs. A single eagle might hunt over a territory of more than 60 square mi.

Mountain goat

MARMOT *(MARMOTA BROWERI)*

Alaska's biggest rodent, marmots are common in the Brooks Range, where they live communally in scree where they can hide easily from predators. Browsing on pretty much anything that grows at that altitude, a marmot can grow to 2 feet in length and weigh 8 pounds or more.

MOUNTAIN GOAT *(OREAMNOS AMERICANOS)*

Living on the high peaks, favoring rocky areas so steep that any predator would slip and fall, mountain goats live in the arc of coastal mountains from roughly Anchorage all the way down through the Panhandle. An adult male goat weighs 250–350 pounds, with females running about 40% smaller. Goats can live up to 18 years, although 12 is the high end of average. They feed on the high alpine plants—grasses, herbs, shrubs—and then in winter will eat whatever is available, favoring blueberry plants, hemlock, and lichens.

Marmot

Golden eagle

EXPERIENCING THE MOUNTAINS

No runway? No problem: bush planes can land anywhere from alpine meadows to snow-covered glaciers.

Alaska has more big mountains than the rest of the country combined.

FLIGHTSEEING

Unless you feel like spending a month or so climbing, the best way to see Alaska's peaks is by plane, and the best place to do that is in Denali. Flightseeing trips leave from Talkeetna; the best travel up Ruth Glacier, into the Great Gorge—an area of dramatic rock and ice—and up around the summit of Mt. McKinley. Although summit is often hidden in clouds, it's still the best ride in Alaska.

HORSEBACK

Encompassing more than 13 million acres of mountains, glaciers, and remote river valleys, **Wrangell–St. Elias National Park and Preserve** is wild and raw with so many big mountains that a lot of them don't even have names. There's no better way to absorb the enormity and natural beauty of this region than on horseback. Centuries-old game trails and networks blazed and maintained by contemporary outfitters wind through lowland spruce forests and into wide-open high-country tundra. From there, horses can take you almost anywhere, over treeless ridgelines and to sheltered campsites on the shores of scenic tarns.

SKIING

Alyeska Resort, located 40 mi south of Anchorage in Girdwood, is Alaska's largest and best-known downhill ski resort. A new high-speed quad lift gets you up the mountain. The resort encompasses 1,000 acres of terrain for all skill levels. Ski rentals are available at the resort. Local ski and snowboard guides teach classes and offer helicopter ski and snowboard treks into more remote sites in the nearby Chugach and Kenai ranges. You probably won't see much wildlife, but you'll see a lot of mountain.

TOP GUIDES

FLIGHTSEEING

There's no question that the top mountain-oriented activity in Alaska for most visitors is flightseeing in Denali National Park. One of the top companies to go with is **K2 Aviation**, out of Talkeetna. They provide thoroughly-narrated tours that vary by length and route; we highly recommend going on the longest one (and thus most expensive one) you can afford. Most people agree that the flight that takes you up over the top of McKinley itself is the best (you guessed it: it's also the priciest).

Alyeska Resort, Girdwood

K2 Aviation is owned by **Rust's Flying Service** (☎ *907/243–1595 or 800/544–2299* ⊕ *www.flyrusts.com*), based in Anchorage, so even if you can't make it up to Talkeetna by land they will help you arrange to experience their tour from your Anchorage base. If you prefer not to head north, they run trips out to the Brooks Range and the mountainous Harding Icefield and Kenai Fjords National Park, among other places.

HIKING

If you are fit and want to immerse yourself in the mountains, consider a trip with **Arctic Treks** (☎ *907/455–6502* ⊕ *www.arctictreksadventures.com*), based in Fairbanks. You don't need experience in the backcountry to go

Watch for golden eagles in the mountains.

on their trips, and they are very highly recommended.

HORSEBACK

Horseback riding is the unsung hero of mountain travel in Alaska; in the warmer months, there's hardly a more pleasant way to travel. **Chena Hot Springs Resort** (☎ *907/451–8104* ⊕ *www.chenahotsprings.com*), east of Fairbanks, can outfit you with a horse and enough instruction to get the previously inexperienced out on the trails and up into the mountains. If you won't have time to travel to the Fairbanks area, consider a guided ride with **Alaska Excursions** (☎ *907/983–4444* ⊕ *www.alaskaexcursions.com*), based in Skagway; they lead very good tours in a more conveniently-located mountain landscape.

MOUNTAINEERING

While serious climbing isn't for everyone, if you are fit and not afraid of heights, Alaska is both a top destination for the pros and a great place for those interested in the sport to try their hand. **Alaska Mountain Guides** (⊕ *www.alaskamountainguides.com*) has offices all over the state and is especially strong in the area of helping first-timers feel comfortable with the sometimes-vertigo-inducing sport.

THE SEA

The most philosophically accurate maps of Alaska are perhaps the nautical charts: they show the sea, in great detail, and only sketch in a few features on land. Anybody who has done much travel in Alaska understands why. Travel on land is arduous. Travel in a boat, unless the weather gets you, is sheer joy.

Alaska's coastline—longer than that of the rest of the United States combined—and adjacent waters range from the deep and smooth inlets and bays of Southeast Alaska to the huge, shallow, and wild waters of the Bering Sea.

The ocean influences almost everything in Alaska, from how people live to the weather they encounter. Fishing has always been one of the state's biggest industries since the Russians who settled here introduced the concept, and fish and other sea creatures had been important sources of food and materials for coastal

communities for thousands and thousands of years before that (in fact, they still are).

And the health of the sea influences not just the adjacent coastal areas but fishing returns hundreds and hundreds of miles inland; if not enough salmon survive in the sea long enough to make it back to the mouth of their home river, it follows that a reduced amount will make it up the length of those rivers to spawn. Subsistence hunters deep in the Brooks Range can face hardship, as well as bears who depend on spawned-out salmon for much of their diet.

Perhaps even more compelling a reason to travel here: the sea is simply where some of Alaska's most beautiful, graceful, dramatic animals spend their time. Whether its rafts of birds covering a dozen acres of sea off the Aleutians, or the slow arc of a whale's back in Southeast, the sea is the center of Alaska's life. However you travel through it, doing so with a knowledgeable guide who can help you better understand what you encounter will increase your enjoyment exponentially.

SAFETY TIP

If you're going to get out onto the water by self-propelled means—a kayak, canoe, or raft—go with a guide; a reputable one will ensure weather and tide conditions align in the chosen paddling spot for the smoothest ride possible (or roughest-while-still-safe, in the case of rafting).

Only consider going it alone if you have serious endurance-paddling experience under your belt and know what information to gather and what equipment to bring to avoid a dangerous situation.

FLORA

Most people go to the beach looking for animals, but there's no shortage of things for plant lovers to see, either. Some of the state's most weird and wonderful living organisms can be found here.

BULL KELP (*NEREOCYSTIS*)

Probably the most common seaweed found on Alaska's beaches, bull kelp is dull brown and has a bulb at one end of its otherwise long, whiplike structure. That's right: snap it just so and it will crack like a whip. Or you can cut the bulb in half and blow the whole thing like a trumpet. One of the fastest growing plants in nature, most strands of bull kelp are around 8 to 15 feet long. If you're kayaking and are feeling puckish, it's generally safe to pick a little (just make sure it looks healthy) and nibble it right there. Some people also bring it home and fry it or put it in a salad.

EELGRASS (*ZOSTERA MARINA*)

Common all along the Alaskan coast, eelgrass can grow up to 6 feet (although it usually doesn't in the short Alaska growing season). Thin, brown, and with roots that are covered with fine hairs, it's a perfect place for spawning herring to lay their eggs. The largest patch of eelgrass in the world is in Bristol Bay, off the west coast of the state (the patch is in Izembek Lagoon and stretches across roughly 34,000 hectares at last measure).

HORSETAIL (*EQUISETUM ARVENSA*)

One of the first plants to come up on beaches and along glacial moraines, horsetails look just like their name, if horses had bushy green tails with segments kind of like bamboo. They might grow to a couple feet tall, and can have a cone, sort of like a pinecone, for spores. Traditionally it is used for helping bladder or kidney issues, and it can also serve as a good natural solution for certain soil moisture imbalances.

SALIX

Salix include willows and several hundred other species of trees. However, along Alaskan beaches, what you are most likely to see are *Salix hookeriana*, or Dune willows, which can have yellow, green, or brown flowers. They like to grow on wet soil and in coastal meadows, often right near spots you might be near while fishing, wildlife-watching, cruising, or kayaking.

Bull kelp

Salix

Horsetail

Eelgrass

FAUNA

Alaska's seas are among the biologically richest in the world—which is why the whales all come here to eat. For things with fins and flippers, this is paradise.

HORNED PUFFIN (*FRATERCULA CORNICULATA*)
Named for the black, fleshy projections above each eye, horned puffins spend most of their life on water, coming to land only for nesting. They are expert swimmers, using their wings to "fly" underwater and their webbed feet as rudders. Horned puffins have large orange-red and yellow bills.

HUMPBACK WHALE (*MEGAPTERA NOVAEANGLIAE*)
Humpbacks are most commonly seen in the Southeast. Humpback whales grow to 50 feet, but most are closer to 40, weighing up to 80,000 pounds. They are distinguished by the way they swim and their shape at the waterline: their back forms a right angle as they dive. Whales do not generally show their tails above water unless they are sounding or diving deep. Baleen whales, humpbacks feed on krill and plankton, using the baleen to filter their food from the sea water. Most of Alaska's humpbacks winter in Hawaii, but there are a couple small year-round populations, most notably near Sitka.

SALMON
Alaska has five species of salmon: pink (humpie), chum (dog), coho (silver), sockeye (red), and the king, or Chinook. All salmon share the trait of returning to the waters in which they were born to spawn and die. During the summer months this means rivers are clogged with dying fish, and a lot of very happy bears.

SEA OTTER (*ENHYDRA LUTRIS*)
Sea otters don't have blubber; instead, air trapped in their dense fur keeps their skin dry. Beneath their outer hairs, the underfur ranges in density from 170,000 to 1 million hairs per square inch. Not surprisingly, the otter spends much of every day grooming. Otters also eat about 14 crabs a day, or ¼ of their body weight.

STELLER SEA LION (*EUMETOPIAS JUBATUS*)
Its ability—and tendency—to roar is what gives the sea lion its name. Because they can rotate their rear flippers and lift their bellies off the ground, sea lions can get around on land much more easily than seals can. They are also much larger, the males reaching up to 9 feet and weighing up to 1,500 pounds. They feed primarily on fish, but will also eat sea otters and seals.

Humpback Whale

Salmon

Horned Puffin

Sea otter

2

EXPERIENCING THE SEA

Whale-watching trips are one of the most rewarding ways to experience the waters of Alaska.

To really see the sea, you're going to need a boat.

INSIDE PASSAGE AMH FERRY

The Alaska Marine Highway runs ferries from Bellingham, Washington, to as far out as Dutch Harbor, in the Aleutians. But there are also some island areas, where the land meets the sea, that offer a great chance for spotting wildlife.

WILDLIFE-WATCHING CRUISE

The best whale-watching is in Southeast Alaska: a lot of humpbacks hang out close to Juneau, making it the easiest place to start from. Frederick Sound is famous for its huge humpback population, as is Icy Strait, near the entrance to Glacier Bay.

Glacier Bay itself is one of the richest marine environments in the state: humpbacks, orcas, seals, porpoise, and more.

TRIP TO REMOTE PACIFIC ISLANDS

For migratory birds and Northern Pacific seals, the place to go is the Pribilof Islands. Approximately 200 species of birds have been sighted on the twin islands of St. Peter and St. Paul, out in the middle of the Bering Sea, but you will almost certainly need to be part of a guided tour to get there. The Pribilofs are also home to the world's largest population of fur seals.

AMH FERRY TO THE ALEUTIANS

A little more accessible, the Aleutians—particularly Dutch Harbor—are also spots for adding to the life list, since many vagrants appear. Take the Alaska Marine Highway from Kodiak for the three-day run to Dutch. Along the way, you'll likely see humpbacks, fin whales, orcas, and more puffins, murres, and auklets than you knew the planet could hold.

TOP GUIDES

WILDLIFE-WATCHING EXCURSIONS

If you have the opportunity to travel to Sitka, **Otter Quest** is a great guide company for spotting not just otters but the whole spectrum of wildlife.

Believe it or not, there's an excellent snorkel outfitter in Ketchikan that facilitates trips most experienced snorkelers give an enthusiastic two thumbs up to. **Snorkel Alaska** (⊠ *S. Tongass Hwy. and Roosevelt Dr.* ☎ *907/247–7783* ⊕ *www. snorkelalaska.com.*) will provide a wetsuit for protection against the water temperatures; you'll likely get an up-close view of such fascinating tidal sea creatures as giant sunflower stars, bright blood stars, and sea cucumbers.

If you want to get down to water level but aren't so keen on outright submersion, **Southeast Sea Kayaks** (☎ *907/ 225–1258 or 800/287–1607* ⊕ *www. kayakketchikan.com*) specializes in day trips that still take you to some of the remotest inlets in Southeast.

Orca Enterprises (with Captain Larry) (☎ *907/789–6801 or 888/733–6722* ⊕ *www.alaskawhalewatching.com*) out of Juneau is a favorite Southeast whale-watching guide company; Captain Larry notes his whale-spotting success rate is 99.9% during the summer months. Hi success rate is due in part

Sea otter floating in Tutka Bay, Kenai Peninsula

to the speediness of his boat; he's able to cover more ground than some of the larger vessels.

If you've only got a few hours, **Weather Permitting Alaska** (☎ *907/209–4221* ⊕ *www.weatherpermittingalaska.com*) can get you out and back in about 4 hours. Their ship is luxury-level with delicious food served, an added plus.

WILDLIFE TOURS FARTHER AFIELD

If you can afford the trip out in terms of time and money, and if you have even just a slight interest in birds, travel to the Pribilofs with **Wilderness Birding Adventures**. The guides with Wilderness Birding lead trips here regularly and are well-versed in most details you would ever want to know about the many different ways the birds and other animals come from across the sea to breed here. Because of the wildlife that comes here, it's one of the most unique seascapes you could hope to experience in the state. Wilderness Birding also runs trips to other parts of the state; among other combinations, you could match a tour to the Pribilofs with another trip to the Brooks Range to immerse yourself in the mountains.

Steller Sea Lions

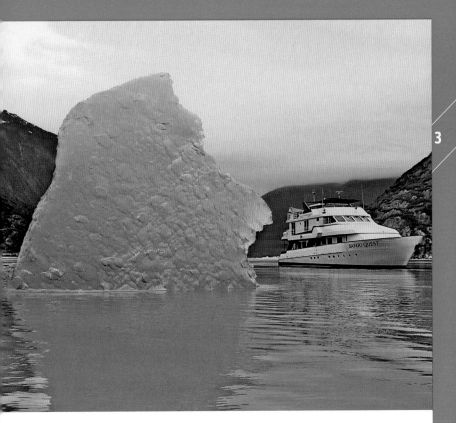

Choosing Your Cruise

WORD OF MOUTH

"Part II of our trip was the Island Princess 7-day one-way cruise from Vancouver to Anchorage. The mini-suite was much larger than we expected, with plenty of room for everything. The food was delicious. The views in Glacier Bay and College Fjord were outstanding (2400 pictures later . . .)."

—musictub

By Linda Coffman

Alaska is one of cruising's showcase destinations. Itineraries give passengers more choices than ever before—from traditional loop cruises of the Inside Passage, round-trips from Vancouver or Seattle, to one-way Inside Passage–Gulf of Alaska cruises.

Though Alaska cruises have generally attracted an older-passenger demographic, more young people and families are setting sail for the 49th state and children are a common sight aboard ship. Cruise lines have responded with youth programs and shore excursions with appeal for youngsters and their parents. Shore excursions have become more active, too, often incorporating activities families can enjoy together, such as bicycling, kayaking, and hiking. Many lines also offer pre- or postcruise land tours as an optional package trip, and onboard entertainment and learning programs are extensive. Most also hire Alaska Native speakers, naturalists, or local personalities to lead discussions stimulated by the local environment.

Cruise ships may seem like floating resorts, but you can't check out and go elsewhere if you don't like your ship. The one you choose will be your home—it determines the type of accommodations you have, what kind of food you eat, what style of entertainment you see, and even the destinations you visit. If you don't enjoy your ship, you probably won't enjoy your cruise. That is why the most important choice you'll make when booking a cruise is the combined selection of cruise line and cruise ship.

CRUISING IN ALASKA

Which cruise is right for you depends on numerous factors, notably your budget, the size and style of ship you choose, and the itinerary.

ITINERARIES

Cruise ships typically follow one of two itineraries in Alaska: round-trip Inside Passage loops and one-way Inside Passage–Gulf of Alaska cruises. Itineraries are usually seven days, though some lines offer longer trips. ■ TIP→ Keep in mind that the landscape along the Inside Passage changes dramatically over the course of the summer cruise season. In May and June, you'll see snowcapped mountains and dramatic waterfalls from snowmelt cascading down the cliff faces, but by July and August most of the snow and some waterfalls will be gone.

The most popular Alaskan ports of call are Haines, Juneau, Skagway, Ketchikan, and Sitka. Lesser-known ports in British Columbia, such as Victoria and the charming fishing port of Prince Rupert, have begun to see more cruise traffic.

Small ships typically sail within Alaska, setting sail from Juneau or other Alaskan ports, stopping at the popular ports as well as smaller, less visited villages. Some expedition vessels focus on remote beaches and fjords, with few, if any, port calls.

ROUND-TRIP INSIDE PASSAGE LOOPS
A seven-day cruise typically starts and finishes in Vancouver, British Columbia, or Seattle, Washington. The first and last days are spent at sea, traveling to and from Alaska along the mountainous coast of British Columbia. Once in Alaska waters, most ships call at a different port on each of four days, and reserve one day for cruising in or near Glacier Bay National Park or another glacier-rich fjord.

ONE-WAY INSIDE PASSAGE–GULF OF ALASKA ITINERARIES
These cruises depart from Vancouver, Seattle, or, occasionally, San Francisco or Los Angeles, and finish at Seward or Whittier, the seaports for Anchorage (or vice versa). They're a good choice if you want to explore Alaska by land, either before or after your cruise. For this itinerary, you'll need to fly into and out of different cities (into Vancouver and out of Anchorage, for example), which can be pricier than round-trip airfare to and from the same city.

SMALL-SHIP ALASKA-ONLY ITINERARIES
Most small ships and yachts home port in Juneau or other Alaskan ports and offer a variety of one-way and round-trip cruises entirely within Alaska. A typical small-ship cruise is a seven-day, one-way or round-trip from Juneau, stopping at several Inside Passage ports—including smaller ports skipped by large cruise ships.

SMALL-SHIP INSIDE PASSAGE REPOSITIONING CRUISES
Alaska's small cruise ships and yachts are based in Juneau or other Alaskan ports throughout the summer. In September they sail back to their winter homes in the Pacific Northwest; in May they return to Alaska via the Inside Passage. These repositioning trips are usually about 11 days and are often heavily discounted, because they take place during the shoulder season.

OTHER ITINERARIES

Although mainstream lines stick to the popular seven-day Alaskan itineraries, some smaller excursion lines add more exotic options. For example, you may find an occasional voyage across the Bering Sea to Japan and Asia. You can also create your own itinerary by taking an Alaska Marine Highway System ferry to ports of your choosing.

FERRY TRAVEL

The cruise-ship season is over by October, but for independent, off-season ferry travel November is the best month. After the stormy month of October, it's still relatively warm on the Inside Passage (temperatures will average about 40°F), and it's a good month for wildlife-watching. In particular, humpback whales are abundant off Sitka, and bald eagles congregate by the thousands near Haines.

> **TIP**
>
> Although most other kinds of travel are booked over the Internet nowadays, cruises are a different story. Your best bet is still to work with a travel agent who specializes in cruises. Agents with strong relationships with the lines have a much better chance of getting you the cabin you want, and possibly even extras.

CRUISE TOURS

Most cruise lines offer the option of independent, hosted, or fully escorted land tours before or after your cruise. Independent tours give you a preplanned itinerary with confirmed hotel and transportation arrangements, but you're free to follow your interests in each town. Hosted tours are similar, but tour-company representatives are available along the route for assistance. On fully escorted tours you travel with a group, led by a tour director. Activities are preplanned (and typically prepaid), so you have a good idea of how much your trip will cost (not counting meals and incidentals) before departure. Most lines offer cruise tour itineraries that include a ride aboard the Alaska Railroad.

Running between Anchorage, Denali National Park, and Fairbanks are Holland America Line's *McKinley Explorer*, Princess Tours' *Denali Express* and *McKinley Express,* and Royal Caribbean's *Wilderness Express,* which offer unobstructed views of the passing terrain and wildlife from private glass-domed railcars. Princess Cruises and Holland America Line have the most extensive Alaska cruise tours, owning and operating their own coaches, railcars, and lodges.

In addition to rail trips to Denali, Holland America offers tours into the Yukon, as well as river cruises on the Yukon River. Princess's cruise tours include trips to the Yukon and the Kenai Peninsula. Both lines offer land excursions across the Arctic Circle to Prudhoe Bay. Several cruise lines also offer pre- and postcruise tours of the Canadian Rockies. Of the traditional cruise-ship fleets, Carnival Cruise Lines, Norwegian Cruise Line and Disney Cruise Line do not currently offer cruise-tour packages in Alaska. Many cruise lines also offer pre- or postcruise hotel and sightseeing packages in Vancouver, Seattle, or Anchorage lasting one to three days.

SMALL SHIP LINES

Most small-ship lines offer hotel add-ons, but not land tours.

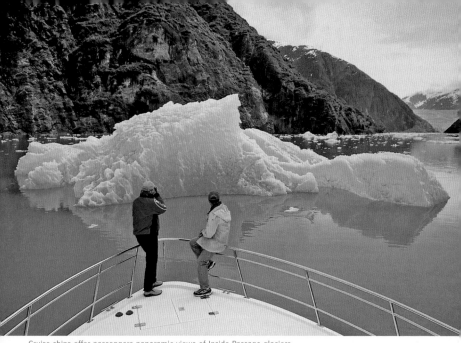
Cruise ships offer passengers panoramic views of Inside Passage glaciers.

DO-IT-YOURSELF LAND SEGMENTS

Independent travel by rental car or RV before or after a cruise is another option. Passengers generally begin or end their cruise in Anchorage, the most practical port city to use as a base for exploring Alaska. Almost any type of car or recreational vehicle can be rented here.

WHEN TO GO

Cruise season runs from mid-May to late September. The most popular sailing dates are from late June through August, when warm days are apt to be most plentiful. In spring, wildflowers are abundant, and you'll likely see more wildlife along the shore because the animals haven't yet migrated to higher elevations. May and June are traditionally drier than July and August. Alaska's early fall brings the splendor of autumn hues and the first snowfalls in the mountains. Animals return to low ground, and shorter days bring the possibility of seeing the northern lights. Daytime temperatures in May, June, and September are in the 50s and 60s. July and August averages are in the 60s and 70s, with occasional days in the 80s. Cruising in the low and shoulder seasons provides other advantages besides discounted fares: availability of ships and particular cabins is greater, and ports are almost completely free of tourists.

BOOKING YOUR CRUISE

As a rule, the majority of cruisers plan their trips four to six months ahead of time. It follows then, that a four- to six-month window should give you the pick of sailing dates, ships, itineraries, cabins, and flights to

Cabin Cruising

INSIDE CABINS

An inside cabin is just that: a stateroom that's inside the ship with no window. These are always the least expensive cabins and are ideal for passengers who would rather spend on excursions than on upgraded accommodations. Inside cabins are generally as spacious as outside cabins, and decor and amenities are similar. Many ships locate cabins accommodating three or more passengers on the inside. ■TIP➜ For passengers who want a very dark room for sleeping, an inside cabin is ideal.

OUTSIDE CABINS

Outside cabins have either a picture window or porthole. To give the illusion of more space, these cabins might rely on the generous use of mirrors. Outside cabins are the better choice for those prone to motion sickness. ■TIP➜ Check to make sure your view of the sea is not obstructed by a lifeboat. The ship's deck plan will help you figure it out.

BALCONY CABINS

A balcony—or veranda—cabin is an outside cabin with floor-to-ceiling glass doors that open onto a private deck. Balconies are sometimes cut out of the cabin's square footage (depending on the ship). ■TIP➜ If you have small children, a veranda cabin isn't the best choice. Accidents can happen, even on balconies with solid barriers beneath the railing.

SUITES

Suites are the most lavish accommodations. Although they're always larger than regular cabins, they don't always have separate rooms for sleeping. The most expansive (and expensive) have large living rooms and separate bedrooms and may also have huge private outdoor sundecks with hot tubs and dining areas.

the port city. If you're looking for a standard itinerary and aren't choosy about the vessel or dates, you could wait for a last-minute discount, but they are harder to find than in the past.

If particular shore excursions are important to you, consider booking them when you book your cruise to avoid disappointment later.

CRUISE COSTS

Average fares for Alaskan itineraries vary dramatically depending on when you sail, which ship and grade of cabin you choose, and when you book. Published rates are highest during June, July, and August; you'll pay less, and have more space on ship and ashore, if you sail in May or September.

Whenever you choose to sail, remember that the brochure price is the highest fare the line can charge for a given cruise. Most lines offer early-booking discounts. Although these vary tremendously, many lines will offer at least 10% off if you book ahead of time, usually by the end of January for a summer cruise. Sometimes you can book a discounted last-minute cruise if the ship hasn't filled all its cabins, but you won't get your pick of ships, cabins, or sailing dates. However, since most cruise

CLOSE UP

Before You Book

If you've decided to use a travel agent, ask yourself these 10 simple questions, and you'll be better prepared to help the agent do his or her job.

1. Who will be going on the cruise?

2. What can you afford to spend for the entire trip?

3. Where would you like to go?

4. How much vacation time do you have?

5. When can you get away?

6. What are your interests?

7. Do you prefer a casual or structured vacation?

8. What kind of accommodations do you want?

9. What are your dining preferences?

10. How will you get to the embarkation port?

lines will, if asked, refund the difference in fare if it drops after you've paid your deposit and before you make your final payment, there's little advantage in last-minute booking.

SOLO TRAVELERS

Single cabins for solo travelers are nonexistent on most ships; taking a double cabin can cost as much as twice the advertised per-person rates (which are based on two people sharing a room). Some cruise lines will find roommates of the same sex for singles so that each can travel at the regular per-person rate.

EXTRAS

Cruise fares typically include accommodation, onboard meals and snacks, and most onboard activities. Not normally included are airfare, shore excursions, tips, soft drinks, alcoholic drinks, or spa treatments. Port fees, fuel surcharges, and sales taxes are generally added to your fare at booking.

PLANNING

What to Wear: When preparing for your Alaska cruise, remember this first rule of Alaskan thumb: be an onion. Never leave the ship without dressing in layers. Your first layer should be thin and airy so that if it gets warm your skin can breathe. Every layer over that, however, should aim to keep you warm and dry. In Alaska it is quite common for a hot and sunny day to abruptly change. For onboard dress, follow your cruise line's suggestions regarding what to bring for the evening or two you might need to wear something formal to dinner.

What to Pack: Don't forget your valid passport; American and Canadian citizens are now required to provide proof of citizenship regardless of whether their Alaska cruise is crossing international boundaries. Although disposable and small digital cameras are very handy for candid shots, they are not much good for catching wildlife from afar. A good zoom lens can be heavy, but can make all the difference. Even if you have a quality camera, pack binoculars for everyone. Be sure to take bug spray during the summer months, as the mosquitoes are large, plentiful, and fierce.

TIP

Notify the cruise line of any dietary restrictions when booking your cruise, and follow up on the arrangements a couple of months before embarking.

3

Getting to the Port: Most cruise-ship passengers fly to their port of embarkation. If you book your cruise far enough in advance, you'll be given the opportunity to purchase an air-and-sea package, which can save you money on your flight. With this option a uniformed cruise-line agent will meet you at the airport to smooth your way to the pier. Without the package you can still access the cruise's transfer service, but it might cost more than a cab or shuttle.

Boarding: The lines at check-in can be long (up to an hour of wait time) if you are boarding a large cruise ship. You'll be issued a boarding card that doubles as your stateroom key and shipboard charge card. Either before you enter the check-in area or before proceeding to the ship, you and your hand luggage will pass through a security checkpoint. Once you're on board, you'll produce your boarding card once more before heading to your cabin. On a small-ship cruise, embarkation is much more relaxed and relatively line-free.

Restaurant Seating: Restaurant seating is a major consideration for most cruisers as they choose which line they'll travel with. Some cruise ships have traditional assigned dinner seatings, where you will choose between early or late seating and be assigned a table for the entire trip. Early seating is generally scheduled between 6 and 6:30 pm, while late seating can begin from 8:15 to 8:45 pm. Families with young children or older passengers often choose an early seating. Early diners are not encouraged to linger too long as the dining room needs to be prepared for the late seating, which is viewed by some passengers as more romantic and less rushed. Some lines offer open seating; you'll dine whenever you want within service hours and sit wherever you please. Still other cruise lines strike a balance of options with alternatives like à la carte restaurants and casual dinner menus in the buffet facilities.

Paying for Things on Board: Because cashless society prevails on cruise ships, during check-in an imprint is made of your credit card or you place a cash deposit for use against your onboard charges. Most onboard expenditures are charged to your shipboard account (via a swipe of your key card) with your signature as verification, with the exception of some casino gaming.

You'll get an itemized bill listing your purchases at the end of the voyage, and any discrepancies can be discussed at the purser's desk. To save time, check the balance of your shipboard account before the last day by requesting an interim printout of your bill from the purser to insure accuracy. On some ships you can even access your account on your stateroom television.

Will I Get Seasick? Many first-time passengers are anxious about whether they'll be stricken by seasickness, but there is no way to tell until you

ON-BOARD EXTRAS

As you budget for your trip, keep these likely additional costs in mind.

Cocktails: $5.75–$9

Wine by the glass: $6–$9

Beer: $5–$6

Bottled water: $2.50–$4

Specialty ice cream and coffee: $4–$6

Laundry: $1–$10 per piece (where self-launder facilities are unavailable)

Spa treatments: $100–$175

Salon services: $30–$100

Casino Gambling: 5 cents to $10 for slot machines; $5 and up for table games

Bingo: $5–$10 per card for multiple games in each session

actually sail. Modern vessels are equipped with stabilizers that eliminate much of the motion responsible for seasickness. On an Alaska cruise you will spend most of your time in calm, sheltered waters, so unless your cruise includes time out in the open sea (say, between San Francisco and Vancouver) you may not even feel the ship's movement—particularly if your ship is a megaliner. You may feel slightly more movement on a small ship, but not by much as these ships ply remote bays and coves that are even more sheltered than those traveled by regular cruise ships.

If you have a history of seasickness, don't book an inside cabin. For the terminally seasick, it will begin to resemble a moveable coffin in short order. If you do become seasick, you can use common drugs such as Dramamine and Bonine. Some people find anti-seasickness wristbands helpful; these apply gentle pressure to the wrist in lieu of drugs. Worn behind the ear, the Transderm Scop patch dispenses a continuous metered dose of medication, which is absorbed into the skin and enters the bloodstream. Apply the patch four hours before sailing and it will continue to be effective for three days.

KEEPING IN TOUCH

Rates for your in-room direct-dial phone vary from $5 to as much as $15 *per minute*; most passengers reserve it for emergency use only. Some cruise ships are wired to act as cell towers, so depending on your provider and roaming charges, you might be able to somewhat-affordably use your device throughout your trip uninterrupted (though we encourage you not to—you're on vacation!). In addition to the 75¢–$1 per minute Internet fee, you might also need to pay a one-time connection charge, and the connection might be maddeningly slow. For each port, we list a less-expensive Internet option or two.

OTHER CONSIDERATIONS

Children's programs: Virtually every line has children's programs and Disney Cruise Line's entry into Alaska gives parents a superior option; however, high-end lines generally only offer supervised programs when enough children are aboard to warrant them or during school holidays. Small ships are less likely to offer kids' programs; however, some do schedule a few family-friendly sailings. Check whether the available shore excursions include activities that will appeal to kids.

Dining: Some cruise lines offer traditional assigned dining, meaning you will dine each evening at the same table with the same companions. Others offer open seating, allowing you to dine whenever and with whomever you like; still others offer a choice between the two systems. Most traditional cruise ships have at least one restaurant in addition to the main dining room; some have more. Most ships offer vegetarian and heart-healthy or low-carb options.

Ports of call: You'll want to know where and when you will be stopping. Will there be enough time in port to do what you want to do there? Will it be the right time of day for your chosen activity? Will you tender to shore by boat or moor up at the dock? This is important, as tendering can take some time away from your port visit.

Onboard activities: Your cruise will likely include one or two full days at sea. Think about how you'd like to fill the time. Do you want great workout facilities or a spa? What about educational opportunities or shopping? If seeing Alaska itself is your priority, choose a ship with lots of outdoor *and* indoor viewing space.

ABOUT THE SHIPS

CRUISE SHIPS

Large cruise lines account for the majority of passengers sailing to Alaska. These typically have large cruise ships in their fleets with plentiful deck space and, often, a promenade deck that allows you to stroll the ship's perimeter. In the newest vessels, traditional meets trendy with resort-style innovations; however, they still feature cruise-ship classics, like afternoon tea and complimentary room service. The smallest cruise ships carry as few as 400 passengers, while the biggest can accommodate between 1,500 and 3,000 passengers—enough people to outnumber the residents of many Alaskan port towns. Large ships are a good choice if you're looking for nonstop activity and lots of options; they're especially appealing for groups and families with older kids. If you prefer a gentler pace and a chance to get to know your shipmates, try a smaller ship.

SMALL SHIPS

Compact expedition-type vessels bring you right up to the shoreline to skirt the face of a glacier and pull through narrow channels where big ships don't fit. These cruises focus on Alaska, and you'll see more wildlife and call into smaller ports, as well as some of the better-known towns. Enrichment talks—conducted by naturalists, native Alaskans, and other experts in the state's natural history and native cultures—are

CRUISE SHIPS AT A GLANCE

Cruise Lines/Ships	Cabins	Double Occupancy	Decks	Restaurants	In-Cabin VCR/DVD Players	Wi-Fi	Pools	Hot Tubs	Bars	Cinema	Library	Showrooms	Children's Program	Dance Clubs
American Cruise Line														
American Star Class	48	100	4	1	DVD	no	no	no	no	no	yes	no	no	no
American Safari Line														
Safari Explorer	18	36	3	1	DVD	no	no	1	1	no	no	no	no	no
Safari Quest	11	21	4	1	DVD	no	no	1	1	no	yes	no	no	no
Safari Spirit	6	12	4	1	DVD	no	no	1	1	no	no	no	no	no
Carnival Cruise Lines														
Carnival Spirit	1023	2124	12	3	VCR (some)	yes	3	4	7	no	yes	1	ages 2-17	2
Celebrity Cruises														
Celebrity Infinity	1023	2046	11	3	VCR (some) DVD (some)	yes	3	6	7	yes	yes	1	ages 3-17	1
Celebrity Millennium	1079	2158	11	3	VCR (some) DVD (some)	yes	3	6	7	yes	yes	1	ages 3-17	1
Celebrity Century	875	1750	10	3	VCR (some) DVD (some)	yes	2	5	7	yes	yes	1	ages 3-17	1
Disney Cruise Line														
Disney Wonder	877	1754	11	5	DVD (some)	yes	3	4	6	yes	no	2	ages 3-17	2
Holland America Line														
Amsterdam	690	1380	9	3	DVD	yes	2	2	6	yes	yes	1	ages 3-17	1
Zuiderdam/Oosterdam/Westerdam	958	1916	11	3	DVD	yes	2	5	9	yes	yes	1	ages 3-17	2
Volendam/Zaandam	716	1432	10	3	DVD	yes	2	2	6	yes	yes	1	ages 3-17	1
Statendam	675	1350	10	3	DVD	yes	2	2	9	yes	yes	1	ages 3-17	1
Inner Seas Discoveries														
Wilderness Adventurer	30	60	3	1	no	no	no	no	1	1	no	no	no	no
Wilderness Discoverer	38	76	3	1	no	no	no	no	2	1	no	no	no	no

Lindblad Expeditions

National Geographic Sea Bird/Sea Lion	31	62	3	1	no	yes	no	no	1	no	yes	no	no	no
Norwegian Cruise Line														
Norwegian Pearl	1197	2394	15	10	DVD (some)	yes	2	6	9	yes	yes	1	ages 2-17	2
Norwegian Jewel	1188	2376	15	10	DVD (some)	yes	2	6	9	yes	yes	1	ages 2-17	2
Oceania Cruises														
Regatta	342	684	9	2	DVD (some)	yes	1	3	4	no	1	1	no	1
Princess Cruises														
Sea Princess	975	1950	10	3	DVD (some)	yes	3	5	7	no	yes	2	ages 3-17	1
Coral/Island Princess	985	1970	11	5	DVD (some)	yes	3	5	7	no	yes	2	ages 3-17	2
Diamond/Sapphire Princess	1337	2670	13	8	DVD (some)	yes	4	8	11	no	yes	2	ages 3-17	2
Star/Golden Princess	1300	2600	14	6	DVD (some)	yes	4	9	9	no	yes	2	ages 3-17	2
Regent Seven Seas Cruises														
Seven Seas Navigator	245	490	8	3	DVD	yes	1	1	4	no	yes	1	ages 5-17	1
Royal Caribbean Intl														
Radiance of the Seas	1071	2139	12	5	DVD (some)	yes	2	3	11	yes	yes	1	ages 3-17	1
Rhapsody of the Seas	999	1998	11	2	DVD (some)	yes	2	6	6	no	yes	1	ages 3-17	1
Silversea Cruises														
Silver Shadow	191	382	7	3	DVD	yes	1	2	3	no	yes	1	no	1

All large ships on this list have in-cabin safes, in-cabin refrigerators in most categories, laundry service, hair salons, gyms and fitness classes, spas, saunas, steam rooms or thermal suites (for which there is a charge), casinos, dance clubs, and showrooms; many ships have dry-cleaning service.

LARGE CRUISE LINES

SHIP	EMBARKATION PORT	DURATION IN NIGHTS	ITINERARY AND PORTS OF CALL
Carnival Cruise Lines			
Carnival Spirit	Seattle	7	Round-trip: Juneau, Skagway, Ketchikan, Victoria, BC, Sawyer Glacier
Celebrity Cruises			
Celebrity Infinity	Seattle	7	Round-trip: Ketchikan, Juneau, Skagway, Victoria, BC, Sawyer Glacier
Celebrity Century	Vancouver	7	Round-trip: Ketchikan, Juneau, Icy Strait Point, Hubbard Glacier
Celebrity Millennium	Vancouver	7	Northbound: Skagway, Juneau, Ketchikan, Icy Strait Point, Hubbard Glacier
	Seward	7	Southbound: Skagway, Juneau, Ketchikan, Icy Strait Point, Hubbard Glacier
Disney Cruise Line			
Disney Wonder	Seattle	7	Round-trip: Ketchikan, Juneau, Skagway, Sawyer Glacier, Victoria, BC
Holland America Line			
Amsterdam	Seattle	14	Round-trip: Ketchikan, Anchorage, Kodiak, Juneau, Icy Strait Point, Victoria, BC, Hubbard Glacier, Sawyer Glacier
Oosterdam	Seattle	7	Round-trip: Juneau, Sitka, Ketchikan, Victoria, BC, Sawyer Glacier
Statendam	Vancouver	7	Northbound: Skagway, Juneau, Ketchikan, Glacier Bay
	Seward	7	Southbound: Haines, Juneau, Ketchikan, Glacier Bay
Volendam	Vancouver	7	Round-trip: Skagway, Juneau, Ketchikan, Sawyer Glacier, Glacier Bay
Westerdam	Seattle	7	Round-trip: Juneau, Sitka, Ketchikan, Victoria, BC, Hubbard Glacier
Zaandam	Vancouver	7	Northbound: Juneau, Skagway, Ketchikan, Glacier Bay
	Seward	7	Southbound: Juneau, Haines, Ketchikan, Glacier Bay
Zuiderdam	Vancouver	7	Round-trip: Skagway, Juneau, Ketchikan, Sawyer Glacier, Glacier Bay
Norwegian Cruise Line			
Norwegian Pearl	Seattle	7	Round-trip: Juneau, Skagway, Ketchikan, Victoria, BC, Glacier Bay
Norwegian Jewel	Seattle	7	Round-trip: Juneau, Skagway, Ketchikan, Victoria, BC, Sawyer Glacier
Princess Cruises			
Coral Princess	Vancouver	7	Northbound: Ketchikan, Juneau, Skagway, Glacier Bay, College Fjord
	Whittier	7	Southbound: Ketchikan, Juneau, Skagway, Glacier Bay, Hubbard Glacier
Diamond Princess	Vancouver	7	Northbound: Ketchikan, Juneau, Skagway, Glacier Bay, College Fjord
	Whittier	7	Southbound: Ketchikan, Juneau, Skagway, Glacier Bay, Hubbard Glacier
Golden Princess	Seattle	7	Round-trip: Juneau, Skagway, Ketchikan, Victoria, BC, Glacier Bay or Sawyer Glacier

Ship	Port	Nights	Itinerary
Island Princess	Vancouver	7	Northbound: Ketchikan, Juneau, Skagway, Glacier Bay, College Fjord
	Whittier	7	Southbound: Ketchikan, Juneau, Skagway, Glacier Bay, Hubbard Glacier
Sapphire Princess	Vancouver	7	Northbound: Juneau, Skagway, Ketchikan, Glacier Bay, College Fjord
	Whittier	7	Southbound: Juneau, Skagway, Ketchikan, Glacier Bay, Hubbard Glacier
Star Princess	Seattle	7	Round-trip: Juneau, Skagway, Ketchikan, Victoria, BC, Sawyer Glacier
Sea Princess	San Francisco	10	Round-trip: either Juneau, Ketchikan, Victoria, BC, either Skagway or Haines, either Sawyer Glacier or Glacier Bay
Regent Seven Seas Cruises			
Seven Seas Navigator	Vancouver	7	Northbound: Sitka, Juneau, Skagway, Ketchikan, Hubbard Glacier, Sawyer Glacier
	Seward	7	Southbound: Sitka, Juneau, Skagway, Ketchikan, Hubbard Glacier, Sawyer Glacier
	San Francisco	12	Northbound: Astoria OR, Ketchikan, Juneau, Skagway, Sitka, Hubbard Glacier, Victoria BC, Vancouver BC
	Vancouver	12	Southbound: Sitka, Icy Strait Point, Ketchikan, Juneau, Skagway, Hubbard Glacier, Victoria BC, Astoria, OR, San Francisco, CA
Royal Caribbean International			
Radiance of the Seas	Vancouver	7	Northbound: Ketchikan, Juneau, Skagway, Icy Strait Point, Hubbard Glacier
	Seward	7	Southbound: Ketchikan, Juneau, Skagway, Icy Strait Point, Hubbard Glacier
Rhapsody of the Seas	Seattle	7	Round-trip: Juneau, Skagway, Victoria BC, Sawyer Glacier
Silversea Cruises			
Silver Shadow	Vancouver	10	Round-trip: Skagway, Juneau, Sitka, Ketchikan, Sawyer Glacier, Prince Rupert, BC, Victoria, BC
	Vancouver	11	Round-trip: Skagway, Juneau, Sitka, Ketchikan, Wrangell, Sawyer Glacier, Prince Rupert, BC, Victoria, BC
	Vancouver	7	Northbound: Ketchikan, Juneau, Skagway, Sitka, Sawyer Glacier, Hubbard Glacier
	Seward	7	Southbound: Ketchikan, Juneau, Skagway, Sitka, Sawyer Glacier, Hubbard Glacier

SMALL CRUISE-SHIP LINES

SHIP	EMBARKATION PORT	DURATION IN NIGHTS	ITINERARY AND PORTS OF CALL
American Cruise Lines			
American Spirit or American Star	Juneau	7	Round-trip: Skagway, Glacier Bay, Icy Strait Point, Sitka, Petersburg, Dawes Glacier
	Seattle	11	Northbound: Anacortes, WA, Friday Harbor, WA, Ketchikan, Wrangell, Petersburg, Tracy Arm, Angoon, Icy Strait Point, Juneau
	Juneau	11	Southbound: Ketchikan, Wrangell, Petersburg, Tracy Arm, Angoon, Icy Strait Point, Anacortes, WA, Friday Harbor, WA, Seattle
American Safari Line			
Safari Explorer, Safari Quest, Safari Spirit	Juneau	7	Round-trip: Glacier Bay (2 or 3 days), Icy Strait, Admiralty Island, Endicott Arm
	Seattle	14	Northbound: Prince Rupert, BC or Misty Fjords, Ketchikan, Meyer's Chuck, Petersburg, Glacier Bay, Juneau
	Juneau	14	Southbound: Glacier Bay, Petersburg, Wrangell, Ketchikan, Prince Rupert, BC or Misty Fjords, Seattle
InnerSea Discoveries			
Wilderness Adventurer, Wilderness Discoverer	Ketchikan	7	Northbound: Klawock Native Village, Baranof Island, Frederick Sound, Dawes Glacier, Juneau
	Juneau	7	Southbound: Frederick Sound, Baird Glacier, Wrangell, Misty Fjords, Ketchikan
	Seattle	14	Northbound: San Juan Islands, Misty Fjords, Ketchikan, Klawock Native Village, Baranof Island, Frederick Sound, Dawes Glacier, Juneau
	Juneau	14	Southbound: Frederick Sound, Baird Glacier, Wrangell, Misty Fjords, Ketchikan, San Juan Islands, Seattle
Lindblad Expeditions			
National Geographic Sea Bird and Sea Lion	Sitka	7	Northbound: Point Adolphus, Glacier Bay, Petersburg, Frederick Sound, Sawyer Glacier, Juneau
	Juneau	7	Southbound: Sawyer Glacier, Petersburg, Frederick Sound, Glacier Bay, Point Adolphus, Sitka
	Seattle	11	Northbound: San Juan Islands, Alert Bay, Misty Fjords, Petersburg, Glacier Bay, Point Adolphus, Sitka
	Sitka	11	Southbound: Point Adolphus, Glacier Bay, Juneau, Petersburg, Misty Fjords, Alert Bay, San Juan Islands, Seattle

SMALL SHIP CRUISES

We cover the most recognized small-ship lines sailing in Alaska, but that is by no means exhaustive. Other great small ships sailing the Inside Passage include Fantasy Cruises' *Island Spirit* (⊕ *www.smallalaskaship.com*), owned and operated by Captain Jeff Behrens. Captain Behrens is committed to rapport-building with and respect for the area's smallest communities; as a result, 32-passenger *Island Spirit* can make off-the-beaten-path port calls like Tenakee Springs (⊕ *www.tenakeespringsak.com*), Five Finger Lighthouse (⊕ *www.5fingerlighthouse.com*), and Baranof Warm Springs, in addition to scenic anchorages like Ford's Terror that only small ships can access. Charters and photography-focused cruises are also available.

Alaska Sea Adventures (⊕ *www.yachtalaska.com*) focuses on charters and single-theme cruises on wildlife photography, birding, research, archaeology, whale migration, or fish spawning. Its two ships, *Northern Song* and *Alaska Legend*, can accommodate up to 8 passengers each.

the norm. Cabins on expedition ships can be tiny, usually with no phone or TV, and bathrooms are often no bigger than cubbyholes. The dining room and lounge are usually the only public areas on these vessels; however, some are luxurious with cushy cabins, comfy lounges and libraries, and hot tubs. You won't find much nightlife aboard, but what you trade for space and onboard diversions is a unique and unforgettable glimpse of Alaska.

Many small ships are based in Juneau or another Alaska port and sail entirely within Alaska. Twice annually, some offer an Inside Passage cruise as the ships reposition to and from their winter homes elsewhere.

Small-ship cruising can be pricey, as fares tend to be inclusive (except for airfare), but with few onboard charges, and, given the size of ship and style of cruise, fewer opportunities to spend on board.

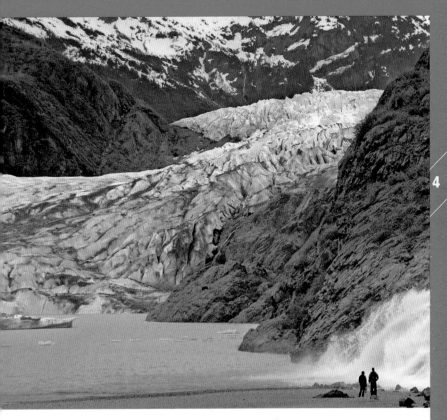

Southeast Alaska

INCLUDING KETCHIKAN, JUNEAU, HAINES, SITKA, AND SKAGWAY

WORD OF MOUTH

"We hiked to the tongue of the Mendenhall Glacier to find this roaring waterfall crashing into the bay. It gave us a perspective on man's insignificance next to Mother Nature."

—Chris Marlow, Photo Contest Winner

WELCOME TO SOUTHEAST ALASKA

TOP REASONS TO GO

★ **Native art and culture:** Ancestral home of the Tlingit, Haida, and Tsimshian, Southeast is dedicated to preserving native heritage. Native crafts include totem poles and masks.

★ **Rivers of ice:** Visitors relish the opportunity to walk on Southeast's accessible glaciers or to admire them on flightseeing or kayak trips.

★ **Tongass National Forest:** America's largest national forest is home to bears, bald eagles, Sitka black-tailed deer, wolves, and marine mammals.

★ **Fishing nirvana:** Southeast is an angler's paradise. The region's healthy populations of salmon and halibut—as well as the wealth of charter boats and fishing lodges—make this a premier fishing destination.

★ **Taking the ferry:** The Alaska Marine Highway is the primary means of transportation here. It's a low-cost, high-adventure alternative to cruising, and an easy way to spend time talking to Alaskans.

1 Ketchikan and Vicinity. The self-proclaimed "Salmon Capital of the World," Ketchikan is the doorway to Southeast. Be sure to check out the area's charter-fishing opportunities and wealth of local art. Ketchikan is a jumping-off point for Misty Fiords National Monument and visits to the Indian community of Metlakatla.

2 Wrangell and Petersburg. These towns provide access to the magnificent Stikine River. Wrangell, which welcomes some of the smaller cruise ships, is the primary hub for those who want to travel to the Anan Bear & Wildlife Observatory to see both brown and black bears fishing for salmon. Petersburg has a vibrant fishing community and stellar access to fishing, whale watching, and hiking.

3 Sitka. With its mixed history of Tlingit, Russian, and American rule, Sitka is home to a lively community, an excellent park system (including Sitka National Historical Park), and outdoor activities.

It's a must-see for anyone traveling in Southeast and a must-paddle for kayakers of all experience levels.

4 Juneau and Vicinity. Cruise passengers flock by the hundreds of thousands to take in the state capital's historic charm, artsy community, and natural beauty, including world-famous Mendenhall Glacier. But with a number of hotels and B&Bs, Juneau also welcomes independent travelers. The city is also the access point for surrounding attractions, including Admiralty Island National Monument, home to Southeast's largest population of brown bears.

5 Glacier Bay National Park and Preserve. Southeast's signature attraction, Glacier Bay is home to the continent's largest collection of tidewater glaciers, which make for incredible viewing. The park's remote, undeveloped location—Gustavus, the closest town, isn't really a town at all—ensures that travelers in search of quiet repose will not be disappointed.

GETTING ORIENTED

As remote as it is, Southeast Alaska shares a few traits with heavily populated regions. It has skyscrapers (the towering peaks of the Coast Range), traffic jams (try to swim through a salmon creek in midsummer), and sprawl (the rain forests cover hundreds of thousands of acres). The area's settlements offer plenty of attractions, from Skagway's flashy gold-rush delights to Glacier Bay's isolated fjords.

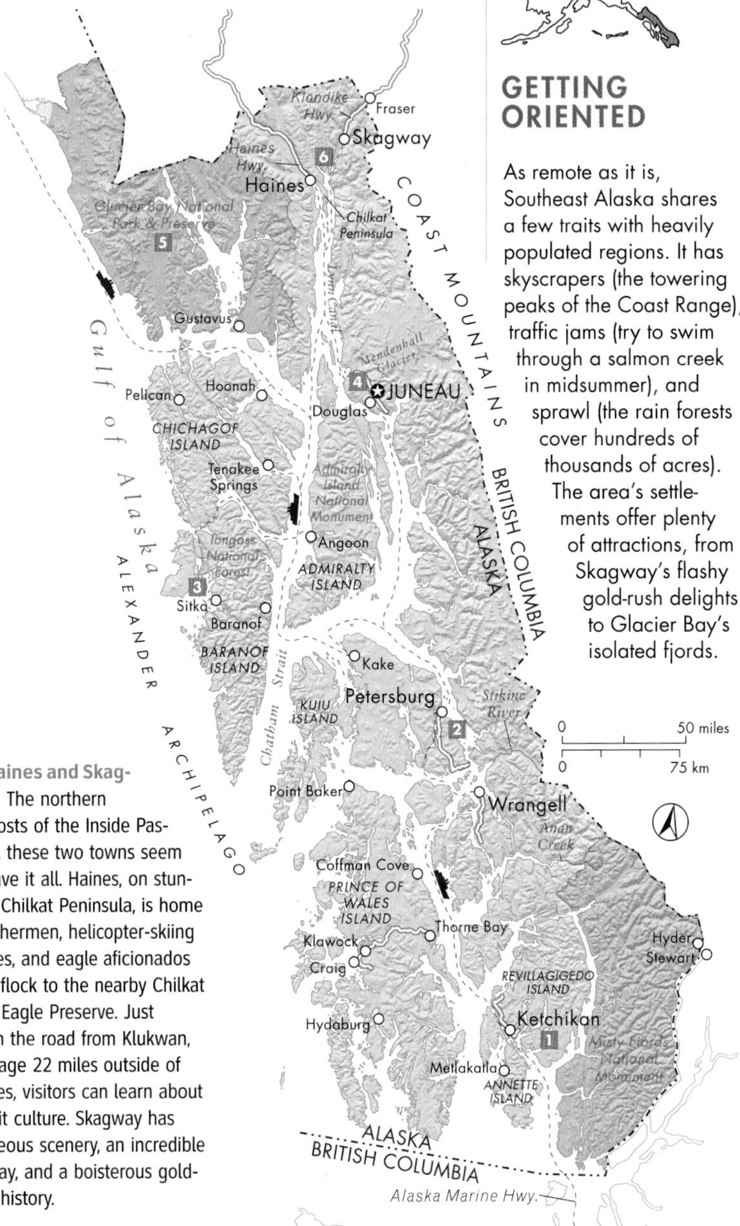

4

6 Haines and Skagway. The northern outposts of the Inside Passage, these two towns seem to have it all. Haines, on stunning Chilkat Peninsula, is home to fishermen, helicopter-skiing guides, and eagle aficionados who flock to the nearby Chilkat Bald Eagle Preserve. Just down the road from Klukwan, a village 22 miles outside of Haines, visitors can learn about Tlingit culture. Skagway has gorgeous scenery, an incredible railway, and a boisterous gold-rush history.

0 50 miles

0 75 km

Updated by
Jenna Schnuer

Southeast Alaska stretches down from the rest of the state like the tail of a kite. It is a world of soaring glaciers, steep-shouldered islands, cliff-rimmed fjords, and snowcapped peaks. Glacier Bay National Park and Preserve, one of the region's most prized attractions, is home to the largest concentration of coastal glaciers on earth.

Lush stands of spruce, hemlock, and cedar blanket thousands of islands. The region's myriad bays, coves, lakes, and swift, icy rivers provide some of the continent's best fishing grounds. Many of Southeast Alaska's wildest and most pristine landscapes are within Tongass National Forest, comprised of nearly 17 million acres—almost three-quarters of the Panhandle's land.

Southeast lacks only one thing: connecting roads. The lack of pavement between the area's communities presents obvious challenges to four-wheeled transport. The isolation and the wet weather keep people from moving in; otherwise Southeast Alaska would probably be as densely populated as Seattle. To help remedy the transportation question, Alaskans created the Alaska Marine Highway System, a network of passenger and vehicle ferries, some of which have staterooms, observation decks, video theaters, arcades, cafeterias, cocktail lounges, and heated, glass-enclosed solariums.

Southeast's natural beauty and abundance of wildlife have made it one of the world's fastest-growing cruise destinations. About 25 big cruise ships ply the Inside Passage—once the traditional route to the Klondike goldfields and today the centerpiece of many Alaska cruises—during the height of summer. A number of smaller ships—some locally owned—also cruise through. Regular air service to Southeast is available from the Lower 48 states and other parts of Alaska.

Three groups of Native peoples inhabit Southeast coastal region: the Tlingit (*klink*-it), Haida, and Tsimshian (*sim*-shee-ann). Because their cultures were once in danger of being lost, there's an ever-growing focus in Southeast on preserving Native traditions and teaching visitors about their history. Efforts are underway in many towns to teach the often tricky-to-master Native languages in schools and through other programs. Visitors to Southeast benefit from these programs, since local teens often work as guides at cultural institutions. The Tlingit, Haida, and Tsimshian, like their coastal neighbors in British Columbia, have rich traditions of totemic art, including carved poles, masks, baskets, and ceremonial objects. At villages like Klukwan, outside of Haines, there's been a push to help residents learn these art forms and keep them alive for generations to come.

Residents—some from other states, some who can trace their ancestors back to the gold-rush days, and some whose ancestors came over the Bering Land Bridge from Asia thousands of years ago—are an adventurous bunch. The rough-and-tumble spirit of Southeast often combines with a worldly sophistication: those who fish for a living might also be artists, Forest Service workers may run a bed-and-breakfast on the side, and homemakers may be native dance performers.

Southeast Panhandle stretches some 500 mi from Yakutat at its northernmost point to Ketchikan and Metlakatla at its southern end. At its widest point, the region measures only 140 mi, and in the upper Panhandle just south of Yakutat, at 30 mi across, it's downright skinny by Alaska standards. Most of the Panhandle consists of a sliver of mainland buffered on the west by islands and on the east by the imposing peaks of the Coast Mountains.

Those numerous coastal islands—more than 1,000 throughout the Inside Passage—collectively constitute the Alexander Archipelago. Most of them present mountainous terrain with lush covers of timber, though large clear-cuts are also common. Most communities are on islands rather than on the mainland. The principal exceptions are Juneau, Haines, and Skagway, plus the hamlets of Gustavus and Hyder. Island outposts include Ketchikan, Wrangell, Petersburg, Sitka, and the villages of Craig, Pelican, Metlakatla, Kake, Angoon, and Hoonah. Bordering Alaska just east of the Panhandle lies the Canadian province of British Columbia.

PLANNING

WHEN TO GO

The best time to visit is from May through September, when weather is mildest, rain is less frequent, daylight hours are longest, wildlife is most abundant, and festivals and visitor-oriented activities are in full swing. But remember: Southeast sits in a rain forest, so rain can rule the day. There's a reason why XtraTuf waterproof boots are nicknamed "Southeast sneakers." Summertime high temperatures hover around the low to mid-60s, with far warmer days interspersed throughout. Shoulder-season temperatures are cooler, and the region is less crowded. Bring rain gear, layered clothing, sturdy footwear, a hat, and binoculars.

Allow yourself at least a week here. Plenty of adventures await ambitious independent travelers who plan ahead and ride state ferries.

If strolling through downtown shopping districts and museum-hopping is your idea of a perfect afternoon, journey to Ketchikan, Haines, Skagway, Sitka, or Petersburg. For a wilderness experience in a peaceful, remote location, consider booking a multiple-night stay at one of Southeast's remote fly-in lodges.

GETTING HERE AND AROUND

AIR TRAVEL

Southeast Alaska is best explored by ship or plane. **Alaska Airlines** (☎ 800/252–7522 ⊕ www.alaskaair.com) operates several flights daily from Seattle and other Pacific Coast and Southwestern cities to Ketchikan, Wrangell, Petersburg, Sitka, Glacier Bay, and Juneau. The carrier also connects Juneau to the northern Alaska cities of Yakutat, Cordova, Anchorage, Fairbanks, Nome, Kotzebue, and Prudhoe Bay. Unless your destination is Haines, Skagway, or Hyder, forget about driving to Southeast. Cars don't do much for travelers, as roads typically run just a few miles out from towns and villages, then dead-end. Many people elect to transport their vehicles (and themselves) via the ferries of the Alaska Marine Highway System. Serious cyclists bring their bikes along. Visitor information centers are generally open mid-May through August, daily 8 to 5, with additional hours when cruise ships are in port; between September and mid-May they're typically open weekdays 8 to 5.

FLIGHTSEEING

There's no better way to view Southeast's twisting channels, towering mountains, and gleaming glaciers than from one of the region's many small-aircraft flights.

At least four services offer daily flights between Southeast's larger towns—Juneau, Haines, Skagway, Ketchikan, Sitka, Petersburg, and Wrangell—in addition to the bevy of helicopter flightseeing services that specialize in short, scenic flights. Tops among the fixed-wing carriers are **Air Excursions** (☎ 800/354–2479 ⊕ www.airexcursions.com) and **Wings of Alaska** (☎ 907/789–0790 ⊕ www.wingsofalaska.com), both of which offer connecting flights and scenic air tours of Southeast landmarks.

Flying between destinations in Southeast—while significantly more expensive—is an experience you won't forget. If your itinerary includes an extra day or two in Southeast (particularly in Juneau), consider spending a day flying to and from a neighboring community. Round-trip tickets from Juneau to Skagway, for instance, start at around $250, as compared to approximately $170 for a one-hour flightseeing trip in and around Juneau.

A host of floatplane services offer access to remote cabins and remote freshwater fishing destinations. Check out **Southeast Aviation** (☎ 888/359–6478 ⊕ www.flymisty.com) for flight details.

CRUISE AND FERRY TRAVEL

Southeast Alaska includes a number of popular ports of call for cruise ships (⇨ *Chapter 3, Choosing Your Cruise*). For those looking to avoid cruise travel or for more flexibility, the **Alaska Marine Highway** (☎ 907/465–3941 or 800/642–0066 ⊕ www.ferryalaska.com) allows you to

BEST BETS FOR DIFFERENT TRAVELERS

For travelers who are also taking a cruise:

■ Get up close and personal with the sea life in Ketchikan with Snorkel Alaska

■ Kayak across Mendenhall Lake at the beginning or end of your cruise

For those who are traveling in a family group with children:

■ Take the tram up Mt. Roberts in Juneau

■ Explore Skagway's Klondike Gold Rush National Historical Park

■ Dog sled on Denver Glacier, outside Skagway, or Juneau's Mendenhall Glacier

For travelers interested in luxury over rustic, but who still want an authentic Alaska experience:

■ Stay in McFarland's Floatel: all the seclusion of a beachfront cabin, plus the security of a main resort building floating right in the bay

■ Fly out to Waterfall Resort, out of Ketchikan, one of the most luxurious remote fishing lodges in the state

For those who want to see the wildlife up close in their natural habitat:

■ Visit Anan Wildlife Observatory, which many argue is the best bear-viewing spot in the state—in terms of both proximity and quantity

4

construct an itinerary that is all your own; it's quite popular with budget-conscious, adventurous visitors. Ferry ports of call and landings in Southeast include Yakutat, Skagway, Haines, Pelican, Gustavus, Juneau, Hoonah, Tenakee, Angoon, Sitka, Kake, Petersburg, Wrangell, Ketchikan, and Metakatla.

HEALTH AND SAFETY

Southeast is, as we've mentioned, wet. Make sure you bring raingear. No sense catching cold on vacation. New to catching seafood yourself? Consider hiring a guide to help you find the safest spots—Alaska's waters are powerful. Also, don't rent a boat and go out solo—even a skiff—if you don't have boating experience. Shifts in weather, tides, and lots of other factors can turn a pleasant kayaking experience into something far less fun.

MONEY MATTERS

While most towns—especially the cruise ship-heavy towns—are loaded with ATMS, it doesn't hurt to have some cash in your wallet, especially if you're visiting some of the smaller towns of Prince of Wales Island.

RESTAURANTS

From scallops to king salmon, fresh seafood dominates menus in Southeast. Juneau, Sitka, and Ketchikan all have a variety of ethnic eateries, along with notable gourmet restaurants. Many towns also have good greasy spoons or roadhouses where you can get a serving of local gossip along with your breakfast or slice of pie.

HOTELS

Lodging choices along the Inside Passage range from remote Forest Service cabins to top-end hotels. In general, the latter are a pricey option, but rates drop in the off-season (mid-September to mid-May).

Budget travelers will find hostels in many of the larger towns. Fine hotels are found in Ketchikan and Juneau, and luxurious fishing lodges attract anglers on Prince of Wales Island and in other places in Southeast. Bed-and-breakfasts are also popular in the Inside Passage.

CABINS

U.S. Forest Service Cabins are scattered throughout Tongass National Forest. With more than 150 rustic sites on offer, the cabins make for a charming and cheap escape (up to $45 per night per cabin). ■ TIP→ Almost all must be reserved in advance, either in person, by mail, or online; in some cases nominal service fees may be charged for cancellations. Popular with local Alaskans and return visitors, many cabins book up long before summer arrives. However, if you haven't arranged a cabin before hitting town, check at the local Forest Service office; there's always a good chance of finding something, although it may not be in one of the most popular locations. Still, every view in Alaska is great. Most are reached by floatplane or boat, but some are accessible by road. They offer bunks for six to eight occupants, tables, stoves, and outdoor privies—but no electricity or running water. You provide your own sleeping bag, food, and cooking utensils. Bedside reading in most cabins includes a diary kept by visitors—add your own adventure. ☎ *877/444–6777 reservations ⊕ www.fs.fed.us/recreation/reservations/.*

But the U.S. Forest Service isn't the only cabin rental game in Southeast. **Alaska State Parks** has a small number of cabins near Ketchikan and Juneau. Again, reservations can be made up to six months in advance. Cabins vary in size, with sleeping capacity ranging from 3 to 10 people. For more information or to reserve a cabin online, contact the Department of Natural Resources Public Information Center in Anchorage. ☎ *907/269–8400 ⊕ www.dnr.state.ak.us/parks/cabins/index.htm.*

EQUIPMENT RENTAL

A few local outfitters rent cabin supplies, including cooking utensils, to travelers. Annahootz Alaskan Adventures in Sitka can outfit you with cabin supplies from lighters and matches to pots and pans. Alaska Wilderness Outfitting in Ketchikan rents cabin supplies like cooking utensils, Coleman stoves, coolers, knives, and hot pads.

Contacts Annahootz Alaskan Adventures (*Sitka* ☎ *907/747–2608 ⊕ www. annahootz.com/gear.php*). **Alaska Wilderness Outfitting** (*Ketchikan* ☎ *907/225–7335 ⊕ www.latitude56.com*).

DINING AND LODGING PRICE CATEGORIES				
	¢	$	$$	$$$	$$$$
Restaurants	under $10	$10–$15	$15–$20	$20–$25	over $25
Hotels	under $75	$75–$125	$125–$175	$175–$225	over $225

Restaurant prices are per person for a main course at dinner. Hotel prices are for two people in a standard double room in high season.

KETCHIKAN

Ketchikan is famous for its colorful totem poles, rainy skies, steep–as–San Francisco streets, and lush island setting. Some 13,000 people call the town home, and, in summer cruise ships crowd the shoreline, floatplanes depart noisily for Misty Fiords National Monument, and salmon-laden commercial fishing boats motor through Tongass Narrows. In the last decade Ketchikan's rowdy, blue-collar heritage of logging and fishing has been softened by the loss of many timber-industry jobs and the dramatic rise of cruise-ship tourism. With some effort, though, visitors can still glimpse the rugged frontier spirit that once permeated this hardscrabble cannery town. Art lovers should beeline for this town. Ketchikan's arts community is very active. Travelers in search of the perfect piece of Alaska art will find an incredible range of pieces to choose from.

The town is at the foot of 3,000-foot Deer Mountain, near the southeast corner of Revillagigedo (locals shorten it to Revilla) Island. Prior to the arrival of white miners and fishermen in 1885, the Tlingit used the site at the mouth of Ketchikan Creek as a summer fish camp. Gold discoveries just before the turn of the 20th century brought more immigrants, and valuable timber and commercial fishing resources spurred new industries. By the 1930s the town bragged that it was the "salmon-canning capital of the world." You will still find some of Southeast's best salmon fishing around here.

This town is the first bite of Alaska that many travelers taste. Despite its imposing backdrop, hillside homes, and many staircases, Ketchikan is relatively easy to walk through. Favorite downtown stops include the Spruce Mill Development shops and Creek Street. A bit farther away you'll find the Totem Heritage Center and Deer Mountain Hatchery. Out of town (but included on most bus tours) are two longtime favorites: Totem Bight State Historical Park and Saxman Totem Pole Park.

GETTING HERE AND AROUND

Ketchikan is a regular stop on cruise-ship and ferry routes, but Alaska Airlines also flies in from Seattle and other Pacific Northwest locations. If you're traveling out of the town on the highway in either direction, you won't go far before you run out of road. The North Tongass Highway ends about 18 mi from downtown, at Settler's Cove Campground. The South Tongass Highway terminates at a power plant about 13 mi from town. Side roads soon end at campgrounds and at trailheads, viewing points, lakes, boat-launching ramps, and private property.

Ketchikan has three bus routes that serve the city and outlying areas. In addition, during the cruise-ship season (May to September) there is a local shuttle bus operating a circular route from Berth 4 and including stops at Eagle Park, Southeast Discovery Center, Creek Street, Totem Heritage Center, Deer Mountain Tribal Hatchery, and Ketchikan Historic Museum. The shuttle service is free.

Arriving at the airport, visitors can take the local Gateway Borough Ferry ($5). This is a vehicle and walk-on ferry that crosses the Tongass Passage, taking about 10 minutes. Ketchikan also has a water taxi that runs from the airport and will drop off visitors at the various marinas or piers along the water-front (cost varies).

> ## WET YET WONDERFUL
>
> Southeast has its drawbacks. For one thing, it rains a lot (though, really, that's to be expected in a rain forest). If you plan to spend a week or more, be prepared for showers during at least a few of those days. Hard-core Southeast residents just throw on slickers and rubber boots and shrug it off (leave your umbrella behind if you don't want to be pegged as a tourist). Their attitude is philosophical: without the rain, there would be no forests; no lakes; no streams running with salmon and trout; and no healthy populations of brown and black bears, moose, deer, mountain goats, and wolves.

ESSENTIALS

Medical Assistance Ketchikan General Hospital (⊠ 3100 Tongass Ave. ☎ 907/225–5171 ⊕ www.peacehealth.org/ketchikan).

Pharmacies Downtown Drugstore (⊠ 300 Front St. ☎ 907/225–3144). Island Pharmacy (⊠ 3526 Tongass Ave. ☎ 907/225–6186).

Visitor Information Ketchikan Visitors Bureau (⊠ 131 Front St. ☎ 907/225–6166 or 800/770–3300 ⊕ www.visit-ketchikan.com). Southeast Alaska Discovery Center (⊠ 50 Main St. ☎ 907/228–6220 ⊕ www.fs.fed.us/r10/tongass/districts/discoverycenter/). U.S. Forest Service (⊠ 648 Mission St. ☎ 907/225–3101 ⊕ www.fs.fed.us/r10/tongass).

EXPLORING
TOP ATTRACTIONS

★ **Creek Street.** This was once Ketchikan's infamous red-light district. During Prohibition, Creek Street was home to numerous speakeasies, and in the early 1900s more than 30 houses of prostitution operated here. Today the small, colorful houses, built on stilts over the creek waters, have been restored as trendy shops.

The Falls at Salmon Falls Resort. Get out your camera and set it for high speed at the fish ladder, a series of pools arranged like steps that allow fish to travel upstream around a dam or falls. When the salmon start running from June onward, thousands of fish leap the falls (or take the easier fish-ladder route). They spawn in Ketchikan Creek's waters farther upstream. Many can also be seen in the creek's eddies above and below the falls. The falls, fish ladder, and a large carving of a jumping salmon are just off Park Avenue on Married Man's Trail. The trail was

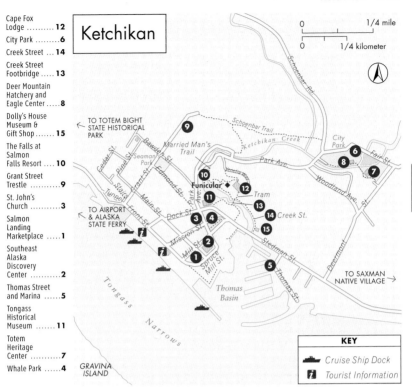

4

once used by married men for discreet access to the red-light district on Creek Street. ⊠ *Married Man's Trail off Park Ave.*

Southeast Alaska Discovery Center. This impressive public lands interpretive center features exhibits—including one on the rain forest—that focus on the resources, Native cultures, and ecosystems of Southeast Alaska. The U.S. Forest Service and other federal agencies provide information on Alaska's public lands, and a large gift shop sells natural-history books, maps, and videos about the sights in Ketchikan and Southeast. America the Beautiful–National Park and Federal Recreational Land Passes are accepted and sold. ⊠ *50 Main St.* ☎ *907/228–6220* ⊕ *www.fs.fed.us/r10/tongass/districts/discoverycenter* 🖀 *$5 May–Sept., free Oct.–Apr.* ⊙ *May–Sept., weekdays 8–5, weekends 8–4; Oct.–Apr., Thurs.–Sun. 10–4.*

★ **Totem Heritage Center.** Gathered from uninhabited Tlingit and Haida village sites, many of the authentic Native totems in this rare collection are well over a century old—a rare age for cedar carvings, which are frequently lost to decay in Southeast's exceedingly wet climate. The center also features guided tours and displays crafts of the Tlingit, Haida, and Tsimshian cultures. Outside are several more poles carved in the three decades since this center opened. The center offers an annual series of classes, workshops, and seminars related to Northwest Coastal Native

ALASKA TRAVEL SPECIALISTS

Viking Travel (☎ 907/772–3818 or 800/327–2571 ⊕ www.alaskaferry. com) is a reservations service that can help you with your Alaska Marine Highway trip or other Alaska vacation plans. The agency has special airfares that are booked in conjunction with ferry itineraries. Tour specialist **Alaska Bound** (☎ 231/439–3000 or 888/252–7527 ⊕ www.alaskabound.com) helps travelers choose the perfect small- or large-ship cruise through the Inside Passage. **Alaska Tour & Travel**(☎ 907/245–0200 or 800/208–0200 ⊕ www.alaskatravel. com) customizes tour packages to the Fairbanks area as

well as through South Central and Southeast Alaska, and to most of the major National Parks. **Alaska Tours**(☎ 907/277–3000 or 866/317–3325 ⊕ www.alaskatours. com) helps individuals and groups plan Alaska trips from the Southeast to the Northwest (and everything in between).

Adventure-seeking travelers looking for a Southeast-based tour company should consider one of the oldest outfits in the state, **Mountain Travel Sobek** (☎ 888/831–7526 ⊕ www. mtsobek.com). They organize several tours throughout Southeast, as well as in the rest of the state.

art and culture. ⊠ *601 Deermount St.* ☎ *907/225–5900* ⊕ *www.city. ketchikan.ak.us/departments/museums/totem.html* ☎ *$5* ⊙ *May–Sept., daily 8–5; Oct.–Apr., weekdays 1–5.*

WORTH NOTING

Cape Fox Lodge. For the town's best harbor views and one of Southeast Alaska's most luxurious lobbies, walk to the top of steep Venetia Avenue or take the funicular ($2) up from Creek Street. Don't miss the totems and other artwork created by master carvers Nathan Jackson and Lee Wallace. ⊠ *800 Venetia Way* ☎ *907/225–8001 or 800/225–8001* ⊕ *www.capefoxlodge.com.*

City Park. The Deer Mountain Hatchery and Eagle Center leads into this small but charming park, which has picnic tables, a fountain, and paved paths. Ketchikan Creek runs through it. ⊠ *Park and Fair Sts.*

Creek Street Footbridge. Stand over Ketchikan Creek for good salmon viewing when the fish are running. In summer you can see impressive runs of coho, king, pink, and chum salmon, along with smaller numbers of steelhead and rainbow trout heading upstream to spawn. ■ TIP→ Keep your eyes peeled for sea lions snacking on the incoming fish.

Deer Mountain Hatchery and Eagle Center. Tens of thousands of king and coho salmon are raised at this hatchery on Ketchikan Creek owned by the Ketchikan Indian Community. Midsummer visitors can view natural spawning in the creek by pink salmon and steelhead trout as well as workers collecting and fertilizing the salmon eggs for the hatchery. Visitors to the Eagle Center can get a close-up view of eagles, great-horned owls, red-tailed hawks, a falcon, and one turkey vulture. ⊠ *1158 Salmon Rd.* ☎ *907/228–5530 or 800/252–5158* ⊕ *www.kictribe.org*

TAKE THE FERRY

The **Alaska Marine Highway System** operates stateroom-equipped vehicle and passenger ferries from Bellingham, Washington, and from Prince Rupert, British Columbia. Popular among budget-minded travelers, and those seeking an alternative to cruise-ship travel, the Alaska Marine Highway allows passengers to create their own itineraries. In Southeast Alaska the vessels call at Metlakatla, Ketchikan, Wrangell, Petersburg, Kake, Sitka, Angoon, Tenakee, Hoonah, Juneau, Gustavus, Pelican, Haines, Skagway, and Yakutat—though it's possible to take the ferry all the way to South Central and southwestern Alaska.

■TIP➔ In summer, staterooms on the ferries are sold out before sailing time; reserve months in advance. There are common areas on the ferries where you can throw a sleeping bag or sit in a recliner seat. If you are planning to take a car on the ferry, early reservations for vehicle space are also highly recommended. This is particularly true for recreational vehicles. Ferry travel is also an ideal way for bicyclists to hop from town to town. There is a fee of $15 to $50 (depending on your route) to bring a bicycle aboard. A separate ferry, operated by the Inter-Island Ferry Authority, runs between Ketchikan and Hollis (on Prince of Wales Island).

Information Alaska Marine Highway central reservations office (✉ *6858 Glacier Hwy., Juneau* ☎ *907/465–3941 or 800/642–0066* ⊕ *www.ferryalaska.com*). **B.C. Ferries** (✉ *1112 Fort St., Victoria, BC, Canada* ☎ *250/386–3431 or 888/223–3779* ⊕ *www.bcferries. com*). **Inter-Island Ferry Authority** (✉ *Box 470, Klawock 99925* ☎ *907/826–4848 or 866/308–4848* ⊕ *www.interislandferry.com*).

✉ *$12 for hatchery and eagle compound admission* ☉ *Early May–Sept., daily 8–4:30.*

Dolly's House Museum & Gift Shop. Formerly owned by the inimitable Dolly Arthur, this steep-roofed home once housed Creek Street's most famous brothel. The house has been preserved as a museum, complete with furnishings, beds, and a short history of the life and times of Ketchikan's best-known madam. ✉ *Creek St.* ☎ *907/225–6329 (summer only)* ✉ *$5* ☉ *Daily 8–4 when cruise ships are in port; closed in winter.*

Grant Street Trestle. At one time virtually all of Ketchikan's walkways and streets were made from wooden trestles, but now only one of these handsome wooden streets remains, constructed in 1908.

St. John's Church. Built in 1903, this church is the oldest remaining house of worship in Ketchikan. Its interior is formed from red cedar cut in the Native-operated sawmill in nearby Saxman. When cruise ships are in town, a docent is on hand in the church to answer questions. There is also a small gift shop. ✉ *Mission St.* ☎ *907/225–3680* ⊕ *members. tripod.com/~Southeast_Seafarer/stjohns.html.*

Salmon Landing Marketplace. Modeled after 1920s-style cannery architecture, this 6½-acre waterfront complex—much of it built out over the waters of Tongass Narrows—features five buildings filled with a mix

The Aquaculture Debate

Five species of wild Pacific salmon are found in Alaska waters. All are anadromous (they spend part or all of their adult lives in salt water but depart to freshwater streams and rivers to spawn), and all five species have at least two common names: pink (humpback) salmon, chum (dog) salmon, coho (silver) salmon, sockeye (red) salmon, and Chinook (king) salmon. The smallest of these five, the pink salmon, has an average weight of only about 3 or 4 pounds, while king salmon can often tip the scales at more than 25 pounds. King salmon is generally considered the most flavorful, but sockeye and coho are also very highly regarded. Pinks and chum salmon are the mainstay of canneries.

After spending a year or more in the ocean (the length of time varies among the species), Pacific salmon return to their native streams to spawn and die. The annual summertime return of adult salmon is a major event in Alaska, both for the animals (including bears) that depend on this bounty, and for thousands of commercial fishers and sport anglers.

Alaska has long been famous for its seafood, and one of the first acts following statehood in 1959 was to protect fisheries from overharvesting. Today the stocks of salmon and other fish remain healthy, and careful management ensures that they will remain so in the future. In the 1980s and 1990s, aquaculture—fish farming—grew into an enormous international business, particularly in Norway, Chile, the United Kingdom, and British Columbia. Leery of the consequences to wild salmon, Alaska has never allowed any salmon aquaculture.

Pen-raised fish are affordable, available year-round, and of a consistent quality, but controversy surrounds the practice of fish farming. Many people believe it has a disastrous impact on the environment, citing such issues as disease; pollution from the waste of huge concentrations of fish; and the harvesting of non-native species, such as Atlantic salmon.

On the other side of the debate, there are those who believe that fish farming is helping to protect the earth's valuable—and decreasing—populations of salmon. Proponents of fish farms point out that the practice also offers revenue and more jobs. Offshore fish farming in the United States is a highly incendiary topic of debate; those supporting it believe that if the farms are placed in deep ocean pockets, the pollution from and medication given to the pen-raised fish will be scattered better by strong currents. Many environmentalists beg to differ, hoping to establish stringent guidelines before opening the ocean to fish-farming corporations.

One Alaska bumper sticker says: "Friends don't let friends eat farmed salmon." Just across the border, in British Columbia, many people find employment as fish-farm workers. No matter which side you agree with in the aquaculture debate, be sure to enjoy a plate of delicious wild salmon during your visit to Alaska—with luck, it could be a fish you've hooked yourself!

—Don Pitcher

of retail stores, souvenir shops, galleries, and restaurants. Cruise ships moor just a few steps away, filling the shops with tourists all summer long. ⊠ *Mill and Front Sts.*

Thomas Street and Marina. From this street you can see Thomas Basin, the most accessible of Ketchikan's four harbors and home port to pleasure and commercial fishing boats. Old buildings, including the maroon-fronted Potlatch Bar, sit atop pilings, and you can walk out to the breakwater for a better view of busy Tongass Narrows.

4

Tongass Historical Museum. Native artifacts and pioneer relics revisit the mining and fishing eras at this museum in the same building as the library. Exhibits include a big, brilliantly polished lens from Tree Point Lighthouse, well-presented Native tools and artwork, and photography collections. Other exhibits rotate, but always include Tlingit items. ⊠ *629 Dock St.* ☎ *907/225–5600* ⊕ *www.city.ketchikan.ak.us/ departments/museums/tongass.html* 🖃 *$2* ☉ *May–Sept., daily 8–5; Oct.–Apr., Tues.–Fri. 1–5, Sat. 10–4. Closed Sun. and Mon.*

Whale Park. This small park on a traffic island across from St. John's Church is the site of the **Chief Kyan Totem Pole,** now in its third incarnation. The original was carved in the 1890s, but over the decades it deteriorated and it was replaced in the 1960s. The current replica was erected in 1993, and the 1960s version is now housed in the Totem Heritage Center.

OUTDOOR ACTIVITIES AND GUIDED TOURS

CANOPY TOURS

Often associated with rain forests of the tropical sort, canopy tours are Ketchikan's fastest-growing outdoor activity. Featuring a series of zip-lines, aerial boardwalks, and suspension bridges, canopy tours provide an up-close view of the coastal forests. Granted, you won't spend the whole tour admiring the foliage: at **Alaska Canopy Adventures** (☎ *907/225–5503* ⊕ *www.alaskacanopy.com*)—a course at the Alaska Rainforest Sanctuary, 8.4 mi south of town—the longest of the tour's eight zip-lines stretches more than 800 feet, and whisks you along some 130 feet off the ground. Book online or with your cruise line. A rain-forest zip-line and ropes course is offered through **Southeast Exposure** (☎ *907/225–8829* ⊕ *www.southeastexposure.com*), a well-known kayaking outfit in the area.

DRIVING TOURS

Adventure Kart Expedition. There's no faster route to feeling like a kid on a first go-kart outing than spending a few hours in one of Adventure Kart Expedition's cool little off-road vehicles. After choosing a helmet, you'll get a quick lesson in the how-tos of driving one of the vehicles. Then you, and the people in the lineup of ATVs you'll race along with, will put pedal to metal (literally) as you zip down old backcountry timber trails. Wear old clothes: there's no way you're coming back from this one clean. Depending on the weather, the trails will either be dusty or mud-filled, but always fun. ☎ 907/617–6551 ⊕ *www. adventurekarts.com.*

FISHING

Sportfishing for salmon and trout is excellent in the Ketchikan area, in both saltwater and freshwater lakes and streams. As a result, a plethora of local boat owners offer charter and guide services. Contact the **Ketchikan Visitors Bureau** (☎ *907/225– 6166 or 800/770–3300* ⊕ *www. visit-ketchikan.com*) for information on guide services and locations.

HARBOR AND AIR TOURS

Alaska Travel Adventures (☎ *800/323– 5757, 907/247–5295 outside Alaska* ⊕ *www.bestofalaskatravel.com*) runs fun 20-person canoe outings perfect for people just dipping their toe into (very) soft adventure travel. The company's backcountry Jeep trips are also a great deal of fun.

Allen Marine Tours (☎ *907/225–8100 or 888/747–8101* ⊕ *www. allenmarinetours.com*), one of Southeast's largest and best-known tour operators, leads Misty Fiords National Monument catamaran tours throughout the summer. They also offer combo motorcoach and walking tours of Ketchikan sites that end with a water-jet-powered cruise into the Tongass Narrows.

If you want to head out on a floatplane to see the environs, contact **Southeast Aviation** (☎ *907/225–2900 or 888/359–6478* ⊕ *www.flymisty. com*). They offer tours of the glaciers and mountains of Misty Fiords National Monument, bear viewing, and charters.

HIKING

Get details on hiking around Ketchikan from the Southeast Alaska Discovery Center and Ketchikan Visitors Bureau *(⇨ Exploring, above)*. The 3-mi trail from downtown to the 3,000-foot summit of **Deer Mountain** will repay your efforts with a spectacular panorama of the city below and the wilderness behind. The trail officially begins at the corner of Nordstrom Drive and Ketchikan Lake Road, but consider starting on the paved, 1.5-mi scenic walk on the corner of Fair and Deermount streets. Pass through dense forests before emerging into the alpine country. A shelter cabin near the summit provides a place to warm up.

Ward Lake Recreation Area, about 6 mi north of town, has hikes next to lakes and streams and beneath towering spruce and hemlock trees; it

CLOSE UP

Ketchikan's Totem Pole Parks

For the most part, the totem poles in Ketchikan's two biggest totem pole parks are replicas of those brought in from outlying villages as part of a federal project during the late 1930s.

Totem Bight State Historical Park (⊠ N. Tongass Hwy., approx. 10 mi north of town ☎ 907/247–8574 ✉ Free ⊙ Dawn–dusk ⊕ dnr.alaska. gov/parks/units/totembgh.htm) has many totem poles and a hand-hewn Native tribal house; it sits on a scenic spit of land facing the waters of Tongass Narrows. The clan house is open daily in summer. About a quarter of the Ketchikan bus tours include Totem Bight.

A 2.5-mi paved walking path–bike trail parallels the road from Ketchikan to **Saxman Totem Pole Park**

(⊠ S. Tongass Hwy., 2 mi south of town ☎ 907/225–4421 ⊕ www. capefoxtours.com), named for a missionary who helped Native Alaskans settle here before 1900. A totem park dominates the center of Saxman, with poles that represent a wide range of human and animal-inspired figures, including bears, ravens, whales, and eagles. There is a $3 charge to enter.

Saxman's Beaver Clan tribal house is said to be the largest in Alaska. Carvers create totem poles and totemic art objects in the adjacent carver's shed. You can get to the park on foot or by taxi, bicycle, or city bus. You can visit the totem park on your own, but to visit the tribal house and theater you must take a tour. Tickets are sold at the gift shop across from the totems. Call ahead for tour schedules.

also has several covered picnic spots and a pleasant campground. An easy 1.3-mi nature trail circles the lake, which is popular for steelhead and salmon fishing. **Ward Creek Trail** begins from the lake and follows the creek 2.5 mi, with shoreside paths to creek-side platforms. The trail is hard-packed gravel, and is wide and gentle enough for wheelchairs. More ambitious hikers head up the 2-mi **Perseverance Trail,** a challenging set of steps and boardwalk that takes hikers through the open muskeg (peat bog) to a small lake.

LOCAL INTEREST

A Native-owned company, **Cape Fox Tours** (☎ 907/225–4846 ⊕ www. capefoxtours.com), leads tours of Saxman Totem Pole Park and the historic George Inlet Cannery. You can book the cannery tour through your cruise line, and most of the other tours either through your cruise line or at the Ketchikan Visitors Bureau.

SEA KAYAKING

Southeast Exposure (☎ 907/225–8829 ⊕ www.southeastexposure.com) offers a 3½-hour guided Eagle Islands sea-kayak tour and a 4½-hour Tatoosh Islands sea-kayak tour in Behm Canal.

Southeast Sea Kayaks (☎ 907/225–1258 or 800/287–1607 ⊕ www. kayakketchikan.com) leads kayak tours of Ketchikan and Misty Fiords, and offers kayak lessons and rentals. It specializes in remote day trips and guided multinight trips to Misty Fiords. Travelers with just one day to spend on a Ketchikan adventure should consider this company's

WALKING AROUND KETCHIKAN

This walk originates at the helpful **Ketchikan Visitors Bureau** on Front Street. Just a few steps up Mill Street is the **Salmon Landing Marketplace**, filled with shops and restaurants. Next door, learn about Southeast Alaska's wild places at the **Southeast Alaska Discovery Center**. Farther up Mill Street, past minuscule **Whale Park** with its Chief Kyan totem pole, you can follow Stedman Street across the bridge to **Thomas Street**, which overlooks one of Ketchikan's four harbors. Following Deermont Street uphill for several blocks, you'll come across the **Totem Heritage Center** and its collection of ancient totem poles. A footbridge takes you to **Deer Mountain Hatchery and Eagle Center**, where you can see young salmon and rehabilitated bald eagles, and **City Park**. From here, Park Avenue runs parallel to Ketchikan Creek, heading downhill to the fish ladder and the Salmon carving next to the **Falls at Salmon Falls Resort**.

Glance uphill from the falls to see historic **Grant Street Trestle**, where the road becomes a steep plank bridge supported on pilings. It's about a 10-minute walk down Park Avenue from the hatchery.

From the fish ladder, a boardwalk path follows Ketchikan Creek and leads to trendy **Creek Street**. For a good side trip, take the short funicular ($2) to **Cape Fox Lodge** to get a great view of the harbor. Back on the Creek Street boardwalk is former brothel **Dolly's House**. If you retrace your steps up the boardwalk and cross the **Creek Street Footbridge**, you may see salmon during summertime runs. Just in front of you is the Chief Johnson Totem Pole, near the **Tongass Historical Museum**, with interesting relics from the early days of mining and fishing. A left turn onto Bawden Street will take you past historic **St. John's Church**.

combination tour of kayaking through Orcas Cove and flightseeing Misty Fiord National Monument. It's hard to beat a day that includes a transfer from a boat to a floatplane.

SNORKELING

Snorkel Alaska. While signing up to go snorkeling in Alaska may seem like little more than a novelty, it takes just a few seconds in the waters off Ketchikan—don't worry, they'll lend you a wetsuit to keep you warm—to understand that you're about to have an incredibly special experience. The experienced guides provide both novice and experienced snorkelers the information they need to quickly become comfortable and give themselves over to underwater gazing at giant sunflower stars, bright blood stars, sea cucumbers, and more. ⊠ *S. Tongass Hwy. and Roosevelt Dr.* ☎ *907/247–7783* ⊕ *www. snorkelalaska.com.*

WHERE TO EAT

$$$–$$$$ ✕ **Annabelle's Famous Keg and Chowder House.** Nestled into the ground
AMERICAN   floor of the historic Gilmore Hotel, this unpretentious Victorian-style restaurant serves a hearty array of seafood and pastas, including

several kinds of chowder and steamer clams. Prime rib on Friday and Saturday evenings is a favorite, and the lounge with a jukebox adds a friendly vibe. ⊠ *326 Front St.* ☎ *907/225–6009* ⊕ *www. gilmorehotel.com/annabelles.htm.*

$$$$
AMERICAN/
SEAFOOD

★

✕ **Bar Harbor Restaurant.** Though a quick glance at the menu doesn't give the impression that one of Southeast's, if not Alaska's, more inventive chefs owns Bar Harbor, that is indeed the case. Even Southeast standards like fried halibut and chips get a bump from the chef's trained-at-culinary-school ways. He brought all he learned at culinary school back to Ketchikan, and visitors and locals are the better for it. The chef's joy in cooking comes through in every bite of his food. The tiny blue-and-white house on the waterfront makes for a cozy spot to dine, but if you can, try to get a seat on the back deck. Oh, and, inside or out: get the Gorgonzola fries. ⊠ *2813 Tongass Ave.* ☎ *907/225–2813* ⊕ *barharborrestaurantketchikan.com/* ⌂ *Reservations essential.*

$
FILIPINO

✕ **Diaz Café.** Take a break from salmon saturation at this Old Town Ketchikan spot. On historic Stedman Street, Diaz Café serves hearty Filipino cuisine that's a favorite of locals and, especially, of cruise ship staffers hungry for a taste of home. Budget-wary travelers take heart: you don't have to spend much at Diaz to get a really filling meal. And the place is a wonderful time warp; it's straight back to the linoleum-and-tile 1950s inside. ⊠ *335 Stedman St.* ☎ *907/225–2257.*

$-$$
MEXICAN

✕ **Ocean View Restaurant.** This locals' favorite eatery has burgers, steaks, pasta, pizzas, and seafood. They're all fine, but the main draws are authentic and very filling south-of-the-border dishes prepared under the direction of the Mexican-American owners. Three tables in the back have nice views of the Tongass Narrows. ⊠ *1831 Tongass Ave.* ☎ *907/225–7566* ⊕ *www.oceanviewmex.com.*

WHERE TO STAY

For expanded hotel reviews, visit Fodors.com.

$
🛏 **Black Bear Inn.** This isn't a typical B&B; it is, within minutes, your new home. **Pros:** kitchen fully stocked for breakfast and all-day snacks; a phenomenal backyard space. **Cons:** outside of downtown, so a car is helpful, though local buses and taxis can fill in. ⊠ *5528 N. Tongass Hwy.* ☎ *907/225–4343* ⊕ *stayinalaska.com* ⤳ *4 rooms, 1 apartment, 1 cabin* ⌂ *In-room: Wi-Fi. In-hotel: business services, parking.*

B&B RESERVATIONS

Bed-and-breakfasts are exceedingly popular in the Inside Passage, and for good reason. Dozens of regional B&Bs are excellent alternatives to local hotels; they also provide the opportunity to meet fellow travelers, dig into a homemade breakfast (such as smoked-salmon omelets or authentic sourdough pancakes), and learn about the area from local business owners.

Local Agents Alaska Travelers Accommodations (⊕ *www. alaskatravelers.com*). **Ketchikan Reservation Service** (⊕ *www. ketchikan-lodging.com*).

4

DID YOU KNOW?

Being "low on the totem pole" isn't necessarily bad. The most important figure can sit at the base or the top of a totem pole, and sometimes it's even in the middle.

$$$–$$$$ ⌂ **Cape Fox Lodge.** With scenic views of the town and Thomas Basin from 135 feet above Creek Street, Cape Fox Lodge's setting is cozy yet luxurious. **Pros:** complimentary Wi-Fi; on-site artwork by master carvers. **Cons:** rooms are rather plain; hotel has somewhat of a conference property feel. **TripAdvisor:** "rooms are large and clean," "lovely rooms with a view," "staff was very friendly and helpful." ✉ *800 Venetia Way* ☎ *907/225–8001, 866/225–8001 reservations* ⊕ *www.capefoxlodge.com* ⇨ *72 rooms, 2 suites* ⚕ *In-room: Wi-Fi. In-hotel: restaurant, bar, laundry facilities, business center, some pets allowed.*

> **SEAFOOD STOP**
>
> For some of Southeast's best canned, smoked, or frozen salmon and halibut, along with crab and clams, try **Salmon Etc.** on Mission Street. ✉ *322 Mission St., Ketchikan* ☎ *907/225–6008 or 800/354–7256* ⊕ *www.salmonetc. com.*

$–$$ ⌂ **Gilmore Hotel.** Crammed between the large buildings along Front Street, the Gilmore is a boutique hotel with slightly less-than-boutique prices. **Pros:** marina-view rooms are nice, if you can get one; charming property. **Cons:** not handicapped accessible; lots of stairs; lobby could use renovation. **TripAdvisor:** "rooms are tiny but clean," "staff were friendly," "wonderful sense of history." ✉ *326 Front St.* ☎ *907/225–9423 or 800/275–9423* ⊕ *www.gilmorehotel.com* ⇨ *38 rooms, 1 suite* ⚕ *In-room: Wi-Fi. In-hotel: restaurant, bar, business center* ⦿*Breakfast.*

$$–$$$ ⌂ **Inn at Creek Street & New York Hotel.** More than a century old, this quaint hotel is the site one of the nicest eateries in Ketchikan, now run by Ketchikan Coffee Company. **Pros:** loft suites have jetted tubs; rooms have Wi-Fi; standard rooms are reasonably priced. **Cons:** café hours limited Sunday–Thursday. **TripAdvisor:** "quite lovely inside," "very comfortable and great location," "beautifully kept." ✉ *207 Stedman St.* ☎ *907/225–0246, 866/225–0246 outside Alaska* ⊕ *www. thenewyorkhotel.com* ⇨ *8 rooms, 8 suites* ⚕ *In-room: kitchen (some), Wi-Fi. In-hotel: restaurant, bar, business center.*

$$$ ⌂ **The Landing.** Near the ferry terminal, this Best Western property is named for the state ferry landing directly across the road. **Pros:** free shuttle; near airport. **Cons:** somewhat overpriced given its location and amenities; room decor has little personality. **TripAdvisor:** "clean and quiet," "excellent customer service," "room was spacious." ✉ *3434 Tongass Ave.* ☎ *907/225–5166 or 800/428–8304* ⊕ *www. landinghotel.com* ⇨ *107 rooms, 21 suites* ⚕ *In-room: Wi-Fi. In-hotel: 2 restaurants, bar, gym, laundry facilities, business center, parking, some pets allowed.*

$$$–$$$$ ⌂ **The Narrows Inn.** Three miles from the center of town and ¼ mi north of the airport parking lot, the Narrows is a modern lodge where rustic wood trim enlivens the small rooms with simple furniture. **Pros:** great views of Tongass in selected rooms; complimentary continental breakfast; freezer available for fish storage. **Cons:** inconvenient location; not all rooms have good views. ⌂ *Box 8296, 99901* ☎ *907/247–2600 or 888/686–2600* ⊕ *www.narrowsinn.com* ⇨ *44 rooms, 3 suites*

CAMPING IN KETCHIKAN

⚠ **Ward Lake Campgrounds.** Two rain-forest campgrounds are 8 mi north of Ketchikan; turn right onto Revilla Road and follow it to the exceptionally scenic Ward Lake area, popular for fishing, hiking, and picnicking. Both are managed by the Forest Service, with sites reservable through the **National Recreation Reservation Service.** Signal Creek Campground is adjacent to Ward Lake, and Last Chance Campground is a mile farther up Revilla Road. **Pros:** sites can be reserved; surrounded by forest; fishing allowed at Ward Lake. **Cons:** water at Signal Creek is provided during peak season only; most of Signal Creek's sites do not accommodate larger motor homes; no hookups at either campground. ☎ *907/225–2148, reservations 518/885–3639 or 877/444–6777 ⊕ www.fs.fed.us/ r10/tongass; reservations ⊕ www. recreation.gov* 🛏 *Signal Creek: 24 sites. Last Chance: 19 sites* ♿ *Flush toilets.*

♿ *In-room: Wi-Fi. In-hotel: restaurant, bar, business center, some pets allowed* ⊙| *Breakfast.*

NIGHTLIFE

BARS

Ketchikan has quieted down in recent years as the economy shifted from logging to tourism, but it remains something of a party town, especially when crews stumble off fishing boats with cash in hand. You won't have any trouble finding something going on at several downtown bars. **First City Saloon** (⊠ *830 Water St.* ☎ *907/225–1494*) is the main dance spot, with live music throughout the summer. The **Potlatch Bar** (⊠ *126 Thomas Basin* ☎ *907/225–4855*) delivers up music on weekends as well.

SHOPPING

ART GALLERIES

Main Street Gallery. Run by the Ketchikan Area Arts and Humanities Council, the gallery hosts 12 exhibits per year. The gallery showcases established local artists as well as rising national stars. The light and cheery gallery is well worth a visit as you stroll around town, especially if you're itching to discover a new-to-you favorite artist. ⊠ *330 Main St.* ☎ *907/225–2211* ⊕ *ketchikanarts.org* ⊙ *Weekdays 9–5, Sat. 11–3; closed every Sun. and last Sat. of each month.*

In business since 1972, **Scanlon Gallery** (⊠ *318 Mission St.* ☎ *907/247–4730 or 888/228–4730* ⊕ *www.scanlongallery.com*) carries prints from a number of well-known Alaska artists, including Byron Birdsall, John Fehringer, Barbara Lavallee, Rie Muñoz, and Jon Van Zyle.

Design, art, clothing, and collectibles converge in the stylish **Soho Coho Contemporary Art and Craft Gallery** (⊠ *5 Creek St.* ☎ *907/225–5954 or 800/888–4070* ⊕ *www.trollart.com*), where you'll find an eclectic

Ketchikan. "On a cool spring day, after walking on glaciers and seeing so much wildlife in the Tundra and sea coast, Ketchikan is comfortable and warm." —Sandy Cook, Fodors.com photo contest participant

collection of art and T-shirts featuring the work of owner Ray Troll—best known for his wacky fish art—and other Southeast Alaska artists.

BOOKS

Upstairs from the Soho Coho Gallery, **Parnassus Books** (✉ *5 Creek St.* ☎ *907/225–7690* ⊕ *www.ketchikanbooks.com*) is a book lover's bookstore, with creaky floors, cozy quarters, many Alaskan titles, and a knowledgeable staff.

AROUND KETCHIKAN

MISTY FIORDS NATIONAL MONUMENT

40 mi east of Ketchikan by air.

Misty Fiords National Monument. Just east of Ketchikan, Misty Fiords National Monument is a wilderness of cliff-faced fjords (or fiords, if you follow the monument's spelling), mountains, and islands with spectacular coastal scenery, wildlife, and recreation. Small boats provide views of breathtaking vistas. Travel on these waters can be an almost mystical experience, with the green forests reflected in the waters of the monument's many fjords. You may find yourself in the company of a whale, see a bear fishing for salmon along the shore, or even pull in your own salmon for an evening meal. ■ TIP→ Note that the name Misty refers to the weather you're likely to encounter.

Fodor's Choice
★ Most visitors to Misty Fiords arrive on day trips via floatplane from Ketchikan or on board catamarans run by **Alaska Travel Adventures** (☎ *800/323–5757, 907/247–5295 outside Alaska* ⊕ *www. bestofalaskatravel.com*). **Allen Marine Tours** (☎ *907/225–8100 or 888/747–8101* ⊕ *www.allenmarinetours.com*) offers tours of Misty Fiords.

METLAKATLA

12 mi south of Ketchikan.

The village of Metlakatla—the name translates roughly as "saltwater passage"—is on Annette Island, just a dozen miles by sea from busy Ketchikan but a world away culturally. A visit to this quiet community offers visitors a chance to learn about life in a small Inside Passage Native community.

In most Southeast Native villages the people are Tlingit or Haida in heritage. Metlakatla is the exception, as most folks are Tsimshian. They moved to the island from British Columbia in 1887, led by William Duncan, an Anglican missionary from England. The town grew rapidly and soon contained dozens of buildings on a grid of streets, including a cannery, a sawmill, and a church that could seat 1,000 people. Congress declared Annette Island a federal Indian reservation in 1891, and it remains the only reservation in Alaska today. Father Duncan continued to control life in Metlakatla for decades, until the government finally stepped in shortly before his death in 1918.

During World War II the U.S. Army built a major air base 7 mi from Metlakatla that included observation towers for Japanese subs, airplane hangars, gun emplacements, and housing for 10,000 soldiers. After the war it served as Ketchikan's airport for many years, but today the long runways are virtually abandoned save for a few private flights.

GETTING HERE AND AROUND

The **Alaska Marine Highway System** offers daily ferry service from Ketchikan to Metlakatla and back. If you prefer to arrive from above, **ProMech Air** has scheduled floatplane flights between Ketchikan and outlying communities including Metlakatla and Prince of Wales Island. Run by the Metlakatla community, **Metlakatla Tours** leads local tours that include visits to Duncan Cottage, the cannery, and the longhouse, along with a Tsimshian dance performance. Local taxis can take you to other sights around the island, including Yellow Hill and the old Air Force base.

ESSENTIALS

Airplane Contact ProMech Air (☎ *907/225–3845 or 800/860–3845* ⊕ *www. promechair.com*).

Ferry Contact The **Alaska Marine Highway System** (☎ *907/465–3941 or 800/642–0066* ⊕ *www.ferryalaska.com*).

Tour Information Metlakatla Tours (☎ *907/886–8687* ⊕ *www.metlakatla.com*).

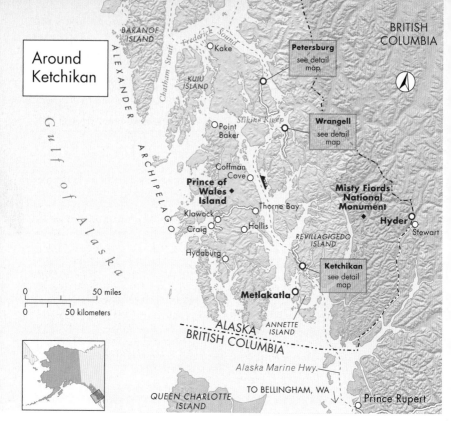

Around Ketchikan

BARANOF ISLAND

Frederick Sound

Kake

Chatham Strait

KUIU ISLAND

ALEXANDER

Petersburg
see detail map

BRITISH COLUMBIA

Gulf of Alaska

Stikine River

Point Baker

Wrangell
see detail map

ARCHIPELAGO

Coffman Cove

Prince of Wales ◆ Island

Thorne Bay

Misty Fiords National Monument

Hyder

Stewart

Klawock

Hollis

Craig

REVILLAGIGEDO ISLAND

Hydaburg

Ketchikan
see detail map

0   50 miles
0   50 kilometers

Metlakatla

ANNETTE ISLAND

ALASKA
BRITISH COLUMBIA

Alaska Marine Hwy.

QUEEN CHARLOTTE ISLAND

TO BELLINGHAM, WA

Prince Rupert

EXPLORING

Metlakatla's religious heritage still shows today. The clapboard **William Duncan Memorial Church**, topped with two steeples, burned in 1948 but was rebuilt several years later. It is one of nine churches in tiny Metlakatla. **Father Duncan's Cottage** is maintained to appear exactly as it would have in 1891, and includes original furnishings, personal items, and a collection of turn-of-the-20th-century music boxes. ⊠ *Corner of 4th Ave. and Church St.* ☎ *907/886–8687* ⊕ *www.metlakatla.com* ✉ *$2* ⊘ *Weekdays 8:30–12:30, or when cruise ships are in port.*

Father Duncan worked hard to eliminate traditional Tsimshian beliefs and dances, but today the people of Metlakatla have resurrected their past; they perform old dances in traditional regalia. The best place to catch these performances is at the traditional **longhouse** (known as *Le Sha'as* in the Tsimshian dialect), which faces Metlakatla's boat harbor. Three totem poles stand on the back side of the building, and the front is covered with a Tsimshian design. Inside are displays of native crafts and a model of the fish traps that were once common throughout the Inside Passage. Native dance groups perform here on Wednesday and Friday in summer. Just next to the longhouse is an **Artists' Village,** where booths display locally made arts and crafts. The village and longhouse open when groups and tours are present.

Two miles from town is a board-walk path that leads up the 540-foot **Yellow Hill.** Distinctive yellow sandstone rocks and panoramic vistas make this a worthwhile detour on clear days.

4

WHERE TO STAY

For expanded hotel reviews, visit Fodors.com.

$ ⌂ **Metlakatla Inn.** This two-story building, decorated with Native art, offers standard motel accommodations with private decks off the upstairs rooms. **Pros:** property has recently been renovated; car rental available on-site. **Cons:** guests share the same phone line; property lacks charm. ⊠ *3rd Ave. and Lower Milton St.* ☎ *907/886–3456* ⊕ *www.metlakatlainn.com* ⤍ *9 rooms, 2 apartments* ⌂ *In-room: kitchen (some), Wi-Fi. In-hotel: business center, some pets allowed.*

$ ⌂ **Tuck'em Inn.** This family-run lodging occupies two separate down-town houses. **Pros:** convenient location; breakfast included. **Cons:** some rooms share bathrooms; rooms don't have much personality. ⊠ *Hillcrest and Western Aves.* ☎ *907/886–6611* ⊕ *www.alaskanow.com/tuckem-inn* ⤍ *6 rooms* ⌂ *In-room: kitchen (some). In-hotel: laundry facilities, business center* ⊫*Breakfast.*

HYDER

90 mi northeast of Ketchikan.

The tiny, nondescript town of Hyder sits at the head of narrow Portland Canal, a 70-mi-long fjord northeast of Ketchikan. The fjord marks the border between Canada and the United States, and Hyder sits just 2 mi from the larger town of Stewart, British Columbia. ■ **TIP→** It's also one of the few Southeast settlements accessible by paved road.

The 1898 discovery of gold and silver in the surrounding mountains brought a flood of miners to the Hyder area, and the town eventually became a major shipping port. Mining remained important for decades, but a devastating 1948 fire destroyed much of the town, which had been built on pilings over the water. A small amount of mining still takes place here, but the beauty of the area, while not any more interesting than Ketchikan, attracts a respectable number of tourists. Today Hyder calls itself "the friendliest ghost town in Alaska," a claim that may be based more on marketing than reality.

GETTING HERE AND AROUND

From Stewart, in Canada, Highway 37A continues over spectacular Bear Pass to Hyder and connects the town with the rest of Canada. **Taquan Air** has year-round service between Ketchikan and Hyder every Monday and Thursday.

ESSENTIALS

Airplane Contact Taquan Air (☎ 907/225–8800 or 800/770–8800 ⊕ www.taquanair.com).

Visitor and Tour Information
Stewart-Hyder Chamber of Commerce (✉ Box 306, Stewart, BC V0T 1W0 ☎ 250/636–9224 ⊕ www. stewart-hyder.com).

EXPLORING

The **Stewart Historical Society Museum**, housed in the town's former fire hall, contains wildlife displays and exhibits on the region's mining history. Pop culture buffs will enjoy movie props from films made in the area, including Insomnia. ✉ 6th and Columbia Sts. ☎ 250/636–2568 ⊠ $5 ⊙ May, June, and Sept., weekends 10–6; July and Aug., daily 10–6.

> ### HYDER TIPS
>
> The somewhat lackluster town of Hyder is small and has only a handful of tourist-oriented businesses, a post office, and a library. Nearby Stewart has slightly more to offer, including a museum, hotels, restaurants, and camping. You will need to check in at Canadian customs (open 24 hours) before crossing the border from Hyder into Stewart, a process that has unfortunately become more difficult. Canadian money is primarily used in Hyder, but greenbacks are certainly accepted.

Six miles north of Hyder on Salmon River Road is the **Fish Creek Wildlife Observation Site** (⊕ www.fs.fed.us/r10/ro/naturewatch/southeast/fish_creek/fishcreek.htm). From late July to early September, a large run of salmon attracts black and brown bears, which, in turn, attract more than a few photographers. The creek produces some of the largest chum salmon anywhere.

Twenty-five miles east of Stewart on Highway 37A is the imposing **Bear Glacier**. The glacier sits across a small lake that is often crowded with icebergs.

A dirt road from Hyder into Canada leads 17 mi to remote **Salmon Glacier**, one of the few glaciers accessible by road in Southeast Alaska.

Getting "Hyderized" (which involves drinking and drinking-related silliness) is a term that you will hear upon arrival in the area. You can get Hyderized at **Glacier Inn** (✉ Main St. ☎ 250/636–9248), where the walls are papered with thousands of signed bills. The tradition supposedly began when prospectors would tack a dollar bill on the wall in case they were broke when they returned.

WHERE TO EAT AND STAY

For expanded hotel reviews, visit Fodors.com.

$$$ ✕ **Bitter Creek Café**. This bustling Stewart café serves a variety of cuisines,
CAFÉ   including a wide selection of salads, gourmet steaks, lasagna, seafood, and even Mexican dishes. It's all made in-house, including the freshly baked breads and desserts. The quirky interior is adorned with a fun collection of antiques as well as a 1930 Pontiac. Relax on the outside deck on a summer afternoon. ✉ 5th Ave., Stewart ☎ 250/636–2166 ⊕ bittercreek.homestead.com ⊙ Closed Oct.–Apr. No lunch.

$ 🛏 **Ripley Creek Inn**. Stewart's best lodging option covers five historic downtown buildings. **Pros:** nice decks and views from rooms. **Cons:**

somewhat noisy; not much to do in immediate area. ✉ *306 5th Ave., Stewart* ☎ *250/636–2344* ⊕ *www.ripleycreekinn.com* ⇥ *32 rooms* ⚷ *In-room: kitchen (some), Wi-Fi. In-hotel: business center, some pets allowed.*

PRINCE OF WALES ISLAND

43 mi northwest of Ketchikan.

Prince of Wales Island stretches more than 130 mi from north to south, making it the largest island in Southeast Alaska. Only two other American islands—Kodiak in Alaska and Hawaii in the Hawaiian chain—are larger. Prince of Wales (or "P.O.W." as locals call it) has a diversity of landforms, a plethora of wildlife, and exceptional sportfishing, especially for steelhead, salmon, and trout anglers, with the Karta and Thorne rivers among the favorites.

The island has long been a major source of timber, both from Tongass National Forest lands and those owned by native corporations. While much of the native land has been cut over, environmental restrictions on public lands have greatly reduced logging activity. The island's economy is now supported by small-scale logging operations, tourism, and commercial fishing.

Approximately 4,500 people live full-time on Prince of Wales Island, scattered in small villages and towns. A network of 1,500 mi of roads—nearly all built to access clear-cuts—crisscrosses the island, providing connections to even the smallest settlements.

GETTING HERE AND AROUND

The **Inter-Island Ferry Authority** operates a daily vehicle and passenger ferry between Ketchikan and Prince of Wales Island. The ferry terminal is in the tiny settlement of Hollis, 31 mi from Craig on a paved road.

Paved roads link Craig and Hollis. The relative abundance of roads, combined with ferry and air access from Ketchikan, makes it easy to explore this island. It's a shame that more people don't do so.

ESSENTIALS

Ferry Information Inter-Island Ferry Authority (☎ *907/826–4848 or 866/308–4848* ⊕ *www.interislandferry.com*).

Visitor Information Prince of Wales Chamber of Commerce (✉ *Box 490, Klawock 99921* ☎ *907/775–2626* ⊕ *www.princeofwalescoc.org*).

EXPLORING

The primary commercial center for Prince of Wales is **Craig**, on the island's western shore. This town of 1,500 retains a hard-edged aura fast disappearing in many Inside Passage towns, where tourism now holds sway. Although sightseeing attractions are slim, the town exudes a frontier spirit, and its small-boat harbors buzz with activity.

A half-dozen miles from Craig is the Tlingit village of **Klawock** (☎ *907/755–2345*), with a sawmill, cannery, hatchery, and the island's only airport. The town is best known for its striking totem poles in **Totem Park.** Several of these colorful poles were moved here in the 1930s; others are more recent carvings. You can watch carvers restoring old totems at the carving shed, across the road from the grocery store. Klawock is also home to **Prince of Wales Hatchery** (☎ *907/755–2231* ⊕ *www.powha.org* ⊘ *Tours June–Aug., Mon.–Sat. 1–5*), one of the state's most effective hatcheries. It's open for summertime tours ($2), and it also has a small visitor center with an aquarium full of young coho salmon.

Along the bay you'll find **St. John's by the Sea Catholic Church,** with stained-glass windows picturing Native Alaskans.

The Haida village of **Hydaburg,** approximately 40 mi south of Klawock (via chip-sealed road), lies along scenic Sukkwan Strait. A small collection of **totem poles** occupies the center of this Haida settlement, the only one in Alaska. Originally from British Columbia's Queen Charlotte Island, the Haida settled here around 1700.

A number of large natural caverns pockmark northern Prince of Wales Island. The best known of these, **El Capitan Cave,** has one of the deepest pits in the United States and is open to the public. Paleontologists have found a wealth of black bear, brown bear, and other mammal fossils in the cave's 13,000 feet of passageways, including some that date back more than 12,000 years. The Forest Service leads free El Capitan tours several times a week in summer. Tours take about two hours. It takes some work to get to the mouth of the cave but, if you're up for a 1,100-foot hike up a 367-step stairway, it's well worth the effort. The rangers don't rush, and give visitors plenty of time to catch their breath along the way by discussing the intensely lush forest that surrounds the cave area. Reservations are required at least two days in advance, and no children under age 7 are permitted. Bring a flashlight and wear hiking boots or rubber boots. A light jacket is also helpful, as the cave gets quite cool. ⊠ *Mi 51 along North Prince of Wales Rd.* ☎ *907/828–3304* ⊕ *www.fs.fed.us/r10/tongass/districts/pow/recreation/rogs/elcap.shtml.*

WHERE TO STAY

For expanded hotel reviews, visit Fodors.com.

$–$$ ⌇ **Inn of the Little Blue Heron.** With sweeping water views, cozy rooms, and outdoor decks tailored for simultaneous coffee drinking and wildlife viewing, the Little Blue Heron is a favorite among regular visitors to Craig. **Pros:** both locations offer wireless Internet; can rent out whole inn or suite for large groups. **Cons:** rooms at the South Cove location are small. ⊠ *406 9th St. and 403 Beach Rd., Craig* ☎ *907/826–3608* ⊕ *www.littleblueheroninn.com* ⟿ *6 rooms, 1 suite* △ *In-room: kitchen (some), Wi-Fi. In-hotel: some age restrictions* ⦶ *Breakfast.*

$$$$ ⌇ **McFarland's Floatel.** At this quiet resort 2 mi across the bay from the logging town of Thorne Bay on the eastern side of Prince of Wales, each of the four beachfront log cabins sleeps up to six people and includes a loft, woodstove, full kitchen, and private bath. **Pros:** nightly rate covers up to four guests; quiet setting. **Cons:** restaurant is open only to hotel guests; location is remote. ⌂ *Box 19149, Thorne Bay 99919* ☎ *907/828–3335 or 888/828–3335* ⊕ *www.mcfarlandsfloatel.com* ⟿ *4 cabins* △ *In-room: kitchen, no TV, Wi-Fi. In-hotel: laundry facilities, business center* ⊘ *Closed Oct.–mid-Apr.*

$$$$ 🏨 **Rock Haven.** A few minutes' boat ride from the shores of the fishing-centric Coffman Cove, Rock Haven is instant peace and relaxation. Pros: stunning setting; owners clearly enjoy running a lodge; lodge pets are a friendly bunch Cons: there's no way to just pop out for a quick bite to eat; even if the property weren't a boat ride from Coffman Cove, the town doesn't offer much in the way of restaurants; you need to be handy with a skiff if you want to motor out to the lodge on your own—there are some widowmaker rocks in the water ⊠ *Across bay, Coffman Cove* ☎ *907/329–2003* ⊕ *www.rockhavenalaska.com* ➴ *3 rooms, 1 one-bedroom apartment with kitchenette* ⚭ *In-room: Wi-Fi.*

$–$$ 🏨 **Ruth Ann's Hotel.** Victorian-style furnishings and details flavor this tasteful gingerbread hotel. **Pros:** honeymoon suite is perfect for romantic travelers. **Cons:** rooms are up the hill and not on the water. ⊠ *505 Water St., Craig* ☎ *907/826–3378* ➴ *17 rooms, 1 suite* ⚭ *In-room: kitchen (some). In-hotel: restaurant, bar, some pets allowed* ⊙ *Restaurant closed Jan.*

$$$$ 🏨 **Shelter Cove Lodge.** Tall windows front the water at this modern lodge along the South Boat Harbor in Craig. **Pros:** price is all-inclusive; lodge was renovated in 2008. **Cons:** expensive rate in comparison to similar properties; no elevator. ⊠ *703 Hamilton Dr., Craig* ☎ *907/826–2939 or 888/826–3474* ⊕ *www.sheltercovelodge.com* ➴ *10 rooms* ⚭ *In-room: Wi-Fi. In-hotel: restaurant, bar, water sports, laundry facilities* ⊙ *Restaurant closed Sept.–May* ❙◯❙ *All-inclusive.*

$$$$
Fodor's Choice
★
🏨 **Waterfall Resort.** At this upscale fishing lodge guests can choose from several accommodation styles, eat bountiful meals with all the trimmings, and fish from custom-built 25-foot cabin cruisers under the care of expert fishing guides. **Pros:** plenty of saltwater fishing; opportunity to spot wildlife. **Cons:** most kitchens in the condos aren't used, since meals are provided by the resort; remote location. ⊡ *Box 6440, Ketchikan 99901* ☎ *907/225–9461 or 800/544–5125* ⊕ *www.waterfallresort.com* ➴ *10 lodge rooms, 4 suites, 4 condos, 26 cabins* ⚭ *In-room: kitchen (some), no TV. In-hotel: restaurant, bar, laundry facilities, business center, some age restrictions* ⊙ *Closed Sept.–late May* ❙◯❙ *All meals.*

WRANGELL

87 mi north of Ketchikan.

A small, unassuming timber and fishing community, Wrangell sits on the northern tip of Wrangell Island, near the mouth of the fast-flowing Stikine River—North America's largest undammed river. The Stikine plays a large role in the life of many Wrangell residents, including those who grew up homesteading on the islands that pepper the area. Trips on the river with local guides are highly recommended as they provide, basically, an insider's guide to the Stikine and a very Alaskan way of life. Like much of Southeast, Wrangell has suffered in recent years from a declining resource-based economy. But locals are working to build tourism in the town. Bearfest, which started in 2010, celebrates Wrangell's proximity to Anan Creek, where you can get a close-up view of both brown and black bears.

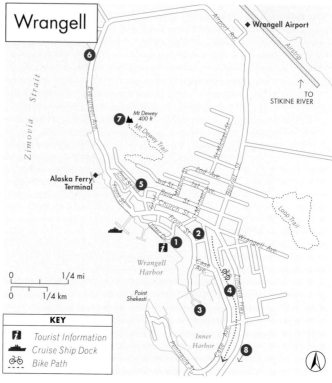

Wrangell has flown three different national flags in its time. Russia established Redoubt St. Dionysius here in 1834. Five years later Great Britain's Hudson's Bay Company leased the southern Alaska coastline, renaming the settlement Ft. Stikine. It was rechristened Wrangell when the Americans took over in 1867; the name came from Baron Ferdinand Petrovich von Wrangel, governor of the Russian-American Company.

The rough-around-the-edges town is off the track of the larger cruise ships, so it does not get the same seasonal traffic that Ketchikan and Juneau do. Hence, it is nearly devoid of the souvenir shops that dominate so many other nearby downtown areas. But the gift shops and art galleries that are here do sell locally created work, and the town is very welcoming to visitors; independent travelers would do well to add a stop in Wrangell to their Southeast wanderings.

GETTING HERE AND AROUND

Although you probably won't get to Wrangell on a cruise ship (though some small ship lines do sail here), ferries connect the town to other Southeast Alaska ports via the **Alaska Marine Highway.** The town is fairly compact, and most sights are within walking distance of the city dock or ferry terminal. Alaska Airlines provides two daily jet stops connecting from Seattle and Juneau.

A GOOD WALK

Bone up on local history and biology at the **Wrangell Museum in the Nolan Center,** which houses informative and surprisingly entertaining exhibits, a well-stocked gift shop, and a helpful visitor center. Farther along Front Street, check out **Kik-setti Totem Park** before turning onto Shakes Street to see the town's prized attraction, **Chief Shakes Island.** You may want to spend time here just soaking in the harbor view and examining the old totem poles. **Chief Shakes's grave site** is on the hill overlooking Wrangell Harbor. Get here from Chief Shakes Island by turning right on Case Avenue. From the grave site, head up Church Street

to the **Irene Ingle Public Library.** About 0.6 mi north of the ferry terminal along Evergreen Avenue you'll find **Petroglyph Beach,** where ancient etchings are visible along the shore. Be prepared to leave the observation deck behind: most of the best petroglyphs are scattered across the rocky beach. For a woodsy hike, climb **Mt. Dewey,** the hill right behind town. Farther afield (5 mi south of town) is the fun hike to **Rainbow Falls.**

It is a 1.5-mi walk between Petroglyph Beach and Chief Shakes Island, so you should plan at least three hours to complete the walk and sightseeing around town.

4

ESSENTIALS

Ferry Contact The **Alaska Marine Highway System** (☎ *907/465–3941 or 800/642–0066* ⊕ *www.ferryalaska.com*).

Medical Center **Wrangell Medical Center** (✉ *310 Bennett St.* ☎ *907/874–7000* ⊕ *www.wrangellmedicalcenter.com*).

Pharmacy **Stikine Drug** (✉ *202 Front St.* ☎ *907/874–3422* ⊕ *www.stikinedrug.com*).

Visitor Information **Wrangell Visitor Center** (✉ *296 Campbell Dr., in Nolan Center* ✇ *Box 1350, Wrangell 99929* ☎ *907/874–2829 or 800/367–9745* ⊕ *www.wrangellalaska.org*).

EXPLORING
TOP ATTRACTIONS

★ **Chief Shakes Island.** This small island sits in the center of Wrangell's protected harbor, and is accessible by a footbridge from the bottom of Shakes Street. Seven totem poles surround a traditionally styled tribal house, built in the 1930s as a replica of one that was home to many of the various Shakes and their peoples. ✉ *Off Shakes St.* ☎ *907/874–3481* 💳 *$3.50* ☉ *Daily when cruise ships are in port (ask at Wrangell Visitor Center) or by appointment.*

★ **Nolan Center.** Wrangell's museum moved into a building that acts as a centerpiece for cultural life in Wrangell. Exhibits provide a window on the region's rich history. Featured pieces include the oldest known Tlingit house posts dating from the late 18th century, decorative posts from Chief Shakes's clan house, petroglyphs, century-old spruce-root and cedar-bark baskets, masks, gold-rush memorabilia, and a fascinating photo collection. If you're spending any time in town, don't pass this up.

WORTH THE DETOUR

Fodor's Choice ★ **Anan Creek Wildlife Observatory.** About 30 mi southeast of Wrangell in the Tongass National Forest, Anan is one of Alaska's premier black- and brown-bear–viewing areas. Each summer, from early July to late August, as many as 30 to 40 bears gather at this Southeast stream to feed on huge runs of pink salmon. On an average visit of about three hours you might spot bears while strolling the ½-mi viewing boardwalk. Once on the platform, you will likely see many bears at the same time. There is a photo blind accessible from the viewing platform. Five people at a time can use the photo blind for 30-minute intervals, which provides photo opportunities of bears at less than 11 yards. The photo blind provides stream-level photo-ops of bears catching salmon. Forest Service interpreters are on hand to answer questions. The site is accessible only by boat or floatplane.

From July 5 to August 25 you must have a pass to visit Anan; the U.S. Forest Service places a limit on the number of people who can visit the site each day. Unless you have experience navigating the Stikine by boat and in walking through bear country, it's highly recommended that you go to Anan with a local guide. The guide companies provide passes to Anan for their guests.

The following Wrangell-based guide companies are all authorized to run trips to Anan. **Alaska Charters and Adventures** ☎ 888/993–2750 ⊕ www.alaskaupclose.com. **Alaska Vistas** ☎ 907/874–3006 or 888/874–3006 ⊕ www.alaskavistas. com. **Alaska Waters** (☎ 907/874–2378 or 800/347–4462 ⊕ www. alaskawaters.com). For additional details, contact the **Tongass National Forest Wrangell Ranger District** (☎ 907/874–2323 ⊕ www. fs.fed.us/r10/tongass).

Also in the building are the town's **Civic Center** (☎ 907/874–2829 or 800/367–9745 ⊕ www.wrangellalaska.org), a 200-seat movie theater/performance space/convention center, and the **Wrangell Visitor Center.** The latter is staffed when the museum is open, and has details on local adventure options. ✉ 296 Outer Dr. ☎ 907/874–3770 ☉ May–Sept., Tues.–Sat. 10–5, and when ferry or cruise ships are in port; Oct.–Apr., Tues.–Sat. 1–5.

Petroglyph Beach State Historic Park. Scattered among other rocks at this public beach are three dozen or more large stones bearing designs and pictures chiseled by unknown ancient artists. No one knows why the rocks at this curious site were etched the way they were, or even exactly how old these etchings are. You can access the beach via a boardwalk, where you'll find signs describing the site along with carved replicas of the petroglyphs. Most of the petroglyphs are to the right between the viewing deck and a large outcropping of rock in the tidal beach area. Because the original petroglyphs can be damaged by physical contact, only photographs are permitted. But you are welcome to use the replicas to make a rubbing from rice paper and charcoal or crayons (available in local stores). ✉ 0.6 mi north of ferry terminal off Evergreen Ave.

WORTH NOTING

Chief Shakes's Grave Site. Buried here is Shakes V, who led the local Tlingit during the first half of the 19th century. A white picket fence surrounds the grave, and two killer-whale totem poles mark his resting spot overlooking the harbor. Find the grave on Case Avenue. ⊠ *Case Ave.*

Irene Ingle Public Library. The library, behind the post office, has two ancient petroglyphs out front and is home to a large collection of Alaskan books, computers with free Internet access, and a helpful staff. ⊠ *124 2nd St.* ☎ *907/874–3535.*

Kik-setti Totem Park. You'll find several recently carved totem poles at this pocket-size park with Alaska greenery. ⊠ *Front St.*

Mt. Dewey. Despite the name, this landmark is more a hill than a peak. Still, it's a steep 15-minute climb up the John Muir Trail from town to the top through a second-growth forest. The trail begins from 3rd Street behind the high school, and an observation platform on top provides a viewpoint for protected waterways and islands named from its Russian history, including Zarembo, Vank, and Woronkofski. The trail is named for naturalist John Muir, who, in 1879, made his way up the trail and built a campfire. Locals didn't realize there was anybody up on Mt. Dewey and the campfire light caused quite a commotion below.

Rainbow Falls. The trail to this scenic waterfall starts across the road from Shoemaker Bay, 5 mi south of Wrangell. A ¾-mi trail climbs uphill through the rain forest, with long stretches of boardwalk steps, ending at an overlook just below the falls. Hikers with more stamina can continue another 3 mi and 1,500 vertical feet to Shoemaker Bay Overlook.

OUTDOOR ACTIVITIES AND GUIDED TOURS

AIR CHARTER

Sunrise Aviation (☎ *907/874–2319 or 800/874–2311* ⊕ *www.sunriseflights. com*) is a charter-only air carrier that flies to the Anan Creek Wildlife Observatory, LeConte Glacier, or Forest Service cabins.

BICYCLING

A waterfront trail connects Wrangell with Shoemaker Bay Recreation Area, 4½ mi south of town. The trail is mainly flat; more adventurous souls can brave the dozens of miles of logging roads that crisscross the island.

BOATING

Mark Galla of **Alaska Peak & Seas** (☎ *907/874–2454* ⊕ *www. wedoalaska.com*) guides wildlife trips, Stikine jet-boat tours, and boat trips to surrounding areas. **Alaska Vistas and Stikine Wilderness Adventures** (☎ *907/874–3006 or 866/874–3006* ⊕ *www.alaskavistas.com*) has jet-boat trips to Anan Creek Wildlife Observatory that depart from Wrangell, plus a variety of guided sea-kayak adventures and rafting trips. They also offer custom tours and itinerary planning. **Breakaway Adventures** (☎ *907/874–2488 or 888/385–2488* ⊕ *www. breakawayadventures.com*) leads a variety of jet-boat trips, including a tour to Chief Shakes Glacier and the nearby hot springs. You can catch one of its water taxis to Petersburg or Prince of Wales Island.

FISHING

Numerous companies schedule salmon- and trout-fishing excursions ranging in length from an afternoon to a week. Contact the **Wrangell Visitor Center** (☎ *800/367–9745* ⊕ *www.wrangellalaska.org*) for information on guide services and locations.

GOLF

Muskeg Meadows Golf Course (☎ *907/874–4653* ⊕ *www.wrangellalaskagolf.com*), Southeast Alaska's first USGA regulation links, is a well-maintained, 2,950-yard 9-hole course with a driving range. Situated in a wooded area ½ mi from town, the course is easily accessible, and golf clubs and pull carts can be rented on-site. The course is, most likely, one of the only ones in the world with a "Ravens Rule," which states that "a ball stolen by a raven may be replaced, with no penalty, provided there is a witness."

NATURAL HISTORY

Alaska Charters and Adventures (☎ *888/993–2750* ⊕ *www.alaskaupclose. com*) offers wildlife viewing, bear photography trips, fishing, glacier tours, and a Stikine River jet-boat wilderness tour.

Alaska Vistas. This company does regular float trips on the Stikine, which rises in British Columbia and flows through the edges of the Stikine Icefield. This historic river, once an alternate route to the goldfields, is like nothing else in the state. ☎ *907/874–3006 or 866/874–3006* ⊕ *www.alaskavistas.com.*

WHERE TO EAT

$

DINER

✕**Diamond C Cafe.** The big breakfasts at the Diamond C are just part of the attraction. The café also serves as the gathering place for a group of local guys and, really, it's fun to just sit back and listen. As you dig into the breakfast hash and other goodies, though, there's a chance you'll only have eyes for your plate. ✉ *223 Front St.* ☎ *907/874–3677* ☾ *Breakfast and lunch only.*

$$–$$$

AMERICAN

✕**Stikine Inn Restaurant.** With views overlooking the water, the restaurant at the Stikine Inn is, easily, the prettiest place to dine in town. Considering the sparse number of restaurants in town, the Stikine could just serve a get-by menu, but the restaurant's salads, pizzas, burgers, and hearty soups go far beyond. They serve seriously tasty dishes. Portions tend to be oversize, especially on the dessert front. Consider splitting that dessert you eyeballed on the menu with at least one other person (if not two). The Stikine also has a full bar, and for those who enjoy their beverages caffeinated serves good coffee drinks. ✉ *107 Stikine Ave.* ☎ *907/874–4388* ⊕ *www.stikineinn.com/dining.html.*

$$–$$$

AMERICAN

✕**Zak's Cafe.** Though Zak's has a no-frills look about it, it's worth a visit (especially since there aren't a huge number of dining choices in town). The restaurant serves good food at reasonable prices. Check out the day's specials or try the steaks, chicken, seafood, and salads. At lunch the menu includes burgers, sandwiches, fish-and-chips, and wraps. ✉ *314 Front St.* ☎ *907/874–3355.*

WHERE TO STAY

For expanded hotel reviews, visit Fodors.com.

$ **Alaskan Sourdough Lodge.** Formerly Bruce Harding's Old Sourdough Lodge, this rambling inn on the south side of the harbor, five blocks from downtown, began life as a construction camp, and traces of its rough-hewn origins remain today. **Pros:** excellent home-style dining; continental breakfast included with room rate. **Cons:** tight hallways and sparse furnishings; pets are not allowed. **TripAdvisor:** "homey feel is phenomenal," "room was comfortable and clean," "casual and pleasant." ✉ *1104 Peninsula St.* ☎ *907/874–3613 or 800/874–3613* ⊕ *www.akgetaway.com/HardingsLodge* ⏎ *15 rooms, 1 suite* ⚘ *In-room: Internet, Wi-Fi (some). In-hotel: restaurant, bar, water sports, laundry facilities, business center* ⊖*Breakfast.*

$–$$ **Grand View Bed & Breakfast.** Two miles from town—perhaps within walking distance for avid pedestrians—this unassuming beachfront home provides spectacular views across Zimovia Strait. **Pros:** expert sightseeing tours provided by owners; visitors get the inside scoop from a true local; complimentary Wi-Fi. **Cons:** 2 mi from town; no credit cards accepted. ✉ *Mi 2, Zimovia Hwy.* ⏎ *Box 927, 99929* ☎ *907/874–3225* ⊕ *www.grandviewbnb.com* ⏎ *3 rooms* ⚘ *In-hotel: laundry facilities, business center* ⊟ *No credit cards* ⊖*Breakfast.*

$ **Rooney's Roost Bed & Breakfast.** This century-old home—easily Wrangell's most charming digs—is just a block from downtown. **Pros:** large, delicious breakfast; owned by a local who grew up in Wrangell. **Cons:** with just four rooms, you should book early. **TripAdvisor:** "very quaint and cozy," "friendly and homey," "rooms were spacious and beautifully decorated." ✉ *206 McKinnon St.* ⏎ *Box 552, Wrangell 99929* ☎ *907/874–2026* ⊕ *www.rooneysroost.com* ⏎ *4 rooms* ⚘ *In-room: Wi-Fi* ⊖*Breakfast.*

¢ **Shakes Slough Cabins.** If you're a hot springs or hot tub enthusiast, these Forest Service cabins on the Stikine River, accessible from Wrangell, are worth checking out. **Pros:** open-air hot tub; stunningly beautiful and remote location. **Cons:** cabins have no electricity or water; hard to get to if you don't hire a local boat guide to bring you to the cabins; popular with locals and return visitors, and tend to fill in advance. ✉ *Forest Service, 525 Bennett St., Wrangell* ☎ *907/874–2323, 877/444–6777 National Recreation Reservation Service* ⊕ *www.recreation.gov* ⏎ *2 cabins.*

$–$$ **Stikine Inn.** After some down years, Wrangell's largest inn is on the upswing; the rooms and lobby have been remodeled, and the Stikine Inn's in-house restaurant and wine bar may be the best in town. **Pros:** scenic waterfront location; good restaurant; 100% smoke-free. **Cons:** decor won't win any design awards. **TripAdvisor:** "friendly and helpful proprietors," "warm people and beautiful views," "very comfortable."

✉ 107 Stikine Ave. ☎ 907/874–3388 or 888/874–3388 🌐 www.stikineinn.com ↬ 34 rooms, 3 suites ♁ In-room: kitchen (some), Wi-Fi. In-hotel: restaurant, some pets allowed.

SHOPPING

Garnet Ledge, a rocky ledge at the mouth of the Stikine River, is the source for garnets sold by local children for 25¢ to $50. The site was deeded to the Boy Scouts in 1962 and to the Presbyterian Church in Wrangell in 2006, so only children can collect these colorful but imperfect stones, the largest of which are an inch across. You can purchase garnets at a few covered shelters near the city dock when cruise ships are in, at the Wrangell Museum, or at the ferry terminal when a ferry is in port.

Local artist **Brenda Schwartz-Yeager** (✉ *7 Front St.* ☎ *907/874–3508* 🌐 *www.marineartist.com*) creates watercolor scenes of the Alaskan coast on navigational charts of the region. Schwartz-Yeager, who grew up in Wrangell, is also a boat captain and local guide who, with her husband, owns Alaska Charters and Adventures.

PETERSBURG

22 mi north of Wrangell.

Getting to Petersburg is an experience, whether you take the "high road" by air or the "low road" by sea. Alaska Airlines claims one of the shortest jet flights in the world, from takeoff at Wrangell to landing at Petersburg. The schedule calls for 20 minutes of flying, but it's usually more like 15. At sea level only ferries and smaller cruisers can squeak through Wrangell Narrows with the aid of more than 50 buoys and range markers along the 22-mi waterway, which takes almost four hours. But the inaccessibility of Petersburg is also part of its charm: you'll never be overwhelmed here by hordes of cruise passengers; only smaller ships can reach the town.

The Scandinavian heritage is gradually being submerged by the larger American culture, but you can occasionally hear Norwegian spoken, especially during the Little Norway Festival, held here each year on the weekend closest to May 17. If you're in town during the festival, be sure to take part in one of the fish feeds that highlight Syttende Mai, or, the Norwegian Constitution Day, celebration. You won't find better folk dancing and beer-batter halibut outside Norway.

One of the most pleasant things to do in Petersburg is to roam among the fishing vessels tied up dockside in the town's expanding harbor. This is one of Alaska's busiest, most prosperous fishing communities, with an enormous variety of seacraft. You'll see small trollers, big halibut vessels, and sleek pleasure craft. By watching shrimp, salmon, or halibut catches being brought ashore (though be prepared for the pungent aroma), you can get a real appreciation for this industry.

On clear days Petersburg's scenery is second to none. Across Frederick Sound the sawlike peaks of the Stikine Ice Cap scrape clouds from the

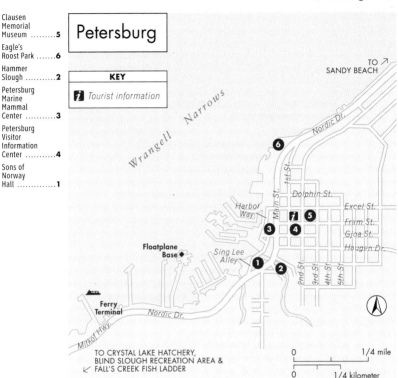

sky, looking every bit as malevolent as their monikers suggest. (Some of the most wickedly named summits include Devil's Thumb, Kate's Needle, and Witch's Tit.) **LeConte Glacier,** Petersburg's biggest draw, lies at the foot of the ice cap, about 25 mi east of town. Accessible only by water or air, the LeConte is the continent's southernmost tidewater glacier and one of its most active, often calving off so many icebergs that the tidewater bay at its face is carpeted shore to shore with floating bergs.

Although Petersburg is nice to explore, commercial fishing is more important than tourism—in other words, you'll find more hardware stores than jewel merchants. But that's also a big part of its charm. The main attractions are the town's Norwegian heritage, its vibrant community, and its magnificent mountain-backed setting. The country around Petersburg provides an array of outdoor fun, from whale-watching and glacier-gazing to hiking and fishing.

GETTING HERE AND AROUND

Once you arrive in Petersburg by ferry on the **Alaska Marine Highway** or by airplane, a host of outdoor activities await you. **Kaleidoscope Cruises** conducts whale-watching and glacier-ecology boat tours led by a professional naturalist, and **Tongass Kayak Adventures** leads day and overnight tours to the icebergs in LeConte Glacier Bay and to see the whales of Frederick Sound. You can also see the Stikine River and LeConte Glacier from above on a flightseeing tour with the locally popular air-taxi operator **Pacific Wings** or rent a boat at **Scandia House** or **Jensen Boat Rentals**. For help finding more tours of the environs, contact travel agency **Viking Travel** or visit the **Petersburg Visitor Information Center**.

ESSENTIALS

Ferry Contact Alaska Marine Highway System (☎ 907/465-3941 or 800/642-0066 ⊕ www.ferryalaska.com).

> ## FISH AND FLOWERS
>
> Petersburg evokes Norway: tidy white buildings line the streets, bright-color leaf and flower designs (called rosemaling) decorate older homes, and row upon row of sturdy fishing vessels pack the harbor. No wonder—this community was founded by Norwegian Peter Buschmann in 1897.

Medical Assistance Petersburg Medical Center (⊠ 103 Fram St. ☎ 907/772-4291 ⊕ www.pmc-health.com).

Pharmacy Rexall Drugs (⊠ 215 N. Nordic Dr. ☎ 907/772-3265 ⊕ www.petersburgrexall.com).

Tour Information Jensen Boat Rentals (☎ 907/772-4635 ⊕ www.jensensboatrentals.com). **Kaleidoscope Cruises** (☎ 907/772-3736 or 800/868-4373 ⊕ www.petersburglodgingandtours.com). **Pacific Wing** (⊠ 1500 Haugen Dr. ☎ 907/772-9258). **Tongass Kayak Adventures** (☎ 907/772-4600 ⊕ www.tongasskayak.com). **Viking Travel** (☎ 907/772-3818 or 800/327-2571 ⊕ www.alaskaferry.com).

Visitor Information Petersburg Visitor Information Center (⊠ 1st and Fram Sts. ⌂ Box 649, Petersburg 99833 ☎ 907/772-4636 ⊕ www.petersburg.org).

EXPLORING

Clausen Memorial Museum. The museum's exhibits explore commercial fishing and the cannery industry, the era of fish traps, the social life of Petersburg, and Tlingit culture. Don't miss the museum shop; the 126.5-pound king salmon—the largest ever caught commercially—as well as the Tlingit dugout canoe; the Cape Decision lighthouse station lens; and *Earth, Sea and Sky,* a 3-D wall mural outside. ⊠ 203 Fram St. ☎ 907/772-3598 ⊕ www.clausenmuseum.net ⌘ $3 ⊗ May–early Sept., Mon.–Sat. 10–5; early-Sept.–late-Dec., Tues.–Sat. 10–2.

Eagle's Roost Park. Just north of the Petersburg Fisheries cannery, this small roadside park is a great place to spot eagles, especially at low tide. On a clear day you will also discover dramatic views of the sharp-edged Coast Range, including the 9,077-foot summit of Devil's Thumb.

Hammer Slough. Houses on high stilts and the historic Sons of Norway Hall border this creek that floods with each high tide, creating a photogenic reflecting pool.

Petersburg Marine Mammal Center. Visitors to this nonprofit research and learning center can share and gather information on marine mammal sightings, pick up reference material, and have fun with the interactive educational kiosk. ⊠ Gjoa St. and Sing Lee Alley, behind Viking Travel ☎ 907/772-4170 summer only ⊕ www.psgmmc.org ⌘ Free ⊗ Mid-June–Aug., Mon.–Sat. 9–5.

Petersburg Visitor Information Center. This small office is a good source for local information, including maps and details on tours, charters, and nearby outdoor recreation opportunities. ✉ *1st and Fram Sts.* ☎ *907/772–4636 or 866/484–4700* ⊕ *www.petersburg.org* ⊗ *May–Sept., Mon.–Sat. 9–5, Sun. noon–4; Oct.–Apr., weekdays 10–2.*

Sons of Norway Hall. Built in 1912, this large, barnlike structure that stands just south of the Hammer Slough is the headquarters of an organization devoted to keeping alive the traditions and culture of Norway. The window shutters are decorated with colorful Norwegian rosemaling designs. Outside sits a replica of a Viking ship that is a featured attraction in the annual Little Norway Festival each May. On the south side of the building is the **Bojer Wikan Fisherman's Memorial,** where deceased local fishermen are honored with a bronze statue. ✉ *23 S. Sing Lee Alley* ☎ *907/772–4575.*

OFF THE BEATEN PATH

Falls Creek Fish Ladder. Coho and pink salmon migrate upstream in late summer and early fall at this fish ladder south of town. Fish head up the ladder to get around a small falls. ✉ *Mi 10.8, Mitkof Hwy.*

Blind Slough Recreation Area. This recreation area includes a number of sites scattered along the Mitkof Highway 15–20 mi south of Petersburg. **Blind River Rapids Trail** is a wheelchair-accessible 1-mi boardwalk that leads to a three-sided shelter overlooking the river—one of Southeast's most popular fishing spots—before looping back through the muskeg. Not far away is a bird-viewing area where several dozen trumpeter swans spend the winter. In summer you're likely to see many ducks and other waterfowl. At Mile 18 the state-run **Crystal Lake Hatchery** releases thousands of king and coho salmon each year. The kings return in June and July, the coho in August and September. Nearby is a popular picnic area. Four miles south of the hatchery is a Forest Service campground. ☎ *907/772–4772* ⊕ *www.fs.fed.us/r10/ro/naturewatch/southeast/blind_slough/blind_slough.htm.*

Other popular day adventures include a kayaking trip up **Petersburg Creek** or a hike on the **Three Lakes Loop Trail.**

OUTDOOR ACTIVITIES

HIKING

For an enjoyable loop hike from town, follow Dolphin Street uphill from the center of town. At the intersection with 5th Street, a boardwalk path leads 900 feet through forested wetlands to the baseball fields, where a second boardwalk takes you to 12th Street and Haugen Drive. Turn left on Haugen and follow it past the airport to **Sandy Beach Park,** where picnickers can sit under log shelters and low tide reveals remnants of ancient fish traps and a number of petroglyphs. From here you can return to town via Sandy Beach Road or hike the beach when the tide is out. Along the way is the charming **Outlook Park,** a covered observatory with binoculars to scan for marine life. A pullout at Hungry Point provides views to the Coast Range and Frederick Sound. Across the road the half-mile **Hungry Point Trail** takes you back to the baseball fields—a great spot for panoramic views of the mountains—where you can return downtown on the nature boardwalk. Plan on an hour and a half for this walk.

For something more strenuous, a 4-mi trail begins at the airport and climbs 1,600 feet in elevation to **Raven's Roost Cabin**. Along the way you take in a panorama that reaches from the ice-bound Coast Range to the protected waters and forested islands of the Inside Passage far below. The two-story Forest Service cabin is available for rent ($35 per night); contact the **National Recreation Reservation Service** (☎ *518/885–3639 or 877/444–6777* ⊕ *www.recreation.gov*). Get details on these and other hikes from the Petersburg Visitor Information Center or from the **Petersburg Ranger District** (✉ *12 N. Nordic Dr.* ☎ *907/772–3871* ⊕ *www.fs.fed.us/r10/tongass*).

WHERE TO EAT

¢–$ ✕ **Coastal Cold Storage.** This busy little seafood deli in the heart of Peters-
SEAFOOD   burg serves daily lunch specials, including fish chowders and halibut beer bits (a local favorite), along with grilled-chicken wraps, steak sandwiches, breakfast omelets, and waffles. It's a great place for a quick bite en route to your next adventure; there isn't much seating in the shop's cramped interior. On sunny days, place your order and then grab a seat at one of the tables set up out front on the sidewalk. Live or cooked crab is available for takeout, and the shop can process your sport-caught fish. ✉ *306 N. Nordic Dr.* ☎ *907/772–4177 or 877/257–4746.*

¢   ✕ **Helse Restaurant.** Locals flock to this modest mom-and-pop place for
AMERICAN   lunch. It's the closest thing to home cooking Petersburg has to offer, and most days it's open from 8 to 5, even in winter. A couple of dozen sandwiches grace the menu, as do rotating soups and homemade bread. The daily specials are a good bet, and the gyros are decent as well. Helse also doubles as an ice cream and espresso stand. ✉ *13 Sing Lee Alley* ☎ *907/772–3444.*

$ ✕ **Papa Bear's Pizza.** Although it has a few tables, this often-crowded
PIZZA   pizza joint primarily specializes in take-out pizzas, pizza by the slice, hamburgers, submarine sandwiches, and giant calzones. It also serves ice cream. ✉ *301 S. Nordic Dr.* ☎ *907/772–3727.*

WHERE TO STAY

For expanded hotel reviews, visit Fodors.com.

$$–$$$ ⊞ **A Guest House at Water's Edge.** Along the shore of Frederick Sound, 2 mi north of Petersburg, this two-bedroom, family-run guesthouse offers one creek- and one beachside room. **Pros:** quiet location; waterfront view. **Cons:** property is not disability-friendly; breakfast is not served; three-night minimum stay. ✉ *705 Sandy Beach Rd.* ☎ *907/772–3736 or 800/868–4373* ⊕ *www.petersburglodgingandtours.com* ⤶ 2

rooms ♿ *In-room: kitchen, Wi-Fi. In-hotel: laundry facilities, some age restrictions.*

$$ ⌂ **The Lucky Loon.** Sitting on a beautiful piece of waterfront property, the two-bedroom house, fitted with two double beds and two queen-size beds, feels like instant home from the moment you walk in. ⊠ *181 Frederick Dr.* ☎ *907/772–2345* ⊕ *www.theluckyloon.com* ⬎ *2 bedrooms* ♿ *In-room: kitchen, Internet. In-hotel: laundry facilities.*

$$–$$$ ⌂ **Scandia House.** This hotel on Petersburg's main drag, a fixture since 1910, was rebuilt following a 1995 fire. **Pros:** some pets allowed; airport and ferry shuttle. **Cons:** fourth-floor rooms aren't accessible by elevator. **TripAdvisor:** "perfect location and clean rooms," "great harbor location," "friendly place." ⊠ *110 Nordic Dr.* ☎ *907/772–4281 or 800/722–5006* ⊕ *www.scandiahousehotel.com* ⬎ *33 rooms, 3 suites* ♿ *In-room: kitchen (some), Wi-Fi. In-hotel: water sports, some pets allowed* ⏐⊙⏐ *Breakfast.*

$ ⌂ **Sea Level B&B.** The views from the large picture windows at this small B&B, a home on stilts above the Wrangell Narrows, are worth the 10 or 15 minutes it takes to walk to town. **Pros:** excellent view of narrows; excellent chance of spotting a whale from the house. **Cons:** B&B is a 10- to 15-minute walk from downtown. ⊠ *913 N. Nordic Dr.* ☎ *907/772–3240* ⊕ *www.sealevelbnb.com* ⬎ *2 rooms* ♿ *In-room: kitchen (some), Wi-Fi* ⊟ *No credit cards* ⏐⊙⏐ *Breakfast.*

$ ⌂ **Tides Inn.** The Tides, Petersburg's largest hotel, is a block uphill from the town's main thoroughfare. **Pros:** views of the boat harbor from the newer rooms. **Cons:** rooms in the old wing are dark and dated. **TripAdvisor:** "staff is very friendly and helpful," "quiet and comfortable," "great breakfasts." ⊠ *307 N. 1st St.* ☎ *907/772–4288 or 800/665–8433* ⊕ *www.tidesinnalaska.com* ⬎ *45 rooms* ♿ *In-room: kitchen (some), Wi-Fi. In-hotel: some pets allowed* ⏐⊙⏐ *Breakfast.*

NIGHTLIFE

All bars and restaurants in Petersburg are now smoke-free. The **Harbor Bar** (⊠ *310 N. Nordic Dr.* ☎ *907/772–4526*), with ships' wheels, nautical pictures, and a mounted red snapper, is true to the town's seafaring spirit. A separate outside entrance leads to the bar's liquor store. Sample the brew and blasting music at **Kito's Kave** (⊠ *Sing Lee Alley* ☎ *907/772–3207*), a popular hangout among rowdy local fishermen. La Fonda, a Mexican restaurant, leases space inside the bar.

SHOPPING

BOOKSTORE

Off an alley in a big, beautiful white house that served as a boardinghouse to fishermen and schoolteachers, **Sing Lee Alley Books** stocks books on Alaska, best sellers, cards, and gifts. ⊠ *11 Sing Lee Alley* ☎ *907/772–4440.*

SEAFOOD

At **Tonka Seafoods,** across the street from the Sons of Norway Hall, check out the gift shop, and sample smoked or canned halibut and salmon. Be sure to taste the white king salmon—an especially flavorful type of Chinook that the locals swear by. Tonka will also ship. ⊠ *22 Sing Lee Alley* ☏ *907/772–3662 or 888/560–3662* ⊕ *www.tonkaseafoods.com.*

Outside of downtown, consider stopping in at **Northern Lights Smokeries** for owner Thomas Cumps' hot-smoked white king, red king, and sockeye salmon, or a local favorite, cold-smoked black cod. Northern Lights also ships. It's best to call ahead to make sure he'll be around before you stop by. ☏ *907/772–4608* ⊕ *www.nlsmokeries.com.*

SITKA

110 mi west of Petersburg.

It's hard not to like Sitka, with its eclectic blend of Native Alaskan, Russian, and American history and its dramatic and beautiful open-ocean setting. This is one of the best Inside Passage towns to explore on foot, with such sights as St. Michael's Cathedral, Sheldon Jackson Museum, Castle Hill, Sitka National Historical Park, and the Alaska Raptor Center topping the town's must-see list.

Sitka was home to the Kiksádi clan of the Tlingit people for centuries prior to the 18th-century arrival of the Russians under the direction of territorial governor Alexander Baranof. Baranof believed the region was ideal for the fur trade. The governor also coveted the Sitka site for its beauty, mild climate, and economic potential; in the island's massive timber forests he saw raw materials for shipbuilding. Its location offered trading routes as far west as Asia and as far south as California and Hawaii. In 1799 Baranof built St. Michael Archangel—a wooden fort and trading post 6 mi north of the present town.

Strong disagreements arose shortly after the settlement. The Tlingits attacked the settlers and burned their buildings in 1802. Baranof, however, was away in Kodiak at the time. He returned in 1804 with a formidable force—including shipboard cannons—and attacked the Tlingits at their fort near Indian River, site of the present-day 105-acre Sitka National Historical Park, forcing many of them north to Chichagof Island.

By 1821 the Tlingits had reached an accord with the Russians, who were happy to benefit from the tribe's hunting skills. Under Baranof and succeeding managers, the Russian-American Company and the town prospered, becoming known as the Paris of the Pacific. The community built a major shipbuilding and repair facility, sawmills, and forges, and even initiated an ice industry, shipping blocks of ice from nearby Swan Lake to the booming San Francisco market. The settlement that was the site of the 1802 conflict is now called Old Sitka. It is a state park and listed as a National Historic Landmark.

The town declined after its 1867 transfer from Russia to the United States, but became prosperous again during World War II, when it served as a base for the U.S. effort to drive the Japanese from the

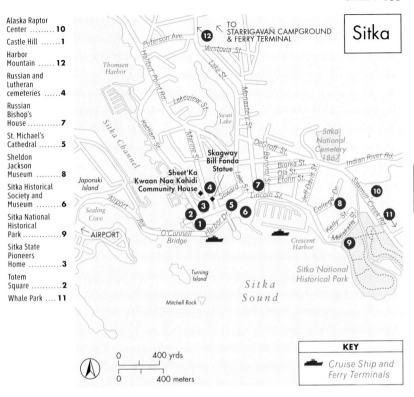

Aleutian Islands. Today its most important industries are fishing, government, and tourism.

GETTING HERE AND AROUND

Sitka is a common stop on cruise routes for smaller ships and a regular stop along the **Alaska Marine Highway System. Alaska Airlines** also operates flights from Seattle and other Pacific Coast and Southwestern cities to Sitka. The best way to see the town's sights is on foot.

ESSENTIALS

Airline Contact Alaska Airlines (☎ 800/252–7522 ⊕ www.alaskaair.com).

Ferry Contact Alaska Marine Highway System (☎ 907/465–3941 or 800/642–0066 ⊕ www.ferryalaska.com). **Sitka Ferry Terminal** (☎ 907/747–8737).

Internet Highliner Café (✉ 327 Seward St., in Seward Square Mall ☎ 907/747–4924).

Medical Assistance Sitka Community Hospital (✉ 209 Moller Ave. ☎ 907/747–3241 ⊕ www.sitkahospital.org).

Pharmacy Harry Race Pharmacy (✉ 106 Lincoln St. ☎ 907/747–8006). **White's Pharmacy** (✉ 705 Halibut Point Rd. ☎ 907/747–5755).

A GOOD WALK

Most folks begin their tours of Sitka under the distinctive onion dome of **St. Michael's Cathedral**, right in the town center. A block behind the cathedral along Harbor Drive is **Harrigan Centennial Hall**, a low-slung convention hall that houses the smallish **Sitka Historical Society and Museum** and an information desk that opens when cruise ships are in port. A block east, along Lincoln Street, you'll find the **Russian Bishop's House**, one of the symbols of Russian rule. Continue out on Lincoln Street along the bustling boat harbor to Sheldon Jackson College, where the worthwhile **Sheldon Jackson Museum** is packed with Native cultural artifacts. Another ½ mi out along gently curving Metlakatla Street is the **Sitka National Historical Park**, where you can chat with Native artisans as they craft carvings and silver jewelry. Behind the main building a network of well-signed paths takes you through the rain forest past more than a dozen totem poles and to the site of a Tlingit fort from the battle of 1804. A signed trail crosses the Indian River (watch for spawning salmon in late summer) and heads across busy Sawmill Creek Road to the **Alaska Raptor Center**, for an up-close look at bald eagles.

Return to town along Sawmill Creek Road. On your right, you'll see the white headstones of the small Sitka National Cemetery. Back downtown, you can browse the many shops or walk along Harbor Drive and take the path to the summit of **Castle Hill**, where Russia transferred Alaska to American hands—these are the best views in town. If you follow the path down the other side of the hill, check out the impressive **Sitka State Pioneers Home**, with the statue of pioneer "Skagway Bill" Fonda. Across the street is **Totem Square**, with its tall totem pole and three ancient anchors. Adjacent to the Pioneers Home is the **Sheet'ka Kwaan Naa Kahidi** community house. Native dances take place here in summer. End your walk at the haunting (not haunted) **Russian and Lutheran cemeteries** that fill the dark woods along Marine Street a block from the blockhouse. The grave of Princess Maksoutoff, a member of the Russian royal family, is here.

Sitka has many attractions, and you can easily spend a full day exploring this culturally rich area. You can accomplish the walk in two to three hours if you do not spend much time at each stop. You can pound the pavement around town in an hour or so.

Visitor Information Sitka Convention and Visitors Bureau (✉ *303 Lincoln St.* 🖂 *Box 1226, Sitka 99835* ☎ *907/747–5940* ⊕ *www.sitka.org*).

EXPLORING

TOP ATTRACTIONS

☾ ★ **Alaska Raptor Center.** The only full-service avian hospital in Alaska, the Raptor Center rehabilitates 100 to 200 birds each year. Situated just above Indian Creek, the center is a 20-minute walk from downtown. Well-versed guides provide an introduction to the rehabilitation center (including a short video), and guests are able to visit with one of these majestic birds. The Raptor Center's primary attraction is an enclosed

20,000-square-foot flight training center, built to replicate the rain forest, where injured eagles relearn survival skills, including flying and catching salmon. Visitors watch through one-way glass windows. A large deck out back faces an open-air enclosure for eagles and other raptors whose injuries prevent them from returning to the wild. Additional mews with hawks, owls, and other birds are along a rain-forest path. The gift shop sells all sorts of eagle paraphernalia, the proceeds from which fund the center's programs. ⊠ *1000 Raptor Way, off Sawmill Creek Rd.* ☎ *907/747–8662 or 800/643–9425* ⊕ *www.alaskaraptor. org* 🖾 *$12* ⊙ *Mid-May–Sept., daily 8–4.*

★ **St. Michael's Cathedral.** This cathedral, one of Southeast Alaska's best-known national landmarks, is treasured by visitors and locals alike—so treasured that in 1966, as a fire engulfed the building, townspeople risked their lives and rushed inside to rescue the cathedral's precious Russian icons, religious objects, and vestments. Using original blueprints, an almost exact replica of onion-dome St. Michael's was completed in 1976. Today you can see what could possibly be the largest collection of Russian icons in the United States, among them the much-prized *Our Lady of Sitka* (also known as the *Sitka Madonna*) and the *Christ Pantocrator* (*Christ the World Judge*), displayed on the altar screen. ⊠ *240 Lincoln St.* ☎ *907/747–8120* ⊕ *www.nps.gov/akso/cr/ akrcultural/CulturalMain/2ndLevel/NHL/NHLStMichael.htm* 🖾 *$2 requested donation* ⊙ *May–Sept., daily 8:30–4; Oct.–Apr., hrs vary.*

★ **Sheldon Jackson Museum.** Near the campus of the former **Sheldon Jackson College,** this octagonal museum, which dates from 1895, contains priceless Native Alaskan items collected by Dr. Sheldon Jackson (1834–1909), who traveled the remote regions of Alaska as an educator and missionary. This state-run museum features artifacts from every Native Alaska culture; on display are carved masks, Chilkat blankets, dogsleds, kayaks, and even the impressive helmet worn by Chief Katlean during the 1804 battle against the Russians. The museum's small but well-stocked gift shop, operated by the Friends of the Sheldon Jackson Museum, carries books, paper goods, and handicrafts created by Alaska Native artists. ■TIP➔ Don't be shy. Open the drawers under the glass cases all around the main room of the musem. They hold on-exhibit artifacts, too. ⊠ *104 College Dr.* ☎ *907/747–8981* ⊕ *www.museums. state.ak.us/sheldon_jackson/sjhome.html* 🖾 *$4 mid-May–mid-Sept., $3 mid-Sept.–mid-May* ⊙ *Mid-May–mid-Sept., daily 9–5; mid-Sept.–mid-May, Tues.–Sat. 10–4.*

Fodor'sChoice **Sitka National Historical Park.** The main building at this 113-acre park
★ houses a small museum with fascinating historical exhibits and photos of Tlingit native culture. Highlights include a brass peace hat given to the Sitka Kiksádi by Russian traders in the early 1800s and Chilkat robes. Head to the theater to watch a 12-minute video about Russian-Tlingit conflict in the 19th century. Ask a ranger to point you toward the Centennial Totem Pole, installed in honor of the park's 100th anniversary in 2011. Also here is the **Southeast Alaska Indian Cultural Center,** where Native artisans demonstrate silversmithing, weaving, wood carving, and basketry. Make sure you strike up a conversation (or two) with the artists; they're there to showcase and talk about their

work as well as Tlingit cultural traditions. At the far end of the building are seven totems (some more than a century old) that have been brought indoors to protect them from decay. Behind the center a wide, 2-mi path takes you through the forest and along the shore of Sitka Sound. Scattered along the way are some of the most skillfully carved native totem poles in Alaska. Keep going on the trail to see spawning salmon from the footbridge over Indian River. Park Service rangers lead themed walks in summer, which focus on the Russian-Tlingit conflict, the area's natural history, and the park's totem poles. ✉ *106 Metlakatla St.* ☎ *907/747–6281, 907/747–8061 gift shop* ⊕ *www.nps. gov/sitk* 🎫 *$4* ☉ *May–Sept., daily 8–5; Oct.–Apr., closed Sun.*

WORTH NOTING

Castle Hill. On this hill Alaska was formally handed over to the United States on October 18, 1867, and the first 49-star U.S. flag was flown on January 3, 1959, signifying Alaska's statehood. To reach the hill, take the first right off Harbor Drive just before O'Connell Bridge; then go into the **Baranof Castle Hill State Historic Site** entrance. A paved path switchbacks to the top, where you can read the interpretive signs on the area's Tlingit and Russian history and take in the views of Crescent Harbor and downtown Sitka. On a clear day, look for the volcanic flanks of Mt. Edgecumbe on the horizon.

Harbor Mountain. During World War II the U.S. Army constructed a road to the 2,000-foot level of Harbor Mountain, a perfect spot from which to watch for invading Japanese subs or ships (none were seen). This road has been improved over the years, and it is possible to drive 5 mi to a spectacular summit viewpoint across Sitka Sound. A trail climbs uphill from the parking lot, and then follows the ridge 2.5 mi to a Forest Service shelter. From there ambitious hikers could continue downhill another 3.5 mi to Sitka via the **Gavan Hill Trail.** ⊕ *dnr.alaska. gov/parks/aktrails/ats/se/gavin.htm.*

Russian and Lutheran cemeteries. Most of Sitka's Russian dignitaries are buried in these sites off Marine Street, which, thanks to their wooded locations, require a bit of exploring to locate. The most distinctive (and easily accessible) grave belongs to Princess Maksoutoff (died 1862), wife of the last Russian governor and one of the most illustrious members of the Russian royal family to be buried on Alaska soil.

Russian Bishop's House. A registered historic landmark, this house facing the harbor was constructed by the Russian-American Company for Bishop Innocent Veniaminov in 1842 and completed in 1843. Inside the house, one of the few remaining Russian-built log structures in Alaska, are exhibits on the history of Russian America, including several places where portions of the house's structure are peeled away to expose Russian building techniques. The ground level is a free museum, and Park Service rangers lead guided tours of the second floor, which houses the residential quarters and a chapel. ✉ *501 Lincoln St.* ☎ *907/747–0135* ⊕ *www.nps.gov/sitk* 🎫 *Tours $4* ☉ *May–Sept., daily 8:30–5; Oct.–Apr. by appointment.*

Sitka Historical Society and Museum. A Tlingit war canoe sits beside this brick building, farmally named Harrigan Centennial Hall. Check out the museum's collection of Tlingit, Victorian-era, and Alaska-purchase historical artifacts; there's an auditorium for New Archangel Dancers performances, which take place when cruise ships are in port. ⊠ *330 Harbor Dr.* ☎ *907/747–6455 museum, 907/747–5940 Visitors Bureau* ⊕ *www.sitkahistory.org* ⊠ *$2* ☉ *Museum mid-May–mid-Sept., daily 9–4:30; mid-Sept.–mid-May, Tues.–Sat. 10–4.*

Sitka State Pioneers Home. Known locally as just the Pioneers Home, this large, red-roof home for elder Alaskans has an imposing 14-foot statue in front symbolizing Alaska's frontier sourdough spirit ("sourdough" generally refers to Alaska's American pioneers and prospectors); it was modeled by an authentic prospector, William "Skagway Bill" Fonda. Adjacent to the Pioneers Home is **Sitka Tribal Tours' Sheet'ka Kwaan Naa Kahidi** community house, where you can watch Native dance performances throughout the summer. ⊠ *Lincoln and Katlian Sts.* ☎ *907/747–7290 for Sitka Tribal Tours reservations.*

Totem Square. On this grassy square directly across the street from the Pioneers Home are three anchors discovered in local waters and believed to be of 19th-century British origin. Look for the double-headed eagle of czarist Russia carved into the cedar of the totem pole in the park.

☾ ▶ **Whale Park.** This small waterside park sits in the trees 4 mi east of Sitka right off Sawmill Creek Road. Boardwalk paths lead to five viewing platforms and steps take you down to the rocky shoreline. A gazebo next to the parking area contains signs describing the whales that visit Silver Bay, and you can listen to their sounds from recordings and an offshore hydrophone here. ▪**TIP**➔ **Tune your radio to FM 88.1 anywhere in Sitka to hear a broadcast of humpback whale sounds picked up by the hydrophone.**

SPORTS, THE OUTDOORS, AND GUIDED TOURS

BICYCLING

If it isn't raining, rent a high-quality mountain bike from **Yellow Jersey Cycle Shop** (⊠ *329 Harbor Dr.* ☎ *907/747–6317* ⊕ *www. yellowjerseycycles.com*) and head out on the nearby dirt roads and trails. Staffers know Sitka's many mountain- and road-bike routes well.

BOAT AND KAYAK TOURS

Alaska Travel Adventures (☎ *800/323–5757, 907/747–5295 outside Alaska* ⊕ *www.bestofalaskatravel.com*) leads a three-hour kayaking tour in protected waters south of Sitka. The tour includes friendly guides, basic kayak instruction, and snacks at a remote cabin on the water.

Allen Marine Tours (☎ *907/747–8100 or 888/747–8101* ⊕ *www. allenmarinetours.com*), one of Southeast's largest and best-known tour operators, leads different boat-based Sitka Sound tours throughout the summer. The Wildlife Quest tours are a fine opportunity to view humpback whales, sea otters, puffins, eagles, and brown bears in a spectacular setting. When seas are calm enough, it offers a tour to the bird sanctuary at **St. Lazaria Islands National Wildlife Refuge.**

Sitka Sound Ocean Adventures. The guide company's waterfront operation is easy to find: just look for the big blue bus they use as their base at Crescent Harbor next to Centennial Hall & Convention Center. Sitka Sound runs a variety of guided kayak trips through the mysterious and beautiful outer islands off the coast of Sitka. Experienced paddlers who want to go it on their own can rent gear from the company. Sitka Sound's guides quickly help new-to-the-area paddlers understand its wonders (and, for day trips, they pack a great picnic). ✉ *Harbor Dr. at Centennial Hall* ☎ 907/752–0660 ⊕ *www.kayaksitka.com.*

> **NEED ADVICE?**
>
> The Harrigan Centennial Hall has a volunteer-staffed information desk provided by the **Sitka Convention and Visitors Bureau** (✉ *303 Lincoln St.* ☎ *907/747–5940* ⊕ *www.sitka.org*), whose headquarters are a short walk away on Lincoln Street.

BUS TOURS AND HISTORICAL WALKS

Sitka Tours (☎ 907/747–8443) meets ferries and cruise ships and leads both bus tours and historical walks.

Tribal Tours (☎ 907/747–7290 or 888/270–8687 ⊕ *www.sitkatours.com*) emphasizes Sitka's rich Native culture, with bus or walking tours and dance performances at the Tribal Community House.

FISHING

Sitka is home to a fleet of charter boats. The Sitka Convention and Visitors Bureau Web site (⊕ *www.sitka.org*) has descriptions of and Web links to several dozen sportfishing operators. A good one is **Sitka's Secrets** (✉ *500 Lincoln St., Suite B-9* ☎ 907/747–5089 ⊕ *www.sitkasecret.com*), operated by naturalists who combine wildlife-viewing with fishing.

The Boat Company (☎ 360/697–4242 ⊕ *www.theboatcompany.com*) offers multiday wildlife-watching and fishing trips departing from Sitka and Juneau.

FOUR-WHEELED FUN

Alaska ATV Tours (☎ 907/966–2301 or 877/966–2301 ⊕ *www.alaskaatvtours.com*) offers half-day tours of remote Kruzof Island aboard two-person Yamaha ATVs. Stops include Iris Meadows Estuary, a black-sand beach, and one of Kruzof's numerous salmon-laden creeks. The tour, which departs from Sitka, includes a scenic 30-minute boat transfer through the islands and channels of Sitka Sound.

HIKING AND BIRD-WATCHING

Seven miles north of Sitka, **Starrigavan Recreation Area** is a peaceful, end-of-the-road place to explore the rain forest. The state ferry terminal is less than a mile from Starrigavan, and a popular Forest Service campground is also here. Several easy trails lead hikers through the area, including the ¼-mi boardwalk **Estuary Life Trail.** It circles a small estuary and includes a bird-viewing shelter and access to a nearby artesian well. The ¾-mi **Forest and Muskeg Trail** winds through a spruce-hemlock forest and traverses a muskeg, with interpretive signs along the way. Across the road is the delightful 1.25-mi loop **Mosquito**

Cove Trail, which skirts the rocky shoreline to Mosquito Cove before returning through thickly forested hills. Get a map of local trails from **Sitka Trail Works** (✉ *801 Halibut Point Rd.* ☎ *907/747–7244* ⊕ *www. sitkatrailworks.org*).

UNDERWATER ACTION

Sea Life Tours (☎ *907/966–2301* or *877/966–2301* ⊕ *www. sealifediscoverytours.com*) operates a semisubmersible tour vessel with large underwater windows that provide views of kelp forests, fish, crab, sea urchins, anemones, and starfish. Divers with underwater cameras zoom in for close-up views via the video monitor.

WHERE TO EAT

$ ✕ **Little Tokyo**. Sitka probably isn't the first place you expect to find
JAPANESE Japanese food, but Little Tokyo delivers great rolls and *nigiri*. It's not fancy, but this small restaurant has a sushi bar where the chefs prepare all the standards, plus Alaska rolls (with smoked salmon and avocado). Udon noodle soups are popular on rainy afternoons, and bento-box dinners—complete with katsu entrées, California rolls, tempura, pot stickers, miso soup, and salad—hover around $10. ✉ *315 Lincoln St.* ☎ *907/747–5699.*

$$$–$$$$ ✕ **Ludvig's Bistro**. This remarkably creative eatery used to escape detec-
MEDITERRANEAN tion by most tourists (much to the pleasure of Sitkans). It's now almost
Fodor's Choice always packed with food lovers from all corners of the globe anxious
★ to try chef-owner Colette Nelson's food, so be prepared for a wait—but rest assured that Ludvig's is worth it. The interior evokes an Italian bistro, with rich yellow walls and copper-topped tables. Seafood (particularly king salmon and scallops) is the specialty, and organic ingredients are used whenever possible. You'll also find Caesar salads, vegetarian specials, Angus filet mignon, and one of the state's best wine lists. ✉ *256 Katlian St.* ☎ *907/966–3663* ۩ *Closed mid-Feb.–Apr.*

$–$$ ✕ **Nugget Restaurant**. Travelers flying out from Sitka head here while
AMERICAN hoping their jet will make it through the pea-soup fog outside. The setting is standard, and the menu encompasses burgers (15 kinds), sandwiches, tuna melts, salads, steaks, pasta, seafood, and Friday-night prime rib. There's a big breakfast menu, too, but the real attraction is the range of homemade pies, which are known throughout Southeast Alaska. ■ TIP➔ Get a slice à la mode, or buy a whole pie to take with you. The lemon custard is a local favorite. Reservations are recommended. ✉ *Sitka Airport Terminal* ☎ *907/966–2480.*

$$–$$$ ✕ **Van Winkle & Sons**. This restaurant's somewhat lackluster ambience
SEAFOOD (Formica tabletops, paper napkins, vinyl swivel-chair seating) doesn't quite match up to the gorgeous water views and upscale fare but, really, you won't mind. One of Sitka's largest eateries, it bills itself as "Frontier Cuisine," which translates to a seafood-heavy menu. But Van Winkle also serves pizzas, chicken, and duck. The create-your-own pastas are excellent (a half order is plenty for normal-size appetites), and the rich desserts necessitate sharing. There's no elevator to the restaurant's second-floor location, but a stair lift assists disabled customers. The water view is good. ✉ *205 Harbor Dr.* ☎ *907/747–7652.*

WHERE TO STAY

For expanded hotel reviews, visit Fodors.com.

$$$–$$$$ ☒ **Alaska Ocean View Bed & Breakfast.** Carole Denkinger, who runs
★ this cozy B&B out of the home she shares with her husband Bill, is
an extremely personable host who enjoys talking about the area and
prides herself on never serving anyone the same breakfast twice. **Pros:**
large, varied breakfasts. **Cons:** only three rooms. **TripAdvisor:** "very
comfortable with wonderful breakfasts," "very nice owners," "room
was immaculate and tastefully designed." ⌷ *1101 Edgecumbe Dr.*
☎ *907/747–8310 or 888/811–6870* ⊕ *www.sitka-alaska-lodging.com*
↶ *3 rooms* ⚮ *In-room: Internet. In-hotel: business center, some pets
allowed* ▯○▯ *Breakfast.*

$ ☒ **Alaska Swan Lake Bed & Breakfast.** This is one of the best B&Bs in
☾ town, with a quiet, lakeside setting, attractively appointed rooms with
private baths, and friendly owners. **Pros:** quiet, convenient location.
Cons: bathrooms are small. ⌷ *206½ Lakeview Dr.* ☎ *907/747–5746*
↶ *4 rooms* ⚮ *In-room: Wi-Fi. In-hotel: laundry facilities* ▯○▯ *Breakfast.*

$$$$ ☒ **Baranof Wilderness Lodge.** This cozy fishing lodge is nestled in Warm
Springs Bay, 20 air mi from Sitka on the wild east side of Baranof Island.
Pros: rate is all-inclusive from Sitka. **Cons:** rate is expensive in compari-
son to similar accommodations. ⌂ *Box 2187, 99835* ☎ *907/738–3597
or 800/613–6551* ⊕ *www.flyfishalaska.com* ↶ *1 room, 7 cabins* ⚮ *In-
room: no TV. In-hotel: water sports, some pets allowed* ▭ *No credit
cards* ⊙ *Closed Oct.–May* ▯○▯ *All-inclusive.*

$$ ☒ **Fairweather Vacation Rentals.** These cozy rental apartments are located
downtown close to the harbor. **Pros:** accommodations are private; group
has the entire property; laundry facilities are one block away. **Cons:** few
amenities. ⌷ *308 Monastery St.* ☎ *907/747–8601* ↶ *3 apartments (1
one-bedroom, 2 studios)* ⚮ *In-room: kitchen. In-hotel: Internet, Wi-Fi,
parking, some pets allowed.*

$$$–$$$$ ☒ **Rockwell Lighthouse.** On an island 1 mi from town, Burgess Bauder (a
★ local veterinarian and lovable curmudgeon) rents out his 1,600-square-
foot four-story lighthouse, which was hand-built in the 1980s with
coastal woods and a light at the top installed to Coast Guard specifica-
tions. **Pros:** accommodations are private; group has the entire property.
Cons: staff is not always friendly; not much to do in immediate area;
group must rent entire property. ⌂ *Box 277, 99835* ☎ *907/747–3056*
↶ *4 rooms* ⚮ *In-room: kitchen. In-hotel: laundry facilities, some pets
allowed* ▭ *No credit cards.*

$$$ ☒ **Shee Atiká Totem Square Inn.** On Totem Square in downtown Sitka,
this inn is one of the town's better-run outfits. **Pros:** convenient loca-
tion for fishermen; complimentary airport shuttle service, Wi-Fi, and
continental breakfast. **Cons:** rooms without harbor view overlook a
particularly unattractive parking lot. **TripAdvisor:** "room was clean,"
"location was great," "big beds and all amenities." ⌷ *201 Katlian St.*
☎ *907/747–3693 or 866/300–1353* ⊕ *www.totemsquareinn.com* ↶ *68
rooms* ⚮ *In-room: Internet, Wi-Fi. In-hotel: gym, laundry facilities,
business center, some pets allowed* ▯○▯ *Breakfast.*

$ ☒ **Sitka Hotel.** This noisy but comfortable, old-fashioned downtown
hotel was built in 1939. **Pros:** good views from most rooms; decent price.

KEEPERS OF THE DEEP:
A LOOK AT ALASKA'S WHALES

It's unforgettable: a massive, barnacle-encrusted humpback breaches skyward from the placid waters of an Alaskan inlet, shattering the silence with a thundering display of grace, power, and beauty. Welcome to Alaska's coastline.

Alaska's cold, nutrient-rich waters offer a bounty of marine life that's matched by few regions on earth. Eight species of whales frequent the state's near-shore waters, some migrating thousands of miles each year to partake of Alaska's marine buffet. The state's most famous cetaceans (the scientific classification of marine mammals that includes whales, dolphins, and porpoises) are the humpback whale, the gray whale, and the Orca (a.k.a. the killer whale).

(top) A breaching humpback (left) An Orca whale

BEST REGIONS TO VIEW WHALES

Whales can be viewed throughout the world; after all, they are migratory animals. But thanks to its pristine environment, diversity of cetacean species, and jaw-dropping beauty, Alaska is perhaps the planet's best whale-watching locale.

Mutually curious!

From April through October, humpbacks visit many of Alaska's coastal regions, including the Bering Sea, the Aleutian Islands, and Prince William Sound. The **Inside Passage,** though, is the best place to see them: it's home to a migratory population of up to 600 humpbacks. Good bets for whale-viewing include taking a trip on the **Alaska Marine Highway,** spending time in **Glacier Bay National Park,** or taking a day cruise out of any of Southeast's main towns. While most humpbacks return to Hawaiian waters in the winter, some spend the whole year in Southeast Alaska.

Gray whales favor the coastal waters of the Pacific, which terminate in the Bering Sea. Their healthy population—some studies estimate that 30,000 gray whales populate the west coast of North America—make

THE HUMPBACK: Musical, Breaching Giant

Humpbacks' flukes allow them to breach so effectively that they can propel two-thirds of their massive bodies out of the water.

Known for their spectacular breaching and unique whale songs, humpbacks are captivating. Most spend their winters in the balmy waters off the Hawaiian Islands, where females, or sows, give birth. Come springtime, humpbacks set off on a 3,000-mile swim to their Alaskan feeding grounds.

Southeast Alaska is home to one of the world's only groups of bubble-net feeding humpbacks. Bubble-netting is a cooperative hunting technique in which one humpback circles below a school of baitfish while exhaling a "net" of bubbles, causing the fish to gather. Other humpbacks then feed at will from the deliciously dense group of fish.

The Song of the Humpback

All whale species communicate sonically, but the humpback is the most musical. During mating season, males emit haunting, songlike calls that can last for up to 30 minutes at a time. Most scientists attribute the songs to flirtatious, territorial, or competitive behaviors.

QUICK FACTS:

Scientific name: *Megaptera novaeangliae*

Length: Up to 50 ft.

Weight: Up to 90,000 pounds (45 tons)

Coloring: Dark blue to black, with barnacles and knobby, lighter-colored flippers

Life span: 30 to 40 years

Reproduction: One calf every 2 to 3 years; calves are generally 12 feet long at birth, weighing up to 2,000 pounds (1 ton)

them relatively easy to spot in the spring and early summer months, especially around **Sitka** and **Kodiak Island** and south of the **Kenai Peninsula**, where numerous whale-watching cruises depart from Seward into **Resurrection Bay.**

Orcas populate nearly all of Alaska's coastal regions. They're most commonly viewed in the **Inside Passage** and **Prince William Sound**, where they reside year-round. A jaunt on the Alaska Marine Highway is one option, but so is a kayaking or day-cruising trip out of **Whittier** to Prince William Sound.

When embarking on a whale-watching excursion, don't forget rain gear, a camera, and binoculars!

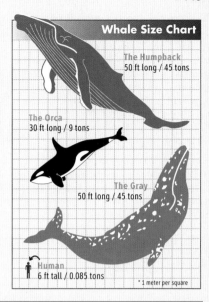

Whale Size Chart

The Humpback
50 ft long / 45 tons

The Orca
30 ft long / 9 tons

The Gray
50 ft long / 45 tons

Human
6 ft tall / 0.085 tons

* 1 meter per square

THE GRAY WHALE: Migrating Leviathan

Though the average lifespan of a gray whale is 50 years, one individual was reported to reach 77 years of age—a real old-timer.

While frequenting Alaska during the long days of summer, gray whales tend to stay close to the coastline. They endure the longest migration of any mammal on earth—some travel 14,000 mi each way between Alaska's Bering Sea and their mating grounds in sunny Baja California.

Gray whales are bottom-feeders that stir up sediment on sea floor, then use their baleen—a comblike collection of long, stiff hairs inside their mouths—to filter out sediment and trap small crustaceans and tube worms.

Their predilection for near-shore regions, coupled with their easygoing demeanor—some "friendly" gray whales have even been known to approach small tour boats—cements their spot on the short list of Alaska's favorite cetacean celebrities. (Gray whales aren't always in such amicable spirits: whalers dubbed mother gray whales "devilfish" for the fierce manner in which they protected their young.)

QUICK FACTS:

Scientific name:
Eschrichtius robustus

Length: Up to 50 ft.

Weight: Up to 90,000 pounds (45 tons)

Coloring: Gray and white, usually splotched with lighter growths and barnacles

Life span: 50 years

Reproduction: One calf every 2 years; calves are generally 15 feet long at birth, weighing up to 1,500 pounds (3/4 ton)

AN AGE-OLD CONNECTION

Nearly every major native group in Alaska has relied on whales for some portion of its diet. The Inupiaq and Yup'ik counted on whales for blubber, oil, meat, and intestines to survive. Aleuts used whale bones to build their semisubterranean homes. Even the Tlingit, for whom food was perennially abundant, considered a beached whale a bounty.

Subsistence whaling lives on in Alaska: although gray-whale hunting was banned in 1996, the Eskimo Whaling Commission permits the state's native populations to harvest 50 bowhead whales every year.

Other Alaskan whale species:
Bowhead, northern right, minke, fin, and beluga whales also inhabit Alaskan waters.

barnacles

BARNACLES These ragged squatters of the sea live on several species of whales, including humpbacks and gray whales. They're conspicuously absent from smaller marine mammals, such as Orcas, dolphins, and porpoises. The reason? Speed. Scientists theorize that barnacles are only able to colonize the slowest-swimming cetacean species, leaving the faster swimmers free from their unwanted drag.

THE ORCA: Conspicuous, Curious Cetacean

Why the name killer whale? Perhaps for this animal's skilled and fearsome hunting techniques, which are sometimes used on other, often larger, cetaceans.

Perhaps the most recognizable of all the region's marine mammals, Orcas (also called killer whales) are playful, inquisitive, and intelligent whales that reside in Alaskan waters year-round. Orcas travel in multigenerational family groups known as pods, which practice cooperative hunting techniques.

Orcas are smaller than grays and humpbacks, and their 17-month gestation period is the longest of any cetacean. They are identified by their white-and-black markings, as well as by the knifelike shape of their dorsal fins, which, in the case of mature males, can reach 6 feet in height.

Pods generally adhere to one of three common classifications: **residents,** which occupy in-shore waters and feed primarily on fish; **transients,** which occupy larger ranges and hunt sea lions, squid, sharks, fish, and whales; and **offshores,** about which little is known.

QUICK FACTS:

Scientific name: *Orcinus orca*

Length: Up to 30 ft.

Weight: Up to 18,000 pounds (9 tons)

Coloring: Smooth, shiny black skin with white eye patches and chin and white belly markings

Life span: 30 to 50 years

Reproduction: One calf every 3 to 5 years; calves are generally 6 feet long at birth, weighing up to 400 pounds (0.2 ton)

Cons: noisy location; sparse amenities. **TripAdvisor:** "room was huge and comfortable," "total immersion in local flavor," "a bit noisy." ✉ *118 Lincoln St.* ☎ *907/747–3288* ⊕ *www.sitkahotel.net* ⥹ *60 rooms* ♨ *In-room: Wi-Fi. In-hotel: restaurant, bar, laundry facilities, business center, some pets allowed.*

$$$–$$$$ ⊡ **Westmark Sitka.** Sitka's nicest hotel has large rooms, many overlooking Crescent Harbor; the best are the corner suites. **Pros:** nice views; big rooms. **Cons:** no ferry shuttle; breakfast not offered. **TripAdvisor:** "room is very spacious and clean," "food is awesome," "staff is helpful and pleasant." ✉ *330 Seward St.* ☎ *907/747–6241 or 800/544–0970 in U.S., 800/999–2570 in Canada* ⊕ *www. westmarkhotels.com* ⥹ *100 rooms, 3 suites* ♨ *In-room: kitchen (some), Wi-Fi. In-hotel: restaurant, bar, business center.*

¢ ⊡ **White Sulphur Springs Cabin.** This Tongass National Forest public-use cabin is 65 mi northwest of Sitka. **Pros:** good views of Pacific Ocean; beautiful surroundings. **Cons:** guests must bring own bedding and cooking utensils; requires boat ride to location. ☎ *907/747–6671 information, 877/444–6777 reservations* ⊕ *www.fs.fed.us/r10/tongass/cabins/ sitka/whitesulphur.shtml or www.recreation.gov* ⥹ *1 cabin.*

CAMPING IN SITKA

⛺ **Starrigavan Recreation Area.** Seven miles north of town and ¾ mi from the ferry terminal, this popular Tongass National Forest year-round campground has a mix of sites for car campers, backpackers, and RV travelers. All sites have tree cover, and facilities include tables, grills, potable water, and vault toilets. Everything is fully ADA accessible, and group sites include a covered cooking shelter. Snow may limit vehicle access in winter. Pros: separate tent areas; pleasant amphitheater. Cons: no hookups; no dump station on-site. ☎ *907/747–4216 information, 877/444–6777 reservations* ⊕ *www.recreation. gov or www.fs.fed.us/r10/ tongass/recreation/rec_facilities/ sitkacamp.shtml.*

NIGHTLIFE AND THE ARTS

BARS

As far as the locals are concerned, a spot in one of the limited green-and-white-vinyl booths at **Pioneer Bar** (✉ *212 Katlian St.* ☎ *907/747–3456*), across from the harbor, is a fine destination. It's vintage Alaska, with hundreds of pictures of local fishing boats, rough-hewn locals clad in Carhartts and XtraTuf boots, occasional live music, and pool tables. Regulars, mostly local fishermen, swear by the submarine sandwiches and hot dogs.

DANCE

★ The **New Archangel Dancers of Sitka** is an all-female troupe of local Sitka women dedicated to preserving Alaska's Russian history that has performed since 1969. Seasonal performances showcase authentic dances from Russia and the surrounding regions. Tickets are $10, and are sold a half-hour before performances. A **recorded message** (☎ *907/747–5516* ⊕ *www.newarchangeldancers.com*) gives the schedule a week in advance. Performances are 30 minutes long and take place in Harrigan Centennial Hall.

Sheet'ka Kwaan Naa Kahidi Dancers (☎ 907/747–7290 or 888/270–8687 ⊕ *www.sitkatours.com*) perform Tlingit dances in full native regalia at the Sheet'ka Kwaan Naa Kahidi community house on Katlian Street. The dance schedule is listed on the board at Harrigan Centennial Hall.

FESTIVALS

Southeast Alaska's major chamber-music festival is the annual **Sitka Summer Music Festival** (☎ 907/277–4852 or 907/747–6774 ⊕ *www. sitkamusicfestival.org*), a three-week June celebration of concerts and special events that attracts musicians from as far away as Europe and Asia. All performances are held in Harrigan Centennial Hall. The **Sitka WhaleFest** (☎ 907/747–7964 ⊕ *www.sitkawhalefest.org*) is held around town in early November, when the whales are plentiful (as many as 80) and tourists are not.

SHOPPING

ART GALLERIES

Fairweather Gallery and Gifts (✉ 209 *Lincoln St.* ☎ 907/747–8677 ⊕ *www.fairweatherprints.com*) sells tops, dresses, and other clothing featuring hand-painted and printed Alaska-inspired designs, as well works by local artists.

Fishermen's Eye Fine Art Gallery (✉ 239 *Lincoln St.* ☎ 907/747–6080 ⊕ *www.fishermenseye.com*) is a tasteful downtown gallery that prides itself on its vibrant collection of made-in-Sitka art, including silver jewelry, native masks, and carved bowls. Housed within a Victorian-style 1895 home next to the Bishop's House, **Sitka Rose Gallery** (✉ 419 *Lincoln St.* ☎ 907/747–3030 or 888/236–1536 ⊕ *www.sitkarosegallery. com*) is the town's most charming shop, and features Alaskan paintings, sculptures, Native art, and jewelry.

BOOKSTORE

Old Harbor Books (✉ 201 *Lincoln St.* ☎ 907/747–8808) has an impressive collection of Alaska titles, along with a knowledgeable staff. Directly behind the bookstore is a cozy left-wing hangout called the **Backdoor Café** (☎ 907/747–8856), with excellent espresso and fresh-baked pastries.

GIFTS

Fresh Fish Company (✉ 411 *DeGroff St.* ☎ 907/747–5565, 888/747–5565 *outside Alaska*) sells and ships fresh locally caught salmon, halibut, and shrimp. Located in the old pulp mill building 5 mi east of Sitka, **Theobroma Chocolate Company** (☎ 907/966–2345 or 888/985–2345 ⊕ *www. theobromachocolate.com*) produces a range of rich treats, including chocolates shaped like halibut and salmon. Tours of this gourmet chocolate factory are available daily. Behind the Sitka Rose Gallery, **WinterSong Soap Company** (✉ 419 *Lincoln St.* ☎ 907/747–8949 or 888/819–8949 ⊕ *www.wintersongsoap.com*) sells colorful and scented soaps that are handcrafted on the premises.

JUNEAU

100 mi northeast of Sitka.

Juneau, Alaska's capital and third-largest city, is on the North American mainland but can't be reached by road. The city owes its origins to two colorful sourdoughs (Alaskan pioneers)—Joe Juneau and Richard Harris—and to a Tlingit chief named Kowee, who led the two men to rich reserves of gold at Snow Slide Gulch, the drainage of Gold Creek around which the town was eventually built. That was in 1880, and shortly thereafter a modest stampede resulted in the formation of a mining camp, which quickly grew to become the Alaska district government capital in 1906. The city may well have continued under its original appellation—Harrisburg, after Richard Harris—were it not for Joe Juneau's political jockeying at a miner's meeting in 1881.

For some 60 years after Juneau's founding gold was the mainstay of the economy. In its heyday the AJ (for Alaska Juneau) Gold Mine was the biggest low-grade ore mine in the world. It was not until World War II, when the government decided it needed Juneau's manpower for the war effort, that the AJ and other mines in the area ceased operations. After the war mining failed to start up again, and government became the city's principal employer. Juneau's mines leave a rich legacy, though; the AJ Gold Mine alone produced more than $80 million in gold.

Perhaps because of its colorful history, Juneau is full of contrasts. Its dramatic hillside location and historic downtown buildings provide a frontier feeling, but the city's cosmopolitan nature comes through in fine museums, noteworthy restaurants, and a literate and outdoorsy populace. Here you can enjoy the Mt. Roberts Tramway, plenty of densely forested wilderness areas, quiet bays for sea kayaking, and even a famous drive-up glacier.

Along with the Alaska State Museum and Mt. Roberts Tramway, make time for a tour to Mendenhall Glacier and the Macaulay Salmon Hatchery. Douglas (which at one point was a bigger outpost than Juneau) is across the Gastineau Channel to the west. For goings on, pick up the *Juneau Empire* (⊕ *www.juneauempire.com*), which keeps tabs on state politics, business, sports, and local news.

GETTING HERE AND AROUND

Juneau is an obligatory stop on the Inside Passage cruise and ferry circuit. Hence, the town has an overabundance of visitors in midsummer. **Alaska Airlines** also flies here. Downtown Juneau is compact enough so that most of its main attractions are within walking distance of one another. Note, however, that the city is very hilly, so your legs will get a real workout. Look for the 20 signs around downtown that detail Juneau's fascinating history.

ESSENTIALS

Airline Contact Alaska Airlines (☎ 800/252–7522 ⊕ www.alaskaair.com).

Internet Heritage Coffee Company (✉ 174 S. Franklin St. ✉ 216 2nd S. ☎ 907/586–1087 ⊕ www.heritagecoffee.com). **Juneau Public Library** (✉ 292 Marine Way ☎ 907/586–5249 ⊕ www.juneau.org/library).

Medical Assistance **Bartlett Regional Hospital** (✉ 3260 Hospital Dr. ☎ 907/586–2611 ⊕ www.bartletthospital.org).

Pharmacy **Juneau Drug Co.** (✉ 202 Front St. ☎ 907/586–1233). **Ron's Apothecary Shoppe** (✉ 9101 Mendenhall Mall Rd., in Mendenhall Mall next to Super Bear market ☎ 907/789–0458 ⊕ www.ronsapothecary.com).

Post Office and Shipping **U.S. Postal Service** (✉ 709 W. 9th St. ✉ 9491 Vintage Blvd. ⊕ www.usps.gov). **DHL** (✉ Drop box: 8th fl. lobby, State Office Bldg., 333 Willoughby Ave. ☎ 800/225–5345 ⊕ www.dhl-usa.com). **FedEx** (✉ 9203 Bonnett Way ☎ 800/463–3339 ⊕ www.fedex.com). **UPS** (✉ 1900 Renshaw Way ☎ 800/742–5877 ⊕ www.ups.com).

Visitor Information **Alaska Department of Fish & Game** (🗋 Box 115525, Juneau 99811 ☎ 907/465–4180 sportfishing seasons and regulations; 907/465–2376 license information ⊕ www.adfg.state.ak.us). **Alaska Division of Parks** (✉ 400 Willoughby Ave.99801 ☎ 907/465–4563 ⊕ www.alaskastateparks.org). **Juneau Convention and Visitors Bureau** (✉ 1 Sealaska Plaza, Suite 305 99801 ☎ 907/586–1737 or 800/587–2201 ⊕ www.traveljuneau.com).

EXPLORING
TOP ATTRACTIONS

☺ ★ **Alaska State Museum.** This is one of Alaska's finest museums. Those interested in Native cultures will enjoy examining the 38-foot walrus-hide *umiak* (an open, skin-covered Inupiaq boat). Natural-history exhibits include preserved brown bears and a two-story-high eagle-nesting tree. Russian-American and gold-rush displays and contemporary art complete the collection. ■**TIP**➔ **Be sure to visit the gift shop (run by the Friends of the Alaska State Museum) and its extraordinary selection of Native art, including baskets, carvings, and masks.** ✉ 395 *Whittier St.* ☎ 907/465–2901 ⊕ *www.museums.state.ak.us* 🎟 *$5 summer, $3 winter* ☉ *Mid-May–mid-Sept., daily 8:30–5:30; mid-Sept.–mid-May, Tues.–Sat. 10–4.*

☺ ★ **Mt. Roberts Tramway.** One of Southeast Alaska's most popular tourist attractions, this tram whisks you from the cruise terminal 1,800 feet up the side of Mt. Roberts. After the six-minute ride you can take in a film on the history and legends of the Tlingits, visit the nature center, go for an alpine walk on hiking trails (including the 5-mi round-trip hike to Mt. Roberts's 3,819-foot summit), purchase Native crafts, or enjoy a meal while savoring mountain views. A local company leads guided wilderness hikes from the summit, and the bar serves locally brewed beers. ☎ 907/463–3412 or 888/461–8726 ⊕ *www.goldbelttours.com* 🎟 *$27* ☉ *May–Sept., hrs vary; closed in winter.*

South Franklin Street. The buildings on South Franklin Street (and neighboring Front Street), among the oldest and most inviting structures in the city, house curio and crafts shops, snack shops, and two salmon shops. Many reflect the architecture of the 1920s and 1930s. When the small **Alaskan Hotel** opened in 1913, Juneau was home to 30 saloons; the Alaskan gives today's visitors the most authentic glimpse of the town's whiskey-rich history. The barroom's massive, mirrored oak back bar is accented by Tiffany lights and panels. Topped by a wood-shingled turret, the 1901 **Alaska Steam Laundry Building** now houses

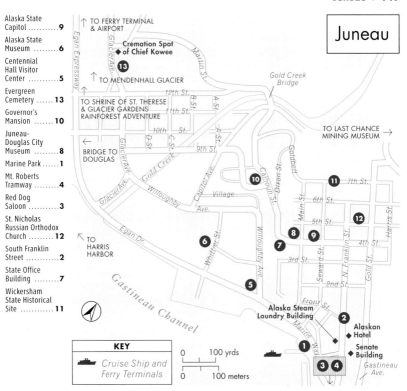

a coffeehouse and other stores. The **Senate Building,** another of South Franklin's treasured landmarks, is across the street.

WORTH NOTING

Alaska State Capitol. Completed in 1931 and remodeled in 2006, this rather unassuming building houses the governor's office and hosts state legislature meetings in winter, placing it at the epicenter of Alaska's increasingly animated political discourse. Historical photos line the upstairs walls. Feel free to stroll right in. ■TIP➜ You can pick up a self-guided tour brochure as you enter. Complimentary guided tours available daily mid-May through mid-Sept. ⊠ *Corner of Seward and 4th Sts.* ☎ *907/465–4648* ⊕ *w3.legis.state.ak.us/misc/capitol.php.*

Centennial Hall Visitor Center. Here you can get complete details on Juneau sights and activities, plus walking-tour maps. You can find out about hiking trails and other activities on nearby Tongass National Forest lands. ⊠ *101 Egan Dr.* ☎ *907/586–2201 or 888/581–2201* ⊕ *www. traveljuneau.com* ☉ *May–Sept., weekdays 8:30–5, weekends 9–5; Oct.–Apr., weekdays 9–4.*

Evergreen Cemetery. Many Juneau pioneers, including Joe Juneau and Richard Harris, are buried here. Juneau (1836–99), a Canadian by birth, died in Dawson City, Yukon, but his body was returned to the city that bears his name. Harris (1833–1907), whose name can be found

A GOOD WALK

The most common starting spot is **Marine Park**, situated right along the cruise-ship dock. For an introduction to Alaska's human and natural history, head to the engaging **Alaska State Museum**. From here, circle back along Willoughby Avenue to the **State Office Building**. Catch the elevator to the eighth-floor atrium, which features an observation deck with vistas across the Gastineau Channel. The snug but cheery **Juneau-Douglas City Museum**, a local treasure that's slightly off the beaten path, sits a short distance away at 4th and Main streets. The looming, banklike building across the street is the **Alaska State Capitol**. For a far more attractive example of governmental architecture, walk past the **Governor's Mansion**, a few minutes uphill on Calhoun Street. If you have the time and energy, you may want to continue along Calhoun, across the Gold Creek Bridge, and then down along 12th Street to the quiet **Evergreen**

Cemetery, where town fathers Joe Juneau and Richard Harris, as well as Chief Kowee, are buried.

Back in downtown, the **Centennial Hall Visitor Center** isn't far from the historic buildings and busy shops of downtown Juneau, particularly those along **South Franklin Street**. Check out the Alaskan Hotel, the Alaska Steam Laundry Building, and the Senate Building before dipping inside the terminally crowded **Red Dog Saloon** at the intersection of South Franklin Street and Admiralty Way. Try a microbrew, and then continue down the street to the **Mt. Roberts Tramway**, a popular way to reach alpine country for a hike overlooking Juneau and the Gastineau Channel.

To cover downtown Juneau's many interesting sights, you should allow at least three or four hours for exploring. Add at least another hour if you're a museum fan, or if you plan to ride the Mt. Roberts Tramway.

on downtown's Harris Street, died here. A meandering gravel path leads through the graveyard, and at the end of it is the monument commemorating the cremation spot of Chief Kowee.

Governor's Mansion. Completed in 1912, this stately colonial-style home overlooks downtown Juneau. With 14,400 square feet, 6 bedrooms, and 10 bathrooms, it's no miner's cabin. Out front is a totem pole that tells three tales: the history of man, the cause of ocean tides, and the origin of Alaska's ubiquitous mosquitoes. Unfortunately, tours of the residence are not permitted. ⊠ *716 Calhoun Ave.*

☾ **Juneau-Douglas City Museum.** Among the exhibits interpreting local mining and Tlingit history are an Assay Lab diorama, a reconstructed Tlingit fish trap and video of excavation, historic photos, and pioneer artifacts, including a century-old store and kitchen. Digital story kiosks highlight Alaska's government, civil rights in Alaska, Alaska's quest for statehood, and cultures of Juneau. Youngsters will appreciate the hands-on room, where they can try on clothes similar to ones worn by the miners or look at gold-rush stereoscopes. Guided historic walking tours are offered May to September. ⊠ *114 4th St.* ☎ *907/586–3572* ⊕ *www.*

Mendenhall Glacier, Juneau. Kayak along this receding glacier just 13 mi outside of the city.

juneau.org/parksrec/museum ✉ *$4 summer, free winter* ☉ *May–Sept., weekdays 9–5, weekends 10–5; Oct.–Apr., Tues.–Sat. 10–4.*

OFF THE
BEATEN
PATH

Last Chance Mining Museum. A 1.5-mi hike or taxi ride behind town, this small museum is housed in the former compressor building of Juneau's historic AJ Gold Mine. The collection includes old mining tools, rail-cars, minerals, and a 3-D map of the ore body. The surrounding country is steep and wooded, with trails leading in all directions, including one to the summit of Mt. Juneau. ✉ *1001 Basin Rd.* ☏ *907/586–5338* ✉ *$4* ☉ *Mid-May–mid-Sept., daily 9:30–12:30 and 3:30–6:30; closed in winter.*

Marine Park. On the dock where the cruise ships "tie up" is a little urban oasis with benches, shade trees, and shelter. It's a great place to enjoy an outdoor meal from one of Juneau's street vendors, and on Friday evenings in summer it features live performances by Juneau musicians. A visitor kiosk is staffed according to cruise-ship schedules.

Red Dog Saloon. The frontierish quarters of the Red Dog have housed an infamous Juneau watering hole since 1890. Nearly every conceivable surface in this two-story bar is cluttered with graffiti, business cards, and memorabilia, including a pistol that reputedly belonged to Wyatt Earp, who failed to reclaim the piece after checking it in at the U.S. Marshall's office on June 27, 1900. The saloon's food menu includes halibut, reindeer sausage, potato skins, burgers, and locally brewed Alaskan beers. A little atmospheric sawdust covers the floor as well. Musicians pump out ragtime piano tunes when cruise ships are docked. ✉ *278 S. Franklin St.* ☏ *907/463–3658* ⊕ *www.reddogsaloon.com.*

St. Nicholas Russian Orthodox Church. It's the oldest Russian church in Southeast Alaska. Built in 1894 by newly baptized Orthodox Natives and Siberian gold miners, the church was refurbished in the late 1970s and is a national historic landmark. The quaint, onion-dome white-and-blue church has services sung in Slavonic, English, and Tlingit on Saturday and Sunday. ⊠ *326 5th St.* ☎ *907/845–2288* ⊕ *www. stnicholasjuneau.org.*

State Office Building. The building's sprawling eighth-floor patio, which faces the Gastineau Channel and Douglas Island, is a popular lunch destination for state workers and assorted residents. On most Fridays at noon, concerts inside the four-story atrium feature a grand old theater pipe organ, a veteran of the silent-movie era. Also here are the historic old witch totem pole; the Alaska State Library, with a fine collection of historical photos; and computers with public Internet access. If you're having trouble finding the building, just ask for directions to the "S.O.B."—the locals are fond of acronyms. ⊠ *4th and Calhoun Sts.*

Wickersham State Historical Site. At the top of the hill behind the capitol, on a rise sometimes known as "Chicken Ridge," stands the former residence of James Wickersham, pioneer judge, delegate to Congress, prolific author, and gutsy outdoorsman. The white New England–style home, constructed in 1898, contains memorabilia from the judge's travels throughout Alaska—from rare native basketry and ivory carvings to historic photos and a Chickering grand piano that came "'round the Horn" to Alaska in the 1870s. The tour provides a glimpse into the life of this dynamic man. At this writing the state is considering renovations of the site, so it's best to call ahead to make sure it's open when you plan to visit. ⊠ *213 7th St.* ☎ *907/586–9001* ⊕ *www.dnr.state.ak.us/ parks* ⊡ *Free* ⊗ *Mid-May–Sept., Mon.–Sat. 10–4.*

WHERE TO EAT

$$–$$$
AMERICAN

✕ **Douglas Café.** In the heart of quiet Douglas, across the bridge and a couple of miles from downtown Juneau, this family eatery has Formica tables and a three-meals-a-day menu (breakfast on weekends only) that includes omelets, sandwiches, kids' favorites, and a bundle of different kinds of burgers, which are often cited as the best in the city. It's a good choice for those seeking an alternative to downtown Juneau's occasional midsummer crowds. ⊠ *916 3rd St., Douglas* ☎ *907/364–3307* ⊗ *Closed Mon.*

$$$$
SEAFOOD

✕ **Gold Creek Salmon Bake.** Trees, mountains, and the rushing water of Salmon Creek surround the comfortable, canopy-covered benches and tables at this authentic salmon bake. Fresh-caught salmon is cooked over an alder fire and served with a succulent sauce. For $42 there are all-you-can-eat salmon, pasta, and chicken along with baked beans, rice pilaf, salad bar, corn bread, and blueberry cake. Wine and beer are extra. After dinner you can pan for gold in the stream, wander up the hill to explore the remains of the Wagner gold mine, or roast marshmallows over the fire. A round-trip bus ride from downtown is included. ⊠ *1061 Salmon Lane Rd.* ☎ *907/789–0052 or 800/323–5757* ⊕ *www. bestofalaskatravel.com* ⊗ *Closed Oct.–Apr.*

$$–$$$
ECLECTIC
✕ The Hangar on the Wharf. Crowded with locals and travelers, the Hangar occupies the building where Alaska Airlines started business. Flight-theme puns dominate the menu (i.e., "Pre-flight Snacks" and the "Plane Caesar"), but the comfortably worn wood and vintage airplane photos create a casual dining experience that outweighs the kitsch. Every seat has views of the Gastineau Channel and Douglas Island. On warm days, outdoor seating is offered. This Juneau hotspot makes a wide selection of entrées, including locally caught halibut and salmon, filet mignon, great burgers, and daily specials. They serve more than 100 beers, including a few dozen on tap. On Friday and Saturday nights jazz or rock bands take the stage. For travelers who have had enough salmon, the Hangar is known for its prime rib. ✉ *2 Marine Way, Merchants Wharf Mall* ☎ *907/586–5018* ⊕ *www.hangaronthewharf.com.*

¢
CAFÉ
✕ Heritage Coffee Company. Juneau's favorite coffee shop is a downtown institution, with locally roasted coffees, gelato, fresh pastries, and all sorts of specialty drinks. ■ TIP➔ **The window-front bar is good for people-watching while you sip a chai latte.** The same folks also operate several other coffee outposts, including the **Glacier Cafe** in Mendenhall Valley, which boasts a bigger menu that includes breakfast burritos and omelets, along with lunchtime paninis, wraps, soups, salads, and burgers, plus various vegetarian dishes. ✉ *174 S. Franklin St.* ☎ *907/586–1087* ✉ *216 2nd St.* ☎ *907/586–1752* ✉ *Mendenhall Mall Rd.* ☎ *907/789–0692* ⊕ *www.heritagecoffee.com* ☾ *No dinner.*

$–$$
PIZZA
✕ Island Pub. The Island Pub in Douglas has fast service, views of the Gastineau Channel, a full bar, occasional live music, and good times, making it one of the area's coolest restaurants. There are salads, sandwiches, and wraps, but the real draw is the pizza: thin, 13-inch focaccia crusts are prepared fresh daily, topped with creative ingredients, and baked in a copper wood-fired oven. Customers are encouraged to build their own pizzas, and the best of their creations end up on the menu. (An unexpected but excellent pizza topping: pine nuts.) The menu is therefore in a state of constant flux. If you've got room, try one of the chef's dessert pizzas—bizarre, but surprisingly good. ✉ *1102 2nd St., Douglas* ☎ *907/364–1595* ⊕ *www.theislandpub.com.*

¢
VEGETARIAN
✕ Rainbow Foods. This crunchy natural foods market is a popular lunch-break destination for downtown workers. Organic produce, coconut-milk ice cream, and vitamin supplements fill the shelves, but the real attraction is the weekday buffet, with various hot entrées, salads, soups, and deep-dish pizzas. Arrive before 11 am for the best choices. Self-serve coffee and freshly baked breads are available, along with a few inside tables. ✉ *224 4th St.* ☎ *907/586–6476* ⊕ *www.rainbow-foods.org.*

$$–$$$
SEAFOOD
✕ Twisted Fish Company. Juneau's liveliest downtown eatery serves up creative pan-Asian seafood and Alaska classics. Housed in a log-frame waterfront building adjacent to the Taku Store and the base of the Mt. Roberts Tramway, Twisted's fish is as fresh as you'll find. Grab a seat on the deck for prime-time Gastineau Channel gazing and a bowl of

Captain Ron's chowder. Inside, you'll find a dining room with a roaring river-rock hearth and flame-painted salmon, porpoises, marlin, and tuna decorating the walls. ⊠ *550 S. Franklin St.* ☎ *907/463–5033* ⊕ *twisted-fish.hangaronthewharf.com* ⊘ *Closed Oct.–Apr.*

$$$–$$$$ ✕ **Zephyr.** One of Juneau's more upscale restaurants, Zephyr distin-
MEDITERRANEAN guishes itself by remaining faithfully Mediterranean. The Greco-Roman menu features Spanish, Greek, Italian, and Middle Eastern specialties such as hummus spread on pita toast points, lamb kebabs, and Aegean pasta with feta and sun-dried tomatoes. The restaurant's excellent beer and wine list, along with its two bars—one on the ground floor and another on the upstairs mezzanine level—make it a great place to meet friends for an aperitif. ⊠ *200 Seward St.* ☎ *907/780–2221.*

WHERE TO STAY

For expanded hotel reviews, visit Fodors.com.

¢–$ ⬚ **Alaskan Hotel.** This historic 1913 hotel in the heart of downtown
★ Juneau sits over the popular bar of the same name; be prepared for noise Thursday through Saturday nights when bands are playing. **Pros:** historic property with quaint furnishings; the bar downstairs is a good time. **Cons:** some rooms are noisy; can smell a bit musty. **TripAdvisor:** "as historic as a hotel comes," "in the center of the action," "old furniture but decent bathroom." ⊠ *167 S. Franklin St.* ☎ *907/586–1000* *or 800/327–9347* ⊕ *www.thealaskanhotel.com* ⋺ *44 rooms, 22 with bath* ⅏ *In-room: kitchen (some), no TV (some), Wi-Fi (some). In-hotel: bar, laundry facilities, some pets allowed.*

$$$$ ⬚ **Alaska's Capital Inn.** Gold-rush pioneer John Olds built this Ameri-
Fodor's Choice can foursquare home in 1906, and a major restoration transformed it
★ into Juneau's most elegant B&B. **Pros:** beautiful restoration to 1906 mansion; nice antiques. **Cons:** the inn sits atop a steep—but walkable—incline from the main section of downtown; room rates are a little high. **TripAdvisor:** "warm and relaxing," "nice rooms and good beds," "wonderful hosts." ⊠ *113 W. 5th St.* ☎ *907/586–6507* *or 888/588–6507* ⊕ *www.alaskacapitalinn.com* ⋺ *5 rooms, 2 suites* ⅏ *In-room: Internet, Wi-Fi. In-hotel: business center, some age restrictions* ⊺⊙⊦ *Breakfast.*

$$ ⬚ **Aspen Suites Hotel.** This all-suite hotel is Juneau's newest property. **Pros:** well-equipped kitchens; complimentary Wi-Fi. **Cons:** not near downtown attractions; housekeeping is weekly, not daily. ⊠ *8400 Airport Blvd.* ☎ *907/500–7700* ⊕ *www.aspenhotelsak.com* ⋺ *78 rooms* ⅏ *In-room: kitchen, Wi-Fi. In-hotel: gym, laundry facilities, business center, parking.*

$–$$ ⬚ **Driftwood Lodge.** This workaday downtown motel is one of Juneau's best values, with a central location and well-maintained rooms, some of which include kitchenettes stocked with dishes, silverware, pots, and pans. **Pros:** most units are spacious; all rooms have private bathrooms. **Cons:** not handicapped-accessible; decor is spare. **TripAdvisor:** "friendly front desk staff," "very clean," "very noisy." ⊠ *435 Willoughby Ave.* ☎ *907/586–2280 or 800/544–2239* ⊕ *www.driftwoodalaska.com* ⋺ *21 rooms, 41 suites* ⅏ *In-room: kitchen (some), Internet. In-hotel: laundry* facilities, business center, parking, some pets allowed.

$–$$ ☷ **Extended Stay Deluxe.** This corporate-style inn is within walking distance of the airport and 9 mi from downtown. **Pros:** all rooms have kitchenettes; pet friendly. **Cons:** rooms are not as clean as they could be; charge for Wi-Fi. **TripAdvisor:** "very close to the airport," "clean and fairly quiet," "dirty room and comfortable bed." ✉ *1800 Shell Simmons Dr.* ☎ *907/790–6435 or 800/ 398–7829* ⊕ *extendedstayhotels. com* ⇆ *94 rooms* ⚲ *In-room: kitchen, Wi-Fi. In-hotel: pool, gym, laundry facilities, business center, some pets allowed* ¶ *Breakfast.*

$$ ☷ **Frontier Suites Airport Hotel.** Near the airport in Mendenhall Valley, 9 mi from Juneau, this rambling hotel is great for families. **Pros:** large rooms; full kitchens. **Cons:** long distance from downtown; not a lot of character to hotel. **TripAdvisor:** "loved the spacious rooms," "nice and clean," "big rooms and incredible service." ✉ *9400 Glacier Hwy.* ☎ *907/790–6600 or 800/544–2250* ⊕ *www.frontiersuites.com* ⇆ *104 rooms, 32 suites* ⚲ *In-room: safe, kitchen, Internet. In-hotel: restaurant, bar, gym, laundry facilities, some pets allowed.*

$$$ ☷ **Goldbelt Hotel Juneau.** A high-rise by local standards, the seven-story Goldbelt is one of Juneau's better lodging places, with decent (if somewhat overpriced) rooms with basic amenities, including local coffee. **Pros:** large rooms; free Wi-Fi. **Cons:** street-side rooms are very noisy; a little pricy. **TripAdvisor:** "very friendly and accommodating staff," "hotel is clean and staff are helpful," "great location." ✉ *51 W. Egan Dr.* ☎ *907/586–6900 or 888/478–6909* ⊕ *www.goldbelttours.com* ⇆ *105 rooms* ⚲ *In-room: Wi-Fi. In-hotel: restaurant, bar, parking.*

$$$ ☷ **Grandma's Feather Bed.** This charming Victorian-style hotel—the smallest property in the Best Western chain—is less than a mile from the airport in Mendenhall Valley. **Pros:** delicious breakfasts; deluxe suites with in-room whirlpool baths. **Cons:** outside of downtown; hotel fills quickly, so book ahead. **TripAdvisor:** "bed was very comfortable," "great location and friendly staff," "rooms are beautiful." ✉ *2358 Mendenhall Loop Rd.* ☎ *907/789–5566 or 888/781–5005* ⇆ *14 rooms* ⚲ *In-room: Wi-Fi. In-hotel: restaurant, laundry facilities* ¶ *Breakfast.*

$$$$ ☷ **Pearson's Pond Luxury Inn and Adventure Spa.** On a small pond near Mendenhall Glacier, this large, jaw-droppingly landscaped home may be Alaska's finest B&B. **Pros:** private balconies offer excellent views; guest use kayaks and bicycles. **Cons:** two-night minimum during summer season; limited convenient public transportation. **TripAdvisor:**

Fodor's Choice
★

CAMPING IN JUNEAU

⚠ **U.S. Forest Service Campgrounds.** Forest Service–maintained campgrounds are scattered around Tongass National Forest and are accessible from Juneau, Sitka, Ketchikan, Hollis, and Klawock. All have pit toilets and sites for RVs and tents, but not all provide drinking water. Space is generally available without a reservation. **Pros:** many sites have access for the disabled; reservations are available. **Cons:** most Tongass campsites do not have hookups; cell-phone service is limited. ✉ *Juneau Ranger District, 8465 Old Dairy Rd.* ☎ *907/586– 8800, 877/444–6777 reservations* ⊕ *www.recreation.gov.*

"accommodations are excellent," "beautiful and peaceful," "impeccable service." ⊠ *4541 Sawa Circle* ☎ *907/789–3772* ⊕ *www.pearsonspond. com* ⤶ *5 suites* ⚲ *In-room: kitchen, Internet, Wi-Fi. In-hotel: gym, spa, water sports, laundry facilities, business center, some age restrictions* ¡○¡ *Breakfast.*

$$ ⌂**Prospector Hotel.** A short walk west of downtown and next door to the Alaska State Museum, this nicely appointed but visually unremarkable hotel is frequented by business travelers and legislators during the winter legislative session. **Pros:** convenient location; friendly staff. **Cons:** very lackluster exterior and lobby; rooms could use some updating. **TripAdvisor:** "room was homey and clean," "beer is the coldest in Juneau," "reasonably quiet." ⊠ *375 Whittier St.* ☎ *907/586–3737, 800/331–2711 outside Alaska, 800/478–5866 in Alaska* ⊕ *www. prospectorhotel.com* ⤶ *56 rooms, 7 suites* ⚲ *In-room: Wi-Fi. In-hotel: restaurant, bar, parking, some pets allowed.*

$$$ ⌂**Silverbow Inn.** Conveniently located in Juneau's historic downtown, the expanded Silverbow combines a downstairs bakery and café with 11 contemporary hotel rooms on the two upper levels. **Pros:** new flat-screen televisions in rooms; nice historic location. **Cons:** no laundry facilities; parking is limited. **TripAdvisor:** "so friendly and helpful," "tastefully decorated," "comfortable and clean." ⊠ *120 2nd St.* ☎ *907/586–4146 or 800/586–4146* ⊕ *www.silverbowinn.com* ⤶ *11 rooms* ⚲ *In-room: Wi-Fi. In-hotel: restaurant, bar, parking* ¡○¡ *Breakfast.*

¢ ⌂**U.S. Forest Service Cabins.** Scattered throughout Tongass National **Fodor'sChoice** Forest, these rustic cabins offer a charming and cheap escape. ⊠ *Ju-* ★ *neau Ranger District, 8465 Old Dairy Rd., Juneau* ☎ *907/586–8800; 877/444–6777 reservations* ⊕ *www.recreation.gov* ⤶ *150 cabins.*

$$–$$$$ ⌂**Westmark Baranof Hotel.** The Baranof has long been Juneau's most prestigious address; it's as close to a big-city downtown boutique hotel as you're going to find in Southeast Alaska. **Pros:** elegant art deco public areas; excellent in-house hotel and bar. **Cons:** lower floors are noisy. ⊠ *127 N. Franklin St.* ☎ *907/586–2660 or 800/544–0970* ⊕ *www.westmarkhotels.com* ⤶ *195 rooms and suites* ⚲ *In-room: kitchen (some), Wi-Fi. In-hotel: restaurants, bar, gym, parking, some pets allowed.*

NIGHTLIFE AND THE ARTS

BARS

If you're a beer fan, look for **Alaskan Brewing Company** (⊠ *5429 Shaune Dr.* ☎ *907/780–5866* ⊕ *www.alaskanbeer.com*). These tasty brews, including Alaskan Amber, Pale Ale, IPA, Stout, Alaskan Summer Ale, and Smoked Porter, are brewed and bottled in Juneau. You can visit the brewery (and get free samples of the goods) 11 to 6 daily May through September, with 20-minute tours every half hour. Between October and April tours take place Thursday through Saturday 11 to 6. ∎**TIP**➔This is no designer brewery—it's in Juneau's industrial area, and there is no upscale café/bar attached—but the gift shop sells T-shirts and beer paraphernalia.

The **Alaskan Hotel Bar** (✉ *167 S. Franklin St.* ☎ *907/586–1000*) is Juneau's most historically authentic watering hole, with flocked-velvet walls, antique chandeliers, and vintage Alaska frontier-brothel decor. The atmosphere, however, is anything but dated, and the bar's live music and open-mike night draw high-spirited crowds. Past visitors to Juneau may recall the **Imperial Saloon** (✉ *241 Front St.* ☎ *907/586–1960*) as one of the downtown dives, but a major remodeling transformed it into a favorite place to drink, shoot pool, and meet singles. The divey decor hasn't all disappeared—the walls still feature mounted moose and bison heads. There's also the original pressed-tin ceiling. When the ships are in, the music at **Red Dog Saloon** (✉ *278 S. Franklin St.* ☎ *907/463–3658*) is live and the crowd gets livelier. Just down Front Street is the **Viking Lounge** (✉ *218 Front St.* ☎ *907/586–2159*), which sells more alcohol than any other bar in Southeast. Cruise-ship workers love it for its DJ, dance floor, karaoke nights, and general rowdy vibe, and billiards enthusiasts appreciate the bar's eight pool tables.

MUSIC FESTIVALS

The annual weeklong **Alaska Folk Festival** (☎ *907/463–3316* ⊕ *www. akfolkfest.org*) is staged each April in Juneau, drawing singers, banjo masters, fiddlers, and even cloggers from all over the state and beyond, many of whom congregate at the Alaskan Hotel, the Festival's unofficial rallying point. Each May Juneau is the scene of **Juneau Jazz & Classics** (☎ *907/463–3378* ⊕ *www.jazzandclassics.org*), which celebrates music from Bach to Brubeck.

SYMPHONY

The **Juneau Symphony** (☎ *907/586–4676* ⊕ *www.juneausymphony. org*), directed by Kyle Wiley Pickett, performs classical works October through June in the high school auditorium and local churches.

THEATER

Alaska's only professional theater company, the nationally renowned **Perseverance Theatre** (✉ *914 3rd St., Douglas* ☎ *907/463–8497* ⊕ *www. perseverancetheatre.org*) performs a wide range of classics and new productions, regularly promoting Alaska artists and staging world premieres. The company tours extensively, bringing its unique productions such as its all-Tlingit version of Shakespeare's *Macbeth* to audiences everywhere. Perseverance's season runs from September through May, giving travelers another good reason to visit Alaska during shoulder season.

SHOPPING

ART GALLERIES

Annie Kaill's Gallery (✉ *244 Front St.* ☎ *907/586–2880* ⊕ *www. anniekaills.com*) displays a mix of playful and whimsical original prints, pottery, jewelry, and other arts and crafts from Alaska artists.

A surprising exception to the cheesy-airport-gift-shop epidemic, Juneau's airport gift shop, **Hummingbird Hollow** (☎ *907/789–4672* ⊕ *www.hummingbirdhollow.net*), is another fine place for authentic Native art, including a diverse selection of jewelry, baskets, and Eskimo dolls. The cooperatively run **Juneau Artists Gallery** (☎ 907/586–9891 ⊕ *www.juneauartistsgallery.com*), on the first floor of the old Senate Building at 175 South Franklin Street, sells a nice mix of watercolors, jewelry, oil and acrylic paintings, etchings, photographs, art glass, ceramics, fiber arts, and pottery from more than 20 local artists.

Rie Muñoz, of the **Rie Muñoz Gallery** (✉ *2101 N. Jordan Ave.* ☎ *907/789–7449 or 800/247–3151* ⊕ *www.riemunoz.com*) is one of Alaska's best-known artists. She's the creator of a stylized, simple, and colorful design technique that is much copied but rarely equaled. The gallery is located in Mendenhall Valley, a convenient 10-minute walk from the airport. In downtown Juneau, see Rie Muñoz's paintings and tapestries at **Decker Gallery** (✉ *233 S. Franklin St.* ☎ *907/463–5536 or 800/463–5536*). Located upstairs through a separate entrance next to Heritage Coffee, **Wm. Spear Design** (✉ *174 S. Franklin St.* ☎ *907/586–2209* ⊕ *www.wmspear.com*) is an interesting store, where this lawyer-turned-artist produces a fun and colorful collection of enameled pins and zipper pulls.

SEAFOOD

Taku Store (✉ *550 S. Franklin St.* ☎ *907/463–5319 or 800/582–5122* ⊕ *www.takustore.com*), at the south end of town near the cruise-ship docks and Mt. Roberts Tramway, processes nearly 6 million pounds of fish a year, mostly salmon. ■ TIP➔ The smoked sockeye fillets make excellent gifts. You can view the smoking procedure through large windows and then purchase the packaged fish in the deli-style gift shop or have some shipped back home.

SIDE TRIPS FROM JUNEAU

A few miles outside this ever-expanding city are some great day trips. The area's undisputed champion of visitor attractions is Mendenhall Glacier. Admiralty Island is also popular—it has hikes through rain forest, excellent bear viewing, and secluded sea kayaking.

NATIVE CULTURE NEARBY

If you're interested in seeing how many Alaska Natives of Southeast Alaska live today, you can fly or take one of the Alaska Marine Highway's ferries (☎ *907/465–3941 or 800/642–0066*) to **Kake, Angoon,** or **Hoonah**. Hoonah's historic cannery building has been beautifully restored, and serves as part of Huna Totem Corporation's **Icy Strait Point** (⊕ *www.icystraitpoint.com*) cruise port. Hoonah and Icy Strait Point's proximity to Point Adolphus—a favorite whale spot—means that trips from here maximize whale-watching time by cutting out extra travel time. There are daily trips into the strait, but book well in advance whether you're coming via cruise or not.

Independent travelers won't find much organized touring in Kake or Angoon, but you will find hotels (advance reservations strongly suggested), and guided fishing and natural-history trips can be arranged by asking around.

In Kake, contact the **Keex' Kwaan Lodge** (☎ *907/785–3434* ⊕ *www.kakealaska.com*).

In Angoon, try the all-inclusive **Favorite Bay Luxury Wilderness Resort** (☎ 907/788–3344 or 866/788–3344 ⊕ *www.favoritebay.com*).

In Hoonah, **Icy Strait Lodge** (☎ 866/645–3636 ⊕ *www.icystraitnow.com*) provides very comfortable on-the-water accommodations.

MACAULAY SALMON HATCHERY

3 mi northwest of downtown Juneau.

Macaulay Salmon Hatchery. Watch through an underwater window as salmon fight their way up a fish ladder from mid-June to mid-October. Inside the busy hatchery, which produces almost 125 million young salmon annually, you will learn about the environmental considerations of commercial fishermen and the lives of salmon. A retail shop sells gifts and salmon products. ✉ *2697 Channel Dr.* ☎ *907/463–4810 or 877/463–2486* ⊕ *www.dipac.net* 🖃 *$3.25 including short tour* ⊙ *Mid-May–mid-Sept., weekdays 10–6, weekends 10–5; Oct.–mid-May by appointment.*

GLACIER GARDENS RAINFOREST ADVENTURE

6½ mi northwest of Juneau.

Glacier Gardens Rainforest Adventure. Spread over 50 acres of rain forest, the family-owned Glacier Gardens has ponds, waterfalls, hiking paths, a large atrium, and gardens. The roots of fallen trees, turned upside down and buried in the ground, act as bowls to hold planters that overflow with begonias, fuchsias, and petunias. Guided tours in covered golf carts lead you along the 4 mi of paved paths, and a 580-foot-high overlook provides dramatic views of the Mendenhall wetlands wildlife refuge, Chilkat mountains, and downtown Juneau. A café and gift shop are here, and the conservatory is a popular wedding spot. ■ TIP→ The Juneau city bus, which departs from multiple locations in downtown Juneau, stops right in front of Glacier Gardens. ✉ *7600 Glacier Hwy.* ☎ *907/790–3377* ⊕ *www.glaciergardens.com* 🖃 *$24.95 including guided tour* ⊙ *May–Sept., daily 9–6; closed in winter.*

MENDENHALL GLACIER

13 mi north of Juneau.

Mendenhall Glacier. Alaska's most-visited drive-up glacier spans 12 mi and is fed by the massive Juneau Icefield. Like many other Alaska glaciers, it is retreating up the valley, losing more than 100 feet a year as massive chunks of ice calve into the small lake separating Mendenhall from the Mendenhall Visitor Center. The center has highly interactive exhibits on the glacier, a theater and bookstore, educational exhibits, and panoramic views. It's a great place for children to learn the basics of glacier dynamics. Nature trails lead along Mendenhall Lake and into the mountains overlooking Mendenhall Glacier; the trails are marked by posts and paint stripes delineating the historic location of the glacier, providing a sharp reminder of the Mendenhall's hasty retreat. An elevated viewing platform allows visitors to look for spawning sockeye and coho salmon—and the bears that eat them—at Steep Creek, ½ mi south of the visitor center along the Moraine Ecology Trail. Several companies lead bus tours to the glacier. A glacier express bus leaves from the cruise-ship terminal and heads right out to Mendenhall Glacier; ask at the

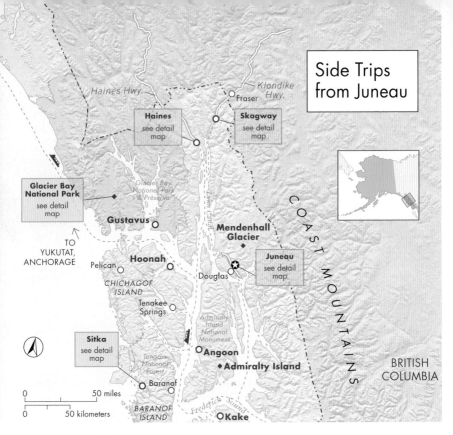

visitor information center there. ⊠ *End of Glacier Spur Rd. off Mendenhall Loop Rd.* ☎ *907/789–0097* ⊕ *www.fs.fed.us/r10/tongass/districts/mendenhall* ⊠ *Visitor center $3 in summer, free in winter* ☉ *May–Sept., daily 8–7:30; Oct.–Apr., Thurs.–Sun. 10–4.*

SHRINE OF ST. THERESE

23 mi northwest of downtown Juneau.

Shrine of St. Therese. Built in the 1930s, this beautiful stone church and its 15 stations of the cross are the only structures on a serene tiny island accessible via a 400-foot-long pedestrian causeway. Visitors enjoy the Merciful Love Labyrinth, the black-granite Shrine Columbarium, and the floral gardens along the Good Shepherd Rosary Trail. Sunday services are held at 1:30 pm from June through August. For those wishing to explore the area for more than a few hours, the shrine offers a lodge and four rental cabins that run the gamut from rustic to resplendent. ■ **TIP**➔ A round-trip taxi ride may cost $60 or more. ⊠ *415 6th St., #300* ☎ *907/780–6112* ⊕ *www.shrineofsainttherese.org.*

ADMIRALTY ISLAND

40 mi south of Juneau.

Admiralty Island. The island is famous for its lush old-growth rain forest and abundant wildlife, including one of the largest concentrations of brown bears anywhere on the planet. Native Tlingit inhabitants called it Kootznoowoo, meaning "fortress of the bears." Ninety miles long, with 678 mi of coastline, Admiralty—the second-largest island in Southeast Alaska—is home to an estimated 1,600 bears, almost one per square mile.

The Forest Service's **Admiralty Island National Monument** (⊕ *www.fs.fed. us/r10/tongass/districts/admiralty*) has a system of 14 public-use cabins, a canoe route that crosses the island via a chain of lakes and trails, the world's highest density of nesting bald eagles, large concentrations of humpback whales, and some of the region's best sea kayaking and sportfishing.

Fodor's Choice More than 90% of Admiralty Island is preserved within the Kootznoowoo Wilderness. Its chief attraction is **Pack Creek**, where you can watch brown bears feeding on salmon. One of Alaska's premier bear-viewing sites, Pack Creek is co-managed by the U.S. Forest Service and the Alaska Department of Fish and Game. Permits are required during the main viewing season, from June 1 through September 10, and only 24 people per day are allowed to visit Pack Creek from July 5 through August 25. If you're headed to Pack Creek without a guide or an experienced visitor, be sure to cover the basics of bear safety before your trip. ■TIP➔ At this writing, from January 2012 onward permits will be processed through www.recreation.gov. ☎ 907/586–8800 ⊕ *www.fs.fed. us/r10/tongass/districts/admiralty* 🗐 $20–$50.

OUTDOOR ACTIVITIES AND GUIDED TOURS

BIKING

Drop by the Centennial Hall Visitor Center for details on local trails open to bikes. Nearby is **Driftwood Lodge** (⊠ 435 *Willoughby Ave.* ☎ 907/586–2280 ⊕ *www.driftwoodalaska.com*), which has basic bikes for rent.

BOATING, CANOEING, AND KAYAKING

Above & Beyond Alaska (☎ 907/364–2333 ⊕ *www.beyondak.com*) guides day and overnight camping, ice climbing, Mendenhall Glacier trips, and sea-kayaking trips in the Juneau area.

★ **Adventure Bound Alaska** (☎ 907/463–2509 or 800/228–3875 ⊕ *www. adventureboundalaska.com*) offers all-day trips to Sawyer Glacier within Tracy Arm in summer.

Alaska Boat and Kayak Rental (☎ 907/789–6886 ⊕ *www.juneaukayak. com*) rents kayaks, canoes, and camping equipment at the Auke Bay boat harbor 12 mi north of Juneau. The company also provides water-taxi services for kayakers looking to access remote paddling terrain.

Alaska Discovery (☎ 510/594–6000 or 800/586–1911 ⊕ *www.akdiscovery.com*) leads 9- and 12-day trips down the Tatshenshini and Alsek rivers.

Alaska Travel Adventures (☎ 800/323–5757, 907/789–0052 *outside Alaska* ⊕ *www.bestofalaskatravel.com*) leads Mendenhall River floats and numerous other tours throughout the Juneau area.

DID YOU KNOW?

On the Trail of Time, see the physical signs of Mendenhall Glacier's history. Dark (old) and light (new) green vegetation meet at the highest point reached by the glacier's ice.

The **Juneau Steamboat Company** (☎ *907/723–0372* ⊕ *www.juneausteamboat.com*) offers scenic tours of the Gastineau Channel aboard an authentic wood-fired steam launch, similar to those used around Juneau in the late 1800s and early 1900s. Tours come with entertaining narration about the historic mines of the area.

CLIMBING GYM

If it's pouring down rain—and in Juneau, it often is—head south of town to the **Rock Dump** (✉ *1310 Eastaugh Way* ☎ *907/586–4982* ⊕ *www.rockdump.com*). The Dump has climbing walls for all abilities from beginner to expert; day passes are $13.

CROSS-COUNTRY SKIING

Find groomed cross-country ski trails near the Eaglecrest Ski Area and at Mendenhall Campground in the winter. You can rent skis and get advice about touring the trails and ridges around town from **Foggy Mountain Shop** (✉ *134 N. Franklin St.* ☎ *907/586–6780* ⊕ *www.foggymountainshop.com*). The shop also outfits hikers and climbers in summer.

In winter the **Parks and Recreation Department** (☎ *907/586–5226, 907/586–0428 24-hr information* ⊕ *www.juneau.org/parksrec*) sponsors a group ski and snowshoe outing each Wednesday and Saturday when there's sufficient snow.

DOWNHILL SKIING

Southeast Alaska's only downhill ski area, **Eaglecrest** (☎ *907/790–2000, 907/586–5330 recorded ski information* ⊕ *www.juneau.org/eaglecrest*), is on Douglas Island, 30 minutes from downtown Juneau. The resort typically offers late-November to mid-April skiing and snowboarding on 620 acres of well-groomed and off-piste terrain. Amenities include four double chairlifts, cross-country trails, a beginner's platter pull, a ski school, a ski-rental shop, a cafeteria, and a tri-level day lodge. Enjoy the northern lights while you night ski from January through mid-March.

FISHING

Sportfishing is an exceedingly popular activity in the Juneau area, and many charter boats depart from local harbors. **Alaska Trophy Fishing** (☎ *907/321–5859 or 866/934–7466* ⊕ *www.alaskatrophyfishing.com*) offers tailor-made fishing vacations and charters. **Juneau Sportfishing & Sightseeing** (☎ *907/586–1887* ⊕ *www.juneausportfishing.com*) has fishing trips aboard luxury boats.

The **Juneau Convention and Visitors Bureau** (☎ *907/586–1737 or 800/587–2201* ⊕ *www.traveljuneau.com*) Web site has a complete list of operators and several companies that lead whale-watching trips from Juneau.

FLIGHTSEEING

Several local companies operate helicopter flightseeing trips to the spectacular glaciers flowing from Juneau Icefield. Most have booths along the downtown cruise-ship dock. All include a touchdown on a glacier, providing guests of almost all ages and abilities a chance to romp on these rivers of ice. Some also lead trips that include a dogsled ride on the glacier, an increasingly popular tourist pastime. Helicopter tours in Juneau have a controversial history due to noise complaints from residents. Note that though we recommend the best companies, even some of the most experienced pilots have had accidents; always ask a carrier about its recent safety record before booking a trip.

Coastal Helicopters (☎ *907/789–5600 or 800/789–5610* ⊕ *www.coastalhelicopters.com*) lands on several glaciers within the Juneau Icefield.

Flying out of Douglas, **ERA Helicopters** (☎ *907/586–2030 or 800/843–1947* ⊕ *www.flightseeingtours.com*) has a fully narrated one-hour trip that includes landing on the Norris or Taku Glacier. **NorthStar Trekking** (☎ *907/790–4530* ⊕ *www.northstartrekking.com*) has three levels of excellent glacier hikes. The lowest level includes a one-hour interpretive walk while the highest consists of a four-hour hike that includes the chance to practice basic climbing and rope techniques. No experience is necessary.

Temsco Helicopters (☎ *907/789–9501 or 877/789–9501* ⊕ *www.temscoair.com*), the self-proclaimed pioneers of Alaska glacier helicopter touring, offers glacier tours, dogsled adventures, and year-round flightseeing. **Ward Air** (☎ *907/789–9150 or 800/478–9150* ⊕ *www.wardair.com*) conducts flightseeing trips to Glacier Bay, the Juneau Icefield, Tracy Arm, and Pack Creek.

★ **Wings Airways and Taku Glacier Lodge.** This Juneau-based company specializes in tours of the surrounding ice fields and the Taku Flight & Feast ride, on which a salmon feast awaits you at a classic Alaskan cabin, complete with glacier views—one of the best day trips out of the state capital. ☎ *907/586–6275* ⊕ *www.wingsairways.com*.

GOLD PANNING

Gold panning is fun, especially for children, and Juneau is one of Southeast's best-known gold-panning towns. Sometimes you actually discover a few flecks of the precious metal in the bottom of your pan. You can buy a pan at almost any Alaska hardware or sporting-goods store. **Alaska Travel Adventures** (☎ *800/323–5757, 907/789–0052 outside Alaska* ⊕ *www.bestofalaskatravel.com*) has gold-panning tours near the famous Alaska-Juneau Mine.

GOLF

Juneau's par-3, 9-hole **Mendenhall Golf Course** (✉ *2101 Industrial Blvd.* ☎ *907/789–1221*) is a modest layout but has views that any exclusive private course would die for. Club rentals are available.

A BREATHTAKING JOURNEY

Taku Glacier Lodge (☎ *907/586–6275* ⊕ *www.takuglacierlodge.com*) is a remote, historic lodge south of Juneau along Taku Inlet. Hole-in-the-Wall Glacier is directly across the inlet from the lodge, and nature trails wind through the surrounding country, where black bears and bald eagles are frequently sighted. Floatplanes fly from Juneau on a scenic trip to the lodge for a delicious lunch or dinner, followed by a flight back two hours later. No overnight stays are available.

4

HIKING

Gastineau Guiding (☎ 907/586–8231 ⊕ www.stepintoalaska.com) leads a variety of hikes in the Juneau area. Especially popular are their walks from the top of the tram on Mt. Roberts. The **Parks and Recreation Department** (☎ 907/586–5226, 907/586–0428 24-hr information ⊕ www.juneau.org/parksrec) in Juneau sponsors a group hike each Wednesday morning and on Saturday in summer. Hikers can contact the **U.S. Forest Service** (☎ 907/586–8790) for trail books and maps.

SIGHTSEEING AND GLACIERS

Former miners lead three-hour tours of the historic **AJ Gold Mine** (☎ 907/463–5017) south of Juneau. The tour includes a gold-panning demonstration and time in the old tunnels that lace the mountains. Mine tours depart from downtown by bus. The **Juneau Convention and Visitors Bureau** (☎ 907/586–1737 or 800/587–2201 ⊕ www.traveljuneau. com) has a list of other companies that provide tours to Mendenhall Glacier. **Alaska Coach Tours** (☎ 907/586–7433 ⊕ www.juneautrolley. com) operates the Historic Juneau Trolley, providing a 45-minute tour of Alaska's capital city. **Mighty Great Trips** (☎ 907/789–5460 ⊕ www. mightygreattrips.com) leads guided bus tours that include a visit to Mendenhall Glacier. The company also offers helicopter tours, river rafting, and whale-watching.

WHALE-WATCHING

Alaska Whale Watching (☎ 907/321–5859 or 888/432–6722 ⊕ www. akwhalewatching.com) offers small-group excursions (up to 12 guests) aboard a luxury yacht with an onboard naturalist. The company also offers a whale-watching/fishing combination tour, which is popular with multigenerational groups. Several companies lead whale-watching trips from Juneau. **Juneau Sportfishing & Sightseeing** (☎ 907/586–1887 ⊕ www. juneausportfishing.com) has been around for many years, and its boats carry a maximum of six passengers, providing a personalized trip.

★ **Orca Enterprises (with Captain Larry)** (☎ 907/789–6801 or 888/733–6722 ⊕ www.alaskawhalewatching.com) offers whale-watching tours via jet boats designed for comfort and speed. The operator boasts a whale-sighting success rate of 99.9% between May 1 and October 15.

Fodor's Choice
★ **Weather Permitting Alaska** (☎ 907/209–4221 ⊕ www.weatherpermit tingalaska.com) runs small-boat luxury whale-watching trips that last four hours, including van travel. Visitors get plenty of time to view whales and to look for other animals, including orcas, bears, sea lions, eagles, and porpoises, all while enjoying dramatic scenery. There are never more than six customers on a trip, making this one of the most flexible, intimate, and comprehensive whale-watches anywhere. The boat is stable and roomy. All trips include generous snacks featuring shrimp or salmon and homemade brownies along with nonalcoholic beverages. There is a

money-back guarantee for whale viewing. The boat captain is a certified Wilderness First Aid Responder and is certified in Swift Water Rescue and Proficiency in Survival Craft.

GLACIER BAY NATIONAL PARK AND PRESERVE

60 mi northwest of Juneau.

Fodor's Choice ★ **Glacier Bay National Park and Preserve.** Near the northern end of the Inside Passage, Glacier Bay National Park and Preserve is one of America's most magnificent national parks. Visiting Glacier Bay is like stepping back into the Little Ice Age—it's one of the few places in the world where you can approach such a variety of massive tidewater glaciers. Sounding like cannon fire, bergs the size of 10-story office buildings come crashing from the "snout" of a glacier, each cannon blast signifying another step in the glacier's steady retreat. The calving iceberg sends tons of water and spray skyward, propelling mini–tidal waves outward from the point of impact. **Johns Hopkins Glacier** calves so often and with such volume that large cruise ships can seldom come within 2 mi of its face.

Glacier Bay is a still-forming body of water fed by the runoff of the ice fields, glaciers, and mountains that surround it. In the mid-18th century, ice floes so covered the bay that Captain James Cook and then Captain George Vancouver sailed by and didn't even know it. At the time of Vancouver's sailing in 1794, the bay was still hidden behind and beneath a vast glacial wall of ice, which was more than 20 mi across and in places more than 4,000 feet in depth. It extended more than 100 mi north to its origins in the St. Elias Mountain Range, the world's tallest coastal mountains. Since then, the face of the glacial ice has melted and retreated with amazing speed, exposing 65 mi of fjords, islands, and inlets.

In 1879, about a century after Vancouver's sail-by, one of the earliest white visitors to what is now Glacier Bay National Park and Preserve came calling. The ever-curious naturalist John Muir, who would become one of the region's earliest proponents, was drawn by the flora and fauna that had followed in the wake of glacial withdrawals; he was also fascinated by the vast ice rivers that descended from the mountains to tidewater. Today the naturalist's namesake glacier, like others in the park, continues to retreat dramatically: the Muir Glacier's terminus is now scores of miles farther up the bay from the small cabin he built at its face during his time there.

Glacier Bay is a marvelous laboratory for naturalists of all persuasions. Glaciologists, of course, can have a field day. Animal lovers can hope to see the rare glacial "blue" bears of the area, a variation of the black bear, which is here along with the brown bear; whales feasting on krill; mountain goats in late spring and early summer; and seals on floating icebergs. Birders can look for the more than 200 species that have already been spotted in the park, and if you're lucky, you may witness bald eagles engaging in aerobatics.

A remarkable panorama of plants unfolds from the head of the bay, which is just emerging from the ice, to the mouth, which has been ice-free for more than 200 years. In between, the primitive plants— algae, lichens, and mosses—that are the first to take hold of the bare, wet ground give way to more-complex species: flowering plants such as the magenta dwarf fireweed and the creamy dryas, which in turn merge with willows, alders, and cottonwood. As the living plants mature and die, they enrich the soil

> ### FAIRWEATHER FOLLY
>
> It was Vancouver who named the magnificent snow-clad **Mt. Fairweather**, which towers over the head of the bay. Legend has it that Vancouver named Fairweather on one of Southeast's most beautiful blue days—and the mountain was not seen again during the following century. Overcast, rainy weather is certainly the norm here.

and prepare it for new species to follow. The climax of the plant community is the lush spruce-and-hemlock rain forest, rich in life and blanketing the land around **Bartlett Cove.** ☏ 907/697–2230, 907/697–2627 *boating information* ⊕ *www.nps.gov/glba.*

GUSTAVUS

50 mi west of Juneau, 75 mi south of Skagway.

For airborne visitors, Gustavus is the gateway to Glacier Bay National Park and Preserve. The long, paved jet airport, built as a refueling strip during World War II, is one of the best and longest in Southeast Alaska, all the more impressive because of its limited facilities at the field. Alaska Airlines, which serves Gustavus daily in summer, has a new terminal at the site. Smaller, light-aircraft companies that serve the community out of Juneau also have on-site shelters. A summer ferry, operated on Friday and Sunday by Aramark (☏ 907/264–4600 *or 888/229–8687* ⊕ *www.visitglacierbay.com*), runs between Juneau and Bartlett Cove.

■ **TIP→** Before you get too excited about visiting this remote outpost, be forewarned: Gustavus has no downtown. In fact, Gustavus is not really a town at all. Instead, it's a scattering of homes, farmsteads, a craft studio, fishing and guiding charters, an art gallery, and other tiny enterprises peopled by hospitable individualists. Visitors enjoy the unstructured outdoor activities in the area, including beach- and trail-hiking in the Nature Conservancy's Forelands Preserve.

OUTDOOR ACTIVITIES AND GUIDED TOURS

Glacier Bay is best experienced from the water, whether from the deck of a cruise ship, on a tour boat, or from the level of a sea kayak. National Park Service naturalists often come aboard to explain the great glaciers and to help spot bears, mountain goats, whales, porpoises, and birds.

BOATING AND LOCAL INTEREST **Huna Totem Corporation/Aramark** (☏ 907/264–4600 *or 888/229–8687* ⊕ *www.visitglacierbay.com*) provides daily summertime boat tours from the dock at Bartlett Cove, near Glacier Bay Lodge. These eight-hour trips into Glacier Bay have a Park Service naturalist aboard a high-speed

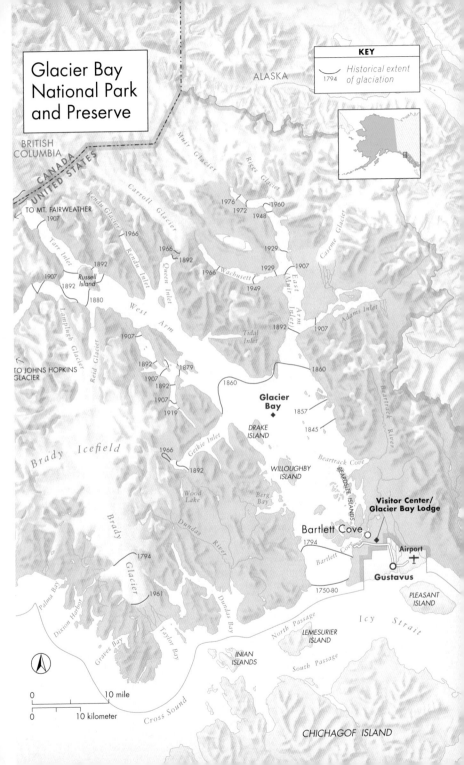

Glacier Bay National Park and Preserve

ALASKA

KEY
1794 *Historical extent of glaciation*

BRITISH COLUMBIA

CANADA
UNITED STATES

TO MT. FAIRWEATHER
1907

Muir Glacier

Riggs Glacier

Carroll Glacier

Rendu Glacier

1976
1972
1948
1960

Casement Glacier

Tarr Inlet
1892

1907
1892
Russell Island
1880

1966

1966
1892

1929

Queen Inlet

Wachusett
1966

1929
1949

1907

Lamplugh Glacier

West Arm

Rendu Inlet

East Muir Arm Inlet

TO JOHNS HOPKINS GLACIER

1907

Reid Glacier

1892
1907
1892
1907
1919

1879

1860

1892

Tidal Inlet

Adams Inlet
1907

1907

Beartrack River

Glacier Bay
1857

1845

1860

DRAKE ISLAND

Brady Icefield

1966
1892

Geikie Inlet

WILLOUGHBY ISLAND

Beartrack Cove

BEARDSLEE ISLANDS

Visitor Center/ Glacier Bay Lodge

Wood Lake

Berg Bay

Bartlett Cove ○

1794

Bartlett Cove

Airport ✝

Gustavus ○

Dundas River

1750-80

PLEASANT ISLAND

Brady Glacier
1794

1961

Palma Bay

Dixon Harbor

Taylor Bay

Dundas Bay

North Passage

Icy Strait

LEMESURIER ISLAND

South Passage

Graves Bay

INIAN ISLANDS

0   10 mile
0   10 kilometer

Cross Sound

CHICHAGOF ISLAND

155-passenger catamaran. A light lunch is included. Campers and sea kayakers heading up the bay ride the same boat.

FLIGHTSEEING **Air Excursions** (☎ 907/697–2375, 800/354–2479 *in Alaska* ⊕ *www. airexcursions.com*) offers daily scheduled air service year-round between Juneau, Gustavus/Glacier Bay, Hoonah, Haines, and Skagway, plus flightseeing tours and charters to other destinations in Southeast Alaska.

HIKING Glacier Bay's steep and heavily forested slopes aren't the most conducive to hiking, but there are several short hikes that begin at the Glacier Bay Lodge. Among the most popular is the **Forest Loop Trail**, a pleasant 1-mi jaunt that begins in a forest of spruce and hemlock and finishes on the beach. Also beginning at the lodge is the **Bartlett River Trail**—a 5-mi round-trip hike that borders an intertidal lagoon, culminating at the Bartlett River estuary. The **Bartlett Lake Trail**, part of a 6-mi walk that meanders through rain forest, ends at the quiet lakeshore. The entire Gustavus beachfront was set aside by the Nature Conservancy, enabling visitors to hike the shoreline for miles without getting lost. The beachfront is part of the **Alaska Coastal Wildlife Viewing Trail** (⊕ *wildlife. alaska.gov*). The spring and fall bird migrations are exceptional on Gustavus estuaries, including Dude Creek Critical Habitat Area, which provides a stopover before crossing the ice fields for sandhill cranes. Maps and wildlife viewing information are available from the **Alaska Division of Wildlife Conservation** (⊕ *wildlife.alaska.gov*).

SEA KAYAKING The most adventurous way to explore Glacier Bay is by paddling your own kayak through the bay's icy waters and inlets. But unless you're an expert, you're better off signing on with the guided tours. You can book a five-day guided expedition through **Alaska Discovery** (☎ 510/594–6000 or 800/586–1911 ⊕ *www.akdiscovery.com*). Alaska Discovery provides safe, seaworthy kayaks and tents, gear, and food. Its guides are tough, knowledgeable Alaskans, and they've spent enough time in Glacier Bay's wild country to know what's safe and what's not. **Spirit Walker Expeditions** (☎ 907/697–2266 or 800/529–2537 ⊕ *www. seakayakalaska.com*) leads 1- to 7-day sea-kayaking trips from Gustavus to various parts of Icy Strait. Trips to Glacier Bay and other remote areas of Southeast Alaska, including Ford's Terror and West Chichagof, are also offered on a limited basis.

Alaska Mountain Guides (☎ 907/766–3396 or 800/766–3396 ⊕ *www. alaskamountainguides.com*) offers day kayaking trips for whale-watching at Point Adolphus, a premier humpback gathering spot, as well as multiday sea-kayaking expeditions next to tidewater glaciers in Glacier Bay National Park.

Kayak rentals for Glacier Bay exploring and camping can be arranged through **Glacier Bay Sea Kayaks** (✉ *Bartlett Cove* ☎ 907/697–2257 ⊕ *www.glacierbayseakayaks.com*). You will be given instructions on handling the craft plus camping and routing suggestions for unescorted trips. Guided day trips are available in Bartlett Cove. The company is an official NPS concession for guided day kayak trips.

WHALE- Step aboard the **M/V TAZ** (☎ 907/321–2302 or 888/698–2726 ⊕ *www. WATCHING taz.gustavus.com*) and check out Icy Strait and Point Adolphus, near

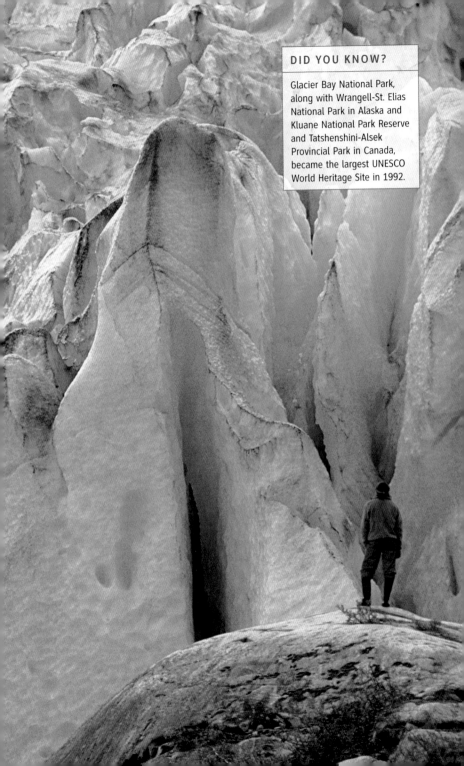

QUAKE HAPPY IN GLACIER BAY

Glacier Bay's impressive landscape is the result of plate tectonics. The region sits directly above a chaotic intersection of fault lines—resulting in a 100-million-year-old crunchfest.

While this movement can be credited for creating the region's stunning topography, it has also wreaked some havoc. On September 10, 1899, the area was rocked by a massive temblor registering 8.4 on the Richter scale. The quake, which had its epicenter in Yakutat Bay, rattled Glacier Bay so much that the entire bay was choked with icebergs.

On July 9, 1958, a tremendous earthquake—a 7.9 on the Richter scale—triggered a landslide of epic proportions in nearby Lituya Bay: 40 million cubic yards of rock tumbled into the bay, and created a tidal wave that reached 1,720 feet.

the entrance to Glacier Bay, for awesome views of humpback whales and many other marine mammals. All tours out of Gustavus include binoculars, snacks, and hot beverages. Half-day tours and custom charters accommodating up to 23 passengers are offered, as well as "Weddings with Whales," where you can get married while surrounded by humpbacks.

WHERE TO STAY

For expanded hotel reviews, visit Fodors.com.

$$$–$$$$ 🏨 **Annie Mae Lodge.** This quiet two-story lodge, one of the few Gustavus places open year-round, faces the Good River, has beautiful grounds, and is a five-minute walk from the beach. **Pros:** beautiful grounds; good views. **Cons:** property is not on the beach; no televisions in rooms. 🏠 *Box 55, 99826* 🕿 *907/697–2346 or 800/478–2346* ⊕ *www.anniemae.com* 🛏 *11 rooms, 9 with bath* ♿ *In-room: no TV. In-hotel: laundry facilities* ⵏ◯ⵏ *Breakfast, all meals.*

$$$$ 🏨 **Bear Track Inn.** Built of spruce logs, this inn sits on a 97-acre property facing Icy Strait. **Pros:** delicious meals at restaurant; a favorite with locals. **Cons:** high room rate; no room TVs. **TripAdvisor:** "staff is marvelous," "rooms are spacious and inviting," "log cabin design is spectacular." ✉ *255 Rink Creek Rd.* 🕿 *907/697–3017 or 888/697–2284* ⊕ *www.beartrackinn.com* 🛏 *14 rooms* ♿ *In-room: no TV. In-hotel: restaurant, water sports, business center* ⊘ *Closed Oct.–Apr.* ⵏ◯ⵏ *All meals.*

$$$–$$$$ 🏨 **Glacier Bay Lodge.** Within the national park, this lodge is constructed of massive timbers and blends well into the thick rain forest surrounding it on three sides. **Pros:** ample hiking trails nearby; good local seafood at restaurant. **Cons:** dining options are all on the property; location is somewhat remote. **TripAdvisor:** "amazing nature experience," "stunning views," "awesome location." ✉ *199 Bartlett Cove Rd.* 🕿 *907/264–4600 or 888/229–8687* ⊕ *www.visitglacierbay.com* 🛏 *49 rooms* ♿ *In-room: no TV. In-hotel: restaurant, bar, water sports, some pets allowed* ⊘ *Closed mid-Sept.–mid-May* ⵏ◯ⵏ *All meals.*

$$$ 🏨 **Gustavus Inn.** Built in 1928 and established as a hotel in 1965, this inn continues a tradition of gracious Alaska rural living. **Pros:** wonderful food in the dining room; nicely decorated rooms. **Cons:** only one

Fodor's Choice
★

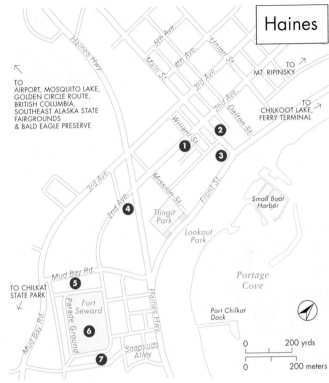

dinner seating; no phones in rooms. **TripAdvisor:** "fantastic service,"
"oasis of charm and comfort," "food is fabulous." ✉ *Mi 1, Gustavus
Rd.* ⬧ *Box 60, Gustavus 99826* ☎ *907/697–2254 or 800/649–5220*
⊕ *www.gustavusinn.com* ⇆ *13 rooms, 11 with bath* ⬧ *In-room: no
TV, Wi-Fi. In-hotel: restaurant, water sports, laundry facilities, business
center* ☾ *Closed mid-Sept.–mid-May* ⦿ *All meals.*

HAINES

75 mi north of Gustavus, 80 mi northwest of Juneau.

Haines encompasses an area that has been occupied by Tlingit peoples
for centuries on the collar of the Chilkat Peninsula, a narrow strip of
land that divides the Chilkat and Chilkoot inlets. Missionary S. Hall
Young and famed naturalist John Muir were intent on establishing a
Presbyterian mission in the area, and, with the blessing of local chiefs,
they chose the site that later became Haines. It's hard to imagine a more
beautiful setting—a heavily wooded peninsula with magnificent views
of Portage Cove and the snowy Coast Range. Unlike most other towns
in Southeast Alaska, Haines can be reached by the 152-mi Haines Highway, which connects at Haines Junction with the Alaska Highway. It's
also accessible by the state ferry (☎ *907/465–3941 or 800/642–0066*)

and by scheduled plane service from Juneau. The Haines ferry terminal is 4½ mi northwest of downtown, and the airport is 4 mi west.

Haines is an interesting community: its history contains equal parts enterprising gold-rush boomtown and regimented military outpost. The former is evidenced by Jack Dalton, who in the 1890s maintained a toll route from the settlement of Haines into the Yukon, charging $1 for foot passengers and $2.50 per horse. His Dalton Trail later provided access for miners during the 1897 gold rush to the Klondike.

The town's military roots are visible at Fort William Henry Seward, located at Portage Cove just south of town. For 17 years (1923–39) prior to World War II, the post, renamed Chilkoot Barracks in commemoration of the gold-rush route, was the only military base in the territory. The fort's buildings and grounds are now part of a National Historic Landmark.

Today the Haines–Fort Seward community is recognized for the Native dance and art center at Fort Seward; the Haines Public Library (which, in 2005, was named Best Small Library in the United States); as well as for the superb fishing, camping, and outdoor recreation to be found at Chilkoot Lake, Portage Cove, Mosquito Lake, and Chilkat State Park on the shores of Chilkat Inlet. Northwest of the city is the Alaska Chilkat Bald Eagle Preserve. Thousands of eagles come here each winter to feed on a late run of chum salmon, making it one of Alaska's premier bird-watching sites.

The downtown area feels as small as a postage stamp, and the town exudes a down-home friendliness. Perhaps this is because Haines sees fewer cruise ships, or maybe it's the grand landscape and ease of access to the mountains and sea. Whatever the cause, visitors should be prepared for a relative lack of souvenir and T-shirt shops compared to other ports. Local weather is drier than in much of Southeast Alaska.

Haines has adopted a no-smoking ordinance that went into effect in 2010. Smoking is banned in all businesses, including bars, restaurants, and shops. Accommodations are allowed to have smoking rooms; be sure to reserve a smoking room if it is needed.

GETTING HERE AND AROUND

Haines is connected to other towns in Southeast Alaska by the **Alaska Marine Highway,** and from here you can connect with smaller vessels serving Bush communities. It is also one of the few towns in Southeast Alaska that is accessible by road; be aware that the weather and wildlife in this area present hazards on the highway. Take the Alaska Highway to Haines Junction and then drive on southwest on the Haines Highway to the Alaska Panhandle. The town is a delightful place to explore on foot. In addition to regional connections, **Air Excursions** offers flightseeing tours of Glacier Bay. Housed a few doors up the street from the visitor center, **Mountain Flying Service** leads flightseeing trips to nearby Glacier Bay National Park. **Wings of Alaska** has scheduled service to Juneau and Skagway.

ESSENTIALS

Medical Assistance **Haines Medical Clinic** (⊠ *131 1st Ave. N, next to Convention and Visitors Bureau* ☎ *907/766–6300).*

WALKING AROUND HAINES

A walk through downtown Haines is best started at the helpful **Haines Convention and Visitors Bureau** on 2nd and Willard streets, where you can pick up a walking-tour brochure. To learn a bit about the area's natural and cultural history, head to the **Sheldon Museum and Cultural Center** on Main Street. From here, you can see the busy docks of Portage Cove, filled with commercial fishing boats and pleasure craft. Head down the hill (turning right on Front Street) to follow the shoreline 0.25 mi to Lookout Park, a fine place to take in the view on a sunny day—which, in Haines, occurs more often than you might guess. Just up the hill from here is a small cemetery with graves dating from the 1880s. From the cemetery, steps emerge on Mission Street; follow it to 2nd Avenue, where a left turn will bring you to **American Bald Eagle Foundation**, a museum and research center for these majestic birds. Another 0.3 mi out 2nd Avenue is perhaps the most interesting sight in Haines: **Ft. William H. Seward National Historic Landmark.** As you enter the grounds, you'll pass **Hotel Halsingland**, originally the commanding officers' quarters. Circle the parade ground if you like, passing the line of officers' homes along the top, stopping in at **Alaska Indian Arts,** housed within the old fort hospital.

4

Tour Information Air Excursions (☎ 907/766–3800 ⊕ www.airexcursions. com). **Earth Center Adventures** (☎ 907/766–3679 ⊕ www.flydrake.com). **Mountain Flying Service** (☎ 907/766–3007 or 800/954–8747 ⊕ www. glacierbayflightseeing.com). **Wings of Alaska** (☎ 907/789–0790 ⊕ www. wingsofalaska.com).

Visitor Information Haines Convention and Visitors Bureau (✉ 2nd Ave. near Willard St. ☝ Box 530, Haines 99827 ☎ 907/766–2234 or 800/458–3579 ⊕ www.haines.ak.us).

EXPLORING

☯ **Alaska Indian Arts.** Dedicated to the revival of Tlingit art, this nonprofit organization is housed in the former fort hospital, on the south side of the parade ground. You can watch artisans doing everything from carving totem poles to creating delicate silver jewelry. ✉ *Ft. Seward* ☎ *907/766–2160* ⊕ *www.alaskaindianarts.com* 🗩 *Free* ☉ *Weekdays 9–5.*

☯ **American Bald Eagle Foundation.** The main focuses here are bald eagles and associated fauna of the Chilkat Preserve, explored in lectures, displays, and videos. A taxidermy-heavy diorama also shows examples of local animals. Opened in summer of 2010, a raptor center features live presentations and an aviary displaying live eagles. The gift shop sells natural-history items. ✉ *Haines Hwy. at 2nd Ave., Box 49* ☎ *907/766–3094* ⊕ *www.baldeagles.org* 🗩 *$3–$10* ☉ *May–Nov., Daily 9–5.*

★ **Ft. William H. Seward National Historic Landmark.** Circle the sloping parade grounds of Alaska's first U.S. army post, where stately clapboard homes

A SCENIC DRIVE

The breathtaking **Haines Highway** (☎ 907/767–5510), a National Scenic Byway, starts at Mile 0 in Haines and continues 152 mi to Haines Junction. You don't have to drive the entire length to experience its beauty, as worthwhile stops are all along the route. At about Mile 6 a delightful picnic spot is near the Chilkat River. At Mile 9.5 the view of Cathedral Peaks, part of the Chilkat Range, is magnificent. Though at Mile 9 the Alaska Chilkat Bald Eagle Preserve begins, the best viewing is between Mile 19 and Mile 21. At Mile 33 is a roadside restaurant called, aptly, **33-Mile Roadhouse**, where you fill your tank and coffee mug and grab a burger and, most importantly, a piece of pie. Do not leave without trying the pie. The United States–Canada border lies at Mile 42; stop at Canadian customs and set your clock ahead one hour.

In winter, the Alaska Chilkat Bald Eagle Preserve (☎ 907/766–2292), on Mile 19–Mile 21 of the Haines Highway, harbors the largest concentration of bald eagles in the world. In November and December, more eagles gather outside of Haines than live in the continental United States. Thousands come to feast on the late run of salmon in the clear, ice-free waters of the Chilkat River, heated by underground warm springs.

stand against a mountain backdrop. The Haines Convention and Visitors Bureau provides a walking-tour brochure of the fort.

Haines Convention and Visitors Bureau. At this helpful tourist office you can pick up hiking- and walking-tour brochures, learn about lodging and attractions, and check out menus from local restaurants. ⊠ *122 2nd Ave. S, Box 530* ☎ *907/766–2234 or 800/458–3579* ⊕ *www.haines. ak.us* ⊗ *Mid-May–mid-Sept., weekdays 8–5, weekends 9–4; mid-Sept.– mid-May, weekdays 8–5.*

The **Hammer Museum** (⊠ *108 Main St.* ☎ *907/766–2374* ⊕ *www. hammermuseum.org*). The owner started his collection decades ago and founded the Hammer Museum—the world's first—in 2001. Among his impressive collection of 1,800 hammers are a Roman battle hammer and 6-foot-long posting hammers used to secure advertisements to local outside walls.

Hotel Halsingland. In Ft. Seward, wander past the huge, gallant, white-columned former commanding officers' home, now a part of the hotel on Officers' Row.

Sheldon Museum and Cultural Center. Steve Sheldon began assembling native artifacts, items from historic Ft. Seward, and gold-rush memorabilia, such as Jack Dalton's sawed-off shotgun, in the 1880s, and started an exhibit of his finds in 1925. Today his collection is the core of the museum's impressive array of artifacts, including Chilkat Blankets, a model of a Tlingit tribal house, and the original lens from the Eldred Rock lighthouse just south of Haines on the Lynn Canal. Repatriated Bear Clan items such as an 18th-century carved ceremonial Murrelet Hat are are on display, thanks to loans to the museum. ⊠ *11 Main St.* ☎ *907/766–2366* ⊕ *www.sheldonmuseum.org* 🖃 *$3*

⊙ *Mid-May–mid-Sept., weekdays 10–4, weekends 1–4; mid-Sept.–mid-May, Mon.–Sat. 1–4.*

OFF THE
BEATEN
PATH

Chilkat State Park. This park on the Chilkat Inlet has beautiful and accessible viewing of both the Davidson and Rainbow glaciers along with public campgrounds. The Seduction Point Trail, about 7 mi one-way, takes hikers to the very tip of the peninsula upon which Haines sits. ☎ 907/766–2292 ⊕ *www.dnr.state.ak.us/parks.*

Dalton City. An 1890s gold-rush town was re-created for the movie *White Fang* and moved to the **Southeast Alaska State Fairgrounds** (☎ 907/766–2476), less than a mile from downtown. The movie-set buildings now house local businesses, including the **Haines Brewing Company** (☎ 907/766–3823). The four-day-long **Southeast Alaska State Fair,** held the last week of July, is one of several official regional blowouts, and thanks to its homespun feel it's a must for state fair fans. In addition to the usual collection of barnyard animals, the fair has live music, rides on a vintage 1920 Herschal-Spillman carousel, local culinary arts, native dances, totemic crafts, art, and photography. ☎ 907/766–2476 ⊕ *www.seakfair.org* ⊠ *$7.*

SPORTS, THE OUTDOORS, AND GUIDED TOURS

BICYCLING

Sockeye Cycle Company (⊠ *24 Portage St., Box 829* ☎ *907/766–2869 or 877/292–4154* ⊕ *www.cyclealaska.com*) specializes in guided mountain- and road-bike tours along the roads and trails of Haines, including the breathtaking 360-mi Golden Circle route that connects Haines and Skagway via the Yukon Territory. The outfit also rents, services, and sells bikes.

BOATING AND FISHING

Alaska Fjordlines (☎ *907/766–3395 or 800/320–0146* ⊕ *www. alaskafjordlines.com*) operates a high-speed catamaran from Skagway and Haines to Juneau and back throughout the summer, stopping along the way to watch sea lions, humpbacks, and other marine mammals. One-way service is also available. **Haines-Skagway Fast Ferry** (☎ *907/766–2100 or 888/766–2103* ⊕ *www.hainesskagwayfastferry.com*) provides a passenger catamaran ferry between Skagway and Haines, with special package rates for visitors who book a ride on Skagway's White Pass Summit Train. The service is offered several times a day in summer, and the trip takes 45 minutes each way.

The jet-boat tours offered by **River Adventures** (☎ *907/766–2050 or 800/478–9827* ⊕ *www.jetboatalaska.com*) are a great way to experience the bald eagle preserve in majestic Chilkat River valley.

For information on numerous sportfishing charter boats in Haines, contact the **Haines Convention and Visitors Bureau** (☎ *907/766–2234 or 800/458–3579* ⊕ *www.haines.ak.us*).

HIKING

Alaska Mountain Guides (☎ *907/766–3396 or 800/766–3396* ⊕ *www. alaskamountainguides.com*), a guide service and rock-climbing school, leads a variety of hiking and mountaineering trips from Haines, ranging from half-day trips to 90-day expeditionary courses for hiking, sea kayaking, fly-fishing, ice climbing, rock climbing, skiing, and mountaineering. Sea-kayak rentals are also available.

Battery Point Trail is a fairly level path that hugs the shoreline for 2 mi, providing fine views across Lynn Canal. The trail begins a mile east of town, and a campsite can be found at Kelgaya Point near the end. For other hikes, pick up a copy of "Haines Is for Hikers" at the Haines Convention and Visitors Bureau.

NATURE AND SKI TOURS

Fodor'sChoice **Alaska Nature Tours** (☎ 907/766–2876 ⊕ www.alaskanaturetours.net) con-
★ ducts bird-watching and natural-history tours through the Alaska Chilkat Bald Eagle Preserve, operates brown bear–watching excursions in July and August, and leads hiking treks in summer and ski tours in winter.

The Chilkat Valley is a powdery heli-skier's paradise, and **Southeast Alaska Backcountry Adventures** (☎ 907/766–2009 ⊕ www.skiseaba.com) lifts skiers and snowboarders by helicopter and Sno-Cat. The company also offers packages that include lodging.

WHERE TO EAT

$–$$ ✕ **Bamboo Room.** Pop culture meets greasy spoon in this unassuming
AMERICAN coffee shop with red-vinyl booths, which has been in the same family for more than 50 years. The menu doesn't cater to light appetites—it includes sandwiches, burgers, fried chicken, chili, and halibut fish-and-chips, but the place really is at its best for an all-American breakfast (available until 3 pm). The adjacent bar has pool, darts, a big-screen TV, and a jukebox. ⊠ 2nd Ave. near Main St. ☎ 907/766–2800 ⊕ www. bamboopioneer.net.

$–$$ ✕ **Mosey's.** The fare at this Mexican restaurant just one block up from
MEXICAN the cruise-ship dock is on the spicy side—owner Martha Stewart (yes, that's her real name) travels to New Mexico each year and brings back bushels of roasted green chilies, the signature ingredient. If your taste buds can handle the kick, you'll be rewarded: the food is bursting with fresh flavors, and the atmosphere is a cheery south-of-the-border alternative to the rest of Haines's more mainstream offerings. Order lunch at the counter or sit down for table service in the evening. ⊠ Soap Suds Alley, Ft. Seward ☎ 907/766–2320 ⊕ www.moseyscantina.com.

¢–$ ✕ **Mountain Market.** Meet the locals over espresso, brewed from fresh-
AMERICAN roasted beans, and a fresh-baked pastry at this busy corner natural-foods store, deli, café, wine-and-spirits shop, de facto meeting hall, and hitching post. But Mountain Market is great for lunchtime sandwiches, wraps, soups, and salads. Friday is pizza day, but come early, since it's often gone by early afternoon. ⊠ 3rd Ave. and Haines Hwy. ☎ 907/766–3340.

WHERE TO STAY

For expanded hotel reviews, visit Fodors.com.

$ ▥ **Alaska Guardhouse.** Conveniently located near the docks, this unpre-
☾ tentious B&B in the Fort Seward area used to be the area's jail. **Pros:**

near the docks; good views. **Cons:** limited amenities; only three rooms. ⊠ *15 Seward Dr., Fort Seward* ☎ *907/766–2566 or 866/290–7445* ⊕ *www.alaskaguardhouse.com* ⇆ *3 rooms, 2 with bath* ⌂ *In-room: kitchen (some), Wi-Fi. In-hotel: some pets allowed* �’❙*Breakfast.*

$ ⌑ **Captain's Choice Motel.** In summer overflowing flower boxes surround this downtown Haines motel. **Pros:** beautiful grounds; continental breakfast includes locally made raisin bread and muffins. **Cons:** the hotel's airport shuttle is unreliable; room amenities are limited; there's a charge for Wi-Fi. **TripAdvisor:** "view was very special," "clean room and comfortable bed," "conveniently located downtown." ⊠ *108 2nd Ave. N, Box 392* ☎ *907/766–3111 or 800/478–2345* ⊕ *www.capchoice. com* ⇆ *40 rooms, 4 suites* ⌂ *In-room: Wi-Fi. In-hotel: bar, laundry facilities, some pets allowed* ❙❙*Breakfast.*

¢–$ ⌑ **Hotel Halsingland. Pros:** elegant, historic property; rental cars on-site. **Cons:** small showers; small rooms. **TripAdvisor:** "part of historic Ft. Seward," "room was spacious and certainly clean," "vintage room fixtures." ⊠ *Ft. Seward* ☎ *907/766–2000 or 800/542–6363* ⊕ *www.hotelhalsingland.com* ⇆ *58 rooms, 52 with bath* ⌂ *In-room: Wi-Fi (some). In-hotel: restaurant, bar, some pets allowed* ❂ *Closed mid-Nov.–Mar.*

NIGHTLIFE AND THE ARTS

NIGHTLIFE

Locals might rule the pool tables at **Fogcutter Bar** (⊠ *122 Main St.* ☎ *907/766–2555*), but they always appreciate a little friendly competition. Like many bars in Southeast Alaska, the Fogcutter sells drink tokens that patrons often purchase for their friends; you'll notice folks sitting at the bar with a small stack of these tokens next to their beverage. The Fogcutter's embossed metal tokens are among Southeast's most ornate. Purchase one for a keepsake—or for later use. **Haines Brewing Company** (⊠ *108 Whitefang Way* ☎ *907/766–3823*), a microbrewery among the Dalton City buildings at the fairgrounds, sells beer by the sample glass, pint glass, or liter growlers to go. Commercial fisherfolk gather nightly at **Harbor Bar** (⊠ *Front St. at harbor* ☎ *907/766–2444*), which dates from 1907. You might catch some live music here in summer, or take in one of its poker tournaments. Inside one of the oldest buildings in town (it was once a brothel), the **Pioneer Bar** (⊠ *2nd Ave. near Main St.* ☎ *907/766–3443*) has historical photographs on the walls, a large-screen television for sports, and occasional bands.

SHOPPING

GALLERIES AND GIFTS

A surprising number of artists live in the Haines area, and you will find their works in several local galleries. Tresham Gregg's **Sea Wolf Gallery** (⊠ *Ft. Seward* ☎ *907/766–2540* ⊕ *www.tresham.com*) sells wood carvings, silver jewelry, prints, and T-shirts with his Native-inspired designs. Haines's most charming gallery, the **Wild Iris Gallery** (⊠ *Portage St.* ☎ *907/766–2300*), displays attractive jewelry, prints, and fashion wear created by owner Fred Shields and his daughter Melina. Other

LEARN ABOUT TLINGIT CULTURE

Jilkat Kwaan Cultural Tours. Built near Klukwan, a Native village 23 mi up the road from Haines, this site offers visitors the chance to learn about the Tlingit, including their arts, language, and traditions. Visit the site's Long House, built using traditional methods; find out about traditional Native crafts, including wood carving and beading; learn about the Chilkat Blanket, the symbol of the local people; see the process for smoking salmon; and much more. A small but well-stocked gift shop sells crafts made by Klukwan locals. ☎ 907/767–5797 ⊕ *www. visitklukwan.com.*

local artists are also represented. It's just up from the cruise-ship dock, and its summer gardens alone are worth the visit.

Birch Boy Products (☎ 907/767–5660 or 877/769–5660 ⊕ *www.birchboy. com*) produces tart and tasty birch syrup; it's sold in local gift shops.

SKAGWAY

14 mi northeast of Haines.

Located at the northern terminus of the Inside Passage, Skagway is only a one-hour ferry ride from Haines. By road, the distance is 359 mi, as you have to take the Haines Highway up to Haines Junction, Yukon, then take the Alaska Highway 100 mi south to Whitehorse, and then drive a final 100 mi south on the Klondike Highway to Skagway. North-country folk call this sightseeing route the Golden Horseshoe or Golden Circle tour, because it passes a lot of gold-rush country in addition to spectacular lake, forest, and mountain scenery.

However you get to Skagway, you'll find the town an amazingly preserved artifact from North America's biggest, most-storied gold rush. Most of the downtown district forms part of the Klondike Gold Rush National Historical Park, a unit of the national park system dedicated to commemorating and interpreting the frenzied stampede of 1897 that extended to Dawson City in Canada's Yukon.

Nearly all the historic sights are within a few blocks of the cruise-ship and ferry dock, allowing visitors to meander through the town's attractions at whatever pace they choose. Whether you're disembarking from a cruise ship, a ferry, or a dusty automobile fresh from the Golden Circle, you'll quickly discover that tourism is the lifeblood of this town. Unless you're visiting in winter or hiking into the backcountry on the Chilkoot Trail, you aren't likely to find a quiet Alaska experience around Skagway.

GETTING HERE AND AROUND

Skagway offers one of the few opportunities to drive in the region. Take the Alaska Highway to the Canadian Yukon's Whitehorse and then drive on Klondike Highway to the Alaska Panhandle. Southeast

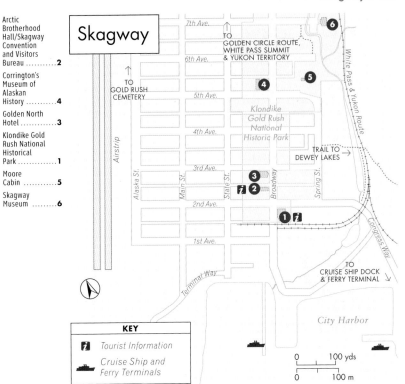

KEY

7 *Tourist Information*

Cruise Ship and Ferry Terminals

Alaska's only railroad, the **White Pass and Yukon Route,** operates several different tours departing from Skagway, Fraser, British Columbia, and on some days, Carcross, Yukon. The tracks follow the historic path over the White Pass summit—a mountain-climbing, cliff-hanging route of as far as 67.5 mi each way. Bus connections are available at Fraser to Whitehorse, Yukon. While the route is primarily for visitors, some locals use the service for transportation between Skagway and Whitehorse.

ESSENTIALS

Internet **Port of Call** (✉ *2nd and Broadway* ☎ *907/983–2411*).

Medical Assistance **Skagway Dahl Memorial Clinic** (✉ *310 14th Ave., between State and Broadway* ☎ *907/983–2255*).

Visitor and Tour Information **Skagway Convention and Visitors Bureau** (✉ *Box 1029, Skagway 99840* ☎ *907/983–2854 or 888/762–1898* ⊕ *www. skagway.com*). **Klondike Gold Rush National Historical Park** (✉ *Visitor center, 2nd Ave. and Broadway* ✉ *Box 517, Skagway 99840* ☎ *907/983–2921* ⊕ *www. nps.gov/klgo*). **White Pass and Yukon Route** (☎ *907/983–2217 or 800/343–7373* ⊕ *www.wpyr.com*).

EXPLORING

★ **Arctic Brotherhood Hall.** The Arctic Brotherhood was a fraternal organization of Alaska and Yukon pioneers. Local members of the Brotherhood built the building's (now renovated) false front out of 8,833 pieces of driftwood and flotsam gathered from local beaches. The result: one of the most unusual buildings in all of Alaska. The AB Hall now houses the **Skagway Convention and Visitors Bureau,** along with public restrooms. ⊠ *Broadway between 2nd and 3rd Aves., Box 1029* ☏ *907/983–2854, 888/762–1898 message only* ⊕ *www.skagway.com* ☉ *May–Sept., daily 8–6; Oct.–Apr., weekdays 8–noon and 1–5.*

Corrington's Museum of Alaskan History. Inside a gift shop, this impressive (and free) scrimshaw museum highlights more than 40 exquisitely carved walrus tusks and other exhibits that detail Alaska's history. Dennis Corrington, a one-time Iditarod Race runner, and the founder of the museum, is often present. A bright flower garden decorates the exterior. ⊠ *5th Ave. and Broadway* ☏ *907/983–2579* ☏ *Free* ☉ *Open when cruise ships are in port.*

Golden North Hotel. Built during the 1898 gold rush, the Golden North Hotel was—until closing in 2002—Alaska's oldest hotel. Despite the closure, the building has been lovingly maintained, and still retains its gold rush–era appearance; a golden dome tops the corner cupola. Today the downstairs houses shops. ⊠ *3rd Ave. and Broadway.*

★ **Klondike Gold Rush National Historical Park.** Housed in the former White Pass and Yukon Route Depot, this wonderful museum contains exhibits, photos, and artifacts from the White Pass and Chilkoot trails. It's a must-see for anyone planning on taking a White Pass train ride, driving the nearby Klondike Highway, or hiking the Chilkoot Trail. Films, ranger talks, and walking tours are offered. Special free Robert Service poetry performances by Buckwheat Donahue—a beloved local character and head of the Skagway Convention and Visitors Bureau—occasionally take place at the visitor center. ⊠ *2nd Ave. at Broadway* ☏ *907/983–2921 or 907/983–9224* ⊕ *www.nps.gov/klgo* ☏ *Free* ☉ *Visitor Center open May–Sept., weekdays 7:30–7, weekends 8–6; Museum open May–Sept., daily 7:30–6; Oct.–Apr., daily 8–5.*

Moore Cabin. Built in 1887 by Captain William Moore and his son Ben Moore, the tiny cabin was the first structure built in Skagway. An early homesteader, Captain Moore prospered from the flood of miners, constructing a dock, warehouse, and sawmill to supply them, and selling land for other ventures. Next door, the larger **Moore House** (1897–98) contains interesting exhibits on the Moore family. Both structures are maintained by the Park Service, and the main house is open daily in summer. ⊠ *5th Ave. between Broadway and Spring St.* ☏ *907/983–2921* ☉ *Memorial Day–Labor Day, daily 10–5.*

Skagway Museum. This nicely designed museum—also known as the Trail of '98 Museum—occupies the ground floor of the beautiful building that also houses Skagway City Hall. Inside, you'll find a 19th-century Tlingit canoe (one of only two like it on the West Coast), historic photos, a red-and-black sleigh, and other gold rush–era artifacts, along with a healthy collection of contemporary local art and post–gold rush

GOLD! GOLD! GOLD!

At the end of the 19th Century, scoundrels and starry-eyed gold seekers alike made their way from Alaska's Inside Passage to Canada's Yukon Territory, with high hopes for heavy returns.

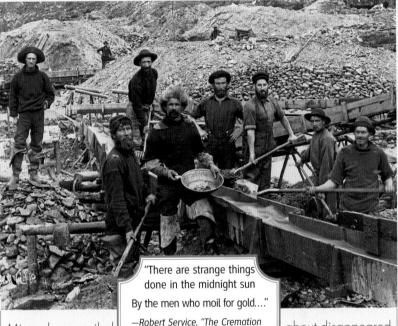

"There are strange things done in the midnight sun
By the men who moil for gold...."

—*Robert Service, "The Cremation of Sam McGee"*

Miners have moiled for gold in the Yukon for many centuries, but the Klondike Gold Rush was a particularly strange and intense period of history. Within a decade, the towns of Skagway, Dyea, and Dawson City appeared out of nowhere, mushroomed to accommodate tens of thousands of people, and just about disappeared again. At the peak of the rush, Dawson City was the largest metropolis north of San Francisco. Although only a few people found enough gold even to pay for their trip, the rush left an indelible mark on the nation's imagination.

An 1898 photograph shows bearded miners using a gold pan and sluice as they search for riches.

A GREAT STAMPEDE

Historians squabble over who first saw the glint of Yukon gold. All agree that it was a member of a family including "Skookum" Jim Mason (of the Tagish tribe), Kate and George Carmack, and Dawson Charlie, who were prospecting off the Klondike River in 1896. Over the following months, word spread and claims were quickly staked. When the first boatload of gold reached Seattle in July 1897, gold fever ignited with the *Seattle Post-Intelligencer's* headline: "GOLD! GOLD! GOLD! Sixty-Eight Rich Men On the Steamer Portland." Within six months, 100,000 people had arrived in Southeast Alaska, intent upon making their way to the untold riches.

Skagway had only a single cabin standing when the gold rush began. Three months after the first boat landed, 20,000 people swarmed its raucous hotels, saloons, gambling houses, and dance halls. By spring 1898, the town was labeled "little better than a hell on earth." When gold was discovered in Nome the next year and in Fairbanks in the early 1900s, Skagway's population dwindled to 700 souls.

(above) Rush hour on Broadway, Skagway, 1898.

A GRITTY REALITY

To reach the mining hub of Dawson City, prospectors had to choose between two risky routes from the Inside Passage. From Dyea, the Chilkoot Trail was steep and bitterly cold. The longer, bandit-ridden White Pass Trail from Skagway killed so many pack animals that it earned the nickname Dead Horse Trail. After the mountains, there were still over 500 mi to travel. For those who arrived, dreams were quickly washed away, as most promising claims had already been staked by the Klondike Kings. Many ended up working as labor. The disappointment was unbearable.

KLONDIKE KATE

The gold rush was profitable for clever entrepreneurs. Stragglers, outfitters, and outlaws took advantage of every opportunity to make a buck. Klondike Kate, a brothel keeper and dance-hall gal, had an elaborate song-and-dance routine that involved 200 yards of bright red chiffon.

TWO ENEMIES DIE IN A SKAGWAY SHOWDOWN

CON ARTIST "SOAPY" SMITH

Claim to Fame: Skagway's best-known gold-rush criminal, Soapy was the de facto leader of the town's loosely organized network of criminals and spies.

Cold-Hearted Snake: Euphemistically referred to as "colorful," he ruthlessly capitalized on the naïveté of prospectors.

Famous Scheme: Soapy charged homesick miners $5 to wire a message home in his counterfeit Telegraph Office (the wires ended in a tangled pile behind a shed).

Shot Through the Heart: In 1898, just days after he served as grand marshal of Skagway's 4th of July parade, Soapy barged in on a meeting set up by his rival, Frank Reid. There was a scuffle, and they shot each other.

Famous Last Words: When he saw Reid draw his gun, Soapy shouted, "My God, don't shoot!"

R.I.P.: Soapy's tombstone was continually stolen by vandals and souvenir seekers; today's grave marker is a simple wooden plank in Skagway's Gold Rush Cemetery.

GOOD GUY FRANK REID

Claim to Fame: Skagway surveyor and all-around good fellow, Frank Reid was known for defending the town against bad guys.

The Grid Man: A civil engineer, Reid helped to make Skagway's streets wide and gridlike.

Thorn in My Side: Reid set up a secret vigilante meeting to discuss one very thorny topic: Soapy Smith.

In Skagway's Honor: Reid killed Soapy during the shootout on the city docks, breaking up Soapy's gang and freeing the town from its grip.

Dyin' Tryin': Reid's heroics cost him his life—he died some days later from the injuries he sustained.

R.I.P.: The town built a substantial monument in Reid's memory in the Gold Rush Cemetery, which you can visit to this day; the inscription reads: "He gave his life for the honor of Skagway."

(above) Soapy Smith (front), so named for his first con, which involved selling "lucky soap," stands with five friends at his infamous saloon.

FOLLOWING THE GOLD TRAIL TODAY

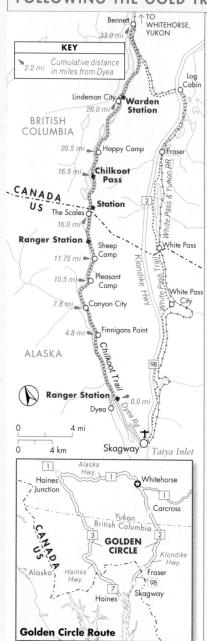

KEY

2.2 mi — Cumulative distance in miles from Dyea

Bennett → TO WHITEHORSE, YUKON
33.0 mi

Log Cabin

Lindeman City **Warden Station**
26.0 mi

BRITISH COLUMBIA

20.5 mi — Happy Camp
Fraser

16.5 mi — **Chilkoot Pass**

CANADA US

Station

The Scales
16.0 mi

Ranger Station
Sheep Camp
11.75 mi

10.5 mi — Pleasant Camp

White Pass
White Pass City

7.8 mi — Canyon City

4.8 mi — Finnigans Point

ALASKA

White Pass & Yukon RR
Klondike Hwy
White Pass Trail
2
98

Ranger Station
0.0 mi
Dyea
Dyea Rd.

0 — 4 mi
0 — 4 km

Skagway — *Taiya Inlet*

Golden Circle Route

1 — Alaska Hwy.
Haines Junction
1 — Whitehorse
1 — Carcross
Yukon
British Columbia
CANADA US
3 — **GOLDEN CIRCLE** — 2
Klondike Hwy.
Alaska
Haines Hwy.
Fraser
7 — Haines — 98 Skagway

THE HISTORIC CHILKOOT TRAIL

If you're an experienced backpacker, consider hiking the highly scenic Chilkoot Trail, the 33-mi route of the 1897–98 prospectors from Skagway into Canada. Most hikers will need four to five days. The trail is generally in good condition, with primitive campsites strategically located along the way. Expect steep slopes and wet weather, along with exhilarating vistas at the summit. Deep snow often covers the pass until late summer. The trail stretches from Dyea (just outside of Skagway) to Lake Bennett. The National Park Service maintains the American side of the pass as part of **Klondike Gold Rush National Historical Park;** the Canadian side is part of the **Chilkoot Trail National Historic Park.** A backcountry permit is required.

■**TIP→** To return to Skagway, hikers usually catch the White Pass & Yukon Route train from Lake Bennett. The fare is $165 to Skagway; the train runs Sunday through Friday and Monday in the summer, departing at 2 pm.

For more details, including backcountry permits (C$55), contact the summer-only **Chilkoot Trail Center** ☎ 907/983–9234 ⊕ www.nps.gov/klgo. Or you can call Parks Canada ☎ 800/661–0486 ⊕ www.pc.gc.ca/chilkoot.

GOLDEN DRIVES

The Golden Circle Route starts in Skagway on the Klondike Highway, then travels to Whitehorse. The route continues to Haines Junction, and then south to Haines. On the much longer Klondike Loop, you'll hop on the Klondike Highway, following the White Pass railway as it travels toward Whitehorse. The highway meets the Alaska Highway, ending at Dawson City on the banks of the Klondike River. From start to finish, it covers 435 mi. If you're taking the Klondike Highway north from Skagway, you must stop at Canadian customs, Mile

(top left) Trekking the Chilkoot Trail (right) White Pass & Yukon Route (bottom left) A bridge on Chilkoot Trail

22. If you're traveling south to Skagway, check in at U.S. Customs, Mile 6.

WHITE PASS & YUKON ROUTE

You can travel the gold-rush route aboard the historic White Pass & Yukon Route (WP & YR) narrow-gauge railroad. The diesel locomotives tow vintage-style viewing cars up steep inclines, hugging the walls of precipitous cliffs with views of craggy peaks, forests, and plummeting waterfalls. It's open mid-May to late September only, and reservations are highly recommended.

■ **TIP→** Most of the commentary is during the first half of the trip and relates to sights out of the left side of the train, so sit on this side. A "seat exchange" at the summit allows all guests a canyonside view.

Several options are available, including a fully narrated 3-hour round-trip excursion to White Pass summit (fare: $112). Sights along the way include Bridal Veil Falls, Inspiration Point, and Dead Horse Gulch. Through service to Whitehorse, Yukon (4 hours), is offered daily as well—in the form of a train trip to Fraser, where bus connections are possible on to Whitehorse (entire one-way fare to Whitehorse: $119). Also offered are the Chilkoot Trail hikers' service and a 4-hour roundtrip to Fraser Meadows on Saturday and Sunday (fare: $155).

Call ahead or check online for details and schedules. ☎ 907/983–2217 or 800/343–7373 ⊕ www.wpyr.com.

history exhibits. ⊠ *7th Ave. and Spring St.* ☎ *907/983–2420* 🖃 *$2* ⊙ *Mid-May–Sept., weekdays 9–5, weekends 10–4; Oct.–mid-May, hrs vary.*

OUTDOOR ACTIVITIES AND GUIDED TOURS

BIKING

Sockeye Cycle Company (☎ *907/983–2851* ⊕ *www.cyclealaska.com*), based in Haines, and, in summertime, in Skagway, specializes in guided bike tours in the area, including a train/bike ride combo. Sockeye also rents bikes for independent explorers.

BOATING

Alaska Fjordlines (☎ *907/766–3395 or 800/320–0146* ⊕ *www.alaskafjordlines.com*) operates a popular day tour from Skagway and Haines to Juneau and back. Passengers board a high-speed catamaran at 8 am and stop along the way to watch sea lions, humpbacks, and other marine mammals. The boat gets to Juneau at 11 am, where a bus transports visitors into town and to Mendenhall Glacier, returning to the boat at 5:30 pm for the ride back to Skagway, where the boat returns at 8:15 pm. One-way service is also available. **Haines-Skagway Fast Ferry** (☎ *907/766–2100 or 888/766–2103* ⊕ *www.hainesskagwayfastferry. com*) provides a fast passenger catamaran ferry between Skagway and Haines, with service several times a day in summer. The trip is about 45 minutes each way.

LOCAL INTEREST BY BUS

Skagway Street Car Company (☎ *907/983–2908* ⊕ *www.skagwaystreetcar. com*) revisits the gold-rush days in modern restorations of the bright-yellow 1920s sightseeing buses. Costumed conductors lead these popular two-hour tours, but advance reservations are recommended for independent travelers, since most seats are sold aboard cruise ships. Call a week ahead in peak season to reserve a space.

OUTDOOR ADVENTURE

Alaska Excursions (☎ *907/983–4444* ⊕ *www.alaskaexcursions.com*) leads wheeled (no snow) sled-dog tours, horseback-riding tours, and golfing day trips. Booking independently with this service can be difficult, as cruise-ship groups reserve the bulk of available slots. **Packer Expeditions** (☎ *907/983-3005* ⊕ *www.packerexpeditions.com*) offers guided hikes on wilderness trails not accessible by road. One trip includes a helicopter flight, a 2-mi hike toward the Laughton Glacier, and a one-hour ride back to town on the White Pass Railroad. A longer hike on

ALL THAT GLIMMERS

Old false-front stores, saloons, and brothels—built to separate gold-rush prospectors from their grubstakes going north or their gold pokes heading south—have been restored, repainted, and refurbished by the federal government and Skagway's citizens. The town feels a little like a Disney theme park in spots, and it's made all the more surreal by the surrounding mountains. But the scene today is not appreciably different from what the prospectors saw in the days of 1898, except that the street is now paved to make exploring easier.

WALKING AROUND SKAGWAY

Skagway's rowdy history is memorialized at the corner of 1st Avenue and Main Street, where a marker notes the infamous 1898 gun battle between Soapy Smith and Frank Reid. From the marker, head two blocks east along 1st Avenue and turn left on Broadway into the heart of the town. Inside the old White Pass and Yukon Railroad Depot at 2nd Avenue and Broadway, you'll find the **Klondike Gold Rush National Historical Park** visitor center, one of Southeast's best museums.

The next block north on Broadway—the heart of historical Skagway—contains several of the town's best-known buildings. The two-centuries-old Red Onion Saloon remains a favorite place to imbibe under the watchful eyes of "working girl" mannequins. Next door is the **Arctic Brotherhood Hall**, the facade of which is constructed entirely of driftwood. Inside, you'll find the helpful **Skagway Convention and Visitors Bureau**, which is full of friendly faces and useful local information. The golden dome of the **Golden North Hotel**, built in 1898, sits across the street from the old Mascot Saloon. ■TIP→ There are also public restrooms here. Keep going up Broadway for **Corrington's Museum of Alaskan History**, with its large collection of scrimshaw (carved ivory) art. A right turn on

5th Avenue brings you to the Park Service's **Moore Cabin**, Skagway's oldest structure. The beautifully restored Skagway City Hall is housed in the same granite-front building as the **Skagway Museum**. Return to Broadway and follow it to 6th Avenue, where you can see *The Days of '98 with Soapy Smith* show inside historic Eagles Hall.

If you are up for a longer walk, continue 2 mi out of town along Alaska Street to the **Gold Rush Cemetery**, where you'll find the graves of combatants Soapy Smith and Frank Reid. The cemetery is also the trailhead for the short walk to Lower Reid Falls, an enjoyable jaunt through the valley's lush forest. (A city bus takes you most of the way to the cemetery for $2 each direction.) No tour of Skagway is complete without a train ride on the famed **White Pass and Yukon Route**. Trains depart from the corner of 2nd Street and Broadway several times a day in summer.

The six blocks that compose the heart of downtown Skagway can be explored in a half hour, but budget two hours to see the Park Service's historic buildings and the Skagway Museum. (If you include the 4-mi round-trip walk to the Gold Rush Cemetery, plan on three to four hours.) Leave some time to explore Skagway's many shops, restaurants, and other attractions.

the same trail uses the train for access in both directions and includes time hiking on the glacier.

Temsco Helicopters (☎ *907/983–2900 or 866/683–2900* ⊕ *www. temscoair.com*) will fly you to Denver Glacier for an hour of learning about mushing and riding on a dogsled.

DYEA

Once a bustling town filled with miners-to-be preparing to head up the Chilkoot Trail, Dyea is quite a bit quieter these days. At its height, Dyea had 48 hotels. Now? There are a few people still living in the area, but for the most part Dyea functions as both a fascinating historic site and a stunning place of beauty. The mud flats and sky play tricks on the eyes—the land looks like it stretches on endlessly. Dyea is part of Klondike Gold Rush National Historical Park and the National Park Service offers tours of area. Or, for those who really want to experience Dyea's quiet, consider camping there. Visit the small cemeteries; the headstones tell the stories of those who once called Dyea home.

WHERE TO EAT

⊄
CAFÉ
✕ **Glacial Smoothies and Espresso.** This local hangout is the place to go for a breakfast bagel or a lunchtime soup-and-sandwich combo. Prices are steeper than at some coffee shops, but the ingredients are fresh and local, and nearly everything on the menu is made on-site. Customers can cool down with a Mango Madness or Blueberry Blues smoothie, and soft-serve ice cream in summer. ⊠ *3rd Ave. between Main and State Sts.* ☎ *907/983–3223* ⊕ *www.glacialsmoothies.com* ☉ *No dinner.*

$–$$
PIZZA
✕ **Skagway Pizza Station.** Housed in a former gas station, this year-round restaurant is known for its comfort-food specials. The huge calzones are stuffed and served piping hot with sides of house marinara and ranch dressing—build your own or choose one of the chef's creations, like the Chicken Hawk Squawk with pineapple and jalapeños. Or do as the Skagwegians do and wash down one of the 14-inch pizzas with a pint or two of Alaskan Summer Ale. For dog-tired travelers who can't walk another block, the Pizza Station delivers for free. ⊠ *4th Ave. between Main and State Sts.* ☎ *907/983–2200.*

$$–$$$
CAFÉ
✕ **Stowaway Cafe.** Always crowded, this harborside café is just a few steps from the cruise-ship dock. Seafood is the attraction—including wasabi salmon and glacé de poisson—but you can also eat steaks, chicken, or smoked ribs. "Café" is an understated description of the restaurant; this is one of Skagway's finest restaurants. While reservations are not required, they're certainly recommended. ⊠ *205 Congress Way* ☎ *907/983–3463* ☉ *Closed Oct.–Apr. No lunch.*

WHERE TO STAY

For expanded hotel reviews, visit Fodors.com.

$–$$
☷ **Mile Zero Bed & Breakfast.** In a quiet residential area a few blocks from downtown, this comfortable B&B has spacious and well-insulated guest rooms, all with private entrances, phones, and baths. **Pros:** all rooms have televisions and phones; communal areas are comfortable and clean. **Cons:** limited room amenities; not much view. ⊠ *9th Ave. and Main St.* ☎ *907/983–3045* ⊕ *www.mile-zero.com* ➳ *7 rooms*

⚙ *In-room: Wi-Fi. In-hotel: business center* ⦿ *Breakfast.*

$ ⛁ **Sgt. Preston's Lodge.** This four-building lodge—which feels more like a motel—occupies a former army barracks. **Pros:** convenient to the cruise-ship and ferry docks; has a handicapped-accessible room; pets allowed for a small fee. **Cons:** some rooms are shaped oddly; some rooms are small. **TripAdvisor:** "room was spacious and clean," "very comfortable," "décor was quaint." ⊠ *370 6th Ave., Box 538* ☎ *907/983–2521 or 866/983–2521* ⊕ *sgtprestonslodge.com* ⋐ *40 rooms* ⚙ *In-room: Wi-Fi. In-hotel: business center, some pets allowed* ⦿ *No meals.*

$$–$$$ ⛁ **Skagway Inn Bed & Breakfast.** Each room in this family-friendly downtown Victorian inn (once a not-so-family-friendly bordello) is named after a different gold-rush gal. **Pros:** large breakfast served; nicely remodeled. **Cons:** floors are creaky; walls are thin; some rooms without private bathrooms. ⊠ *655 Broadway* ☎ *907/983–2289 or 888/752–4929* ⊕ *www.skagwayinn.com* ⋐ *10 rooms, 4 with bath* ⚙ *In-room: no TV, Wi-Fi. In-hotel: restaurant, business center* ☾ *Closed Oct.–Apr.* ⦿ *Breakfast.*

$$ ⛁ **White House.** This B&B is about two blocks from downtown Skagway. **Pros:** conveniently located. **Cons:** no pets allowed. **TripAdvisor:** "very cozy rooms," "staff are friendly and helpful," "a wonderful home atmosphere." ⊠ *8th Ave. and Main St.* ☎ *907/983–9000* ⊕ *www.atthewhitehouse.com* ⋐ *10 rooms* ⚙ *In-room: Wi-Fi. In-hotel: laundry facilities* ⦿ *Breakfast.*

OUT AND ABOUT

If you are up for a long walk, head 2 mi out of town along Alaska Street to the **Gold Rush Cemetery**, where you'll find the graves of combatants Soapy Smith and Frank Reid. The cemetery is also the trailhead for the short walk to Lower Reid Falls, an enjoyable jaunt through the valley's lush forest. (A city bus takes you most of the way to the cemetery for $2 each direction.) No tour of Skagway is complete without a train ride on the famed **White Pass and Yukon Route**. Trains depart from the corner of 2nd Street and Broadway several times a day in summer.

NIGHTLIFE AND THE ARTS

BARS

Whereas Skagway was once host to dozens upon dozens of watering holes in its gold-rush days, the **Red Onion Saloon** (⊠ *Broadway at 2nd Ave.* ☎ *907/983–2222* ⊕ *www.redonion1898.com*) is pretty much the sole survivor among them. The upstairs was Skagway's first bordello, and you'll find a convivial crowd of Skagway locals and visitors among the scantily clad mannequins who represent the building's former illustrious tenants. A ragtime pianist tickles the keys in the afternoons, and local musicians strut their stuff on Thursday nights. The saloon closes up shop for winter.

THEATER

★ Since 1927 locals have performed a show called *The Days of '98 with Soapy Smith* at Eagles Hall. You'll see cancan dancers (including Molly Fewclothes, Belle Davenport, and Squirrel Tooth Alice), learn a little local history, and watch desperado Soapy Smith being sent to his reward. At the evening show you can enjoy a few warm-up rounds of mock gambling with Soapy's money. Performances of Robert Service poetry start a half hour before showtime. ⊠ *Broadway and 6th Ave.* ☎ *907/983–2545 May–mid-Sept., 808/328–9132 mid-Sept.–Apr.* ⊠ *$20* ⊙ *Mid-May–mid-Sept., daily at 10:30, 2:30, and 8.*

SHOPPING

Corrington's Alaskan Ivory (⊠ *525 Broadway* ☎ *907/983–2579*) is the destination of choice for scrimshaw seekers; it has one the state's best collections of ivory art. For those in search of locally produced silver jewelry, watercolor prints, and other handmade crafts, the artist-owned **Alaska Artworks** (⊠ *555C Broadway* ☎ *907/983–3443* ⊕ *www.skagwayartworks.com*) can't be beat. **Skaguay News Depot & Books** (⊠ *264 Broadway* ☎ *907/983–3354*), its moniker a throwback to the town's old spelling, is a small but quaint bookstore that carries books on Alaska, magazines, children's books, maps, and gifts.

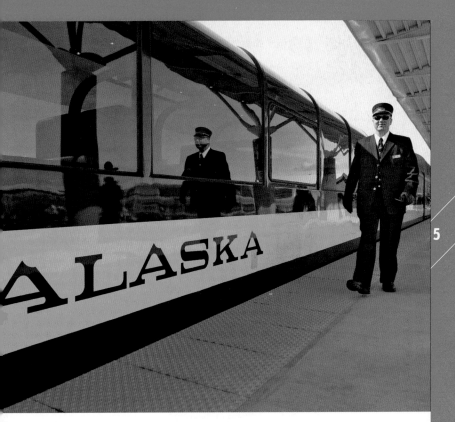

Anchorage

WORD OF MOUTH

"On our first day in Anchorage we ate breakfast at Snow City Cafe, which we can thoroughly recommend, and walked around downtown Anchorage. We also walked the Tony Knowles trail from Downtown to Earthquake Park, hoping to see Moose, but no luck. Dinner that night was at Humpy's Great Alaskan Alehouse where we ate good pub food."

—threadies

WELCOME TO ANCHORAGE

TOP REASONS TO GO

★ **Tackling a 50-pound salmon:** Anglers can cast for huge king salmon or feisty silvers while wading among reflections of skyscrapers at Ship Creek.

★ **Winter celebrations:** Beginning in late February, locals celebrate the two-week Fur Rendezvous. Events—from the blanket toss to the Running of the Reindeer, Alaska's spin on Pamplona's tradition—lead up to the start of the Iditarod Trail Sled Dog Race in early March.

★ **Shopping:** Shops and vendors at the Saturday and Sunday markets sell everything from kid-friendly tchochtkes to elegant Native crafts and locally produced foods.

★ **Seafood:** Dining out in Anchorage means local halibut, salmon, king-crab legs, scallops, and oysters. Many of the city's finest restaurants hide in not-so-pretty strip malls.

★ **Hiking and biking:** Laced with more than 120 mi of paved urban trails, Anchorage is a paradise for hikers and bicyclists. Rugged paths lead from town into the Chugach Mountains.

1 Downtown. The city's cultural center has a festive atmosphere on summer afternoons, with flowers hung from street lamps and the smell of grilled onions and hot dogs in the air along 4th Avenue. The streets are lined with art galleries and shops; the weekend markets promise good hunting for shoppers seeking souvenirs.

2 Midtown. Some 3 mi east of the airport, Midtown is a newer neighborhood with an assortment of restaurants, shopping centers, and large hotels. The city's main library branch and a major movie-theater complex are located a short walk from most hotels.

3 **Tony Knowles Coastal Trail and Kincaid Park.** An 11-mi ribbon of asphalt beginning Downtown and stretching to Kincaid Park, the popular Tony Knowles Coastal Trail traverses tidal marshes, moose-inhabited greenbelts, and bluffs overlooking the inlet, Mt. Susitna, and the distant Alaska Range. Kincaid Park offers 40 mi of trails for biking, hiking, and cross-country skiing.

4 **Spenard.** Sandwiched between the airport and Midtown, Spenard is one of Anchorage's oldest neighborhoods, and also one of its up and comers. Home to the Anchorage location of outdoor gear giant REI, Spenard is also home to some of the city's hippest restaurants. The neighborhood has a youthful, outdoorsy vibe about it.

GETTING ORIENTED

Founded in 1915 as a railroad camp, Anchorage has grown into Alaska's largest city and main travel hub. It's connected to the state's road network by the Seward and Glenn highways and remains the headquarters for the Alaska Railroad, which runs from Seward to Fairbanks. The city is bordered to the east by the Chugach foothills, to the west by Cook Inlet, to the south by Potter Marsh, and to the north by military bases. Sled-dog races are still among the most revered events held here; moose and occasionally bears roam city bike trails, and spectacular wilderness is a short drive away.

Updated by
Jenna Schnuer

By far Alaska's largest and most sophisticated city, Anchorage is situated in a truly spectacular location. The permanently snow-covered peaks and volcanoes of the Alaska Range lie to the west of the city, part of the craggy Chugach Range is actually within the eastern edge of the municipality, and the Talkeetna and Kenai ranges are visible to the north and south. On clear days Mt. McKinley looms on the northern horizon, and two arms of Cook Inlet embrace the town's western and southern borders.

Anchorage is Alaska's medical, financial, and banking center, and home to the executive offices of most of the Native corporations. The city has a population of roughly 277,000, approximately 40%, of the people in the state. The relative affluence of this white-collar city—with a sprinkling of olive drab from nearby military bases—fosters an ever-growing range of restaurants and shops, first-rate entertainment, and sporting events.

Incorporated in 1920, Anchorage is a young city. Nearly everything has been built since the 1970s—an Anchorage home dating from the 1950s almost merits historic status. The city got its start with the construction of the federally built Alaska Railroad, completed in 1917, and traces of its railroad heritage remain today. The city's architecture is far from memorable—though it has its quirky and charming moments—but the surrounding mountains more than make up for it.

Boom and bust periods followed major events: an influx of military bases during World War II; a massive buildup of Arctic missile-warning stations during the Cold War; reconstruction following the devastating Good Friday earthquake of 1964; and in the late 1960s the biggest jackpot of all—the discovery of oil at Prudhoe Bay and the construction of the Trans-Alaska Pipeline. Not surprisingly, Anchorage positioned itself as the perfect home for the pipeline administrators and support industries, and it continues to attract a large share of the state's oil-tax dollars.

PLANNING

WHEN TO GO

Located between the coast and several mountain ranges, Anchorage is a meteorologist's nightmare. Fickle weather patterns change less by the day than by the hour. Generally, fair-weather visitors should plan trips between the last week of May and mid-August.

Of the snow-free months, May is typically the driest, August and September the wettest. July is the warmest month, with an average temperature of 58.4°F, and May the coolest at 46.6°F. But don't be fooled by statistics. Late-May temperatures can exceed 70°F, and "hot" July and August days sometimes break 80°F. Of course, rainy low-pressure systems from the Gulf of Alaska can skulk in at any time, bringing wet and cool weather.

So how to plan for such vagaries? Do as the locals do: come prepared to go with the flow. That means packing light rain jackets and layers as well as tank tops and sunblock, and allowing for some flexibility with your planning.

GETTING HERE AND AROUND

AIR TRAVEL

Ted Stevens Anchorage International Airport is 6 mi from downtown Anchorage on International Airport Road. Several carriers, including ERA, Frontier Flying Service, and PenAir, connect Anchorage with smaller Alaskan communities. Floatplane operators and helicopters serve the area from Lake Hood, which is adjacent to and part of Anchorage International Airport. A number of smaller air taxis and air-charter operations are at Merrill Field, 2 mi east of downtown on 5th Avenue.

Taxis queue up at the lower level of the airport terminals outside the baggage-claim areas. They are on a meter system, and it costs about $20, not including tip, for a ride to Downtown. An Alaska Railroad station in the airport has direct service to Downtown. Most of the larger hotels provide free airport shuttle services.

Airport **Ted Stevens Anchorage International Airport** (☎ *907/266–2526* ⊕ *www.anchorageairport.com*).

BOAT TRAVEL

Cruise ships sailing the Gulf of Alaska and the Alaska Marine ferries call in Seward, two hours by train or bus south of Anchorage.

BUS TRAVEL

The municipal People Mover bus system covers the whole Anchorage Bowl. A one-way fare is $1.75 for rides outside the Downtown area; day passes good for unlimited rides are $5. ■**TIP**➔ Get schedules and information from the central bus depot at 6th Avenue and G Street.

Contact **People Mover** (☎ *907/343–6543* ⊕ *www.peoplemover.org*).

CAR TRAVEL

The Glenn Highway enters Anchorage from the north and becomes 5th Avenue near Merrill Field; this route will lead you directly into Downtown. Gambell Street leads out of town to the south, becoming New Seward Highway at about 20th Avenue. South of town, it becomes the Seward Highway. If you bring your RV or rent one on arrival, know that parking an RV downtown on weekdays is challenging. There's a big parking lot on 3rd Avenue between C and E streets. Parking is usually not a problem in other parts of town.

TAXI TRAVEL

If you need a taxi, call one of the cab companies; it's not common to hail one. Prices are $2 to $3 for pickup, plus an additional $2.50 for each mile. Allow 20 minutes for arrival of the cab during morning and evening rush hours. Alaska Cab has taxis with wheelchair lifts. In the snow-free months a network of paved trails provides good avenues for in-city travel for bicyclists and walkers.

Contact **Alaska Cab** (☎ 907/563–5353).

TOUR TRAVEL

Tour Anchorage and the surrounding mountains and glaciers of South Central Alaska by land or by air with one of the many sightseeing companies in the region. The Log Cabin and Visitor Information Centers have brochures for Anchorage bus tours, and for a one-hour overview, hop on a trolley with **Anchorage City Trolley Tours Gray Line of Alaska** has a city tour ($54) that lasts 3½ hours.

Any air-taxi company can arrange for a flightseeing trip over Anchorage and environs. The fee is determined by the length of time you are airborne, number of passengers, and size of the plane. Tours of about an hour and a half generally cost around $200 per person. Three-hour flights over Mt. McKinley from **Rust's Flying Service**, including a landing on a remote lake or a stop in Talkeetna, run $375 per person.

Contacts **Anchorage City Trolley Tours** (☎ 907/276–5603 ⊕ www.alaskatrolley.com). **Gray Line of Alaska** (☎ 907/277–5581 or 888/452–1737 ⊕ www.graylinealaska.com). **Rust's Flying Service** (☎ 907/243–1595 or 800/544–2299 ⊕ www.flyrusts.com).

TRAIN TRAVEL

From mid-May through September, the Alaska Railroad runs daily between Anchorage and Seward; daily between Anchorage and Fairbanks via Talkeetna and Denali National Park and Preserve; and daily between Anchorage and Whittier, Portage, Spencer Whistle Stop, and Grandview. Winter service is available once each month from Anchorage to Talkeetna and, weekly, a round-trip from Anchorage to Fairbanks and back. Call for schedule and fare information.

Contact **Alaska Railroad** (☎ 907/265–2494 or 800/544–0552 ⊕ www.akrr.com).

DINING AND LODGING PRICE CATEGORIES				
¢	$	$$	$$$	$$$$
Restaurants	under $10	$10–$15	$15–$20	$20–$25	over $25
Hotels	under $100	$100–$150	$150–$200	$200–$250	over $250

Restaurant prices are per person for a main course at dinner. Hotel prices are for two people in a standard double room in high season.

HEALTH AND SAFETY

Though most areas populated by tourists are safe to wander, Anchorage is a city, so it's best just to stay aware as you walk around town. That definitely holds true if you choose to hike any local trails—even those within the city limits. Before Anchorage was a paved city, it was wild. Most locals have stories of surprise visits by a moose or bear during a morning bathrobe run to get the newspaper. Moose and other animals walk the trails, too. As you walk along, make some noise, either by singing or talking to a friend. But the award for the biggest pest of all goes to the unofficial state bird, the mosquito. Bring mosquito repellent with you for all day hikes.

Alaska Regional Hospital (⊠ 2801 DeBarr Rd., East Anchorage ☎ 907/276–1131 ⊕ www.alaskaregional.com). **Physician Referral Service** (☎ 888/254–7884 Alaska Regional Hospital, 907/261–2945 Providence Alaska Medical Center). **Police, fire, and ambulance** (☎ 911). **Providence Alaska Medical Center** (⊠ 3200 Providence Dr., East Anchorage ☎ 907/562–2211 ⊕ www.providence.org/alaska).

VISITOR INFORMATION

Alaska sees more than 1.5 million visitors each summer and, of that total, more than 40 percent spend at least one night in Anchorage. The tourist-friendly city offers a wealth of information and services to help visitors along the way. In addition to the Log Cabin and Visitor Information Center downtown, there are two visitor information centers in Ted Stevens Anchorage International Airport: one in the north terminal (open mid-May through Sept.) and one in the south terminal in the C Concourse baggage claim area (open year-round).

Alaska Department of Fish & Game (⊠ 333 Raspberry Rd., Midtown ☎ 907/267–2100 ⊕ www.adfg.state.ak.us). **Alaska Public Lands Information Center** (⊠ 4th Ave. and F St., Downtown ☎ 907/271–2737 🖶 907/271–2744 ⊕ www.nps.gov/aplic). **Anchorage Convention and Visitors Bureau** (ACVB ⊠ 524 W. 4th Ave., Downtown ☎ 907/276–4118, 800/478–1255 to order visitor guides ⊕ www.anchorage.net). **Anchorage Downtown Partnership** (⊠ 333 W. 4th Ave., Downtown ☎ 907/279–5650 ⊕ www.anchoragedowntown.org). **Log Cabin and Visitor Information Center** (⊠ 4th Ave. and F St., Downtown ☎ 907/274–3531 ⊕ www.anchorage.net).

BEST BETS FOR DIFFERENT TRAVELERS

If you're on your way to a cruise (or are just back from one):

■ Stretch your sea legs and take a walk along the Tony Knowles Coastal Trail, or venture just south of town and hike Flattop Mountain. Either way, you'll get views of Cook Inlet, Mt. Susitna, and the Alaska Range.

■ Shop at the Anchorage Market and Festival any Saturday or Sunday during the warm months for souvenirs at some of the best prices going.

If you have kids in tow:

■ The Anchorage is a can't-miss spot; head to the hands-on science exhibits.

■ Watch the planes come and go at Lake Hood's seaplane base.

If you're looking for some pampering and fine-dining:

■ The Sheraton Anchorage Hotel and Spa features Ice Spa, one of the best places for a treatment in Anchorage (with mountain views to boot).

■ Marx Bros. Café, downtown, has real Alaskan atmosphere and will likely serve you one of the best meals you'll have while in Alaska.

EXPLORING ANCHORAGE

Anchorage is a pedestrian- and bike-friendly city. Downtown Anchorage's flower-lined streets are easily explored on foot, and several businesses rent bicycles. The grid plan was laid out by the Army Corps of Engineers, and streets and avenues run exactly east–west and north–south, with numbers in the first direction and letters of the alphabet or Alaska place-names (Barrow, Cordova, Denali, etc.) in the other. The only aberration is the absence of a J Street—a concession, some say, to the city's early Swedish settlers, who had difficulty pronouncing the letter. You'll need a car for longer stays, expeditions, and to reach some of the city's better restaurants without relying on taxis.

Outside Downtown, Anchorage is composed of widely scattered neighborhoods and large shopping malls clustered along busy thoroughfares. And although there's no shortage of excellent restaurants Downtown, many of the town's best places are found in cheesy strip malls. Also, you're never more than a block or two from a good espresso stand or shop.

Once you're done wandering the shops Downtown, consider heading south to Midtown. The neighborhood has some of Anchorage's best restaurants. It's also a good neighborhood to stay in if you would rather be slightly outside the main tourist fray.

The next neighborhood heading away from Downtown is South Anchorage. Until recently South Anchorage was more of a local spot, but with several new restaurants opening there's been a growing tourist presence in the area. South Anchorage also has a large mall.

Another neighborhood worth exploring is Spenard, just west of Midtown (Spenard Road is considered to be the dividing line). The neighborhood—which celebrates its annual Spenardi Gras every March—has an artsy hip vibe and is home to some of the city's best casual restaurants, a good farmers' market, and Anchorage's largest independent bookstore.

You'll find plenty to do year-round in Anchorage, though most visitors, particularly first-timers, might be happiest in June, July, or August, when the days are longer—up to 19 hours, 21 minutes during the summer solstice—and the temperatures warmer. If you must choose one of the shoulder seasons, choose fall. There's less chance of rain; the snow has not yet arrived on trails except in the highest mountain passes; and there's an excellent chance for warm, sunny days, cool nights, and dazzling color changes in the trees and tundra. But if you choose fall, pack a few extra layers as a just-in-case for early snow (or be prepared to visit one of Anchorage's many gear shops): the city's earliest measurable dose of snow fell on September 20, 1947.

5

DOWNTOWN

TOP ATTRACTIONS

Alaska Center for the Performing Arts. The distinctive stone-and-glass building overlooks an expansive park filled with brilliant flowers all summer. Look inside for upcoming events, or relax amid the blossoms on a sunny afternoon. The Center—which has four theaters—is home to eight resident performing arts companies, including Alaska Dance Theatre, Anchorage Opera, and the Anchorage Symphony Orchestra. ⊠ *621 W. 6th Ave., at G St., Downtown* ☏ *907/263–2787, 877/278–7849 tickets* ⊕ *www.myalaskacenter.com* ✉ *Tours by appointment only.*

☾ **Alaska Public Lands Information Center**. Stop here for information on all
★ of Alaska's public lands, including national and state parks, national forests, and wildlife refuges. You can plan a hiking, sea-kayaking, bear-viewing, or fishing trip; find out about public-use cabins; learn about Alaska's plants and animals; or head to the theater for films highlighting different parts of the state. The bookstore sells maps and nature books. Guided walks to historic Downtown sights detail the role Captain James Cook played in Alaska's history. Tours depart daily throughout the summer at 11 am and 2:30 pm. ⊠ *605 W. 4th Ave., No. 105, at F St., Downtown* ☏ *907/271–2737* ⊕ *www.alaskacenters.gov* ☾ *Memorial Day–Labor Day, daily 9–5; Labor Day–Memorial Day, weekdays 10–5.*

☾ **Anchorage Museum**. This is no just-in-case-of-a-rainy-day attraction.
Fodor's Choice An extensive renovation in 2008–09 made the Anchorage Museum an
★ essential stop for visitors. There's no better way to deepen your understanding of the state's history, people, and, thanks to an impressive collection of paintings and photographs, beauty. The postrenovation star of the museum is the Smithsonian Arctic Studies Center, featuring more than 600 objects from Native cultures, short films that teach visitors about modern-day Native life, and much more. If you have a strong interest in history, art, or culture, leave extra time for the center—though it's just one large room, you might end up staying for hours. A good follow-up: wander the galleries filled with paintings and other art that showcases Alaska landscape and history through the talents

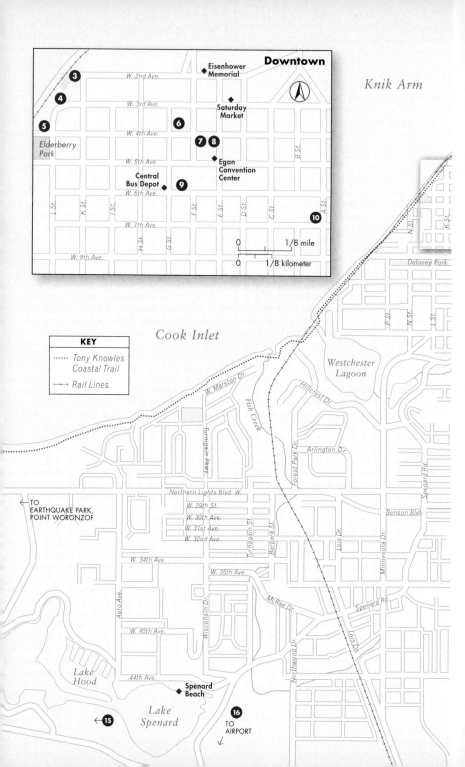

Anchorage

of painters and other artists. The Alaska Gallery's dioramas and other traditional museum exhibits focus on the state's history. Cap the visit in the Imaginarium Discovery Center. Kids and their parents—and, ok, adults without kids, too—won't want to leave the museum once they step into the 9,000-square-foot center loaded with hands-on science exhibits. There's also a planetarium. In summer the first-floor atrium is the site of free daily presentations by local artists and authors. Muse restaurant, a bright and modern spot operated by local favorite the Marx Bros. Café, serves delicious lunches, dinners, and cocktails. The gift shop is one of Anchorage's best places to buy Alaska Native art and other souvenirs. Book lovers beware (or you may spend your vacation budget all at once): the shop's book department runs the gamut from Alaska fiction to history, cookbooks, and beyond. ⊠ *625 C St., Downtown* ☎ *907/929–9201, 907/929–9200 recorded information* ⊕ *www.anchoragemuseum.org* ⊐ *$10* ⊘ *Mid-May–mid-Sept., daily 9–6, until 9 on Thurs.; mid-Sept.–mid-May, Tues.–Sat. 10–6, Sun. noon–6.*

Fodor's Choice ★ **Tony Knowles Coastal Trail.** Strollers, runners, bikers, dog walkers, and in-line skaters cram this recreation trail on sunny summer evenings, particularly around Westchester Lagoon. In winter cross-country skiers take to it by storm. The trail begins off 2nd Avenue, west of Christensen Drive, and curls along Cook Inlet for approximately 11 mi to Kincaid Park, beyond the airport. In summer you might spot beluga whales offshore in Cook Inlet. Access points are on the waterfront at the ends of 2nd, 5th, and 9th avenues and at Westchester Lagoon.

WORTH NOTING

Alaska Railroad Historic Depot. Totem poles and a locomotive built in 1907 are outside the station, the headquarters of the Alaska Railroad since 1915. A monument in front of the depot relates the history of the railroad, which brought an influx of people into the city during the early 1900s. During February's Fur Rendezvous festival, model-train buffs set up their displays here. ⊠ *411 W. 1st Ave., Downtown* ☎ *907/265–2494 or 800/544–0552* ⊕ *www.alaskarailroad.com* ⊘ *Daily, depending on train schedules.*

Historic City Hall. Offices of the Anchorage Convention and Visitors Bureau now occupy this 1936 building. A few exhibits and historic photos are right inside the lobby. Out front, take a look at the marble sculpture of William Seward, the secretary of state who engineered the purchase of Alaska from Russia. ⊠ *524 W. 4th Ave., Downtown.*

Log Cabin and Downtown Visitor Information Center. A giant jade boulder stands outside the downtown visitor information center. Housed in a Bush-style log cabin, the center's sod roof is festooned with huge hanging baskets of flowers. Anchorage calls itself the "Air Crossroads of the World." It's a major stopping point for cargo jets en route to Asia, and a signpost out front marks the mileage to many international destinations. ■TIP➔ After a stop in the cabin, step out the back door to the more spacious visitor center stocked with brochures. There are also two visitor information centers in Ted Stevens Anchorage International Airport, one in the north terminal and one in the south terminal in the C Concourse baggage claim area. ⊠ *4th Ave. and F St., Downtown* ☎ *907/257–2363*

⊕ *www.anchorage.net*   ⊙ *June–Aug., daily 8–7; May and Sept., daily 8–6; Oct.–Apr., daily 9–4.*

Oscar Anderson House Museum. City butcher Oscar Anderson built Anchorage's first permanent frame house in 1915, at a time when most of Anchorage consisted of tents. Swedish Christmas tours are held the first two weekends of December. Guided 45-minute tours are

available whenever the museum is open. ⊠ *420 M St., in Elderberry Park, Downtown* ☎ *907/274–2336* ☞ *$3* ⊙ *June–mid-Sept., weekdays noon–5; group tours (maximum 10 participants per group) must be arranged in advance.*

Resolution Park. This tiny park has a cantilevered viewing platform dominated by a monument to Captain Cook, whose explorations in 1778 led to the naming of Cook Inlet and many other geographic features in Alaska. Mt. Susitna, known as the Sleeping Lady, is the prominent low mountain to the northwest, and Mts. Spurr and Redoubt, active volcanoes, are just south of Mt. Susitna. Mt. McKinley, Mt. Foraker, and other peaks of the Alaska Range are often visible from more than 100 mi away. ⊠ *3rd Ave. at L St., Downtown.*

☺ **Ship Creek.** The creek is dammed right here in downtown, with a footbridge across the dam and access from either bank. You'll see a waterfall; salmon running upstream from June through August; anglers; and, above it all, downtown Anchorage. Farther upstream (follow Whitney Road and turn left on Post Road) is the newly renamed William Jack Hernandez Sport Fish Hatchery—during the runs you can see salmon in the clear, shallow water as they try to leap up the falls. ⊠ *Whitney Rd., Downtown.*

MIDTOWN

★ **Alaska Heritage Museum at Wells Fargo.** More than 900 Alaska Native artifacts are the main draw in the quiet, unassuming lobby of a large midtown bank—it's reputed to be one of the largest private collections of Native artworks in the country. You'll also find paintings by Alaskan artists, a library of rare books, and a 46-troy-ounce gold nugget. ⊠ *Wells Fargo Bank, 301 W. Northern Lights Blvd., at C St., Midtown* ☎ *907/265–2834* ⊕ *www.wellsfargohistory.com/museums/museum_anchorage.html* ☞ *Free* ⊙ *Late May–early Sept., weekdays noon–5; early Sept.–late May, weekdays noon–4.*

GREATER ANCHORAGE

EAST ANCHORAGE

☺ **Alaska Botanical Garden.** The garden showcases perennials hardy enough to make it in South Central Alaska in several large display gardens, a pergola-enclosed herb garden, and a rock garden amid 110 acres of mixed boreal forest. There's a 1-mi nature trail loop to Campbell Creek, with views of the Chugach Range and a wildflower trail between the display gardens. Interpretive signs guide visitors and identify plants along the trail. Children can explore the garden with an activity-filled duffel bag Tuesday–Saturday 1–4 pm. Docent tours are available at 1 pm daily June through August, or by appointment between June 1 and September 15. The gift shop and retail nursery are open 10–4 Tuesday–Sunday late May to mid-September. ⊠ *4601 Campbell Airstrip Rd., East Anchorage ⊕ Off Tudor Rd. (park at Benny Benson School)* ☎ *907/770–3692* ⊕ *www.alaskabg.org* ☜ *$5* ☉ *Daily during daylight hrs.*

ⓒ **Alaska Native Heritage Center.** On a 26-acre site facing the Chugach
Fodor's Choice Mountains, this facility provides an introduction to Alaska's Native
★ peoples. The spacious Welcome House has interpretive displays, artifacts, photographs, demonstrations, Native dances, storytelling, and films, along with a café and an upgraded gift shop selling museum-quality crafts and artwork. Step outside for a stroll around the adjacent lake, where you will pass seven village exhibits representing the 11 Native cultural groups through traditional structures and exhibitions. As you enter the homes, you can visit with the culture hosts, hear their stories, and experiment with some of the tools, games, and utensils used in the past. ■ TIP→ The Heritage Center provides a free shuttle from the downtown Log Cabin and Visitor Information Center several times a day in summer. You can also hop a bus at the downtown transit center; Route 4 (Glenn Highway) will take you to the Heritage Center's front door. There's also a Culture Pass Joint Ticket for $28.95 that provides admission here and to the Anchorage Museum downtown; it's available at either location. ⊠ *8800 Heritage Center Dr. (Glenn Hwy. at Muldoon Rd.), East Anchorage* ☎ *907/330–8000 or 800/315–6608* ⊕ *www.alaskanative.net* ☜ *$24.95, $10 Alaska residents* ☉ *Mid-May (Mother's Day)–Sept., daily 9–5; Oct.–mid-May, Sat. 10–5.*

SOUTH ANCHORAGE

ⓒ **Alaska Zoo.** Roam the trails and visit with the polar bears, caribou, brown and black bears, seals, tigers, snow leopards, moose, wolves, lynx, and a large array of birds that call the Alaska Zoo home. Along with a major facility upgrade with a new entrance cabin and gift shop in 2009, the zoo has also upgraded its mission statement to concentrate on promoting the conservation of arctic and subarctic animal species. Daily two-hour tours, led throughout the summer, include two behind-the-scenes stops. ⊠ *4731 O'Malley Rd., South Anchorage ⊕ 2 mi east of New Seward Hwy.* ☎ *907/346–3242* ⊕ *www.alaskazoo.org* ☜ *$12, $6 kids 3–17, free kids 2 and under* ☉ *June–Sept. 14, daily 9–6 (June–Aug., until 9 on Tues. and Fri. with special programs starting at 7 pm); Sept. 15–Oct. 31, daily 10–5; Nov. and Feb., daily 10–4:30; Dec. and Jan., daily 10–4; Mar. and Apr., daily 10–5; winter closing hrs may vary with conditions.*

ⓒ **Potter Marsh.** Sandhill cranes, trumpeter swans, and other migratory birds, as well as the occasional moose or beaver, frequent this marsh about 10 mi south of Downtown on the Seward Highway. An elevated boardwalk makes viewing easy, and in summer there are salmon runs in the creek beneath the bridge. The **Potter Section House,** an old railroad service building just south of the marsh, operates as a state park office. Out front is an old engine with a rotary snowplow that was used to clear avalanches. ⊠ *Seward Hwy., South Anchorage* ☎ *907/269–8400* ⊕ *www.adfg.alaska.gov/index.cfm?adfg=viewinglocations.pottermarsh.*

WEST ANCHORAGE

☾ **Alaska Aviation Heritage Museum.** The state's unique aviation history is presented with 25 vintage aircraft—seven have been completely restored—three theaters, an observation deck along **Lake Hood,** the world's busiest seaplane base, a flight simulator, and a gift shop. Highlights include a Stearman C2B, the first plane to land on Mt. McKinley back in the early 1930s. Volunteers are working to restore a 1931 Fairchild Pilgrim aircraft and make it flyable and are eager to talk shop. A free shuttle to and from Anchorage Airport is available. ⊠ *4721 Aircraft Dr., West Anchorage* ☎ *907/248–5325* ⊕ *www.alaskaairmuseum. org* ☜ *$10* ⊙ *May 11–Sept. 15, daily 9–5; Sept. 16–May 10, Wed.–Sun. 9–5.*

SPORTS AND THE OUTDOORS

Few American cities feel as connected to the outdoors as Anchorage. From the in-town Tony Knowles Coastal Trail to a nearly endless supply of trails and other outdoor adventures in the Chugach National Forest and on nearby waterways, Anchorage is an outdoor-lover's playground. And that doesn't just hold true for the warmer months; a nearby ski resort offers downhill delights and there's plenty of dog mushing and ice climbing and other wintry sports to try. Up for some spectator sports instead? Anchorage doesn't disappoint: minor-league baseball, the start of the Iditarod, and a hardcore hockey team are waiting for you.

PARTICIPATORY SPORTS

BICYCLING, RUNNING, AND WALKING

Anchorage has more than 120 mi of paved bicycle trails, and many streets have marked bike lanes. Although busy during the day, Downtown streets are uncrowded and safe for cyclists in the evening. ■ TIP→ Pick up a guide to local trails at the **Alaska Public Lands Information Center** (⊠ *4th Ave. and F St., Downtown* ☎ *907/644–3661 or 866/869-6887* 🖷 *907/271–2744* ⊕ *www.alaskacenters.gov*) or at area bookstores. At the far west end of Raspberry Road in South Anchorage the 43 mi of trails at **Kincaid Park** (☎ *907/343–6397* ⊕ *www.muni. org/Departments/parks/Pages/parkdistrictsw.aspx)* wind through 1,400 acres of mixed spruce and birch forest. Mountain bikers will find easy-to-moderate riding along with some challenging hills. Be advised that Kincaid Park is home to a sizable moose population, as well as the occasional bear, so stay alert at all times. Considered one of the best places for Nordic skiing in the United States, the park remains popular throughout the year. The Kincaid Outdoor Center—locally called Kincaid Chalet—is available for a fee for social functions such as weddings, receptions, and meetings. The park also has a climbing wall. The **Tony Knowles Coastal Trail** (⊕ *dnr.alaska.gov/parks/aktrails/ats/anc/knowlsct.*

htm) and other bike trails in Anchorage are used by runners, cyclists, in-line skaters, and walkers. It begins Downtown off 2nd Avenue and is also easily accessible from Westchester Lagoon near the west end of 15th Avenue. The trail runs from the lagoon 2 mi to Earthquake Park and then continues an additional 7 mi to Kincaid Park, where several unpaved trails provide for more adventurous biking and hiking. Those who prefer the off-road experience should pick up a copy of Mountain Bike Anchorage, by Rosemary Austin.

Alaskabike. Starting in Anchorage, these multiday touring packages explore South Central and nearby scenic highways. ☎ *907/245–2175* ⊕ *www.alaskabike.com.*

A number of popular running events are held annually in Anchorage, including the **Alaska Run for Women** (⊕ *www.akrfw.org*) in early June, which raises money for the fight against breast cancer. The late-April **Heart Run** (⊕ *www.heartrun.com*) is a fund-raiser for the American Heart Association's work to prevent heart disease. Alaska's biggest and most famous running event is the **Mayor's Midnight Sun Marathon** (⊕ *www.mayorsmarathon.com*), held on the summer solstice in mid- to late June. Just a short pedal away from a Tony Knowles Coastal Trail access point, rent adult and children's bicycles, as well as trailers and baby seats, at **Alaska Pablo's Bicycle Rentals** (⊠ *501 L St., Downtown* ☎ *907/250–2871 or 866/445–9801* ⊕ *www.pablobicyclerentals. com* ☉ *Mon.–Sun. 8–7*). Rental rates begin at $7 per hour. Discounts available for groups of five or more. **Downtown Bicycle Rental** (⊠ *333 W. 4th Ave., Downtown* ☎ *907/279–5293* ⊕ *www.alaska-bike-rentals. com*) has an inventory of more than 100 bikes of all types, as well as clip-in pedals and shoes. The minimum rental rate is $16 for 3 hours, which includes free lock, helmet, and map. Located five blocks from the Coastal Trail, the company also offers combo hike and bike trips that include a shuttle van ride to the Flattop trailhead. The **Arctic Bicycle Club** (☎ *907/566–0177* ⊕ *www.arcticbike.org*) organizes races and tours.

Just 30 mi north of Anchorage, **Lifetime Adventures** operates out of the state park campground at Eklutna Lake. Lifetime rents bikes, trailers, and kayaks. You can take the popular Paddle & Pedal package in which you paddle in one direction and pedal your way back. ☎ *800/952–8624* ⊕ *www.lifetimeadventures.net.*

BIRD-WATCHING

Popular bird-watching places include the Tony Knowles Coastal Trail, which provides access to Westchester Lagoon and nearby tide flats, along with Potter Marsh on the south end of Anchorage. The Anchorage chapter of the **Audubon Society** (⊕ *www.anchorageaudubon.org*) offers a downloadable list of the "Birds of Anchorage" on their Web site, and can refer you to local birders who will advise you on the best bird-watching spots. The society also hosts bird-watching classes and field trips. The society's Upper Cook Inlet Bird Report Hotline (☎ *907/338–2473*) tracks the latest sightings in town. Naturalists Lisa Moorehead and Bob Dittrick of **Wilderness Birding Adventures** (☎ *907/694–7442* ⊕ *www.wildernessbirding.com*) offer backcountry birding, wildlife, and natural-history trips to remote parts of Alaska, as well as village-based, birding-focused trips to some of Alaska's birding hot spots.

CANOEING AND KAYAKING

Local lakes and lagoons, such as Westchester Lagoon, Goose Lake, and Jewel Lake, have favorable conditions for canoeing and kayaking. More adventurous paddlers should head to Whittier or Seward for sea kayaking. Take a guided trip in sea kayaks from **Kayak Adventures Worldwide** (⊠ *Box 2249, Seward* ☎ *907/224–3960* ⊕ *www. kayakak.com*), which offers half-day trips to Resurrection Bay and a variety of full-day trips to Resurrection Bay and Aialik Bay. Kayak-

ing classes teach basic sea-kayaking skills. It also runs multiday trips in Kenai Fjords and offers customized booking dates and a B&B out of a home in Seward. **Alaska Rafts & Kayak** (⊠ 401 W. Tudor Rd., *Midtown* ☎ 907/561–7238 ⊕ *www.alaskaraftandkayak.com*) rents or, if you're in the market, sells a flotilla's worth of small boats, including kayaks, canoes, inflatable rafts, and one-man fishing pontoons. Float tubes, too.</R> **REI** (⊠ 1200 W. Northern Lights Blvd., *Spenard* ☎ 907/272–4565 ⊕ *www.rei.com*) sells and rents all sorts of outdoor gear, including canoes and sea kayaks.

FISHING

Nearly 30 local lakes are stocked with catchable game fish. ∎**TIP→** You must have a valid Alaska sport fishing license to fish in the state. Fishing licenses may be purchased at any Fred Meyer or Carr's/Safeway grocery or local sporting goods store, or online at ⊕ https://www.admin.adfg.state. ak.us/buyonline. Nonresidents can buy an annual license for extended stays or a 1-, 3-, 7-, or 14-day permit. A separate king salmon stamp is required to fish for the big guys. Rainbow trout, arctic char, landlocked salmon, Dolly Varden, grayling, and northern pike are among the species found in waters like Jewel Lake in South Anchorage and Mirror and Fire lakes near Eagle River. Coho salmon return to Ship Creek (downtown) in August, and king salmon are caught there between late May and early July. Campbell Creek and Bird Creek just south of town are also good spots for coho—locally called silver—salmon. At times, Bird Creek has had some issues with local brown bears encroaching on anglers, so be bear aware if you fish or hike near there. Contact the **Alaska Department of Fish and Game** (☎ 907/267–2218 ⊕ *www.adfg.alaska.gov/*) for licensing information. For information about Anchorage-area lakes, go to the Web site; click on Sport Fishing, the South Central portion of the "Fisheries by Area" map, and then Anchorage.

CRUISE KENAI

Give your arms a rest, soak up glacier views, and spot the abundant wildlife of Kenai Fjords National Park from a cruise boat. **Alaska Heritage Tours Reservations** (⊠ 509 W. 4th Ave., Downtown ☎ 877/777–2805 ⊕ www. kenaifjords.com), with Kenai Fjord Tours, offers day packages to Kenai Fjords National Park April through November. The company offers transportation via coach and train between Anchorage and Seward. ∎TIP→ Check the Web site for special deals.

5

"This picture harnesses the energy from my first hike to the top of Flat Top Mountain just outside of Anchorage. The hike is great for all skill levels." —Clay W. Padgett, Fodors.com photo contest winner

FLIGHTSEEING

This area is the state's air-travel hub. Plenty of flightseeing services operating out of city airports and floatplane bases can take you on spectacular tours of **Mt. McKinley**, the **Chugach Range, Prince William Sound, Kenai Fjords National Park**, and the **Harding Icefield.** Anchorage hosts the greatest number and variety of services, including companies operating fixed-wing aircraft, floatplanes, and helicopters.

Fodor's Choice ★ **Rust's Flying Service.** An Anchorage company in business since 1963, Rust's will take you on narrated flightseeing tours of Mt. McKinley and Denali, Columbia Glacier, and Prince William Sound, as well as on flights to the peninsula for bear viewing. Rust's recently started offering three- and five-night fly-in hiking trips to Denali National Park and Lake Clark National Park. The company also owns Talkeetna-based **K2 Aviation.** ☎ *907/243–1595 or 800/544–2299 ⊕ www.flyrusts.com.*

GOLF

Anchorage is Alaska's golfing capital, with several public courses. They won't compare to offerings in Phoenix or San Diego, but courses are open until 10 pm on long summer days, and at some courses the mountain views put most other courses to shame. **Anchorage Golf Course** (⊠ *3651 O'Malley Rd., South Anchorage* ☎ *907/522–3363 ⊕ www. anchoragegolfcourse.com*) has 18 holes and, as of the 2011 season, a new pro shop and bar. Golf carts and clubs are available for rent. The city-run **Russian Jack Springs Park** (⊠ *5200 DeBarr Rd., South Anchorage* ☎ *907/343–6992 ⊕ www.anchorageparkfoundation.org/directory/ russianjack.htm*) is generally open May through September. It has 9 holes and clubs for rent. **Tanglewood Lakes Golf Club** (⊠ *11701 Brayton*

Dr., South Anchorage ☎ 907/345–
4600 ⊕ www.alaskagolflinks.com/
tanglewoodrates.html) is a 9-hole
course in South Anchorage, and
home to the Tanglewood Lakes
Golf Dome, an indoor driving
range open year round. For information on other courses around
the state, check out ⊕ www.
alaskagolflinks.com.

TIP

If you choose to travel by rail
independently, the Alaska Railroad
cars also have onboard guides
and glass-domed observation
cars, and make the trip between
Anchorage and Fairbanks hooked
up to the same engines as the
cruise-line cars. Alaska Railroad's
Web site (⊕ www.akrr.com) has
details.

ICE-SKATING

Ice-skating is a favorite wintertime
activity in Anchorage, with several
indoor ice arenas, outdoor hockey
rinks, and local ponds opening when temperatures drop. Though Alaska's early winters and cold temperatures often allow for pond skating as
early as mid-November, consider calling the Visitor's Center or asking
an in-the-know local before stepping out onto pond ice.

Ben Boeke Ice Arena (⊠ 334 E. 16th Ave., Midtown ☎ 907/274–5715
⊕ www.benboeke.com) is a city-run indoor ice arena with open skating and skate rentals year-round. An indoor ice rink at Dimond Mall,
the **Dimond Ice Chalet** (⊠ 800 E. Dimond Blvd., South Anchorage
☎ 907/344–1212 ⊕ www.dimondicechalet.com) is open to the public
daily. In winter, **Westchester Lagoon**, 1 mi south of downtown, is a favorite outdoor family (and competitive) skating area, with smooth ice and
piles of firewood next to the warming barrels. Other pond skating possibilities include **Cheney Lake, Goose Lake, Jewel Lake,** and **Spenard Lake.**

RAFTING

Based in Girdwood, **Chugach Powder Guides** (✉ Box 641, Girdwood
99587 ☎ 907/783–4354 ⊕ www.alaskanrafting.com) leads scenic floats
on the Placer, Twentymile, and Portage rivers, along with white-water
trips on the Talkeetna River and summer Tordrillo Mountain packages.
Alaska's oldest adventure and wilderness guiding company (in business
since 1975), **Nova** (✉ Box 1129, Chickaloon 99674 ☎ 800/746–5753
⊕ www.novalaska.com) provides both scenic and white-water wilderness rafting trips statewide, including day trips in the Anchorage, Kenai
Peninsula, and Mat-Su areas, multiday trips in remote areas, and glacier
hikes on the Mat-Su Glacier.

SKIING

★ Cross-country skiing is extremely popular in Anchorage. Locals ski on
trails in town at Kincaid Park or Hillside and farther away at Girdwood Valley, Turnagain Pass, and Chugach State Park. Downhill skiing is convenient to downtown. A number of cross-country ski events
are held annually in Anchorage. The **Alaska Ski for Women** (⊕ www.
alaskaskiforwomen.org), held on Super Bowl Sunday in early February, is the biggest women's ski race in North America, attracting more
than 1,500 skiers. Many of the skiers don crazy costumes for the event.
The **Nordic Skiing Association of Anchorage** (⊕ www.anchoragenordicski.
com) sponsors many other ski races and events throughout winter, from

wooden-ski classics to the highly competitive Besh Cup series. Biggest of all is the **Tour of Anchorage** (⊕ *www.tourofanchorage.com*), a grueling 50-km (31-mi) race in early March. If you're not up to doing 50k, there are 25k (16-mi) and 40k (25-mi) competitions as well. **Alyeska Ski Resort** (☎ *907/754–1111 or 800/880–3880, 907/754–7669 recorded information and snow conditions, 907/753–2275 ticket office* ⊕ *www. alyeskaresort.com*), at Girdwood, 40 mi south of the city, is Alaska's premier destination resort, where snowfall averages 643 inches annually. Alyeska features a day lodge, hotel, restaurants, nine lifts, a tram, a vertical drop of 2,500 feet, and 73 runs for all abilities. Lift tickets cost $60 for adults; $40 for night skiing. The tram ($18) is open in summer, providing access to the Seven Glaciers restaurant and hiking trails. Alyeska picks up skiers and snowboarders from Anchorage on weekend days. The service costs $65 and includes a lift ticket. **Alyeska Accommodations** (☎ *907/783–2000 or 888/783–2001* ⊕ *www. alyeskaaccommodations.com*) can set you up in a privately owned cabin or condo. **Alpenglow at Arctic Valley** (✉ *Mi 7, Arctic Valley Rd. off Glenn Hwy., just past Muldoon Exit* ☎ *907/428–1208* ⊕ *www.skialpenglow. com*) is a small ski area just north of Anchorage. On the eastern edge of town, **Hilltop Ski Area** (✉ *Abbott Rd. near Hillside Dr., East Anchorage* ☎ *907/346–1446* ⊕ *www.hilltopskiarea.org*) is a favorite ski area with families.

On 1,400 acres of rolling, timbered hills and bordered on the west by Cook Inlet, **Kincaid Park** (✉ *Main entrance at far west end of Raspberry Rd., Southwest Anchorage* ☎ *907/343–6397* ⊕ *www.muni.org/parks/ parkdistrictsw.cfm*) is a scenic treasure with maintained trails groomed for diagonal and skate-skiing. National cross-country skiing events (including U.S. Olympic team qualifying events and national masters championships) are held each winter along the 60 km (37 mi) of interwoven trails—including 20 km (12 mi) that are lighted for night skiing. The park is open year-round: for skiing in winter; and for mountain biking, hiking, and other outdoor activities in summer. The Raspberry Road parking lot is open 10 am–11 pm daily; lots inside the park are open 10 am–10 pm daily. The locally owned outdoors shop **Alaska Mountaineering and Hiking** (✉ *2633 Spenard Rd., Midtown* ☎ *907/272– 1811* ⊕ *www.alaskamountaineering.com*) has a highly experienced staff and plenty of cross-country skis for sale or rent. Ski sales and rentals are available from **REI** (✉ *1200 W. Northern Lights Blvd., Midtown* ☎ *907/272–4565* ⊕ *www.rei.com/stores/16*).

SPECTATOR SPORTS

Wintertime brings hockey, dog mushing, and ski races, and long summer days provide the chance to watch a semipro baseball game and still have time to watch the sun go down at midnight. **Sullivan Arena** (✉ *334 E. 16th Ave., Midtown* ☎ *907/566–1596*) is Anchorage's primary venue for large events, from ice hockey to boat shows. **Mulcahy Stadium** (✉ *E. 16th Ave. at Cordova St., Midtown*) is the center for semipro baseball in Anchorage.

BASEBALL

Two summer collegiate baseball teams play at Mulcahy Stadium next to the Sullivan Arena. The games played here are intense—many players have gone on to star in the major leagues. The **Anchorage Bucs** (☎ 907/561–2827 ⊕ *www.anchoragebucs.com*) have a dozen or so former players who went on to the majors, including standouts Wally Joyner, Jeff Kent, and Bobby Jones. The most famous player on the **Glacier Pilots** (☎ 907/274–3627 ⊕ *www.glacierpilots.com*) was Mark McGwire, but many other pre–major leaguers have played for them over the years, including Dave Winfield, Randy Johnson, and Reggie Jackson.

FOOTBALL

Alaska's entry in the Intense Football League playing indoor arena-style ball is the **Alaska Wild** (☎ 907/771–9400 ⊕ *goalaskawild.com*). The season runs from March through June, with home games in Anchorage.

HOCKEY

Hockey is in the blood of any true Alaskan, and kids as young as age 4 crowd local ice rinks in hopes of becoming the next Scott Gomez (who, along with playing for the New York Rangers, backs an eponymously-named foundation that provides "opportunities and assistance for youth hockey in Alaska").

The East Coast Hockey League's **Alaska Aces** (☎ 907/258–2237 ⊕ *www.alaskaaces.com*) play minor-league professional hockey in the Sullivan Arena. The **University of Alaska Anchorage** (☎ 907/786–1293 ⊕ *www.goseawolves.com*) has a Division I NCAA hockey team that draws several thousand loyal fans to home games at the Sullivan Arena.

WHERE TO EAT

Anchorage's dining scene has, to the relief of repeat visitors and, even more so, locals, been on the rise for the past several years. Established (and still highly recommended) restaurants like Jen's and Marx Brothers Café have been joined by the likes of the small-plate and wine-focused Crush Wine Bistro and Cellar and the Pacific Rim cuisine-focused Ginger. No matter the restaurant, the local catch is a frequent star. Beware: eating salmon or halibut in-state may ruin the experience for most other restaurants in the Lower 48. Anchorage also offers up plenty of worldy flavors thanks to the city's ethnic diversity. And, of course, nobody should leave Anchorage without trying the local fast-food specialty: a reindeer hot dog or sausage from the cart in front of the courthouse on 4th Ave. Smoking is not allowed in Anchorage restaurants.

DOWNTOWN

$$$$ ✕ **Club Paris.** Alaska's oldest steak house has barely changed since open-
STEAK ing in 1957. The restaurant has dark wood and an old-fashioned feel, and serves tender, flavorful steaks of all kinds, including a 4-inch-thick filet mignon. If you have to wait for a table, have a martini at the bar and order the hors d'oeuvres platter ($32)—a sampler of top sirloin steak, cheese, and prawns that could be a meal for two. For dessert,

try a slice of tart key lime or sweet-potato pie. Dinner reservations are advised. ⊠ *417 W. 5th Ave., Downtown* ☎ *907/277–6332* ⊕ *www. clubparisrestaurant.com* ⊗ *No lunch Sun.* ✛ *C2.*

$$$$ ✕ **Corsair Restaurant.** This fine-dining establishment specializes in con-
CONTINENTAL tinental and American cuisine with an emphasis on traditional French haute cuisine, and has earned an international reputation for its steak and seafood. More than 800 wine selections from its 10,000-bottle cellar have won the Corsair recognition from *Wine Spectator* magazine. ⊠ *944 W. 5th Ave., Downtown* ☎ *907/278–4502* ⊕ *www. corsairrestaurant.com* ⊗ *Closed Sun. and holidays* ✛ *A2.*

$$$$ ✕ **Crow's Nest Restaurant.** In the Hotel Captain Cook, American and
CONTINENTAL French cuisine are the order of the day, along with the best view in Anchorage—the Chugach Mountains to the east, the Alaska Range to the north, and the sprawling city of Anchorage 20 stories below. Equally impressive are the 10,000-bottle wine cellar and hefty portions. The waitstaff presents a menu of seafood, along with beef, pork, and lamb, served in an elegant setting with plenty of starched linen, brass, and teak. ⊠ *Hotel Captain Cook, 20th fl., 5th Ave. and K St., Downtown* ☎ *907/343–2217* ⊕ *www.captaincook.com/dining/crows-nest* ⚑ *Reservations essential* ⊗ *Closed Sun. and Mon. in winter. No lunch* ✛ *A2.*

$$$ ✕ **Crush Wine Bistro and Cellar.** The conversation-friendly combo of
ECLECTIC sharing-friendly small plates and an extensive wine list make Crush Anchorage's go-to when you want to discuss adventures already lived or the ones to come. The restaurant could probably coast on that combo alone but, luckily, the owners aren't into coasting. They brought on chef Christopher Vane, nominated for a 2011 James Beard Award, to head up an inventive—but budget-friendly—menu that ranges from $5 plates of blue cheese-stuffed Medjool dates to $8 servings of sherried portobello and spinach polenta, and beyond. Though it's more fun to share, diners who prefer a plate of their own can also opt for one of the daily dinner specials. Along with a world's worth of wines, Crush also serves a wide range of top-flight beers and some seriously beautiful espresso drinks. Housed in a building that could easily be a setting for a 1970's-era sci-fi flick, the interior is far warmer and more inviting than its curvy porthole-ish exterior. ⊠ *343 W. 6th Ave., Downtown* ☎ *907/865–9198* ⊕ *www.crushak.com* ⊗ *Closed Sun.* ✛ *C2*

$$ ✕ **Downtown Deli.** Perfect for a quick meal break, this café is across the
AMERICAN street from the Log Cabin and Visitor Information Center. Although you can choose from familiar sandwiches like the French dip or the chicken teriyaki, this deli also has Alaskan favorites like grilled halibut and reindeer stew. The dark, rich chicken soup comes with either noodles or homemade matzo balls, and breakfasts range from omelets and homemade granola to cheese blintzes. You can sit in one of the wooden booths for some privacy or out front at the sidewalk tables for some summertime people-watching. ⊠ *525 W. 4th Ave., Downtown* ☎ *907/276–7116* ⚑ *Reservations not accepted* ⊗ *No dinner Oct.–May* ✛ *C1.*

$$$$ ✕ **Ginger.** Thanks to beautifully crafted dishes that focus on cuisines
ASIAN from the Pacific Rim as well as popular Asian dishes like Pad Thai, Ginger was a welcome addition to the local dining scene when it opened

in 2007. The menu offers dishes that will please both the adventurous and more traditional diners. Ginger also keeps vegetarians happy with dishes including grilled tofu over a cold Israeli couscous salad. Decorated in beautiful woods and warm tones, the interior complements the menu perfectly. Alaska local chef Guy Conley was nominated for a 2010 James Beard Award in the best chef/northwest category. The restaurant also has a bar area but the dining space gets the go-to nod; it's prettier. ⊠ *425 W. 5th Ave., Downtown* ☎ *907/929–3680* ⊕ *www.gingeralaska.com* ⊗ *No lunch weekends* ♣ *C2.*

$$$ ✗ **Glacier BrewHouse.** The scent of hops permeates the cavernous, wood-
AMERICAN beam BrewHouse, where a dozen or so ales, stouts, lagers, and pilsners are brewed on the premises. Locals mingle with visitors in this noisy, always-busy heart-of-town restaurant, where dinner selections range from thin-crust, 10-inch pizzas to chipotle shrimp cocktail and from barbecue pork ribs to fettuccine jambalaya and fresh seafood (in season). The bacon-laced seafood chowder is a must on cooler days. For dessert, don't miss the wood-oven-roasted apple-and-currant bread pudding (though, really, you can't go wrong with the peanut-butter pie either). You can watch the hardworking chefs in the open kitchen. The brewery sits behind a glass wall, and the same owners operate the equally popular Orso, next door. ⊠ *737 W. 5th Ave., Downtown* ☎ *907/274–2739* ⊕ *www.glacierbrewhouse.com* ♣ *B2.*

$$$$ ✗ **Marx Bros. Cafe.** Inside a little frame house built in 1916, this nation-
CONTINENTAL ally recognized 14-table café opened in 1979 and is still going strong.
Fodor's Choice The menu changes frequently, and the wine list encompasses more than
★ 700 international choices. For an appetizer, try the black-bean-and-duck soup or fresh Kachemak Bay oysters. The outstanding made-at-your-table Caesar salad is a superb opener for the baked halibut with a macadamia-nut crust served with coconut-curry sauce and fresh mango chutney. And if the sweet potato–and-pecan pie is on the menu, get it! ⊠ *627 W. 3rd Ave., Downtown* ☎ *907/278–2133* ⊕ *www.marxcafe.com* ⊛ *Reservations essential* ⊗ *Closed Sun. and Mon. No lunch* ♣ *C1.*

¢–$ ✗ **New Sagaya's City Market.** Stop at one of the two New Sagaya's for
ECLECTIC quick lunches and Kaladi Brothers espresso. The in-house bakery, L'Aroma, makes specialty breads and a wide range of snack-worthy pastries, and the international deli and grocery serves California-style pizzas, Chinese food, lasagna, rotisserie chicken, salads, and even stuffed cabbage. At the downtown market, you can eat inside on the sheltered patio or grab an outside table on a summer afternoon. New Sagaya's has one of the best seafood counters in town, and will even box and ship your fish. The grocery stores carry an extensive selection of Asian foodstuffs, and the produce and meat selections are excellent. ⊠ *900 W. 13th Ave., Downtown* ☎ *907/274–6173, 907/274–9797, or 800/764–1001* ⊠ *3700 Old Seward Hwy., Midtown* ☎ *907/562–9797* ⊕ *www.newsagaya.com* ♣ *E3, G5.*

$$$$ ✗ **Orso.** Upon entering Orso ("bear" in Italian), you'll feel, to a certain
ITALIAN degree, as though you've stepped out of Anchorage and into a Tuscan villa. Alaskan touches flavor rustic Mediterranean dishes that include traditional pastas, fresh seafood, and locally famous desserts—most notably a delicious molten chocolate cake. Be sure to ask about the daily

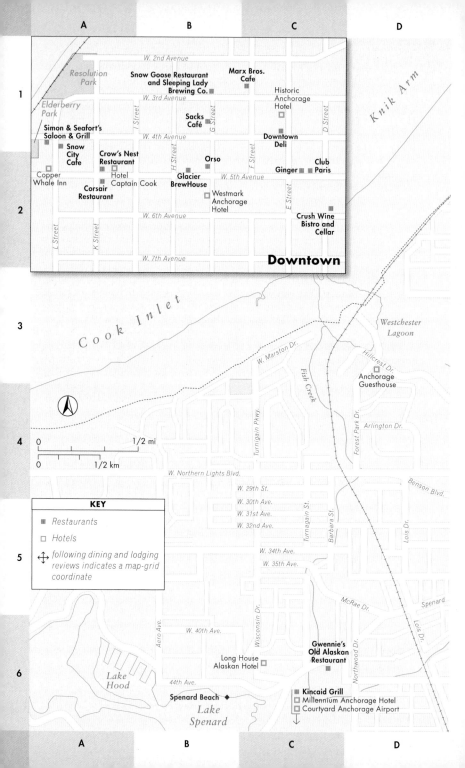

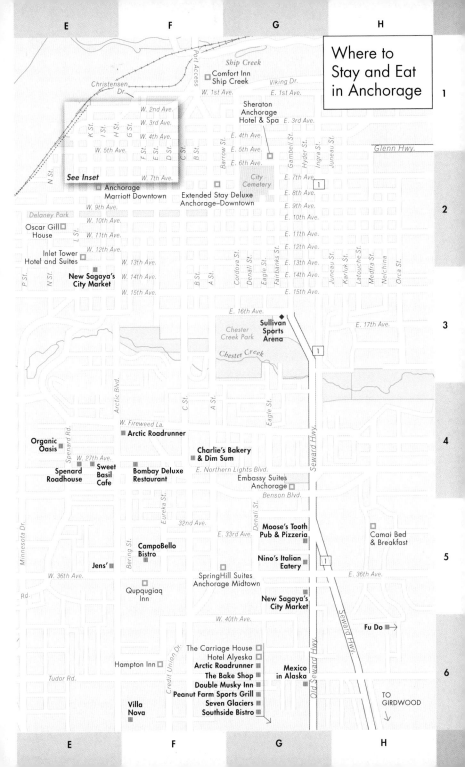

Where to Stay and Eat in Anchorage

E **F** **G** **H**

1

Ship Creek

Comfort Inn
Ship Creek
Christensen
Dr.
Port Access
W. 1st Ave.
E. 1st Ave.
Viking Dr.

Sheraton
Anchorage
Hotel & Spa
E. 3rd Ave.
Glenn Hwy.

W. 2nd Ave.
W. 3rd Ave.
E. 4th Ave.
W. 4th Ave.
E. 5th Ave.
W. 5th Ave.
E. 6th Ave.

K St.
I St.
H St.
G St.
F St.
E St.
D St.
C St.
B St.
Barrow St.
Gambell St.
Hyder St.
Ingra St.
Juneau St.

City
Cemetery
E. 7th Ave.

See Inset
W. 7th Ave.

2

Anchorage
Marriott Downtown
Extended Stay Deluxe
Anchorage–Downtown
E. 8th Ave.
E. 9th Ave.

W. 9th Ave.
Delaney Park
W. 10th Ave.
E. 10th Ave.
Oscar Gill
House
L St.
W. 11th Ave.
E. 11th Ave.
E. 12th Ave.

Inlet Tower
Hotel and Suites
W. 12th Ave.
W. 13th Ave.
E. 13th Ave.
Juneau St.
Karluk St.
Latouche St.
Medfra St.
Nelchina
Orca St.

P St.
N St.
New Sagaya's
City Market
W. 14th Ave.
B St.
A St.
Cordova St.
Denali St.
Eagle St.
Fairbanks St.
E. 14th Ave.
W. 15th Ave.
E. 15th Ave.

3

E. 16th Ave.
Chester
Creek Park
Sullivan
Sports
Arena
E. 17th Ave.

Chester Creek

Arctic Blvd.
C St.
A St.
Eagle St.
Seward Hwy.

4

W. Fireweed La.
Arctic Roadrunner

**Organic
Oasis**
Spenard Rd.
W. 27th Ave.
**Sweet
Basil
Cafe**
**Charlie's Bakery
& Dim Sum**

**Spenard
Roadhouse**
**Bombay Deluxe
Restaurant**
E. Northern Lights Blvd.
Embassy Suites
Anchorage
Benson Blvd.
Denali St.

5

Minnesota Dr.
Eureka St.
32nd Ave.
**Moose's Tooth
Pub & Pizzeria**
Camai Bed
& Breakfast

Bering St.
**CampoBello
Bistro**
E. 33rd Ave.
**Nino's Italian
Eatery**

Jens'
W. 36th Ave.
**Qupqugiaq
Inn**
SpringHill Suites
Anchorage Midtown
E. 36th Ave.

Rd.
New Sagaya's
City Market
W. 40th Ave.

6

Old Seward Hwy.
Seward Hwy.
Fu Do

The Carriage House
Hotel Alyeska
Hampton Inn
Credit Union Dr.
Arctic Roadrunner
The Bake Shop
Double Musky Inn
Peanut Farm Sports Grill
Seven Glaciers
Southside Bistro
**Mexico
in Alaska**

Tudor Rd.
**Villa
Nova**
TO
GIRDWOOD

E **F** **G** **H**

Alaska's Well-Worn Trail

Since 1973 mushers and their sled-dog teams have raced more than 1,000 mi across Alaska in the Iditarod Trail Sled Dog Race, the longest sled-dog race in the world.

After a ceremonial start in downtown Anchorage on the first Saturday in March, dog teams wind through Alaska, battling almost every imaginable winter challenge. Iditarod mushers and dogs endure extreme cold, deep snow, gale-force winds, whiteouts, river overflow, and moose attacks, not to mention fraying tempers. Less than 10 days later, the front-runners in the "Last Great Race" cross under the burled-wood arch finish line in Nome, on the Bering Sea coast.

The Iditarod's origins can be traced to two events: an early 1900s long-distance race called the All-Alaska Sweepstakes and the delivery of a lifesaving serum to Nome by dog mushers during a diphtheria outbreak in 1925.

Fascinated with the trail's history, Alaskan sled-dog enthusiasts Dorothy Page and Joe Redington Sr. staged the first race in 1967 to celebrate the role of mushing in Alaska's history. Only 50 mi long and with a purse of $25,000— no small amount at that time—it attracted the best of Alaska's competitive mushers. Enthusiasm waned in 1969, however, when the available winnings fell to $1,000. Instead of giving up, Redington expanded the race.

In 1973, after three years without a race, he organized a 1,000-mi race from Anchorage to Nome, with a then-outrageous purse of $50,000. Critics scoffed, but 34 racers entered. First place went to a little-known musher named Dick Wilmarth, who finished in 20 days. Redington then billed the Iditarod as a 1,049-mi race to symbolize Alaska, the 49th state. While still the official distance, the race really covers more than 1,150 mi.

The race actually begins in Wasilla, the Iditarod's headquarters, a 50-mi drive north of Anchorage. The first few hundred miles take mushers and dogs through wooded lowlands and hills, including Moose Alley.

Teams then cross the Alaska Range and enter Interior Alaska, with Athabascan villages and gold-rush ghost towns, including Iditarod. Next, the trail follows the frozen Yukon River, then cuts over to the Bering Sea coast for the final 270-mi "sprint" to Nome. It was here, in 1985, that Libby Riddles drove her team into a blinding blizzard en route to a victory that made her the first woman to win the race. After that, Susan Butcher won the race four times, but the all-time record holder is Rick Swenson, with five victories. Lance Mackey holds the record for most consecutive wins, with his back to backs from 2007 to 2010. The fastest time was recorded in 2011, when Alaska native John Baker finished in 8 days, 18 hours, and 46 minutes.

specials. If you can't get a table at dinner (reservations are advised), you can select from the same menu at the large bar. Upstairs you'll find a cozier, quieter space. For lighter bites or drinks, consider the restaurant's daily happy hour, which features half-price appetizers and drink specials on wine, cocktails, and Glacier BrewHouse beers. ⊠ *737 W. 5th Ave., at G St., Downtown* ☎ *907/222–3232* ⊕ *www.orsoalaska.com* ✛ *B2.*

"Along with native bears, moose, and other animals, all of the residents at the sanctuary are native to Alaska." —Amy Dawson, Fodors.com photo contest participant

$$$-$$$$
ECLECTIC
★

✕ **Sacks Café.** This downtown spot serves a world's worth of flavors from chicken and scallops over udon noodles to cider-brined pork tenderloin with Alaska purple potato salad. The kitchen relies on local produce when available. There's always something new to try at Sacks. When Anchorage weather turns gray, the colorful interior and art provide respite. The monthly wine flights, normally with three different selections of 3-ounce pours with information sheets on each wine, don't hurt either. Be sure to ask about the daily specials, particularly the fresh king salmon and halibut. Singles congregate along a small bar, sampling wines from California, Australia, and France. The café is especially crowded during lunch, served from 11 to 2:30, and dinner begins at 5. The weekend brunch menu, one of the best Downtown, includes eggs Benedict, a Mexican scrambled egg dish called *migas*, and various salads and sandwiches. ✉ *328 G St., Downtown* ☎ *907/276–3546 or 907/274–4022* ⊕ *www.sackscafe.com* ⌲ *Reservations essential* ⊹ *B1.*

$$$$
SEAFOOD

✕ **Simon & Seafort's Saloon & Grill.** Windows overlooking Cook Inlet vistas, along with the high ceilings and a classic brass-and-wood interior, have long made this an Anchorage favorite. The menu includes prime rib (aged 28 days) and other steak-house favorites, but the main attraction is seafood: fish is blackened, grilled, fried, or prepared any other way you like it. Try the king crab legs or the seafood linguine, and for dessert the Brandy Ice: vanilla ice cream whipped with brandy, Kahlúa, and crème de cacao. The bar is a great spot for microbrews, single-malt scotch, and martinis; the best tables are adjacent to tall windows facing the water. ✉ *420 L St., Downtown* ☎ *907/274–3502*

⊕ *simonandseaforts.com/page/home* ⌆ *Reservations essential* ⊘ *No lunch weekends* ⊹ *A1.*

¢–$ ✕ **Snow City Cafe.** On summer days, Snow City attracts some serious
ECLECTIC crowds—and for good reason. This modern but unassuming café, con-
Fodor's Choice venient to many of the downtown hotels, serves one of Anchorage's
★ best (and reasonably priced) breakfasts. Oh, lunch, too. If you're not
an early riser, be prepared to wait. Put your name down with the hostess, grab a coffee at the to-go stand, and hang out with everybody else
outside until your table is ready. While waiting, consider writing a haiku
to add to the restaurant's customer-penned haiku collection. Service is
fast in the chipper and family-friendly restaurant. The breakfast menu,
served all day, features inventive spins on eggs Benedict, including one
topped with king crab cakes; omelets; pancakes; and more. Snow City's
lunch menu consists of hot or cold sandwiches, fresh soups, and salads,
and has lots of vegetarian options. Meat eaters need look no further
than the excellent meatloaf sandwich; since Snow City offers a refrigerator case filled with to-go sandwiches, the meatloaf is also a perfect picnic
or hiking companion. ⊠ *4th Ave. at L St., Downtown* ☎ 907/272–2489
⊕ *www.snowcitycafe.com* ⊘ *No dinner.*

$ ✕ **Snow Goose Restaurant and Sleeping Lady Brewing Company.** Although
AMERICAN you can dine indoors at this comfortable edge-of-downtown eatery, the
real attraction in summer is alfresco dining on the back deck and on
the rooftop. On clear days you can see Mt. McKinley on the northern
horizon and the Chugach Mountains to the east. The menu emphasizes
Alaskan takes on classic pub fare, including fish tacos and reindeer-
stuffed mushrooms, but the award-winning beer and the view are the
best reasons to visit. To sample the specialty beers, gather around oak
tables in the upstairs bar for a brewed-on-the-premises ale, India Pale
Ale, stout, barley wine, or porter. Several of the beers, including the Portage Porter and 49er, an amber ale, pay homage to Alaska. The restaurant also hosts a range of events in its theater, including improv comedy
nights and live music. ⊠ *717 W. 3rd Ave., Downtown* ☎ 907/277–7727
⊕ *www.alaskabeers.com* ⊹ *B1.*

MIDTOWN

¢–$ ✕ **Arctic Roadrunner.** Every year when locals vote for Anchorage's best
AMERICAN burger joint, Arctic Roadrunner comes out on top. The no-frills decor
is mostly 1950s Formica, but if you prefer made-to-order burgers to
industrial fast food then this is the place for you. Eat in or drive through
at the Arctic Boulevard location and head to nearby Valley of the Moon
Park for a sack lunch with the kids. Ultrathick milk shakes and crunchy
onion rings are also on everybody's list of favorites. The South Anchorage location has an outdoor deck on Campbell Creek, and in midsummer you can watch spawning salmon swim past. ⊠ *2477 Arctic Blvd.,
Midtown* ☎ 907/279–7311 ⊠ *5300 Old Seward Hwy., South Anchorage* ☎ 907/561–1245 ▭ *No credit cards* ⊘ *Closed Sun.* ⊹ *F4.*

$$ ✕ **Bombay Deluxe Restaurant.** Anchorage's first Indian restaurant is
INDIAN housed in a collection of international shops at the Valhalla Center
strip mall. Dinners include such spicy standards as lamb korma, chicken
vindaloo, *palak paneer* (spinach and cheese), and 8 different types of

Indian breads—from tandoori roti to garlic naan. The restaurant is especially popular for weekday lunch, when the big buffet provides a sampling of Indian favorites, including several vegetarian offerings. ⊠ *555 W. Northern Lights Blvd., Midtown* ☎ *907/277–1200* ⊕ *www. bombaydeluxe.com* ✛ *F4.*

$$$ ✕ **CampoBello Bistro.** CampoBello has surprisingly sophisticated Ital-
ITALIAN ian entrées and sinful desserts, considering its location in a mall in Midtown. Step inside for a romantic lunch or dinner surrounded by splashes of modern art on the walls and candles on the tables. Specialties include ample servings of seafood crepes, wild-mushroom cannelloni, veal saltimbocca, homemade four-cheese ravioli, and shrimp and scallops Florentine. Service is attentive, and the wine list—particularly the Italian choices—is impressive. Dinner reservations are advised. ⊠ *601 W. 36th Ave., Midtown* ☎ *907/563–2040* ⊘ *Closed Sun. No lunch Sat. No dinner Mon.* ✛ *F5.*

¢ ✕ **Charlie's Bakery & Dim Sum.** Tucked away in a Midtown strip mall, this
CHINESE little gem serves some of the finest authentic Chinese food in Anchorage—and at bargain prices. The atmosphere at this popular lunch spot is casual; order at the counter, take a number for your table, and wait for your meal to be delivered. Dinner is served from 5 to 8:30, and the place closes at 9. Dishes like the vibrant spicy shrimp, loaded with vegetables and hot sauce, make this eatery worth a visit. ⊠ *2729 C St., Midtown* ☎ *907/677–7777* ⊘ *Closed Sun.* ✛ *F4.*

$ ✕ **Fu Do.** This is one of the oldest and best Chinese restaurants in Alaska.
CHINESE Although it's surrounded by fast-food spots and gas stations, when you step inside Fu Do, the deep red Chinese wallpaper and lanterns, ultra-friendly staff, and Asian music take you to another continent. All the standards are available on the enormous menu, including beef with oyster sauce, kung pao chicken, sweet-and-sour pork, and various vegetable entrées. Portions are huge, and include soup, kimchi, rice, egg roll, and tea. Lunch specials are an even better deal, and free delivery for orders over $20 is offered if you don't want to leave your hotel. ⊠ *2600 E. Tudor Rd., Midtown* ☎ *907/561–6610* ⊕ *www. fudochineserestaurant.net* ⊘ *Closed Mon.* ✛ *H6.*

$$$$ ✕ **Jens'.** Don't let the Midtown strip mall that houses Jens' put you
CONTINENTAL off: this is one of Anchorage's best fine-dining establishments. The light and airy restaurant has a playful, energetic feel; chef-owner Jens Haagen Handsen's outsized personality has a lot to do with it. Colorful paintings grace red walls, and the incredibly friendly waiters make guests feel like they're the only ones that matter. The menu changes frequently, but usually includes Alaskan salmon, halibut, and rockfish, along with such specialties as rack of lamb, tenderloin of veal, and an "almost world-famous" pepper steak. Chef Hansen's heritage reveals itself at lunch (when the Danish specials appear) and on the dessert menu; Danish berry pudding served with cream is a delightful way to cap a meal. For a light evening meal, sample the appetizers at the wine bar, where Jens holds court. Reservations are suggested, but Jens' can usually accommodate drop-ins. ⊠ *701 W. 36th Ave., at Arctic Blvd., Midtown* ☎ *907/561–5367* ⊕ *www.jensrestaurant.com* ⊘ *Closed Sun. and Jan. No lunch Sat., no dinner Mon.* ✛ *E5.*

5

$ ✕ **Moose's Tooth Pub & Pizzeria**. Always the top pick when local news-
PIZZA papers rate Anchorage pizzerias, Moose's Tooth is packed all week,
despite the ample seating (in the order of 300 guests). The reason for
the popularity is obvious: creative pizzas and handcrafted beers from its
own brewery. More than a dozen ales, ambers, porters, and stouts are
the order of the day, and homemade root beers, cream sodas, and ginger
ales are also available. You can match these brews with one of a seemingly endless roster of pizzas topped with standards like mushrooms and
roasted red peppers or inventive options like jalapeños, cream cheese,
halibut, or capers. If you're so inclined, check out the daily pizza specials for some pretty exotic topping combinations, such as southern
pork barbecue and Samui shrimp. Those who prefer non-pizza fare can
choose from soups, sandwiches, and salads. ⊠ *3300 Old Seward Hwy.,
Midtown* ☎ *907/258–2537* ⊕ *www.moosestooth.net* ✛ *G5*.

$$$ ✕ **Nino's Italian Eatery**. Nino's achieved near-instant success with its rea-
ITALIAN sonably priced southern Italian menu and traditional pizza. Choose
from old favorites like chicken parmigiana or eggplant rollatini. Nino's
also offers a good selection of Italian wines, imported bottled beer, and
local drafts. No reservations are taken, but it's worth the wait. ⊠ *831
36th Ave., Midtown* ☎ *907/336–6466* ⊕ *www.ninositalianeatery.com*
⊘ *Closed Mon.* ⊲ *Reservations not accepted* ✛ *G5*.

¢–$ ✕ **Sweet Basil Cafe**. Recently moved from its Downtown location to Mid-
CAFÉ town, this family-run café has hot and cold lunchtime sandwiches on
freshly baked sweet basil bread accompanied by a choice of homemade
soups. Fresh pastas, salads, wraps, fish tacos, smoothies, pastries, and
light breakfasts fill out the menu, but the daily specials are often your
best bet. There's also a nice variety of dinners to go, including wild-
mushroom–and–chicken–filled crepes and a roasted-veggie-and-goat-
cheese lasagna. ■**TIP**➔ **The juice bar is one of a handful in Anchorage.**
⊠ *1021 W. Northern Lights Blvd., Midtown* ☎ *907/274–0070* ⊕ *www.
sweetbasilak.com* ⊘ *Closed Sun. No dinner* ✛ *E4*.

$$$ ✕ **Villa Nova**. This standby restaurant is popular for its authentic Italian
ITALIAN cuisine including veal, lamb, chicken, steak, and seafood entrées. Dim
lighting, linen tablecloths, and fresh flowers create a romantic ambience
(though dress is casual). The bar has domestic and imported liquors,
wines, and beers, and handcrafted desserts that change daily. Make reservations for dinner. ⊠ *5121 Arctic Blvd., Midtown* ☎ *907/561–1660*
⊕ *www.villanovaalaska.com* ⊘ *Closed Sun. and Mon.* ✛ *F6*.

SPENARD

$ ✕ **Gwennie's Old Alaskan Restaurant**. Historic Alaskan photos, stuffed
AMERICAN animals, and memorabilia adorn this old family favorite just south of
city center toward the airport. Lunch and dinners are available, but the
restaurant is best known for its old-fashioned breakfasts, available all
day. Try the sourdough pancakes, reindeer sausage and eggs, or crab
omelets. Portions are very generous—a serving of fries alone can feed
a small family. Don't expect anything fancy; this is diner food in an
Alaskana-filled setting. ⊠ *4333 Spenard Rd., Spenard* ☎ *907/243–2090*
⊕ *www.gwenniesrestaurant.com* ✛ *C6*.

$ ✕ **Organic Oasis**. Just across the street from Chilkoot Charlie's, this popu-
CAFÉ   lar café is part eatery and part community center–event space. The menu
offers plenty of healthy (or, at least, healthy-sounding) fare, including
fresh-squeezed juices, smoothies, organic sandwiches, espresso drinks,
pizza, fresh vegan soups, and tempeh burgers. They bake their own
bread and buns. Vegans and vegetarian visitors to Anchorage should
put a giant star on Organic's location on the city map. But that doesn't
mean omnivores will be left in the cold. The menu also includes buffalo
burgers, chicken, salmon, and grilled Buffalo New York strip steaks.
There's even organic beer and wine. There's live music many nights each
week and free Wi-Fi access anytime. Service can be slow at times. If this
place could somehow manage to acquire a more hippie vibe, it'd float
to Berkeley unassisted. ✉ *2610 Spenard Rd., Spenard* ☎ *907/277–7882*
⊕ *www.organicoasis.com* ✛ *E4.*

$$–$$$ ✕ **Spenard Roadhouse**. Though it pays homage to the roadhouses that dot
AMERICAN   Alaska—and the state's history—Spenard Roadhouse is by no means
just a place to grab a quick meal while traveling. Settle in; order some
wine, a cocktail, a house-made infused vodka, or one of the 30-plus
bourbons on hand, and enjoy. The warm and inviting restaurant features art that will delight the eyes as the menu is a treat for the taste-
buds. Owned by the folks behind super popular mainstays Snow City
Café and Sacks Café, Spenard Roadhouse serves lunch and dinner daily
and a weekend breakfast menu you'll dream about the rest of the week.
The weekend breakfast "hair o'the dog" cocktails alone are worth getting out of bed for. Try the house-infused habanero Bloody Mary. Lunch
and dinner menus offer plates both light and mighty hearty, from a spin-
ach and goat cheese salad to the belly-busting bacon jam burger. (Yes,
bacon jam.) Other options include pizzas, sandwiches, small plates, and
seafood-laden pastas. Of course, you'll need to finish the meal off with
a s'more or a slice of chocolate peanut-butter pie. Better yet: go with
friends and order a few of each. Whether traveling with a pack of people
or solo, service is friendly and accommodating. A perfect complement
to the meal for those who need to catch up on email (or Facebook): the
restaurant offers free Wi-Fi. ✉ *1049 W. Northern Lights Blvd., Spenard*
☎ *907/770–7623* ⊕ *www.spenardroadhouse.com* ✛ *E4.*

GREATER ANCHORAGE

SOUTH ANCHORAGE

$$$$ ✕ **Kincaid Grill**. This out-of-the-way restaurant provides a respite after a
CONTINENTAL   summertime hike or wintertime ski in nearby Kincaid Park. Chef and
owner Al Levinsohn worked his way up through some of Alaska's finest
restaurants, and the experience shines through in his diverse and creative menu. The upscale setting is lively, with old-time jazz spilling from
the speakers, the buzz of conversation, and artistically presented meals.
If traveling solo, consider taking a seat at the wine bar, where you can
sample a microbrew or vintages from around the globe. The menu, with
a focus on Alaska regional cuisine, seafood, and game meats, changes
every few weeks. Menu mainstays include filet mignon, grilled Hawaiian game fish, Alaskan salmon or halibut, and a rich seafood gumbo.

The chocolate bourbon soufflé dessert is well worth the 15-minute wait. ✉ *6700 Jewel Lake Rd., South Anchorage* ☎ *907/243–0507* ⊕ *www. kincaidgrill.com* ⌲ *Reservations essential* ⊙ *Closed Sun. and Mon. No lunch* ✛ *C6.*

$$ ✕**Mexico in Alaska**. Owner Maria-Elena Ball befriends everyone, par-
MEXICAN ticularly young children, at this authentic Mexican restaurant. Favor-
ite dishes include lime-marinated fried chicken, *chilaquiles* (tortilla casserole with mole sauce), and *entremesa de queso* (melted cheese, jalapeños, and onions with homemade tortillas). A vegetarian menu is available. The restaurant is several miles south of downtown, so you'll need to drive or catch the city bus. ✉ *7305 Old Seward Hwy., South Anchorage* ☎ *907/349–1528* ⊕ *www.mexicoinalaska.com* ⊙ *Closed Sun.* ✛ *G6.*

$ ✕**Peanut Farm Sports Grill**. At 20,000 square feet, the mega sports bar has
AMERICAN room for athletic fans of every stripe, from hockey (of course) to mush-
ing and beyond. Peanut Farm has 70 TV screens, pool tables, darts, an outdoor deck on the bank of Campbell Creek, a heated deck overlook-ing the creek, and a large and varied menu. The hot wings are the best in town, and you can slake your thirst with one of 30 draft beers. The Farm opens at 6 for breakfast every day. ✉ *5227 Old Seward Hwy., South Anchorage* ☎ *907/563–3283* ⊕ *www.wemustbenuts.com* ✛ *G6.*

$$$ ✕**Southside Bistro**. Established in South Anchorage, the Southside
CONTINENTAL (another in a long list of great Anchorage restaurants tucked away in
nondescript strip malls) quickly became a local favorite for its artful treatments of Alaska seafood—the fresh scallop and risotto cake is deli-cious, as are veal, venison, and rack of lamb. A hardwood brick oven produces flatbreads and pizzas; cheesecakes, pastries, and ice creams are decorated with hand-painted designs. The wine list includes more than 100 mostly American wines, and the impressive beer menu includes brews made locally as well as beers from the Lower 48 and the rest of the world. If you're watching your budget, grab a seat on the bistro side of the restaurant and order from the bar menu—choose burg-ers, pizzas, appetizers, or one of our favorites, an excellent angel-hair pasta. Reservations are highly recommended. ✉ *1320 Huffman Park Dr., South Anchorage* ☎ *907/348–0088* ⊕ *www.southsidebistro.com* ⊙ *Closed Sun. and Mon.* ✛ *G6.*

WHERE TO STAY

While other cities see new hotels pop up, seemingly, out of nowhere, the Anchorage hotel scene tends to stay rather consistent. Most of the major chains have a place in town, and there are some strong indepen-dents as well. If you're traveling without a car, consider staying Down-town, where the hotels are just steps away from shops and restaurants. Anchorage is also home to many B&Bs. Go that route if you want to hop right into learning about the Alaskan way of life—it's hard to find a local who doesn't have good stories to tell. For a listing of hotels, contact the Anchorage Convention & Visitors Bureau. Reservations are must for the major hotels, especially during the summer months.

For expanded hotel reviews, visit Fodors.com.

DOWNTOWN

$$$$ ▦ **Anchorage Marriott Downtown.** One of Anchorage's biggest lodgings, the brightly decorated Marriott appeals to business travelers, tourists, and corporate clients. **Pros:** one of the newest hotels in town; modern, up-to-date facilities. **Cons:** no free Wi-Fi; pricey valet parking; cruise-ship crowds at times in summer. **TripAdvisor:** "room was very spacious," "comfy and had a nice room," "great location downtown." ⊠ *820 W. 7th Ave., Downtown* ☎ *907/279–8000 or 800/228–9290* ⊕ *www.marriott.com* ⏎ *390 rooms, 3 suites* ⑆ *In-room: Wi-Fi. In-hotel: restaurant, bar, pool, gym, spa, parking* ⊹ *E2.*

> **ADDITIONAL HOTEL INFO**
>
> **Anchorage B&Bs.** Find a range of accommodations on the Web site for Anchorage B&Bs (⊕ *www.anchorage-bnb.com*).

$$–$$$ ▦ **Comfort Inn Ship Creek.** The namesake Ship Creek gurgles past this popular family hotel, a short walk northeast of the Alaska Railroad Historic Depot. **Pros:** pet-friendly; pool; good location for fishing or watching the fisherfolk; free Wi-Fi. **Cons:** if you're not into the fishing opportunity at Ship Creek, the location is a problem; the walk into the downtown area is an uphill climb; rooms are a bit noisy at times. **TripAdvisor:** "location is pretty good," "staff was very nice," "great breakfast and all day coffee." ⊠ *111 Ship Creek Ave., Downtown* ☎ *907/277–6887 or 800/424–6423* ⊕ *www.choicehotels.com/hotels/ak006* ⏎ *88 rooms, 12 suites* ⑆ *In-room: kitchen (some), Wi-Fi. In-hotel: pool, gym, some pets allowed* ❙❂❙ *Breakfast* ⊹ *F1.*

$$–$$$ ▦ **Copper Whale Inn.** A view across Cook Inlet to Sleeping Lady and other mountains is a bonus at this small inn on the edge of Downtown. **Pros:** excellent breakfast; convenient downtown location; responsive and attentive staff. **Cons:** some rooms are small; some shared baths. **TripAdvisor:** "very comfortable and quiet," "great location," "inn is adorable." ⊠ *440 L St., Downtown* ☎ *907/258–7999* ⊕ *www.copperwhale.com* ⏎ *14 rooms, 12 with bath* ⑆ *In-room: no a/c (some), Wi-Fi. In-hotel: business center* ❙❂❙ *Breakfast* ⊹ *A2.*

$$–$$$ ▦ **Extended Stay Deluxe Anchorage—Downtown.** Formerly the Aspen Hotel, the Extended Stay Deluxe features large rooms comfortably furnished with one king or two queen beds, a writing table, 27-inch TV, DVD player, mini-refrigerator, and microwave. **Pros:** very good rates available online; nice facilities for long stays; airport shuttle available; fitness center. **Cons:** fee for Internet and laundry use; parking can be a hassle. **TripAdvisor:** "delicious but limited continental breakfast," "room was clean and basically comfortable," "great location." ⊠ *108 E. 8th Ave., Downtown* ☎ *907/868–1605* ⊕ *www.extendedstay.com* ⏎ *75 rooms, 14 suites* ⑆ *In-room: kitchen, Wi-Fi. In-hotel: pool, gym, business center* ❙❂❙ *Breakfast* ⊹ *F2.*

$$$–$$$$ ▦ **Historic Anchorage Hotel.** The little building has been around since
★   1916, and experienced travelers call it the only hotel in Anchorage with charm: the original sinks and tubs have been restored, and upstairs hallways are lined with Old Anchorage photos. **Pros:** excellent staff; new TVs; very convenient downtown location; kids under 12 are

free. **Cons:** rooms are small; no airport shuttle. **TripAdvisor:** "room was comfy and quiet," "friendly and helpful," "so much history." ⊠ *330 E St., Downtown* ☎ *907/272–4553 or 800/544–0988* ⊕ *www. historicanchoragehotel.com* ⤵ *16 rooms, 10 junior suites* ⌂ *In-room: no a/c, Wi-Fi. In-hotel: gym, some pets allowed* ⍾⃝ *Breakfast* ✛ *C1.*

$$–$$$ ⊡ **Hotel Captain Cook.** Recalling Captain Cook's voyages to Alaska and
★   the South Pacific, dark teak paneling lines the hotel's interior, and a nautical theme continues into the guest rooms. **Pros:** staff very well trained and accommodating; excellent lobby bar. **Cons:** fixtures and furnishings a bit dated; no air-conditioning in rooms; hallways can be dark. ⊠ *4th Ave. and K St., Downtown* ☎ *907/276–6000 or 800/843–1950* ⊕ *www. captaincook.com* ⤵ *547 rooms, 96 suites* ⌂ *In-room: Wi-Fi. In-hotel: 4 restaurants, pool, gym* ✛ *A2.*

$$–$$$ ⊡ **Inlet Tower Hotel & Suites.** Built in 1952 in a residential areas a few
★   blocks south of Downtown, this 14-story building was Alaska's first high-rise; windows overlook either the Chugach Mountains, Cook Inlet, or downtown Anchorage. **Pros:** excellent restaurant on-site; complimentary parking and in-room Wi-Fi; New Sagaya's market is but a stone's throw away; airport shuttle available. **Cons:** downtown attractions are a bit of a hike; hallways narrow, and can be dark. **TripAdvisor:** "formal as an apartment building," "rooms were clean and fairly modern," "well cleaned and maintained." ⊠ *1200 L St., Downtown* ☎ *907/276– 0110 or 800/544–0786* ⊕ *www.inlettower.com* ⤵ *140 rooms, 24 suites* ⌂ *In-room: kitchen (some), Wi-Fi. In-hotel: restaurant, gym, laundry facilities, business center, parking* ✛ *E2.*

$ ⊡ **Oscar Gill House.** Originally built by Gill in the settlement of Knik (north of Anchorage) in 1913, this historic home has been transformed into a comfortable B&B in a quiet neighborhood along Delaney Park Strip, with Downtown attractions a short walk away. **Pros:** great breakfast; very hospitable owners in a bit of Old Anchorage history. **Cons:** shared bath in two of the rooms; walk to downtown might be a bit of a hike for some. **TripAdvisor:** "a beautifully restored historic B&B," "rooms were clean and cozy," "extremely accommodating." ⊠ *1344 W. 10th Ave., Downtown* ☎ *907/279–1344* ⊕ *www.oscargill.com* ⤵ *3 rooms, 1 with bath* ⌂ *In-room: Wi-Fi* ⍾⃝ *Breakfast* ✛ *E2.*

$$$–$$$$ ⊡ **Sheraton Anchorage Hotel & Spa.** A glass-canopy lobby with a jade-tile staircase, acres of new marble, and guest rooms where you can pick up voice mail, iron a suit, and brew your own coffee make this 16-story hotel one of the city's best. **Pros:** nice, modern renovation; great views from the upper floors. **Cons:** fees for parking and Internet access. **TripAdvisor:** "staff was very friendly," "rooms were comfortable," "great workout facility." ⊠ *401 E. 6th Ave., Downtown* ☎ *907/276–8700 or 800/325–3535* ⊕ *www.sheraton.com* ⤵ *370 rooms, 3 suites* ⌂ *In-room: Wi-Fi. In-hotel: 2 restaurants, bar, gym, business center, parking, some pets allowed* ✛ *G2.*

$$$–$$$$ ⊡ **Westmark Anchorage Hotel.** Each comfortable room in this 13-story hotel has a small private balcony and modern furnishings. **Pros:** the restaurant gets high marks; central Downtown location gives you walking access to other great eating spots and tourist attractions; private balconies in every room. **Cons:** noise, both from other rooms and

outside, is a problem; few frills; no airport shuttle. **TripAdvisor:** "beds were comfortable," "great view of the ocean," "good location." ⊠ *720 W. 5th Ave., Downtown* ☎ *907/276–7676 or 800/544–0970* ⊕ *www. westmarkhotels.com* ⤳ *188 rooms, 12 suites* ⚹ *In-room: Wi-Fi. In-hotel: restaurant, bar, gym, parking.*

MIDTOWN

¢ ⚏ **Anchorage Guest House.** Popular with young outdoorsy travelers, this adventure travel accommodation in a residential neighborhood near Downtown has private rooms as well as dorm-style accommodations with bunks (know, though, that all rooms share the same three bathrooms). **Pros:** affordable rooms for adventurous travelers; great chance to meet an eclectic clientele; complimentary Wi-Fi. **Cons:** basic, no-frills accommodations not for everyone; shared baths, even for the regular rooms. **TripAdvisor:** "clean and quiet," "home away from home," "well stocked with quality provisions." ⊠ *2001 Hillcrest Dr., Midtown* ☎ *907/274–0408* ⊕ *www.akhouse.com* ⤳ *3 rooms, 1 dorm room* ⚹ *In-room: kitchen, no TV. In-hotel: laundry facilities, business center* ⦿| *Breakfast* ✛ *D3.*

$$–$$$ ⚏ **Courtyard Anchorage Airport.** Business travelers pack this modern hotel near the airport; some rooms have a whirlpool bath and king-size bed, and all have a coffeemaker, two phones, microwave, refrigerator, and hair dryer. **Pros:** close to airport; free Wi-Fi and airport shuttle. **Cons:** there's a fee for breakfast; location is noisy; not convenient for restaurants and sights. **TripAdvisor:** "clean room with a very comfortable bed," "staff were very attentive," "modern style and great beds." ⊠ *4901 Spenard Rd., Midtown* ☎ *907/245–0322 or 877/729–0197* ⊕ *www.marriott.com* ⤳ *148 rooms, 6 suites* ⚹ *In-room: Wi-Fi. In-hotel: restaurant, pool, gym* ✛ *C6.*

$$$$ ⚏ **Embassy Suites Anchorage.** Opened in June 2008, this is the latest addition to the Anchorage upscale hotel inventory; in addition to the long list of amenities, a hot cooked-to-order breakfast and an afternoon manager's reception featuring complimentary hors d'oeuvres and cocktails are both included. **Pros:** top-of-the-line facilities; freebies at manager's reception; great breakfast. **Cons:** neighborhood is a high-traffic area; only some rooms have a (distant) mountain view. **TripAdvisor:** "staff were very friendly and helpful," "great service and room," "very clean and comfortable." ⊠ *600 E. Benson Blvd., Midtown* ☎ *907/332–7000 or 800/362–2779* ⊕ *embassysuites1.hilton.com* ⤳ *169 suites* ⚹ *In-hotel: restaurant, bar, pool, gym, laundry facilities, business center, parking* ✛ *G4.*

$$$$ ⚏ **Hampton Inn.** Midway between the airport and Downtown, the Hampton has all the standard features, and a few that are better than average, such as designer furnishings, an indoor swimming pool, and a spa. **Pros:** shuttle will take you into town; great beds; excellent breakfast. **Cons:** some rooms near the pool can be noisy and smell of chlorine; basic chain-hotel ambience. **TripAdvisor:** "quiet hotel with helpful and friendly staff," "great location," "clean and spacious with modern décor." ⊠ *4301 Credit Union Dr., Midtown* ☎ *907/550–7000*

5

or 800/426–7866 ⊕ *www. hamptoninn.com* ⥴ *97 rooms* ☒ *In-room: Wi-Fi. In-hotel: pool, gym, spa, business center* ⏚ *Breakfast* ✛ *F6.*

$$ ⏚ **Long House Alaskan Hotel.** Five minutes from the airport, this hotel consists of three log-covered two-story buildings; rooms are large and comfortable (though they won't win any design awards). **Pros:** free shuttle; close to airport; friendly staff. **Cons:** no elevator to second-floor rooms; pretty basic amenities. **TripAdvisor:** "location is very good," "old but seemed pretty clean," "staff was helpful and friendly." ⊠ *4335 Wisconsin St., Midtown* ☎ *907/243–2133 or 800/243–2133* ⊕ *www. longhousehotel.com* ⥴ *54 rooms, 3 suites* ☒ *In-room: Wi-Fi. In-hotel: parking* ⏚ *Breakfast* ✛ *C6.*

$$$$ ⏚ **Millennium Anchorage Hotel.** Perched on the shore of Lake Spenard, the
★ extensively renovated Millennium Anchorage Hotel is one of the city's best spots to watch planes come and go; the lobby resembles a hunting lodge with its stone fireplace, trophy heads, and mounted fish on every wall. **Pros:** close to the airport; old Alaska hunting-lodge feel; an airport shuttle is available. **Cons:** furnishings and facilities getting worn; airplane noise from Lake Hood can be a problem in summer; fee for Wi-Fi use. **TripAdvisor:** "staff is very nice," "beds were comfortable," "food and drinks were really good." ⊠ *4800 Spenard Rd., Midtown* ☎ *907/243–2300 or 800/544–0553* ⊕ *www.millennium-hotels.com/ anchorage* ⥴ *243 rooms, 4 suites* ☒ *In-room: Internet. In-hotel: restaurant, bar, gym, spa, business center, parking, some pets allowed* ✛ *F3.*

¢–$ ⏚ **Qupqugiaq Inn.** A bland, boxy exterior disguises this cross between a motel and a hostel with an unpronounceable name; the interior architecture of "Q Inn" is distinctive, with flowing, asymmetrical curves, handmade tiles, handcrafted furniture, and an international theme in each room. **Pros:** good value for your travel dollar; unique architecture and ambience; family-friendly hostel rooms. **Cons:** eco-hippie vibe could be a problem for some; room quality varies considerably. **TripAdvisor:** "rooms were clean," "very warm innkeepers," "soft beds but small rooms." ⊠ *640 W. 36th Ave., Midtown* ☎ *907/563–5633* ⊕ *www.qupq. com* ⥴ *25 rooms, 12 with bath* ☒ *In-room: no a/c, Wi-Fi. In-hotel: restaurant, business center* ✛ *F5.*

$$$$ ⏚ **SpringHill Suites Anchorage Midtown.** Spacious one-room suites have separate living and sleeping areas and either a king bed or two double beds with a pullout sofa, plus microwave, mini-refrigerator, and flat-screen TV. **Pros:** complimentary parking; 24-hour airport shuttle. **Cons:** small laundry facilities for such a large hotel; most restaurants within easy walking distance are national chains. **TripAdvisor:** "staff is very friendly," "beds were comfortable," "very clean rooms." ⊠ *3401 A St., Midtown* ☎ *907/562–3247 or 877/729–0197* ⊕ *www.springhillsuites. com* ⥴ *101 suites* ☒ *In-room: Wi-Fi. In-hotel: pool, gym, laundry facilities* ⏚ *Breakfast* ✛ *E5.*

GREATER ANCHORAGE

EAST ANCHORAGE

$ 🛏 **Camai Bed & Breakfast.** This elegant B&B is Anchorage's oldest; two of the suites have private entries and plenty of space for families. **Pros:** private entries a real plus; quiet residential neighborhood; very experienced hosts. **Cons:** a relatively long way from Downtown restaurants; lack of credit-card payment option can be a bother. **TripAdvisor:** "hosts were very welcoming," "breakfast was great and beautifully presented," "spacious and clean." ✉ *3838 Westminster Way, East Anchorage* 📞 *907/333–2219* 🌐 *www.camaibnb.com* 🛏 *3 suites* 🛁 *In-room: no a/c, Wi-Fi. In-hotel: business center* 🚫 *No credit cards* 🍴 *Breakfast* ✚ *H5.*

NIGHTLIFE AND THE ARTS

NIGHTLIFE

Anchorage does not shut down when it gets dark. Bars here—and throughout Alaska—open early (in the morning) and close as late as 3 am on weekends. There's a ban on smoking in bars and bingo parlors, as well as in restaurants. The listings in the *Anchorage Daily News* entertainment section, published on Friday, and in the free weekly *Anchorage Press* (🌐 *www.anchoragepress.com*) range from concerts and theater performances to movies and a roundup of nightspots featuring live music.

BARS AND NIGHTCLUBS

Though locals say it isn't what it used to be (but, really, what is?), **Bernie's Bungalow Lounge** (✉ *626 D St., Downtown* 📞 *907/276–8808*) still pulls in plenty of twentysomethings looking to dance, drink, and make eyes at the cutie across the room. The best spot in the house: the outdoor patio.

Fodor's Choice ★ **Chilkoot Charlie's** (✉ *2435 Spenard Rd., Spenard* 📞 *907/272–1010* 🌐 *www.koots.com*), a rambling timber building with sawdust floors, multiple bars, three dance floors, loud music (rock or swing bands and DJs) nightly, two DJs every Thursday, Friday, and Saturday, and rowdy customers, is where young Alaskans go to get crazy. This legendary bar has many unusual nooks and crannies, including a room filled with Russian artifacts where vodka is the drink of choice, plus a reconstructed version of Alaska's infamous Birdhouse Bar. If you haven't been to 'Koots, you haven't seen Anchorage nightlife at its wildest.

Lots of old-timers favor the dark bar of **Club Paris** (✉ *417 W. 5th Ave., Downtown* 📞 *907/277–6332* 🌐 *www.clubparisrestaurant.com*). The Paris mural and French street lamps hanging behind the bar have lost some luster, but there's still a faithful clientele. The jukebox favors swing. **Rumrunners** (✉ *501 W. 4th Ave., Downtown* 📞 *907/278–4493* 🌐 *www.rumrunnersak.com*) is right across from Old City Hall in the center of town. A pub-grub menu brings the lunch crowd, but when evening comes the big dance floor gets packed as DJs spin the tunes. A trendy place for the dressy "in" crowd, the bar at **Simon & Seafort's Saloon & Grill**

STOP FOR A MINUTE

First-timers to Anchorage are often surprised by the number of places one can grab a cup of Joe around town. Yes, it's true: Anchorage residents easily rival Seattleites for their devotion to java. But, of course, some cups of coffee are better than others. Some places to start your day (or hang out between adventures): a local favorite since opening its first spot in 1986, **Kaladi Brothers Coffee** has espresso, lattes, baked goods, and more at 10 locations around town, most with free Wi-Fi access. For a list, go to the Web site. ⊠ *621 W. 6th Ave.* ☎ *907/277-1881* ⊕ *www.kaladi.com.*

In South Anchorage, coffee's next wave is brewing. **SteamDot Coffee**

and **Espresso Lab** treats coffee lovers to quite the coffee brewing show at its "slow bar." This is not the place to go if you're in the mood for syrup-heavy espresso drinks. SteamDot is all about the flavor of coffee. ⊠ *10950 O'Malley Center* ☎ *907/344-4422* ⊕ *www.steamdot.com.*

If you prefer the focus of your coffee break to be on the baked goods, pop into **Alaska Cake Studio** downtown. From creative cupcakes—the flavor of the month always surprises—to cookies, croissants, and, of course, cakes, sweet treat fans can't go wrong. ⊠ *608 W. 4th Ave.* ☎ *907/272-3995* ⊕ *www.alaskacakestudio.com.*

(⊠ *420 L St., Downtown* ☎ *907/274-3502* ⊕ *www.simonandseaforts. com*) has stunning views of Cook Inlet, a special single-malt scotch menu, and a wide selection of imported beers. **Snow Goose Restaurant** (⊠ *717 W. 3rd Ave., Downtown* ☎ *907/277-7727* ⊕ *www.alaskabeers. com*) is a good place to unwind with a beer inside or on the airy outside deck overlooking Cook Inlet. There's decent food, too.

GAY AND LESBIAN BARS

Anchorage's gay nightlife centers on a pair of bars, both of which attract a mixed crowd. **Mad Myrna's** (⊠ *530 E. 5th Ave., Downtown* ☎ *907/ 276-9762* ⊕ *www.alaska.net/~madmyrna*) has country line dancing Wednesday, karaoke Thursday, and drag shows (and more karaoke) every Friday. The **Raven** (⊠ *708 E. 4th Ave., Downtown* ☎ *907/276-9672*) is a neighborhood hangout where you'll meet regulars over a game of billiards or darts.

LIVE MUSIC

See the "Play" section in Friday editions of the *Anchorage Daily News* for complete listings of upcoming concerts and other performances, or get the same entertainment information online at ⊕ *www.adn.com.*

Chilkoot Charlie's (⇨ *see Bars and Nightclubs*) is an exceptionally popular party place, with live music every night of the week. Fans of salsa, merengue, and other music crowd the dance floor at the downtown **Club Soraya** (⊠ *333 W. 4th Ave., Downtown* ☎ *907/276-0670* ⊕ *www.akswing.com/clubsoraya.htm*). There are dance classes several nights a week, followed by live bands. One of Anchorage's favorite bars, **Humpy's Great Alaskan Alehouse** (⊠ *610 W. 6th Ave., Downtown* ☎ *907/276-2337* ⊕ *www.humpys.com*) serves up rock, blues, and folk five nights a week, including open mike on Monday, along with dozens of microbrews (more than 40 beers are on tap) and surprisingly tasty pub grub—we especially like the smoked salmon spread. Trivia buffs should head to Humpy's on Tuesday nights for the weekly pub quiz.

The Tap Root. Locals say this is one of the best places in town for live music. Folk, bluegrass, and jam bands rule the stage most nights. Beer and whiskey fans will rejoice over the extensive menu of their favorite beverages. The club, formerly in South Anchorage, recently tripled in size when it moved into the space that used to house the now-defunct Fly By Night Club. The Tap Root has a full bar and serves a better-than-expected menu of sandwiches, salads, bar snacks, and entrées including halibut tacos and baby back ribs. ✉ *3300 Spenard Rd., Spenard* ☎ *907/345–0282* ⊕ *www.taprootalaska.com.*

> ### MUSIC ALFRESCO
>
> On most summertime Saturdays **open-air concerts** (✉ *E St. and W. 4th Ave., Downtown*) are presented in Peratrovich Park. A range of performers plays at the **Anchorage Market and Festival** (✉ *3rd Ave. and E St., Downtown* ☎ *907/272-5634* ⊕ *www. anchoragemarkets.com*) every Saturday and Sunday from late May to mid-September.

THE ARTS

Anchorage often surprises visitors with its variety—and high quality—of cultural activities. In addition to top-name touring groups and performers, a sampling of local productions, including provocative theater, children's shows, improvisational troupes, Buddhist lectures, photography exhibits, poetry readings, and Native Alaskan dance performances, is always going on around town. The Friday entertainment section of the *Anchorage Daily News* is packed with events and activities. **CenterTix** (☎ *907/263–2787 or 877/278–7849* ⊕ *alaskapac.centertix.net/*) sells tickets by phone or from their Web site for a wide variety of cultural events throughout South Central Alaska.

The **Alaska Center for the Performing Arts** (✉ *621 W. 6th Ave., at G St., Downtown* ☎ *907/263–2900* ⊕ *www.myalaskacenter.com*) has four theaters. The arts complex is home to many local performing groups and also showcases traveling production companies. The lobby box office (weedays 9–5, Saturday noon–5) sells tickets to the productions and is a good all-around source of cultural information.

FILM

The popular **Bear Tooth Theatrepub** (✉ *1230 W. 27th Ave., Spenard* ☎ *907/276–4200*) screens films—from art house to blockbuster—for only $3.50 ($5 for reserved seating) and also serves tasty pizzas, sandwiches, burritos, salads, and beer while you watch.

OPERA AND CLASSICAL MUSIC

The **Anchorage Opera** (☎ *907/279–2557* ⊕ *www.anchorageopera. org*) produces three operas during its November through March season. The **Anchorage Symphony Orchestra** (☎ *907/274–8668* ⊕ *www.*

Continued on page 237

THE GLORIOUS AND RELENTLESS MIDNIGHT SUN

The side-lit afternoons seeping into late evening. The unforgettable sunsets streaking the sky with swaths of neon. The 9 PM golf tee offs and midnight baseball games. The black-out curtains and sleep masks. The bloodshot eyes. The madness of it all: Alaska's tilted life.

The light (and lack thereof) is one of Alaska's most dramatic characteristics. Long summer days goad visitors to sightsee well into the evening, while record-breaking vegetables (read: cabbages the size of coffee tables) grow in the fields. The feeble, or just plain absent, winter sun allows snow to recharge glaciers while the aurora borealis (a.k.a. the northern lights) dances above hibernating bears and humans alike.

Remember that the farther north you go in Alaska, the more pronounced the midnight sun will be. If you make it to Barrow, you'll experience nightless days in summer. Heading south means a less extreme case of the midnight sun, but often just as much revelry celebrating its presence. Summertime simply has a different feeling in Alaska—enjoy the local fairs and festivals, and the stunning mixture of persistent daylight, snow-capped mountains, and miles of vibrant wildland.

(above) A brave Midnight Sun runner
(right) How does *your* garden grow?

THE MIDNIGHT SUN: HOW IT WORKS

The Earth spins on a slightly tilted axis as it rotates around the sun. The northern hemisphere is tilted toward the sun in summer and away from it in winter. So how does this explain Alaska's midnight sun? The globe's most northern areas, including much of Alaska, are tilted so far toward the sun in summer that there's continuous light.

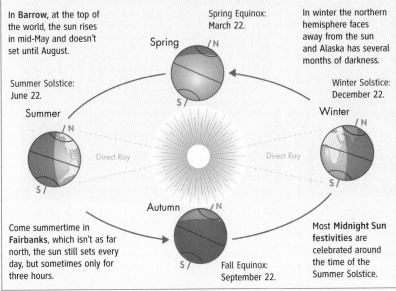

In **Barrow**, at the top of the world, the sun rises in mid-May and doesn't set until August.

Spring Equinox: March 22.

In winter the northern hemisphere faces away from the sun and Alaska has several months of darkness.

Summer Solstice: June 22.

Winter Solstice: December 22.

Come summertime in **Fairbanks**, which isn't as far north, the sun still sets every day, but sometimes only for three hours.

Fall Equinox: September 22.

Most **Midnight Sun** festivities are celebrated around the time of the Summer Solstice.

TIPS FROM AN ALASKAN

Coping with the Midnight Sun

- Close your shades a few hours before bedtime. Bring a sleep mask or use the black-out curtains in your hotel room!

- Bring antihistamines to soothe the mosquito bites we *promise* you'll get—the added bonus is the drowsiness.

- You can always count sheep. Or count microbrews! Alaska has many to enjoy, including Silver Gulch, Sleeping Lady, Kodiak Brewery, and Moose's Tooth.

- If all else fails, go out and enjoy the eerie light. Many people find that they simply need less sleep in summer.

Surviving the Polar Winter

- Get what sunlight you can. Make sure you're up and at 'em whenever the sun is.

- Take your vitamins, especially vitamin D, and eat plenty of fruit.

- Some Alaskans go that extra step and visit tanning salons to boost their mood—and, of course, for a little color!

- Fool your body into thinking the sun is out: sip your morning coffee near a lamp (preferably full-spectrum).

- Did we mention Alaska's many excellent microbrews?

MIDNIGHT SUN REVELRY

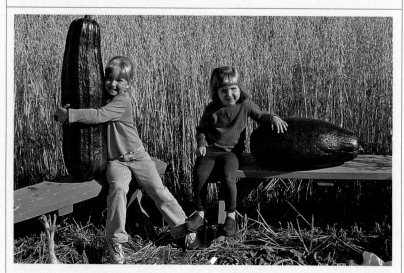

During the peak of the midnight sun season, June and early July, there's almost no end to the special activities and festivals celebrating the light. It's a good thing, too—you may have trouble falling asleep!

■ Taking place the Saturday closest to the summer solstice, the **Mayor's Marathon and Half Marathon in Anchorage** attract runners from all over the country. (⊕ www.mayorsmarathon.com)

■ The much less formal 10-km **Midnight Sun Run is held in Fairbanks** every June on the weekend closest to the summer solstice. The run starts at 10 pm. (⊕ fairbanks-alaska.com/midnight-sun-run.htm)

■ The **midnight sun baseball game in Fairbanks** is the best-known midnight sun activity in Alaska. The Alaska Goldpanners are the stars of the Alaska League, comprised of college athletes from around the country. Every summer solstice, the

Goldpanners host the "high noon at midnight" classic, a tradition since 1906. The first pitch is thrown at 10:30 pm, and the entire game is played without the use of artificial lights. (They haven't worked since they were struck by lightning years ago!) (⊕ www.goldpanners.com)

■ If you'd rather steer clear of festivals and find a spot of your own, **drive out of Fairbanks** along Steese Highway or Chena Hot Springs Road for the unforgettable nighttime view.

■ Almost every Alaskan town has a special event on or near the summer solstice, but one of the best is the **Nome Midnight Sun Festival,** which celebrates 22 hours of direct sunlight with parades, barbecues, and folk music. (⊕ www.visitnomealaska.org)

■ The **Alaska State Fair** runs for 12 days before Labor Day in the town of Palmer, 40 mi northeast of Anchorage. Check out the giant midnight sun–grown vegetables on display and colorful vending booths selling an array of goods from cookies to jewelry. (⊕ www.alaskastatefair.org)

anchoragesymphony.org) performs classical concerts October through April. The box office of the Alaska Center for the Performing Arts sells tickets for both.

THEATER

The **Alaska Center for the Performing Arts** stages major theater performances, and hosts the Anchorage Opera and the Anchorage Symphony Orchestra. The **Anchorage Community Theater** (⊠ *1133 E. 70th Ave.* ☎ *907/344–4713* ⊕ *actalaska. org*) has a year-around schedule of locally produced plays, and also offers training for prospective thespians of all ages and skill levels. **Cyrano's Off-Center Playhouse** (⊠ *4th Ave. and D St., Downtown* ☎ *907/274–2599* ⊕ *www.cyranos. org*) mounts innovative productions in a cozy theater connected to a namesake café and bookstore. **Out North Contemporary Art House** (⊠ *1325 Primrose St., just west of Bragaw Rd. off DeBarr Rd., East Anchorage* ☎ *907/279–3800* ⊕ *www.outnorth.org*), whose productions are thought-provoking and, at times, controversial, often earns critical acclaim from local reviewers. Student productions from the **University of Alaska Anchorage Theater** (⊠ *3211 Providence Dr., East Anchorage* ☎ *907/786–4849* ⊕ *theatre.uaa.alaska.edu*) are timely and well done. The theater is intimate, with seating on three sides.

SHOPPING

Stock up for your travels around Alaska in Anchorage, where there's no sales tax. The weekend markets are packed with Alaskan-made products of all types, and you're likely to meet local artisans.

MALLS AND DEPARTMENT STORES

Anchorage's **5th Avenue Mall** occupies a city block at 5th Avenue and A Street, and contains dozens of stores, including nationally known brands like JC Penney and Banana Republic, and a few local stores, like Alaska Wild Berry Products, perfect for one-stop gift shopping. Just across 6th Avenue, and connected by a skywalk to the 5th Avenue Mall, is Alaska's only **Nordstrom**. The city's largest shopping mall, **Dimond Center**, is on the south end of town at Dimond Boulevard and Old Seward Highway. In addition to dozens of shops, Dimond Center has a movie theater and an ice-skating rink. Nearby are several big-box discount stores, including Costco, Best Buy, and Walmart.

MARKETS

Fodor's Choice   On weekends throughout the summer the **Anchorage Market and Festival**
★   (☎ 907/272–5634 ⊕ *www.anchoragemarkets.com*) opens for business
(and loads of fun) in the parking lot at 3rd Avenue and E Street. More
than 300 vendors offer Alaskan-made crafts, ethnic imports, and deliciously fattening food. Stock up on birch candy and salmon jerky to
snack on while traveling or as perfect made-in-Alaska gifts for friends
back home. The open-air markets run from mid-May to mid-September,
weekends 10–6. A smaller market sells local produce and crafts July
through August, on Wednesday from 9 to 4, at Northway Mall in East
Anchorage.

SPECIALTY SHOPS

ART

The Anchorage **First Friday Arts Walk** is a popular monthly (and year-
round) event, with 15 or so galleries offering a chance to sample hors
d'oeuvres while looking over the latest works by regional artists.

    Artic Rose Gallery (✉ *420 L St., Downtown* ☎ *907/279–3911* ⊕ *www.
articrosegallery.com*) is in the same building as Simon and Seafort's
restaurant. Alaska's oldest gallery, **Artique** (✉ *314 G St., Downtown*
☎ *907/277–1663* ⊕ *www.artiqueltd.com*), sells paintings, prints, and
jewelry by prominent Alaskan artists. The **International Gallery of Contemporary Art** (✉ *427 D St., Downtown* ☎ *907/279–1116* ⊕ *www.
igcaalaska.org*) is Anchorage's premier fine-arts gallery, with changing
exhibits monthly. **4th Avenue Market Place** (✉ *411 W. 4th Ave., Downtown*) in Ship Creek Center houses several shops that showcase and
sell Alaska Native crafts, including exquisite handwoven baskets and
delicately-beaded jewelry. Two you shouldn't miss: **Two Spirits Gallery**
and **One People Gallery.** Many artists work on-site, so the Market Place
should be considered a go-to for anybody interested in meeting the
people behind the crafts.

BOOKS AND MUSIC

Easily the largest independent bookstore in Alaska, **Title Wave Books**
(✉ *1360 W. Northern Lights Blvd., Midtown* ☎ *907/278–9283 or*
888/598–9283 ⊕ *www.wavebooks.com*) fills a 30,000-square-foot
space at the other end of the REI strip mall. The shelves are filled with
used titles across more than 1,600 categories and a large section of
Alaska-focused books; the staff is very knowledgeable. **Kaladi Brothers
Coffee** (✉ *1340 W. Northern Lights Blvd., Midtown* ☎ *907/258–9283*
⊕ *www.kaladi.com*), right near Title Wave Books, will caffeinate you
and provide free Wi-Fi access to boot.

GIFTS

★   Several downtown shops sell quality Native Alaskan artwork, but the
best buys can be found in the gift shop at the **Alaska Native Medical Center**
(✉ *4315 Diplomacy Dr., at Tudor and Bragaw Rds., East Anchorage*
☎ *907/563–2662*), which is open weekdays 10–2 and 11–2 on the first
and third Saturday of the month. It doesn't take credit cards.

The gift shop at **Alaska Native Heritage Center** (✉ 8800 Heritage Center Dr., Glenn Hwy. at Muldoon Rd., East Anchorage ☎ 907/330–8000 or 800/315–6608 ⊕ www.alaskanative.net) sells Native crafts. **Laura Wright Alaskan Parkys,** now owned by Wright's granddaughter Sheila Ezelle, an Alaskan Inupiaq, sells distinctive Eskimo-style "parkys" (parkas) and will custom sew one for you. They're available at **Heritage Gifts** (✉ 333 W. 4th Ave., No. 227, at D St., Downtown ☎ 907/274–4215). **Oomingmak** (✉ 6th Ave. and H St., Downtown ☎ 907/272–9225 or 888/360–9665 ⊕ www.qiviut.com), a Native-owned cooperative, sells items made of qiviut, the warm undercoat of the musk ox. Scarves, shawls, and tunics are knitted in traditional patterns.

Although furs may not be to everyone's taste or ethics, a number of Alaska fur companies have stores and factories in Anchorage. One of the city's largest and best-known furriers is **David Green Master Furrier** (✉ 130 W. 4th Ave., Downtown ☎ 907/277–9595 ⊕ www.davidgreenfurs.com). **Alaska Fur Exchange** (✉ 4417 Old Seward Hwy., Midtown ☎ 907/563–3877 ⊕ www.alaskafurexchange.com) has a large Midtown store that sells both furs and Native artwork.

JEWELRY

The **Kobuk Valley Jade Co.** (✉ Olympic Circle, Girdwood ☎ 907/783–2764), at the base of Mt. Alyeska, sells hand-polished jade pieces as well as Native masks, baskets, and jewelry.

SPORTS AND OUTDOOR EQUIPMENT

If you get to Alaska and discover you've left some critical camping or outdoor recreation gear behind, **REI** (✉ 1200 W. Northern Lights Blvd., Spenard ☎ 907/272–4565 ⊕ www.rei.com) rents camping, skiing, and paddling equipment. It also gives weekly seminars on season-specific outdoors subjects, and the salespeople are very knowledgeable about local conditions and activities, and the gear required to get you out and back safely. **Sportsman's Warehouse** (✉ 8681 Old Seward Hwy., South Anchorage ☎ 907/644–1400 ⊕ www.sportsmanswarehouse.com) is a big-box outdoors store with all manner of fishing, hiking, and camping gear. Prices are lower than at most places in town, and the selection is great, but you won't find the personal attention and knowledgeable staff that the more high-end places specialize in.

Mt. View Sports Center. If you're looking for brand names like Abel, Sims, Filson, Patagonia, Kimber, and Mountain Hardwear, Mt. View is your place. It is pretty much fly-fishing central in Anchorage, and you can find expert advice and guidance for your prospective fishing and hunting adventures. There's also an excellent book section that covers all sorts

Finger Lake Checkpoint. Sled dogs start the Iditarod in Anchorage and stop here, 194 mi into the 1,150-mi trek.

of outdoor activities in Alaska. ✉ *3838 Old Seward Hwy., Midtown* ☎ *907/563–8600* ⊕ *www.mtviewsports.com*

Alaska Mountaineering & Hiking. This place is the go-to specialist for any gear having to do with, aptly, mountaineering or hiking. Whether you're setting out on a series of day hikes or you're planning a serious climb, the knowledgable staff can help you choose the right equipment for the task. ✉ *2633 Spenard Rd., Spenard* ☎ *907/272–1811* ⊕ *www.alaskamountaineering.com.*

SIDE TRIPS FROM ANCHORAGE

GIRDWOOD

40 mi southeast of Anchorage.

A ski resort, summer vacation spot, and home to an eclectic collection of locals, the town of Girdwood sits in a deep valley and is surrounded by tall mountains on three sides as well as Turnagain Arm, one of the most photogenic sites in South Central. Originally called Glacier City (a name we're rather fond of), Girdwood got its start as a gold-mining town. The town was renamed for James Girdwood, an Irish linen merchant who had four gold claims. But the name wasn't the only thing that changed over the years; the town itself was moved 2½ mi from its original site after the 1964 earthquake.

Today Girdwood's main attraction is the Mt. Alyeska Ski Resort, the largest ski area in Alaska. Besides enjoying the obvious winter

SLED DOG RACES AND WINTER FUN

World-championship races are run in February, with three consecutive 25-mi heats through downtown Anchorage, out into the foothills, and back. People line the route with cups of coffee in hand to cheer on their favorite mushers.

The three-day races are part of the annual **Fur Rendezvous Festival**, one of the largest winter festivals in the United States. Other attractions include a snow-sculpture competition, car races, Eskimo blanket toss (a holdover from earlier days when dozens of people would team up to grasp a round walrus hide blanket and launch a hunter high into the air, trampoline-style, in an effort to spot distant seals, walrus, and whales), dog weight–pulling contests (where canines of all breeds and sizes compete to see which can pull the most weight piled on a sled), a carnival, and even snowshoe softball. Fur Rondy (as the Fur Rendezvous Festival is more commonly known) events take place from late February to the start of the Iditarod in early March. The Fur Rondy office (⊠ *400 D St., No. 200, Downtown* ☎ *907/274–1270* ⊕ *www.furrondy.net*) has a guide to the festival's events.

In March mushers and their dogs compete in the 1,150-mi **Iditarod Trail Sled Dog Race** (☎ *907/376–5155; 800/545–6874 Iditarod Trail Headquarters* ⊕ *www.iditarod. com*). The race commemorates the delivery of serum to Nome by dog mushers during the diphtheria epidemic of 1925. The serum run was the inspiration for the animated family film *Balto*. Dog teams leave downtown Anchorage and wind through the Alaska Range, across the Interior, out to the Bering Sea coast, and on to Nome. Depending on weather and trail conditions, winners can complete the race in nine days (⇨ *see Alaska's Well-Worn Trail Close-Up box*).

attractions, you can hike up the mountain, rent a bike, or visit several restaurants (our favorite is Seven Glaciers) and gift shops open all year. Girdwood is wetter than Anchorage; it often rains or snows here while the sun shines to the north.

GETTING HERE AND AROUND

Though it's 40 mi from Ted Stevens Anchorage International Airport, consider adding extra time if you make the drive to Girdwood—but not because of any traffic concerns. The drive down the New Seward Highway is stunning—oh, that Turnagain Arm—and photo ops abound. Other options include a ride on the **Alaska Railroad**'s *Coastal Classic* or *Glacier Discovery* trains (☎ *907/265–2494 or 800/544–0552* ⊕ *www. alaskarailroad.com*), or reserve a spot on the Magic Bus (☎ *907/230–6773* ⊕ *www.themagicbus.com*), which runs between Anchorage and Girdwood year-round. Alyeska also runs a ski and snowboard bus from Anchorage to Girdwood weekend days throughout ski season; purchase tickets online at www.alyeskaresort.com, at the Carrs/Safeway on Huffman Road, or at an Alyeska Resort ticket office. Once in town, you'll need to rely on your own car, the Alyeska Resort shuttle service, or foot power.

WHEN TO GO

Though Girdwood is best known for its winter ski activities, there's plenty to do year-round. The town's restaurants remain popular with locals—snow or no snow—and the area offers some of Anchorage's best hiking trails, fishing, and much more.

EXPLORING

Girdwood Center for Visual Arts. Though you'll go to Girdwood to ski or hike, you'll end up spending time perusing the crafts and artwork at this non-profit co-op gallery. With pieces from 40 atists on display, there's plenty to look at—and you might end up taking care of any gift needs (from the trip or for the holidays) in one fell swoop. ⊠ *Olympic Mountain Loop, Girdwood* ☎ *907/783–3209* ⊕ *www.gcvaonline.org* ⊘ *Closed Mon. and Tues.*

WHERE TO EAT

¢–$

AMERICAN

✕ **The Bake Shop.** The atmosphere is vintage 1975 at this old-time Girdwood favorite where you order at the counter and wait for servers to bring your meal. Breakfasts are filling, with piles of sourdough pancakes, fluffy omelets (we heartily recommend the farmer's omelet), and homemade pastries. Skiers and snowboarders drop by for a fast lunch or dinner of homemade soups, sandwiches, or garden-fresh pizzas. Get a loaf of the hearty sourdough or one of the huge cinnamon buns to go. Dine out front in summer, surrounded by hanging baskets filled with begonias, lobelia, and impatiens. ⊠ *Olympic Mountain Loop, Girdwood* ☎ *907/783–2831* ⊕ *www.thebakeshop.com* ⊟ *No credit cards* ⊘ *Sun.–Fri. 7–7, Sat. 7–8* ✛ *G6.*

$$$$

SOUTHERN

✕ **Double Musky Inn.** Anchorage residents say eating at this award-winning spot is well worth the one-hour drive south to Girdwood and the inevitable wait for dinner—you can usually find a spot at the bar, order an appetizer while you wait, and choose from the extensive martini menu or the local draft beers. It's very noisy, and the interior is completely covered with tacky art and Mardi Gras souvenirs of all types, but the windows frame views of huge Sitka spruce trees. The diverse menu mixes hearty Cajun-style meals with such favorites as garlic seafood pasta, rack of lamb, French pepper steak, and lobster kebabs. For dessert lovers, the biggest attraction is the gooey, chocolate-rich Double Musky pie. The restaurant and lounge are smoke-free. ⊠ *Crow Creek Rd., Girdwood* ☎ *907/783–2822* ⊕ *www.doublemuskyinn.com* ⌁ *Reservations not accepted* ⊘ *Closed Mon. and late Oct.–Dec. 10. No lunch* ✛ *G6.*

$$$$

CONTINENTAL

✕ **Seven Glaciers.** A 60-passenger aerial tram (free with dinner reservations, otherwise $18 round-trip) carries you to this refined yet relaxing mountainside Girdwood restaurant perched at the 2,300-foot level on Mt. Alyeska. The comfortable dining room overlooks seven glaciers. The kitchen, led by Chef Jason Porter, creates an ever-changing menu that relies, as much as possible, on local produce, seafood, and meat. À la carte prices are high; consider the six-course chef's tasting menu ($85 per person) instead. The restaurant also caters to special diets and offers a gluten-free menu. Both tram and restaurant are wheelchair accessible. ⊠ *Hotel Alyeska, 1000 Arlberg Rd., Girdwood*

☎ *907/754-2237* ⊕ *www.alyeskaresort.com* ⌂ *Reservations essential* ⊙ *Closed Mon.-Wed., Thurs., dinner only. Nov.-May* ⊹ *G6.*

WHERE TO STAY

For expanded hotel reviews, visit Fodors.com.

$ ⊡ **The Carriage House.** This Girdwood B&B is across from the Double Musky restaurant and close to Alyeska Resort's downhill ski slopes. **Pros:** elegant furnishings; very nice breakfast spread. **Cons:** location can be a bit remote for some; restaurant traffic is bothersome. ⊠ *Mi 0.2, Crow Creek Rd., Girdwood* ☎ *907/783-9464 or 888/961-9464* ⊕ *www.thecarriagehousebandb.com* ↩ *4 rooms* ⌂ *In-room: kitchen, Internet* ⏐⊙⏐ *Breakfast* ⊹ *G6.*

$$$$ ⊡ **The Hotel Alyeska.** Lush forests surround this large and luxurious
Fodor's Choice hotel at the base of Alyeska Ski Resort in Girdwood, an hour south of
★ Anchorage. **Pros:** great views; rooms remodeled in 2007. **Cons:** smallish rooms; service can be uneven. **TripAdvisor:** "very good restaurants and friendly staff," "beautiful views," "rooms were extremely comfortable and large." ⊠ *1000 Arlberg Rd., Box 249, Girdwood* ☎ *907/754–1111 or 800/880–3880* ⊕ *www.alyeskaresort.com* ↩ *304 rooms, 12 suites* ⌂ *In-room: safe. In-hotel: 5 restaurants, bar, pool, gym* ⊹ *G6.*

SPORTS AND THE OUTDOORS

Alaska Backcountry Access. This outfitter zips people out of town for jetboat rides up Twentymile River, kayaking, and much more. Families with kids six and over might enjoy the slightly adventurous Girdwood Trekker trips, a naturalist-led day trip that includes a hike, panning for gold, and a cable hand tram trip across Glacier Creek. ⊠ *New Girdwood Townsite* ☎ *907/783–3600 or 800/783–3005* ⊕ *www. akback.com.*

Alyeska Resort. Located 40 mi south of Anchorage in Girdwood, Alyeska Resort is Alaska's largest and best-known downhill ski resort. A high-speed quad lift gets you up the mountain faster. The resort encompasses 1,000 acres of terrain for all skill levels. Ski rentals are available at the resort. Local ski and snowboard guides teach classes on the mountain and offer helicopter ski and snowboard treks into more remote sites in the nearby Chugach and Kenai ranges. ☎ *907/754–7669* ⊕ *www. alyeskaresort.com.*

Chugach Powder Guides. Founded in 1997, this helicopter-ski and Sno-Cat operation focuses on backcountry skiing and snowboarding in the Chugach Range out of Girdwood and Seward; Alaska Range adventures are also featured. When you see films of extreme helicopter skiing in Alaska, it's usually these guys. ☎ *907/783–4354* ⊕ *www. chugachpowderguides.com.*

5

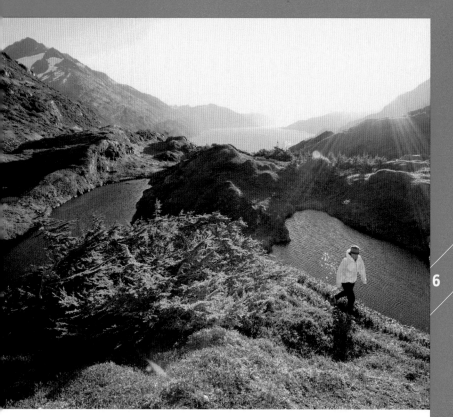

South Central Alaska

INCLUDING PRINCE WILLIAM SOUND, HOMER, AND THE KENAI PENINSULA

WORD OF MOUTH

"Homer is a cute place with plenty to do to keep you busy for a couple of days—my favorite thing was taking a ferry to Halibut Cove and dining at the Saltry—reservations required—it is a beautiful place."

—sunburn1944

WELCOME TO SOUTH CENTRAL ALASKA

TOP REASONS TO GO

★ **The fishing:** In summer salmon fill the rivers, which you can fish with a guide, from your own boat, or from the bank. Fishing for halibut and rockfish is also possible from charter boats out of Homer or Seward.

★ **The wildlife:** Urban moose, black and brown bears, sea lions, Dall sheep, gray whales, and bald eagles are all common in the region. Keep your eyes open and you're likely to see numerous animals, whether within town or city limits or in the backcountry.

★ **The scenery:** South Central doesn't scrimp on grandiose scenes. Boasting views of volcanoes and mountains that fall right into the water, the Kenai Peninsula is a buffet for the eyes, while Prince William Sound offers calving glaciers and narrow inlets uninhabited by anything but sea life.

★ **The access:** With a network of roads and ferries, all of the above are easily accessible. No matter where you go in the region, you're only a few steps away from the wilderness.

1 Prince William Sound. Spanning 15,000 square mi, Prince William Sound is made up of remote coves, glaciers that curve right into the sea, and small islands topped with sea lions and puffins. The sound is easily accessible from Anchorage via Whittier or Valdez.

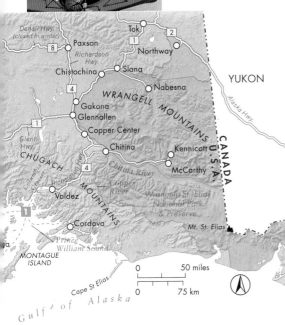

YUKON

CANADA
U.S.A.

WRANGELL MOUNTAINS

CHUGACH MOUNTAINS

Denali Hwy.
(closed in winter)
Paxson
Tok
Northway
Richardson Hwy.
Chistochina
Slana
Nabesna
Gakona
Glennallen
Copper Center
Chitina
Kennicott
McCarthy
Glenn Hwy.
Chitina River
Copper River
Wrangell-St. Elias National Park & Preserve
Valdez
Cordova
Mt. St. Elias
Prince William Sound
MONTAGUE ISLAND
Cape St Elias
Gulf of Alaska

0   50 miles
0   75 km

GETTING ORIENTED

South Central is the epicenter of Alaska's population and commerce. The Mat-Su Valley, just 15 mi north of Anchorage, is the fastest-growing region in America. South Central is populated for a reason: the entire region is rich with awe-inspiring natural attractions and superb recreational opportunities. Geographical features include four mountain ranges, three national parks, the country's second-largest national forest, and more glaciers, rivers, and lakes than one person could visit in a lifetime.

6

2 Kenai Peninsula.
Anchorage is called "the best base camp in the world." One look at the peninsula and all the recreation available, and you'll understand why. The Kenai has world-class recreation opportunities that include fishing, hiking, canoeing, and whale-watching.

3 Homer. Literally the end of the road, Homer is an alluring blend of commercial fishermen, artists, bohemians, and tourists. With bluffs sloping down to Kachemak Bay, it's hard to find a spot in town without a view of

the ocean or mountains. Be sure to try the excellent restaurants and sip a locally brewed beer.

4 Mat-Su Valley and Beyond. Just north of Anchorage, the Matanuska-Susitna Valley is a mixture of bedroom communities, agricultural concerns, and recreation options. It's also the gateway to the Interior. Several spectacular mountain ranges converge here: the Chugach, the Talkeetna, and the Alaska, with rivers and streams full of trophy-class salmon and trout.

Updated by
Teeka A. Bal-
las and Lisa
Hupp

There are few places in America that offer such a diverse array of natural beauty as South Central Alaska. From whales to glaciers, there is something to satiate every nature lover's appetite. Unlike those of most of Alaska, the wonders of South Central are traversable or viewable by car. There are roads to a majority of the beloved spots in the region.

Most visitors to South Central tend to begin and end their visit in Anchorage, the region's transportation hub. During the summer months this is where planes, trains, buses, and automobiles depart on a daily basis. RV rentals are also popular in Anchorage, and can be seen in droves along the Seward Highway along Cook Inlet. Most highways in South Central are two lanes and paved, but summertime traffic can be frustrating. Be wary of impatient drivers trying to get around slow-moving RVs, and always be aware of wildlife as well. Every year motorists kill hundreds of moose, and in turn there are many driver fatalities. South Central Alaska is bordered on the south and the west by ocean waters: the Gulf of Alaska, Prince William Sound, and Cook Inlet. This region is lined with a smattering of quaint port towns. From Kodiak, a commercial-fishing port, to Homer, a funky laid-back artists' colony, each town has its own personality. Inland, the remnants of mining towns continue to grow and prosper in different ways. Talkeetna, a small village on the northern edge of the region, is a starting point for many mountaineers, as it's located at the base of Mt. McKinley. Most locals refer to the 20,320-foot mountain by its original Athabascan name, Denali, which means "the High One." In the center of South Central is Alaska's farmland, the Matanuska-Susitna Valley (generally referred to as the "Mat-Su Valley," the "Matsu," or just "the Valley"). The region boasts 75-pound cabbages and gigantic award-winning rhubarb.

All of South Central is wrapped in the embrace of several mountain ranges. In a crescent shape south and east of Anchorage is the 300-mi-long Chugach Mountain Range. It bends all the way around the gulf to Valdez, where it meets the Wrangell-St. Elias National Park. The

Chugach, St. Elias, and Wrangell mountain ranges are so immense that they are often referred to, collectively, as the "mountain kingdom of North America."

The mountain peaks don't end there, however. Across Cook Inlet, easily viewed from Anchorage, is a small part of the Alaska Range, known as the Pacific Ocean's great Ring of Fire, snowcapped volcanoes still known to occasionally blow off steam and lava. The Alaska Range is a narrow 400-mi-long range that embraces the highest peak in North America, Mt. McKinley.

Whether you're hoping to explore mountains or ocean, tundra, taiga, or forest, each climate zone and ecosystem is available in South Central. From the coastal rain forests around Seward and Kodiak to the rough Arctic chill of glaciers flowing off the Harding Icefield, the region offers it all.

PLANNING

WHEN TO GO

Summer is the peak season all over the state. In South Central this means it is rarely too hot or too cold, particularly along the coast, although rainfall occurs often and without warning. Long daylight hours make it possible to enjoy the beauty and the bounty of Alaska at all hours. However, if you're hoping to catch more hours of darkness, there are always the shoulder seasons. Unfortunately, the weather in spring and fall tends to be more unpredictable than in summer, with random appearances of snow and dramatic drops in temperature. Autumn starts early, with the deciduous trees beginning to show color in mid-August. Visitor services stay open until the end of September.

GETTING HERE AND AROUND

BOAT AND FERRY TRAVEL

With its glaciers, mountains, fjords, and sea mammals, the South Central coast is great to see by ferry. The ferries between Valdez and Whittier run by way of Columbia Glacier in summer, where it is not unusual to witness giant fragments of ice calving from the face of the glacier into Prince William Sound.

The **Alaska Marine Highway**, the state-run ferry operator, has scheduled service to Valdez, Cordova, Whittier, Homer, and Seldovia on the mainland; to Kodiak and Port Lions on Kodiak Island; and to the port of Dutch Harbor in the Aleutian Islands. These connect to the ferries that operate in Southeast Alaska, but the two systems connect only on once-a-month sailings. Ferries operate on two schedules; summer (May–September) sailings are considerably more frequent than fall and winter service. Check your schedules carefully: ferries do not stop at all ports every day. Reservations are required on all routes and should be made as far in advance as possible.

Alaska Marine Highway (☎ *907/465-3941 or 800/642-0066 ⊕ www. ferryalaska.com*).

BUS TRAVEL

For bus service in the region, contact Alaska Direct Bus Lines, Homer Stage Line, Park Connection Motor Coach, or Seward Bus Line.

Contacts **Alaska Direct Bus Lines** (☎ *800/770-6652*). **Homer Stage Line** (☎ *907/868-3914*). **Park Connection Motor Coach** (☎ *800/266-8625*). **Seward Bus Line** (☎ *907/563-0800 or 907/224-3608*).

CAR TRAVEL

Car is definitely the way to go in South Central; the road system is more developed than most other regions, and is also mostly paved. It's also got some of the coolest drive routes that involve putting your car on a ferry. If you're renting, know that not all rental companies will let you do this (start with the larger chains, which are more likely to have a seaworthy rental policy available), so if this is part of your travel plan, aim to get your ducks in a row about two or three months in advance before the ferry-friendly rental agencies are all booked for your dates.

TRAVEL TIMES FROM ANCHORAGE

DESTINATION	TIME
Chugach State Park	20 mins–1 hr by car, depending on section of park
Cordova	1 hr to Whittier by car, then 3 hrs by ferry
Denali State Park	3 hrs by car
Glennallen	4 hrs by car
Homer	4–5 hrs by car
Kenai/Soldotna	2–3 hrs by car
Lake Clark	1–2 hrs by air taxi
Portage Glacier	50 mins by car
Seward	2–2½ hrs by car
Wrangell–St. Elias	6–8 hrs by car

RAILROAD TRAVEL

Anchorage is the region's hub, connected by rail and road to major ports in South Central. To the east, you can reach McCarthy and Valdez by an indirect but scenic drive on the Glenn and Richardson highways. The Seward and Sterling highways connect to nearly every town on the Kenai Peninsula. The **Alaska Railroad Corporation** operates the Alaska Railroad, which runs 470 mi between Seward and Fairbanks via Anchorage. There's daily service between Anchorage and Fairbanks in summer, and in winter there's one round-trip per week. Service to Seward from Anchorage runs every weekend from mid-May to September.

Contacts **Alaska Railroad Corporation** (☎ *800/544-0552 ⊕ www.akrr.com*).

HEALTH AND SAFETY

In South Central, it's important to stick to basic principles of Alaska safety: hiring a guide for anything outside your comfort zone might just prove to be the most important investment you've ever made. Follow bear safety rules; especially down the Kenai Peninsula, know that moose can be the more-dangerous encounter, so use extreme respect.

MONEY MATTERS

Nothing is too surprising on the financial front here: try to bring cash if you're traveling to a small town, and even if you've pre-paid for a guide's services, remember to bring a little something to tip with at the end of the day or trip.

RESTAURANTS

The best way to describe the hospitality industry in Alaska is "informal," and this applies as much to South Central as it does anywhere else. Don't worry if you still have your hiking clothes on when you go out to eat. Every kind of food is available, especially in larger towns, but options decline considerably from mid-September through April.

HOTELS

Accommodations in Alaska, particularly in the sparsely populated areas can be quite rugged. You will find a lot of establishments have only shared bathrooms, and most amenities like a coffee pot, television, and Internet are scant, although the latter is beginning to find its way even into remote villages. In the most rural of places it is not entirely unheard-of to find no bathrooms in the establishment, but rather a "honey bucket" out back. If such things are important to you, it's wise to inquire in advance.

DINING AND LODGING PRICE CATEGORIES				
	¢	$	$$	$$$	$$$$
Restaurants	under $10	$10–$15	$15–$20	$20–$25	over $25
Hotels	under $75	$75–$125	$125–$175	$175–$225	over $225

Restaurant prices are per person for a main course at dinner. Hotel prices are for two people in a standard double room in high season.

PRINCE WILLIAM SOUND

Tucked into the east side of the Kenai Peninsula, the sound is a peaceful escape from the throngs of people congesting the towns and highways. Enhanced with steep fjords, green enshrouded waterfalls, and calving tidewater glaciers, Prince William Sound is a stunning arena. It has a convoluted coastline, in that it is riddled with islands, which makes it hard to discern just how vast the area is. The sound covers almost

BEST BETS FOR DIFFERENT TRAVELERS

If you're also taking a cruise:

■ Get down to Homer and across Kachemak Bay to Seldovia; this area will let you experience the crowdless kayaking, small town feel, and (if you go to Seldovia) off-road-system tranquility your cruise may have been lacking.

If you're traveling with kids:

■ Alaska SeaLife Center, in Seward, features enough hands-on displays and sea creature-viewing areas to keep both the young and young-at-heart occupied for hours.

If you want to get up close and personal with the wildlife:

■ Out of Seward, take a full-day cruise into Kenai Fjords National Park; this fascinating landscape is also chock-full of sea lions, birds, and other fjord-dwelling creatures.

If you want both a comfortable retreat experience and easy access to fishing the storied waters of the Kenai:

■ Stay at the Kenai Princess Wilderness Lodge, right on the Russian River; they'll help you get set up to fish in this gorgeous location famous for huge (and delicious) salmon.

15,000 square mi—more than 12 times the size of Rhode Island—and is home to more than 150 glaciers. The sound is vibrantly alive with all manner of marine life, including salmon, halibut, humpback and orca whales, sea otters, sea lions, and porpoises. Bald eagles are easily seen soaring above, and often brown and black bears, Sitka black-tailed deer, and gray wolves can be spotted on the shore.

Unfortunately, the *Exxon Valdez* oil spill in 1989 heavily damaged parts of the sound, and oil still washes up on shore after high tides and storms. The original spill had a devastating effect on both animal and human lives. What lasting effect this lurking oil will have on the area is still being studied and remains a topic of much debate.

■TIP→ Bring your rain gear—Prince William Sound receives more than 150 inches of rain per year.

The sound is best explored by charter boat or guided excursion out of Whittier, Cordova, or Valdez. Even though the waters are mostly protected, open stretches are common, and the fickle Alaska weather can fool even experienced boaters. From the road system, Whittier and Valdez are your best bets for finding charter outfits.

CHUGACH STATE PARK

Bordering Anchorage to the east.

GETTING HERE AND AROUND

The Chugach forms the backdrop of Anchorage, and trailheads are accessible at the top of O'Malley, Huffman, and DeArmoun roads, south of Anchorage at Potter Valley, McHugh Creek, and Bird Ridge on the Seward Highway, and to the north of town at Arctic Valley Road (6 mi out) and Eagle River Road (13 mi out).

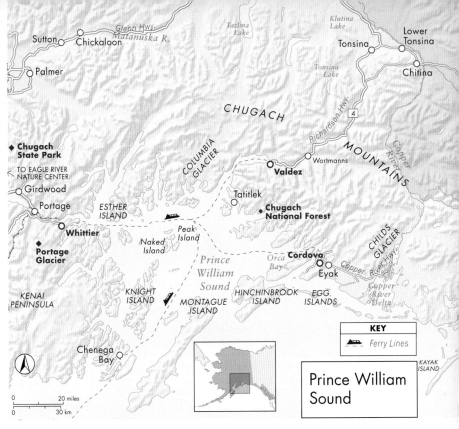

Prince William Sound

KEY
🛥 Ferry Lines

ESSENTIALS

Visitor Information Park Headquarters (✉ Mi 115, Seward Hwy. 📇 HC 52, Box 8999, Indian 99540 ☎ 907/345-5014 🌐 www.dnr.alaska.gov/parks/units/chugach).

EXPLORING

Comprising nearly a half-million acres, **Chugach State Park** is the third-largest state park in America. Just on the edge of Anchorage, the park is Alaska's most accessible wilderness. It has nearly 30 trails for all types of hikes and hikers. Totaling more than 150 mi, the hiking trails range from 2 mi to 30 mi long. Although the park is technically an urban park, in that it is connected to the largest city in Alaska, it is far from being a typical urban setting. Chugach State Park is anything but tame; it's real wilderness, home to Dall sheep, mountain goats, brown bears, moose, and several packs of wolves.

Miners who sought the easiest means of traversing the mountain peaks and passes initially blazed most of the trails within the park. Today those same trails are restored every spring and maintained by park rangers and various volunteer groups. Trailheads are scattered around the park's perimeter from Eklutna Lake, 30 mi north of Anchorage, to the trailhead for the Crow Pass Trail near Girdwood, 37 mi to the south. It is free to hike in the park, whether you're there for an afternoon or a week; however, several of the more popular trailheads charge a $5 daily parking fee.

The park offers some truly intoxicating views, and depending on what perch you're looking down from, you can see across the bay to the looming white mountains of the Alaska Range, the great tides of Cook Inlet, and, on clear days, Mt. McKinley in all her glory. One of the best and most easily accessible places to try for such a view is from Flattop Mountain on the park's western edge. The peak is the most popular destination within Chugach Park. It is a 1-mi-long hike to the top, and hikers of all abilities make the trek. Be advised, however, that although you may see people hiking in flip-flops up to the peak, it is strenuous and can be very challenging. Wear sturdy hiking shoes and proper attire. The trail up can be exhausting, and the way down can be very taxing on the knees. It's always wise to hike with trekking poles; they help relieve the stress on the back and the knees. Carry water and a snack, and as always, be prepared for sudden weather changes. Every year people are rescued from this trail because they have underestimated its potential for calamity, so be prepared.

Eagle River Road leads 12 mi into the mountains from the bedroom community of Eagle River. The **Eagle River Nature Center**, at the end of Eagle River Road, has wildlife displays, telescopes for wildlife spotting, and 9 mi of hiking trails within the center's perimeters, and there are volunteers to answer questions, lead hikes, and host naturalist programs throughout the year. A cabin that sleeps eight and a pair of yurts (round insulated tents) that sleep four and six are available to rent. The cost is $65 per night, and a 1.5 mi hike in is required. Amenities include woodstoves, firewood, and outdoor latrines. The center is also the trail end for the Crow Pass Trail, a 26-mi section of the Historic Iditarod Trail. ✉ *32750 Eagle River Rd., Eagle River* ☎ *907/694–2108* ⊕ *www.ernc.org* 🅿 *Parking $5* ⊙ *May–Sept., Tues.–Sun. 10–5; Oct.– Apr., Fri.–Sun. 10–5.*

OUTDOOR ACTIVITIES AND GUIDED TOURS

The **Little Rodak Trail** is less than 1 mi long and has a viewing platform that overlooks the Eagle River valley. **Albert Loop Trail** behind the nature center has markers that coordinate with a self-guided hike along its 3-mi route; pick up a brochure at the Eagle River Nature Center.

HIKING　Several trailheads along the edge of Anchorage lead into the park and its 3,000- to 5,000-foot-tall peaks. The park's most popular day climb is **Flattop Mountain,** which towers 3,500 feet above sea level. It's reached via the Glen Alps Trailhead off Upper Huffman Road on Anchorage's Hillside. A 1-mi trail climbs 1,300 feet from the Glen Alps parking area to the top. On a bright summer day you'll encounter plenty of company. Bring along a day pack with plenty of water and energy bars, a rainproof jacket, good hiking boots, and trekking poles.

MOUNTAIN　Mountain biking has become very popular in the park, and most, but
BIKING　not all, trails are open to bikes; check the signs and symbols at the trailheads if in doubt. The Powerline Pass trail from the Glen Alps parking lot is wide and well maintained for bikes and offers a great view from the pass, as well as opportunities to spot moose, Dall sheep, bears, and

maybe even wolves. **Sunshine Fitness and Sports** (⊠ *123 E. Fireweed La., Anchorage* ☎ *907/272–6444* ⊕ *www.sunshinefitness.com*) rents mountain bikes.

CHUGACH NATIONAL FOREST

40 mi east of Anchorage.

GETTING HERE AND AROUND

The Seward Highway between Anchorage and Seward has a number of trail access points. (Check the highway for mile markers, with the distance measured from Seward.) At Mile 63.7, just south of Turnagain Pass, is the turnoff to the Johnson Pass Trail, a relatively flat trail to walk. Seven miles farther south, take the Hope Highway 18 mi to its end and find the Porcupine Campground. From there the Gull Rock Trail follows the shore of Turnagain Arm for 5 mi, offering scenic views across the arm and the chance to spot beluga whales foraging for salmon. Farther south on the Seward Highway, at Mile 23.1, the Ptarmigan Creek Trail starts at the campground and climbs 3.5 mi into the mountains, ending next to a lake surrounded by snowy peaks. Your best bet for getting around the area is by rental car.

ESSENTIALS

Visitor Information Alaska Public Lands Information Center (☎ 907/644–3661 or 866/869–6887 ⊕ www.alaskacenters.gov). **Forest Headquarters** (☎ 907/743–9500 Anchorage ⊕ www.fs.fed.us/r10/chugach).

EXPLORING

Sprawling east of Chugach State Park, **Chugach National Forest** encompasses nearly 6 million acres. The forest covers most of the Kenai Peninsula and parts of Prince William Sound, and is the second-largest national forest in the United States, exceeded in size only by the Tongass in Southeast Alaska.

The forest has abundant recreational opportunities: hiking, camping, backpacking, fishing, boating, mountain biking, horseback riding, hunting, and flightseeing. South Central Alaska is not the best terrain for rock climbing (aside from Mt. McKinley), as the rock is predominantly composed of hardened ocean sediments that are weak and crumbly. There are, however, some places for great bouldering, and in the wintertime ice climbing is quite popular, as are snowshoeing, skiing, snowmachining, and dog mushing.

Hiking trails offer easy access into the heart of the forest. You can spend a day hiking or looking for wildlife, or you can embark on a multiday backpacking excursion. At all but the most popular trailheads a five-minute stroll down a wooded trail can introduce you to the sights, smells, and tranquillity of backcountry Alaska.

⚠ Be prepared to be self-sufficient when entering Chugach Forest. Trailheads typically offer nothing more than a place to park and perhaps an

---

CLIMB IT

Every summer solstice (in 2012: June 20), locals climb to the top of Flattop Mountain to celebrate the longest day of the year. If you're in town for this event, it's great fun; there's even an impromptu concert by musicians who lug their instruments to the top of the mountain. Parking spots are at a premium, so arrive early.

6

CAMPING IN CHUGACH STATE PARK

⚠ **Alaska State Park Campgrounds.** You'll find three road-accessible campgrounds in Chugach Park: at Eklutna Lake, Bird Creek, and Eagle River. All are within a short drive of Anchorage, and sites are available on a first-come, first-served basis. The Eklutna Lake site has a ranger station, and hiking trails of varying degrees abound in the area. Eagle River has running water and a dump station. Fishing is best at Bird Creek during the annual silver salmon run in July and August, but be prepared for crowds. Online reservations are available. **Pros:** most of the campsites have ample room to move about; some semblance of privacy; amenities are clean and looked after. **Cons:** only three campgrounds in the immediate area for a lot of traffic; grounds book up quickly; a lot of loud reveling—but tempered by the strict curfew; bears frequent the campsites. ⌂ *Alaska State Parks, HC 52, Box 8999, Indian 99540* ☎ *907/345-5014* ⊕ *www. dnr.ak.gov/parks/aspunits/index.htm* ⇋ *135 sites* ⚐ *Pit toilets, drinking water, fire grates, picnic tables* ☾ *Closed roughly Oct.–Apr.*

outhouse. Running water, trail maps, and other amenities are not available. Also, be "bear aware" whenever you travel in bear country—and all of Alaska is bear country. In recent years urban and rural bear attacks have been on the rise in South Central. Try to hike in groups or pairs. Pay attention to your surroundings, and make noise when traveling, especially in areas of reduced visibility. Bears will most likely make themselves scarce with some advance warning of your arrival.

OUTDOOR ACTIVITIES

★ **Crow Pass Trail** is a 26-mi-long backpacking trail that begins outside Girdwood and ends in Eagle River at the nature center. The trail is part of the Historic Iditarod Trail and is a truly great hike. The first 3 mi of this trail are the most strenuous, but after that the worst things hikers have to contend with are snow above the tree line and icy-cold river crossings. In Alaska during the summer it is wise to cross through rivers only in the morning in order to avoid the rising waters throughout the day as snow and glaciers melt under the many hours of sunshine.

In addition to offering splendid views, Crow Pass Trail winds around the front of the amazing Raven Glacier terminus. The glacier is ½ mi wide and more than 2 mi long, with many deep crevasses. You can camp anywhere along the trail, though it's important to know that camping anywhere near the glacier, even at the peak of summer, is a chilly endeavor. There is one cabin available along the trail at 3,500 feet. The cabin is above the tree line, just across from rich crystalline-blue Crystal Lake. It is almost always booked at least six months in advance. Contact forest headquarters.

★ **Resurrection Pass Trail**, a 38-mi-long backpacking trail through the Chugach National Forest, draws hikers and backpackers for its colorful wildflowers in summer. There's also a chance to spot wildlife: moose, caribou, Dall sheep, mountain goats, black and brown bears, wolves,

CAMPING IN CHUGACH NATIONAL FOREST

⚠ **U.S. Forest Service Campgrounds.** The Forest Service maintains 18 campgrounds, 14 of them road accessible, within Chugach National Forest. The campgrounds do not have hookups for RVs, but the four that have road access are otherwise suitable for both RVs and tents. The Russian River Campground has a three-day limit during salmon-fishing season in June and July. Reservations (for a fee) are accepted at five campgrounds—Cooper Creek South, Ptarmigan Creek, Russian River, Trail River, and Williwaw. **Pros:** camping is inexpensive; there are numerous campgrounds in South Central. **Cons:** popular campgrounds can be crowded and loud during fishing season; not very enjoyable if the weather is crummy. ☎ 877/444–6777 ⊕ *www.recreation.gov* ⤴ *414 RV/tent sites* ♿ *Pit toilets, drinking water, fire grates, picnic tables.*

coyotes, and lynx all traverse the forest. Carry binoculars for the best wildlife-viewing opportunities.

The northern end of the trail starts south of the town of Hope, and follows an old mining trail through the Kenai Mountains to its end near Cooper Landing. The trail branches off at one point to the Devil's Pass trailhead along the Seward Highway. Besides cabins, the U.S. Forest Service has provided several "official" campsites along the trail, where you'll find a cleared patch of ground and a fire ring. You are free, however, to pitch your tent wherever you like.

WHERE TO STAY

For expanded hotel reviews, visit Fodors.com.

¢ 🏚 **U.S. Forest Service Cabins.** Along trails, near wilderness alpine lakes, in coastal forests, and on saltwater beaches, these rustic cabins offer retreats for the solo hiker or a group of friends. **Pros:** remote; cheap; beautiful. **Cons:** too remote for some; extremely basic; often booked months in advance for summer; mice frequent the establishment. ☎ 877/444–6777 *reservations* ⊕ *www.recreation.gov* ⤴ *41 cabins.*

PORTAGE GLACIER

54 mi southeast of Anchorage.

GETTING HERE AND AROUND

Gray Line of Alaska leads summer boat tours (from mid-May to mid-September) along the face of Portage Glacier aboard the 200-passenger *Ptarmigan* for $79. The view of Portage Lake and the surrounding peaks and hanging glaciers (the high-up glaciers that terminate at the tops of cliffs) is spectacular, especially on a sunny day when the icy-blue hues of the glaciers shine through.

ESSENTIALS

Visitor and Tour Information Begich-Boggs Visitor Center (☎ 907/783–2326 ⊕ *www.fs.fed.us/r10/chugach/chugach_pages/bbvc* ⊗ *Mid Sept.–early May*). **Gray Line of Alaska** (☎ 907/277–5581 or 800/478–6388 ⊕ *www.graylinealaska.com*).

EXPLORING

Portage Glacier is one of Alaska's most frequently visited tourist destinations. A 6-mi side road off the Seward Highway leads to the Begich-Boggs Visitor Center, on the shore of Portage Lake and named after two U.S. congressmen who disappeared on a small-plane journey out of Anchorage in 1972. The center is staffed by Forest Service personnel, who can help plan your trip and explain the natural history of the area. A film on glaciers is shown hourly, and icebergs sometimes drift down to the center from Portage Glacier. Due to global climate change, Portage Glacier, like most of the glaciers in Alaska, has receded from view in recent years.

The mountains surrounding Portage Glacier are covered with smaller glaciers. A 1-mi hike west brings you to the **Byron Glacier** overlook. The glacier is notable for its accessibility—it's one of the few places where you can hike onto a glacier from the road system. In summer, naturalists lead free weekly treks in search of microscopic ice worms.

Several hiking trails are accessible from the Seward Highway, including the steep paths up Falls Creek and Bird Ridge. Both offer spectacular views of **Turnagain Arm,** where explorer Captain Cook searched for the Northwest Passage. Local lore has it that the arm is so named because Cook entered it repeatedly, only to be forced to turn back by the huge tide. The tide is so powerful it sometimes rushes up the arm as a tidal bore—a wall of water that goes up an inlet. An increasingly popular, yet somewhat dangerous, sport is windsurfing the tidal bore. To view the bore tide, station yourself at one of the turnoffs along the arm about 2½ hours after low tide in Anchorage—tide books are available at sporting goods shops, grocery stores, and bookstores, or you can find tide information on the Web.

During the summer months beluga whales are frequent visitors to the arm as they patrol the muddy waters in search of salmon and hooligan, a variety of smelt. The whales travel in pods of adult and juvenile animals, the adults distinguishable by their bright white color. They're smaller than other whales that frequent Alaska's coastal waters, reaching only 15 feet in length and weighing up to a ton. During high tide from July to August, when the surface of the water is calm, belugas are often spotted from the highway, frequently causing traffic jams as tourists and residents pull off the road for a chance to view the whales as they travel up and down the shoreline. It's an increasingly special thing to spot a beluga here; for reasons that are still unclear to scientists, South Central's beluga population has declined from 1,300 in 1980 to fewer than 375 in 2010.

Alaska Wildlife Conservation Center is a 144-acre drive-through wildlife center just before the Portage Glacier turnoff. Moose, bison, elk, caribou, Sitka black-tailed deer, musk ox, great horned owls, a brown bear, and a bald eagle, many of them orphaned in the wild, now live in the park. There are also snack and gift shops. ⊠ *Mi 79, Seward Hwy., Portage* ☎ *907/783–2025* ⊕ *www.alaskawildlife.org* ⌦ *$10* ☉ *Jan. and Feb., weekends only 10–6; Mar.–May 14, daily 10–6; May 16–Sept. 13, daily 8–8; Sept. 14–Dec., daily 10–6.*

Little remains of the community of **Portage** as a result of the 1964 earthquake. The ghost forest of dead spruce in the area was created when the land subsided by 6 to 10 feet after the quake and saltwater penetrated inland from Turnagain Arm, killing the trees.

EN ROUTE

On your way to Portage, look for **Indian Valley Meats** (✉ *Huot Circle, 23 mi south of Anchorage on Seward Hwy. at Mi 104, Indian* ☎ *907/653–7511* ⊕ *www.indianvalleymeats.com*). This is a popular place for Alaskans to have their game processed. There is a shop on the premises where workers sell smoked salmon and musk ox, reindeer, and buffalo sausage made on the premises. They'll also smoke, can, and package the fish you've caught and arrange for shipping.

OUTDOOR ACTIVITIES AND GUIDED TOURS

COMBINATION TRIPS

NOVA (✉ *Mi 76.2, Glenn Hwy., Chickaloon* ☎ *800/746–5753* ⊕ *www.novalaska.com*) has been guiding residents and visitors since 1975. The company conducts river rafting, glacier hiking, fishing, and backcountry combo trips from its office in tiny Chickaloon between Palmer and Glennallen.

ROCK AND ICE CLIMBING

For information about rock- and ice-climbing activities, check with the **Alaska Rock Gym** (✉ *4840 Fairbanks St., Anchorage* ☎ *907/562–7265* ⊕ *www.alaskarockgym.com*). It's got a great indoor gym, and staff can point you to where local climbers have set routes along the Seward Highway south of town that are close to Anchorage.

6

WHITTIER

60 mi southeast of Anchorage.

The entryway to Whittier is unlike any other: a 2½-mi drive atop railroad tracks through the Anton Anderson Memorial Tunnel, cut through the Chugach Mountain Range. Once on the other side of the tunnel, you enter the mysterious world of Whittier, the remnants of a military town developed in World War II. The only way to get to Whittier was by boat or train until the tunnel opened to traffic in 2000.

This quaint hamlet, nestled at the base of snow-covered peaks at the head of Passage Canal on the Kenai Peninsula, has an intriguing history. During World War II the U.S. Army constructed a port in Whittier and built the Hodge and Buckner buildings to house soldiers. These enormous monoliths are eerily reminiscent of Soviet-era communal apartment buildings. The Hodge Building (now called Begich Towers) houses almost all of Whittier's 180 year-round residents. The town averages 30 feet of snow in the winter, and in summer gets a considerable amount of rainfall. Whittier's draw is primarily fishing, but there are a number of activities to be had on Prince William Sound, including kayaking and glacier tours with some of the best glacier viewing in South Central Alaska.

Whittier is very small, and there is not much to look at in town, but the location is unbeatable. Surrounding peaks cradle alpine glaciers, and when the summer weather melts the huge winter snow load you can catch glimpses of the brilliant blue ice underneath. Sheer cliffs drop into Passage Canal and provide nesting places for flocks of black-legged kittiwakes, while sea otters and harbor seals cavort in the small-boat harbor and salmon return to spawn in nearby streams. A short boat ride out into the sound reveals tidewater glaciers, and an alert wildlife watcher can catch sight of mountain goats clinging to the mountainsides and black bears patrolling the beaches and hillsides in their constant search for food.

■TIP→ Many companies' phones in Whittier are disconnected from October through April. If you can't get through to a number with prefix 472, check the company's Web site for an alternate number.

GETTING HERE AND AROUND

Unless you come in on a cruise ship, ferry, or other boat, your only way in and out of Whittier is through the tunnel. Its access, however, is limited by the railroad schedule, so it's not always possible to breeze in and out of town. ■TIP→ For current tunnel information and schedules, check the tunnel's Web site. Tolls are $12 for passenger vehicles and $20 to $35 for RVs and trailers; waits of up to an hour are possible, and summer hours are from 6 am until 11 pm.

ESSENTIALS

Tunnel Information **Anton Anderson Memorial Tunnel** (⊕ www.dot.state. ak.us/creg/whittiertunnel/index.shtml).

OUTDOOR ACTIVITIES AND GUIDED TOURS

BOATING AND WILDLIFE VIEWING

Alaska Sea Kayakers (☎907/472–2534 or 877/472–2534 ⊕www. alaskaseakayakers.com) can supply sea kayaks and gear for exploring Prince William Sound and also conducts guided day trips, multiday tours, instruction, and boat-assisted and boat live-aboard kayaking trips. The company practices a leave-no-trace camping ethos, and is very conscientious about avoiding bear problems. All guides are experienced Alaskan paddlers, and group sizes are kept small. Trips are May through mid-September.

The small fleet of boats at **Lazy Otter Charters** (☎800/587–6887 ⊕www. lazyottercharters.com) is available for private charter, sightseeing, and sea-kayak drop-offs. Groups of up to 22 people can join trips through Prince William Sound; you can also get transport to Cordova and Valdez. Customized sightseeing trips run from four or five hours to eight or nine hours.

Major Marine Tours (☎907/274–7300 or 800/764–7300 ⊕www. majormarine.com) runs a five-hour cruise from Whittier that visits two tidewater glaciers. The waters of Prince William Sound are well protected and relatively calm, making this a good option if you're inclined toward queasiness. Seabirds, waterfowl, and bald eagles are always present, and the chance to get close to the enormous walls of ice of the glaciers is not to be missed. The cruise is $107 per person, and runs from mid-May to mid-September. For an additional $19 every cruise features a freshly prepared all-you-can-eat salmon and prime rib meal and reserved table seating for every guest inside the heated cabin.

From Whittier, tours with **Prince William Sound Glacier Cruises** (✉Pier 1, Whittier ☎877/777–4054 ⊕www.princewilliamsound.com) travel through the sheltered bays, fjords, and canals of Prince William Sound.

You can view glaciers, seabirds, and wildlife such as seals, sea lions, sea otters, whales, bears, and mountain goats. The company can arrange transportation from Anchorage to Whittier by bus or rail, or you can drive to Whittier in your own vehicle. Prices vary according to length of trip and travel options; cruises take place mid-May through mid-September.

Retired marine biologist Gerry Sanger runs full-day photo tours limited to 3 people in his 30-foot boat with **Sound Eco Adventures** (☏ 888/471–2312 ⊕ *www.soundecoadventure.com*) from March through October.

Phillips' Cruises & Tours has been running the **26 Glacier Cruise** (☏ *907/276–8023 or 800/544–0529* ⊕ *www.26glaciers.com*) through Prince William Sound for many years. The high-speed catamaran covers 135 mi of territory in 4½ hours, leaving Whittier and visiting Port Wells, Barry Arm, and College and Harriman fjords. The boat is a very stable platform, and even visitors prone to seasickness can take this cruise with no ill effects. The heated cabin has large windows, upholstered booths, and wide aisles, and all seats are pre-reserved. There's a snack bar and a saloon on board, and wildlife encounters are commonplace. You can drive to Whittier and catch the boat at the dock, or you can arrange with the company to travel from Anchorage by rail or bus. The trip is $139 per person, plus tax, and includes a hot lunch of cod or chicken; tours are given May through September.

WHERE TO EAT AND STAY
For expanded hotel reviews, visit Fodors.com.

$ ✕**China Sea**. This restaurant offers a great array of flavors. The menu is
CHINESE filled with the standard Chinese fare, but there are a significant number of fresh, local seafood dishes that make this place a stand-out choice. Try the excellent grilled halibut (or, for non–fish lovers, the Mongolian beef). ⊠ *Harbor* ☏ *907/472–3663* ⊘ *Closed mid-Sept.–May.*

¢ ✕**Lazy Otter Café & Gifts**. Amid the summer shops and docks this little
AMERICAN café offers warm drinks, an array of soups, sandwiches, and fresh-baked pastries, along with an Alaskan favorite: soft-serve ice cream. The busy shop only offers a couple of indoor seats, but there's outdoor seating that overlooks the harbor and is pleasant on sunny days. ⊠ *Lot 2, Whittier Harbor* ☏ *907/472–6887.*

$ ✕**Varly's Ice Cream & Pizza**. Even though ice cream hardly seems like the
PIZZA thing you'd seek when in Alaska, hot days (and even not-so-hot days) beg for Varly's. If the weather's cold and rainy, pizza is the alternative fare. If you're not sure which way to lean, we wouldn't blame you if you opted for a little of each. The owners (of Varly's Swiftwater Seafood Café fame) take great pride in what they do, and it shows: the delicious pizza is homemade and something to write home about. It might sound frightening, but trust us when we say the Kraut—a pizza topped with sauerkraut and pepperoni (no kidding!)—is the best. ⊠ *Lot 1A Triangle Lease Area* ☏ *907/472–2547.*

$$ ✕**Varly's Swiftwater Seafood Café**. This is a great place to get the feel of
SEAFOOD Whittier. Place your order at the window and then grab a seat at the counter and wait for your food. There's outdoor seating that overlooks the small-boat harbor. Menu items include homemade chowders,

hand-battered seafood, peel-and-eat shrimp, burgers, and chicken. A smoked prime rib dinner is served on Friday and Saturday nights. ⊠ *Harbor Loop* ☎ *907/472–2550* ⊘ *Closed mid-Sept.–May.*

$$$$
Fodor'sChoice
★

⌖ **Inn at Whittier.** This first-class luxury hotel sits right on the water overlooking the harbor. **Pros:** every room has a great view. **Cons:** no kitchen amenities. **TripAdvisor:** "well decorated," "wonderful views," "room was clean and very nice." ⊠ *5a Harbor Rd., Whittier* ☎ *907/472–3200* ⊕ *www.innatwhittier.com* ⌁ *24 rooms* ☖ *In-room: Wi-Fi. In-hotel: some pets allowed* ⫶⊙⫶ *Breakfast.*

$$$–$$$$

⌖ **June's Whittier Condo Suites.** June's rents out 10 condominiums in the Begich Towers building, half with bay views, half with mountain views. **Pros:** private condos in Penthouse area of Begich Towers; lovely view. **Cons:** old building is a little rough outside. ⊠ *Begich Towers, Kenai St.* ⌂ *Box 715 99693* ☎ *888/472–6001* ⊕ *www.whittiersuitesonline. com* ⌁ *10 rooms* ☖ *In-room: kitchen. In-hotel: parking* ⫶⊙⫶ *Continental breakfast.*

VALDEZ

6 hrs northeast of Whittier by water, 304 mi east of Anchorage.

Valdez (pronounced val-*deez*) is the largest of the Prince William Sound communities. This year-round ice-free port was the entry point for people and goods going to the Interior during the gold rush. Today that flow has been reversed, as Valdez Harbor is the southern terminus of the Trans-Alaska Pipeline, which carries crude oil from Prudhoe Bay and surrounding oil fields nearly 800 mi to the north. This region, with its dependence on commercial fishing, is still feeling the aftereffects of the massive oil spill in 1989. Much of Valdez looks modern, because the business area was relocated and rebuilt after its destruction by the 1964 Good Friday earthquake. Even though the town is younger than the rest of developed Alaska, it's acquiring a lived-in look.

Many Alaskan communities have summer fishing derbies, but Valdez may hold the record for the number of such contests, stretching from late May into September for halibut and various runs of salmon. If you go fishing, by all means enter the appropriate derby. Every summer the newspapers run sob stories about tourists who landed possible prizewinners but couldn't share in the glory (or sizable cash rewards) because they hadn't forked over the five bucks to officially enter the contest. The **Valdez Silver Salmon Derby** is held the entire month of August. Fishing charters abound in this area of Prince William Sound, and for good reason: these fertile waters provide some of the best saltwater sportfishing in all of Alaska.

GETTING HERE AND AROUND

Valdez is road-accessible, and the 304-mi drive from Anchorage is stunning if a bit long to do in one day. The Richardson Highway portion of the drive takes you through Thompson Pass, high alpine country with 360-degree views. As you approach the town, the road descends into a steep canyon with rushing waterfalls—a popular ice-climbing destination in winter. Valdez's port is a stop on the Alaska Marine Highway, from which you can also sail to Cordova and Whittier. There's also a commercial airport.

The downtown is above the harbor, and two main avenues—Hazelet and Meals—run north–south with smaller streets branching off.

ESSENTIALS

Medical Assistance Providence Valdez Community Hospital (⊠ *911 Meals Ave.* ☎ *907/835–2249*).

Visitor and Tour Information Valdez Convention and Visitors Bureau (⊠ *200 Chenega St.* ↴ *Box 1603, Valdez 99686* ☎ *907/835–2984* ⊕ *www. valdezalaska.org*).

EXPLORING

The **Valdez Museum** explores the lives, livelihoods, and events significant to Valdez and surrounding regions. Exhibits include a restored 1880s Gleason & Baily hand-pump fire engine, a 1907 Ahrens steam fire engine, a 19th-century saloon, information on the local native peoples, and a recently-updated exhibit on the 1989 oil spill. Every summer the museum hosts an exhibit of quilts and fiber arts made by local and regional artisans. At a separate site, a 35- by 40-foot model of **Historical Old Town Valdez** (⊠ *436 S. Hazlet Ave.*) depicts the original town, which was devastated by the 1964 earthquake. There's also an operating seismograph and an exhibit on local seismic activity. A Valdez History Exhibits Pass includes admission to both the museum and the annex. ⊠ *217 Egan Dr.* ☎ *907/835–2764* ⊕ *www.valdezmuseum.org* ⬤ *$7* ☉ *May–Sept. (through Labor Day), Mon.–Sat. 1–5.*

OFF THE BEATEN PATH

A visit to **Columbia Glacier**, which flows from the surrounding Chugach Mountains, should certainly be on your Valdez agenda. Its deep aquamarine face is 5 mi across, and it calves icebergs with resounding cannonades. This glacier is one of the largest and most readily accessible of Alaska's coastal glaciers. The state ferry travels past the face of the glacier, and scheduled tours of the glaciers and the rest of the sound are available by boat and aircraft from Valdez, Cordova, and Whittier.

OUTDOOR ACTIVITIES AND GUIDED TOURS

ADVENTURE If you want a taste of backcountry snowmachining action (what snowmobiling is called in Alaska), **Alaska Snow Safaris** (⊠ *17435 Marcus Baker Dr., Palmer* ☎ *888/414–7669* ⊕ *www.snowmobile-alaska.com*) has an enormous winter playground near Valdez. From November to the end of April they'll take you into the wilderness on your machine or theirs to explore mile after mile of untouched, ungroomed snow. The trips are tailored to all levels of experience.

Anadyr Adventures (☎ *907/835–2814 or 800/865–2925* ⊕ *www. anadyradventures.com*) has 20 years' experience leading sea-kayak trips into Alaska's most spectacular wilderness, Prince William Sound. Guides will escort you on day trips, multiday camping trips, "mother ship" adventures based in a remote anchorage, or lodge-based trips for the ultimate combination of adventure by day and comfort by night. If you're already an experienced kayaker, it'll outfit you and you can travel on your own. Also available are guided hiking and glacier trips, ice caving at Valdez Glacier, soft-adventure charter-boat trips in the sound, and water-taxi service to or from anywhere on the eastern side of the sound.

Whether you're looking for a full-on winter backcountry heli-ski excursion (in winter) or a half-day walk on a glacier, **H2O Guides** (☎ *907/835–8418* 🌐 *www.h2oguides.com*) can hook you up. For most visitors, the day trips to Worthington Glacier State Park will suffice. It can set up any level of icy adventure you desire, from a half-day walk on the glacier to a multi-day ice-climbing trip. The company is in the Mountain Sky hotel, and can arrange fishing, flightseeing, multiday, multisport, and otherwise-customized trips as well.

CAMPING IN VALDEZ

⛺ **Bayside RV Park.** This full-service RV park with a few tent sites has a panoramic view of the mountains. The staff can help you book fishing and sightseeing trips with local charter outfits. **Pros:** close to the water; free hot unmetered showers. **Cons:** no trees between campsites; can get a little crowded. ✉ *230 E. Egan Dr.* ☎ *907/835–4425 or 888/835–4425* 🌐 *www.baysiderv.com* *110 RV/tent sites* *In-room: Internet, flush toilets, full hookups, dump station, drinking water, guest laundry, showers, picnic tables, electricity, public telephone* *Closed Sept.–Apr.*

BOATING AND WILDLIFE VIEWING

Valdez-based **Lu-Lu Belle** (☎ *800/411–0090* 🌐 *www.lulubelletours.com*) leads small-group whale-watching and wildlife-viewing cruises, and sailings past the Columbia Glacier, the largest glacier in Prince William Sound. The 1 pm departure boards promptly at 12:45.

Stan Stephens Glacier & Wildlife Cruises (☎ *866/867–1297* 🌐 *www.stanstephenscruises.com*) leads Prince William Sound glacier and wildlife-viewing cruises to Columbia and Meares glaciers from mid-May through mid-September. Trips include narration on local commercial-fishing operations, as well as commentary on the Alyeska Pipeline terminal and history of defunct gold mines.

Anadyr Adventures (☎ *907/835–2814 or 800/865–2925* 🌐 *www.anadyradventures.com*), in business since 1989, offers an array of kayaking and glacier adventures in Prince William Sound.

WHERE TO EAT

$ SEAFOOD

✕ **MacMurray's Alaska Halibut House.** At this very casual family-owned establishment you order at the counter, sit at the Formica-covered tables, and check out the photos of local fishing boats. The battered halibut is excellent—light and not greasy. Other menu items include homemade clam chowder, but if you're eating at the Halibut House, why try anything else? ✉ *208 Meals Ave.* ☎ *907/835–2788.*

$$ AMERICAN

✕ **Mike's Palace Ristorante.** Across from the scenic boat harbor, Mike's is a local favorite. The menu offers the world: from the standard America hamburger and Greek gyros to Mexican dishes and Italian pastas, there's a little bit of everything for every type of palate. There is an excellent selection of salads (a rarity throughout Alaska), steaks, and seafood. ✉ *201 N. Harbor Dr.* ☎ *907/835–2365.*

WHERE TO STAY

If you roll into town without reservations, especially if it's after hours, stop at the Valdez Convention and Visitor's Bureau on the corner of Fairbanks. It posts vacancies in bed-and-breakfasts on the window when it closes for the day.

For expanded hotel reviews, visit Fodors.com.

The state of Alaska publishes a free informative guide called **RV Tips: Trip Information Planning Booklet: A practical guide to campgrounds, dump stations, and propane services along Alaska's highways.** It is available online (⊕ *www.dced.state.ak.us/oed/student_info/pub/rvtips.pdf*).

$$ **Best Western Valdez Harbor Inn.** Near the harbor, this hotel has an inlet from the sound, complete with sea otters, seals, and waterfowl right outside the lobby windows and visible from some of the rooms. **Pros:** on an inlet; very clean. **Cons:** just like any Best Western elsewhere. **TripAdvisor:** "room was clean and comfortable," "typical chain hotel," "great location." ⊠ *100 Harbor Dr., Box 468* ☎ *907/835–3434 or 888/222–3440* ⊕ *www.bestwestern.com* ⤳ *88 rooms* △ *In-room: Internet, Wi-Fi. In-hotel: restaurant, gym, laundry facilities, some pets allowed* ⦿ *Breakfast.*

$$$ **Mountain Sky Hotel and Suites.** The hotel is within easy walking distance of shops, restaurants, and the small-boat harbor—the center of summertime activity. **Pros:** has all amenities; very clean. **Cons:** not much personality. **TripAdvisor:** "very gracious hosts," "room was extremely clean and tidy," "centrally located and spacious rooms." ⊠ *100 Meals Ave.* ☎ *907/835–4445* ⊕ *www.mountainskyhotel.com* ⤳ *101 rooms* △ *In-room: Wi-Fi. In-hotel: pool, gym, spa, laundry facilities* ⦿ *Breakfast.*

$$$$ **Prince William Sound Lodge.** This fly-in lodge on a remote shore of northeastern Prince William Sound offers a wide range of vacation activities, including hiking, bird-watching, wildlife viewing, exploring nearby Alaska native villages, and the chance for some of the best silver salmon fishing in the state. **Pros:** delicious meals; incredible location. **Cons:** remote, fly-in location. ⊠ *Ellamar* ⬚ *3900 Clay Products Dr., Anchorage 99517* ☎ *907/248–0909 or 907/440–0909* ⊕ *www. princewilliamsound.us* ⤳ *5 rooms* △ *In-room: no TV. In-hotel: restaurant* ▭ *No credit cards* ⊗ *Closed late Sept.–Apr.* ⦿ *All meals.*

CORDOVA

6 hrs southeast of Valdez by water, 150 mi east of Anchorage by air.

A small town with the spectacular backdrop of snowy Mt. Eccles, Cordova is the gateway to the Copper River delta—one of the great birding areas of North America. Perched on Orca Inlet in eastern Prince William Sound, Cordova began life early in the 20th century as the port city for the Copper River and Northwestern Railway, which was built to serve the Kennicott Copper mines 191 mi away in the Wrangell Mountains. Since the mines and the railroad shut down in 1938, Cordova's economy has depended heavily on fishing. Attempts to develop a road along the abandoned railroad line connecting to the state highway system were dashed by the 1964 earthquake, so Cordova remains isolated. Access is limited to airplane or ferry.

6

GETTING HERE AND AROUND

Take the scenic ferry from either Whittier or Valdez along the **Alaska Marine Highway,** or catch a commercial flight from Anchorage. Once in town, the center is foot-friendly, but you'll want some wheels for heading down the Copper River Highway.

> **TIP**
>
> ■TIP➜ Some of the more-popular lodges need to be booked at least a year in advance. However, last-minute cancellations can create openings even late in the season.

Though there isn't much in the way of paved road in Cordova, you can still drive the remnants of the scenic Copper River Highway, which takes you past Childs Glacier and the Million Dollar Bridge.

ESSENTIALS

Ferry Information Alaska Marine Highway (✉ *6858 Glacier Hwy., Juneau* ☎ *907/465–3941 or 800/642–0066* ⊕ *www.ferryalaska.com*).

Medical Assistance Cordova Medical Center (✉ *602 Chase Ave.* ☎ *907/424–8000*).

Rental Cars Chinook Auto Rentals (✉ *Cordova Airport* ☎ *877/424–5279*).

Visitor Information Cordova Chamber of Commerce (✉ *404 First St., Cordova* ☎ *907/424–7260* ⊕ *www.cordovachamber.com*).

EXPLORING

Exhibits at the **Cordova Museum** tell of early explorers to the area, Native culture, the Copper River and Northwestern Railway/Kennicott Mine era, and the growth of the commercial fishing industry. An informative brochure outlines a self-guided walking tour of the town's historic buildings. Evening programs and regional art exhibits such as "Fish Follies" and "Bird Flew" are sponsored by the historical society. The gift shop features a selection of local postcards, Cordova and Alaskan gifts, and local history books. ✉ *622 1st St.* ☎ *907/424–6665* ⊕ *www. cordovamuseum.org* 🖆 *$1 suggested donation* ☉ *Memorial Day–Labor Day, Mon.–Sat. 10–6, Sun. 2–4; Labor Day–Memorial Day, Tues.–Fri. 10–5, Sat. 1–5.*

Drive out of town along the Copper River Highway and visit the **Copper River delta**. This 700,000-acre wetland is one of North America's most spectacular vistas. The two-lane highway crosses marshes, forests, streams, lakes, and ponds that are home to countless shorebirds, waterfowl, and other bird species. Numerous terrestrial mammals including moose, wolves, lynx, mink, and beavers live here, too, and the Copper River salmon runs are world famous. When the red and king salmon hit the river in spring, there's a frantic rush to net the tasty fish and rush them off to waiting markets and restaurants all over the country.

The **Million Dollar Bridge,** at Mile 48, was a railroad project completed in 1910 for the Copper River and Northwestern Railway to carry copper ore to market from the mines at Kennicott. Soon after construction was completed, the nearby Childs and Miles glaciers threatened to overrun the railroad and bridge. Although the glaciers stopped short of the railroad, the copper market collapsed in 1938, making the route economically obsolete. The far span of the bridge was toppled by the Good Friday earthquake in 1964 and was not rebuilt until 2005.

From the end of the road you can view the **Childs Glacier.** Although there is no visitor center, there is a covered viewing area next to the bridge, where you can see the face of the glacier and wait for a huge chunk of ice to topple into the river. The waves produced by falling ice frequently wash migrating salmon onto the riverbank; the local brown bears have been known to patrol the river's edge looking for an easy meal, so keep your eyes peeled.

OUTDOOR ACTIVITIES AND GUIDED TOURS

Spring migration to the **Copper River delta** provides some of the finest avian spectacles in the world. Species include the western sandpiper, American dipper, orange-crowned warbler, and short-billed dowitcher. Trumpeter swans and dusky Canada geese can also be seen. The **Copper River Delta Shorebird Festival** (☎ 907/424–7260 ⊕ *www.cordovachamber. com*), held the first week of May, includes five days of workshops and guided field trips. As many as 5 million birds, mostly western sandpipers and dunlins, descend on the Copper River delta, feeding and resting on their long migration to their northern nesting grounds. This migration respite is critical for these birds, and the food they gather from the rich mudflats of the delta keeps them alive and healthy.

Alaskan Wilderness Outfitting Co. (☎ 907/424–5552 ⊕ *www. alaskawilderness.com*) operates an air-taxi service out of Cordova and arranges fresh- and saltwater fly-out fishing experiences, from drop-offs to guided tours with lodge accommodations. It also offers floating cabins in Prince William Sound and a full-service lodge for silver salmon on the Tsiu River.

Cordova Air Service (☎ 907/424–3289) leads aerial tours of Prince William Sound on planes with wheels or floats.

Cordova Coastal Outfitters (☎ 907/424–7424 ⊕ *www.cordovacoastal. com*) conducts half- and full-day sea-kayak tours. It rents kayaks, canoes, bikes, small motorboats, and camping and fishing gear, and can arrange custom tours to fit your desired level of activity. It also runs half- and full-day wildlife and natural history tours on a 32-foot commercial fishing boat, as well as a water taxi. If you rent a kayak or bring your own, you can get pick-up and drop-off service anywhere on the road system.

EN ROUTE At Mile 17 there's a turnoff to **Alaganik Slough.** This 5-mi road leads to a wheelchair-accessible boardwalk as well as covered viewing shelters, restrooms, and picnic areas. A dedicated bird-watcher can spend hours peering into the vegetation, seeking out interesting avian species.

WHERE TO EAT

$$
AMERICAN
✕**Ambrosia.** Pastas, hamburgers, and submarine sandwiches are served behind the storefront, but it's the hearty pizzas that have earned this place its reputation among locals. ✉ *410 1st St.* ☎ *907/424–7175* ☺ *Closed Nov.–Jan.*

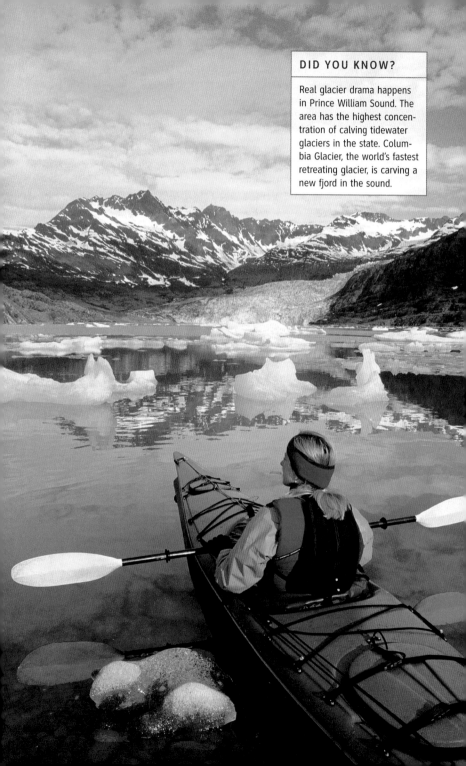

¢–$ ✕ **Killer Whale Café**. Have a breakfast of espresso and baked goods or
CAFÉ an omelet at this café. For lunch you can choose from a deli menu of
soups, salads, and sandwiches, followed by a fresh, homemade dessert.
✉ *507 1st St.* ☎ *907/424–7733* ▭ *No credit cards* ◷ *No dinner; closed
Oct.–May 1.*

$$$ ✕ **Powder House Bar & Restaurant**. On clear summer evenings you can
AMERICAN relax on the deck overlooking Eyak Lake at this roadside bar and enjoy
whatever the cook's in the mood to fix: homemade soups, sandwiches,
sushi, and seasonal seafood are all possibilities. If you're lucky or skill-
ful in your fishing endeavors, the kitchen staff will cook your catch.
Steak and seasonal seafood, including shrimp, scallops, razor clams,
and whatever else is fresh, are available every night. ✉ *Mi 2.1, Copper
River Hwy.* ☎ *907/424–3529.*

WHERE TO STAY

For expanded hotel reviews, visit Fodors.com.

$ ☶ **Cordova Lighthouse Inn**. Two of the rooms have mountain views, but
if at all possible get one of the two with harbor views for the full Alas-
kan fishing-village ambience, or the new large suite with the fireplace.
Pros: in-town location; remodeled in 2008; very nice rooms. **Cons:** must
climb steep stairs to access the four rooms at the top. ✉ *112 Nicholoff
Way, Box 2206* ☎ *907/424–7080* ⊕ *www.cordovalighthouseinn.com*
⤷ *8 rooms* ⚹ *In-room: Wi-Fi. In-hotel: laundry facilities.*

$–$$ ☶ **Cordova Rose Lodge**. This truly unique lodge sits on a barge on the
Prince William Sound breakwater. **Pros:** delicious breakfast; waterfront
location. **Cons:** short walk from town; some folks might want a vehicle.
✉ *1315 Whitshed, Box 1494* ☎ *907/424–7673* ⊕ *www.cordovarose.
com* ⤷ *11 rooms, 2 cabins* ⚹ *In-room: kitchen, no TV (some), Wi-Fi.
In-hotel: business center* ◷ *Closed Oct.–Apr., or until weather is good*
◉⦿ *Breakfast.*

$ ☶ **Northern Nights Inn B&B**. Commanding a dramatic view of Orca Inlet
just a couple of blocks from downtown Cordova, this turn-of-the-20th-
century bed-and-breakfast has roomy suites furnished with antiques.
Pros: big, bright rooms are a great value; some rooms have full kitchens.
Cons: only one ground-floor room for those who have trouble with
stairs. **TripAdvisor:** "great breakfasts cooked to order," "very clean
and comfortable," "great hosts and location." ✉ *500 3rd St., Box 1564*
☎ *907/424–5356* ⊕ *www.northernnightsinn.com* ⤷ *1 room, 3 suites*
⚹ *In-room: kitchen, Wi-Fi. In-hotel: laundry facilities.*

$$$ ☶ **Orca Adventure Lodge**. The list of activities at the lodge goes on and
on: fishing, kayaking, river rafting, hiking, bear-viewing, and flightsee-
ing. **Pros:** spectacular views with sea otters congregating outside. **Cons:**
about 2 mi from town, so some folks might want a vehicle. ✉ *301 Orca
Rd.* ⤶ *Box 2105, 99574* ☎ *907/424–7249 or 866/424–6722* ⊕ *www.
orcaadventurelodge.com* ⤷ *23 rooms, 4 suites* ⚹ *In-room: no TV,
Wi-Fi. In-hotel: restaurant* ◷ *Restaurant closed Oct.–May.*

$$ ☶ **Reluctant Fisherman Inn**. At this waterfront hotel and restaurant you
can watch the commercial-fishing fleet and other maritime traffic sail
by. **Pros:** perfect location in the heart of Cordova. **Cons:** Rooms can be
noisy with nightlife activity. **TripAdvisor:** "incredible scenery," "world
class food," "very comfortable." ✉ *407 Railroad Ave.* ☎ *907/424–3272*

6

or *877/770–3272* ⊕ *www.reluctantfisherman.com* ⤵*41 rooms* ⬧ *In-room: Wi-Fi. In-hotel: restaurant, bar, laundry facilities* ⍥*Breakfast.*

¢ ⊞ **U.S. Forest Service Cabins.** The Cordova Ranger District of the Chugach National Forest maintains a series of 18 backcountry cabins for rent. **Pros:** beautiful and remote. **Cons:** you must be self-sufficient and comfortable in the wilderness. ☎ *877/444–6777* ⊕ *www.recreation. gov* ⤵*17 cabins.*

SHOPPING

Orca Book & Sound Co. (⊠ *507 1st St.* ☎ *907/424–5305* ⊙ *Closed Sun.*) is much more than a bookstore. In addition to books, it sells music, art supplies, children's toys, and locally produced art. The walls often double as a gallery for local works or traveling exhibits, and the store specializes in old, rare, out-of-print, and first-edition books, especially Alaskana. ■**TIP→** In the back is an espresso-smoothie bar; the upstairs area has wireless Internet access for a small fee.

KENAI PENINSULA

The Kenai Peninsula, thrusting into the Gulf of Alaska south of Anchorage, is South Central's playground, offering salmon and halibut fishing, spectacular scenery, and wildlife viewing. Commercial fishing is important to the area's economy; five species of Pacific salmon run up the aqua-color Kenai River every summer. Campgrounds and trailheads for backwoods hiking are strung along the roads. Along the way you can explore three major federal holdings on the peninsula—the western end of the sprawling Chugach National Forest, Kenai National Wildlife Refuge, and Kenai Fjords National Park.

HOPE

39 mi west of Portage, 87 mi south of Anchorage.

The little gold-mining community of Hope sits just across Turnagain Arm from Anchorage. To visit, however, you must drive the 87 mi all the way around the arm. Your reward is a quiet little community that is accessible to but not overrun by tourists. Hope was founded by miners in 1896, and the old log cabins and weathered frame buildings in the town center are favorite photography subjects. You'll find lots of gold-panning, fishing, and hiking opportunities, and the northern trailhead for the 38-mi-long Resurrection Pass Trail is nearby. Contact the U.S. Forest Service for information on campgrounds, cabin rentals, and hikes in the area.

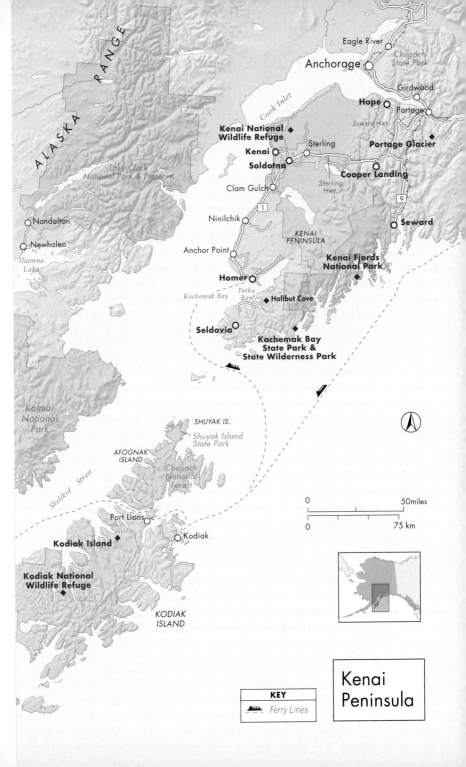

CAMPING IN HOPE

⚠ **Coeur d'Alene Campground.** If you really want to get away from civilization, come here. It sits high above the Resurrection Creek valley, quite literally in mountain-goat country. The drive is up a twisty 6-mi road over areas not recommended for RVs or trailers. There's no water at the site, no reservations are taken, and there's no charge for camping. From Hope, take the Resurrection Creek road for 1.6 mi to the Palmer Creek Road, and head up the mountain. The road is frequently closed due to avalanches until mid- to late May. **Pros:** fantastic views of the mountains. **Cons:** very basic amenities. ⊠ *Mi 2 Palmer Creek Rd.* ☎ *No phone* ⊃ *6 tent sites* ⚲ *Pit toilets, fire pits, picnic tables* ☉ *Closed Oct.–Apr.*

⚠ **Porcupine Campground.** The highway dead-ends into this campground: you're right on the shore of Turnagain Arm, with access to the 5-mi Gull Rock Trail, which runs along the shoreline. Occasionally you can spot the bore tide and beluga whales as they hunt for salmon up and down the coast. Some of the campsites overlook the arm, but you'll have to be quick or lucky to snag one of these. ■**TIP**→ **Although the mudflats look tempting at low tide, under no circumstances should you venture onto them—it's very dangerous out there, and chances for rescue if you're stranded are nil.** **Pros:** well maintained; mostly private sites. **Cons:** can get crowded during peak season. ⊠ *Mi 17.8, Hope Hwy.* ☎ *No phone* ⊃ *24 RV/tent sites* ⚲ *Pit toilets, drinking water, fire pits, picnic tables* ▤ *No credit cards* ☉ *Closed mid-Sept.–Apr.*

WHERE TO EAT

$$ ✕ **Tito's Discovery Cafe.** When the original Tito's restaurant burned down,
AMERICAN uninsured, in 1999, the owner was faced with financial ruin. But this tiny community got together and put Tito back on his feet and rebuilt the restaurant. Today Tito's serves basic American roadhouse food, along with seafood pasta, the ubiquitous halibut, and fresh-baked pies. We highly recommend the reindeer sausage sub. ⊠ *Mi 16.5, Hope Hwy.* ☎ *907/782–3274* ☉ *Open May 2–Sept., daily 7–9.*

WHERE TO STAY

For expanded hotel reviews, visit Fodors.com.

$$$ ▥ **Bowman's Bear Creek Lodge.** Of the five cabins, four are around a pond and one is down by the creek. **Pros:** great restaurant, dinners included in price; nightly campfire around the pond. **Cons:** shared bath. ⊠ *Mi 15.9, Hope Hwy.* ⌑ *Box 4, 99605* ☎ *907/782–3141* ⊕ *www.bowmansbearcreeklodge.com* ⊃ *5 cabins with shared bath* ⚲ *In-room: no TV. In-hotel: restaurant* ☉ *Dinner nightly 4–10.*

¢ ▥ **Seaview Cafe & Bar.** True to its name, this rustic little establishment in the original Hope town site offers great views of the arm and the Chugach. **Pros:** charming historic location. **Cons:** cabins are rustic; food is bar food. ⊠ *Main St., Box 110* ☎ *907/782–3300* ⊕ *www.seaviewcafealaska.com* ⊃ *50 tent sites, 16 RV sites with hookups ($18*

MOUNTAIN BIKING THE KENAI PENINSULA

The Kenai Peninsula offers outstanding opportunities for mountain bikers seeking thigh-busting challenges amid extraordinary scenery. **Crescent Creek Trail** (at Mile 44.9 of Sterling Highway; drive 3 mi to the trailhead at end of gravel road); **Devil's Pass** (at Mile 39.5 of Seward Highway); **Johnson Pass** (at Miles 32.6 and 63.7 of Seward Highway); and the **Resurrection trail systems** offer miles of riding for a wide range of expertise. Cyclists here are subject to highly fickle mountain weather patterns. But remember that you're never really alone in wild Alaska: be sure to bring along bear spray and bug dope (repellent).

For maps and descriptions of trails, visit the state **Department of Natural Resources** Web site (⊕ *www.dnr.state.ak.us/parks/aktrails/ats/ken-ats.htm*).

with electric and $12 without), 2 cabins ♿ In-room: kitchen (some), no TV. In-hotel: restaurant, bar ☉ Closed mid-Sept.–mid-May.

SHOPPING

Sherritt Fine Art Gallery (✉ *2nd St.* ☎ *907/782–3436* ⊕ *www.scottsherritt.com*) This cozy gallery space exhibits Scott Sheritt's Alaska-influenced paintings, as well as those of other artists.

SEWARD

74 mi south of Hope, 127 mi south of Anchorage.

Fodor's Choice ★ It seems hard to believe that such beauty exists as in Seward. Surrounded on all sides by Kenai Fjords National Park, Chugach National Forest, and Resurrection Bay, Seward offers all the quaint realities of a small railroad town with the bonus of jaw-dropping scenery. This little town of fewer than 3,000 citizens was founded in 1903, when survey crews arrived at the ice-free port and began planning a railroad to the Interior. Since its inception, Seward has relied heavily on tourism and commercial fishing. It is also the launching point for excursions into Kenai Fjords National Park, where it is quite common to see marine life and calving glaciers.

GETTING HERE AND AROUND

As a cruise-ship port, Seward has several routes in and out. Arrive by boat via the Alaska Marine Highway or, from Anchorage, take a luxury Ultradome railcar, or drive the 127 mi from Anchorage. Although there's a small airport, only private planes use it. It's possible to walk around town or from the harbor to downtown, but there's also trolley service in summer.

ESSENTIALS

Medical Assistance Providence Seward Medical Center (✉ *417 1st Ave.* ⊕ *907/224–5205*).

Visitor and Tour Information Seward Visitors Bureau (✉ *Mi 2, Seward Hwy.* ✉ *Box 749, Seward 99664* ☎ *907/224–8051* ⊕ *www.sewardak.org*).

EXPLORING

☾ Spend an afternoon at the **Alaska**
Fodor's Choice **SeaLife Center,** with massive cold-
★ water tanks and outdoor viewing
decks as well as interactive displays
of cold-water fish, seabirds, and
marine mammals, including harbor seals and a 2,000-pound sea
lion. A research center as well as
visitor center, it also rehabilitates
injured marine wildlife and provides educational experiences for
the general public. Appropriately,
the center was partially funded with
reparations money from the *Exxon*

WORD OF MOUTH

"We drove to Lowell Point where
we hopped on our water taxi
down Resurrection Bay and up
Ailaik Bay. Found our little island,
and the two of us plus our guide
hopped out and started paddling.
It was amazing—we had the entire
bay to ourselves, save for a couple
of tour boats, which would only
come in to view the glacier for
10–15 minutes, tops." —BostonGal

Valdez oil spill. Films, hands-on activities, a gift shop, and behind-the-
scenes tours ($12 and up) complete the offerings. ⊠ *301 Railway Ave.*
☏ *907/224–6300 or 888/378–2525* ⊕ *www.alaskasealife.org* ✉ *$20*
⊙ *Mid-May–mid-Sept., Mon.–Thurs. 9–6:30, Fri.–Sun. 8–6:30; mid-
Sept.–mid-May, daily 10–5.*

★ A short walk from the parking lot along a paved path will bring you
face to face with **Exit Glacier** *(⇨ see Kenai Fjords National Park),* just
outside Seward. Look for the marked turnoff at Mile 3.7 as you enter
town or ask locals for directions. There's a small walk-in campground
here, a ranger station, and access to the glacier. Exit Glacier is the most
accessible part of the **Harding Icefield.** This mass of ice caps the Kenai
Mountains, covering more than 1,100 square mi, and it oozes more
than 40 glaciers from its edges and down the mountainsides. Reach it
from Mile 3.7. The hike to the ice field from the parking lot is a 9-mi
round-trip that gains 3,000 feet in elevation, so it's not for the timid or
out of shape. But if you're feeling up to the task, the hike and views are
breathtaking. Local wildlife includes mountain goats and bears both
black and brown, so keep a sharp eye out for them. Once you reach the
ice, don't travel across it unless you have the gear and experience with
glacier travel. Glacier ice is notoriously deceptive—the surface can look
solid and unbroken, while underneath a thin crust of snow crevasses
lie in wait for the unwary.

Seward, like Valdez, was badly damaged by the 1964 earthquake. A
movie illustrating the upheaval is shown from Memorial Day until
Labor Day, daily at 2 pm in the **Seward Community Library.** Russian icons
and paintings by prominent Alaskan artists are on exhibit. ⊠ *238 5th
Ave.* ☏ *907/224–4082* ⊕ *www.cityofseward.net/library* ✉ *Movie $3*
⊙ *Mon.–Thurs. 10–8, Fri. and Sat. 10–6, Sun. 1–6.*

The **Seward Museum** displays photographs of the quake's damage, model
rooms and artifacts from the early pioneers, and historical and current information on the Seward area. ⊠ *336 3rd Ave., at Jefferson St.*
☏ *907/224–3902* ✉ *$3* ⊙ *Mid-May–Sept., daily 10–5; Oct.–mid-May,
weekends noon–4. Hrs may vary; call for recorded information.*

Seward. Fishing is an important industry and popular recreational activity in Seward.

The first mile of the historic original **Iditarod Trail** runs along the beach and makes for a nice, easy stroll. There is also a great walking tour designed by the city—maps are available at the visitor bureau, the converted railcar at the corner of 3rd Avenue and Jefferson Street, or the Seward Chamber of Commerce Visitor Center at Mile 2 on the Seward Highway.

For a different view of the town, drive out **Nash Road**, around Resurrection Bay, and look down at Seward, nestled at the base of the surrounding mountains like a young bird in its nest. If you drive south from the SeaLife Center for about 10 minutes, you'll reach **Lowell Point**, a wooded stretch of land along the bay with great access to camping, beach walking, hiking, and kayaking; the spot is great for a day trip.

OUTDOOR ACTIVITIES AND GUIDED TOURS

For more details on Kenai Fjords, flip to the next section.

ADVENTURE AND WILDLIFE VIEWING

Exit Glacier Guides (✉ *Small-boat harbor* ☎ 907/224–5569, 907/491–0552 [Sept.–May] ⊕ *www.exitglacierguides.com*) offers guided tours to Exit Glacier—and not just to the moraine, where most tourists stop. The experienced guides lead travelers onto the glacier. It also offers guided hikes to viewpoints and the Harding Icefield. For those wanting to visit the glacier independently, Exit Glacier Guides runs an hourly shuttle from downtown to the glacier for $10 round-trip.

BOATING

Kenai Fjords Tours (☎ 907/276–6249 *or* 877/777–4051 ⊕ *www.kenaifjords.com*), part of the Native-owned Alaska Heritage Tours, is the oldest and largest company running tours through the park. From March through mid-September it leads 3- to 10-hour cruises, priced from $69 to $189, which includes lunch. In 2007 and 2008 it added catamarans to its fleet, which are less susceptible to the rolling motion that can cause seasickness. Cruise options include exclusive visits to Fox Island, interpretive programs by National Park Service rangers, cruise and kayak combinations, glacier viewing, and opportunities to see whales, puffins, otters, and Steller sea lions. Transportation and overnight options are also available. **Captain's Choice Tour** (☎ 877/777–4051 ⊕ *www.mariahtours.com*), a part of Kenai Fjords Tours, operates smaller boats (with a maximum of 22 passengers per boat) through Kenai Fjords mid-May–August. The tour specializes in birding and photography. Breakfast and lunch are provided.

Major Marine Tours (☎ 907/274–7300 or 800/764–7300 ⊕ *www. majormarine.com*) conducts half-day and full-day cruises of Resurrection Bay and Kenai Fjords National Park. Park cruises are narrated by a National Park Service ranger, and meals of salmon and prime rib are an option. A custom-built catamaran runs daily from March through September. Summer cruises include a three-hour whale-watching tour and a six-hour Kenai Fjords trip, featuring narration by a national park ranger. Major Marine Tours can arrange transportation between Anchorage and Seward.

The Fish House. Operating out of Seward since 1974, this booking agency represents dozens of Resurrection Bay and Kenai Peninsula fishing charters, specializing in silver salmon and halibut, and can hook you up for half-day or full-day charters. ⊠ *Small-boat harbor* ☎ *907/224–3674 or 800/257–7760* ⊕ *www.thefishhouse.net.*

DEEP-SEA FISHING

Crackerjack Sportfishing (✉ *Box 2794, small-boat harbor 99664* ☎ *907/224–2606 or 800/566–3912* ⊕ *www.crackerjackcharters.com*) offers full- and half-day fishing charters as well as two- to five-day fishing expeditions in the Kenai Fjords National Park and beyond. The local captains have been guiding in Seward for 15 years, and offer trips year-round.

HIKING

The **Caines Head Trail** allows easy, flat hiking along the coast, but a large portion of the hike is over tidal mudflats, so care must be taken to time the hike correctly—with tides here running in the 10- to 20-foot range, bad planning isn't just a case of getting your feet wet. It's officially advised that the trail be hiked only when there's a "plus 4-foot tide or greater" in summer. The trail is 4.5 mi, starting from Lowell Point, and two cabins can be rented at Derby Cove and Callisto Canyon.

The **Lost Lake/Primrose Trail** is a 16-mi end-to-end loop through spruce forests and up into the high alpine area. The Lost Lake trailhead is near Mile 5 of the Seward Highway, and the other end is at the Primrose campground at Mile 17. The trails are steep and usually snow-covered through late June, but the views along the Lost Lake valley are worth the climb. Above the tree line you're in mountain-goat country—look for white, blocky figures perched on the precarious cliffs. The lake is a prime spot for rainbow trout fishing. As usual, be bear aware. The Dale Clemens cabin, at Mile 4.5 from the Lost Lake trailhead, has propane heat and a stunning view of Resurrection Bay.

For a comprehensive listing of all the trails, cabins, and campgrounds in the Seward Ranger District of Chugach National Forest, check the Web site of the U.S. Forest Service.

One of the biggest events of the year in Seward is the **Mt. Marathon Race,** run on July 4 since 1915. Folks come from near and far to run, and the entire town comes out to celebrate. It doesn't take the winners very long—44 minutes or so—but the route is straight up the mountain (3,022 feet) and back down to the center of town. Ambitious hikers can hit the Runner's Trail behind Providence Medical Center on Jefferson, while those who prefer a more leisurely (though still steep) climb can take the Hiker's Trail from 1st Avenue. For more information, contact the **Seward Chamber of Commerce** (🕮 *Box 749, Seward 99664* 📠 *907/224–8051* ⊕ *www.sewardak.org*).

WHERE TO EAT

$$$$ ✕ **Chinooks Waterfront Restaurant.** On the waterfront in the small-boat SEAFOOD harbor, Chinooks has a dazzling selection of fresh seafood dishes, beers on tap, a great wine selection, and a stunning view from the upstairs window seats. Pasta dishes and a few beef specialties round out the menu We recommend the seafood sauté. ⊠ *1404 4th Ave.* 📠 *907/224– 2207* ⊕ *www.chinookswaterfront.com* ⊘ *Closed mid-Oct.–May.*

$$$ ✕ **Christo's Palace.** Serving Greek, Italian, Mexican, and seafood meals, ECLECTIC this ornately furnished downtown restaurant is a surprisingly elegant hidden treasure. The nondescript facade belies the high-beamed ceilings, dark-wood accents, ornate chandeliers, and a large, gorgeous mahogany bar reputedly built in the mid-1800s and imported from San Francisco. Portions are generous, desserts are tempting, and there is a small selection of after-dinner cognacs. The grilled halibut portobello is particularly good. ⊠ *133 4th Ave.* 📠 *907/224–5255* ⊕ *www. christospalace.com.*

$$–$$$ ✕ **Le Barn Appétit.** Don't let the name fool you. This little restaurant and FRENCH inn are in fact in an old barn, but this is no run-of-the-mill grub. You'll find some of the finest French cuisine in Alaska. The quiche Lorraine and the crepes are worth writing home about. For dinner, the chicken cordon bleu and the stuffed pork tenderloin are perfect examples of the excellent cuisine to be found here. The on-site B&B offers a very pleasant stay. ⊠ *11786 Old Exit Glacier Rd.* 📠 *907/224–8706* ⊕ *www. lebarnappetit.com.*

¢–$ ✕ **Railway Cantina.** This little hole-in-the-wall in the harbor area is a MEXICAN local favorite. A wide selection of burritos, quesadillas, and great fish tacos incorporates local seafood and is supplemented by an array of hot sauces, many contributed by customers who brought them from their travels. ⊠ *1401 4th Ave.* 📠 *907/224–8226.*

$$$ ✕ **Resurrection Roadhouse.** On a sunny summer evening you'll have to AMERICAN fight locals for seats on the Roadhouse's deck, which overlooks the Resurrection River and the mountains surrounding it. Set off Exit Glacier/Herman Leirer Road, and part of the Seward Windsong Lodge, the Roadhouse gets warm afternoon light that goes well with multiple types of beers on tap and excellent pizzas and sweet-potato fries. ■ TIP➔ The bar and restaurant have different menus—ask to see both, and then decide

6

where to sit. ⊠ *Mi 0.5, Exit Glacier Rd.; 31772 Herman Leirer Rd.* ☎ *907/224–7116 or 877/777–4079* ⊕ *www.sewardwindsong.com.*

WHERE TO STAY

For expanded hotel reviews, visit Fodors.com.

$$$ **Alaska Paddle Inn.** A new building offers beachfront panoramic views out at Lowell Point and access to its own private beach. **Pros:** unobstructed views of Resurrection Bay; waffle irons and mix in rooms. **Cons:** 20 steps up to the High Tide room. **TripAdvisor:** "a lovely location to relax," "room was wonderful," "beautiful accommodations and wonderful hosts." ⊠ *13745 Beach Dr.* ☎ *907/362–2628* ⊕ *www.alaskapaddleinn.com* ⟿ *2 rooms* ⚬ *In-room: kitchen, Wi-Fi* ⦿ *Breakfast.*

$–$$ **Alaska's Treehouse B&B.** Enjoy spectacular views of the Chugach ★   Mountains from the solarium and from the hot tub on the tiered deck at this quiet, rustic retreat. **Pros:** silence, solitude, and nature; modern amenities. **Cons:** a bit out of town; you'll need a car. **TripAdvisor:** "accommodations were spacious and comfortable," "fantastic breakfasts," "hosts were exceedingly generous." ⊠ *14593 Rainforest Circle, 1/2 mi off Seward Hwy., at Mi 7* ⬠ *Box 861 99664* ☎ *907/224–3867* ⊕ *www.virtualcities.com/ak/treehouse.htm* ⟿ *2 suites* ⚬ *In-hotel: restaurant* ▭ *No credit cards* ⦿ *Breakfast.*

$$ **Breeze Inn.** Across the street from the small-boat harbor, this modern hotel is very convenient if you're planning an early-morning fishing trip. **Pros:** directly across from the harbor; walking distance to downtown. **Cons:** rooms are bland and chain motel–like. ⊠ *1306 Seward Hwy.* ⬠ *Box 2147 99664* ☎ *907/224–5237 or 888/224–5237* ⊕ *www. breezeinn.com* ⟿ *100 rooms* ⚬ *In-room: Wi-Fi. In-hotel: 2 restaurants, bar, laundry facilities, some pets allowed.*

$$$–$$$$ **Hotel Edgewater.** The rooms at Seward's newest and snazziest hotel overlook Resurrection Bay, and on clear days the panorama of mountains, glaciers, and the bay is breathtaking. **Pros:** downtown location is convenient to the SeaLife Center, restaurants, and shops. **Cons:** it's not the cheapest waterfront lodging in town. **TripAdvisor:** "great view," "great adventure home base," "room was clean." ⊠ *202 5th Ave.* ☎ *907/224–2700 or 888/793–6800* ⊕ *www.hoteledgewater.com* ⟿ *76 rooms* ⚬ *In-room: Internet. In-hotel: bar* ⊙ *Closed Oct.–Apr.* ⦿ *Breakfast.*

$$$$ **Hotel Seward.** This historic downtown hotel is convenient to res-
Fodor's Choice   taurants, shopping, and the Alaska SeaLife Center. **Pros:** cool historic
★   building; excellent downtown location. **Cons:** no elevator in one wing. **TripAdvisor:** "very friendly and accommodating," "very quaint," "one of the most comfortable beds." ⊠ *221 5th Ave.* ☎ *907/224–2378 or 800/655–8785* ⊕ *www.hotelsewardalaska.com* ⟿ *62 rooms* ⚬ *In-room: Wi-Fi.*

$$$$ **Kenai Fjords Wilderness Lodge.** An hour's boat ride from Seward, this wilderness lodge sits within a quiet, forest-lined cove on Fox Island in Resurrection Bay. **Pros:** solitude; great views; everything's included. **Cons:** its location makes it pricey. ⊠ *Fox Island* ⬠ *1304 4th Ave.* ☎ *907/ 224–8068 or 877/777-4053* ⊕ *www.kenaifjordslodge.com* ⟿ *8 cabins*

 In-room: kitchen, no TV. In-hotel: restaurant ⊙ *Closed Sept.–May* †○| *All meals.*

¢ ⊞ **Miller's Landing.** This sprawling waterfront complex offers cabins, campsites for tents ($26) and RVs ($36), water-taxi service to remote sites, sea-kayak and boat and motor rentals, and a booking service for area B&Bs, fishing trips, dogsled rides, hiking expeditions, sailing tours, and wildlife cruises. **Pros:** one-stop shopping for all your travel needs; a great location. **Cons:** some cabins are very, very basic; the campground can be overcrowded. ⊠ *Lowell Point Rd., Box 81* ☎ *907/224–5739 or 866/541–5739* ⊕ *www.millerslandingak.com* ⤳ *13 cabins, 3 rooms, 29 tent sites, 31 RV sites with hookups.*

$$$ ⊞ **Seward Windsong Lodge.** In a forested setting near the bank of the Resurrection River, the Seward Windsong has rooms and deluxe balcony suites decorated in warm plaids, pine furniture, and Alaskan prints. **Pros:** incredible views of the river valley; Resurrection Roadhouse is right next door. **Cons:** outside town, so you'll want a car, though a complimentary shuttle service is offered. ⊠ *Mi 0.5, Exit Glacier Rd., about 2 mi north of Seward* ⌖ *2525 C St., Anchorage 99503* ☎ *907/265–4501 or 888/959–9590* ⊕ *www.sewardwindsong.com* ⤳ *180 rooms, 16 suites* *In-room: Wi-Fi. In-hotel: restaurant, bar.*

$$ ⊞ **Stoney Creek Inn.** Sandwiched between two streams—one glacial, the other salmon-spawning—this B&B about 6 mi out of Seward offers a quiet respite from the summer buzz. **Pros:** quiet location a perfect distance from town. **Cons:** far enough from town that you'll want a car. ⊠ *33422 Stoney Creek Ave.* ☎ *907/224–3940* ⊕ *www.stoneycreekinn. net* ⤳ *5 rooms* *In-room: Wi-Fi* †○| *Breakfast.*

$$$ ⊞ **Teddy's Inn the Woods Bed & Breakfast.** This lovely bed-and-breakfast
Fodor's Choice is nestled in the woods across from Kenai Lake, surrounded by moun-
★ tains and hiking trails. **Pros:** The setting is superb; basketball courts on the property. **Cons:** You have to go up a flight of stairs. TripAdvisor: "excellent and warm host," "breakfasts are wonderful." ⊠ *29792 Seward Hwy (Mile 23), Seward* ☎ *907/288–3126* ⊕ *www.seward.net/ teddys/* ⤳ *1 cabin (3 twin beds, 1 queen)* *In-room: full kitchen, Wi-Fi, no TV. In-hotel: parking (free), some pets allowed* ⊟ *No credit cards* †○| *Breakfast.*

$–$$ ⊞ **Van Gilder Hotel.** Built in 1916 and listed on the National Register of Historic Places, the Van Gilder is an elegant building steeped in local history. **Pros:** oldest hotel in Seward. **Cons:** shared kitchen. **TripAdvisor:** "old world charm," "super comfortable," "clean and full of character." ⊠ *308 Adams St.* ☎ *907/224–3079 or 800/478-0400* ⊕ *www. vangilderhotel.com* ⤳ *20 rooms, 4 suites* *In-room: no TV, Wi-Fi. In-hotel: parking (free)* †○| *Breakfast.*

SHOPPING

☻ The **Ranting Raven** (⊠ *238 4th Ave.* ☎ *907/224–2228*) is a combination gift shop, bakery, and lunch spot, adorned with raven murals on the side of the building. You can indulge in fresh-baked goods, espresso drinks, and daily lunch specials such as quiche, focaccia, and homemade soups while perusing the packed shelves of local artwork, native crafts, and jewelry. **Resurrect Art Coffeehouse** (⊠ *320 3rd Ave.* ☎ *907/224–7161* ⊕ *www.resurrectart.com*) is a darling coffeehouse and gallery-gift shop.

CAMPING IN SEWARD

⚠ **Waterfront Park.** The city of Seward operates Waterfront Park, a sprawling facility that occupies some of the town's premier real estate. Campsites are all first come, first served except for "caravans" of 10 units or more. The payoff is camping on the shore of Resurrection Bay with an unparalleled view of the waterfront and the mountains across the way. Fishing boats, cruise ships, ferries, pleasure craft, and work boats parade past the park day and night; seals, sea lions, and sea otters cruise past; seabirds, waterfowl, and bald eagles glide overhead; and the fishing from the beach is very good during the silver salmon run that peaks in July. Expect crowds and a limited selection of sites on holiday and salmon derby weekends, and anytime the fishing is especially hot. **Pros:** right in the middle of the action; gorgeous view. **Cons:** right in the middle of the action, so it can stay loud late into the night. ✉ *Ballaine Blvd.* ☏ *City of Seward, SPRD/Parks & Campgrounds, Box 167, 99664-0167* ☏ *907/224–4055* ⊕ *www.cityofseward.net/parksRec/campgrounds.htm* ↪ *500 spaces, 99 with hookups* ⚑ *Pit toilets, full hookups, drinking water, fire pits, picnic tables* ▭ *No credit cards.*

It is housed in a 1932 church, and the ambience and views from the old choir loft are reason enough to stop by. Local art is showcased, and it's a good place to find Alaskan gifts that aren't mass-produced.

KENAI FJORDS NATIONAL PARK

125 mi south of Anchorage.

★ **Kenai Fjords National Park.** Photogenic Seward is the gateway to the 670,000-acre Kenai Fjords National Park. This is spectacular coastal parkland incised with sheer, dark, slate cliffs rising from the sea, ribboned with white waterfalls, and tufted with deep-green spruce. Kenai Fjords presents a rare opportunity for an up-close view of blue tidewater glaciers as well as some remarkable ocean wildlife.

GETTING HERE AND AROUND

The only land route to the park is via Herman Leirer (Exit Glacier) Road, which ends at Exit Glacier. Boats leaving Seward for half-day tours and beyond are ample. Beyond that access is limited unless you charter a boat or airplane, or arrange for a tour with one of the local companies. If you take a day trip on a tour boat out of Seward, it's highly likely you'll see frolicking sea otters, crowds of Steller sea lions lazing on the rocky shelves along the shore, a porpoise or two, bald eagles, and tens of thousands of seabirds. Humpback whales and orcas are sighted occasionally, and mountain goats mull about the seaside cliffs. The park's coastal fjords are a favorite of sea kayakers, who can camp or stay in reserved public-use cabins.

One of the park's chief attractions is Exit Glacier, which can be reached only by the one road that passes into Kenai Fjords. Trails inside the park lead to an overlook of the vast Harding Icefield.

Before venturing out into the far reaches of the park, gather as much data as possible from the locals concerning the weather, tides, and dangerous beaches. Once you leave Seward, you're a long way from help. Backcountry travelers should also be aware that some of the park's coastline has been claimed by local Native organizations and is now private property. Check with park headquarters to avoid trespassing on Native land.

ESSENTIALS
Visitor Information Kenai Fjords Park Office (☎ *907/224–7500* ⊕ *www.nps.gov/kefj).*

OUTDOOR ACTIVITIES AND GUIDED TOURS

BOATING **Major Marine Tours** (☎ *907/274–7300 or 800/764–7300* ⊕ *www.majormarine.com*) runs ranger-led boat tours through the park, with both half- and full-day excursions available.

COMBO TOURS **Exit Glacier Guides** (✉ *411 Port Ave., Seward* ☎ *907/224–5569 or 907/491–0552* ⊕ *www.exitglacierguides.com*) provides a $10 shuttle from town to Exit Glacier, and offers guided hikes to the glacier and Harding Icefield. **Kenai Fjord Tours** (☎ *800/478–8068*) leads day trips into Kenai Fjords National Park. It also conducts combination train–cruise–motor coach trips from Anchorage.

WHERE TO STAY
For expanded hotel reviews, visit Fodors.com.

¢ 🛏 **National Park Service Cabins.** The Kenai Fjords National Park manages four cabins, including three along the coast, favored by sea kayakers and for summer use only. **Pros:** you'll get all the nature you want. **Cons:** a few are accessible by boat or floatplane only. ✉ *1212 4th Ave.* 🗐 *Box 1727, Seward 99664* ☎ *907/224–7500 to reserve winter cabin, 907/271–2737 in Anchorage for summer rentals* ⊕ *www.nps.gov/kefj/index.htm* ⤴ *4 cabins.*

COOPER LANDING

100 mi south of Anchorage.

Centrally located on the Kenai Peninsula, Cooper Landing is within striking distance of some of Alaska's most popular fishing locations. Here the Russian River flows into the Kenai River, and spectacular fishing opportunities abound. Solid lines of traffic head south from Anchorage every summer weekend, and the confluence of the two rivers gets so crowded with enthusiastic anglers that the pursuit of salmon is often referred to as "combat fishing." However, a short walk upstream will separate you from the crowds and afford a chance to enjoy these gorgeous blue rivers.

The Russian River supports two runs of red (sockeye) salmon every summer, and it's the most popular fishery in the state. The Kenai River is famous for its runs of king (Chinook), red, pink, and silver (coho) salmon, as well as large rainbow trout and Dolly Varden char. A number of nearby freshwater lakes, accessible only by hiking trail, also provide excellent fishing for rainbow trout and Dolly Varden.

Continued on page 288

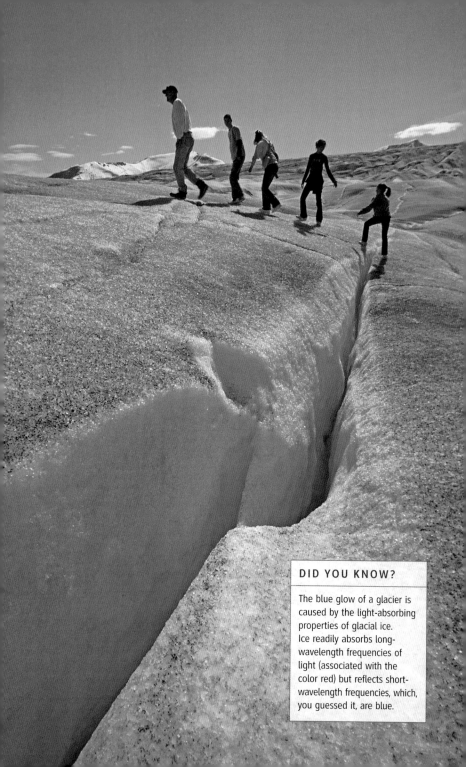

DID YOU KNOW?

The blue glow of a glacier is caused by the light-absorbing properties of glacial ice. Ice readily absorbs long-wavelength frequencies of light (associated with the color red) but reflects short-wavelength frequencies, which, you guessed it, are blue.

ALASKA'S GLACIERS
NOTORIOUS LANDSCAPE ARCHITECTS

(opposite) Facing the Taku Glacier challenge outside of Juneau. (top) River of ice

Glaciers—those massive, blue-hued tongues of ice that issue forth from Alaska's mountain ranges—perfectly embody the harsh climate, unforgiving terrain, and haunting beauty that make this state one of the world's wildest places. Alaska is home to roughly 100,000 glaciers, which cover almost 5% of the state's land.

FROZEN GIANTS

A glacier occurs where annual snowfall exceeds annual snowmelt. Snow accumulates over thousands of years, forming massive sheets of compacted ice. (Southeast Alaska's **Taku Glacier**, popular with flightseeing devotees, is one of Earth's meatiest: some sections measure over 4,500 feet thick.) Under the pressure of its own weight, the glacier succumbs to gravity and begins to flow downhill. This movement results in sprawling masses of rippled ice (Alaska's **Bering Glacier**, at 127 miles, is North America's longest). When glaciers reach the tidewaters of the coast, icebergs calve, or break off from the glacier's face, plunging dramatically into the sea.

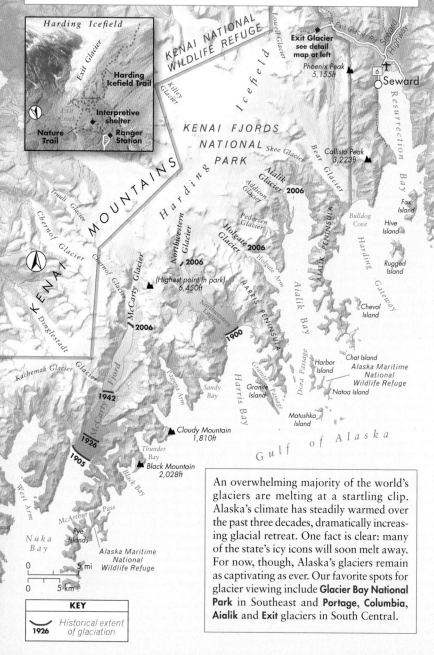

THE RAPIDLY RETREATING GLACIERS IN KENAI FJORDS NATIONAL PARK

Harding Icefield

Exit Glacier

Harding Icefield Trail

Interpretive shelter

Nature Trail

Ranger Station

KENAI NATIONAL WILDLIFE REFUGE

Lowell Glacier

Exit Glacier Rd

Seward Highway

Exit Glacier see detail map at left

Phoenix Peak 5,155ft

6

Seward

Killey Glacier

Icefield

Resurrection Bay

KENAI FJORDS NATIONAL PARK

Skee Glacier

Bear Glacier

Callisto Peak 3,223ft

Fox Island

Atalik Glacier **2006**

Addison Glacier

Pedersen Glacier

Bulldog Cove

Hive Island

Truuli Glacier

Harding

Chernof Glacier

KENAI MOUNTAINS

Chernof Glacier

Northwestern Glacier

Holgate Glacier **2006**

Holgate Arm

AIALIK PENINSULA

Harding Gateway

Rugged Island

2006

(Highest point in park) 6,450ft

HARRIS PENINSULA

Aialik Bay

Cheval Island

Dinglestadt Glacier

McCarty Glacier

Northwestern Lagoon

2006

Kachemak Glacier

1900

Paguna Arm

Dora Passage

Chat Island
Alaska Maritime National Wildlife Refuge

Harbor Island

Granite Passage

Natoa Island

1942

McCarty Fjord

Sandy Bay

Granite Island

Harris Bay

Matushka Island

1926

Gulf of Alaska

1905

Cloudy Mountain 1,810ft

Black Bay

Thunder Bay

Black Mountain 2,028ft

West Arm

McArthur Pass

Nuka Bay

Pye Islands

Alaska Maritime National Wildlife Refuge

0   5 mi
0   5 km

An overwhelming majority of the world's glaciers are melting at a startling clip. Alaska's climate has steadily warmed over the past three decades, dramatically increasing glacial retreat. One fact is clear: many of the state's icy icons will soon melt away. For now, though, Alaska's glaciers remain as captivating as ever. Our favorite spots for glacier viewing include **Glacier Bay National Park** in Southeast and **Portage, Columbia, Aialik** and **Exit** glaciers in South Central.

KEY

1926 Historical extent of glaciation

ICY BLUE HIKES & THUNDEROUS BOATING EXCURSIONS

Glaciers enchant us with their size and astonishing power to shape the landscape. But let's face it: nothing rivals the sheer excitement of watching a bus-size block of ice burst from a glacier's face, creating an unholy thunderclap that resounds across an isolated Alaskan bay.

Most frequently undertaken with a seasoned guide, **glacier trekking** is becoming increasingly popular. Many guides transport visitors to and from glaciers (in some cases by helicopter or small plane), and provide ski excursions, dogsled tours, or guided hikes on the glacier's surface. Striding through the surreal landscape of a glacier, ice crunching underfoot, can be an otherworldly experience. Whether you're whooping it up on a dogsled tour, learning the fundamentals of glacier travel, or simply poking about on a massive field of ice, you're sure to gain an acute appreciation for the massive scale of the state's natural environment.

You can also experience glaciers **via boat**, such as the Alaska Marine Highway, a cruise ship, a small chartered boat, or even your own bobbing kayak. Our favorite out of Seward is the ride with Kenai Fjords Tours. Don't be discouraged by rainy weather. Glaciers often appear even bluer on overcast days. When piloting your own vessel, be sure to keep your distance from the glacier's face.

Taking in the sights at Mendenhall Glacier

DID YOU KNOW?

What do glaciers and cows have in common? They both *calve*. While bovine calving refers to actual calf-birth, the word is also used to describe a tidewater glacier's stunning habit of rupturing icebergs from its terminus. When glacier ice meets the sea, steady tidal movement and warmer temperatures cause these frequent, booming deposits.

GLACIER-VIEWING TIPS

- The most important rule of thumb is never to venture onto a glacier without proper training or the help of a guide.

- Not surprisingly, glaciers have a cooling effect on their surroundings, so wear layers and bring gloves and rain gear.

- Glaciers can powerfully reflect sunlight, even on cloudy days. Sunscreen, sunglasses, and a brimmed hat are essential.

- Warm, thick-soled waterproof footwear is a must.

- Don't forget to bring a camera and binoculars (preferably waterproof).

Don't let the presence of dozens if not hundreds of fellow anglers lull you into a sense of complacency: in recent years the amount of brown bear activity at the Russian River has increased noticeably. This needn't deter you from enjoying yourself, though. Be aware of the posted signs warning of recent bear sightings, observe the local "rules of the road" about fishing and disposing of carcasses, and keep your senses tuned.

Cooper Landing serves as a trailhead for the 38-mi-long Resurrection Pass Trail, which connects to the village of Hope and the Russian Lakes/Resurrection River trails, which run south to Exit Glacier near Seward. The town's central location also affords easy access to saltwater recreation in Seward and Homer.

GETTING HERE AND AROUND

Follow the line of traffic flowing south out of Anchorage on the Seward Highway every Friday; take a right at the "Y" onto the Sterling Highway and soon you'll be there—just don't blink or you'll miss it! Look for the lodges and tackle shops that spring up from the wilderness, dotting either side of the highway. Cooper Landing does not operate a commercial airport.

SPORTS, THE OUTDOORS, AND GUIDED TOURS

FISHING Most lodges in Cooper Landing cater to the fishing crowd; ask when you make your reservation.

For fly-fishing for trout and salmon, **Alaska Troutfitters** (☎ *907/595–1212* ⊕ *www.aktroutfitters.com*) accommodates every level of fisherperson, from rank amateur to seasoned veteran. The company conducts a school covering everything from casting technique to fishing entomology and can arrange package deals with instruction, fishing, transportation, and accommodations.

Alaska Wildland Adventures. From the lodge in Cooper Landing south of Anchorage, these folks provide fishing adventures on the upper and lower Kenai River. ☎ *907/783–2928 or 800/334–8730* ⊕ *www.alaskawildland.com*.

HORSEBACK **Alaska Horsemen Trail Adventures.** This Cooper Landing–based com-
RIDING pany offers multiday pack trips into the Kenai Mountains via Crescent Lake, Resurrection, and other area trail systems. ☎ *907/595–1806 or 800/595–1806* ⊕ *www.alaskahorsemen.com*.

MULTISPORT **Alaska River Adventures.** These Cooper Landing–based guides take small groups fishing throughout the region, with self-professed "well-seasoned old pros." Additionally, they hold rare permits that allow them to offer trips into low-traversed areas. For those who want to experience the tranquil setting of Cooper Landing without having to go fish, they also offer "paddle and saddle" and scenic river-rafting day trips, as well as a gold-panning trip that introduces you to prospecting. ☎ *907/595–2000 or 800/836–9027* ⊕ *www.alaskariveradventures.com*.

WHERE TO EAT

¢–$ ✕ **Sunrise Inn.** On the shore of Kenai Lake, this cheerful little restau-
AMERICAN rant dishes up homemade soups, chowders, and salsas. The eclectic and very reasonably priced menu includes wraps and vegetarian items. Daily specials made from scratch and hand-grated french fries feature

prominently in what the owners describe as a "backwoods bistro." There's a spotting scope in the parking lot for spying on the Dall sheep and mountain goats in the surrounding peaks. The bar hosts live music on Saturday in summer, and there's a great deck for when the weather's warm. ⊠ *Mi 45, Sterling Hwy.* ☎ *907/595–1222* ⊕ *www. alaskasunriseinn.com.*

WHERE TO STAY

For expanded hotel reviews, visit Fodors.com.

$$ 🖬 **Alaska Wildland Adventures' Kenai Riverside Lodge.** This collection of buildings on the bank of the Kenai River offers a "roughing it in authentic comfort" all-inclusive package with renovated cabins that have private baths. **Pros:** beautiful wooded location; great adventure and expedition packages. **Cons:** cabins are a bit small. ⊠ *Mi 50.1, 16520 Sterling Hwy., Cooper Landing* ⬚ *Box 389, Girdwood 99587* ☎ *907/595–1279 or 800/478–4100* ⊕ *www.alaskasportfish.com* ⤳ *8 cabins* ⚅ *In-room: no TV. In-hotel: restaurant* ⊙ *Closed Oct.–mid-May.*

$$$$ 🖬 **Eagle Landing Resort.** Cabins come in three variations—regular, deluxe, and riverfront, all with private baths, heat, and kitchens. **Pros:** accommodations fit any budget; great views; fantastic kitchens. **Cons:** some staircases are steep (although most cabins also have bedrooms downstairs); some upstairs rooms are only semiprivate. ⊠ *Mi 48.1, Sterling Hwy., Box 748* ☎ *907/595–1213 or 866/595–1213* ⊕ *www. eaglelandingresort.net* ⤳ *12 cabins* ⚅ *In-room: kitchen, no TV, Wi-Fi.*

$$$$ 🖬 **Great Alaska Adventure Lodge.** Midway between Seward and Homer,
★ this lodge lives up to its name. **Pros:** all-inclusive; right along the Sterling Highway. **Cons:** right on the Sterling Highway. **TripAdvisor:** "the most amazing adventure," "a trout fishing dream," "lodging was spacious." ⊠ *Mi 82.5, 33881 Sterling Hwy., Sterling* ⬚ *Box 2670, Poulsbo, WA 98370* ☎ *907/262–4515; 800/544–2261; 360/697–6454 in winter* ⊕ *www.greatalaska.com* ⤳ *25 rooms* ⚅ *In-room: no TV. In-hotel: restaurant* ⊙ *Closed Oct.–mid-May.*

$$$ 🖬 **Gwin's Lodge.** Gwin's is the epicenter of much of the activity on the peninsula. **Pros:** get everything you need in one place. **Cons:** some cabins are actually trailers with a log facade. ⊠ *Mi 52, Sterling Hwy.* ☎ *907/595–1266* ⊕ *www.gwinslodge.com* ⤳ *17 rooms* ⚅ *In-room: no TV, Wi-Fi. In-hotel: restaurant, bar* ⊙ *Restaurant closed Oct.–Mar.*

$$ 🖬 **The Inn at Tern Lake.** Although the address is technically in Moose Pass, the Inn at Tern Lake sits right between Cooper Landing and Moose Pass, a few miles south of the "Y" where the Sterling Highway branches off the Seward. **Pros:** babbling springs and terns on the lake complete the Alaska experience. **Cons:** its unique location also means it's a bit far from any amenities. **TripAdvisor:** "spacious and beautiful rooms," "views were breathtaking," "accommodations were spotless." ⊠ *Mi 36, Seward Hwy.* ⬚ *Box 7, Moose Pass 99631* ☎ *907/288–3667* ⊕ *www. ternlakeinn.com* ⤳ *4 rooms* ⚅ *In-room: kitchen, Internet. In-hotel: tennis court, business center* ⎰◉⎱ *Breakfast.*

$$$$ 🖬 **Kenai Princess Wilderness Lodge.** "Elegantly rustic" might best describe
Fodor'sChoice this sprawling complex approximately 45 mi from Seward, on a bluff
★ overlooking the Kenai River. **Pros:** cozy rooms have fireplaces and manage to escape a corporate feel. **Cons:** rooms don't have views of the

6

river, even though the lodge sits right on top of it. **TripAdvisor:** "very nice setting overlooking Kenai River," "charming and rustic Alaskan lodge," "grounds are lovely." ⊠ *Mi 47.7, Sterling Hwy., Cooper Landing 99572* ☎ *907/595–1425 or 800/426–0500* ⊕ *www.princesslodges. com/kenai_lodge.cfm* ⇲ *86 rooms* ⌂ *In-hotel: restaurants, bar, gym, laundry facilities* ☉ *Closed mid-Sept.–May.*

KENAI NATIONAL WILDLIFE REFUGE

95 mi northwest of Kenai Fjords National Park, 150 mi southwest of Anchorage

Kenai National Wildlife Refuge. Its nearly 2 million acres include a portion of the Harding Icefield as well as two large and scenic lakes, Skilak and Tustumena. The refuge is not only the finest moose habitat in the region, but its waterways are great for canoeing and kayaking. The refuge maintains two visitor centers. The main center, in Soldotna, has wildlife dioramas, free films and information, and a bookstore and gift shop. There's also a seasonal "contact" center at Mile 57.8 of the Sterling Highway, open from mid-June to mid-August.

Wildlife is plentiful even by Alaskan standards: the refuge was originally established to protect the Kenai moose. Although caribou seldom appear near the road, Dall sheep and mountain goats live on the peaks near Cooper Landing, and black and brown bears, wolves, coyotes, lynx, beavers, and lots of birds reside here as well.

The refuge also contains a canoe trail system through the Swan Lake and Swanson River areas. Covering more than 140 mi on 100 lakes and the Swanson River, this route is an underused portion of the refuge that escapes the notice of most visitors and residents alike. This series of lakes linked by overland portages offers fantastic access to the remote backcountry, well away from what passes for civilization in the subarctic. The fishing improves exponentially with distance from the road system, and opportunities for undisturbed wildlife viewing are nearly unlimited.

GETTING HERE AND AROUND

■**TIP**→ You must paddle into the refuge; access is generally by canoe. Road access to the canoe trailheads is off the Swanson River Road at Mile 83.4 of the Sterling Highway. Other than canoeing, the only way to get into the far reaches of the refuge is by airplane. Floatplane services in Soldotna, where the refuge is headquartered, can fly you into the backcountry. The refuge office maintains lists of transporters, air taxis, canoe rentals, and big-game guides that are permitted to operate on refuge lands. To reach the main visitor center/refuge office on Ski Hill Road, turn south on Funny River Road in Soldotna just west of the Kenai River Bridge, and follow the signs.

ESSENTIALS

Visitor Information **Kenai National Wildlife Refuge Visitor Center** (⊠ *Ski Hill Rd., Soldotna* ☎ *907/262–7021* ⊕ *fws.gov/refuges/profiles/index. cfm?id=74525*).

SPORTS, THE OUTDOORS, AND GUIDED TOURS

BIKING **Alaska Backcountry Bike Tours.** Guided day and multiday hiking-mountain biking combo trips are a great way to get into the Kenai NWR wilderness. Contact Alaska Backcountry Bike Tours to set something up. ⊕ *www.mountainbikealaska.com.*

CANOEING The best way to experience the refuge's backcountry is by canoe. The **Swan Lake Canoe System** and the **Swanson River Canoe System** are accessed from the road system at the turnoff at Mile 83.4 of the Sterling Highway. Several loop trips enable visitors to fish, hike, and camp away from the road system and motorized boat traffic. Fishing for trout, salmon, and Dolly Varden is excellent, and the series of lakes and portages offer access to more than 100 mi of waterways. The Kenai National Wildlife Refuge Visitor Center has a list of canoeing outfitters.

HIKING Hiking trails branch off from the Sterling Highway and the Skilak Lake Loop. Degree of difficulty ranges from easy half-mile walks to strenuous climbs to mountain lakes. Bring topographic maps, water, food, insect repellent, and bear awareness. You won't find toilets, water fountains, or signposts. Remember: brown and black bears are numerous on the Kenai Peninsula.

WHERE TO STAY
For expanded hotel reviews, visit Fodors.com.

$$$$ ⬛ **Kenai Backcountry Lodge.** A trip to the Kenai Backcountry Lodge involves much more than driving up to the door and booking a room—in fact, that's not even an option. **Pros:** gets you to the backcountry without roughing it too much. **Cons:** shared bathrooms. ⬒ *Box 389, Girdwood 99587* ☎ *800/334–8730* ⊕ *www.alaskawildland.com/ kenaibackcountrylodge.htm* ⬏ *4 log cabins, 6 tent cabins* ⬙ *In-room: no TV. In-hotel: restaurant* ⊙ *Closed Sept.–May.*

¢ ⚠ **USFWS Cabins.** These cabins are in remote areas of the refuge accessible only by air or boat. The reservation system is a bit cumbersome, but can be done over the phone. However, if you're willing to overcome these hurdles, you'll find tranquillity and true wilderness, and won't have to worry about your tent springing a leak. **Pros:** the true experience of being off the grid. **Cons:** making a reservation is no easy feat; no amenities. ⬒ *Kenai National Wildlife Refuge, Attn: Cabin Reservation, Box 2139, Soldotna 99669* ☎ *907/262–7021 or 877/285–5628* ⊕ *kenai. fws.gov/visitorseducators/cabin/reserve.htm* ⬏ *11 cabins.*

KENAI AND SOLDOTNA

116 mi northwest of Seward, 148 mi southwest of Anchorage.

The towns of Kenai and Soldotna are mentioned almost interchangeably due to their proximity. Soldotna, with its strategic location on the peninsula's northwest coast, is the commercial and sportfishing hub of the Kenai Peninsula. Along with its sister city, Kenai, whose onion-dome

CAMPING IN KENAI NWR

🔥 **Kenai National Wildlife Refuge Campgrounds.** The U.S. Fish and Wildlife Service maintains 14 road-accessible campgrounds in the Kenai Refuge. None have hookups, and only two of the campgrounds (Hidden Lake and Upper Skilak Lake) charge fees for camping. All but three campgrounds have drinking water; all have nearby hiking trails and fishing. The maximum length of stay is 14 consecutive days, with a few exceptions—the Russian River Ferry site limit is three days, and the Hidden Lake and Upper Skilak limit is seven days. **Pros:** the refuge is your playground. **Cons:** road-accessible means crowd-accessible. 🖂 *Kenai National Wildlife Refuge, Box 2139, Soldotna 99669-2139* ☎ *907/262–7021* ⊕ *kenai.fws.gov* ⤳ *130 sites (110 suitable for RVs)* ♿ *flush toilets, drinking water (some), fire pits, picnic tables* 🔥 *Reservations not accepted* ▭ *No credit cards.*

Holy Assumption Russian Orthodox Church highlights the city's old town, it is home to Cook Inlet oil-field workers and their families. Soldotna's commercial center stretches along the Sterling Highway, making this a stopping point for those traveling up and down the peninsula. The town of Kenai lies near the end of the road that branches off the Sterling Highway in Soldotna. Near Kenai is Captain Cook State Recreation Area, one of the least-visited state parks on the road system. This portion of the peninsula is level and forested, with numerous lakes and streams pocking and crisscrossing the area. Trumpeter swans return here in spring, and sightings of moose are common.

GETTING HERE AND AROUND

As you're driving either north or south on the Sterling Highway from Cooper Landing or Homer, you'll know you've hit Soldotna when you're suddenly stuck in traffic in between strip malls. Kenai is 11 mi up the Kenai Spur Highway, which originates in central Soldotna. Commercial flights are available to Kenai from Anchorage.

ESSENTIALS

Medical Assistance **Central Peninsula General Hospital** (🖂 *250 Hospital Pl., Soldotna* ☎ *907/714–4404*).

Visitor Information **Kenai Visitor and Convention Bureau** (🖂 *11471 Kenai Spur Hwy., Kenai* ☎ *907/283–1991*).

EXPLORING

ℭ In addition to fishing, clam digging is also popular at **Clam Gulch**, 24 mi south of Soldotna on the Sterling Highway. This is a favorite of local children, who love any excuse to dig in the muddy, sloppy goo. Ask locals on the beach how to find the giant razor clams (recognized by their dimples in the sand). Ask for advice on how to clean the clams—cleaning is pretty labor intensive, and it's easy to get into a clam-digging frenzy when the conditions are favorable, only to regret your efforts when cleaning time arrives. The clam digging is best when tides are minus 4 or 5 feet. ■ TIP→ A sportfishing license, available at grocery stores, sporting-goods shops, and drugstores, is required for clam diggers 16 years old and over.

OUTDOOR ACTIVITIES AND GUIDED TOURS

FISHING Anglers from around the world come for the salmon-choked streams and rivers, most notably the Kenai River and its companion, the Russian River.

Knowledgeable fishery professionals figure it's only a matter of time before someone with sportfishing gear catches a 100-pounder. There are two runs of kings up the Kenai every summer. The first run starts in mid-May and tapers off in early July, and the second run is from early July until the season ends on July 31. Generally speaking, the first run has more fish, but they tend to be smaller than second-run fish. Smaller, of course, has a whole different meaning when it comes to these fish. Fifty- and 60-pounders are unremarkable here, and 40-pound fish are routinely tossed back as being "too small." The limit is one king kept per day, five per season, no more than two of which can be from the Kenai. In addition to a fishing license, you must obtain a special Alaska king salmon license stamp and a harvest record. These can be purchased on the Alaska Department of Fish and Game Web site (⊕ *www. adfg.alaska.gov*), or check with your guide, as most guides sell them. The river also supports two runs of red (sockeye) salmon every year, as well as runs of silver (coho) and pink (humpback) salmon. Rainbow trout of near-mythic proportions inhabit the river, as do Dolly Varden char. ■ TIP➔ Fishing pressure is heavy, so don't expect a wilderness experience, especially in the lower river near Soldotna.

Farther up the river, between Kenai Lake in Cooper Landing and Skilak Lake, motorboats are banned, so a more idyllic experience can be had. Scores of guide services ply the river, and if you're inexperienced at the game, consider hiring a guide for a half-day or full-day trip. Deep-sea fishing for salmon and halibut out of Deep Creek is challenging Homer's position as the preeminent fishing destination on the southern Kenai Peninsula. This fishery is unusual in that tractors launch boats off the beach and into the Cook Inlet surf. The local campground and RV lot is packed on summer weekends.

Area phone books list some 300 fishing charters and guides, all of whom stay busy during the hectic summer fishing season.

Alaska Wildland Adventures. Head down the Kenai River and learn about the surroundings and wildlife with these guides. One of the oldest and largest outfitters on the peninsula, it has trips to suit anyone. ☎ *800/478–4100* ⊕ *www.alaskarivertrips.com.*

Hi Lo Charters (☎ *907/283–9691* ⊕ *www.hilofishing.com*) is a family-operated outfit that's been in business for more than 20 years. It's a full-service guide outfitter that specializes in hooking king salmon. The **Sports Den** (☎ *907/262–7491* ⊕ *www.alaskasportsden.com*) arranges fishing trips on the river, on the saltwater, or to a remote fly-in location for salmon, trout, or halibut.

MULTISPORT' This region is known for its outstanding kayaking, canoeing, and fishing. **Alaska Canoe & Campground** (☎ 907/262–2331 ⊕ *www.alaskacanoetrips. com*) outfits cabins, offers instruction, and shuttles to put-in and take-out points. They also outfit for fishing adventures.

WHERE TO EAT

$$–$$$ ✕**The Duck Inn**. With pizzas, burgers, chicken, steaks, and seafood,
AMERICAN there's something for everyone. Portions are generous, and the prices are reasonable. Locally caught halibut is a specialty, prepared in enough different ways to stave off halibut overload. There's also lots of artwork featuring ducks. ✉ *43187 Kalifornsky Beach Rd., Soldotna* ☎ *907/262–2656.*

$ ✕**Sal's Klondike Diner**. In Sterling, between Cooper Landing and Sol-
AMERICAN dotna, Sal's has a true diner atmosphere. It's open 24 hours, and the portions are large; there's even a sign on the wall that says, "If you're still hungry, tell us." Burgers, sandwiches, fish-and-chips, halibut, salmon, and some steaks are available, along with homemade bread and pies baked every day. You can buy loaves of sourdough, white, or wheat bread. It's a favorite spot for locals. ✉ *44619 Sterling Hwy., Sterling* ☎ *907/262–2220.*

$ ✕**St. Elias Brewing Company**. Everything at St. Elias is homemade: the
AMERICAN ever-rotating beers, the stone-fired rustic pizza, the sandwiches, and the desserts. The Mt. Redoubt chocolate cake with a molten center is simply divine. This is a great place to check out the locals; the patrons are just as friendly as the staff. ✉ *434 Sharkathmi Ave., Sterling* ☎ *907/260–7837.*

WHERE TO STAY

For expanded hotel reviews, visit Fodors.com.

$$ ⌂ **Aspen Hotel Soldotna**. The Soldotna hostelry sits on a bluff overlooking the Kenai River, and if you get a river-view room you'll have a front-row seat for the fishing action during salmon runs. **Pros:** hot tub; swimming pool; river frontage. **Cons:** bland, corporate feel. **TripAdvisor:** "very helpful and friendly," "very clean with everything needed," "clean and modern." ✉ *326 Binkley Circle, Soldotna* ☎ *907/260–7736 or 888/308–7848* ⊕ *www.aspenhotelsak.com* ↰ *63 rooms* ⌂ *In-room: Wi-Fi. In-hotel: pool, spa, laundry facilities, business center* ❢ *Breakfast.*

$$ ⌂ **Best Western King Salmon Motel**. This Best Western has large rooms, including some with kitchenettes. **Pros:** meticulously cleaned. **Cons:** surrounded by strip malls. **TripAdvisor:** "very spacious and comfortable room," "everyone was very accommodating," "comfy and clean." ✉ *35546-A Kenai Spur Hwy., Soldotna* ☎ *907/262–5857 or 888/262– 5857* ⊕ *www.bestwestern.com* ↰ *49 rooms* ⌂ *In-room: kitchen (some), Internet. In-hotel: restaurant, laundry facilities.*

HOMER

77 mi south of Soldotna, 226 mi southwest of Anchorage.

At the southern end of the Sterling Highway lies the city of Homer, at the base of a narrow spit that juts 4 mi into beautiful Kachemak Bay. Glaciers and snowcapped mountains form a dramatic backdrop across the water.

GOOD ALASKAN READS

Travelers at Fodors.com weigh in on the best reads to inspire you before your trip to Alaska and to introduce you to a bit of the history and culture of the state:

"I enjoyed Peter Jenkins' *Looking For Alaska*. He spent time in several towns. One interesting part was about people who live miles from a main road so a trip to town might be a 60-mile snowmobile trip. The Pratt Museum in Homer has a short video about homesteading in the 50s." —dfrostnh

"I enjoyed the novel *Alaska* by James Michener." —Connie

"*Coming into the Country* by John Mcphee is my favorite. *Last Light Breaking: Living Among Alaska's Inupiat Eskimos* by Nick Jans—he lived in a small village (Ambler, I think) teaching at a native school and exploring in his spare time, and writes beautifully. He also writes a popular monthly column for *Alaska Magazine*." —Bill_H

"My choice would also be *Coming into the Country*—pushing 30 years old but still as evocative. And now for something completely different,

have a go at Michael Chabon's amazing *The Yiddish Policemen's Union*, a mystery set in an alternate-history Southeast Alaska populated by Jews following the collapse of Israel in the War of Independence. Fabulous read." —Gardyloo

"*Good Time Girls*, by Lael Morgan—the true account of the 'ladies of the night' who migrated to the Klondike (Dawson City) and on to Fairbanks. Lots of photos and interesting stories. If you like mysteries, anything by Sitka resident John Straley, Alaska's 'Novelist Laureate' for 2007. *The Last Run: the True Story of Rescue and Redemption on Alaska's Seas*, by Todd Lewan, is a gripping and very readable account of a rescue by the Coast Guard. You'll learn a lot about Southeast Alaska, the life of a fisherman, and helicopters. Amazing." —enzian

"*Drop City* by T.C. Boyle is on the list of 1,001 books you must read before you die. It's about the clash/interaction of a hippie community and the Alaskan residents. Interesting reading and provided interesting color on life in the interior." —keymom

Founded in the late 1800s as a gold-prospecting camp, this community was later used as coal-mining headquarters. Chunks of coal are still common along local beaches; they wash into the bay from nearby slopes where the coal seams are exposed. Today the town of Homer is an eclectic community with most of the tacky tourist paraphernalia relegated to the Spit (though do note the Spit has plenty else to recommend it, not the least of which is the 360-degree view of the surrounding mountains); the rest of the town is full of local merchants and artisans. The community is an interesting mix of fishermen, actors, artists, and writers. Much of the commercial fishing centers on halibut, and the popular Homer Jackpot Halibut Derby is often won by enormous fish weighing more than 300 pounds. The local architecture includes everything from dwellings that are little more than assemblages of driftwood to steel commercial buildings and magnificent homes on the hillside overlooking the surrounding bay, mountains, forests, and glaciers.

GETTING HERE AND AROUND

The Sterling Highway ends in Homer, and the drive in is beautiful. Once there, you'll see signs on your left for Pioneer Avenue, Homer's commercial district. On the right is the historic town center, and if you keep to the road you'll hit the spit. Homer also operates a commercial airport, with flights daily to and from Anchorage, Seldovia, and elsewhere. If you're traveling on the Marine Highway system, ferries to Kodiak and beyond dock several times a week in summer.

ESSENTIALS

Medical Assistance **South Peninsula Hospital** (⊠ *4300 Bartlett St.* ☎ *907/235–8101*).

Visitor Information **Homer Chamber of Commerce** (⊠ *201 Sterling Hwy.* ✑ *Box 541, Homer 99603* ☎ *907/235–7740* ⊕ *www.homeralaska.org*).

EXPLORING

Start your visit with a stop at the Homer Chamber of Commerce's **Visitor Information Center**, where racks are filled with brochures from local businesses and attractions. ⊠ *201 Sterling Hwy.* ☎ *907/235–7740* ⊕ *www.homeralaska.org* ☉ *Memorial Day–Labor Day, weekdays 9–7, weekends 10–6; early Sept.–late May, weekdays 9–5.*

Directly across from the end of Homer Spit is **Halibut Cove**, a small artists' community. Spend a relaxing afternoon or evening meandering along the boardwalk and visiting galleries. The cove is lovely, especially during salmon runs, when fish leap and splash in the clear water. Several lodges are on this side of the bay, on pristine coves away from summer crowds. The *Danny J* ferries people across from Homer Spit, with a stop at the rookery at Gull Island and two or three hours to walk around Halibut Cove, for $50 apiece. The ferry makes two trips daily: the first leaves Homer at noon and returns at 5 pm, and the second leaves at 5 pm and returns at 10 pm. Central Charters and the Saltry Restaurant handle all bookings. *(⇨ See Outdoor Activities and Guided Tours and Where to Eat below.)*

ⓒ Protruding into Kachemak Bay, **Homer Spit** provides a sandy focal point
Fodor's Choice for visitors and locals. A paved path stretches most of the 4 mi and is
★ great for biking or walking. A commercial-fishing-boat harbor at the end of the path has restaurants, hotels, charter-fishing businesses, sea-kayaking outfitters, art galleries, and on-the-beach camping spots. Fly a kite, walk the beaches, drop a line in the Fishing Hole, or just wander through the shops looking for something interesting; this is one of Alaska's favorite summertime destinations.

ⓒ **Islands and Ocean Center** provides a wonderful introduction to the Alaska
★ Maritime National Wildlife Refuge. The refuge covers some 3.5 million acres spread across some 2,500 Alaskan islands, from Prince of Wales Island in the south to Barrow in the north. Opened in 2003, this 37,000-square-foot facility with towering windows facing Kachemak Bay is a must-see for anyone interested in wild places—and it's free! A film takes visitors along on a voyage of the Fish and Wildlife Service's research ship, the MV *Tiglax*. Interactive exhibits detail the birds and marine mammals of the refuge (the largest seabird refuge in America),

and one room even re-creates the noisy sounds and pungent smells of a bird rookery. In summer, guided bird-watching treks and beach walks are offered. ⊠ *95 Sterling Hwy.* ☎ *907/235–6961* ⊕ *www. islandsandocean.org* ⊠ *Free* ⊘ *Memorial Day–Labor Day, daily 9–6; Labor Day–Sept. 30, Tues.–Sun. 10–5; Oct.–May, Tues.–Sat. noon–5; May–Memorial Day, daily 10–5.*

Kachemak Bay abounds with wildlife, including a large population of puffins and eagles. Tour operators take you past bird rookeries or across the bay to gravel beaches for clam digging. Most fishing charters include an opportunity to view whales, seals, porpoises, and birds close up. At the end of the day, walk along the docks on Homer Spit and watch commercial fishing boats and charter boats unload their catch.

> **HOMER FESTIVALS**
>
> Early-summer visitors to Homer join thousands of migrating shorebirds for the **Kachemak Bay Shorebird Festival** on the second weekend in May. Experts offer bird-watching trips and photography demonstrations, and a simultaneous Wooden Boat Festival provides a chance to meet some of Alaska's finest boatbuilders. Various kids' events add to the fun. During the first weekend of August the **KBBI Concerts on the Lawn** (☎ *907/235-7721* ⊕ *www.kbbi.org*) bring an array of folk and rock music performers to Karen Hornaday Park.

Across Kachemak Bay from Homer Spit lies 400,000-acre **Kachemak Bay State Park** (☎ *907/235-7024* ⊕ *www.alaskastateparks.org*), one of the largest coastal parks in America. *Flip ahead to the next section of this chapter for more information about this park.* The park encompasses a line of snowcapped mountains and several large glaciers; the prominent one visible from the spit is called Grewingk Glacier. One of the most popular trails leads 2 mi, ending at the lake in front of Grewingk Glacier. Several state park cabins can be rented for $50–$65 a night, and a number of luxurious private lodges occupy remote coves. Park access is primarily by water taxi from the spit; contact **Mako's Water Taxi** (☎ *907/235-9055* ⊕ *www.makoswatertaxi.com*).

The **Pratt Museum** is an art gallery and natural history museum rolled into one. It has a saltwater aquarium, an exhibit on the 1989 *Exxon Valdez* oil spill, botanical gardens, nature trails, a gift shop, and pioneer, Russian, and Alaska Native displays. You can spy on wildlife with robotic video cameras set up on a seabird rookery and at the McNeil River Bear Sanctuary. A refurbished homestead cabin and outdoor summer exhibits are along the trail out back. ⊠ *Bartlett St. off Pioneer Ave.* ☎ *907/235-8635* ⊕ *www.prattmuseum.org* ⊠ *$4–$8* ⊘ *Mid-May–mid-Sept., daily 11–6; mid-Sept.–mid-May, Tues.–Sun. noon–5.*

OUTDOOR ACTIVITIES AND GUIDED TOURS

BOATING AND FISHING

Homer is a major commercial fishing port (especially for halibut) and a popular destination for sport anglers in search of giant halibut or feisty king and silver salmon. Near the end of the Spit, Homer's famous **Fishing Hole** is a small bight stocked with king and silver salmon smolt (baby fish) by the Alaska Department of Fish and Game. The salmon then head out to sea, returning several years later to the Fishing Hole, where they are easy targets for wall-to-wall bank-side anglers throughout summer. The Fishing Hole isn't anything like casting for salmon along a remote stream, but your chances are good and you don't need to drop $800 for a flight into the wilderness. Fishing licenses and rental poles are available from fishing-supply stores on the Spit.

Quite a few companies offer charter fishing in summer, from about $250 to $350 per person per day, including bait and tackle. The pricing is usually based on how many different types of fish you're fishing for.

Central Charters & Tours (⊠ *4241 Homer Spit Rd.* ☎ *907/235–7847* ⊕ *www.centralcharter.com*) can arrange fishing trips in outer Kachemak Bay and Lower Cook Inlet—areas known for excellent halibut fishing. Boat sizes vary considerably; some have a six-person limit, whereas others can take up to 16 passengers. They can also arrange non-fishing tours.

Homer Ocean Charters (☎ *800/426–6212* ⊕ *www.homerocean.com*) on the Spit sets up fishing and sightseeing trips, as well as sea-kayaking and water-taxi services and remote-cabin rentals. Some of its most popular cruises go to the **Rookery Restaurant** at Otter Cove Resort. Also try **Inlet Charters** (☎ *800/770–6216* ⊕ *www.halibutcharters.com*) for fishing charters, water-taxi services, sea-kayaking, and wildlife cruises.

Anyone heading out on a halibut charter is advised to buy a $10 ticket for the **Homer Jackpot Halibut Derby** (☎ *907/235–7740* ⊕ *www.homerhalibutderby.com*); first prize for the largest halibut is more than $40,000.

SEA KAYAKING   Several local companies offer guided sea-kayaking trips to protected coves within Kachemak Bay State Park and nearby islands. **True North Kayak Adventures** (☎ *907/235–0708* ⊕ *www.truenorthkayak.com*) has a range of such adventures, including a six-hour paddle to Elephant Rock for $130 and an all-day boat and kayak trip to Yukon Island for $150 (both trips include round-trip water taxi to the island base camp, guide, all kayak equipment, and bakery lunch). For something more unusual, book an overnight trip to Kasitsna Bay through the beautiful **Across the Bay Tent & Breakfast** (☎ *907/235–3633, 907/345–2571 Sept.–May* ⊕ *www.tentandbreakfastalaska.com*). Grounds are gorgeous, facilities are basic, and guests can take kayak tours, rent a mountain bike, or just hang out on the shore and participate in workshops on topics like fish-skin basketry, wildlife photography, and permaculture design.

BEAR WATCH

Homer is a favorite departure point for viewing Alaska's famous brown bears in Katmai National Park. **Emerald Air Service** (☎ *907/235–4160 or 877/235–9600* ⊕ *www.emeraldairservice. com*) is one of several companies offering all-day and custom photography trips starting around $625 per person. **Hallo Bay Wilderness** (☎ *907/235–2237 or 888/535–2237* ⊕ *www.hallobay. com*) offers guided close-range viewing without the crowds. Day trips are offered, but it's the two- to seven-day stays at this comfortable coastal location that provide the ultimate in world-class bear- and wildlife-viewing.

WHERE TO EAT

$$$ ✕ **Café Cups.** It's hard to miss this place as you drive down Pioneer
ECLECTIC Avenue—look for the huge namesake cups on the building's facade. A
longtime Homer favorite, this café serves dinners that make the most
of the locally abundant seafood, complemented by a terrific wine list.
The menu includes hand-cut steaks, a "twisted fettuccine" that blends
seafood, raspberries, and chipotle in an Alfredo cream sauce. Be sure
to make a reservation, as this place gets quite busy during the summer
months. ■ TIP→ Locals know to ignore the menu and just ask to hear the
day's specials. Vegetarian options are also offered, and singles mix at
the hand-carved wine bar. ✉ *162 W. Pioneer Ave.* ☎ *907/235–8330*
☯ *Closed Sun. and Mon.*

$$$$ ✕ **Captain Pattie's Seafood Restaurant.** A favorite with hard-to-please
SEAFOOD locals, Captain Pattie's offers a wide array of fresh local seafood, along
with beachfront views of Kachemak Bay. The appetizer menu alone is
worth the wait, which can be considerable during the summer rush. The
clam chowder is excellent, and the staff is friendly and efficient. There's
a good wine selection, and local beer on tap. If you get lucky on your
fishing excursion, the restaurant will cook your catch to your liking.
Try the great desserts, too. ✉ *4241 Homer Spit Rd.* ☎ *907/235–5135*
☯ *Closed Oct.–Mar.*

$$ ✕ **Fat Olives Restaurant.** Pumpkin-color walls, light streaming through
MEDITERRANEAN tall front windows, and a playful collection of Italian posters add to
the appeal of this fine Tuscany-inspired bistro. The menu encompasses
enticing appetizers, salads, sandwiches, calzones, and pizzas throughout the day, along with oven-roasted chicken, fresh seafood, pork loin,
and other fare in the evening. If you're in a hurry, just get a giant slice
of the thin-crust cheese pizza to go for $5. You can order meals at the
bar, where there is a great wine selection, and there's always something
decadent for dessert. ✉ *276 Olson La.* ☎ *907/235–8488.*

$$$ ✕ **Fresh Sourdough Express Bakery & Café.** This place was the first certified
CAFÉ green restaurant in Alaska, and proud of it. It features regional, organic
☺ ingredients, baked goods made with hand-ground grain, and fresh sea-
food in season. You can get box lunches for your all-day fishing or sight-
seeing trips—even order them online for next-day pickup. There's a small
gift shop and a play area outside for kids. ✉ *1316 Ocean Dr.* ☎ *907/235–
7571* ⊕ *www.freshsourdoughexpress.com* ☯ *Closed Nov.–Mar.*

¢ ✕ **Fritz Creek General Store.** Directly across the road from the Homestead
ECLECTIC Restaurant is this old-fashioned country store, gas station, liquor store,
post office, video-rental shop, and deli. The latter is the primary reason
for stopping at Fritz's. The food is amazingly good, from the hot and
fattening turkey sandwiches to incredible freshly baked breads and
pastries, pizza by the slice, veggie burritos, tamales, and ribs to go. Pull
up a chair at a table crafted from an old cable spool and join the back-
to-the-land crowd as they drink espresso, talk Alaskan politics, and pet
the cats. ✉ *55770 E. End Rd. (Mi 8.2)* ☎ *907/235–6753.*

$$$–$$$$ ✕ **Homestead Restaurant.** This former log roadhouse 8 mi from town
CONTINENTAL is a favorite of locals who appreciate artfully presented food served
Fodor's Choice amid contemporary art. The Homestead specializes in seasonal fish
★ and shellfish prepared with garlic, citrus fruits, or spicy ethnic sauces,

as well as steak, rack of lamb, and prime rib. Epic views of the bay, mountains, and hanging glaciers are yours for the looking. Homestead has an extensive wine list and locally brewed beer on tap. ⊠ *Mi 8.2, E. End Rd., Homer* ☎ *907/235–8723* ⊕ *www.homesteadrestaurant.net* ⊗ *Closed Nov.–Mar. 8.*

$$$
SEAFOOD
Fodor's Choice
★

✕ **Saltry Restaurant.** On a hill overlooking Halibut Cove, this is a wonderful place to soak up a summer afternoon. Local seafood is the main attraction, prepared as everything from curries and pastas to sushi. They also serve fresh-baked bread, and their salads are made of freshly harvested greens from their gardens. The restaurant is small, and although the tables aren't exactly crowded together, it's definitely intimate. When weather permits, get a table on the deck. Dinner seatings are at 6 and 7:30; before or after dinner you can stroll around the boardwalks at Halibut Cove and visit the art galleries or just relax on the dock. Sea otters often play just offshore. Reservations are essential for the ferry ($30 round-trip), which leaves Homer Spit at 5 pm. A noon ferry ($50) will take you to the Saltry for lunch (¢–$), stopping along the way for wildlife-viewing. ⊠ *9 W. Ismilof Rd.* ☞ *Box 6410, Halibut Cove 99603* ☎ *907/399–2683* ⊜ *Reservations essential* ⊕ *www.thesaltry.com* ⊗ *Closed Labor Day–Memorial Day.*

¢
CAFÉ

✕ **Two Sisters Bakery.** This very popular café is a short walk from both Bishops Beach and the Islands and Ocean Center. In addition to fresh breads and pastries, Two Sisters specializes in deliciously healthful lunches, such as vegetarian focaccia sandwiches, homemade soups, quiche, and salads. Sit on the wraparound porch on a summer afternoon, or take your espresso and scone down to the beach to watch the waves roll in. ■**TIP→** Upstairs are three comfortable guest rooms ($), all with private baths. Your latte and Danish pastry breakfast is served in the café. ⊠ *233 E. Bunnell Ave.* ☎ *907/235–2280* ⊕ *www.twosistersbakery.net.*

WHERE TO STAY

For expanded hotel reviews, visit Fodors.com.

$$$

▦ **Alaskan Suites.** These modern log cabins offer million-dollar views from a hilltop on the west side of Homer. **Pros:** crow's-nest views; highway location with no highway noise. **Cons:** not within walking distance of anything. **TripAdvisor:** "cabin was beautiful," "excellent location," "view of the mountains was great." ⊠ *3255 Sterling Hwy.* ☎ *907/235–1972 or 888/239–1972* ⊕ *www.alaskansuites.com* ⬎ *5 cabins* ⬧ *In-room: kitchen. In-hotel: some pets allowed.*

$$$$

▦ **Driftwood Inn.** The Driftwood seeks to accommodate all travelers, with an RV park, two deluxe lodges, a cottage, and a historic inn. **Pros:** accommodation for every budget. **Cons:** the ship's quarters are tight. **TripAdvisor:** "staff was very friendly," "rooms are clean and cozy," "great views and wonderful service." ⊠ *135 W. Bunnell Ave.* ☎ *907/235–8019 or 800/478–8019* ⊕ *www.thedriftwoodinn.com* ⬎ *22 rooms, 14 with bath; 1 cottage* ⬧ *In-room: Wi-Fi. In-hotel: laundry facilities, some pets allowed.*

$$

▦ **Land's End Resort and Lodges.** This sprawling complex at the end of Homer Spit has wide-open views of the bay. **Pros:** the Spit-end location puts you 5 mi out into the bay. **Cons:** you might be disappointed if you get a room without a view. **TripAdvisor:** "experience of a lifetime,"

CAMPING ON HOMER SPIT

⚠️ **Homer Spit Campground.** Homer's 4-mi-long Spit is popular not just as a jumping-off point for fishing, kayaking, and other adventures, but also because it provides great camping with a view. Find a spot on the sand between the other tents and RVs and pay your fee at the city's camping office. The beach is often windy—make sure your tent poles are sturdy—and it's not far from the road. Still, it's hard to beat the spectacular setting. A few campsites are open year-round. **Pros:** fantastic view, campground feel, just down the road from town. **Cons:** smells like fish, high wind area, lots of people. ✉ *4535 Homer Spit Rd.* ☎ *907/235–8206* ⮑ *122 RV sites, 25 tent sites* ♿ *Flush toilets, partial hookups, dump station, drinking water, guest laundry, showers, grills, picnic tables, electricity, public telephone.*

"condo was clean and well appointed," "spectacular views." ✉ *4786 Homer Spit Rd.* ☎ *907/235–0400 or 800/478–0400* ⊕ *www.lands-end-resort.com* ⮑ *108 rooms, 24 2-room suites, 34 lodges* ♿ *In-room: kitchen (some), Wi-Fi. In-hotel: restaurant, bar, pool, spa, laundry facilities.*

$ 🏨 **Old Town Bed & Breakfast.** Bright and cozy, the Old Town B&B is housed in the oldest commercial building in Homer. **Pros:** warm, inviting, and friendly, breakfast is divine. **Cons:** some rooms have shared baths; white curtains invite plenty of midnight summer sunlight. **TripAdvisor:** "quaint and cozy," "felt more like a historical art museum," "lovely old style rooms." ✉ *106 W. Bunnell St. in Old Inlet Trading Post* ☎ *907/235–7558* ⊕ *www.oldtownbedandbreakfast.com* ⮑ *3 rooms, 1 with bath* ♿ *In-room: no TV* ⭐ *Breakfast.*

$$$$ 🏨 **Tutka Bay Wilderness Lodge.** On a small cove 9 mi by boat (the trip is included in the price) from Homer Spit, this luxurious small resort is adjacent to Kachemak Bay State Park. **Pros:** location, location, location. **Cons:** because of its location, it's a bit pricey. ⌂ *Box 960, 99603* ☎ *907/235–3905 or 800/606–3909* ⊕ *www.tutkabaylodge.com* ⮑ *4 cabins, 2 suites* ♿ *In-room: TV, Wi-Fi* ⭐ *All meals.*

NIGHTLIFE

★ Dance to lively bands on weekends at **Alice's Champagne Palace** (✉ *195 E. Pioneer Ave.* ☎ *907/235–6909*). The bar attracts nationally known singer-songwriters on a regular basis.

The members of **Pier One Theater** (☎ *907/235–7333* ⊕ *www.pieronetheatre.org*) perform plays on weekends throughout the summer. Find them in the old barnlike building on the Spit.

The Spit's infamous **Salty Dawg Saloon** (✉ *4380 Homer Spit Rd.* ☎ *907/235–6718*) is a tumbledown lighthouse of sorts, sure to be frequented by a carousing fisherman or two, along with half the tourists in town.

SHOPPING

ART AND GIFTS   A variety of art by the town's residents can be found in the galleries on and around Pioneer Avenue. The **Bunnell Street Gallery** (✉ *106 W. Bunnell St. on corner of Main St.* ☎ *907/235–2662* ⊕ *www.bunnellstreetgallery. org*) displays innovative contemporary art, all of it produced in Alaska. The gallery, which occupies the first floor of a historic trading post, also hosts workshops, lectures, musical performances, and other community events.

The gift shop at the **Pratt Museum** (✉ *3779 Bartlett St. off Pioneer Ave.* ☎ *907/235–8635*) stocks natural-history books, locally crafted or inspired jewelry, note cards, and gifts for children. **Ptarmigan Arts** (✉ *471 E. Pioneer Ave.* ☎ *907/235–5345*) is a cooperative gallery with photographs, paintings, pottery, jewelry, woodworking, and other pieces by local artisans.

CLOTHING   **Homer's Jeans** (✉ *564 E. Pioneer Ave., Suite 1* ☎ *907/235–6234*) offers name-brand outdoor wear in addition to more utilitarian gear. Buy your cute shoes or your hiking boots here. **Nomar** (✉ *104 E. Pioneer Ave.* ☎ *907/235–8363 or 800/478–8364* ⊕ *www.nomaralaska.com*) creates Polarfleece garments and other rugged Alaskan outerwear, plus duffels, rain gear, and children's clothing. The company manufactures equipment and clothing for commercial fishermen.

FOOD   **Alaska Wild Berry Products** (✉ *528 E. Pioneer Ave.* ☎ *907/235–8858* ⊕ *www.alaskawildberryproducts.com*) sells chocolate-covered candies, jams, jellies, sauces, and syrups made from wild berries handpicked on the Kenai Peninsula, as well as Alaska-theme gifts and clothing. Drop by for free samples of the chocolates. Homer is famous for its halibut, salmon, and Kachemak Bay oysters. For fresh fish, head to **Coal Point Trading Company** (✉ *4306 Homer Spit Rd.* ☎ *907/235–3877 or 800/325–3877* ⊕ *www.welovefish.com*). Coal Point can also package and ship fish that you catch.

Fritz Creek Store (✉ *Mi 8.2, E. End Rd.* ☎ *907/235–6753*) sells fresh, homemade food in an old log building. **Two Sisters Bakery** (✉ *233 E. Bunnell Ave.* ☎ *907/235–2280*) serves fresh-baked bread as well as coffee, muffins, soup, and pizza.

KACHEMAK BAY STATE PARK AND STATE WILDERNESS PARK

10 mi southeast of Homer.

GETTING HERE AND AROUND
Kachemak Bay State Park and State Wilderness Park are accessible by boat or bush plane.

ESSENTIALS
Visitor Information **Kenai State Parks Office** ☎ *907/262–5581 or 907/235–7024* ⊕ *www.dnr.alaska.gov/parks/units/kbay/kbay.htm.*

EXPLORING
Kachemak Bay State Park and State Wilderness Park protects more than 350,000 acres of coast, mountains, glaciers, forests, and wildlife on the lower Kenai Peninsula. Recreational opportunities include boating, sea

CAMPING ON KACHEMAK BAY

⚠ **Alaska State Parks Campsites.** Twenty primitive, free campsites with pit toilets and fire rings are scattered along the shores of Kachemak Bay across from Homer and are accessible by boat (water taxis operate here daily in summer). The sites are available on a first-come, first-served basis, and camping is allowed nearly everywhere in the park, not restricted to developed sites. **Pros:** free; away from the tourism bustle. **Cons:** can be pricey to get to. ✉ *Alaska State Parks Kenai Office, Box 1247, Soldotna 99669* ☎ *907/235–7024 or 907/262–5581* ⊕ *www.dnr.alaska.gov/parks/units/kbay/kbay.htm* 🔄 *6 campgrounds with 20 tent sites* ⚿ *Pit toilets (some), fire pits (some), picnic tables (some)* 🚫 *Reservations not accepted.*

kayaking, fishing, hiking, and beachcombing. Facilities are minimal, but include 20 primitive campsites, five public-use cabins, and a system of trails accessible from Kachemak Bay.

WHERE TO STAY

For expanded hotel reviews, visit Fodors.com.

¢ 🏕 **Alaska State Parks Cabins.** Three public-use cabins are within Kachemak Bay's Halibut Cove Lagoon area, another is near Tutka Bay Lagoon, and a fifth is at China Poot Lake. **Pros:** solitude; views. **Cons:** remote locations with no amenities. ✉ *Alaska State Parks Kenai Office, Box 1247, Soldotna 99669* ☎ *907/262–5581* ⊕ *www.dnr.alaska.gov/parks/cabins/kenai.htm* 🔄 *5 cabins* ▬ *No credit cards.*

$$$$ 🏕 **Kachemak Bay Wilderness Lodge.** Across Kachemak Bay from Homer,
★ this luxurious lodge provides wildlife-viewing opportunities and panoramic mountain and bay vistas in an intimate setting for up to 14 guests. **Pros:** extraordinary facility in a stunning location; sauna and outdoor hot tub. **Cons:** its remote location makes the lodge fairly pricey. ✉ *Box 956, Homer 99603* ☎ *907/235–8910* ⊕ *www.alaskawildernesslodge.com* 🔄 *4 cabins, 1 room in lodge* ⚿ *In-room: no TV. In-hotel: restaurant, business center* ⊗ *Closed Oct.–Apr.* 🍽 *All meals.*

SELDOVIA

16 mi south of Homer.

The town of Seldovia is another off-the-road-system settlement on the south side of Kachemak Bay that retains the charm of an earlier Alaska. The town's Russian bloodline shows in its onion-dome church and its name, which means "herring bay." For many years this was the primary fishing town on the bay, but today the focus is on tourism. The town was heavily damaged in the 1964 earthquake, but a few stretches of old boardwalk survive and houses stand on stilts along Seldovia Slough. Seldovia has several restaurants and lodging places, plus a small museum and a hilltop Russian Orthodox church. The area abounds with hiking, mountain-biking, and sea-kayaking options.

GETTING HERE AND AROUND

Access is via the Alaska Marine Highway ferry (twice weekly from Homer), aboard a water taxi ($40–$50), or by air from Homer ($65).

WHERE TO STAY

For expanded hotel reviews, visit Fodors.com.

$$–$$$ ⊞ **Across the Bay Tent & Breakfast Adventure Co.** A step up the comfort ladder from camping, this beachfront establishment is reachable via water taxi from Homer. **Pros:** friendly owners; excellent food; beautiful grounds. **Cons:** although comfortable, you're still sleeping in a tent. ⊠ *Mi 8, Jakalof Bay Rd., 8 mi east of Seldovia* ⬧ *In winter: Box 112054, Anchorage 99511* ⬧ *In summer: Box 81, Seldovia 99663* ☎ *907/235–3633 in summer, 907/345–2571 in winter* ⊕ *www.tentandbreakfastalaska.com* ⬧ *6 tents* ⬧ *In-room: no TV, Wi-Fi. In-hotel: restaurant, beach* ⊗ *Closed Labor Day–Memorial Day.*

$–$$ ⊞ **Seldovia Boardwalk Hotel.** This hotel with a fabulous view of the harbor has immaculate modern rooms, half of which face the water. **Pros:** in-town location. **Cons:** few on-site amenities. ⊠ *Main St.* ⬧ *Box 72, 99663* ☎ *907/234–7816* ⊕ *www.theseldoviaboardwalkhotel.com* ⬧ *14 rooms* ⬧ *In-room: no TV, Wi-Fi* ⧈ *Breakfast.*

KODIAK

248 mi southwest of Anchorage by air.

Russian explorers discovered Kodiak Island in 1763, and the city of Kodiak served as Alaska's first capital until 1804, when the government was moved to Sitka. Situated as it is in the northwestern Gulf of Alaska, Kodiak has been subjected to several natural disasters. In 1912 a volcanic eruption on the nearby Alaska Peninsula covered the town site in knee-deep drifts of ash and pumice. The 1964 earthquake and resulting tsunami destroyed the island's large fishing fleet and smashed Kodiak's low-lying downtown area.

Today commercial fishing is king in Kodiak. Despite its small population—about 13,500 people scattered among the several islands in the Kodiak group—the city is among the busiest fishing ports in the United States. The harbor is also an important supply point for small communities on the Aleutian Islands and the Alaska Peninsula.

Visitors to the island tend to follow one of two agendas: either immediately fly out to a remote lodge for fishing, kayaking, or bear viewing; or stay in town and access whatever pursuits they can reach from the limited road system. If the former is too pricey an option, consider combining the two: driving the road system to see what can be seen inexpensively, then adding a fly-out or charter-boat excursion to a remote lodge or wilderness access point.

Floatplane and boat charters are available from Kodiak to numerous remote attractions. Chief among these areas is the 1.6-million-acre Kodiak National Wildlife Refuge *(see full section below)*, lying partly on Kodiak Island and partly on Afognak Island to the north, where spotting the enormous Kodiak brown bears is the main goal of a trip. Seeing the bears, which weigh a pound at birth but up to 1,500 pounds when fully grown, is worth the trip to this rugged country. The bears are spotted easily in July and August, feeding along salmon-spawning streams. Chartered flightseeing trips go to the area, and exaggerated tales of encounters with these impressive beasts are frequently heard.

GETTING HERE AND AROUND

Access to the island is via the Alaska Marine Highway (which makes several stops a week) or by plane. A few roads stretch out of town, perfect for a day of sightseeing. The action, however, is in town. Kodiak is the entry point for Kodiak National Wildlife Refuge.

Your first stop in exploring the island should be the Kodiak Island Convention & Visitors Bureau. Here you can pick up brochures, pamphlets, and lists of all the visitor services on Kodiak and the surrounding islands, and get help with planning your adventures. If you want to strike out and hike the local trails, there's an informative *Hiking and Birding Guide* published by the Kodiak Audubon Society.

ESSENTIALS

Medical Assistance **Providence Kodiak Island Medical Center** (✉ *1915 E. Rezanof Dr.* ☎ *907/486–3281*).

Visitor Information **Kodiak Island Convention & Visitors Bureau** (✉ *100 Marine Way, Suite 200* ☎ *907/486–4782 or 800/789–4782* ⊕ *www.kodiak.org*).

EXPLORING

★ The **Alutiiq Museum and Archaeological Repository** is home to one of the largest collections of Alaska Native materials in the world, and contains archaeological and ethnographic items dating back 7,500 years. The museum displays only a fraction of its more than 150,000 artifacts, including harpoons, masks, dolls, stone tools, seal-gut parkas, grass baskets, and pottery fragments. The museum store sells Native arts and educational materials. ✉ *215 Mission Rd., Suite 101* ☎ *907/486–7004* ⊕ *www.alutiiqmuseum.org* ☜ *$5* ⊘ *June–Aug., weekdays 9–5, Sat. 10–5, Sun. by appointment; Sept.–May, Tues.–Fri. 9–5, Sat. noon–4.*

The **Baranov Museum** presents artifacts from the area's Russian past. On the National Register of Historic Places, the building was built in 1808 by Alexander Baranov to warehouse precious sea-otter pelts. W.J. Erskine made it his home in 1911. On display are samovars, a collection of intricate native basketry, and other relics from the early Native Koniags and the later Russian settlers. A collection of 40 albums of archival photography portrays various aspects of the island's history. Contact the museum for a calendar of events. ✉ *101 Marine Way* ☎ *907/486–5920* ⊕ *www.baranovmuseum.org* ☜ *$5* ⊘ *June–Aug., Mon.–Sat. 10–4, Sun. noon–4; Sept.–May, Tues.–Sat. 10–3.*

As part of America's North Pacific defense in World War II, Kodiak was the site of an important naval station, now occupied by the Coast Guard fleet that patrols the surrounding fishing grounds. Part of the old military installation has been incorporated into **Fort Abercrombie State Historical Park**, 3½ mi north of Kodiak on Rezanof Drive. Self-guided tours take you past concrete bunkers and gun emplacements. There's a spectacular scenic overlook, great for bird- and whale-watching, and there are 13 campsites suitable for tents or small RVs (no hookups), with pit toilets, drinking water, fire grates, and picnic tables ⊠ *Mi 3.7, Rezanof Dr.* ♨ *Alaska State Parks, Kodiak District Office, 1400 Abercrombie Dr., 99615* ☎ *907/486–6339* ⊕ *www.dnr.alaska.gov/parks/units/ kodiak/ftaber.htm* ⌨ *Park free, campsites $10* ▬ *No credit cards.*

The ornate **Holy Resurrection Russian Orthodox Church** is a visual feast, both inside and out. The cross-shape building is topped by two onion-shape blue domes, and the interior contains brass candelabra, distinctive chandeliers, and numerous icons representing Orthodox saints. Three different churches have stood on this site since 1794. Built in 1945, the present structure is on the National Register of Historic Places. ⊠ *385 Kashevaroff Rd.* ☎ *907/486–3854 parish priest* ⌨ *Donations accepted* ☺ *By appointment.*

> **LOCAL BREW**
>
> The **Kodiak Island Brewing Co.** (⊠ *338 Shelikof Ave.* ☎ *907/486– 2537* ⊕ *www.kodiakbrewery.com*) sells fresh-brewed, unfiltered beer in liters, growlers, pigs, and kegs, so you can stock up for your wilderness expedition and avoid beer withdrawal. Brewer Ben Millstein will also give you a tour of the facility on request. It's open noon–7 daily; drop on by for a couple of pints in the tasting room.

☾ **Kodiak National Wildlife Refuge Visitor Center.** Whether you're spending time in the Kodiak National Wildlife Refuge itself, make sure you stop by the new Kodiak National Wildlife Refuge Visitor Center (located a block from the downtown ferry dock). Wander through exhibits about Refuge flora and fauna, attend an interpretive talk, and marvel at the complete 36-foot hanging skeleton of a male gray whale on the second floor. ⊠ *402 Center Ave.* ☎ *907/487–2626* ⊕ *kodiak.fws.gov.*

OUTDOOR ACTIVITIES AND GUIDED TOURS

Kodiak Adventures Unlimited (☎ *907/486–8766* or *907/539–8767* ⊕ *www. kodiakadventuresunlimited.com*) books charter and tour operators for all of Kodiak. Find their summer kiosk in St. Paul Harbor across from Wells Fargo.

Memory Makers Tour and Guide Service (☎ *907/486–7000* ⊕ *www. memorymakersinak.com*) specializes in angling day trips on the local Kodiak road system; guide Dake Schmidt's knowledge and passion for fishing the 15 local rivers are a real find for those not flying off to remote lodges. Fishing gear, lunch, and a comfy van provided, with sightseeing, wildlife-viewing, and photography tours also available.

WHERE TO EAT

$$–$$$
AMERICAN
✕ **Henry's Great Alaskan Restaurant.** Henry's is a big, boisterous, friendly place at the plaza near the small-boat harbor. The menu is equally big, ranging from fresh local seafood and barbecue to pastas and even some Cajun dishes. Dinner specials, a long list of appetizers, salads, rack of lamb, and a tasty dessert list round out the choices. ⊠ *512 E. Marine Way* ☎ *907/486–8844* ⊕ *www.henryskodiak.com* ☺ *Closed Sun. Oct.–Apr.*

¢
CAFÉ
✕ **Java Flats.** This great coffee shop represents the true essence of Kodiak life. Fantastic breakfast burritos, vegetarian sandwiches, and excellent

coffee make this the perfect place to stock up on coffee beans before embarking on exciting bear-watching and salmon-fishing adventures. ⊠ *11206 W. Rezanof Dr.* ☎ *907/487–2622* ⊕ *www.javaflats.com* ⊗ *No dinner. Closed Mon.*

¢–$ ✕ **Mill Bay Coffee & Pastries.** Serving breakfast, lunches and fabulous pas-
CAFÉ tries, this charming little shop is well worth a visit. The coffee is freshly roasted on-site every other day. Inside, elegant antique furnishings are complemented by local artwork and handicrafts. ⊠ *3833 Rezanof Dr. E* ☎ *907/486–4411* ⊕ *www.millbaycoffee.com* ⊗ *No dinner. Closed Tues.*

$$–$$$ ✕ **Old Powerhouse Restaurant.** This converted powerhouse facility allows
SEAFOOD a close-up view of Near Island and the channel connecting the boat harbors with the Gulf of Alaska. Enjoy fresh sushi and sashimi while watch-
ing the procession of fishing boats gliding past on their way to catch or deliver your next meal. Keep your eyes peeled for sea otters, seals, sea lions, and eagles, too. The menu also features tempura, *yakisoba* (fried noodles), and rice specials. ⊠ *516 E. Marine Way* ☎ *907/481–1088* ⊗ *Closed Mon.*

WHERE TO STAY

For expanded hotel reviews, visit Fodors.com.

$ 🏠 **A Channel View Bed & Breakfast.** Owned and operated by a fifth-
generation Kodiak Alaskan, this emerald-isle favorite has sea views and is conveniently located less than 1 mile from downtown Kodiak. **Pros:** channel views; very hospitable owners **Cons:** slightly inconve-
nient if you don't have a car and aren't keen on a 20-minute walk into town (but Mary and Ron can help you call a cab). **TripAdvisor:** "an exquisite example of pure Alaskan hospitality," "exceptionally kind and thoughtful hosts," "beautiful place and excellent views." ⊠ *1010 Stellar Way* ☎ *907/486–2470* ⊕ *www.kodiakchannelview.com* ⟿ *4 rooms* ⬠ *In-room: Wi-Fi. In-hotel: laundry facilities.* ⏀ *Breakfast.*

$$ 🏠 **Best Western Kodiak Inn.** Rooms here have soothing floral decor, and some overlook the harbor. **Pros:** downtown location. **Cons:** harbor-view rooms are on the street; quieter rooms are in the back. **TripAdvisor:** "comfortable rooms," "bed was great," "housekeeping was extraordi-
narily excellent." ⊠ *236 W. Rezanof Dr.* ☎ *907/486–5712 or 888/563–
4254* ⊕ *www.kodiakinn.com* ⟿ *82 rooms* ⬠ *In-room: Wi-Fi. In-hotel: restaurant, bar, some pets allowed* ⏀ *Breakfast.*

$$ 🏠 **Cliff House B&B.** Perched on Kodiak's rocky coastline, this newly-built custom house hosts a suite of 3 rooms with common sitting area, private entrance, shared bath, and kitchen facilities complete with home-
made granola and a "bottomless cookie jar." **Pros:** excellent views; we repeat: bottomless cookie jar; cozy library for rainy-day relaxation **Cons:** shared bath for some rooms ⊠ *1223 W Kouskov* ☎ *907/486–
5079* ⊕ *www.kodiak-alaska-dinner-cruises.com/kodiak-bed-breakfast.
html* ⟿ *4 rooms, 2 baths* ⬠ *In-room: Wi-Fi. In-hotel: laundry facilities* ⏀ *Breakfast.*

$$ 🏠 **Comfort Inn Kodiak.** This recently remodeled hotel is a five-minute
★ walk from the main terminal at the airport, about 4½ mi from down-
town (but free airport transportation is provided). **Pros:** fish for salmon in the river out back. **Cons:** a bit out of town, so you might want a vehicle. **TripAdvisor:** "treated me like family," "great breakfast,"

6

CAMPING ON KODIAK'S ROAD SYSTEM

There are three Alaska State Parks–run road-accessible campgrounds (Ft. Abercrombie, Buskin River, and Pasagshak) on Kodiak Island, with a total of 48 tent sites. All have toilets, drinking water, and fishing; two have nearby hiking trails. Camping at Pasagshak is free; the campgrounds at Ft. Abercrombie and Buskin River charge $10–$15 a night. Camping limits are 15 consecutive nights at Buskin River and Pasagshak, seven nights at Ft. Abercrombie. Each site has its appeal, but Ft. Abercrombie, set in an old military base, complete with the ghosts of gun emplacements, has fantastic views; however,

it's exposed enough that campers should be sure to stake their tents down tight if the wind starts to howl. **Pros:** some campgrounds have electricity and cold pressurized water; subsistence is allowed, so when the food you pack in runs out, you don't become a featured news story. **Cons:** the water is very cold; far from creature comforts. ⊠ *Alaska State Parks, Kodiak District Office, 1400 Abercrombie Dr., Kodiak* ☎ *907/486–6339* ⤳ *48 tent sites* ⚬ *Portable toilets, drinking water, bear boxes, picnic tables* ⚬ *Reservations not accepted* ⊜ *No credit cards.*

"room was clean and comfortable." ⊠ *1395 Airport Way* ☎ *907/487–2700 or 800/544–2202* ⊕ *www.comfortinn.com/hotel-kodiak-alaska-AK025?promo=gglocal* ⤳ *50 rooms* ⚬ *In-room: Wi-Fi. In-hotel: restaurant, bar, business center, some pets allowed* ⏮ *Breakfast.*

$ 🛏 **Hilltop B&B**. This spacious, split-level home features 7 bedrooms and 3.5 bathrooms, with a private entrance, kitchenette, deck with BBQ grill, and plenty of parking space. **Pros:** wood-burning stove, close to grocery shopping. **Cons:** away from downtown, so rental car advisable. ⊠ *993 Hilltop St.* ☎ *907/539–2325* ⊕ *www.kodiakhilltopbnb.com* ⤳ *7 rooms* ⚬ *In-room: Wi-Fi. In-hotel: laundry facilities.*

KODIAK NATIONAL WILDLIFE REFUGE

50 mi south of Katmai National Park, 300 mi southwest of Anchorage.

GETTING HERE AND AROUND

The refuge is on Kodiak Island and is therefore accessible only by boat or plane. The Alaska Marine Highway stops at the town of Kodiak several times a week in the summer months. From there the Visitor's Bureau can provide lists of the numerous guides, outfitters, and air taxis that service the refuge.

ESSENTIALS

Visitor Information **Kodiak National Wildlife Refuge** (⊠ *1390 Buskin River Rd., MS 559, Kodiak* ☎ *907/487–2600 or 888/408–3514* ⊕ *kodiak.fws.gov*).

EXPLORING

The 1.9-million-acre **Kodiak National Wildlife Refuge** lies mostly on Kodiak Island and neighboring Afognak and Uganik islands, in the Gulf of Alaska. All are part of the Kodiak Archipelago, separated from Alaska's mainland by the stormy Shelikof Strait. Within the refuge are rugged mountains, tundra meadows and lowlands, thickly forested hills that are enough different shades of green to make a leprechaun cry, plus lakes, marshes, and hundreds of miles of pristine coastland. No place in the refuge is more than 15 mi from the ocean. The weather here is generally wet and cool, and storms born in the North Pacific often bring heavy rains.

Dozens of species of birds flock to the refuge each spring and summer, including Aleutian terns, horned puffins, black oystercatchers, ravens, ptarmigan, and chickadees. At least 600 pairs of bald eagles live on the islands, building the world's largest bird nests on shoreline cliffs and in tall trees. Seeing the Kodiak brown bears alone is worth the trip to this rugged country. When they emerge from their dens in spring, the bears chow down on some skunk cabbage to wake their stomachs up, have a few extra salads of sedges and grasses, and then feast on the endless supply of fish when salmon return. About the time they start thinking about hibernating again the berries are ripe (they may eat 2,000 or more berries a day). Kodiak brown bears, the biggest brown bears anywhere, sometimes topping out at more than 1,500 pounds, share the refuge with only a few other land mammals: red foxes, river otters, short-tailed weasels, and tundra voles.

Six species of Pacific salmon—chums, kings, pinks, silvers, sockeyes, and steelhead—return to Kodiak's waters from May to October. Other resident species include rainbow trout, Dolly Varden (an anadromous trout waiting for promotion to salmon), and arctic char. The abundance of fish and bears makes the refuge popular with anglers, hunters, and wildlife-watchers.

SPORTS, THE OUTDOORS, AND GUIDED TOURS

BEAR VIEW-
ING AND
SPORTFISHING

Rohrer Bear Camp (☎ 907/486–5835 ⊕ *www.sportfishingkodiak.com*) guides both bear viewers and visitors who come to Kodiak seeking the island's abundant sportfishing opportunities.

WHERE TO STAY

For expanded hotel reviews, visit Fodors.com.

¢ ⌸ **Kodiak Refuge Public-Use Cabins.** Some of the Park Service's lesser-known wonders are the fantastic cabins that it has scattered all over Alaska. **Pros:** true Alaska wilderness, all to yourself. **Cons:** the chance of getting weathered in for a couple of days means a loose schedule is a necessity; less likely is getting picked for the lottery. ⊠ *1390 Buskin River Rd., Kodiak* ☎ *907/487–2600* ⊕ *www.dnr.alaska.gov/parks/cabins/kodiak.htm* ⤵ *8 cabins* ⚱ *Reservations essential* ☰ *No credit cards.*

MAT-SU VALLEY AND BEYOND

Giant homegrown vegetables and the headquarters of the best-known dogsled race in the world are among the most prominent attractions of the Matanuska-Susitna (Mat-Su) Valley. The valley, lying an hour north of Anchorage by road, draws its name from its two largest rivers, the Matanuska and the Susitna, and is bisected by the Parks and Glenn highways. Major cities are Wasilla (on the Parks Highway) and Palmer (on the Glenn Highway). To the east the Glenn Highway connects to the Richardson Highway by way of several high mountain passes sandwiched between the Chugach Mountains to the south and the Talkeetnas to the north. ■TIP→ At Mile 103 of the Glenn Highway you can view the massive Matanuska Glacier from the road.

LAKE CLARK NATIONAL PARK AND PRESERVE

100 mi southwest of Anchorage by air.

GETTING HERE AND AROUND

There's no road access to the park, so all visits are via small plane. There are no roads within the park, nor are any groceries or camping supplies available. Most people fly into Port Alsworth, where lodging and supplies are available; while you're there sign in at the visitor center.

ESSENTIALS

Visitor Information **Lake Clark Administrative Headquarters** ⌖ *Administrative Headquarters: 240 W. 5th Ave., Suite 236, Anchorage 99501* ☎ *907/644–3626* ✉ *Park visitor center: 1 Park Pl., Port Alswortht* ☎ *907/781–2218* ⊕ *www.nps. gov/lacl.*

EXPLORING

When the weather is good, an idyllic choice beyond the Mat-Su Valley is the 3.4-million-acre **Lake Clark National Park and Preserve**, on the Alaska Peninsula and a short flight from Anchorage or Kenai and Soldotna. The parklands stretch from the coast to the heights of two grand volcanoes: Mt. Iliamna and Mt. Redoubt (which made headlines in 2009 when it erupted, sending ash floating over the region), both topping out above 10,000 feet. The country in between holds glaciers, waterfalls, and turquoise-tinted lakes. The 50-mi-long Lake Clark, filled by runoff waters from the mountains that surround it, is an important spawning ground for thousands of red (sockeye) salmon.

The river-running is superb in this park. You can make your way through dark forests of spruce and balsam poplars or hike over the high, easy-to-travel tundra. The animal life is profuse: look for bears, moose, Dall sheep, wolves, wolverines, foxes, beavers, and mink on land; seals, sea otters, and white (or beluga) whales offshore. Wildflowers embroider the meadows and tundra in spring, and wild roses bloom in the shadows of the forests. Plan your trip to Lake Clark for the end of June or early July, when the insects may be less plentiful. Or consider late August or early September, when the tundra glows with fall colors.

SPORTS   **Castle Mountain Outfitters.** Based in Chickaloon, north of Anchorage in
AND THE   Matanuska Valley, this outfitter conducts a variety of trips ranging from
OUTDOORS   guided hour-long horseback rides to one-week expeditions. ☎ *907/745–6427* ⊕ *www.mtaonline.net/~cmoride/index.html.*

WHERE TO STAY

For expanded hotel reviews, visit Fodors.com.

$$$ ▦ **Farm Lodge.** Near park headquarters in Port Alsworth, the farm was built as a homestead back in the 1940s and has been a lodge since 1977. **Pros:** at the headquarters of Lake Clark National Park; renowned flight service; family-friendly. **Cons:** removed from road system. ⌖ *Box*

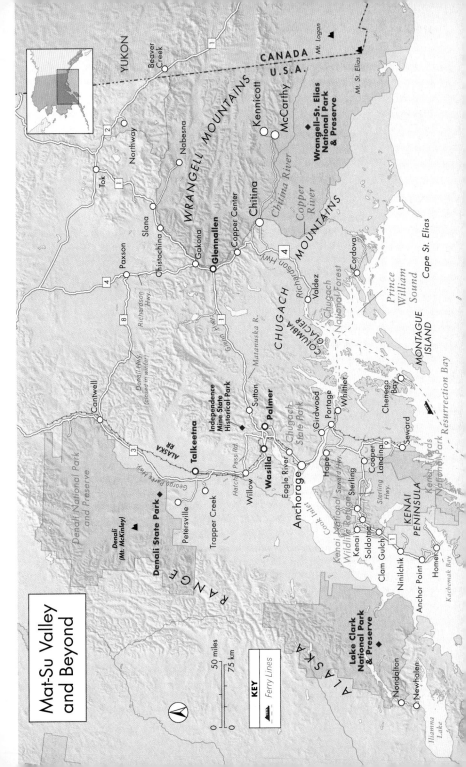

Mat-Su Valley and Beyond

KEY

Ferry Lines

0   50 miles

0   75 km

YUKON

Beaver Creek

CANADA

U.S.A.

Mt. Logan

Mt. St. Elias

Northway

Nabesna

WRANGELL MOUNTAINS

Kennicott

McCarthy

Wrangell–St. Elias National Park & Preserve

Tok

Slana

Chistochina

Gakona

Copper Center

Chitina

Chitina River

Copper River

CHUGACH MOUNTAINS

Paxson

Glennallen

Richardson Hwy.

Richardson Hwy.

Valdez

Chugach National Forest

Columbia Glacier

Cordova

Prince William Sound

Cape St. Elias

Cantwell

Denali Hwy. (closed in winter)

Matanuska R.

Glenn Hwy.

CHUGACH

COLUMBIA GLACIER

MONTAGUE ISLAND

Denali National Park and Preserve

Denali (Mt. McKinley)

Denali State Park

Talkeetna

Independence Mine State Historical Park

Sutton

Palmer

Chugach State Park

Girdwood

Portage

Whittier

Resurrection Bay

RANGE

ALASKA RR

George Parks Hwy.

Hatcher Pass Rd.

Wasilla

Eagle River

Anchorage

Hope

Cooper Landing

Chenega Bay

Seward

Kenai Fjords National Park

Petersville

Trapper Creek

Willow

Cook Inlet

Kenai National Wildlife Refuge

Sterling

Sterling Hwy.

Kenai

Soldotna

KENAI PENINSULA

Kenai National Seward Hwy.

Clam Gulch

Ninilchik

Anchor Point

Homer

Kachemak Bay

ALASKA

Lake Clark National Park & Preserve

Nondalton

Newhalen

Iliamna Lake

1, Port Alsworth 99653 ☎ *888/440–2281* ⊕ *www.lakeclarkair.com/ farm_lodge.html* ⇨ *13 rooms* ☼ *In-room: no TV. In-hotel: restaurant* ⊘ *All meals.*

PALMER

40 mi northeast of Anchorage.

With mountain-ringed farms, Palmer is charming and photogenic. This is the place to search for 100-pound cabbages and fresh farm cheese. Historic buildings are scattered throughout the Matanuska-Susitna Valley (often just referred to as the "Mat-Su Valley" or simply "the Valley"); in 1935 the federal government relocated about 200 farm families from the Depression-ridden Midwest to the Mat-Su Valley. Now it has developed into the state's major agricultural region. Good growing conditions of rich soil combined with long hours of summer sunlight result in some huge vegetables.

GETTING HERE AND AROUND

The Glenn Highway heads north out of Anchorage and right through Palmer. The Chugach Range lines both sides of Palmer's valley, and if you continue past the town you'll find yourself smack in the middle of the mountains.

ESSENTIALS

Medical Assistance **Mat-Su Regional Medical Center** (⊠ *2500 S. Woodworth Loop* ☎ *907/861–6000*).

Visitor Information **Mat-Su Convention & Visitors Bureau** (⊠ *7744 E. Visitors View Ct.* ☎ *907/746–5000* ⊕ *www.alaskavisit.com*). **Palmer Chamber of Commerce** (⊠ *723 S. Valley Way* ☎ *907/745–2880* ⊕ *www.palmerchamber.org*).

EXPLORING

ⓒ On a sunny day the town of Palmer looks like a Swiss calendar photo, with its old barns and log houses silhouetted against craggy Pioneer Peak. On nearby farms (on the Bodenburg Loop off the old Palmer Highway) you can pay to pick your own raspberries and other fruits and vegetables. The peak picking time at **Pyrah's Pioneer Peak Farm** (⊠ *Mi 2.6, Bodenburg Loop* ☎ *907/745–4511* ⊕ *www.pppfarm.net*), which cultivates 35 kinds of fruits and vegetables, occurs around mid-July.

ⓒ Fifty or so animals roam at the **Musk Ox Farm**, which conducts 30-minute guided tours from May to September. There's a hands-on museum and a gift shop featuring hand-knitted items made from the cashmere-like underfur (qiviut) combed from the musk ox. The scarves, caps, and more are made by Oomingmak, an Alaskan Native collective. ⊠ *Mi 50.1, Glenn Hwy.* ☎ *907/745–4151 or 907/745–2353* ⊕ *www.muskoxfarm. org* ⊡ *$9* ⊘ *May–Sept., daily 10–6; Oct.–Apr., by appointment only.*

★ Gold mining was an early mainstay of the Mat-Su Valley's economy. You can tour the long-dormant **Independence Mine** on the Hatcher Pass Road, a loop that in summer connects the Parks Highway just north of Willow to the Glenn Highway near Palmer. The road to Independence Mine from the Palmer side was paved in the summer of 2003. The remainder of the roadway to Willow is gravel. In the 1940s as many as

"The Hatcher Pass road was paved a little way off Highway 3, then became a narrow gravel road, which led to the abandoned Independence Mine. The scenery was awesome." —Tom Wells, Fodors.com photo contest participant.

200 workers were employed by the mine. Today it is a 271-acre state park and a cross-country ski area in winter. Only the wooden buildings remain; one of them, the red-roof manager's house, is now used as a visitor center. Guided tours are given on weekdays at 1:30 and 3:30. ⊠ *Independence Mine State Historical Park, 19 mi from Glenn Hwy. on Hatcher Pass Rd.* ☎ *907/745–3975* ⊕ *www.dnr.alaska.gov/parks/ units/indmine.htm* ✉ *$5 tours* ☉ *Visitor center early June–Labor Day, daily 11–7; grounds year-round. Guided tours start June 20, daily at 1 and 3. There is a day-use parking fee and a separate tour fee.*

WHERE TO STAY

For expanded hotel reviews, visit Fodors.com.

$ ⬛ **Colony Inn.** All guest rooms in this lovingly restored historic building are tastefully decorated with antiques and quilts. **Pros:** quiet; charming; centrally located. **Cons:** front desk a five-minute walk away at Valley Hotel; rooms are small. **TripAdvisor:** "no frills but lots of character," "a charming and comfortable place," "takes you back in time." ⊠ *325 E. Elmwood Ave.* ☎ *907/745–3330, 800/478–7666 in Alaska* ⮡ *12 rooms* ⬥ *In-room: Wi-Fi. In-hotel: restaurant, laundry facilities.*

$–$$ ⬛ **Hatcher Pass Lodge.** This lodge has spectacular views and can serve as a base camp for hiking, berry-picking, and—in fall and winter—skiing. **Pros:** views and nature right out your door. **Cons:** no kitchens and a bit far from town, so dining options are limited. ⊠ *Mi 17, Hatcher Pass Rd., Box 763* ☎ *907/745–5897 or 907/745–1200* ⊕ *www. hatcherpasslodge.com* ⮡ *3 rooms, 9 cabins with shared showers* ⬥ *In-room: no TV, Wi-Fi. In-hotel: restaurant, bar, some pets allowed.*

$ 🏨 **Valley Hotel.** Built in 1948 and run by the same folks as the Colony Inn, this three-story budget hotel was remodeled in 2008. **Pros:** centrally located. **Cons:** small rooms make the hotel less family-friendly than other venues. **TripAdvisor:** "quaint old Alaskan hospitality," "clean and well appointed," "food is pretty good." ⊠ *606 S. Alaska St.* 🕾 *907/745–3330, 800/478–7666 in Alaska* ⇄ *43 rooms* ♿ *In-room: Wi-Fi. In-hotel: restaurant, bar, laundry facilities.*

> **MEGA STATE FAIR**
>
> Giant vegetables (a 105-pound cabbage, a 300-plus-pound summer squash that took four people to carry) are big attractions at Palmer's **Alaska State Fair** (⊠ *Mi 40.2, Glenn Hwy.* 🕾 *907/745–4827 or 800/850–3247* ⊕ *www.alaskastatefair.org*). Shop for Alaskan-made gifts and crafts, and whoop it up with midway rides, livestock and 4-H shows, bake-offs, home-preserved produce contests, food, and live music. The fair runs 12 days, ending on Labor Day. Admission is $9–$11.

WASILLA

42 mi north of Anchorage, 10 mi west of Palmer.

Wasilla made national news in 2008 when Sarah Palin, the former governor of the state and resident and former mayor of the town, was picked to be the Republican vice presidential candidate. Wasilla is one of the valley's original pioneer communities, and over time has served as a supply center for farmers, gold miners, and mushers. Today fast-food restaurants and strip malls line the Parks Highway. ■ TIP→ **It's the best place for stocking up if you're heading north to Talkeetna or Denali.** Rolling hills and more scenic vistas can be found by wandering the area's back roads.

GETTING HERE AND AROUND

Wasilla is accessible by car. Going north along the Glenn Highway, turn off just before Palmer and head west. Not far from there you'll come across the sleepy town of Wasilla. It's not known for glamour or beauty, but strolling through town you'll find some quaint shops and quiet streets that make for great, character-rich photographs.

ESSENTIALS

Visitor Information Wasilla Chamber of Commerce (⊠ *415 E. Railroad Ave.* 🕾 *907/376–1299* ⊕ *www.wasillachamber.org*).

EXPLORING

♻ The **Iditarod Trail Headquarters** displays dogsleds, mushers' clothing, and trail gear, and you can catch video highlights of past races. The gift shop sells Iditarod items. Dog-sled rides are available year-round; in summer rides on wheels are available for $10. ⊠ *Mi 2.2, Knik Rd.* 🕾 *907/376–5155* ⊕ *www.iditarod.com* 🎫 *Free* ☉ *Mid-May–mid-Sept., daily 8–7; mid-Sept.–mid-May, weekdays 8–5 (during week of Fur Rondy, open daily).*

On a 20-acre site, the **Museum of Alaska Transportation and Industry** exhibits some of the machines that helped develop Alaska, from dogsleds to jet aircraft and everything in between. The Don Sheldon Building houses aviation artifacts as well as antique autos, trains, and photographic displays. There is also a snowmachine (Alaskan for snowmobile) exhibit. ✉ *From Parks Hwy., turn south onto Neuser Rd. at Mi 47, follow road ¾ mi to end* ☎ *907/376–1211* ⊕ *www.museumofalaska. org* 🎟 *$8* ◷ *May–Sept., daily 10–5; Sept.–May, Tues. 10–2.*

WHERE TO EAT

$ ✕**Cadillac Café**. Hearty fare fills the menu at this diner-style café, includ-
CAFÉ   ing homemade pies; big, juicy burgers; exotic pizzas turned out of a stone, wood-fired oven; and Southwestern-style Mexican food. The owner describes the decor as "Alaska minimalist," but the booths are plush and comfortable, and hand-rubbed wood is evident. Breakfast is served only on weekends. ✉ *Mi 49, Parks Hwy. at Pittman St., in the Tesoro Bldg.* ☎ *907/357–5533.*

$$–$$$ ✕**Evangelo's Restaurant**. The food is good and the servings are ample at
ITALIAN   this spacious local favorite on the Parks Highway. Try the garlic-sautéed shrimp in a white-wine butter sauce or a mammoth calzone. The pizzas are loaded with goodies, and a salad bar provides a fresh selection. ✉ *Mi 40, Parks Hwy.* ☎ *907/376–1212.*

WHERE TO STAY

For expanded hotel reviews, visit Fodors.com.

$$$ 🛏 **Best Western Lake Lucille Inn**. This well-maintained resort on Lake Lucille provides easy access to several recreational activities, including boating in summer and ice-skating and snowmobiling in winter. **Pros:** beautiful lakefront property. **Cons:** the sound of powerboats whizzing by. **TripAdvisor:** "comfortable rooms and friendly staff," "nice lake views," "fantastic restaurant." ✉ *1300 W. Lake Lucille Dr. Mi 43.5, Parks Hwy.* ☎ *907/373–1776 or 800/528–1234* ⊕ *www.bestwestern. com/lakelucilleinn* 🛌 *50 rooms, 4 suites* ♿ *In-room: Wi-Fi. In-hotel: gym, laundry facilities, some pets allowed* ❙❍❙ *Breakfast.*

$$ 🛏 **Pioneer Ridge Bed and Breakfast Inn**. Each of the spacious, log-
★   partitioned rooms in the converted old Fairview Dairy barn and award-winning inn is decorated according to a theme. **Pros:** cozy and warm; views you can't stop staring at. **Cons:** not handicapped-friendly— although it's only one story, the hotel has many steps. **TripAdvisor:** "great family place," "very large and spacious," "quirky in a nice way." ✉ *2221 Yukon Circle, HC31, Box 5083K* ☎ *907/376–7472 or 800/478–7472* ⊕ *www.pioneerridge.com* 🛌 *1 suite; 1 cabin; 4 rooms with private baths; 1 room with separate, unshared bath* ♿ *In-room: no TV, Wi-Fi* ❙❍❙ *Breakfast* ◷ *Closed Sept.–May.*

TALKEETNA

56 mi north of Wasilla, 112 mi north of Anchorage.

Talkeetna lies at the end of a spur road near Mile 99 of the Parks Highway. The town maintains a Wild West vibe with a small, unpaved downtown area surrounding a central green. Lucky is the traveler who gets a few sunny days—Denali looms over the town, begging you to take dramatic photos. Mountaineers congregate here to begin their assaults on Mt. McKinley in Denali National Park; those just off the mountain are recognizable by their tanned faces with sunglasses lines. The

Denali mountain rangers have their climbing headquarters here, as do most glacier pilots who fly climbing parties to the mountain. A carved pole at the town cemetery honors deceased mountaineers.

EXPLORING

The **Talkeetna Historical Society Museum**, across from the Fairview Inn, explores the history of Mt. McKinley climbs. The museum has a scale model of Mt. McKinley and features information on the history of climbing attempts on the continent's highest peak. A Talkeetna walking-tour map points out sites of historical interest. ⊠ *Mi 14.5, Talkeetna Spur and D St.* ☎ *907/733–2487* ⊕ *www. talkeetnahistoricalsociety.org* ⤙ *$3* ☉ *May 15–Sept. 15, daily 10–6.*

> **SMALL-TOWN FLAVOR**
>
> Talkeetna is a must-visit if you're driving between Anchorage and Denali or Fairbanks. A true small town, Talkeetna has a genuine roadhouse (with delicious home-made berry pies), quirky locals, and a pebbly shore along the Susitna with fantastic views of Mt. McKinley on a clear day. If you do come through town, be sure to check out the **West Rib Pub and Grill** (☎ *907/733–3354*), which is in the back of historic Nagley's Store on Main Street (a mini-museum of sorts). Grab a seat out back and wash down the delicious chili, burgers, and fries with a local microbrew.

OUTDOOR ACTIVITIES AND GUIDED TOURS

BOATING, FLOATING, AND FISHING **Mahay's Riverboat Service** (☎ *907/733–2223 or 800/736–2210* ⊕ *www. mahaysriverboat.com*) conducts scenic jet-boat tours and guided fishing charters on the Susitna and Talkeetna rivers.

Tri-River Charters (⊠ *Box 312, 99676* ☎ *907/733–2400* ⊕ *www. tririvercharters.com*) operates fishing trips out of Talkeetna and on the nearby Deshka River, and can provide all the necessary tackle and gear.

FLIGHTSEEING **Talkeetna Aero Services.** Take a twin-engine aerial tour of the mountain. It's the only service that actually flies over the summit of McKinley (weather allowing). ☎ *907/733–2899, 907/683–2899 Denali, or 888/733–2899* ⊕ *www.talkeetnaaero.com.*

Talkeetna Air Taxi. Check out McKinley and environs, then swoop down to a glacier to test your boots. Maybe even land on one ☎ *907/733–2218 or 800/533–2219* ⊕ *www.talkeetnaair.com.*

HIKING **Alaska Mountaineering School.** Whether it's on mountaineering expeditions to McKinley or less extreme treks into the Alaska Range, this Talkeetna company takes the time to train you before heading out to glacier trek or hit the pristine backcountry. ☎ *907/733–1016* ⊕ *www. climbalaska.org.*

WHERE TO STAY

For expanded hotel reviews, visit Fodors.com.

$ ⊡ **Swiss-Alaska Inn.** Family-run since 1976, this rustic-style property is well known among those who come to fish in the Talkeetna, Susitna, and Chulitna rivers. **Pros:** very quiet. **Cons:** about a half-mile from town, so some folks might want a car. ⊠ *East Talkeetna, by boat launch*

☎ 907/733–2424 ⊕ www.swissalaska.com ⇌ 20 rooms ⚷ In-room: no TV. In-hotel: restaurant, business center.

$$$$ ⚏ **Talkeetna Alaskan Lodge.** This luxury hotel has excellent views of
★ Mt. **Pros:** the restaurant is the place to watch the sun set while you also gaze at Mt. McKinley. **Cons:** large and lacking personality. ⊠ Mi 12.5, Talkeetna Spur Rd. ⌖ 2525 C St., Suite 405, Anchorage 99503 ☎ 888/959–9590 ⊕ www.talkeetnalodge.com ⇌ 212 rooms, 3 suites ⚷ In-room: Wi-Fi. In-hotel: restaurant, bar.

¢–$ ⚏ **Talkeetna Roadhouse.** This circa-1917 log roadhouse has a common
★ sitting area and rooms in a variety of sizes, including a hostel-style bunk room with four beds ($21) and two rustic cabins ($99–$147). **Pros:** this is true, down-home Alaska at its best. **Cons:** shared bath. **Trip-Advisor:** "so homey and comfortable," "great atmosphere," "quaint historic building." ⊠ 13550 E. Main St., Box 604 ☎ 907/733–1351 ⊕ www.talkeetnaroadhouse.com ⇌ 5 rooms, 2 cabins, share 5 baths ⚷ In-room: no TV, Wi-Fi. In-hotel: restaurant, laundry facilities, business center, some pets allowed.

DENALI STATE PARK

6

34 mi north of Talkeetna, 132 mi north of Anchorage.

GETTING HERE AND AROUND

The George Parks Highway bisects Denali State Park and offers not only a majestic view of year-round snow-covered mountaintops, but also a mad array of wildlife. The highway is paved, but after the breakup of winter ice it tends to be riddled with potholes. It's always wise when driving in Alaska to have at least one good spare tire.

ESSENTIALS

Visitor Information Alaska State Parks, Mat-Su Area Office (⌖ HC 32, Box 6706, Wasilla 99687 ☎ 907/745–3975).

EXPLORING

Overshadowed by the larger and more charismatic Denali National Park and Preserve, "Little Denali," or **Denali State Park**, offers excellent access, beautiful views of Mt. McKinley, scenic campgrounds, and prime wilderness hiking and backpacking opportunities within a few miles of the road system. Between the Talkeetna Mountains and the Alaska Range, Denali State Park combines wooded lowlands and forested foothills topped by alpine tundra.

OUTDOOR ACTIVITIES

The park's chief attraction, other than views of McKinley, is the 35-mi-long **Curry-Kesugi Ridge**, which forms a rugged spine through the heart of the park that is ideal backpacking terrain. The initial climb to get to the ridge is strenuous, but once you get up high, it's mostly gentle up-and-down terrain. The trail runs from the Troublesome Creek trailhead at Mile 137.3 to the Little Coal Creek trailhead at Mile 163.9. The Byers Lake campground at Mile 147 has a trailhead for a spur trail that intersects the Kesugi Ridge trail, offering an alternative to hiking the entire trail. Views of Mt. McKinley and the Alaska Range from the ridge trail are stunning. ■ TIP→ This is a

CLOSE UP

A Privileged Communion

Between 1903 and 1912 eight expeditions walked the slopes of 20,320-foot Mt. McKinley. But none had reached the absolute top of North America's highest peak. Thus the stage was set for Hudson Stuck, a self-described American amateur mountaineer.

Stuck came to Alaska in 1904, drawn not by mountains but by a missionary calling. As the Episcopal Church's archdeacon for the Yukon River region, he visited Native villages year-round. His passion for climbing was unexpectedly rekindled in 1906, when he saw from afar the "glorious, broad, massive uplift" of McKinley, the "father of mountains."

Five years after that wondrous view, Stuck pledged to reach McKinley's summit—or at least try. For his climbing party he picked three Alaskans experienced in snow and ice travel, though not in mountaineering: Harry Karstens, a well-known explorer and backcountry guide who would later become the first superintendent of Mt. McKinley National Park; Robert Tatum, Stuck's missionary assistant; and Walter Harper, part Native, who served as Stuck's interpreter.

Assisted by two sled-dog teams, the group began its expedition on St. Patrick's Day, 1913, at Nenana, a village 90 mi northeast of McKinley. A month later they began their actual ascent of the great peak's northern side, via the Muldrow Glacier. The glacier's surface proved to be a maze of crevasses, some of them wide chasms with no apparent bottom. Carefully working their way up-glacier, the climbers established a camp at 11,500 feet. From there the team chopped a staircase up several miles—and 3,000 vertical feet—of rock, snow, and ice.

Their progress was delayed several times by high winds, heavy snow, and near-zero visibility.

By May 30 the climbers had reached the top of the ridge (later named in Karstens' honor) and moved into a high glacial basin. Despite temperatures ranging from subzero to 21°F, they kept warm at night by sleeping on sheep and caribou skins and covering themselves with down quilts, camel's-hair blankets, and a wolf robe.

On June 6 the team established its high camp at 18,000 feet. The following morning was bright, cloudless, and windy. Three of the climbers suffered headaches and stomach pains, but given the clear weather everyone agreed to make an attempt. They left camp at 5 am and by 1:30 pm stood within a few yards of McKinley's summit. Harper, who had been leading all day, was the first to reach the top, soon followed by the others. After catching their breath, the teammates shook hands, said a prayer of thanks, made some scientific measurements, and reveled in their magnificent surroundings.

In his classic book *The Ascent of Denali*, Hudson Stuck later reflected, "There was no pride of conquest, no trace of that exultation of victory some enjoy upon the first ascent of a lofty peak, no gloating over good fortune that had hoisted us a few hundred feet higher than others who had struggled and been discomfited. Rather, was the feeling that a privileged communion with the high places of the earth had been granted."

CAMPING IN DENALI STATE PARK

⚠ **Alaska State Parks Campgrounds.** Four roadside campgrounds are within Denali State Park—two at Byers Lake, Lower Troublesome Creek, and Denali Viewpoint North. All are easily accessible from the Parks Highway. The Byers Lake campground has a boat launch, canoe and kayak rentals, and nearby hiking trails. Sites are on a first-come, first-served basis, and there aren't any hookups. **Pros:** easily accessible. **Cons:** roadside camping means you won't be secluded; no hookups. ⌑ *Alaska State Parks, HC 32, Box 6706, Wasilla 99654* ☎ *907/745–3975* ⊕ *www.dnr.alaska. gov/parks/units/denali2.htm* ↪ *143 tent/RV sites* ⚸ *Pit toilets, drinking water, fire pits, picnic tables* ⚶ *Reservations not accepted* ▤ *No credit cards* ◷ *Closed Oct.–May.*

bear-intensive area, especially the Troublesome Creek area in late summer when the salmon runs are in full force.

Another destination favored by backcountry travelers is the **Peters Hills,** accessible from Petersville Road in Trapper Creek. Denali State Park borders the hills, and primitive trails and campgrounds are used year-round. It's especially popular with snowmachiners in winter and mountain bikers in summer.

For lovers of outdoor activities like naturalist hikes and mountain biking, **Denali Backcountry Lodge** (⊕ *www.denalilodge.com*) offers the complete wilderness package.

WHERE TO STAY

For expanded hotel reviews, visit Fodors.com.

¢ 🏚 **Alaska State Parks Cabins.** Three public-use cabins are in Denali State Park, along the shores of Byers Lake. **Pros:** more accessible than most wilderness cabins. **Cons:** very basic; no running water or electricity. ⌑ *Alaska State Parks Information Center, 550 W. 7th Ave., Suite 1260, Anchorage 99501-3557* ✛ *Mi 43.5, Parks Hwy.* ☎ *907/269–8400* ⊕ *dnr. alaska.gov/parks/cabins/matsu.htm* ↪ *3 cabins* ▤ *No credit cards.*

$$–$$$ 🏚 **McKinley Princess Wilderness Lodge.** When the sky is clear and Mt. **Pros:** clean; with everything you might need. **Cons:** huge; somewhat bland. **TripAdvisor:** "nice and clean," "great views and great customer service," "excellent food." ✉ *Mi 133, Parks Hwy., Trapper Creek* ☎ *907/733–2900 or 800/426–0500* ⊕ *www.princesslodges.com* ↪ *460 rooms, 4 suites* ⚸ *In-hotel: 3 restaurants, bars, gym* ◷ *Closed mid-Sept.–mid-May.*

GLENNALLEN

187 mi northeast of Anchorage.

This community of a few more than 500 residents is the gateway to Wrangell–St. Elias National Park and Preserve. It's 124 mi from Glennallen to McCarthy, the last 58 mi on unpaved gravel. This town is also the service center for the Copper River Basin and is a fly-in base for several wilderness outfitters.

GETTING HERE AND AROUND

The Glenn Highway from Anchorage to Glennallen is relatively well maintained all year round. The town's main street, however, is sand and gravel.

ESSENTIALS

Medical Assistance Crossroads Medical Center (✉ Mi 187.5, Glenn Hwy. ☎ 907/822–3203).

Visitor Information Bureau of Land Management (✉ Box 147, Glennallen 99588 ☎ 907/822–3217 ⊕ www.glennallen.ak.blm.gov).

> **WARNING**
>
> Before setting out on McCarthy Road, make sure both you and your car are prepared. Your car should be equipped with a working jack and a properly inflated spare tire, or else potholes, old railroad ties, and occasional railroad spikes may leave you stranded.

WHERE TO STAY

For expanded hotel reviews, visit Fodors.com.

$$ ☷ **Caribou Hotel**. Mauve and sea-green rooms fill this modern hotel. **Pros:** several rooms have hot tubs. **Cons:** some rooms have shared bath. ✉ Mi 186.5, Glenn Hwy. ⌂ Box 329, 99588 ☎ 907/822–3302 or 800/478–3302 ⊕ www.caribouhotel.com ⇶ 83 rooms, 63 with bath; 3 suites; 2 cabins ⌂ In-room: kitchen (some), Wi-Fi. In-hotel: some pets allowed.

WRANGELL–ST. ELIAS NATIONAL PARK AND PRESERVE

77 mi southeast of Glennallen, 264 mi east of Anchorage.

GETTING HERE AND AROUND

The park is accessible from Alaska's highway system, via one of two gravel roads. The unpaved Nabesna Road leaves the Glenn Highway–Tok Cutoff at the village of Slana and takes you 45 mi into the park's northern foothills. The better-known route is McCarthy Road, which stretches 60 mi as it follows an old railroad bed from Chitina to the Kennicott River. At the end of the road you must park and cross the river via a footbridge.

Limited services are available in the end-of-the-road town of McCarthy. Facilities include guest lodges, a B&B, and a restaurant. There's no gas station or post office.

ESSENTIALS

Visitor Information Wrangell–St. Elias Parks Office (✉ Mi 106.8, Richardson Hwy. ⌂ Box 439, Copper Center 99573 ☎ 907/822–5234 ⊕ www.nps.gov/wrst).

EXPLORING

In a land of many grand and spectacularly beautiful mountains, those in the 9.2-million-acre **Wrangell–St. Elias National Park and Preserve** are possibly the finest of them all. This extraordinarily compact cluster of immense peaks belongs to four different mountain ranges. Rising through many ecozones, the Wrangell–St. Elias Park and Preserve is largely undeveloped wilderness parkland on a grand scale. The area is perfect mountain-biking and primitive-hiking terrain, and the rivers invite rafting for those with expedition experience. The mountains attract climbers from around the world; most of them fly in from Glennallen or Yakutat.

Covering a 100 mi by 70 mi area, the **Wrangells** tower above the 2,500-foot-high Copper River Plateau, and the peaks of Mts. Jarvis, Drum, Blackburn, Sanford, and Wrangell rise 15,000 feet to 16,000 feet from sea level.

The white-iced spire of **Mt. St. Elias,** in the St. Elias Range, reaches more than 18,000 feet. It's the fourth-tallest mountain on the North American continent and the crown of the planet's highest coastal range.

The park's coastal mountains are frequently wreathed in snow-filled clouds, their massive height making a giant wall that contains the great storms brewed in the Gulf of Alaska. As a consequence, they bear some of the continent's largest ice fields, with more than 100 glaciers radiating from them. One of these, the **Malaspina Glacier,** is 1,500 square mi—larger than the state of Rhode Island. This tidewater glacier has an incredible pattern of black-and-white stripes made by the other glaciers that coalesced to form it. ■ **TIP→ Look for Malaspina Glacier on the coast north of Yakutat if you fly between Juneau and Anchorage.**

★ The nearby abandoned **Kennicott Mine** is one of the park's main visitor attractions. The open pit mine is reminiscent of ancient Greek amphitheatres, and the abandoned structures are as impressive as the mountains they stand against.

CAMPING IN WRANGELL-ST. ELIAS

Alaska State Parks Campgrounds. The state maintains 23 road-accessible campgrounds in the Matanuska-Susitna–Copper River region. The allowed length of stay varies from 4 to 15 days. **Pros:** most campgrounds have nearby hiking trails. **Cons:** although they can accommodate RVs up to 35 feet, there are no electrical hookups. *Alaska State Parks, Mat-Su Area Office, HC 32, Box 6706, Wasilla 99654* ☎ *907/745–3975* *23 campgrounds* *Flush toilets, drinking water (some), fire pits (some), picnic table (some)* *Reservations not accepted* *No credit cards* *Closed Oct.–May.*

OUTDOOR ACTIVITIES AND GUIDED TOURS

ADVENTURE TOURS

St. Elias Alpine Guides. Based in the town of McCarthy and operating for over three decades, this guide outfit gives introductory mountaineering lessons, leads excursions ranging from half-day glacier walks to month-long backpacking trips, and is the only company contracted by the Park Service to conduct guided tours of historic Kennicott buildings. If you'd rather raft than hike, its Copper Oar rafting outfit (*www.copperoar.com*) has river trips into the heart of the wilderness. ☎ *907/345–9048 or 888/933–5427* *www.steliasguides.com.*

Wrangell Outfitters. This husband-and-wife team from Fairbanks takes visitors on horse-packing trips into the heart of Wrangell–St. Elias National Park and Preserve. ☎ *907/479–5343* *www.wrangelloutfitters.com.*

WHERE TO STAY

For expanded hotel reviews, visit Fodors.com.

6

ECOTOURISM IN ALASKA

Ecotourists aim to travel responsibly. Typically, ecotourism is on a smaller scale and involves more education than traditional tourism; often you are led by guides who know the local natural history and cultures. Itineraries allow you a closer connection to the areas explored. As one Alaska guide says, "Slow down, take a deep breath, feel where you are." The **International Ecotourism Society** (⊕ www.ecotourism.org) is a great resource.

When contacting outfitters, learn about the guides, the nature of the activities they offer, and the area you want to explore. Also be sure to determine how well the guides know the area and how long the company has been in operation. Make it a point to ask for references.

A state-produced *Alaska Vacation Planner* (which also contains information on ecotourism) can be obtained from the **Alaska Travel Industry Association** (☎ 907/929–2842, 800/862–5275 to order vacation planners ⊕ www.travelalaska.com).

The **Alaska Wilderness Recreation and Tourism Association** (☎ 907/258–3171 ⊕ www.awrta.org) can provide information on many businesses and activities across the state.

$$-$$$ ⊡ **Copper River Princess Wilderness Lodge.** At the gateway to the park, this lodge has views of the Wrangell–St. Elias mountain range and the Copper and Klutina rivers. **Pros:** luxurious lodge in the wilderness. **Cons:** little else nearby in the way of amenities. **TripAdvisor:** "beautiful rooms and great views," "eager staff and remote location," "a beautiful and modern lodge." ⊠ *Brenwick Craig Rd., Mi 102, Richardson Hwy., Copper Center* ☎ *907/822–4000; 800/426–0500 reservations* ⊕ *www.princesslodges.com* ⤳ *85 rooms* ⌂ *In-hotel: 2 restaurants, bar* ⊙ *Closed mid-Sept.–mid-May.*

$$-$$$ ⊡ **Kennicott Glacier Lodge.** Artifacts and photos of the era when mining
★ was the main order of business in the ghost town of Kennicott adorn the small rooms in this modern wood lodge. **Pros:** lots of character; delicious food. **Cons:** some rooms have shared bath. ⊠ *5 mi from McCarthy* ⌖ *Box 103940, Anchorage 99510* ☎ *907/258–2350 or 800/582–5128* ⊕ *www.kennicottlodge.com* ⤳ *35 rooms, 10 with bath* ⌂ *In-room: no TV. In-hotel: restaurant* ⊙ *Closed mid-Sept.–mid-May.*

$$$$ ⊡ **Ultima Thule Outfitters.** This remote fly-in-only lodge on the Chitina
★ River in Wrangell–St. **Pros:** adventure and comfort at their best. **Cons:** four-night minimum means it will be an expensive venture. ⌖ *Summer: Box 109, Chitina 99566* ⌖ *Winter: Box 770361, Eagle River 99577* ☎ *907/688–1200* ⊕ *www.ultimathulelodge.com* ⤳ *6 cabins* ⌂ *In-room: no TV. In-hotel: restaurant, business center* ▤ *No credit cards* ⎮⎯⎮ *All meals.*

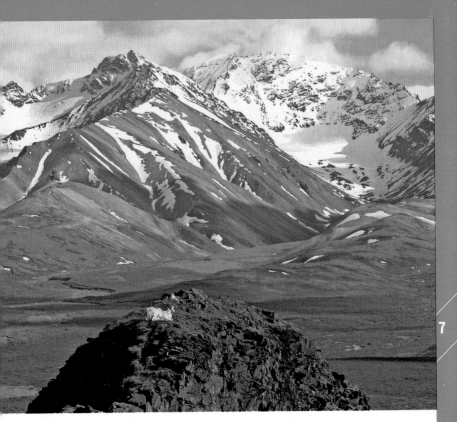

Denali National Park and Preserve

WORD OF MOUTH

"What a view! This Dall sheep was catching some rays, surveying his magnificent kingdom in Denali National Park."
—Chris Marlow, Photo Contest Winner

WELCOME TO DENALI NATIONAL PARK AND PRESERVE

TOP REASONS TO GO

★ **Backcountry hiking:** Getting off the road system and into the park's managed units allows for a true wilderness experience, limited only by time and the strength of your legs. For on-trail hiking try Savage River or Mt. Healy Overlook Trail.

★ **Denali flightseeing:** Soar over river valleys and up glaciers to the slopes of Denali to see the continent's wildest scenery. Some tours also offer landings on Ruth Glacier.

★ **Sled-dog demonstrations:** Watch half-hour demonstrations at the nation's oldest working dogsled kennel. Since the 1920s, sled dogs have been hauling rangers and workers to Denali's interior.

★ **Rafting trip:** Experience Denali through wild rapids or serene flat water.

★ **Bus to Wonder Lake:** It takes all day, but your chances of spotting wildlife are excellent. And from Wonder Lake the view of the massive slopes of Mt. McKinley—Denali—is something you'll never forget.

1 The Entrance. Just outside the park you'll find a strip of hotels, restaurants, and shops; just inside the park are the official visitor's center, the least scenic campsites in Denali, and a level of chaos that does not reflect the park's amazing beauty. Just put all this at your back as soon as you can.

2 Eielson Visitor Center. Deep in the heart of the park, near a favored caribou trail, Eielson offers great mountain views and sweeping vistas of glaciated landscape. If you can't make it to Wonder Lake, at least make it here.

3 The Mountain. Call it Mt. McKinley or Denali or just "the Mountain." It's the highest spot on the continent, a double-edged peak that draws more than 1,000 climbers a year; fewer than half make it to the top. But that's okay: it's easy enough to enjoy the view from below.

4 Wonder Lake. The end of the road for most vehicles, the lake is a full day's ride on one of the park buses. For your time, when the weather allows, you get the best view of the mountain anywhere in the park. And even when the mountain is hiding in the clouds, this is one of the prettiest stretches of landscape in the world.

KEY

⊢—⊣	*Rail Line*
......	*Trail*
▲	*Campground*
🏠	*Lodge*
⛱	*Picnic Area*
🚶	*Ranger Station*
🍴	*Restaurant*
🚌	*Free shuttle bus*

SNOHOMISH HILLS

DENALI NATIONAL PRESERVE

Castle Rocks 2079ft ▲

DENALI NATIONAL PA

COTTONWOOD HILLS

SLOW FORK HILLS

Heart Mtn 6500ft ▲

Mt Russell 11670ft ▲

A L A S K A

Mount Dall 8756ft ▲

DENALI NATIONAL PRESERVE

0   10 miles
0   10 kilometers

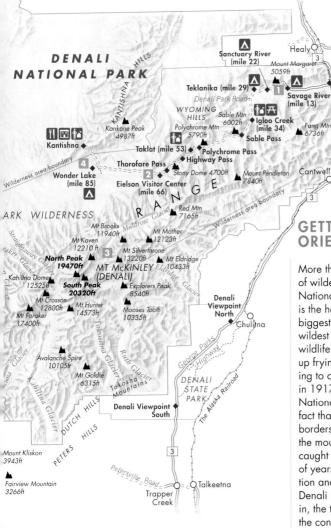

DENALI NATIONAL PARK

KANTISHNA HILLS

Healy

Mount Margaret 5059ft

Sanctuary River (mile 22)

Teklanika (mile 29)

Denali Park Road

Park Entrance & Headquarters

Savage River (mile 13)

Lagoon

WYOMING HILLS

Sable Mtn 6002ft

Igloo Creek (mile 34)

Fang Mtn 6736ft

Kankone Peak 4987ft

Polychrome Mtn 5790ft

Sable Pass

Kantishna

Toklat (mile 53)

Polychrome Pass

Highway Pass

Panorama Mountain 5778ft

Wilderness area boundary

Thorofare Pass

Stony Dome 4700ft

Mount Pendleton 7840ft

Cantwell

Denali Highway

8

Wonder Lake (mile 85)

Eielson Visitor Center (mile 66)

R A N G E

Wilderness area boundary

3

ARK WILDERNESS

Red Mtn 7165ft

Muldrow Glacier

Mt Brooks 11940ft

Mt Mather 12123ft

GETTING ORIENTED

Mt Koven 12210ft

Mt Silverthrone 13220ft

Mt Eldridge 10433ft

North Peak 19470ft

MT McKINLEY (DENALI)

Eldridge Glacier

raker Glacier

Straughaway Glacier

Kahiltna Dome 12525ft

South Peak 20320ft

Explorers Peak 8540ft

Denali Viewpoint North

Mt Crosson 12800ft

Mt Hunter 14573ft

Mooses Tooth 10335ft

Chulitna

Mt Foraker 17400ft

kanit Glacier

Tokositna Glacier

Ruth Glacier

George Parks Highway

DENALI STATE PARK

The Alaska Railroad

Kahiltna Glacier

Avalanche Spire 10105ft

Mt Goldie 6315ft

Tokosha Mountains

Denali Viewpoint South

DUTCH HILLS

Mount Kliskon 3943ft

PETERS HILLS

3

Fairview Mountain 3266ft

Petersville Road

Talkeetna

Trapper Creek

More than 6 million acres of wilderness, Denali National Park and Preserve is the heart of Alaska: the biggest mountains, the wildest rivers, and so much wildlife you'll probably end up frying your camera trying to catch it all. Founded in 1917 as Mt. McKinley National Park (despite the fact that the park's then borders went right across the mountain), government caught up with thousands of years of Native tradition and renamed the park Denali in 1980. One road in, the tallest mountain on the continent, and endless possibilities await you.

7

120 mi south of Fairbanks on the George Parks Hwy.; 240 mi north of Anchorage on the George Parks Hwy.

Updated by
Edward
Readicker–
Henderson

Denali National Park and Preserve is Alaska's most-visited attraction for a reason: the most accessible of Alaska's national parks and one of only three connected to the state's highway system, the 6-million-acre wilderness offers views of mountains so big they seem like a wall on the horizon; endless wildlife, from cinnamon-color Toklat grizzlies to herds of caribou, to moose with antlers the size of coffee tables; glaciers with forests growing on them; autumn tundra the color of a kid's breakfast cereal. Denali is a chance for a visitor to have the wildlife and scenic experience that Yellowstone offered 50 years ago, but Denali has ever so much more as well.

The keystone of the park is Mt. McKinley: more commonly called by its Athabascan name, *Denali,* meaning "the High One," or often referred to by Alaskans simply as "the Mountain," the peak measures in at 20,320 feet, the highest point on the continent. Denali is also the tallest mountain in the world—yes, Mt. Everest is higher, but it sits on the Tibetan plateau, like it was standing on a chair to rise above Denali, which starts barely above sea level.

Unfortunately for visitors on a tight schedule, Denali, like big mountains everywhere, makes its own weather systems, and the simple truth is that the mountain really, really likes clouds: the peaks are wreathed in clouds an average of two out of three days in summer. You can increase your odds of glimpsing Denali's peak by venturing into the heart of the park or staying at a wilderness lodge at the western park boundary. Or get really ambitious: more than 1,000 adventurers climb the mountain's slopes each summer. On average, of those who take the most common route, the West Buttress, just over half make it to the peak. The rest turn back, gasping for breath in the thin air.

Although the mountain is the biggest attraction, you don't need to see it—much less climb it—to appreciate the park; in fact, few people who visit Denali National Park and Preserve will come any closer than 35 mi to the mountain's slopes—and most visitors won't even get that close.

Because even if the mountain is shy, a trip along the park's Denali Park Road offers sights you won't forget: an opportunity to see grizzly bears, wolves, caribou, moose, and Dall sheep—the "big five" of Alaskan animals. And don't miss the soaring golden eagles, clucking ptarmigans, and chattering ground squirrels. If you prefer to take in the scenery without glass between you and the wild, bike or hike along the park road. Or see it all from an eagle's point of view: flightseeing is one of the best ways to gain a full appreciation of the park, especially the wild spires of the Great Gorge along the flanks of Mt. McKinley.

No matter how you come to the park—staying on the bus, flying over the peaks in a small plane, or hiking across the tussocks of the tundra on a route that takes you days away from the nearest person, exploring Denali offers rich rewards: wilderness solitude, a sense of discovery, amazing wildlife encounters, and a chance to truly appreciate the scale, the mystery, and the grandeur of this landscape.

PLANNING

WHEN TO GO

Denali's main season is mid-May into early September. About 90% of the people come in these months, and with good reason: warmish weather, long days, and all the facilities open. Shoulder seasons—early May and late September—can be incredibly beautiful in the park, with few people around; plus, you can often drive your own car a fair way down the park road, since the buses don't run. In winter the only way into the park is on ski or snowshoe or by dogsled. You'll have the place almost entirely to yourself—most of the businesses at the park entrance are closed—and if you're comfortable in deep snow and freezing weather, there is no better time to see Denali.

TIMING

You can do a bus tour of the park in a single day. Allow for all day, and try to go at least as far as Eielson Visitor Center. If you can, go out to Wonder Lake. A few buses go a few miles farther to Kantishna, but the views from Wonder Lake are better; there's no reason to go those last miles unless you're staying at one of the inholding lodges.

If you have more than a single day, the best thing to do is camp in the park. The longer you stay deeper in the park, the better chance you'll have of seeing Mt. McKinley, which, on average, is only visible one day out of three. Again, Wonder Lake is the spot of choice.

It's also easy to fill a day around the park entrance, taking rafting trips on the Nenana River or going on some of the short hikes near the visitor center.

No matter how much time you have, plan ahead. Bus and campsite reservations are available for the summer season beginning December 1. ■TIP➜ Reserve tickets for buses ahead of time; call the numbers provided here or log on to ⊕ www.reservedenali.com. Although you can often just walk up and get on something, it may not be the experience you're after. Advance planning makes for the best trips.

GETTING HERE AND AROUND

The park is 120 mi south of Fairbanks, or 240 mi north of Anchorage, on the George Parks Highway, which is the most common access route.

There is a second, seldom-used road to the park: the Denali Highway leads from Paxon, which is accessible from the Richardson Highway (which connects Fairbanks and Valdez) to Cantwell, coming out just south of the park entrance. This 134-mi road is mostly unpaved, with few services. Only people with high-clearance cars should try it. The Denali Highway is closed in winter.

For those who don't want to drive, Denali National Park is a regular stop on the Alaska Railroad's Anchorage–Fairbanks route. The railway sells packages that combine train travel with hotels and trips into the park.

Only one road penetrates Denali's expansive wilderness: the 92-mi Denali Park Road, which winds from the park entrance to Wonder Lake (as far as the regular buses go) and on the inholding of Kantishna, the historic mining district in the heart of the park, where there are a couple of private lodges. The first 15 mi of the road are paved and open to all vehicles, but beyond the checkpoint at Savage River access is limited to tour buses, special permit holders, and the community members of Kantishna. To get around the park, you need to get on one of the buses (➪ see Transportation chart in this chapter) or start hiking.

Campers with permits for the Teklanika campground can drive to and back out from their campsites at Mile 29, but they cannot tour the park road in their vehicles. Mountain bikes are allowed anywhere on the park road, although you should check with officials before pedaling out; you need to know if there has been a wolf kill or a lot of bear sightings by the road that might limit access.

DINING AND LODGING PRICE CATEGORIES				
¢	$	$$	$$$	$$$$
Restaurants	under $10	$10–$15	$15–$20	$20–$25	over $25
Hotels	under $75	$75–$125	$125–$175	$175–$225	over $225

Restaurant prices are per person for a main course at dinner. Hotel prices are for two people in a standard double room in high season.

HEALTH AND SAFETY

Even if you're not hiking, carry durable rain gear made of a breathable material, and dress in layers. Good, sturdy, broken-in hiking boots, a hat, and warm gloves are a must, as are polypropylene long underwear and layers of wool or fleece for hikers. Avoid cotton. Bring insect repellent, binoculars, and a camera. Park water isn't safe to drink, and past the park entrance there's no food except what you bring in yourself—and don't forget to get a bear-proof container for it from the park headquarters.

EXPLORING DENALI

It's important to reserve tickets for buses ahead of time; call the numbers provided here or log on to ⊕ *www.reservedenali.com.*

With a landmass larger than Massachusetts, Denali National Park and Preserve has too much area for even the most dedicated vacationer to explore in one go. When planning your trip, consider whether you want to strike out on your own as a backcountry traveler or to stay at a lodge nearby and enjoy Denali as a day hiker with the help of a tour or shuttle bus. Either option requires some advance planning, for bus tickets or backcountry permits. But either option also offers a magnificent experience.

PARK BASICS

Admission to Denali is $10 per person or $20 per vehicle ($15 for motorcycles). The **Wilderness Access Center** (⊠ *Mi 1, Park Rd.* ☎ *907/683–9274*) near the park's entrance at Mile 237.3, George Parks Highway, is where you can handle reservations for roadside camping and bus trips into the park. A smaller building nearby is the **Backcountry Information Center,** for those visitors who want to travel and stay overnight in the wilderness. The Backcountry Information Center has backcountry permits and hiking information, including current data on animal sightings (remember the whole park is bear territory), river-crossing conditions, weather, and closed areas. The center is closed in winter (mid-September through mid-May). ■ TIP➔ Free permits are required for overnight backpacking trips, but you won't need one for day hiking.

Open from mid-May to mid-September, the **Denali Visitor Center** (⊡ *Mi 1.5, Park Rd. 99755* ☎ *907/683–2294* ⊕ *www.nps.gov/dena*) exhibits beautiful displays about the park's natural and cultural history, and holds regular showings of *Heartbeats of Denali* in the Karstens Theater. In addition, the center offers a wide variety of interpretive programs and a chance to browse the nearby Denali Bookstore, a great source for wildlife guides, birding guides, and picture books; send some to relatives to make them jealous of your trip. Open year-round with limited vehicle access; the season is mid-May through mid-September, with everything up and running.

Next to the Denali Visitor Center, **Murie Science and Learning Center** (⊠ *Mi 1.5, Park Rd.* ☎ *907/683–1269* ⊕ *www.murieslc.org*) is the foundation of the park's science-based education programs, and also serves as the winter visitor center when the Denali Visitor Center is closed.

At Mile 66 on the Park Road is the **Eielson Visitor Center**, the park's pride and joy. LEED-certified as a green building, Eielson offers amazing views of the mountain, the glaciers, and what happens to a landscape when glaciers go away. Inside is the usual interpretive material. The center offers a daily guided walk at 1 pm, an easy 45-minute or so exploration of the landscape.

> ### FINDING YOUR FOOTING IN DENALI
>
> Denali's entrance area and road corridor (from the highway to Savage River) have plenty of adventure and learning. Besides the visitor and Murie centers, there are sled-dog demonstrations, interpretive walks, and the only maintained trails within the park. Keep an eye out for wildlife, especially moose.

TOUR, SHUTTLE, AND CAMPER BUSES

Don't be alarmed by the crowded park entrance; that gets left behind very quickly. After the chaos of private businesses that line the George Parks Highway and the throngs at the visitor center, there's pretty much nothing else in the park but wilderness. From the bus you'll have the opportunity to see Denali's wildlife in natural settings, as the animals are habituated to the road and vehicles, and go about their daily routine with little bother. In fact, the animals really like the road: it's easier for them to walk along it than to work through the tundra and tussocks.

Bus trips take time. The maximum speed limit is 35 mph, and the buses don't hit that very often. Add in rest stops, wildlife sightings, and slowdowns for passing, and it's an 8- to 11-hour day to reach the heart of the park and the best Denali views from Miles 62–85. *All prices listed below are for adults, and include the $10 park admission fee, unless otherwise noted.* ■TIP➜ If you decide to tour the park by bus, you have two choices: a sightseeing bus tour offered by a park concessionaire or a ride on the shuttle bus. The differences between the two are significant.

Tour buses (☎ *800/622–7275, 907/272–7275 in Alaska or outside U.S.* ⊕ *www.reservedenali.com*) offer a guided introduction to the park. Advance reservations are required for the tour buses and are recommended for the park shuttles. Reservations for the following season become available on December 1, so if you have only a small window to see Denali, plan far ahead. If you're not organized enough to think six months or more out, you can usually get on the bus of your choice with less than a week's notice—and you can almost always get on a shuttle bus within a day or two—but try not to count on that. Work as far ahead as you can to avoid disappointment.

Rides through the park include a five-hour Natural History Tour ($74) a six- to eight-hour Tundra Wilderness Tour ($117.50), and an 11- to 12-hour Kantishna Experience ($169). These prices do not include the park entrance fee. Trips are fully narrated by the driver-guides and include a snack or box lunch and hot drinks. Although the Natural

Continued on page 335

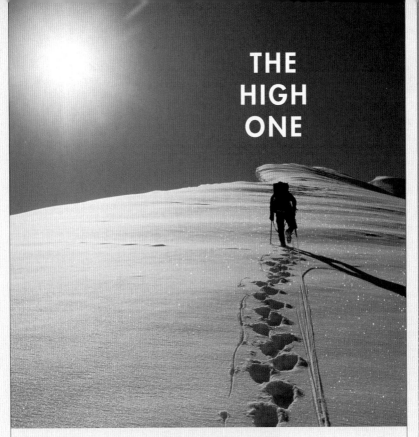

THE HIGH ONE

In the heart of mainland Alaska, within 6-million-acre Denali National Park & Preserve, the continent's most majestic peak rises into the heavens. Officially known as **Mount McKinley,** this 20,320-foot massif of ice, snow, and rock is most commonly referred to by its native name of Denali, or "the High One." Some simply call it "The Mountain." One thing is certain: It's a giant among giants, and the most dominant feature in a land of extremes and superlatives.

Those who have walked McKinley's slopes know it to be a wild, desolate place. As the highest peak in North America, McKinley is a target of mountaineers who aspire to ascend the "seven summits"—the tallest mountains on each continent. A foreboding and mysterious place, it was terra incognita—unclimbed and unknown to most people—as recently as the late 1890s. Among Athabascan tribes, however, the mountain was a revered landmark; many generations regarded it as a holy place and a point of reference.

NAMING TERRA INCOGNITA

Linguists have identified at least eight native Alaskan names for the mountain, including Deenaalee, Doleyka, Traleika, and Dghelay Ka'a. The essence of all the names is "the High One" or "Big Mountain." The first recorded sighting of Mt. McKinley by a foreign explorer was in 1794, when Captain George Vancouver spotted it in the distance. More than a century later, after a summer of gold-seeking, Ivy Leaguer William Dickey reported his experiences in the *New York Sun.* His most significant news was of a massive peak, which he dubbed "Mt. McKinley," after Republican William McKinley of Ohio. Mountaineer Hudson Stuck, who led the first mountaineering team to McKinley's summit, was just one in a long line of Alaskans to protest this name. In Stuck's view, the moniker was an affront to both the mountain and Alaska's native people. For these very reasons, a vast majority of Alaskans call the continent's highest peak by its original name, Denali.

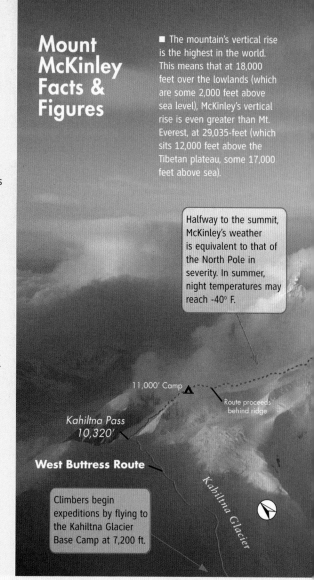

Mount McKinley Facts & Figures

■ The mountain's vertical rise is the highest in the world. This means that at 18,000 feet over the lowlands (which are some 2,000 feet above sea level), McKinley's vertical rise is even greater than Mt. Everest, at 29,035-feet (which sits 12,000 feet above the Tibetan plateau, some 17,000 feet above sea).

Halfway to the summit, McKinley's weather is equivalent to that of the North Pole in severity. In summer, night temperatures may reach -40° F.

11,000' Camp

Route proceeds behind ridge

Kahiltna Pass
10,320'

West Buttress Route

Kahiltna Glacier

Climbers begin expeditions by flying to the Kahiltna Glacier Base Camp at 7,200 ft.

THE WEST BUTTRESS ROUTE

■ The safest route to the summit is the West Buttress. Eighty to 90% of climbers attempting to ascend the peak take this route, with only about half reaching the top.

■ More than 30 people—including some world-class mountaineers—have been killed on the West Buttress.

■ From base camp to high camp, climbers must trek

some 16 miles and 10,000 vertical feet—a trip that takes two to three weeks.

■ The most technically challenging stretch is the ascent to 18,200-foot Denali

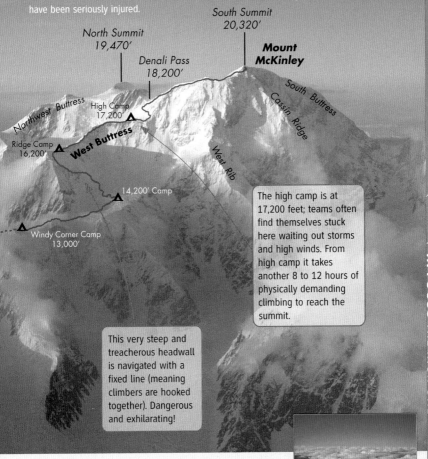

■ In addition to coping with severe weather, climbers face avalanches, open crevasses, hypothermia, frostbite, and high-altitude illnesses. Nearly 100 people have died on the mountain and hundreds more have been seriously injured.

■ McKinley's awesome height and its subarctic location make it one of the coldest mountains on Earth, if not the coldest.

■ Primarily made of granite, McKinley undergoes continual shifting and uplift thanks to plate tectonics (the Pacific plate pushing against the North American Plate); it grows about 1 mm per year.

South Summit
20,320'

Mount
McKinley

North Summit
19,470'

Denali Pass
18,200'

South Buttress

Cassin Ridge

Northwest Buttress

High Camp
17,200'

West Buttress

West Rib

Ridge Camp
16,200'

14,200' Camp

Windy Corner Camp
13,000'

The high camp is at 17,200 feet; teams often find themselves stuck here waiting out storms and high winds. From high camp it takes another 8 to 12 hours of physically demanding climbing to reach the summit.

This very steep and treacherous headwall is navigated with a fixed line (meaning climbers are hooked together). Dangerous and exhilarating!

Pass; climbers must cross a steep snow-covered slope then a shallow bowl called the Football Field.

■ Then, still roped together, climbers ascend an 800-foot snow-and-ice wall to reach the "top of the continent" itself.

Fearless climbers facing the icy challenge at 16,400 feet on the West Buttress Route.

EARLY MILESTONES

Climbing Mt. McKinley in the early 1900s

- In **1903**, two different expeditions made the first attempts to climb Mt. McKinley. The highest point reached? 11,000 feet. Over the next decade, other expeditions would try, and fail, to reach the top.

- Finally, in **1913**, a team led by Hudson Stuck reached the summit. The first person to the top was Walter Harper, a native Alaskan.

- After the Stuck party's success in **1913**, no attempts were made to climb the mountain until **1932**. That year, for the first time, a pilot landed a small plane on one of the mountain's massive glaciers. Another first: a party climbed both the 20,320-foot South Peak and 19,470-foot North Peak. More tragically, the first deaths occurred on the mountain.

- Alaskans Dave Johnston, Art Davidson, and Ray Genet completed the first winter ascent of McKinley in February **1967**. Japanese climber Naomi Uemura completed the first solo ascent of McKinley in **1970**.

A FLIGHT TO REMEMBER

Talkeetna is the home of the popular Denali Flyers. Pilots take you on a variety of air tours into the Alaska Range in small, ski-equipped planes. Flights usually include a passage through the Ruth Glacier's Great Gorge, which is bordered by breathtaking granite spires. Leaving the gorge, you'll enter immense glacial basins of the Don Sheldon Amphitheater (named in honor of the first Denali Flyer). Most trips also include flights past McKinley's southern flanks and show glimpses of its climbing routes. Longer tours circle the mountain, passing among the perennially ice-capped upper slopes, saw-toothed ridges, and vertical rock faces. Flights generally range from 30 minutes to 3 hours and cost $150 to $350 per person.

SHELDON AIR SERVICE is the new incarnation of Hudson Air Service; in 2010 the Talkeetna-based stalwart changed hands and name. The Denali Grand Tour is 90 minutes and costs $280 per person. A glacier landing adds 45 minutes to your flight and costs an additional $75.

☎ 907/733–2321 or 800/478–2321
⊕ www.sheldonairservice. com

K2 AVIATION specializes in flightseeing and glacier landings in the Alaska Range. Prices range from $195 (for a 1-hour flightsee) to $365 (for a 120-minute flightsee with a glacier landing).

☎ 907/733–2291 or 800/764–2291
⊕ www.flyk2.com

TALKEETNA AIR TAXI conducts a breathtaking exploration flight close to massive Mt. McKinley, as well as glacier landings. See Ruth Glacier and the South Face ($195); the base camp ($240); or the Grand Denali Tour ($285). For glacier landings add $75.

☎ 907/733–2218 or 800/533–2219
⊕ www.talkeetnaair.com

BUS	EXPERIENCE	ROUTE	FREQUENCY	COST
Riley Creek Loop	Like taking a bus downtown	Among buildings at park entrance	Continuous	Free
Savage River Shuttle	An easy way to see the wooded areas near the park entrance; good chance of moose	First 14 mi of park road	Hourly in summer	Free
Natural History Tour	Much like the Savage River Shuttle, but with a narrator and a more comfortable bus	First 17 mi of park road	Twice a day	$74 adults; $32 under 14
Tundra Wilderness Tour	From the park entrance to the Toklat River, from a heavily forested area to tundra and the chance of mountain views. Fully narrated.	Cost	Twice a day	$117.50 adults; $53.75 under 14
Kantishna Experience	The grand tour of Denali: from forest to tundra beyond Wonder Lake. Best views of the mountain. Fully narrated.	To the end of the park road	Daily	$169 adults; $79.50 under 14
The Shuttle Bus	The park's own bus: get on and off wherever you want, stay on as long as you feel like paying for. No formal narration, but most of the drivers like to talk and know the park well. This is the most flexible option.	To the end of the park road	Depends on how far out the particular bus goes: every half hour as far as Eielson, every hour to Wonder Lake, four times a day to Kantishna	Round-trip:$24 to Toklat, $30.75 to Eielson, $42.25 to Wonder Lake, $46 to Kantishna
Camper Bus	Transport to all campgrounds inside the park. Like the shuttle bus, no formal narration, but the drivers like to talk and know their stuff.	To Wonder Lake, with stops at all campgrounds along the way	Several times a day	$30.75

History Tour lasts five hours, it goes only 17 mi into the park (2 mi beyond the private-vehicle turn-around), emphasizing Denali's human and natural history. Do not take this tour if you want the best wildlife- or Mt. McKinley–viewing opportunities. You might see a moose or two but not much else. The Tundra Wilderness Tour is a great way to go for a fun, thorough introduction to the park, but if it leaves you wanting more, the Kantishna Experience travels the entire length of the road, features an interpretive guide and ranger, lunch, and some walking. Note, though, that none of the tours allows you to leave the bus without the group or to travel independently through the park.

DENALI'S DINOSAURS

On June 27, 2005, a geologist discovered the track of a theropod, or a three-toed carnivorous dinosaur, in 65- to 70-million-year-old Cretaceous sedimentary rock, just 35 mi west of the park entrance. This is the first hard evidence of dinosaurs in the Interior of Alaska. While the initial discoveries were made by geologists, subsequent finds were uncovered by participants in a teacher workshop with the Murie Science and Learning Center.

The park's own **shuttle buses** (☎ 800/622–7275 or 907/272–7275 ⊕ www.reservedenali.com) don't include a formal interpretive program or food and drink. ■ TIP→ They're less expensive, and you can get off the bus and take a hike or just stop and sightsee almost anywhere you like, then catch another bus along the road. Most of the drivers are well versed in the park's features and will point out plant, animal, and geological sights. The shuttles are less formal than the tour buses, and generally less comfortable (converted school buses). They do stop to watch and photograph wildlife, but with a schedule to keep, time is sometimes limited. Shuttle-bus round-trip fares are $24.50 to the Toklat River at Mile 53; $31.50 to Eielson Visitor Center at Mile 66; and $43.25 to Wonder Lake at Mile 85. They also run a shuttle to Kantishna, for $47.25; the trip takes about 13 hours. Kids 14 and under ride free on the shuttles; 15- to 17-year-olds pay ½ adult fare on all shuttle buses. Obviously, the farther out you're going, the earlier in the day you'll need to be starting; the last bus for Wonder Lake leaves at 10:15 am; the last one for Toklat, at 5 pm. Check with the park for the current schedule.

If you decide to get off the shuttle bus and explore the tundra, just tell the driver ahead of time where you'd like to get out. Some areas are closed to hiking, so check with the rangers at the visitor center before you decide where to go. Some areas are closed permanently, such as Sable Pass, which is heavily traveled by bears; others close as conditions warrant, such as when there's been a wolf kill nearby.

When it's time to catch a ride back, just stand next to the road and wait; it's seldom more than 30 minutes or so between buses. The drivers stop if there is room on board. However, during the mid- and late-summer peak season, an hour or more may pass between stopping buses, as they are more likely to be full. Be prepared to split up if you are in a big group in order to fit on crowded buses during peak times.

Camper buses (☎ *800/622–7275 or 907/272–7275 ⊕ www.reservedenali. com*) serve permitted backpackers and those staying in campgrounds along the road. Seats in the back of the bus are removed for gear storage and there is no formal narration, although the bus drivers aren't likely to let you miss anything important. The $31.50 pass includes transportation anywhere down the road as far as Wonder Lake for the length of the backpacker's stay. Get off and on in the same manner as with the shuttle buses.

GEOLOGY AND TERRAIN

The most prominent geological feature of the park is the Alaska Range, a 600-mi-long crescent of mountains that separates South Central Alaska from the Interior. Mt. Hunter (14,573 feet), Mt. Foraker (17,400 feet), and Mt. McKinley (20,320 feet) are the mammoths of the group. Glaciers flow from the entire Alaska Range.

Another, smaller group of mountains—the Outer Range, north of Denali's park road—is a mix of volcanics and heavily metamorphosed sediments. Though not as breathtaking as the Alaska Range, the Outer Range is popular with hikers and backpackers because its summits and ridges are not as technically difficult to reach.

Several of Denali's most spectacular landforms are deep in the park, but are still visible from the park road. The multicolor volcanic rocks at Cathedral Mountain and Polychrome Pass reflect the vivid hues of the American Southwest. The braided channels of glacially fed streams such as the Teklanika, Toklat, and McKinley rivers serve as highway routes for both animals and hikers. The debris- and tundra-covered ice of the Muldrow Glacier, one of the largest glaciers to flow out of Denali National Park's high mountains, is visible from Eielson Visitor Center, at Mile 66 of the park road. Wonder Lake, a dark and narrow kettle pond that's a remnant from Alaska's ice ages, lies at Mile 85, just a few miles from the former gold-boom camp of Kantishna.

HIKING TERRAIN AND BACKCOUNTRY TRAVEL

You can have one of North America's premier hiking and wilderness experiences in Denali with the proper planning: know your goals; consult park staff before setting out to learn Leave No Trace and bear etiquette; carry proper clothing, food, and water; and don't try to cover too much ground in too short a time.

A big draw for more experienced hikers and backpackers are the foothills and ridges accessible from the park road. As long as you don't go deep into the Alaska Range, it's possible to reach some summits and high ridges without technical climbing expertise. Stamina and physical fitness are required, though. Once up high, hikers find easy walking and sweeping views of braided rivers, tundra benches and foothills, and ice-capped mountains.

LOGISTICS AND DETAILS If you're camping overnight in Denali's wilderness, you need to get a special permit (free of charge) from rangers at the Backcountry Information Center. This must be obtained in person. Advance reservations are not accepted. Only experienced backpackers should try this option. At the center you can look at descriptions of different areas in the park to decide where you want to go. Denali's backcountry is divided into 87 units, and only a limited number of campers are allowed each night in most units. The most desirable units are near the middle of the park, in areas with open tundra and wide-open vistas. These fill up faster than the low-lying areas, many of which are moist and full of mosquitoes in summer. To get time in the best backpacking areas, arrive a couple of days early, stay at one of the facilities near the park entrance (or at the Riley Creek Campground), and check in at the backcountry desk early each morning until your desired unit opens up. Before heading out into the park's wilderness, check the park's Web site in advance (⊕ *www.nps.gov/dena*) and read up on bear and wildlife safety, clean camping, river crossings, and proper food storage (bear-proof canisters are required in many units; you can borrow them, free, from the Backcountry Information Center); when you're at the park, talk with the rangers and tap into their local knowledge. For $31.50 you may ride a camper bus for the duration of your stay (⇨ *see Tour, Shuttle, and Camper Buses, above*).

NATURE TRAILS AND SHORT WALKS

The park offers plenty of options for those who prefer to stay on marked and groomed pathways. The entrance area has more than a half-dozen forest and tundra trails. These range from easy to challenging, so there's something suitable for all ages and hiking abilities. Some, like the **Taiga Loop Trail** and **McKinley Station Loop Trail,** are less than 1½ mi; others, like the **Rock Creek Trail** and **Triple Lakes Trail,** are several miles round-trip, with an altitude gain of hundreds of feet. Along these paths you may see beavers working on their lodges in Horseshoe Lake; red squirrels chattering in trees; red foxes hunting for rodents; sheep grazing on tundra; golden eagles gliding over alpine ridges; and moose feeding on willow.

The **Savage River Trail,** farthest from the park entrance and as far as private vehicles are allowed, offers a 1¾-mi round-trip hike along a raging river and under rocky cliffs. Be on the lookout for caribou, Dall sheep, foxes, and marmots.

The only relatively long, marked trail for hiking in the park, **Mt. Healy Overlook Trail,** is accessible from the entrance area; it gains 1,700 feet in 2.5 mi and takes about four hours round-trip, with outstanding views of the Nenana River below and the Alaska Range, including the upper slopes of Mt. McKinley.

TENT AND RV CAMPING IN DENALI NATIONAL PARK
If you want to camp in the park, either in a tent or an RV, there are five campgrounds, with varying levels of access and facilities. Two of the campgrounds—Riley Creek (near the park entrance, essentially no scenery at all) and Savage River (Mile 13; on a very clear day, you might be able to see the mountain from here, but not much of it)—have spaces that accommodate tents, RVs, and campers. Visitors with private vehicles can also drive to the Teklanika campsite (Mile 29; check for rules about minimum stays, which help keep traffic down), but they must first obtain park-road travel permits; in recent years no tent camping has been allowed at Teklanika, but visitors should check with park

staff for updates. Morino Backpacker Campground (Mile 1.9, about the same as Riley Creek, but tents only), Sanctuary River (Mile 22; the smallest campground in the park, ideal if you want to be alone but can't backpack), Igloo Creek (Mile 43, comparable to Sanctuary River), and Wonder Lake (Mile 85, the cream of the crop in Denali camping—best views of the mountain and great easy hikes) have tent spaces only. The camper buses offer the only access to these sites.

Visitors to the Sanctuary and Igloo Creek campsites should come prepared: both campgrounds lack treated drinking water. All campgrounds have vault toilets and food lockers. Individual sites are beyond sight of the park road, though within easy walking distance.

Fees for individual sites range from $16 to $28 per night. Campsites can be reserved in advance several ways: online, through the Denali National Park Web site (⊕ *www.reservedenali.com*); by faxing a reservation form (form available at ⊕ *www.nps.gov/dena* ☎ *907/ 264–4684*); by calling the reservation service (☎ *800/622–7275 or 907/272–7275*); or by email to reservedenali@aramark.com Reservations can also be made in person at the park. It's best to visit Denali's Web site before making reservations, both to see the reservation form and to learn whether any changes in the reservation system have been made.

Denali National Park Headquarters. ⌂ *Denali National Park Headquarters, Box 9, Denali Park 99755* ☎ *907/683–2294 information, 907/272–7275, 800/622–7275 reservations* ⊕ *www.reservedenali.com* ☉ *All but Riley Creek (no visitor facilities) closed mid-Sept.–late May.*

SPORTS, THE OUTDOORS, AND GUIDED TOURS

FLIGHTSEEING

A flightseeing tour of the park is one of the best ways to get a sense of the Alaska Range's size and scope. Flightseeing is also the best way to get close-up views of Mt. McKinley and its neighboring giants, and maybe even stand on a glacier, all without the hassle of days of hiking and lugging food and gear. Most Denali flightseeing is done out of Talkeetna, a small end-of-the-road town between Anchorage and Denali, and the operators will offer several tours, including a quick fly-by, a summit tour, a glacier landing—something for everybody. We suggest you take the longest, most detailed tour you can afford, so you don't go back home wishing you'd had a chance to see more. *(⇨ See "The High One" in this chapter for more information).*

GUIDED TOURS

In addition to exploring the park on your own, you can take free ranger-guided discovery hikes and learn more about the park's natural and human history. Rangers lead daily hikes throughout summer. Inquire at the visitor center.

Privately operated, narrated bus tours are available through **Denali Park Resorts** (☎ *907/276–7234 or 800/276–7234* ⊕ *www.denaliparkresorts. com*).

KAYAKING AND RAFTING

Several privately owned raft and tour companies operate along the Parks Highway near the entrance to Denali, and they schedule daily rafting, both in the fairly placid areas on the Nenana and through the 10-mi-long Nenana River canyon, which has stretches of Class IV–V rapids—enough to make you think you're on a very wet roller coaster. The Nenana is Alaska's most accessible white water, and if

> ### WORDS OF WISDOM
>
> Keep in mind that, as one park lover put it, "this ain't no zoo." You might hit an off day and have few viewings—enjoy the surroundings anyway. Of course, under no circumstances should you feed the animals (although a mew gull or ground squirrel may very well try to share your lunch).

you don't mind getting a little chilly, a river trip is not just a lot of fun, it's a fantastic way to see a different side of the landscape.

Alaska Raft Adventures books 1½- to 2-hour-long white-water and scenic raft trips along Nenana River through **Denali Park Resorts** (☎ 907/276–7234 or 800/276–7234 ⊕ *www.denaliparkresorts.com*). White-water trips give you two options: do the work and paddle yourself, or sit back and let a guide do the work.

★ **Denali Outdoor Center** (✉ *Mi 0.5 Otto Lake Rd. for main office, Mi 238.9, Parks Hwy.; or Mi 238.9; both offices can help with mountain bikes, river check-in, etc.* ☎ *907/683–1925 or 888/303–1925 ⊕ www. denalioutdoorcenter.com*) has a respected reputation among locals for its scenic rafting trips on the Nenana River and splash-filled trips down the Nenana River canyon's rapids where no river experience is necessary. One of the most challenging trips is a two-hour paddle in inflatable kayaks, called Duckies. They are easy to get out of, stable, and self-bailing. The company also teaches white-water kayaking. All gear is provided, including full dry suits, something you'll appreciate in the splash. Budget travelers can rent canoes or kayaks on Otto Lake for $8 an hour. Camping sites ($8 by the lake), rental cabins ($92) with Wi-Fi in the laundry/shower room, and mountain-bike tours and rentals are also available. Plus, there's a free local shuttle from hotels, lodges, the Alaska Railroad depot, the Denali visitor center, and Otto Lake.

Denali Raft Adventures ☎ *907/683–2234 or 888/683–2234 ⊕ www. denaliraft.com*), Mile 238.6, Parks Highway, launches its rafts several times daily on two- and four-hour scenic and white-water trips on the Nenana River. Gore-Tex dry suits are provided. Guests under the age of 18 must have a release waiver signed by a parent or guardian. Contact the company for copies before the trip. Courtesy pick-up at hotels and the train depot is available witin a seven-mile radius of their location.

MOUNTAIN BIKING

Mountain biking is allowed on the park's dirt road, and no permit is required for day trips. The first 15 mi of the road are paved. Beyond the Savage River checkpoint the road is dirt and gravel, and during the day the road is busy with the park buses, which can leave bikers choking on dust. The road can get really sloppy in the rain, too. The best time to bike is late evening, when the midnight sun is shining and buses have stopped shuttling passengers for the day. When biking on the road, you need to be aware of your surroundings and observe park rules if you decide to leave the road. Off-road riding is forbidden, and some sensitive wildlife areas are closed to hiking. The Sable Pass area is always closed to off-road excursions on foot because of the high bear population, and other sites are posted due to denning activity or recent signs of carcass scavenging. Check current conditions at the visitor center before heading out. **Denali Outdoor Center** (✉ *Mi 0.5, Otto Lake Rd., off Mi 247, Parks Hwy.* ☎ *907/683–1925 or 888/303–1925* ⊕ *www.denalioutdoorcenter.com*) rents mountain bikes by the hour or half or fullday, and conducts guided 2- to 2½-hour tours on trails near the Otto Lake center, complete with bike, helmet, water bottle, and shuttle service.

MOUNTAINEERING

Alaska Mountaineering School (✉ *3rd St., Talkeetna* ☎ *907/733–1016* ⊕ *www.climbalaska.org*) leads backpacking trips in wilderness areas near Talkeetna and elsewhere in the state, including the Brooks Range, and glacier treks that can include overnighting on the ice. It also conducts mountaineering courses that run from 6 to 12 days, expeditions to Mt. McKinley (figure on at least three weeks; prices from $6,000) and other peaks in the Alaska Range, and climbs for all levels of expertise. While you're in Talkeetna, check out its mountain and gear shop on F Street.

Mountain Trip (☎ *866/886–8747 or 970/369–1153* ⊕ *www.mountaintrip. com*) has been guiding climbing expeditions on Mt. McKinley and other Alaska Range peaks since 1973, making it the most senior of the guide companies to operate on the High One. Though the company emphasizes climber safety, most McKinley expeditions reach the summit. Novice to experienced trip levels are offered, and this is the place to call if you're really serious about doing the mountains. Their trips include a Northwest Buttress trip on Denali, which is very rarely attempted, as well as trips around the world. First-class operation, safety first.

WINTER SPORTS

Snowshoers and skiers generally arrive with their own gear and park or camp at the Riley Creek Campground at the park entrance. Dog mushing can also be done with your own team, or you can contact one of the park concessionaires that run day or multiday trips.

Denali West Lodge (☎ *907/674–3112* ✉ *info@denaliwest.com*) is located near the western park boundary, on the shores of Lake Minchumina. Run by Tonya Schlentner, a 1,000-mi Yukon Quest finisher (the Quest is considered a much tougher race than the Iditarod), this fly-in lodge, fueled by alternative energy, offers multiday dog-mushing expeditions from the end of February to March.

Denali Dog Sled Adventures (☎ *907/683–2863* ⊕ *www.earthsonglodge. com* ✉ *info@earthsonglodge.com*) is 4 mi up the Stampede Road. This operation offers one- to four-hour trips, including an "Into the Wild" trip with sites from the book; they also run up to 10-day excursions. Rooms at the lodge—cabins with nice views—start at $155.

DID YOU KNOW?

Breathe deep when climbing Mt. McKinley. The high latitude means there's even less available oxygen at this altitude than at the same height closer to the equator.

A HEALY HIGHLIGHT

One of Healy's greatest attractions is the **Stampede Trail**, perhaps most famous to today's traveler for being where Christopher McCandless of *Into the Wild* fame met his end (and where people who seem to want to replicate it have caused endless problems for Healy's rescue services). On the Stampede Trail you can enter Denali by snowmobile, dogsled, cross-country skis, or mountain bike.

This wide, well-traveled path leads all the way to Kantishna, 90 mi inside the park. To get here, take the George Parks Highway 2 mi north of Healy to Mile 251.1, where Stampede Road intersects the highway. Eight miles west on Stampede Road is a parking lot and the start of the trail.

WHERE TO EAT

IN THE PARK

$ **Canyon Market & Café**. The "only grocery store in Denali" (there's a general store as well, with some groceries) sells fresh fruit, box lunches, and espresso. It has a deli counter, free Wi-Fi, and indoor and outdoor seating. Inside is also Sled Dog Liquor. ⊠ *Mi 238.4, Parks Hwy.* ☎ *907/683–7467* ⊕ *www.canyonmarketcafe.com* ⊗ *Open limited hrs in Apr., daily May through Sept.*

CAFÉ

$ **The Great Alaska Fish & Chip Company**. Stop in for fried halibut, cod, great salad bar, and beer on tap. Or go for the corn fritters, calamari, or -lb., hand-pressed burger with some sweet-potato fries. Recently expanded, it all got so popular. ⊠ *Mi 238, Parks Hwy.* ☎ *907/683–3474* ⊕ *www.alaskafishandchip.com* ⊗ *Mid-May–mid-Sept.*

AMERICAN

$$ **McKinley Creekside Cafe**. This restaurant serves breakfast, lunch, and dinner. Skip right to dessert for one of the famous bakery goods such as "monster" cinnamon rolls and strawberry rhubarb coffee cake, which are made fresh daily on-site. Or for something more substantial, try some of their "homestyle goodness" specialties like the meatloaf, chicken pot pie, ½-lb. hand-formed hamburgers, fish-and-chips, and signature baked halibut. For a hearty, prehike breakfast, try the meat loaf and egg. ■TIP→ At the beginning of each season the café hosts a chili cook-off party for the community with live bluegrass music and $2.50 beers. ⊠ *Mi 238.5, Parks Hwy.* ☎ *907/683–2277* ⊕ *www.mckinleycabins.com* ⊗ *Mid-May–mid-Sept.*

AMERICAN

$$ **Prospector's Historic Pizzeria and Ale House**. Built to have an old-time saloon feel, this restaurant serves handcrafted pizza, salad, soup, salad, pastas, grinder sandwiches, and 49 beers on tap. There's a $10 light lunch special. ⊠ *Mi 238.9, Parks Hwy.* ☎ *907/683–7437* ⊕ *www. prospectorspizza.com* ⊗ *Closed Oct.–Apr.*

AMERICAN

ALONG THE GEORGE PARKS HIGHWAY

¢ **The Denali Doghouse**. It's all about the dog at this casual, dog-decorated and hotdog-theme joint. The local owners put love back into the fast-food burger and hotdog fare. All quarter-pound burger patties are hand pressed, fries and onion rings fresh and hand cut.

AMERICAN

Specialties include bacon, cheese, kraut, slaw, and chili-cheese hot dogs. The Doghouse is a good choice for a quick but filling lunch or dinner in the Glitter Gulch area. ✉ *Mi 238.6, Parks Hwy., Boardwalk* ☎ *907/683–3647* ⊕ *www.denalidoghouse.com* ⊘ *Closed mid-Sept.–mid-May.*

$$ **✕ McKinley/Denali Salmon Bake.**
SEAFOOD Fresh Alaska salmon and seafood bought directly from fishermen top the menu at this rustic spot. It also serves steaks, burgers, and chicken, as well as other breakfast, lunch, and dinner specialties. It's a hot spot with live music and Monday-night poker. Twenty-four-hour shuttle service is provided to area hotels, the park entrance, and Healy, and 12 cabins (8 tent cabins) with shared bath are for rent starting at $79. ✉ *Mi 238.5, Parks Hwy.* ☎ *907/683–2733* ⊕ *www.denaliparksalmonback.com* ⊘ *Closed late Sept.–early May.*

> **THE RANGER KNOWS**

To see things in the park that you'd never notice on your own, take a guided discovery walk with one of Denali's rangers. Rangers will talk about the area's plants, animals, and geological features. Before heading into the wilderness, even on a short hike, check in at the Backcountry Information Center. Rangers will update you on conditions and make route suggestions. Because this is bear country, the Park Service provides backpackers with bear-proof food containers. These containers are mandatory if you're staying overnight in the backcountry.

$$$$ **✕ The Perch.** The bay windows of this fine-dining restaurant, 13 mi south
AMERICAN of the park entrance atop a forested hillside, offer a panoramic view of the surrounding Alaska Range foothills. The Perch serves breakfast and dinner, featuring home-baked breads and desserts along with steak and seafood; don't miss the all-you-can-eat wild Alaska salmon dinner. Next door, the **Panorama Pizza Pub** (☎ *907/683–26233* ⊕ *www.panoramapizzapub.com*) serves hand-tossed brick-oven pizzas, along with soups and sandwiches for dinner and fine Alaskan microbrews. Live music Wednesday—Saturday nights, 5 pm–midnight. Cabin rentals, with creekside and mountain views, are available May–September (starting at $85, with breakfast included), as is complimentary shuttle service for diners and overnighters. Both restaurants have free Wi-Fi. ✉ *Mi 224, Parks Hwy.* ☎ *888/322–2523* ⊕ *www.denaliperchresort.com* ⊘ *Closed mid-Sept.–mid-Apr.*

$$$ **✕ 229 Parks Restaurant and Tavern.** Even if this hot spot didn't serve
AMERICAN amazing food, the graceful timber-frame design, inviting atmosphere,
Fodor's Choice and elaborate elm etchings would be enough to draw in crowds. But
★ just in case, chef and owner Laura Cole directs a scratch kitchen that serves local produce; grass-fed, free-range meat; homemade ice cream and breads; and delectable imports. With their own vegetable gardens and sourcing from small, nearby producers, this is as organic and local as you can get without doing the hunting and gathering yourself. Menus change daily, according to availability. From handmade pappardelle pasta with reindeer sausage and leeks to wild-caught Alaskan weathervane scallops with crisped prosciutto, Laura knows how to make food come to life. Half the restaurant is reservation only—and it books up

7

way in advance; the other half is come and take your chances. ✉ *Mi 229.7, Parks Hwy.* ☎ *907/683–2567* ⊕ *www.229parks.com* ⊗ *No lunch; summer hours, open late May through Oct. 1, closed Sun.; winter hrs, open weekends only, mid-Sept.–mid-May.*

HEALY

$$$$ ✕ **Black Diamond Grill**. For a casual
AMERICAN   and family-oriented atmosphere, dine with a view at this off-the-beaten-path local hangout. The menu features hand-pressed burgers, New York steaks, crab cakes, penne pasta, salads with local and organic greens, and homemade foods, plus fresh baked goodies. To make a day of it, try the ATV tours, horse-drawn carriage rides that end with a barbecue meal at a scenic pavilion, a game of golf (9-hole or mini varieties available), or the fishing at nearby Otto Lake. ✉ *Mi 1, Otto Lake Rd., off Mi 247, Parks Hwy.* ☎ *907/683–4653* ⊕ *www.blackdiamondtourco.com* ⊗ *Closed mid-Sept.–mid-May.*

$$ ✕ **Totem Inn**. Travelers from the George Parks Highway, Healy, and
AMERICAN   Denali come here not so much for the lodging (which is modest at best) as for standard American food at reasonable prices. Steaks, sandwiches, and homemade pizzas are served year-round, while breakfast is served all day. An attached pub and game room allow for swapping stories with the locals, and the free Wi-Fi and Kinect games will help you catch up with the world, or ignore it. Take advantage of the fitness center if you're not getting enough exercise on Denali's trails or a sauna if you are. And, of course, this is the only place around where you can try to ride "The Griz"—a mechanical bull shaped like a grizzly bear. The kitchen is open daily, year-round, 7 am–10 pm. ✉ *Mi 248.7, Parks Hwy.* ☎ *907/683–6500* ⊕ *www.thetoteminn.com.*

RUTH GLACIER

Even the shortest flightseeing trips usually include a passage through the Great Gorge of the **Ruth Glacier**, one of the major glaciers flowing off Denali's south side. Bordered by gray granite walls and gigantic spires, this spectacular chasm is North America's deepest gorge. Leaving the area, flightseers enter the immense, mountain-encircled glacial basins of Ruth Glacier's Don Sheldon Amphitheater. Among the enclosing peaks are some of the range's most rugged and descriptively named peaks, including Moose's Tooth and Rooster Comb. Truly, one of the most beautiful places on the planet.

Mt. McKinley. Alaskans call Mt. McKinley by its original name, Denali, which means "the High One."

WHERE TO STAY

For expanded hotel reviews, visit Fodors.com.

WITHIN THE PARK

If you can afford the price tag, it's worth it to book your stay at a wilderness lodge within Denali, like Camp Denali and North Face Lodge or the Kantishna Roadhouse.

$$$$
Fodor's Choice
★

Camp Denali and North Face Lodge. The legendary, 30-year family-owned-and-operated Camp Denali and North Face Lodge both offer stunning views of Mt. **Pros:** only in-park lodge with a view of Denali; access to canoes; strong emphasis on learning; attention to detail; dedicated staff. Also the only place where you can do guided naturalist walking in the true wilderness heart of Denali. Camp Denali is largely run on renewable energy. **Cons:** alcohol is BYOB; not advisable for families with children under eight; Camp Denali cabins lack private baths (but you can't beat the view from the outhouse). *Box 67, Denali Park, 99755 907/683–2290 www.campdenali.com 18 cabins (Camp Denali) with shared shower, 15 rooms (North Face Lodge) In-room: no a/c, no TV. In-hotel: restaurant No credit cards Closed mid-Sept.–early June All-inclusive.*

$$$$
Kantishna Roadhouse. Run by the Athabascan Doyon Tourism, this establishment at Mile 95 on the Park Road, offers an enriching wilderness getaway. **Pros:** guided hikes with naturalists; all rooms have private baths; home to the only saloon in the Denali backcountry. They'll pick you up at the train station to transport you out. **Cons:** no connection to the outside world besides a phone booth; lacks a direct view of Denali. *Box 130, Denali Park, Kantishna 800/942–7420*

⊕ *www.kantishnaroadhouse.com*
↩ *32 rooms* △ *In-room: no a/c,*
no TV. In-hotel: restaurant, bar
⊙ *Closed mid-Sept.–early June*
†○† *All-inclusive.*

$$ ⚏ **McKinley Creekside Cabins & Creekside Café.** This nice spot sits on 10 acres along Carlo Creek. **Pros:** great location by the water. **Cons:** no TV may lead to withdrawal symptoms in some. ⊠ *Mi 238.5, Parks Hwy.* ☎ *888/533–6254* ⊕ *www.mckinleycabins.com* ↩ *32 cabins* △ *In-room: no a/c, no TV, Wi-Fi. In-hotel: restaurant* ⊙ *Mid-May–mid-Sept.*

$$ ⚏ **Mountain House.** For the true Denali wilderness experience, book an overnight here. **Pros:** the single best view from a bed anywhere near Denali National Park. **Cons:** the final hike up, carrying your food and gear. ⌂ *13756 3rd St. 99676* ☎ *907/733–1016* ⊕ *www.climbalaska.org/mountain-house.html* ↩ *1 house* △ *In-room: no a/c, no TV* ⊙ *Open Mar. 15–July 15, but if you can find someone to fly you in, they'll open it any time.*

ALONG THE GEORGE PARKS HIGHWAY

Hotels, motels, RV parks, campgrounds, and some restaurants are clustered along the highway near the park entrance, which is at Mile 237.3. You can judge distance from the park by mileage markers; numbers increase northward and decrease southward.

$$$$ ⚏ **Denali Princess Wilderness Lodge.** This humongous lodge lies along the Parks Highway in the Glitter Gulch community a mile north of the park entrance. **Pros:** most grandiose lodge in Denali; gym and gift shop on-site. **Cons:** with more than 600 rooms, too big to feel intimate. ⊠ *Mi 238.5, Parks Hwy., 1 mi north of park entrance* ☎ *907/683–2282, 800/426–0500 reservations* ⊕ *www.princesslodges.com* ↩ *656 rooms* △ *In-room: no a/c. In-hotel: 5 restaurants, bars, gym, laundry facilities, business center* ⊙ *Closed mid-Sept.–mid-May.*

$$–$$$ ⚏ **Denali River Cabins and Cedars Lodge.** The cabins, clustered along the glacially fed Nenana River, are next to McKinley Village Lodge, 7 mi south of the park entrance. **Pros:** river views and Finnish sauna; propane grills available. **Cons:** cabins crowded together; property situated near other resorts. **TripAdvisor:** "very polite and helpful," "cabins are quite basic but furnished," "great view of rivers and mountains." ⊠ *Mi 231.1, Parks Hwy.* ☎ *800/230–7275, 907/374–3041 year-round, 907/683–8000 June 1–Sept. 15* ⊕ *www.seedenali.com* ↩ *48 rooms, 54 cabins* △ *In-room: no a/c. In-hotel: restaurant* ⊙ *Closed mid-Sept.–late May* †○† *Breakfast.*

HEALY

$$$ ⊡ **Denali Dome Home.** A 7,200-square-foot modified geodesic dome houses this year-round B&B. **Pros:** thoughtful and knowledgeable owners; unique architecture; attention to detail; DVD and VCR collection. **Cons:** anyone with dog allergies should beware of two Scottish terriers; anyone squeamish about animal hides should be warned that the house is decorated with a few prize trophies. **TripAdvisor:** "rooms were spotlessly clean," "great hosts," "ultra comfortable." ⊠ *137 Healy Spur Rd.* ☎ *907/683–1239 or 800/683–1239* ⊕ *www.denalidomehome.com* ↺ *7 rooms* ⧉ *In-room: no a/c, Wi-Fi. In-hotel: business center* ⎮⊙⎮ *Breakfast.*

$$$ ⊡ **Earthsong Lodge.** Above the tree line at the edge of Denali National Park, Earthsong has views of open tundra backed by peaks of the Alaska Range. **Pros:** each cabin has unique character, as well as hypoallergenic bedding in a totally smoke-free environment; the owners offer a wealth of knowledge. **Cons:** a 17-mi drive from the park entrance; some people might not like the "shoes off" policy in the cabins, but it really does help keep things cleaner. **TripAdvisor:** "clean little cabins with very comfy beds," "fantastic lodging," "excellent hosts." ⊠ *Mi 4, Stampede Rd.* ☎ *907/683–2863* ⊕ *www.earthsonglodge.com* ↺ *12 cabins* ⧉ *In-room: no a/c, no TV, Wi-Fi. In-hotel: restaurant.*

$$ ⊡ **Motel Nord Haven.** Five wooded acres protect this motel from the road, providing a secluded feeling that other accommodations along the George Parks Highway lack. **Pros:** reading and puzzle area with comfy couches; meeting–dining room with large deck and fireplace. **Cons:** lacks character; no stovetops in kitchenettes. **TripAdvisor:** "very accommodating staff," "perfect lodging for exploring Denali," "very clean and quiet." ⊠ *Mi 249.5, Parks Hwy.* ☎ *907/683–4500 or 800/683–4501* ⊕ *www.motelnordhaven.com* ↺ *28 rooms* ⧉ *In-room: no a/c, Wi-Fi. In-hotel: business center.*

CAMPING IN DENALI

⚠ **McKinley RV Park and Campground.** This campground, about 11 mi north of the park entrance on the outskirts of Healy, has a variety of RV sites, from basic two-person tent sites to sites with full electricity, water, and sewer. A dump station, public showers, laundry facilities, deli, ice, gasoline, diesel, and propane are also here. New brew pub just a short walk from the park, with Alaskan beers and food specialties. **Pros:** some sites are wooded and off the highway; numerous services offered. **Cons:** not a scenic location; sites close together. ⊠ *Mi 248.5, Parks Hwy.* ☎ *907/683–2379* ⊕ *www.mckinleyrv.com.*

7

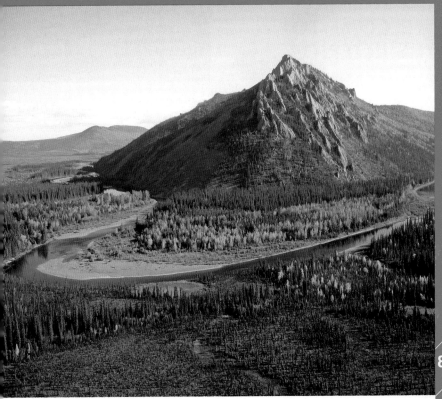

The Interior

WITH FAIRBANKS AND THE YUKON

WORD OF MOUTH

"Riverboat Discovery: I waited 20 years to do it 'cause I thought it was too 'touristy.' But we did it and EVERYONE had a great time. Kids loved it. The Binkley family does a great job."

—zoom907

WELCOME TO THE INTERIOR

TOP REASONS TO GO

★ **Denali National Park and Preserve:** Denali's vertical relief, 18,000 feet, is greater than Mt. Everest's. The park is a stunning place to sample Alaska's natural wonders. (⇨ *See Chapter 7, Denali National Park.*)

★ **Gold-rush heritage:** The frontier spirit of the richest gold rush in Alaska remains alive in Fairbanks. From exploring dredges to panning for gold, chances to participate in the past abound.

★ **Stern-wheeler cruises:** The riverboat *Discovery* is an authentic stern-wheeler that cruises the Chena and Tanana rivers, which served as highways long before there were roads.

★ **The gateway to the Arctic:** Fairbanks is an essential point for connections to northern Alaska—vast land of the midnight sun and the northern lights.

★ **Dog mushing:** The Interior is Alaska's prime mushing spot. Many people live here just so they can spend every free winter moment running sled dogs.

1 Fairbanks. With an area population of about 85,000, Fairbanks is Alaska's northern capital: home to the main campus of the University of Alaska and an important point along the Trans-Alaska oil pipeline. This rough-edged town has a symphony orchestra, Alaska's largest library, and a vibrant local arts scene.

2 North of Fairbanks. The Alaska wilderness is right at Fairbanks's door, with hundreds of miles of subarctic wilderness to explore. Hiking, canoeing, dog mushing, skiing, hot-spring soaking, and fishing are part of daily life. A few roads and isolated villages are the extent of civilization here.

3 Fortymile Country and the Yukon. Fortymile Country yielded some of the first gold discoveries in the state, and today mining operations can be seen along the Taylor Highway. Over the border is Dawson City, the Canadian Klondike Gold Rush boomtown. The Yukon offers countless outdoor activities, such as paddling, climbing, backpacking, and cycling.

GETTING ORIENTED

Interior Alaska is the central part of the state, a vast and broad plateau bordered by the Alaska Range to the south and the Brooks Range to the north. The Yukon River and its many tributaries, including the Tanana River, are dominant features of the landscape. There are few roads, so most of the villages scattered around the Interior are reachable only by aircraft. Fairbanks is the major town in the Interior and serves as the transportation hub for northern and central Alaska, and is the last place to buy supplies before heading into the Bush.

8

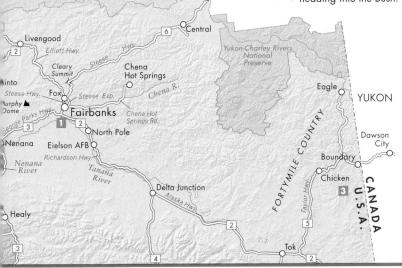

Updated
by Edward
Readicker-
Henderson

Alaska's Interior remains the last frontier, even for the Last Frontier state. The northern lights sparkle above a vast, mostly uninhabited landscape that promises adventure for those who choose to traverse it. Come here for wildlife-rich, pristine land and hardy locals, a rich and quirky history, goldpanning, nonstop daylight in the summer, or ice-sculpting competitions under the northern lights in winter. Outdoor enthusiasts can enjoy hiking, rafting, fishing, skiing, and dogsledding. And don't forget to top off the experience with a soak in the hot springs.

The geology of the Interior played a key role in human history at the turn of the 20th century. The image of early-1900s Alaska, set to the harsh tunes of countless honky-tonk saloons and the clanging of pans, is rooted around the Interior's goldfields. Gold fever struck in Circle and Eagle in the 1890s, spread into Canada's Yukon Territory in the big Klondike Gold Rush of 1898, headed as far west as the beaches of Nome in 1900, then came back to Alaska's Interior when Fairbanks hit pay dirt in 1903. Through it all, the broad, swift Yukon River was the rush's main highway. Flowing almost 2,300 mi from Canada to the Bering Sea, just below the Arctic Circle, it carried prospectors across the north in search of instant fortune.

Although Fairbanks has grown into a small city, many towns and communities in the Interior seem little changed from the gold rush days. While soaking in the water of the Chena Hot Springs Resort you can almost hear the whispers of gold seekers exaggerating their finds and claims, ever alert for the newest strike. When early missionaries set up schools in the Bush, the nomadic Native Alaskan peoples were herded to these regional centers for schooling and "salvation," but that stopped long ago, and today Interior Alaska's Native villages are thriving, with their own schools and a particularly Alaskan blend of modern life and tradition. Fort Yukon, on the Arctic Circle, is the largest Athabascan village in the state.

Alaska's current gold rush—the pipeline carrying (a little less each year) black gold from the oil fields in Prudhoe Bay south to the port of Valdez—snakes its way through the Interior. The Richardson Highway, which started as a gold stampeders' trail, parallels the Trans-Alaska Pipeline on its route south of Fairbanks. And gold still glitters in the Interior: Fairbanks, the site of the largest gold production in Alaska in pre–World War II days, is home to the Fort Knox Gold Mine, which has approximately doubled Alaska's gold production. Throughout the region, as the price of gold continues to climb to record highs on an almost daily basis, hundreds of tiny mines—from one-man operations to full-scale works—are starting up again, proving that what Robert Service wrote more than a hundred years ago still holds true: "There are strange things done in the midnight sun/by the men who moil for gold."

PLANNING

WHEN TO GO

June and July bring near-constant sun (nothing quite like walking out of a restaurant at 11 pm into broad daylight), sometimes punctuated by afternoon cloudbursts. In winter it gets so cold (–30°F or below) that boiling water flung out a window can land as ice particles.

Like most of Alaska, many of the Interior's main attractions are seasonal, May into mid-September. A trip in May avoids the rush, but it can snow in Fairbanks in spring. Late August brings fall colors, ripe berries, active wildlife, and the start of northern lights season. Winter-sports fans should come in March, when the sun's back but there's still plenty of snow.

TRAVEL TIMES FROM FAIRBANKS

DESTINATION	TIME
Anchorage	7 hrs by car; 1 hr by air
Barrow	1½ hrs by air
Dawson City	14 hrs by car
Denali	2 hrs by car
Juneau	3¼ hrs by air
Nome	2 hrs by air
Prudhoe Bay	1½ hrs by air
Seattle	3½ hrs by air
Seward	9½ hrs by car
Skagway	15 hrs by car
Whitehorse	12 hrs by car

GETTING HERE AND AROUND

Interior Alaska is sandwiched between two monumental mountain ranges: the Brooks Range to the north and the Alaska Range to the south. In such a vast wilderness many of the region's residents define their area by a limited network of two-lane highways. You really need a car in the Interior, even if you're based in Fairbanks.

Fairbanks is a sprawling city. Things are too spread out for walking; public transportation is good but service is limited. Hotels run shuttle buses to and from the airport, and you can get around by taxi, but that's going to add up fast. Save yourself some frustration and just rent a car.

AIR TRAVEL

Beyond the highways are many Native villages reached by small airplanes making daily connections out of Fairbanks, which is the regional hub and the thriving commercial center of the Interior.

CAR TRAVEL

The Steese Highway, the Dalton Highway, and the Taylor Highway (which is closed in winter) are well-maintained gravel roads. However, summer rain can make them slick and dangerous. ■TIP→ Rental-car companies have varying policies on whether they allow travel on gravel roads, so check in advance.

The George Parks Highway runs south to Denali National Park and Preserve and on to Anchorage, the state's largest city, 360 mi away on the coast. The Richardson Highway extends to the southeast to Delta Junction before turning south to Valdez, which is 368 mi from Fairbanks.

Two major routes lead north. You can take the Elliott Highway to the Dalton Highway, following the Trans-Alaska Pipeline to its origins at Prudhoe Bay on Alaska's North Slope (you can't drive all the way to the end, but you can get close). Alternatively, explore the Steese Highway to its termination at the Yukon River and the town of Circle.

TOUR TRAVEL

Especially if you're interested in getting out into the wilderness or out to one of the villages, we recommend a tour—it's far less stressful, particularly if you'd otherwise be faced with tasks that you've never undertaken before, things like driving remote unpaved roads without knowing how to change a tire or, worse, wandering the backcountry with limited previous Alaska experience.

Contacts Go North Alaska Adventure Travel Center (☎ 907/479–7271 or 866/236–7271 ⊕ www.gonorthalaska.com). **Northern Alaska Tour Company** (☎ 907/474–8600 or 800/474–1986 ⊕ www.northernalaska.com). **Trans Arctic Circle Treks Ltd.** (☎ 907/479–5451 or 800/336–8735 ⊕ www.arctictreks.com).

CUSTOM SIGHTSEEING **Alaska/Yukon Trails** (☎ 907/479–2277 or 800/770–7275 ⊕ www.alaskashuttle.com).

RIVER TRIPS **Sternwheeler** *Tanana Chief* (⊠ 1020 Hoselton Rd., Fairbanks ☎ 907/452–8687 ⊕ www.sternwheelerak.com). **Riverboat** *Discovery* (⊠ 1975 Discovery Dr., near Fairbanks International Airport, Fairbanks ☎ 907/479–6673 or 866/479–6673 ⊕ www.riverboatdiscovery.com).

SEA AND
LAND TOURS **Denali Park Resorts** (☎ 907/276-7234 or 800/276-7234 ⊕ www. denaliparkresorts.com). **Northern Alaska Tour Company** (☎ 907/474-8600 ⊕ www.northernalaska.com). **Trans Arctic Circle Treks Ltd.** (☎ 907/479-5451 or 800/336-8735 ⊕ www.arctictreks.com).

RESTAURANTS

Even in the most elegant establishments Alaskans sometimes sport sweats or Carhartts. Most restaurants fly in fresh salmon and halibut from the coast. Meat-and-potatoes main courses and the occasional pasta dish fill menus, but most restaurants offer palatable vegetarian choices, too. The food isn't the only thing full of local flavor: walls are usually decked out in some combination of snowshoes, caribou and bear hides, the state flag, and historic photos.

HOTELS

You won't find ultra-luxury hotels, but you can find a range of bed-and-breakfasts, rustic-chic lodges, and national chains, as well as local spots that will please even the most discriminating travelers. For interaction with Alaskans, choose a B&B, as they're usually local-owned; proprietors tend to be eager to provide travel tips or an unforgettable story. The cheapest options are tents or RVs, and there is no shortage of campgrounds here.

DINING AND LODGING PRICE CATEGORIES				
¢	$	$$	$$$	$$$$
Restaurants	under $10	$10–$15	$15–$20	$20–$25	over $25
Hotels	under $75	$75–$125	$125–$175	$175–$225	over $225

Restaurant prices are per person for a main course at dinner. Hotel prices are for two people in a standard double room in high season.

HEALTH AND SAFETY

The Interior really only has two health concerns: hypothermia, and mosquito-induced insanity. To prevent going insane when you're being attacked by a cloud of mosquitoes—and they grow them big in the interior—DEET, and lots of it, is your best bet.

To prevent hypothermia, dress in layers and don't be shy about adding or removing them to maintain a comfortable temperature. For further information on hypothermia, see the Hypothermia box in this chapter.

MONEY MATTERS

ATMs are widely available in all the cities, and most of the towns; if you move out to the villages, though, take cash and don't expect to find much in the way of banking services.

BEST BETS FOR DIFFERENT TRAVELERS

If you're travelling with young ones and want options that involve hands-on, kid-engaging fun:

■ Pioneer Park in Fairbanks

■ Riverboat Discovery in Fairbanks

■ Beringia Centre in Whitehorse

If you want to immerse yourself in the landscape but aren't so keen on roughing it:

■ Soak up Chena Hot Springs (if you're traveling in winter or the shoulder season, you might also see the Northern Lights)

■ Take a Klondike River Float Trip, from Dawson

■ Take an organized trip up the Dalton Highway, the northernmost highway in the country. (Added bonus: great views of the Brooks Range, the tundra, and beyond.)

If you want to experience an Interior few tourists see:

■ Chicken and Eagle in Fortymile Country

■ Dawson in the winter—come when it's a checkpoint for the Yukon Quest, but be ready for temperatures cold enough to make car tires explode

If you want to learn about Alaskan culture beyond the onboard cruise lecture series:

■ Eskimo Olympics in Fairbanks

■ Dawson City Music Festival

FAIRBANKS

At first glance Fairbanks appears to be little more than a sprawling conglomeration of strip malls, chain stores, and other evidence of suburbia (or, as a local writer once put it, "su-brrr-bia"). But look beyond the obvious in the Interior's biggest town and you'll discover why thousands insist that this is the best place to live in Alaska.

The hardy Alaskans who refuse to leave during the cold and dark winters share a strong camaraderie. To live here, you really have to want to live here, which gives the whole city a relaxed, happy vibe. The fight to stave off cabin fever leads to creative festivals, from winter solstice celebrations to an outhouse and snowmachine tug-of-war during Chatanika Days in Chatanika, 28 mi north of town. And isn't there something marvelous about people who, if their car breaks down and it's cold enough to freeze the tires and make them explode, still know what to do?

Many of the old homes and commercial buildings trace their history to the city's early days, especially in the downtown area, with its narrow, winding streets following the contours of the Chena River. Even if each year brings more chain stores, the beautiful hillsides and river valleys remain. And of course there is Fairbanks' fall/winter/spring bonus: being able to see the aurora, or northern lights, an average of 243 nights a year.

These magic lights were a common sight to the Native Alaskans who lived and traveled through Interior Alaska for thousands of years. But people started coming to Fairbanks for the view all because of one guy's bad day: In 1901 E.T. Barnette, a merchant traveling upstream, was forced to leave the boat with all of his trading goods at a wooded spot in the middle of nowhere along the Chena River because the water was too shallow to pass. But while awaiting passage farther east, Barnette's luck took a turn for the wonderful when an Italian prospector discovered gold 12 mi north of Barnette's settlement the next summer. The resulting gold rush created customers for his stockpile of goods and led to the birth of Fairbanks, which for a brief time became the largest and wealthiest settlement in Alaska.

> ### FAIRBANKS GOLD
>
> The gold strike by Felix Pedro in 1902 is commemorated annually in late July with the celebration of Golden Days, marked by a parade and several days of gold rush–inspired activities.

The city's nickname, the Golden Heart, reflects Fairbanks's gold-rush history and its location: it's the gateway to the Far North—the Arctic and the Bering Coast—and to Canada's Yukon Territory.

As you walk the streets of Fairbanks today, it takes a good imagination to envision the rough-and-tumble gold-mining camp that first took shape along the Chena River in the early 1900s. Although a few older neighborhoods have weathered log cabins, the rest is a Western hodgepodge that reflects the urge to build whatever one wants, wherever one wants—a trait that has long been a community standard (and sometimes leads to really interesting roof angles as the house sinks in permafrost).

The city is making some real efforts to preserve what's left of its gold-rush past, most notably in the 44-acre Pioneer Park, where dozens of cabins and many other relics were moved out of the path of progress. Downtown Fairbanks began to deteriorate in the 1970s, before and after the boom associated with the building of the Trans-Alaska Pipeline. But the downward spiral ended long ago and most of downtown has been rebuilt.

For details on all local attractions, historical and otherwise, stop by the downtown Fairbanks Convention and Visitors Bureau in the Morris Thompson Cultural and Visitors Center. We also highly recommend a trip to the campus of the University of Alaska Fairbanks, where the University of Alaska Museum of the North got a makeover in 2006; the new building is full of soothing, swooping lines that evoke glaciers, mountains, and sea life, and one of the best collections of material from around the state that you'll see anywhere.

GETTING HERE AND AROUND

Delta and Northwest Airlines offer seasonal nonstop service from Fairbanks to the Lower 48. Alaska Airlines and ERA Alaska fly the Anchorage–Fairbanks route. There are hotel shuttles, rental cars, and taxis available at the Fairbanks airport.

As for ground transportation, the Alaska Park Connection provides regularly scheduled shuttle service between Seward, Anchorage, and Denali National Park from mid-May to mid-September. Denali Overland Transportation serves Anchorage, Talkeetna, and Denali National

8

Park with charter bus and van service. Alaska/Yukon Trails runs between Fairbanks, Denali, Anchorage, Talkeetna, Whitehorse, and Dawson City.

Between late May and early September, Alaska Railroad's daily passenger service runs between Seward, Anchorage, and Fairbanks, with stops at Talkeetna and Denali National Park and Preserve. Standard trains have dining, lounge, and dome cars, plus the only outdoor viewing platform of its kind. Holland America and Princess offer luxurious travel packages as well.

Make the **Morris Thompson Cultural and Visitors Center** your first stop in Fairbanks, where you can plan your whole trip, from a quick visit to a local attraction or a backcountry adventure. This center is also home to the **Fairbanks Convention and Visitors Bureau** and the **Alaska Public Lands Information Center.** While you're there, browse the free exhibits on Interior Alaska's environment and people, as well as the recently opened fantastic displays of both gold rush and Native history. In the summer, the center hosts Alaska Native art, music, storytelling, and dance. Don't forget to enjoy the free films, use the Wi-Fi and Internet access, or peruse the literature at the Alaska Geographic Bookstore.

ESSENTIALS

Airline Contacts Alaska Airlines (☎ 800/252–7522 ⊕ www.alaskaair.com). **ERA Alaska** (☎ 907/266–8394 or 800/866–8394 ⊕ www.flyera.com).

City Bus Fairbanks MACS Bus System (☎ 907/459–1011 ⊕ www.co.fairbanks. ak.us/transportation ✉ $1.50 a ride or $3 a day).

Commuter Buses Alaska/Yukon Trails (☎ 800/770–7275 ⊕ www. alaskashuttle.com).

Internet College Coffeehouse (✉ 3677 College Rd., Unit 4 ☎ 907/374–0468 ⊕ www.collegecoffeehousefairbanks.com). **Fairbanks Convention and Visitors Bureau** (✉ 101 Dunkel St., Suite 111 ☎ 907/456–5774 or 800/327–5774 ⊕ www.explorefairbanks.com). **Noel Wien Library** (✉ 1215 Cowles St. ☎ 907/459–1020 ⊕ www.library.fnsb.lib.ak.us).

Medical Assistance Fairbanks Memorial Hospital (✉ 1650 Cowles St. ☎ 907/452–8181 ⊕ www.bannerhealth.com). **Fairbanks Urgent Care Center** (✉ 1867 Airport Way, Suite 103B ☎ 907/452–2178). **Tanana Valley Clinic** (✉ 1001 Noble St. ☎ 907/459–3500 ⊕ www.tvcclinic.com).

Post Offices and Shipping U.S. Postal Service (✉ 315 Barnette St. ☎ 907/452–3223 ✉ 4025 Geist Rd. ☎ 907/479–6021). **FedEx** (✉ 418 3rd St., 5A ☎ 907/456–7348 or 800/463–3339 ⊕ www.fedex.com).

Rail Alaska Railroad (☎ 907/458–6025 or 800/544–0552 ⊕ www.akrr.com). **Holland America Tours/Gray Line of Alaska** (☎ 800/544–2206 ⊕ www. graylinealaska.com). **Princess Tours** (☎ 800/426–0500 ⊕ www.princesslodges. com).

Rental Cars Budget Rent-A-Car (☎ 907/474–0855, 800/474–0855 in Alaska ⊕ www.budget.com). **Dollar Rent A Car** (☎ 907/451–4360 or 800/800–4000 ⊕ www.dollar.com). **Hertz** (☎ 907/452–4444 or 800/654–3131 ⊕ www.hertz. com).

Visitor and Tour Information **Alaska Department of Fish and Game** (✉ *1300 College Rd.* ☎ *907/459–7207* ⊕ *www.adfg.state.ak.us*). **Alaska Public Lands Information Center** (✉ *101 Dunkel St., Downtown* ☎ *907/459–3730* ⊕ *www.alaskacenters.gov*). **Fairbanks Convention and Visitors Bureau** (✉ *101 Dunkel St., Downtown* ☎ *907/456–5774, 800/327–5774 recording* ⊕ *www.explorefairbanks. com*). **Morris Thompson Cultural and Visitors Center** (✉ *101 Dunkel St.* ☎ *907/459–3700* ⊕ *www. morristhompsoncenter.org* 🎫 *Free* ⊙ *Summer, daily 8–9; winter, daily 8–5*).

EXPLORING
TOP ATTRACTIONS

★ **Fairbanks Ice Museum.** You'd think that the last thing Fairbanksans would want to hang on to through the too-brief summer is a reminder of the brutal winters. However, the folks at the Ice Museum do just that. Sculptors work behind glass in large freezers where they create intricate sculptures from ice. About 25 sculptures are usually on display. Billed as "the coolest show in town," the Ice Showcase, a large glass-wall display, is kept at 20°F. *Freeze Frame* is a large-screen film demonstrating the techniques of ice sculpture. The museum is in the historic Lacey Street Theater, on the corner of 2nd Avenue and Lacey Street. ✉ *500 2nd Ave., Downtown* ☎ *907/451–8222* ⊕ *www.icemuseum.com* 🎫 *$12* ⊙ *May–Sept., daily 10–9*.

"Fountainhead" Antique Automobile Museum. Located on the property of the Wedgewood Resort, this museum features automobiles from 1898 to 1938—all of which run, the curators taking them out on the roads regularly. The museum also has the first car ever made in Alaska, built in Skagway out of sheet metal and old boat parts, all to impress a girl (didn't work). Alongside the cars are displays of vintage clothing and historical photographs. Widely considered one of the best auto museums in the world, and incredibly interesting, even if you're not interested in old cars. ✉ *212 Wedgewood Dr., Fairbanks* ☎ *907/450–2100* ⊕ *fountainheadmuseum.com* 🎫 *$8; $4 for guests of Wedgewood Resort, Sophie Station Suites, or Bridgewater Hotel* ⊙ *Mid-May–mid-Sept., Sun.–Thurs. 11–10, Fri. and Sat. 11–6; mid-Sept.– mid-May, Sun. noon–6.*

★ **Georgeson Botanical Garden of the Agricultural and Forestry Experiment Station Farm.** When most people think of Alaska vegetation, they conjure up images of flat, treeless tundra, so the amazing variety of native and cultivated flowers on exhibit here is often unexpected. This is where researchers at the University of Alaska Fairbanks study Interior Alaska's unique, short, but intense midnight-sun growing season. The results are

---

SIGHTSEEING TOURS

Gray Line of Alaska (☎ *800/544–2206* ⊕ *www. graylinealaska.com*) runs scenic and informative trips through the Fairbanks area, including a four-hour Discover the Gold sightseeing tour of the *Gold Dredge Number 8,* a stern-wheeler cruise, and a lunch of miner's stew for $114.

Princess Tours (☎ *800/426–0500* ⊕ *www.princesslodges.com*) has a wide variety of tours, including by riverboat, by Hummer, by small planes over the Arctic Circle, and more.

8

spectacular. The grounds feature about 1,000 perennials. The nonstop daylight brings out rich and vibrant colors. The best times to visit are from mid-June to late August. ⊠ *117 W. Tanana Dr.* ✛ *West end of campus, 4 mi west of downtown* ☎ *907/474–6921* ⊒ *$2* ⊘ *May–Sept., daily 8–8; tours Fri. at 2.*

☺ **Large Animal Research Station.** Out on the fringes of the University of
★ Alaska campus is a 134-acre home to about 50 musk ox, 45 caribou, and 40 domestic reindeer (those last two are actually the same animal from most standpoints; they can interbreed, and the main difference comes down to the fact that reindeer, having been domesticated, are lazier and fatter than caribou). Resident and visiting scientists study these large ungulates to better understand their physiologies and how they adapt to Arctic conditions. The station also serves as a valuable outreach program. Most people have little chance to see these animals in their natural habitats, especially the musk ox. Once nearly eradicated from Alaska, these shaggy, prehistoric-looking beasts are marvels of adaptive physiques and behaviors. Their qiviut, the delicate musk ox undercoat of hair that is so soft it makes cashmere feel like steel wool, is combed out (without harming the animals) and made into yarn for scarves, hats, and gloves. The station has this unprocessed wool and yarn for sale to help fund the care of the animals. On tours you visit the pens for a close-up look at the animals and their young, while learning about the biology and ecology of the animals from a naturalist. The tours are a very good deal, and the best way to learn about the animals, but you can also just come by any time of day, and usually see musk ox from the parking lot; they sometimes come quite close to the fence. ⊠ *Yankovich Rd. off Ballaine Rd., behind University of Alaska Fairbanks* ☎ *907/474–7207 tour information* ⊕ *lars.iab.uaf.edu* ⊒ *Tours $10* ⊘ *Free general viewing year-round. Memorial Day–Labor Day 45-min tours daily beginning at 10 am.*

☺ **Pioneer Park.** The 44-acre park is along the Chena River near down-
★ town Fairbanks, and has several museums, an art gallery, theater, civic center, Native village, large children's playground, miniature-golf course, antique merry-go-round, and restaurants. The park also has a re-created gold-rush town with historic buildings saved from urban renewal, log-cabin gift shops, and **Mining Valley,** an outdoor museum of mining artifacts surrounding an indoor-outdoor Alaska Salmon Bake restaurant. The 227-foot stern-wheeler *Nenana* is the second-largest wooden vessel in existence and a national historic landmark. A diorama inside the stern-wheeler details the course the riverboat took on the Yukon and Tanana rivers around the turn of the 20th century. The **Crooked Creek and Whiskey Island Railroad,** a narrow-gauge train, circles the park. The newest addition to the park is a museum housing the first locomotive in Fairbanks, which has been restored to its 1905 condition and is run on special occasions. This is one of the best places in Fairbanks to bring kids and let them run off some energy. ■ TIP➔ No-frills RV camping is available for $12 a night in the west end of the large parking lot on Airport Way. ⊠ *2300 Airport Way (Airport Way and Peger Rd.)* ☎ *907/459–1087* ⊕ *www.fnsb.us/pioneerpark*

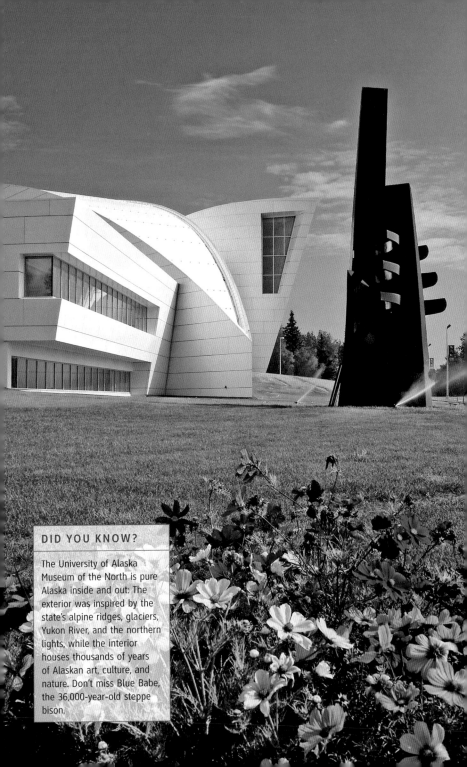

DID YOU KNOW?

The University of Alaska Museum of the North is pure Alaska inside and out: The exterior was inspired by the state's alpine ridges, glaciers, Yukon River, and the northern lights, while the interior houses thousands of years of Alaskan art, culture, and nature. Don't miss Blue Babe, the 36,000-year-old steppe bison.

✉ *Free* ◷ *Park 24 hrs; museum and shops Memorial Day–Labor Day, daily noon–8.*

Fodor's Choice ★ **University of Alaska Museum of the North.** This museum has some of the most distinctive architecture in the state, with sweeping curves and graceful lines that evoke glaciers, mountains, and a fluke of a diving whale. Inside, two-story viewing windows look out on the Alaska Range and the Tanana Valley. Otto, the 8-foot, 9-inch brown bear, greets visitors to the entrance of the Gallery of Alaska, also featuring Blue Babe, a mummified steppe bison that lived 36,000 years ago

> **GARDENS FOR GIANTS**
>
> Interior Alaska gets an extra-large helping of sunlight between May and August. The growing season is short in days, but every day counts because the sun is rarely out of sight. The long daylight hours create intense, vivid colors in flowers, while allowing vegetables to grow to gargantuan dimensions. Cabbages that top 50 pounds and zucchini with telephone-pole-size diameters are common.

during the Pleistocene epoch. The museum has several "please touch" items, including the molars of a mammoth and a mastodon, a gray whale skull, and a 5,495-pound copper nugget. Also in the gallery is a fantastic collection of Native clothes, tools, boats, and more from around the state, offering a chance to see how different groups came to terms with climatic extremes; other dioramas show the state's animals and how they interact. And don't miss the treasured Rose Berry Alaska Art Gallery, representing 2,000 years of Alaska's art, from ancient to modern, or the year-round special exhibits. In the Place Where You Go to Listen, ever-changing light and sound, composed by the real-time movements of the sun, moon, aurora, and seismic activity, create a mesmerizing effect. This is one of the best museums in Alaska, and a can't-miss stop. The gift shop also has one of the better selections of Alaskana in town. ✉ *University of Alaska Fairbanks, 907 Yukon Dr.* ☎ *907/474–7505* ⊕ *www.uaf.edu/museum* ✉ *$10 general admission and additional charges for 30-min summer auditorium shows* ◷ *Mid-May–mid-Sept., daily 9–9; Mon.–Sat. 9–5 rest of year.*

WORTH NOTING

Alaska Range Overlook. Much of the north side of the Alaska Range is visible from this overlook, a favorite spot for time-lapse photography of the midwinter sun just peeking over the southern horizon on a low arc. The three major peaks, called the Three Sisters, are nearly always distinguishable on a clear day. From your left are **Mt. Hayes**, 13,832 feet; **Mt. Hess**, 11,940 feet; and **Mt. Deborah**, 12,339 feet. Much farther to the right, toward the southwest, hulks **Mt. McKinley**, the highest peak in North America. On some seemingly clear days it's not visible at all. At other times the base is easy to see but the peak is lost in cloud cover. ■TIP→ Look for the parking area just east of University of Alaska Museum. ✉ *West Ridge, University of Alaska Fairbanks campus, Yukon Dr.*

♺ **Creamer's Field Migratory Waterfowl Refuge.** Thousands of migrating ducks, geese, and sandhill cranes stop here in spring as they head north to nesting grounds, and in late summer as they head south before the cold hits. It's amazing to watch them gather in huge flocks, with constant take-offs and landings, yet no one ever running into anyone else. This is also a great place to view songbirds and moose. Five miles of nature trails lead through fields, forest, and wetlands, and are open year-round. Don't miss the daily one- to two-hour naturalist walks. Now on the National Register of Historic Places, Creamer's Dairy was the northernmost dairy in North America from 1910 to 1966. The farmhouse is an interpretive center and gift shop open daily 9:30 am–5 pm mid-May to mid-September and Saturday noon–4 pm the rest of the year. Call for listings of year-round events. ⊠ *1300 College Rd.* ☎ *907/459–7307 or 907/452–5162* ⊕ *www.creamersfield.org* ☺ *Walks June–Aug., Mon., Tues., Thurs., and Fri. at 10 am; Wed. at 10 am and 7 pm. Additional walks may be scheduled on request.*

Golden Heart Plaza. This riverside park is the hub of downtown celebrations, including free evening concerts in the park. The plaza is dominated by the towering statue of the Unknown First Family, encircled by plaques containing the names of 4,500 local families who contributed to the building of the plaza.

OUTDOOR ACTIVITIES AND GUIDED TOURS

ADVENTURE TOURS

Northern Alaska Tour Company (☎ *907/474–8600 or 800/474–1986* ⊕ *www.northernalaska.com*) leads year-round half- and full-day excursions to the Arctic Circle and the Yukon River and two- and three-day fly-drive tours to Prudhoe Bay, Barrow, and the Brooks Range. It also has winter aurora-watching trips.

BICYCLING

Bicyclists in Fairbanks use the paved paths from the University of Alaska campus around Farmers Loop to the Steese Highway. Another path follows Geist and Chena Pump roads into downtown Fairbanks. Be warned that many of the trails are in rough shape and suffer from lack of maintenance. A shorter, less strenuous route is the bike path between downtown and Pioneer Park along the south side of the Chena River. Maps showing all the bike paths are available at the Fairbanks Convention and Visitors Bureau. Mountain bikers can test their skills in summer on the ski trails of the University of Alaska Fairbanks and the Birch Hill Recreation Area or on many of the trails and dirt roads around Fairbanks. Stop by the **Alaska Public Lands Information Center** (⊠ *101 Dunkel St., #110* ☎ *907/459–3730* ⊕ *www.alaskacenters.gov*) for mountain-biking information.

BOATING

For relaxing boating in or near Fairbanks, use Chena River access points at Nordale Road east of the city, at the Cushman and Wendell Street bridges near downtown, in Pioneer Park above the Peger River Bridge, at the state campground, and at the University Avenue Bridge.

The Tanana River, with a current that is fast and often shallow, is ideally suited for riverboats. On this river and others in the Yukon River drainage, Alaskans use long, wide, flat-bottom boats powered by one or two large outboard engines. The boats include a lift to raise the engine

Just Outside Fairbanks: Liquid Gold

Trans-Alaska Pipeline. Just north of Fairbanks you can see and touch the famous Trans-Alaska Pipeline. This 48-inch-diameter pipe travels 800 mi from the oil fields on the North Slope of the Brooks Range over three mountain ranges and over more than 500 rivers and streams to the terminal in Valdez. There the crude oil is pumped onto tanker ships and transported to oil refineries in the Lower 48 states. Since the pipeline began operations in 1977, more than 15 billion barrels of North Slope crude have been pumped. Currently the pipe is carrying about 600,000 barrels per day (a number that's decreasing a bit, year by year). The parking lot is right off the Steese Highway and has a sign loaded with information. There's an information kiosk and souvenir stand with Trans-Alaska Pipeline System (TAPS) memorabilia at the Fox Pipeline Viewing Station. ⊠ *Mi 8.4, Steese Hwy.* ⊠ *Free* ⊘ *Information and souvenir stand open Memorial Day–Labor Day.*

a few inches, allowing passage through the shallows, and some of the engines come equipped with a jet unit instead of a propeller to allow more bottom clearance. Arrangements for riverboat charters can be made in almost any river community. Ask at the Fairbanks Convention and Visitors Bureau.

CRUISING AND CANOEING TOURS

Fodor's Choice ★ **Alaska Outdoor Rentals and Guides** (⊠ *Pioneer Park Boat Dock, along Chena River next to Peger Rd.* ☎ *907/457–2453* ⊕ *www.2paddle1.com*) rents gear and arranges pick-ups and drop-offs for the Class I waters of the lower Chena River (the only real challenge for canoeists on the lower river is watching out for powerboats), as well as other local rivers. **Sternwheeler Tanana Chief** (⊠ *1020 Hoselton Rd.* ☎ *907/452–8687* ⊕ *www.sternwheelerak.com*) provides nightly dinner cruises on the Chena River aboard the stern-wheeler *Tanana Chief,* a replica of the riverboats that once plied Interior rivers. The dinner cruise costs $49.95 and boards at 6:30 pm.

Fodor's Choice ★ The city's riverboat history and the Interior's cultural heritage are relived each summer aboard the **Riverboat Discovery** (⊠ *1975 Discovery Dr.* ☎ *907/479–6673 or 866/479–6673* ⊕ *www.riverboatdiscovery. com*), a 3½-hour narrated trip by stern-wheeler along the Chena and Tanana rivers to a rustic Native village on the Tanana River. The cruise provides a glimpse of the lifestyle of the dog mushers, subsistence fishermen, traders, and Native Alaskans who populate the Yukon River drainage. Sights along the way include operating fish wheels, a bush airfield, floatplanes, a smokehouse and cache, log cabins, and dog kennels once tended by the late Susan Butcher, the first person to win the Iditarod four times. The Binkley family, with four generations of river pilots, has run the great rivers of the north for more than 100 years. Cruises are $54.95 and run twice daily (at 8:45 and 2) mid-May to mid-September.

DOG MUSHING

Throughout Alaska, sprint races, freight hauling, and long-distance endurance runs are held in late February and March, during the season when longer days afford enjoyment of the remaining winter snow. Men and women often compete in the same classes in the major races. For children, various racing classes are based on age, starting with the one-dog category for the youngest. The Interior sees a constant string of sled-dog races from November to March, which culminates in the **North American Open Sled-Dog Championship,** attracting international competition to Fairbanks.

In Fairbanks many of the sprint races are organized by the **Alaska Dog Mushers Association** (☎ 907/457–6874 ⊕ *www.sleddog.org*), one of the oldest organizations of its kind in Alaska, and held at its Jeff Studdert Sled Dog Racegrounds at Mile 4, Farmers Loop. The **Yukon Quest International Sled-Dog Race** (☎ 907/452–7954 ⊕ *www.yukonquest.com*) is an endurance race held in February that covers more than 1,000 mi between Fairbanks and Whitehorse, Yukon Territory (the starting point alternates between the two each year), via Dawson and the Yukon River. Considered much tougher and, among mushers, more prestigious than the more famous Iditarod, the Quest goes through more remote lands, with fewer checkpoints. You can get more details from the visitor center in either city or by checking in with the Fairbanks Yukon Quest office, located in the log cabin at 550 1st Avenue.

★ If you want to experience dog mushing for yourself, **Sun Dog Express Dog Sled Tours** (☎ 907/479–6983 ⊕ *www.mosquitonet.com/~sleddog*), with more than 20 years of experience, offers summer and winter tours (weather permitting), demonstrations, and instruction, in addition to a three-day mushing camp.

Offering a mix of trips, **Paws for Adventure Sled Dog Tours** (☎ 907/378–3630 ⊕ *www.pawsforadventure.com* ۞ *Oct.–Apr., weather permitting*) is a good choice. The most adventurous can embark on multiday trips, but other options include a mushing school or a short sled ride.

FISHING

Although a few fish can be caught right in town from the Chena River, the best thing for an avid fishermen to do is hop on a plane or riverboat to get to the best areas for angling. Fishing trips include air charters to Lake Minchumina (an hour's flight from Fairbanks), known for good pike fishing and a rare view of the north sides of Mt. McKinley and Mt. Foraker. Another charter trip by riverboat or floatplane will take you pike fishing in the Minto Flats, west of Fairbanks off the Tanana River, where the mouth of the Chatanika River spreads through miles of marsh and sloughs.

Salmon run up the Tanana River most of the summer, but they're not usually caught on hook-and-line gear. Residents take them from the river with gill nets and fish wheels, using special commercial and subsistence permits. Check the "Outdoors" section in the Friday *Fairbanks Daily News–Miner* for weekly updates on fishing in the Interior. ■ TIP➜ You can purchase fishing licenses (good for one day or longer;

8

MONUMENTAL FORCES

Over the last 100 million years a collage of micro-tectonic plates of igneous and sedimentary rocks collided with and attached itself to the North American continent. The original rocks of these microplates are up to 800 million years old. During these collisions active volcanoes peppered the plates with patches of hard, granitic rock. This tough rock underlies much of the Alaska Range, helping the peaks withstand millions of years of erosion by wind, weather, rivers, and glaciers.

Pressure along the 1,300-mi-long Denali Fault causes uplift throughout the Alaska Range, which continues to rise as fast, in geologic terms, as 1 millimeter per year. Mt. McKinley, at 20,320 feet, the highest peak in North America, was pushed to its towering height by movement along this fault. Today large glaciers pour from the valleys, remnants of the last Ice Age's extensive glaciation, which ended 6,000–7,000 years ago.

Because of the way the ice carved the landscape out as it disappeared, the region is full of thousands upon thousands of lakes and rivers, as well as broad alluvial fans of glacial outwash.

The central part of the Interior was never glaciated; it was, in fact, part of Beringia, a vast, ice-free zone that stretched from the Mackenzie River in the Yukon to as far as the Lena River in Russia, the continents connected by the Bering Land Bridge—which was really more of a subcontinent than a bridge, since it covered as much as 600 mi north to south. Beringia was home to steppe bison (like Blue Babe at the UAF Museum), mammoths, camels, a couple of different kinds of saber-toothed cats, and American lions, as well as horses not much bigger than collies. Beringia disappeared as the ice around it melted, climate change making an entire world disappear.

The Brooks Range was formed by compression generated from a spreading ridge in the Arctic Ocean. The forces stacked and folded Paleozoic and early Mesozoic rock against the northernmost part of the North American continent. Because it is drier and doesn't receive enough moisture to feed glaciers, the Brooks Range to the north was never extensively glaciated.

$20 and up for nonresidents) at many sporting-goods stores and online at ⊕ www.admin.adfg.state.ak.us/license.

Arctic Grayling Guide Service (☎ 907/479–0479 or 907/322–8004 ⊕ *www.wildernessfishing.com*) offers guided and unguided fishing trips via jet boat to a remote fishing spot 60 mi south of Fairbanks to fish for grayling and salmon (May-October). Cabins are available.

GOLF

Chena Bend (☎ 907/353–6223), a well-maintained army course open to civilians, is an 18-hole spread on nearby Ft. Wainwright. The 9-hole course at the **Fairbanks Golf Course** (☎ 907/479–6555) straddles Farmers Loop just north of the university. Summertime midnight golf with a 3 am tee time is considered normal at this course. The 18-hole course at the **North Star Golf Club** (☎ 907/457–4653 ⊕ *www.northstargolf.com*)

PANNING FOR GOLD

The gold information center for Interior Alaska, **Alaskan Prospectors** (✉ *504 College Rd.* ☎ *907/452–7398*) is the oldest mining and prospecting supply store in the state, also featured on the Travel Channel. Stop here for gold pans and books or videos, or to visit the rocks and minerals museum. Employees have valuable advice for the neophyte gold bug.

El Dorado Gold Mine (✉ *Mi 1.3, Elliott Hwy.* ☎ *907/479–6673 or 866/479–6673* ⊕ *www.eldoradogoldmine.com*) conducts two-hour tours ($34.95) of a seasonal mining operation with a ride on a narrow-gauge railroad. Experienced miners Dexter Clark and his wife "Yukon Yonda" demonstrate modern and historical mining techniques and help you pan for gold.

is on the Old Steese Highway, 0.7 mi past Chena Hot Springs Road. It is the northernmost course in the United States, and perhaps the only one where you are encouraged to mark your scorecard with a tally of the wildlife you see. For reservations during the May–September open season, email northstargolf@alaska.net.

HIKING

Creamer's Field Migratory Waterfowl Refuge (⇨ *see Exploring Fairbanks*) has three nature trails within its 1,800 acres on the edge of Fairbanks. The longest trail is 2 mi, and one is wheelchair accessible.

SKIING

CROSS-COUNTRY The Interior has some of the best weather and terrain in the nation for cross-country skiing, especially in late fall and early spring. Among the developed trails in the Fairbanks area, the ones at the **Birch Hill Recreation Area,** on the city's north side, and at the **University of Alaska Fairbanks** are lighted to extend their use into winter nights. Cross-country ski racing is a staple at several courses on winter weekends. The season stretches from October to late March or early April. Other developed trails can be found at **Chena Hot Springs Resort, White Mountains National Recreation Area,** the **Chena Lakes Recreation Area,** and the **Two Rivers Recreation Area.** For more information on skiing, check with the **Alaska Public Lands Information Center** (☎ *907/459–3730*).

DOWNHILL **Birch Hill** (☎ *907/353–7053*), in Ft. Wainwright, has a chairlift and beginner and intermediate runs; it's open November through March, Friday through Sunday. **Mt. Aurora Skiland** (☎ *907/456–7669, 907/389–2314 for office* ⊕ *www.skiland.org*), on the Steese Highway about 20 mi from Fairbanks at Cleary Summit, has a chairlift, rentals, more than 20 runs ranked intermediate to expert, and a 1,100-foot vertical drop. There's lodging in an old gold-camp bunkhouse and aurora viewing. It's open weekends from December to mid-April, if there's enough snow. **Moose Mountain** (☎ *907/479–4732, 907/459–8132 for ski report* ⊕ *www.shredthemoose.com*), off Murphy Dome Road, has 42 runs from two summits for all skiing levels, all accessed by a bus lift system; it's open November through March on weekends, plus school and government holidays.

8

WHERE TO EAT

¢   ✕ **Alaska Coffee Roasting Company.** Fuel up with the university folk,
CAFÉ   where green coffee beans from around the world are roasted and blended. The scratch kitchen also offers flatbread, perfect for one or two, and pastries and desserts like tiramisu, scones, and cheesecake. With its inviting hardwood floors, Tuscan wood oven, and tasteful artwork, this hangout is so popular that a line often curls out the door. ⊠ *4001 Geist Rd., Suite 2, University West* ☎ *907/457–5282* ⊕ *www.alaskacoffeeroasting.com* ✛ *B2.*

$$$$ ✕ **Alaska Salmon Bake.** Salmon cooked over an open fire with a lemon-
SEAFOOD   and-brown-sugar sauce is a favorite at this indoor-outdoor restaurant in
★   Pioneer Park's Mining Valley. Halibut, cod, prime rib, a salad bar, and dessert are also available at the nightly all-you-can-eat dinner. ⊠ *Airport Way and Peger Rd., Pioneer Park* ☎ *907/452–7274 or 800/354–7274* ⊕ *www.akvisit.com/salmon.html* ☽ *No lunch mid-May–mid-Sept.* ✛ *C4.*

$ ✕ **Cookie Jar.** Tucked away in a nondescript neighborhood on a street
AMERICAN   not found on most Fairbanks maps, this restaurant is worth tracking
★   down. The open space features lots of cookie jars, along with plants and artwork. Spanning breakfast, lunch, and dinner, the huge menu includes scads of homemade items, an extensive kids' menu, and vegetarian selections. Entrées range from steak and shrimp to coq au vin. For dessert, try the homemade pies or cookies to match anything your grandma ever baked. Weekend breakfasts are especially popular, so allow extra time. Take Danby Street off the Johansen Expressway; the restaurant is behind Kendall Motors. ⊠ *1006 Cadillac Ct., Aurora* ☎ *907/479–8319* ⊕ *www.cookiejarfairbanks.com* ✛ *B5.*

$$$ ✕ **Gambardella's Pasta Bella.** Locals crowd the family-run Italian restau-
ITALIAN   rant, which has earned a reputation as one of the best in town. The menu includes salads, pasta, pizza, vegetarian entrées, and submarine sandwiches on homemade bread. Its specialties are lasagna, which the *Seattle Times* aptly described as "the mother of all lasagnas," and the tiramisu. The two-story restaurant has outdoor seating on a balcony and at street level. It feels as close to a romantic back-alley restaurant in Italy as you can get in Interior Alaska. ⊠ *706 2nd Ave., Downtown* ☎ *907/456–3417* ☽ *No lunch Sun.* ✛ *B1.*

$$$ ✕ **Geraldo's.** The sign outside will likely contain a plug for the virtues
ITALIAN   of garlic. Rightly so, for no one in Fairbanks puts fresh chopped garlic to better use than Geraldo's, which has gourmet pizza, seafood, pasta, and veal dishes. A painting of Don Corleone hangs on the wall, and Frank Sinatra and Dean Martin provide background music for this cozy and often crowded spot. ⊠ *701 College Rd., Lemeta* ☎ *907/452–2299* ✛ *B5.*

$$$$ ✕ **Ivory Jack's.** Jack "Ivory" O'Brien used to deal Alaskan ivory and
AMERICAN   whalebone out of this small restaurant tucked into the gold-rich hills of the Goldstream Valley on the outskirts of Fairbanks. Crab-stuffed mushrooms are a specialty of this large, open, and airy bar-restaurant. You can choose from more than 15 appetizers as well as burgers, pizza, and entrées such as halibut Dijon and Alaskan king crab. ⊠ *2581 Goldstream Rd., Goldstream* ☎ *907/455–6666* ✛ *A1.*

$$ ⌐**Lavelle's Bistro.** With offerings ranging from rack of lamb and lobster
AMERICAN cakes to halibut and New York steaks, this impressive restaurant has
won a loyal local following. Lavelle's features an extensive 3,000-bottle
wine cellar, and holds regular wine tastings and other events that give
the restaurant sophistication far removed from the frontier image cul-
tivated elsewhere in Fairbanks. This is one of the few places where
Fairbanksans dress up for dinner. ⊠ *SpringHill Suites, 575 1st Ave.,
Downtown* ☎ *907/450–0555* ⊕ *www.lavellesbistro.com* ☯ *No lunch
Sept. 15–May 15* ⊹ *B1.*

$$$ ✕**Pike's Landing.** Enjoy lunch on a huge outside deck (it seats 420) over-
AMERICAN looking the Chena River, or inside in the elegant dining room of an
★ extended log cabin. The meals cost up to $47 for steak and lobster
and rank with the best in the Interior. For a dinner in the $12 range,
relax in the sports bar and catch a view of the river. The palate-pleasing
Sunday brunch has an irresistible dessert table. ⊠ *4438 Airport Way*
☎ *907/479–7113* ⊕ *www.pikeslodge.com* ⊹ *C2.*

$$$$ ✕**Pump House Restaurant.** Alongside the Chena River, this mining pump
AMERICAN station–turned–restaurant claims it's the northernmost oyster bar in
★ the world, and also turns out house specialties such as Alaskan wild
game and seafood chowder. Listed on the National Register of Historic
Places, this pump house, circa 1930s, now houses and utilizes antiques
up to 150 years old. The furnishings and floor are made of rich, polished wood, the pool table dates from 1898, and an Alaskan grizzly
bear in a glass case stands sentry next to the hostess station. Wednesday
night is karaoke night in the bar. In summer, enjoy the midnight sun
on the deck out back by the Chena River. Ask locals where to go for
a nice night out, this is probably where they'll send you. ⊠ *796 Chena
Pump Rd.* ☎ *907/479–8452* ⊕ *www.pumphouse.com* ☯ *No lunch mid-
Sept.–June 1* ⊹ *C1.*

$ ✕**Sam's Sourdough Cafe.** Although Sam's serves meals all day, Fairbank-
AMERICAN sans know it as the best breakfast place in town. Sourdough recipes are
★ a kind of minor religion in Alaska, and Sam's serves an extensive menu
of sourdough specialties, including hotcakes and French toast, as well
as standard meat-and-eggs options, all at reasonable prices. On weekends get here early or be prepared for a wait. The address says Cameron
Street, but it's really fronted on University, just over the railroad tracks.
⊠ *3702 Cameron St.* ☎ *907/479–0523* ⊹ *B3.*

$$ ✕**Silver Gulch Brewing and Bottling Co.** You'll find some unique souvenirs
AMERICAN and an interesting collection of Fairbanks citizens at North America's
northernmost brewery. Founded in 1998, Silver Gulch is probably best
known for its pilsner and lager brews, carried throughout the state.
The brewery is in the Fox Roadhouse building. A preserved section
of the old roadhouse's exterior still stands in the second floor of the
restaurant. This hot spot is 10 mi north of Fairbanks on the Old Steese
Highway, across from the Howling Dog Saloon. After your brewery
tour (make sure to call ahead to arrange it), satisfy your hunger with
I.P.A.–battered fish-and-chips or fresh Alaskan seafood, or enjoy a brew
while sitting in the outdoor beer garden. ⊠ *2195 Old Steese Hwy., Fox*
☎ *907/452–2739* ⊕ *www.silvergulch.com* ⌐ *Free brewery tours avail-
able in summer* ☯ *No lunch weekdays* ⊹ *A6.*

8

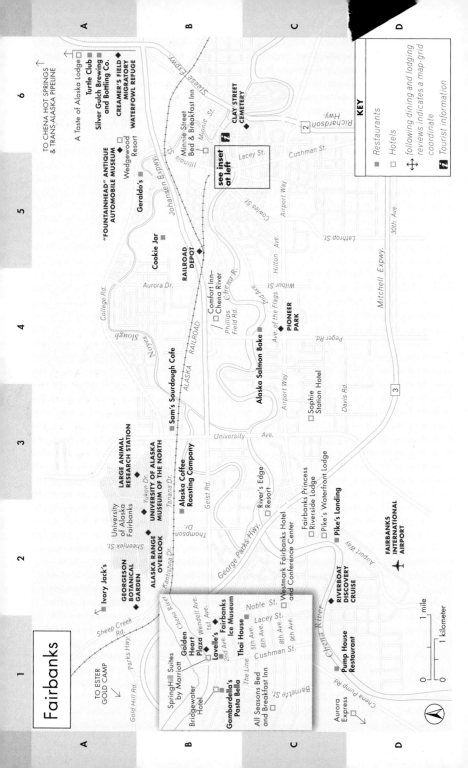

Fairbanks

TO CHENA HOT SPRINGS & TRANS-ALASKA PIPELINE

A Taste of Alaska Lodge
Turtle Club
Silver Gulch Brewing and Bottling Co.
CREAMER'S FIELD MIGRATORY WATERFOWL REFUGE

Wedgewood Resort

Geraldo's

"FOUNTAINHEAD" ANTIQUE AUTOMOBILE MUSEUM

Minnie Street Bed & Breakfast Inn

CLAY STREET CEMETERY

see inset at left

Lacey St.

Cushman St.

Richardson Hwy.

KEY

■ Restaurants
□ Hotels
✛ following dining and lodging reviews indicates a map-grid coordinate
🛈 Tourist information

Cookie Jar

RAILROAD DEPOT

Comfort Inn–Chena River

Phillips Field Rd.

Alaska Salmon Bake

Ave. of the Flags

PIONEER PARK

Airport Way

Sophie Station Hotel

Mitchell Expwy.

30th Ave.

Aurora Dr.

College Rd.

Sam's Sourdough Cafe

LARGE ANIMAL RESEARCH STATION

University of Alaska Fairbanks

UNIVERSITY OF ALASKA MUSEUM OF THE NORTH

ALASKA RANGE OVERLOOK

Alaska Coffee Roasting Company

University Ave.

River's Edge Resort

Fairbanks Princess Riverside Lodge

Pike's Waterfront Lodge

Pike's Landing

FAIRBANKS INTERNATIONAL AIRPORT

Ivory Jack's

GEORGESON BOTANICAL GARDEN

Sheep Creek Rd.

TO ESTER GOLD CAMP

Parks Hwy.

Gold Hill Rd.

RIVERBOAT DISCOVERY CRUISE

George Parks Hwy.

Westmark Fairbanks Hotel and Conference Center

SpringHill Suites by Marriott

Bridgewater Hotel

Gambardella's Pasta Bella

Golden Heart Plaza

Lavelle's

Fairbanks Ice Museum

Thai House

All Seasons Bed and Breakfast Inn

Aurora Express

Pump House Restaurant

Chena Pump Rd.

0   1 mile
0   1 kilometer

¢–$ ✕ **Thai House.** Fairbanks is not known for a wide selection of inter-
THAI national cuisine, but Thai food is an exception, and the Thai House
★ is among the best of the bunch. The prices are astounding, the staff
dress in elaborate Thai silks, and the atmosphere is elegant with hardwood floors and Thai decor on the walls. The restaurant has a loyal
following because the food is authentic. ⊠ *412 5th Ave., Downtown*
☎ *907/452–6123* ✛ *C2.*

$$$$ ✕ **Turtle Club.** Don't go to this windowless and nondescript dining room
AMERICAN expecting great variety. Do go if you are hungry for prime rib, lobster,
prawns, or king crab and have a big appetite. There's a good salad bar,
the service is prompt, and every order comes with homemade bread.
The "Turtle Cut" serving of prime rib, advertised as a "medium portion," weighs a pound. Many of the patrons make this a regular stop
on Friday and Saturday nights, so call ahead for reservations. It's worth
the 10-mi drive north of Fairbanks. ⊠ *Mi 10, Old Steese Hwy., Fox*
☎ *907/457–3883* ⊕ *www.alaskanturtle.com* ✛ *A6.*

WHERE TO STAY

For expanded hotel reviews, visit Fodors.com.

$$$–$$$$ ▦ **A Taste of Alaska Lodge.** The Eberhardt family's lodge is 20 minutes
from Fairbanks, yet far enough away to make you feel like you're on
a wilderness retreat. **Pros:** great view; eclectic collections; quiet loca-
tion. **Cons:** not close to town. **TripAdvisor:** "fantastic room with a
nice view," "hosts were more than gracious," "the perfect Alaskan
lodge experience." ⊠ *551 Eberhardt Rd., Two Rivers* ☎ *907/488–7855*
⊕ *www.atasteofalaska.com* ➹ *8 rooms in lodge, 2 in log house, 1 in
annex* ♿ *In-room: no a/c, kitchen (some), Wi-Fi* ▥ *Breakfast* ✛ *A6.*

$$–$$$ ▦ **All Seasons Bed and Breakfast Inn.** In a quiet residential neighborhood
within walking distance of downtown, this nicely furnished inn pro-
vides relaxation and privacy. **Pros:** close to downtown; clean rooms; trip
planning help available. **Cons:** lacks an Alaskan ambience. **TripAdvisor:**
"immaculately clean," "rooms were nicely decorated," "gracious and
knowledgeable hostess." ⊠ *763 7th Ave., Downtown* ☎ *907/451–6649*
⊕ *www.allseasonsinn.com* ➹ *8 rooms* ♿ *In-room: a/c, Wi-Fi. In-hotel:
laundry facilities, business center* ▥ *Breakfast* ✛ *C1.*

$$–$$$ ▦ **Aurora Express.** It's off the beaten path, but this B&B is unforgettable,
especially for railroad buffs. **Pros:** most unique lodging in the area;
sweeping views of the valley. **Cons:** far from town; phone and TV in com-
mon area only; no kids under 12. ⊠ *1550 Chena Ridge Rd.* ☎ *907/474–
0949 or 800/221–0073* ⊕ *www.fairbanksalaskabedandbreakfast.com*
➹ *7 rooms* ♿ *In-room: no a/c, no TV* ☾ *Closed early Sept.–end of May*
▥ *Breakfast* ✛ *D1.*

$$ ▦ **Bridgewater Hotel.** In the heart of downtown Fairbanks, just above
the Chena River, this hotel has gone through a number of incarna-
tions and is now a thoroughly modern, European-style hotel. **Pros:**
good location; weekend specials available; downtown hotel with the
most character. **Cons:** small and modest rooms; no kitchen or refrigerators; restaurant serves breakfast only. **TripAdvisor:** "staff is awesome,"
"hotel is clean and fresh," "good location but outdated rooms." ⊠ *723*

8

1st Ave., Downtown ☎ *907/452–6661 or 800/528–4916* ⊕ *www. fountainheadhotels.com/bridgewater/bridgewater.htm* ⤴ *94 rooms* △ *In-room: a/c, Wi-Fi. In-hotel: restaurant* ⊙ *Closed mid-Sept.–mid-May* ❖ *Breakfast* ✛ *B1.*

$$$ 🖭 **Comfort Inn–Chena River.** Situated near the banks of the Chena River, directly across the water from Pioneer Park, this hotel has a great vantage point. **Pros:** surrounded by woods; the lounge is equipped with a cozy fireplace. **Cons:** not within easy walking distance of most attractions; the rooms have a chain-hotel feeling. ⊠ *1908 Chena Landings Loop, Railroad Industrial Area* ☎ *907/479–8080 or 800/228–5150* ⊕ *www.choicehotels.com* ⤴ *74 rooms* △ *In-room: a/c, Wi-Fi. In-hotel: pool, some pets allowed* ❖ *Breakfast* ✛ *B4.*

$$$ 🖭 **Fairbanks Princess Riverside Lodge.** An expansive wooden deck facing the Chena River draws a crowd at this luxury lodge in summer. **Pros:** grandiose halls and lounge; next to the Chena River; large gym to work off the steam. **Cons:** caters to large tours; basic rooms, kitchenettes and refrigerators available on request only. **TripAdvisor:** "room was fine," "comfortable bed," "river view was nice and peaceful." ⊠ *4477 Pikes Landing Rd.* ☎ *907/455–4477 or 800/426–0500* ⊕ *www. princesslodges.com* ⤴ *326 rooms* △ *In-room: no a/c, Wi-Fi. In-hotel: 2 restaurants, bar, gym, laundry facilities* ✛ *C2.*

$ 🖭 **Minnie Street Bed & Breakfast Inn.** Martha Stewart would approve of this B&B. **Pros:** luxurious decor; massage available; variety of room styles. **Cons:** not directly downtown; no pets allowed. **TripAdvisor:** "very friendly hosts," "clean and comfortable house," "quiet and well located." ⊠ *345 Minnie St. Downtown* ☎ *907/456–1802 or 888/456–1849* ⊕ *www.minniestreetbandb.com* ⤴ *12 rooms, 3 suites, 1 standalone house* △ *In-room: no a/c, kitchen (some), Wi-Fi. In-hotel: spa, laundry facilities* ❖ *Breakfast* ✛ *B6.*

$$$$ 🖭 **Pike's Waterfront Lodge.** Log columns and beams support the high ceiling in the lobby of this hotel and conference center on the banks of the Chena River. **Pros:** located on the banks of the Chena River; Pike's Landing next door is a hot spot; close to the airport. **Cons:** small gym; cabins are a walk from the restaurant. **TripAdvisor:** "beautiful room with a view," "very comfortable beds," "beautifully decorated." ⊠ *1850 Hoselton Rd.* ☎ *907/456–4500 or 877/774–2400* ⊕ *www. pikeslodge.com* ⤴ *180 rooms, 28 cabins* △ *In-room: a/c, Wi-Fi. In-hotel: restaurant, bar, gym, laundry facilities* ❖ *Breakfast* ✛ *C2.*

$$$ 🖭 **River's Edge Resort.** If you want the privacy of a cottage, a bit of elbow room, and the amenities of a luxury hotel, you can find it along the banks of the Chena River at the River's Edge Resort. **Pros:** prime location along the Chena River; private cabins. **Cons:** no kitchenettes; ½ mi walking distance of nearby shop or bar. **TripAdvisor:** "comfortable rooms," "staff was terrific," "clean and convenient to everything." ⊠ *4200 Boat St., University West* ☎ *907/474–0286 or 800/770–3343* ⊕ *www.riversedge.net* ⤴ *86 cottages, 8 lodge suites* △ *In-room: a/c, Wi-Fi. In-hotel: restaurant, bar, laundry facilities* ⊙ *Closed mid-Sept.– mid-May* ✛ *C2.*

$$$ 🖭 **Sophie Station Hotel.** Its quiet location and helpful staff make this spa-
★   cious hotel near the airport one of Fairbanks's best. **Pros:** complimentary

COME WINTER

The temperature gets down to −40 degrees Fahrenheit every winter in Fairbanks, but school is never canceled, no matter how cold it gets. In recent years, in fact, the only times schools have closed were when rare winter warm spells created icy conditions on the roads that made it too hazardous for bus travel. Young Alaskans are so hardy that outdoor recess takes place down to −20F.

The weather is a great unifying factor among Fairbanks residents.

Winter conditions freeze the pipes of university presidents as well as laborers. After a night of 40 below it's common to see cars bumping along as if the tires were flat; the bottoms of the tires freeze flat, and it takes a quarter mile or so before they warm up and return to round. All cars have an electric plug hanging out front between the headlights because they need to be plugged in during winter to keep running.

newspaper upon arrival; walking distance to grocery stores; equipped with full kitchens. **Cons:** average interior decor; no DVD players or VCRs. **TripAdvisor:** "clean and spacious," "staff was very friendly and helpful," "pleasant and efficient." ✉ *1717 University Ave.* ☎ *907/479–3650 or 800/528–4916* ⊕ *www.fountainheadhotels.com* ⤵ *149 suites* ♿ *In-room: a/c, kitchen, Wi-Fi. In-hotel: restaurant, bar, gym, laundry facilities* ✛ *C3.*

$$$$ 🏨 **SpringHill Suites by Marriott.** At the center of what was once the heart of the commercial district, the SpringHill Suites has 140 comfortable suites, each with a microwave, refrigerator, living-room furniture, and well-lighted work areas. **Pros:** comfortable in-room desk areas; a pool to relax in; home to one of Fairbanks's favorite restaurants. **Cons:** small lounge; no DVD players or VCRs; moderate-size gym. **TripAdvisor:** "breakfast was satisfying," "nice spacious room," "so comfortable and convenient to everything." ✉ *575 1st Ave., Downtown* ☎ *907/451–6552 or 877/729–0197* ⊕ *www.marriott.com/faish* ⤵ *140 suites* ♿ *In-room: a/c, Wi-Fi. In-hotel: restaurant, bar, pool, gym, laundry facilities* ⦿ *Breakfast* ✛ *B1.*

$$ 🏨 **Wedgewood Resort.** Both wild and cultivated flowers adorn the land-

Fodor's Choice scaped grounds of the Wedgewood Resort, which borders on Creamer's

★ Field Migratory Waterfowl Refuge. **Pros:** courteous staff; 4 mi of trails through 76 acres of wildlife sanctuary; antique automobile museum; elegant banquet halls; airport shuttle. **Cons:** a bit far from most of Fairbanks's other attractions. **TripAdvisor:** "large and comfortable," "very quiet," "everything is spotless." ✉ *212 Wedgewood Dr.* ☎ *907/456–3642 or 800/528–4916* ⊕ *www.fountainheadhotels.com* ⤵ *297 suites* ♿ *In-room: a/c, kitchen, Wi-Fi. In-hotel: 2 restaurants, bar, laundry facilities* ✛ *A6.*

$$$ 🏨 **Westmark Fairbanks Hotel and Conference Center.** Built on a courtyard on a quiet street, this full-service and recently expanded complex is within easy walking distance of downtown. **Pros:** on the outskirts of downtown; decent rooms without an overdose of Alaskana. **Cons:** modern, corporate ambience doesn't feel intimate; no spa. **TripAdvisor:** "room was lovely," "nice accommodations but thin walls," "comfortable bed." ⊠ *813 Noble St., Downtown* ☎ *907/456–7722 or 800/544–0970* ⊕ *www.westmarkhotels. com* ↻ *400 rooms* ♿ *In-room: a/c, Wi-Fi (some). In-hotel: restaurant, bar, gym, 2 business centers* ✛ *C2.*

ALL THAT JAZZ

Alaska's premier cultural gathering, the **Fairbanks Summer Arts Festival** (☎ 907/474–8869 ⊕ www.fsaf.org) takes place over two weeks in late July on the University of Alaska Fairbanks Campus. The festivities, which grew from a small jazz festival, now attract visitors worldwide for music, dance, literary arts, healing arts, visual arts, American roots music, and ice-skating instruction. Visitors are encouraged to participate in one- or two-week classes and mini-workshops.

NIGHTLIFE AND THE ARTS

Check the "Kaleidoscope" section in the Thursday *Fairbanks Daily News–Miner* for current nightspots, plays, concerts, and art shows.

THE ARTS

Festivals are a big part of life in Fairbanks, the months of February and March bringing the most revelry.

FESTIVALS **Golden Days** (☎ *907/452–1105* ⊕ *www.fairbankschamber.org*) is the annual celebration of Fairbanks's gold-rush past. Several days of events are capped by a street fair and big parade through the city in late July. **Tanana Valley State Fair** (⊠ *1800 College Rd., Aurora* ⊕ *www. tananavalleyfair.org*) is Interior Alaska's largest annual gathering. It fills a week in early August with attractions such as giant vegetables and the handiwork of local artisans.

The early-February **Yukon Quest** (☎ *907/452–7954* ⊕ *www.yukonquest. com*) calls itself the "toughest sled dog race in the world," passing through historic early-gold-rush territory. In odd-numbered years the 1,000-mi race starts in Whitehorse and in even-numbered years it starts in Fairbanks. The **World Ice Art Championships and U.S. National Championships** (☎ *907/451–8250* ⊕ *www.icealaska.com*) in late February to late March draw ice artists from around the world for an ice-sculpting competition extravaganza. Mid-March brings out a festival goofy enough to cure any case of cabin fever: **Chatanika Days** (☎ *907/389–2164*) feature a snowmachine tug-of-war.

NIGHTLIFE

SALOONS The **Blue Loon** (⊠ *Mi 353.5, Parks Hwy.* ☎ *907/457–5666* ⊕ *www.* ★ *theblueloon.com*), between Ester and Fairbanks, presents year-round entertainment and great grill food. Movies are nightly at 5:30 and 8. Catch national touring bands, comedy, outdoor summer concerts, DJ dancing late nights on weekends, and much more, including free Wi-Fi. The **Howling Dog Saloon** (⊠ *Mi 11, Old Steese Hwy.* ☎ *907/456–4695* ⊕ *www.howlingdogsaloon.com* ⊘ *Closed Nov.–May*) has live music, specializing in blues and rock and roll; a café and bar food; a beer, wine, and liquor menu; and gobs of atmosphere. The clientele is a mix of college students, airline pilots, tourists, miners, and bikers. Out back there are a volleyball court, horseshoe pit, and 10 rustic cabins for rent.

★ Don't be alarmed by the exterior of the **Midnight Mine** (✉ *308 Wendell St.* ☎ *907/456–5348*). It's a friendly neighborhood bar with darts, foosball, a pool table, and a big-screen TV, and it's within walking distance of downtown. Cleo the dog is likely to greet you as you come in—be sure to ask to see her trick. It'll cost you a buck, but it's worth it.

The *Golden Heart Revue* at the **Palace Theatre** (✉ *Pioneer Park, Airport Way and Peger Rd.* ☎ *907/456–5960 or 800/354–7274* ⊕ *www.akvisit. com*) is a musical-comedy show about the founding and building of Fairbanks. It begins at 8:15 nightly from mid-May to mid-September.

The **Senator's Saloon** (✉ *796 Chena Pump Rd.* ☎ *907/479–8452*) at the Pump House Restaurant, is the place to hear easy-listening music alongside the Chena River on a warm summer evening.

SQUARE DANCING   The dancing clubs in Fairbanks, North Pole, Delta Junction, and Tok are all affiliated with the **Northern Lights Council of Dancers** (☎ *907/452– 5699* ⊕ *www.dancealaska.org*), and hold frequent square, contra, and ballroom dances.

SHOPPING

CRAFTS
Known for handwoven rugs, the **Alaska Rag Company** (✉ *603 Lacey St., Downtown* ☎ *907/451–4401* ⊕ *www.alaskaragco.com*) carries the work of many local artists. **Beads and Things** (✉ *537 2nd Ave., Downtown* ☎ *907/456–2323*) sells Native handicrafts from around the state. The **Great Alaskan Bowl Company** (✉ *4630 Old Airport Rd.* ☎ *907/474– 9663* ⊕ *www.woodbowl.com*) sells lathe-turned bowls made out of Alaskan birch.

If Only. a fine store (✉ *215 Cushman St., Downtown* ☎ *907/457–6659*) carries a wide range of unique Alaska items. **A Weaver's Yarn** (✉ *1810 Alaska Way, College* ☎ *907/374–1995*) has musk-ox qiviut to spin.

JEWELRY
In her small, eponymous shop **Judie Gumm Designs** (✉ *3600 Main St., Ester* ☎ *907/479–4568* ⊕ *www.judiegumm.com*) Ms. Gumm fashions stunning (and moderately priced) silver and gold designs best described as sculptural interpretations of Northern images. Ester is 6 mi south of Fairbanks off the George Parks Highway.

Larson's Fine Jewelers (✉ *405 Noble St., Downtown* ☎ *907/456–4141*) has been making Alaskan gold-nugget jewelry and other contemporary designs for six decades. **Taylor's Gold-N-Stones** (✉ *3578-B Airport Way, University Avenue* ☎ *907/456–8369 or 800/306–3589*) uses gemstones mined in Alaska and creates unique gold designs.

OUTERWEAR AND OUTDOOR GEAR
Apocalypse Design (✉ *201 Minnie St.* ☎ *907/451–7555 or 877/521–7555* ⊕ *www.akgear.com*) makes its own specialized cold-weather clothing for dog mushers and other winter adventurers. Travelers from colder areas of the Lower 48 will appreciate the double-layer fleece mittens, among other items. **Beaver Sports** (✉ *3480 College Rd., College* ☎ *907/479–2494* ⊕ *www.beaversports.com*) is equipped with a fine selection of quality backpacking, biking, paddling, and skiing gear; a

8

Celestial Rays of Light: Aurora Borealis

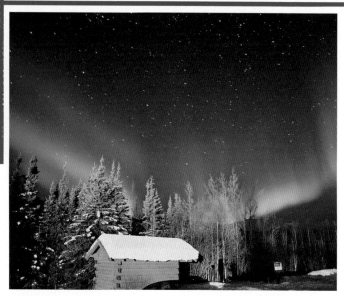

The light show often begins simply, as a pale yellow-green luminous band that arches across Alaska's night sky. Sometimes the band will quickly fade and disappear. Other nights, however, it may begin to waver, flicker, and pulsate. Or the quiescent band may explode and fill the sky with curtains of celestial light that ripple wildly above the northern landscape. Growing more intense, these dancing lights take on other colors: pink, red, blue, or purple. At times they appear to be heavenly flames, leaping across the sky, or perhaps they're exploding fireworks, or cannon fire.

The Fairbanks area is one of the best places in the world to see the aurora borealis—commonly called the northern lights. Here they may appear more than 200 nights per year; they're much less common in Anchorage, partly because of urban glare.

As you watch these dazzling lights spreading from horizon to horizon, it is easy to imagine why many Northern cultures, including Alaska's Native peoples, created myths to explain auroral displays. What start out as patches, arcs, or bands can be magically transformed into vaporous, humanlike figures. Some of Alaska's Native groups have traditionally believed the lights to be spirits of their ancestors. According to one belief, the spirits are celebrating with dance and drumming; another says they're playing games. Yet another tradition says the lights are torches, carried by spirits who lead the souls of recently deceased people to life in the afterworld.

During Alaska's gold-rush era some non-native stampeders supposed the aurora to be reflections of ore deposits. Even renowned wilderness explorer John Muir allowed the northern lights to spark his imagination.

Once, while traveling through Southeast Alaska in 1890, Muir stayed up all night to watch a gigantic, glowing auroral bridge and bands of "restless electric auroral fairies" who danced to music "too fine for mortal ears."

Scientists have a more technical explanation for these heavenly apparitions. The aurora borealis is an atmospheric phenomenon that's tied to explosive events on the sun's surface, known as solar flares. Those flares produce a stream of charged particles, the "solar wind," which shoots off into space. When such a wind intersects with Earth's magnetic field, most of the particles are deflected; some, however, are sent into the upper atmosphere, where they collide with gas molecules such as nitrogen and oxygen. The resulting reactions produce glowing colors. The aurora is most commonly a pale yellowish green, but its borders are sometimes tinged with pink, purple, or blue. Especially rare is the all-red aurora, which appears when charged solar particles collide with oxygen molecules from 50 to 200 mi above Earth's surface.

■ TIP→ Alaska's long hours of daylight hide the aurora in summer, so the best viewing is from September through March. Scientists at the University of Alaska Geophysical Institute give a daily forecast from late fall to spring of when the lights will be the most intense at ⊕ *www.gedds. alaska.edu/auroraforecast* and in the *Fairbanks Daily News–Miner.*

SEEING THE NORTHERN LIGHTS

The **Aurora Borealis Lodge** (✉ *Mi 20.5, Steese Hwy., Cleary Summit* ☎ *907/389–2812* ⊕ *www.auroracabin. com*) has late-night tours to a log lodge on Cleary Summit, with big picture windows to see the sky. The $75–$85 tour includes hot drinks and transportation from Fairbanks. With independent transportation, admission is $25 per person. Four spacious rooms in the two-story building are also available for overnight accommodation (call ahead in the summer season), each with large, north-facing windows, private bath, and kitchen. Aurora tours run from mid-August to mid-April.

About 60 mi northeast of Fairbanks, the **Chena Hot Springs Resort** (✉ *End of Chena Hot Springs Rd., Chena Hot Springs* ☎ *907/451–8104* ⊕ *www.chenahotsprings.com*) treats guests to a Sno-Cat ride to a yurt with a 360-degree panoramic vista of nothing but wilderness. Open every day of the year.

Visitors fill the two warm mountaintop lodges at **Mount Aurora Skiland** (✉ *Mi 20.5, Steese Hwy., Cleary Summit* ☎ *907/389–2314* ⊕ *www.skiland. org*) after 10 pm on winter nights. Images from an aurora Web cam are shown on a large-screen TV. Admission is $25 and includes hot drinks.

Northern Alaska Tour Company (☎ *907/474–8600 or 800/474–1986* ⊕ *www.northernalaska.com*) has a variety of single or multiday winter aurora tours going north to the Arctic Circle and the Brooks Range.

8

big part of Beaver Sports is community involvement, from supporting high school sports teams to facilitating midnight-sun runs.

SPORTS

BASEBALL

★ Scores of baseball players, including Tom Seaver, Dave Winfield, and Jason Giambi, have passed through Fairbanks on their way to the major leagues. The Interior is home to the **Alaska Goldpanners** (☎ *907/451– 0095* ⊕ *www.goldpanners.com*), a member of the Alaska Baseball League, a string of amateur baseball organizations throughout the state. Players are recruited from college teams nationwide, and the summer season (mid-June–late July) generates top-caliber competition. Home games are played at Growden Field, along Lower 2nd Avenue at Wilbur Street, not far from Pioneer Park. The baseball park hosts the **Midnight Sun Baseball Game,** a Fairbanks tradition (2012 is the 107th year) in which the Goldpanners play baseball at midnight of the summer solstice without benefit of artificial lights. This is thrilling (and possibly chilly) to watch on a clear, sunny night when the daylight never ends.

CURLING

Hundreds of Fairbanksans participate each year in curling, a game in which people with brooms play a giant version of shuffleboard on ice. Curlers have an almost fanatical devotion to their sport, and they're eager to explain its finer points to the uninitiated. The **Fairbanks Curling Club** (✉ *1962 2nd Ave.* ☎ *907/452–2875* ⊕ *www.curlfairbanks.org*) hosts an annual Yukon Title *bonspiel* (match) on the first weekend of November and an international bonspiel on the first weekend of April. The club season runs from early October through the middle of April.

RIVERBOAT RACING

A summer highlight is riverboat racing sanctioned by the **Fairbanks Outboard Association** (⊕ *www.yukon800.com*). These specially built 24-foot racing boats are powered by 50-horsepower engines and reach speeds of 75 mph. Weekend races in summer and fall begin and end either at the Chena Pump Campgrounds or at Pike's Landing, just off Airport Way near Fairbanks International Airport. The big riverboat racing event of the season, in late June, is the **Yukon 800 Marathon,** a two-day, 800-mi race between Fairbanks and Galena by way of the Chena, Tanana, and Yukon rivers.

The **Roland Lord Memorial Race,** from Fairbanks to Nenana and back, is held in early August; the **Tanana 440** is held in late July.

NORTH OF FAIRBANKS

When you drive north of Fairbanks you enter territory where people are few and far between. Away from the thin line of the highways spread hundreds of thousands of square miles with few signs of human habitation. Accordingly, driving in the north country involves both nail-biting and jaw-dropping experiences. You might pick up hitchhikers carrying a moose and the smell of having camped for a month. You might see

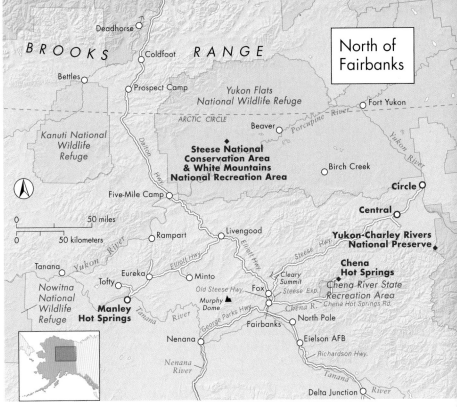

the swirl of musk oxen running from the noise of your car. And you might—probably will—set a personal record for how many cracks your windshield gets in a single day.

On the roads heading east, northeast, and northwest of Fairbanks, the going gets tougher the farther you drive. However, the gravel and other assorted surfaces are worth the trouble of navigating; these roads open up long slivers of the Alaskan wilderness. And since Alaska is so big, the more country you cover, the better your understanding of the place—and the better your chances of understanding the history of each unique road from the stories shared by the people you meet. ■TIP→ Road conditions can be rough, and if you break down, help may be a long way off, so be sure to check your fuel and spare tire before you go. And if you're driving your own car, windshield replacement insurance is the smartest money you'll spend on the trip.

Follow the Chena Hot Springs Road to its end and you'll find a natural hot spring that is among the best in the state. The Steese Highway connects to historic goldfields in Central and Circle, while the Elliott Highway leads northwest and, before shifting to the southwest, connects to the roughly north–south Dalton Highway (built to assist construction of the Trans-Alaska Pipeline System). All three roads provide access to

SIDE TRIP: NENANA, ALASKA

56 road mi southwest of Fairbanks, 75 mi north of Denali National Park, 304 mi north of Anchorage on the George Parks Highway.

For a break from the buzz of the George Parks Highway, take a detour in Nenana (pronounced like banana), a year-round town of approximately 500 people, on the banks of the Tanana River and under the shadow of Toghotthele Hill or, in Athabascan, the "mountain that parallels the river." The downtown avenue seems stuck in time, a relic of the early Alaska Railroad construction heyday from 1915 to 1923.

Nenana has several claims to fame: home to the world's second-largest single-span bridge, 700 feet long; the site where President Warren Harding drove the golden spike into the railroad to commemorate its completion; and the start of the 1925 serum run to Nome. It's also home to the Nenana Ice classic, where Alaskans annually bet on the date and time of the river's spring breakup. Ongoing since 1917, the jackpot sometimes climbs over $300,000.

To get your blood flowing, start with a short walking tour at 5th Street, where you can talk with the staff at the Nenana Visitor Center. Continue north down A Street, past old storefronts, like Coghill's General Store dating from 1916, to the Alaska Railroad Depot, home of the Alaska Railroad Museum, which was built in 1923 and is now on the National Register of Historic Places. It's a fascinating stop, with a lot more inside than just train stuff. One block more along Front Street, peek into St. Mark's Episcopal Church, built upriver in 1905; note its beautiful handcrafted altar and Athabascan moose-hide beadwork inside. Finish the tour along the river at the Alfred Starr Nenana Cultural Center, where you'll find authentic gifts by local artists from within 50 mi of Nenana, or browse the exhibits highlighting history and Athabascan culture of the area.

One of the only places to eat and rent a very basic room is the **Rough Woods Inn & Cafe** (⊠ *2nd and A Sts., Nenana* ☎ *907/832–5299*). This establishment offers roadside food from fresh, deep-fried halibut to Angus charbroiled New York steak, and even breakfast.

countless starting points for hiking, skiing, camping, fishing, canoeing, and other outdoor-oriented adventures.

CHENA HOT SPRINGS

62 mi northeast of Fairbanks.

Chena Hot Springs. The 57-mi paved Chena Hot Springs Road, which starts 5 mi outside Fairbanks, leads to Chena Hot Springs, a favorite playground of many Fairbanks residents. The road passes several attractions, including Chena River State Recreation Area and Chena Hot Springs Resort. If you're heading to the resort, don't skip the hiking, fishing, camping, and canoeing along the way. ■TIP→ The chances of spotting a moose are excellent if you keep a sharp eye on the roadside.

From Mile 26 to Mile 51 the road passes through the **Chena River State Recreation Area,** a diverse wilderness of nearly 400 square mi. You can also stop for a picnic, take a hike for an hour or an extended backpacking trip, fish for the beautiful yet gullible arctic grayling, or rent a rustic backcountry cabin to savor a truly wild Alaskan adventure. Grayling fishing in the Chena River is catch-and-release, single-hook, artificial lure only. There are several stocked lakes along the road affording catch-and-keep fishing for rainbow trout, which are well suited for the frying pan.

OUTDOOR ACTIVITIES AND GUIDED TOURS

DOGSLEDDING **Chena Dog Sled Adventures** (⊠ *Box 16037, Two Rivers* ☎ *907/488–5845* ⊕ *www.ptialaska.net/~sleddogs*) provides winter visitors a chance to drive a dog team or ride in a sled. Ice fishing and snowshoeing are also available. Call ahead for reservations, directions, and accommodations.

HIKING The **Granite Tors Trail,** a 15-mi loop, can be done in a day, and offers a view of the upper Chena Valley and an opportunity to see dramatic "tors" (fingers of rock protruding through grassy meadow) that are reminiscent of the *moai* monuments of Easter Island. The trail is steep, but the views at the top make the climb worthwhile. Although the Interior landscapes lack the impressive mountain views of other parts of the state, the enormous expanse of rolling hills and seemingly endless tracts of forest are every bit as awe-inspiring. However, since there are no mountains here to collect snow and contribute to the water table, water sources along the way are unreliable. ■ TIP→ Bring a couple of quarts of water per person, plus mosquito repellent. Hiking uphill on a hot summer day is dehydrating. Also, weather is fickle here, and a bright, sunny morning can easily turn into an overcast, rainy, and windy afternoon. Come with adequate clothing, including rain gear, no matter how promising the skies look in the morning. A shorter hike is the 3.5-mi Angel Rocks Trail, near the eastern boundary of the area.

PADDLING The **Chena River State Recreation Area** has numerous well-marked river-access points (the Chena Hot Springs Road parallels the Chena River, and canoeists use several put-in points along the way). The lower sections of the river area are placid, but the area above the third bridge, at Mile 44.1, can be hazardous for inexperienced boaters.

Wilderness Enterprises (☎ *907/488–7517* ⊕ *www.wildernessenterprises. com*) has guided fishing for arctic grayling and scenic float trips on the Chena River. Half-day and full-day trips are available. When the temperatures drop, try your hand at ice fishing.

WHERE TO EAT

$$$–$$$$ ✕ **Two Rivers Lodge.** Fairbanksans are known to make the 40-mi round-
SEAFOOD trip for the delicious dinners here, including prime rib, frequent crab
★ specials, and other Alaskan seafood dishes. Don't be discouraged by the building's outward appearance—rustic logs belie the menu's elegance. For a study in Alaskan-style contrasts, stop in the Trapline Lounge first for a predinner refreshment. ⊠ *Mi 16, Chena Hot Springs Rd.* ☎ *907/488–6815* ◷ *No lunch.*

8

Have Your Green and Eat It, Too

Don't feel guilty about leaving on the lights at Chena Hot Springs Resort; most of the energy is geothermal. Since July 2006 the resort has been utilizing the 165F springwater to power three turbines. This feat shocked geothermal experts who claimed that water temperatures must be at least 220 degrees Fahrenheit. This free source of power allows the resort to run greenhouses through the -40 degree Fahrenheit winters.

The daily 2 pm free Renewable Energy tours end at these productive greenhouses, where row upon row of lettuce, up to 25 heads a day, and 5 varieties of tomatoes thrive off a hydroponic, or soil-free, system. Order a salad for dinner and taste the special flavor of local, fresh-picked greens.

WHERE TO STAY

For expanded hotel reviews, visit Fodors.com.

$$$
Fodor's Choice
★

☒ **Chena Hot Springs Resort.** People come in droves to soak in the hot springs—in the hot tubs, the indoor family swimming pool, or the outdoor natural-rock lake (ages 18-plus). **Pros:** it's 95% powered by geothermal energy; there's an activity for every taste. **Cons:** Wi-Fi comes with a daily usage fee at the Aurora Cafe; there are only eight TV channels. **TripAdvisor:** "staff was friendly and helpful," "room was large and clean," "springs are so nice and hot." ☒ *Mi 56.5, Chena Hot Springs Rd.* ☎ *907/451–8104* ⊕ *www.chenahotsprings.com* ⌨ *80 rooms* ⌂ *In-room: no a/c. In-hotel: restaurant, bar, laundry facilities.*

CENTRAL AND CIRCLE

From Fairbanks: 128 mi northeast on the Steese Hwy. to Central, 162 mi on Steese to Circle.

Steese Highway. The Steese Highway follows the Chatanika River and several other creeks along the southern part of the White Mountains. It eventually climbs into weatherworn alpine mountains, peaking at Eagle Summit (3,624 feet), about 100 mi from Fairbanks, and drops back down into forested creek beds en route to Central. At Central you can drive the 30-plus mi on a winding gravel road to Circle, a small town on the Yukon River. The highway is paved to Mile 44 and usually in good shape. A possible exception is in winter, when Eagle Summit is sometimes closed due to drifting snow.

OUTDOOR ACTIVITIES

Tour companies are scarce in the area. Outdoor activities are generally do-it-yourself.

PADDLING The **Chatanika River**, a choice spot for canoeists and kayakers, is still fairly close to Fairbanks. The most northerly **access point** is at Cripple Creek campground, near Mile 60, Steese Highway. Other commonly used access points are at Long Creek (Mile 45, Steese Highway); at the

CAMPING OFF CHENA HOT SPRINGS ROAD

⚠ **Department of Natural Resources Cabins.** Used by adventurers with extensive backcountry experience, these cabins have woodstoves, bunks, and tools for cutting wood. You have to supply everything else—food, bedding, water, cooking utensils. This is basic Alaskan shelter, but it can't be beat for leaving the real world behind. Hiking distances range from 3 to 10 mi, but the North Fork and Chena River cabins are road-accessible. The nightly fee ranges from $25 for the Colorado and Angel Creek cabins to $50 per night for the larger North Fork and Chena River cabins. Wildlife in the area includes moose, porcupines, lynx, fox, pine marten, wolves, coyotes, black bears, and, occasionally, grizzly bears. Facilities vary with each cabin. **Pros:** wilderness is at your doorstep. **Cons:** only amenities are the ones you bring along. ⊠ *Mi 32 to 50, Chena Hot Springs Rd., Chena River State Recreation Area* 🛏 *5 cabins* 🚽 *Pit toilets* ☎ *907/451–2705* ⊕ *www.dnr.alaska.gov* 🛏 *Reservations essential.*

⚠ **Red Squirrel Campground.** If you want to combine easy fishing access with your camping, the grassy Red Squirrel State Campground at Mile Marker 42.8 is your top choice: it's got a pond stocked with grayling. There are two pavilion shelters, and the low number of campsites means quiet evenings (though the fact that it's the farthest trek from Fairbanks out of all the Chena sites might have something to do with that, too). **Pros:** fishing opportunities; fewest campsites means quieter evenings. **Cons:** far from Fairbanks; no river access. ⊠ *Mi 42.8, Chena Hot Springs Rd.* 🛏 *5 sites* 🚽 *Pit toilets, drinking water, fire pits, picnic tables, swimming* 🛏 *Reservations not accepted* ▬ *No credit cards.*

⚠ **Rosehip Campground.** At Mile 27 you'll find these campgrounds; they're very basic but have the essentials for family camping. There's a trail that leads down to the river, which makes it a good put-in and take-out spot for paddlers. It's a shorter drive from Fairbanks than other campgrounds and has river access, but this has helped it grow into the biggest campground near here. **Pros:** close to Fairbanks; river access; small boat launch available. **Cons:** the biggest campground and potentially most crowded of the three. ⊠ *Mi 27, Chena Hot Springs Rd.* 🛏 *37 sites* 🚽 *Pit toilets, drinking water, fire pits, picnic tables* 🛏 *Reservations not accepted* ▬ *No credit cards.*

⚠ **Tors Trail Campground.** Campers at Mile 39.5 are adjacent to the Granite Tors trailhead, a 15-mi loop into the high country. Also across from the campground you'll find a parking area (free for campers) and picnic spot near the river. There are no flush toilets here. **Pros:** close to the popular Granite Tors Trail; scenic picnic locale. **Cons:** no flush toilets; parking isn't free for campers. ⊠ *Mi 39.5, Chena Hot Springs Rd.* 🛏 *24 sites* 🚽 *Pit toilets, drinking water, fire pits, picnic tables* 🛏 *Reservations not accepted* ▬ *No credit cards.*

8

NATIVE ALASKA BY BUSH PLANE

From Fairbanks you can catch a ride on regularly scheduled mail planes to small, predominantly Athabascan villages along the Yukon River on to Eskimo settlements on the Arctic coast. All of the smaller air services operate the mail runs on varying schedules. If you want to visit a particular village, or just have the desire to see a bit of Native Alaska village life, contact any one of the services.

Era Alaska (☎ 907/266-8394, 800/866-8394 in Alaska ⊕ www.

flyera.com) has an extensive roster of scheduled flights to many of the bush villages in northwest Alaska, the Interior, and the North Slope of the Brooks Range. **Warbelow's Air Ventures** (☎ 907/474-0518 or 800/478-0812 ⊕ www.warbelows.com) serves approximately 20 villages. **Wright Air Service** (☎ 907/474-0502, 800/478-0502 in Alaska ⊕ www.wrightair.net) flies from its Fairbanks base to Interior and Brooks Range villages.

state campground, where the Chatanika River crosses the Steese Highway at Mile 39; and at the state's Whitefish Campground, where the river crosses the Elliott Highway at Mile 11. The stream flows into the Minto Flats below this point, and river access is more difficult.

Water in the Chatanika River may or may not be clear, depending on mining activities along its upper tributaries. In times of very low water, the upper Chatanika River is shallow and difficult to navigate. ⚠ **Avoid the river in times of high water,** especially after heavy rains, because of the danger of sweepers, floating debris, and hidden gravel bars. Contact the **Alaska Public Lands Information Center** (☎ 907/459-3730) for the status of the river.

WHERE TO STAY

For expanded hotel reviews, visit Fodors.com.

ȼ ☵ **Chatanika Lodge.** Rocket scientists from the nearby Poker Flat Research Range gather at this cedar lodge, as do mushers (staff can arrange dogsled rides), snowmachiners, and local families. **Pros:** a local favorite; Alaskan character. **Cons:** long drive from Fairbanks; shared bathrooms. ✉ *Mi 28.5, 5760 Steese Hwy.* ☎ *907/389-2164* ⊕ *www.chatanikalodgealaska.com* ⤳ *10 rooms with shared bath* ☖ *In-room: no a/c, Wi-Fi. In-hotel: restaurant, bar, laundry facilities, some pets allowed.*

STEESE AND WHITE MOUNTAINS

30 mi north of Fairbanks via Elliott Hwy.

For those who want to immerse themselves in nature for several days at a time, the **Steese National Conservation Area and the White Mountains National Recreation Area** (☎ 907/474-2200 *Bureau of Land Management [BLM]*) have opportunities for backcountry hiking and paddling. Both areas have road-accessible entry points, but you cannot drive into the Steese Conservation Area. The White Mountains Recreation Area has

CAMPING IN STEESE AND WHITE MOUNTAINS

⚠ **BLM Campgrounds.** The BLM (Bureau of Land Management) manages three road-accessible campgrounds in the Steese Highway area: one at Mile 60 and two off Mile 57 (up 7 mi on the U.S. Creek Road with one at each end of the Nome Creek Road junction). The Cripple Creek Campground at Mile 60, Steese Highway, is the best for RVs, with a dozen sites and a half-dozen places for tents. On the Dalton Highway there are two sites: one undeveloped site at Mile 115 near the Arctic Circle and one at Mile 180, 5 mi north of Coldfoot. The campgrounds are available on a first-come, first-served basis. In addition, you'll find several undeveloped campsites along the Dalton—old gravel pits with no facilities, available free of charge (though they might not be every visitor's first choice). These are really great sites for campfires—and you'll want them, given the particular voraciousness of mosquitoes in and around these parks. ■TIP→ Check the Web site for the most up-to-date information. **Pros:** reservations not required; great place for a campfire. **Cons:** bring the bug spray; first-come, first-served policy means you might be stuck in the gravel pits during high season. ⤳ 5 campgrounds ⚲ Pit toilets, fire pits, picnic tables ☎ 907/474–2251 or 800/437–7021 ⊕ www.blm.gov/ak ⚱ Reservations not accepted ⊟ No credit cards.

limited camping facilities from June to November; reservations are not accepted.

In the Steese National Conservation Area you can take a four- to five-day or 126-mi float trip on the lively, clear-water **Birch Creek**, a challenge with its several rapids; Mile 94 of the Steese Highway is the access point. Along the way you should see plenty of moose, caribou, and dozens of species of birds. This stream winds its way north through the historic mining country of the Circle District. The first take-out point is the Steese Highway Bridge, 25 mi from Circle. Most people exit here to avoid the increasingly winding river and low water. From there Birch Creek meanders on to the Yukon River well below the town. Fairbanks outfitter Alaska Outdoor Rentals and Guides (⇨ *see Boating, above*) arranges these trips.

Rising out of the White Mountains National Recreation Area, **Beaver Creek** makes its easy way north. If you have enough time, it's possible to run its entire length to the Yukon, totaling 360 river miles if done from road to road. If you make a shorter run, you will have to arrange a take-out via small plane. A lot of people make the trip in five or six days, starting from Nome Creek and taking out at Victoria Creek. Contact Alaska Outdoor Rentals and Guides (⇨ *see Cruising and Canoeing Tours under Outdoor Activities and Guided Tours in Fairbanks*) to schedule a trip.

WHERE TO STAY
For expanded hotel reviews, visit Fodors.com.

¢ ⚏ **Public-Use Cabins.** The Bureau of Land Management runs 11 public-use cabins in the White Mountains National Recreation Area and one road-accessible cabin on the Elliot Highway, with 300 mi of interconnecting trails. **Pros:** remote locations allow for an intimate experience with the land. **Cons:** permits required; geared for winter use; no place to take a hot bath. ⊠ *Fairbanks District Office of BLM, 1150 University Ave., Fairbanks* ☎ *907/474–2251 or 800/437–7021* ⊕ *www.blm.gov/ ak* ⚲ *Pit toilets* ⏴ *12 cabins.*

YUKON–CHARLEY RIVERS NATIONAL PRESERVE

20 mi north of Eagle, 100 mi east of Fairbanks.

The 126-mi stretch of the Yukon River running between the small towns of Eagle and Circle—former gold-rush metropolises—is protected in the 2.5-million-acre **Yukon–Charley Rivers National Preserve.** In the pristine Charley River watershed a crystalline white-water stream flows out of the Yukon-Tanana uplands, allowing for excellent river running for expert rafters.

In great contrast to the Charley River, the Yukon River is a powerful stream, dark with mud and glacial silt. The only bridge built across it in Alaska carries the Trans-Alaska Pipeline, north of Fairbanks. The river surges deep, slow, and through this stretch, generally pretty flat, and to travel on it in a small boat is a humbling and magnificent experience. You can drive from Fairbanks to Eagle (via the Taylor Highway off the Alaska Highway) and to Circle (via the Steese Highway), and from either of these arrange for a ground-transportation shuttle back to your starting city at the end of your Yukon River trip. Weeklong float trips down the river from Eagle to Circle, 150 mi away, are possible. For information, contact the **National Park Service** (☎ 907/547–2233) in Eagle. ■ TIP→ Note that there are no developed campgrounds or other visitor facilities within the preserve itself, though low-impact backcountry camping is permitted. ⊠ *National Park Service, 4175 Geist Rd., Fairbanks* ☎ *907/457–5752* ⊕ *www.nps.gov/yuch.*

OUTDOOR ACTIVITIES AND GUIDED TOURS

HIKING The **Alaska Public Lands Information Center** (☎ 907/459–3730) has detailed information about the trails in the Yukon–Charley Rivers National Preserve.

The **Circle-Fairbanks Historic Trail** stretches 58 mi from the vicinity of Cleary Summit to Twelve-Mile Summit. This route, which is not for novices, follows the old summer trail used by gold miners; in winter they generally used the frozen Chatanika River to make this journey. The trail has been roughly marked and cleared, but there are no facilities and water is often scarce. Most of the trail is on state land, but it does cross valid mining claims that must be respected. Although you'll find rock cairns and mileposts while hiking, no well-defined tread exists, so it's easy to become disoriented. ■ TIP→ The State Department of Natural Resources strongly recommends that backpackers on this trail equip themselves with the following USGS topographical maps: Livengood (A-1), Circle (A-6), Circle (A-5), and Circle (B-4).

The Bureau of Land Management maintains the **Pinnell Mountain National Recreation Trail**, connecting Twelve-Mile Summit and Eagle Summit on

HYPOTHERMIA

Hypothermia, the lowering of the body's core temperature, is an ever-present threat in Alaska's wilderness. Wear layers of warm clothing when the weather is cool and/or wet; this includes a good wind- and water-proof parka or shell, warm head- and hand gear, and waterproof or water-resistant boots. Heed the advice of locals who will tell you, "cotton kills." It does nothing to move moisture away from your skin, and can speed the onset of hypothermia. Any time you're in the wilderness, eat regularly to maintain energy, and stay hydrated.

Early symptoms of hypothermia are shivering, accelerated heartbeat, and goose bumps; this may be followed by clumsiness, slurred speech, disorientation, and unconsciousness. In the extreme, hypothermia can result in death. If you notice any of these symptoms in yourself or anyone in your group, stop, add layers of clothing, light a fire or camp stove, and warm up; a cup of tea or any hot fluid also helps. Avoid alcohol, which speeds hypothermia and impairs judgment. If your clothes are wet, change immediately. Be sure to put on a warm hat (most of the body's heat is lost through the head) and gloves. If there are only two of you, stay together: a person with hypothermia should never be left alone. Keep an eye on your traveling companions; frequently people won't recognize the symptoms in themselves until it's too late.

the Steese Highway. This 27-mi-long trail passes through alpine meadows and along mountain ridges, all above the tree line. It has two emergency shelters with water catchment systems, although no dependable water supply is available in the immediate vicinity. Most hikers spend three days making the trip.

RAFTING Rafting trips on the Charley River are for experts only. With access via a small plane, you can put in a raft at the headwaters of the river and travel 88 mi down this exhilarating, bouncing waterway. Contact the National Park Service (⇨ *see above*). The river here is too rough for kayaks and open canoes.

WINTER SPORTS Once past Mile 20 of the Steese Highway you enter a countryside that seems to have changed little in 100 years, even though you're only an hour from downtown Fairbanks. Mountains loom in the distance, and in winter a solid snowpack of 4 to 5 feet makes the area great for snowshoeing, backcountry skiing, and snowmachine riding.

MANLEY HOT SPRINGS

From Fairbanks: 73 mi north on Elliott Hwy. to Livengood, then 79 mi west on Elliott Hwy. to Manley.

The Elliott Highway, which starts in Fox, takes you to the Tanana River and the small community of **Manley Hot Springs**. A colorful, close-knit, end-of-the-road-type place, this town was a trading center for placer miners who worked the nearby creeks. Residents maintain a small public campground across from the Manley Roadhouse. Northern pike are caught in the nearby slough, and a dirt road leads to the Tanana River with its summer runs of salmon. The Manley Hot Springs Resort has closed, but the hot springs are only a short walk from the campground. The highway is paved for 28 mi outside Fairbanks. If you travel here over land, take a moment to reflect on how year-round access to Manley Hot Springs only became available as recently as 1982, when the state decided to start plowing the Elliott highway in winter.

OUTDOOR ACTIVITIES

HIKING   The BLM maintains the moderately difficult 20-mi **Summit Trail**, from the Elliott Highway, near Wickersham Dome, north into the White Mountains National Recreation Area. This nonmotorized trail can be explored as a day hike or in an overnight backpacking trip. It quickly rises into alpine country with 360-degree vistas that include abundant wildflowers and bird-watching in summer, blueberry picking in fall. This is not a loop trail, but ends at Beaver Creek. Be sure to bring water, as sometimes the sources are scarce, and take advantage of the rest shelter at Mile 8. You'll find the parking lot at Mile 28.

WHERE TO STAY

For expanded hotel reviews, visit Fodors.com.

¢–$ 🖼 **Manley Roadhouse.** Built in 1903 in the midst of the gold rush into the Interior, this roadhouse is among the oldest in Alaska. **Pros:** authentically historic building; location near hot springs; decent prices. **Cons:** no rooms have phones and not all have TVs. ✉ *Mi 152, Elliott Hwy.* ☎ *907/672–3161* ⊕ *www.manleyroadhouse.com* ⤴ *13 rooms, 6 with bath; 3 cabins* ⚒ *In-room: a/c (some), no TV (some). In-hotel: restaurant, bar, some pets allowed* ☽ *Closed Oct.–May.*

FORTYMILE COUNTRY

A trip through the Fortymile Country up the Taylor Highway will take you back in time more than a century—when gold was the lure that drew hardy travelers to Interior Alaska. It's one of the few places to see active mining without leaving the road system. In addition, remote wilderness experiences and float trips abound.

The 160-mi **Taylor Highway** runs north from the Alaska Highway at Tetlin Junction, 12 mi east of Tok. It's a narrow rough-gravel road that winds along mountain ridges and through valleys of the Fortymile River. The road passes the tiny community of Chicken and ends in Eagle at the Yukon River. This is one of only three places in Alaska where the Yukon River can be reached by road. A cutoff just south of Eagle connects to the Canadian Top of the World Highway leading to Dawson City in the Yukon Territory, which is the route many Alaskans take to Dawson City—far more scenic, and shorter, than the alternative of taking the Alcan to Whitehorse and then turning north. ⚠ **The highway is not plowed in winter, so it is snowed shut from fall to spring.** Watch for road equipment. If you're roughing it, know that *in addition to the lodging listed below,* the Alaska Bureau of Land Management also maintains three first-come, first-served campsites (as all BLM campsites are) on the Taylor Highway between Tetlin Junction and Eagle at Miles 48.5, 82, and 160.

Continued on page 399

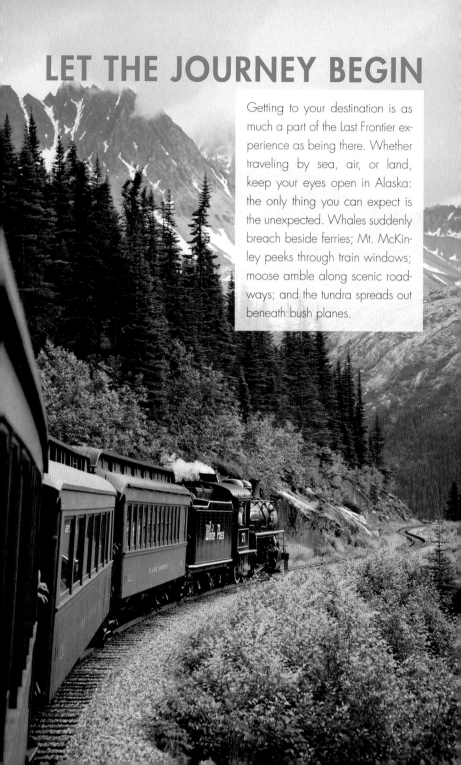

LET THE JOURNEY BEGIN

Getting to your destination is as much a part of the Last Frontier experience as being there. Whether traveling by sea, air, or land, keep your eyes open in Alaska: the only thing you can expect is the unexpected. Whales suddenly breach beside ferries; Mt. McKinley peeks through train windows; moose amble along scenic roadways; and the tundra spreads out beneath bush planes.

ON THE WATER

About 50% of visitors choose to cruise Alaska, but for a real adventure, travel Alaska Marine Highway System ferries. Either way, you'll see glaciers, forests, and maybe a whale or two.

The ferry system operates year-round and has two different routes: Bellingham, Washington to Skagway mimics the most popular cruise ship itinerary; the second route runs from Homer to the Aleutian Chain and Dutch Harbor.

Unlike cruise ships, which follow set itineraries, ferries come and go frequently for added flexibility. Consider, though, that they can arrive at inconvenient times whereas cruises dock for daytrips.

At first glance, the $363 one-way ticket from Bellingham to Skagway is a dream compared to the bare minimum $700 for a cruise ship berth. Add a cabin or bring a vehicle and the price can double or triple—and food isn't included. If you go without amenities, need to bring a car, or want flexibility, the ferry price is right; for those on a budget, an all-inclusive cruise may work better. The AlaskaPass can mitigate ferry costs if adding rail or car travel to a trip. (⇨ *Travel Smart Alaska*)

Ferries might not be as luxurious as cruise ships, but they're comfortable. Each has an observation lounge, and cafeterias serve inexpensive meals. Most cabins have private washrooms. Daring passengers sleep outside on cots beneath the heat lamps free of charge. ■TIP➜ The schedule comes out in January or February, and cabins fill up almost instantly for summer trips; advance booking is essential.

Ferry travel is, with a few exceptions, slow: maximum speed is 16.5 knots, compared with 21 knots or better for a cruise ship. Taking your time has its advantages, though; you'll take in the scenery with the locals who add their own color to the mix.

CONTACTS Alaska Marine Highway (☎ 907/465-3941 or 800/642-0066 ⊕ www.ferry-alaska.com). Pick up tickets at your starting point or have them mailed to you. Alaska-Pass (☎ 206/463-6550 or 800/248-7598 ⊕ www.alaskapass.com).

(left) The White Pass Yukon Route Railroad from Skagway on historic steam Engine 73;
(top right) Passenger stands at stern of Alaska Sate Ferry sailing along Inside Passage under light of midnight sun

ON THE PATH, OR OFF

These maps illustrate major ferry landings, scenic roads, and main rail lines. Beyond Southeast, South Central, and Interior Alaska, you're in the Bush—remote and accessible largely by small plane.

ROADS

With mountains, marine vistas, and miles of open tundra you'll be hard-pressed to find a drive in Alaska that isn't scenic, and not just because there are so few to find. There's always the potential for wildlife encounters, so be alert to something furry darting—or strolling, in the case of moose—out of the roadside brush.

Every year, tourists bring home on the road in RVs. Campgrounds can accommodate trailers, but only private RV parks have hookups. Most drives connect South Central and the Interior, but the Dalton takes adventurers to the Arctic Ocean.

RAILROADS

On Alaska's rails you'll ride history. Relive the Gold Rush on Southeast's only railroad, the cliff-hugging White Pass & Yukon Route, the same trail followed by prospectors.

In South Central, one of the best ways to see Alaska's myriad landscapes is to take the Alaska Railroad from Anchorage to Denali National Park. Don't forget to look for Mt. McKinley; while it's the highest peak in North America, it's frequently hidden in clouds.

PLANES

Bush planes are inextricably part of the Alaskan landscape. To get to that remote wilderness lodge or fly-fishing location, there's often no other choice. The flight you take to a native village off the road system is also a trip on that community's lifeline to the rest of the world.

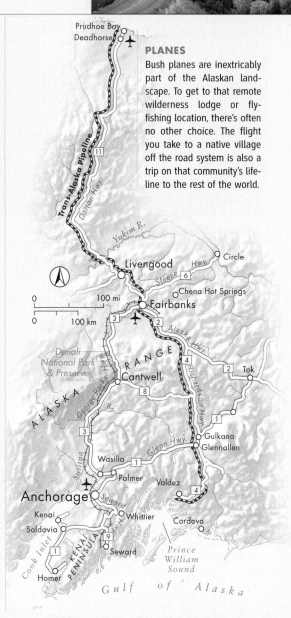

FERRIES

The thin strip of land and hodgepodge of islands that make up Southeast Alaska are best explored by ships or ferries. The Inside Passage is practically the only access point to the region's port towns. Even the state capital, Juneau, is only reached by sea or air.

The Kenai Peninsula and the Aleutian Islands are also popular ship or ferry destinations. If you choose to travel by ferry rather than cruise ship, there won't be endless shipboard entertainment, but on some vessels, forest service naturalists will provide a running commentary on the sights you pass.

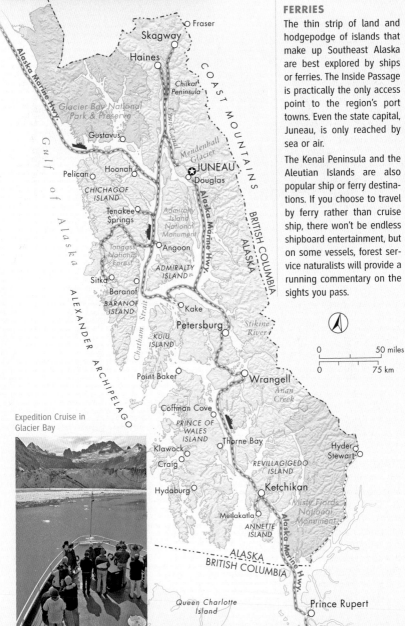

Expedition Cruise in Glacier Bay

0 ————— 50 miles
0 ————— 75 km

IN THE SKIES

No roads, rails, or even airstrips? No problem. Bush planes are meant to go where the trappings of civilization aren't, and pilots deftly land on riverbanks, fields, even water. Lake Hood, outside of Anchorage, is the world's busiest port for seaplanes (and a great place from which to charter a direct flight to remote wilderness spots). One in 78 residents here is a pilot—the most per capita in the U.S.

Bush planes aren't for everyone, though. Extremely nervous fliers should consider how to cope with the effects of updrafts, downdrafts, and even breezes—not to mention the sharp, steeply banked turns pilots make to view wildlife or scenery.

GETTING THERE. Because of the Alaska bypass-mail program (rural towns receive mail and goods at parcel-post rates through regional air carriers), there are more pre-scheduled flights to hidden-away villages than you might think. Flights travel from Anchorage and Fairbanks to regional hubs like Bethel, Nome, Kotzebue, Dillingham,

and Kodiak; you'll transfer at least once (sometimes the following day) to get elsewhere.

If you're on a tight schedule or headed to a location without mail service, charter an air taxi. When arranging a flight, ask for and check references, and inquire about insurance coverage and safety records—any hesitation to fully address your concerns is a sign to move on.

PACK RIGHT. As for what to wear, *always* carry rain gear. If traveling by floatplane, you can buy, borrow, or rent hip waders. Pack in small, soft-sided bags; gear gets stashed in a plane's nooks and crannies. Finally, don't schedule a small-plane pickup for the same day you're flying out of Alaska—weather can delay flights for days.

CONTACTS Commuter lines include Arctic Circle Air (⊕ www.arcticcircleair.com) and Era Alaska (⊕ www.flyera.com). For a list if Alaska air taxis, see ⊕ www.flyalaska.com. The National Transportation Safety Board keeps a database (⊕ www.ntsb.gov/ntsb/query.asp) of air taxi safety records.

(top) de Havilland Turbine Otter on skis near Alaska Range

ALONG THE RAILS

8

Sit back and relax as the train chugs along and the panorama of alpine meadows, snowcapped peaks, and taiga forests unfolds. There's not a bad seat in the house!

Alaska Railroad trains run between Seward and Fairbanks via Anchorage. The *Coastal Classic* goes from Seward to Anchorage in about 4 hours. The *Denali Star* makes the Anchorage to Fairbanks trip in 12 hours. Standard railroad-coach passengers have access to dining cars, lounges, and dome cars (with windows to the ceiling). One-way, peak-season tickets range from $70 to $320, depending on the route and seating class. Service is less expensive but limited off-season.

Princess Tours and Gray Line of Alaska run luxury class service in cars connected to Alaska Railroad trains between Anchorage and Fairbanks. Day- and multiday trips are available.

MOOSE SPOTTING. Conductors may encourage you to give a "moose salute" to passing trains (see photo.) Hold your hands up as though you're being held at gunpoint, and touch your thumbs to your temples to create moose antlers. It's a fun way to say hi to your fellow travelers.

RIDE HISTORY. Since 1923, Alaskans have been flagging down the *Hurricane Turn* much like you'd hail a taxi. One of the last flag-stop trains in America, it still makes unscheduled stops to transport locals to remote cabins in the Interior.

CONTACTS Alaska Railroad Corporation (☎ 907/265–2494 or 800/544–0552 ⊕ www.akrr.com). Gray Line of Alaska (☎ 206/281–3535 or 888/452-737 ⊕ www.graylinealaska.com). Princess Tours (☎ 800/774–6237 ⊕ www.princess.com).

HOW TO HAIL A TRAIN

■ Stand 25 feet from the tracks and wave a large, white cloth above your head.
■ The conductor will acknowledge you by blowing the train whistle.
■ When the train stops and the conductor opens the door (and not before), proceed toward the train.
■ Hop aboard with fellow homesteaders, hikers, and anglers.

(top) Friendly moosing—Seymour Levy, Fodors.com photo-contest winner

ON THE ROAD

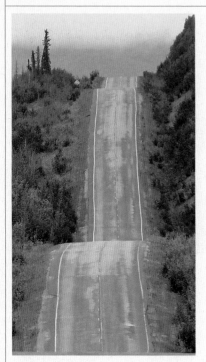

Alaska's highways may only reach a fraction of the state, but they get high marks for natural beauty, cultural and historic significance, and recreational opportunites. Here are our top picks.

SEWARD HIGHWAY
(127 mi, Anchorage to Seward)
Region: South Central (⇨ Ch. 6)
Points of Interest: This All-American Highway (the highest designation for a National Scenic Byway) shoulders Turnagain Arm and Chugach National Forest. Dall sheep roam the mountainsides, and beluga whales swim Cook Inlet. Just north of Seward is the easily accessible Exit Glacier.

GLENN HIGHWAY
(328 mi, Anchorage to Glennallen, Gakona Junction to Tok)
Region: South Central (⇨ Ch. 6)

Points of Interest: Chugach and Talkeetna mountains, Matanuska-Susitna Valley. At Mile 50, stop at the Musk Ox Farm to learn about the animal's rare underwool (*qiviut*); head to Matanuska Glacier at Mile 101.

GEORGE PARKS HIGHWAY
(358 mi, Wasilla to Fairbanks)
Regions: South Central and Interior (⇨ Chs. 6 & 7)
Points of Interest: Enter Denali National Park & Preserve at Mile 237. At the Mile 135 turnout get an exceptional view of Mt. McKinley and access Denali State Park.

RICHARDSON HIGHWAY
(364 mi, Fairbanks to Valdez)
Regions: South Central and Interior (⇨ Chs. 6 & 7)
Points of Interest: Wrangell–St. Elias National Park and Preserve. Mile 28 provides an eyeful of Worthington Glacier near Thompson Pass. See the tumbling waterfalls and rock walls of Keystone Canyon, 15 mi north of Valdez.

DALTON HIGHWAY
(414 mi, starting 84 miles north of Fairbanks near Livengood to Deadhorse)
Regions: Interior and the Bush (⇨ Chs. 7 & 8)
Points of Interest: Watch for caribou ducking under the above-ground portion of the Trans-Alaska Pipeline. Don't get so distracted you that miss Coldfoot— your last chance to get supplies before trekking the last 234 mi to Deadhorse.

FOR MORE INFO

The Milepost (⊕ *http://milepost.com*), an extensive guide to Alaska's roadways, is an absolute must. At the end of this book, you'll find safety tips and road rules in *Travel Smart Alaska*.

(top) Taylor Highway—Som Vembar, Fodors.com photo-contest participant

TOK

12 mi west of Tetlin Junction, 175 mi southwest of Dawson City.

Loggers, miners, old sourdoughs (Alaskan for "colorful local curmudgeons"), and hunting guides who live and work along Tok's streams or in the millions of acres of spruce forest nearby come here for supplies, at the junction of the Glenn Highway and the Alaska Highway. Each summer the city, with a resident population of fewer than 1,500, becomes temporary home to thousands of travelers, including adventurers journeying up the Alaska Highway from the Lower 48.

After crossing into Alaska from the Yukon Territory on the Alaska Highway, the first vestiges of what passes for civilization in the Far North are found in the town of Tok. Here you'll find a visitor center (one of the biggest in Alaska, since it serves as a center for roads branching across the state), food, fuel, hotels, and a couple of restaurants, and the need to make a decision.

Staying on the Alaska Highway and heading roughly west will take you into the Interior and to Fairbanks, whereas heading south on the Tok Cutoff will aim you toward South Central Alaska and the population center of Anchorage. Or you can make a huge loop tour, covering most of the paved highway in the state, taking in much of the terrific variety of landscapes and terrain that the 49th state has to offer. Head down the Tok Cutoff to the Richardson Highway (no one in Alaska uses the highway route numbers, and if you try to, you'll most likely just get blank stares), and then keep going south to Valdez. From there, catch the ferry to Whittier, Cordova, or Seward, explore the Kenai and Anchorage, then head north on the Seward Highway to the parks, to Denali, Fairbanks, and beyond. Loop back to Tok and you've seen most of what can be seen from the road system.

The **Tetlin National Wildlife Refuge** parallels the Alaska Highway for the first 65 highway mi after leaving Canada and offers two basic and seasonal campgrounds at Mileposts 1,249 and 1,256, or take a break from driving at Mile 1,240 and hike 1 mi over a raised-plank boardwalk to Hidden Lake. This 700,000-acre refuge has most of the charismatic megafauna that visitors travel to Alaska to see, including black and grizzly bears, moose, Dall sheep, wolves, caribou, and tons of birds. The visitor center at Mile 1,229 has a large deck with spotting scopes, and inside are maps, wildlife exhibits, books, and interpretive information, as well as a board with information on current road conditions. ⊠ *Mi 1,229, Alaska Hwy.* ☎ *907/883–5312* ⊕ *tetlin.fws.gov* 🖼 *Free* ☽ *Closed mid-Sept.–mid-May.*

To help with your planning, stop in at the **Tok Main Street Visitors Center** (⊠ *Mi 1,314, Alaska Hwy.* ☎ *907/883–5775* ⊕ *www.tokalaskainfo.com*), which has travel information covering the entire state, as well as wildlife and natural-history exhibits. The staff is quite helpful.

ESSENTIALS

Medical Assistance **Public Health Clinic** (⊠ *1,314 Alaska Hwy.* ☎ *907/883–4101*)

CLOSE UP

The Dalton Highway

Dalton Highway. Plenty of hardy, adventurous visitors are choosing to "do the Dalton," a 414-mi gravel highway that connects Interior Alaska to the oil fields at Prudhoe Bay on the Beaufort Sea. Alaska's northernmost highway, the Dalton was built in the mid-1970s so that trucks could haul supplies to Prudhoe and Trans-Alaska Pipeline construction camps in Alaska's northern reaches.

The pipeline is the main attraction for many who make it up this way: stretching 800 mi across the 49th state from Prudhoe Bay to Valdez, it's both an engineering marvel and a reminder of Alaska's economic dependence on oil production. It carries crude oil across three mountain ranges, 34 major rivers—including the Yukon—and hundreds of smaller creeks. It crosses permafrost regions and three major fault lines, too; half of the pipeline runs aboveground and is held aloft by 78,000 vertical supports that proved their ability to withstand sudden, violent ground shifts as recently as 2002 in a 7.9 magnitude quake along the Denali Fault.

Thousands of 18-wheelers still drive the formerly private Dalton each year, but since 1994 they've shared it with sightseers, anglers, and other travelers. That doesn't mean the Dalton is an easy drive. The road is narrow, often winding, and has several steep grades. Sections may be heavily potholed, and its coarse gravel is easily kicked up into headlights and windshields by fast-moving trucks. If you drive the Dalton in your own car, make sure you have windshield replacement insurance, because you positively will be making a claim when you get home. There are few visitor facilities along the way, and almost nowhere to get help if something goes

wrong. And with tow-truck charges of up to $5 per mile (both coming and going), a vehicle breakdown can cost hundreds of dollars even before repairs. Thus, before setting out, check everything you can in your car to make sure it's all working properly, and know how to change tires. Public access ends at **Deadhorse**, just shy of the Arctic coast. This town exists mainly to service the oil fields of Prudhoe Bay.

Unless you're an experienced outdoors person, areas off the Dalton Highway are best explored on a guided adventure tour. The only lodging options are down-at-the-heels motels or wilderness camping.

At **Coldfoot**, more than 250 mi north of Fairbanks, the Arctic Interagency Visitor Center (☎ 907/678–5209) provides information on road and backcountry conditions, along with recent wildlife spottings. A picnic area and a large, colorful sign mark the spot where the road crosses the Arctic Circle. ⚠ There are no services between Coldfoot and Prudhoe Bay, a distance of nearly 250 mi.

Oil-field tours (☎ 907/659–2368 or 866/659–2368 ⊕ www.arcticcaribouinn. com) and shuttles to the Arctic Ocean leave daily from the Arctic Caribou Inn in Deadhorse. The trips, through Tatqaani Tours, include a video presentation on the oil field and a tour of the grounds with a stop at the Arctic Ocean, providing a good sense of how industrialization has come to Alaska's North Slope. Tours run from mid-May to mid-September and require a minimum 24-hour advance reservation. For security reasons, you will need a valid photo ID (driver's license, state ID, or passport). Children must be accompanied by their legal guardian. The inn offers overnight accommodations, buffet-style breakfast, lunch, and dinner, Wi-Fi, cable TV, and tire repair.

TIPS FOR DOING THE DALTON:

■ Slow down and move to the side of the road for trucks.

■ Always leave your headlights on.

■ Yield on one-lane bridges.

■ Pull to the side of the road when stopping for pictures.

■ Carry at least one spare tire.

■ Consider bringing extra gas.

■ Purchase a citizens band (CB) radio.

Note: Not all car-rental companies allow their vehicles on this highway; check in advance.

OUTDOOR ACTIVITIES AND GUIDED TOURS

Although this is not a prime fishing area, fish, mostly grayling, populate the streams along the Dalton. You'll do better the farther you hike from the road, where less-motivated fishermen are weaned out. Lakes along the road contain grayling, and some have lake trout and arctic char. The Alaska Department of Fish and Game's pamphlet "Sport Fishing along the Dalton Highway" is available at the Alaska Public Lands Information Center (⇨ *Fairbanks Essentials, above*).

Alaskan Arctic Turtle Tours (☎ 907/457–1798 or 888/456–1798 ⊕ www.wildalaska.info) specializes in Dalton Highway–area trips, with tours in 15-passenger vans.

Coyote Air (✉ Mi 175, Dalton Hwy., Coldfoot ☎ 907/678–5995, 800/252–0603 mid-May–mid-Sept., 907/479–5995 in winter ⊕ www.flycoyote.com) is a family-run bush-plane service that

specializes in scenic flights, backcountry trip support, and fall hunting trips in the Brooks Range.

Marina Air Fly-In Fishing (✉ 1195 Shypoke Dr., Fairbanks ☎ 907/479–5684 ⊕ www.akpikefishing.com) has fly-in trips to remote lakes for northern pike, rainbow trout, grayling, and silver salmon. Overnight packages with a cabin are $200.

Northern Alaska Tour Company (☎ 907/474–8600 or 800/474–1986 ⊕ www.northernalaska.com) is the most established Dalton Highway tour company. It has numerous trips to the Arctic Circle and beyond, some with fly-drive options that operate year-round.

WHERE TO STAY

For expanded hotel reviews, visit Fodors.com.

Here are the most accessible options for the trip north. *For details on options in Prudhoe Bay or Deadhorse, see Prudhoe Bay.*

$$$ ☷ **Coldfoot Camp.** Fuel, tire repairs, and towing are available here. **Pros:** guided outdoor activities available. **Cons:** basic rooms; greasy road food. ✉ Mi 175, Dalton Hwy., Coldfoot ☎ 866/474–3400 ⊕ www.coldfootcamp.com ⌑ 106 rooms ⌂ In-room: no a/c, no TV. In-hotel: restaurant, bar, laundry facilities.

$$$ ☷ **Yukon River Camp.** You'll find a motel, a tire-repair shop, and gasoline, diesel, and propane here. **Pros:** tire-repair shop. **Cons:** no private bath. ✉ Mi 56, Dalton Hwy. ☎ 907/474–3557 ⊕ www.yukonrivercamp.com ⌑ 42 rooms without private baths ⌂ In-room: no a/c, no TV. In-hotel: restaurant, laundry facilities ☉ Closed Oct.–Apr.

8

WHERE TO EAT

$$$
AMERICAN
✕ **Fast Eddy's Restaurant.** It's much better than the name would indicate: the chef makes his own noodles for chicken noodle soup, and the homemade hoagies and pizza are a welcome relief from the roadhouse hamburgers served by most Alaska Highway restaurants. It's open late, but the soup is usually gone by 5. ⊠ *Mi 1,313.3, Alaska Hwy.* ☎ *907/883–4411.*

WHERE TO STAY

For expanded hotel reviews, visit Fodors.com.

ON THE DEFENSIVE

Ft. Greely, which is 5 mi south of Tok toward Valdez, contains a growing number of underground silos with missiles that are part of the Ballistic Missile Defense System. The missiles are connected to tracking stations elsewhere and would be launched to try to shoot down enemy missiles in space if the United States were ever so attacked.

$$ **Cleft of the Rock Bed & Breakfast.** With options for larger families and couples, this B&B offers either picturesque private cabins or comfortable rooms. **Pros:** cabins with all the comforts of home; on-site basketball courts; close to town. **Cons:** no guided activities; no air-conditioning. ⊠ *Box 245, 0.5 Sundog Trail, off Mi 1,316.5 of Alaska Hwy.* ☎ *907/883–4219* ⊕ *www.cleftoftherock.net* ⤳ *5 cabins, 3 rooms* ⚘ *In-room: no a/c, Wi-Fi (some). In-hotel: some pets allowed* ⊙ *Cabins closed end Sept.–mid-May, rooms open year-round* ⏐○⏐ *Breakfast,*

¢   **Gateway Salmon Bake RV Park.** Behind the former Gateway Salmon Bake are a full-service RV park and a very clean shower facility if you need to hose off the road dust from the long drive. ⊠ *Mi 1,313.1, Alaska Hwy.* ☎ *907/883–5578* ⊙ *Closed Sept.–mid-May.*

$ **Westmark Tok.** Made up of a series of interconnected buildings, the hotel has been updated and has decent accommodations for this remote part of Alaska. **Pros:** satellite TV; margaritas to get lost in; some pets allowed. **Cons:** not for those looking for lots of in-room character. **TripAdvisor:** "friendly and welcoming," "basic but clean and comfortable," "very nice restaurant." ⊠ *Junction of Alaska and Glenn Hwys., Tok* ☎ *907/883–5174 or 800/544–0970* ⊕ *www.westmarkhotels.com* ⤳ *92 rooms* ⚘ *In-room: a/c. In-hotel: restaurant, bar, laundry facilities, business center, some pets allowed* ⊙ *Closed mid-Sept.–mid-May.*

SHOPPING

The **Burnt Paw** (⊠ *Mi 1,314.3, Alaska Hwy.* ☎ *907/883–4121* ⊕ *www. burntpawcabins.com*) sells Alaska jade, gold, Native crafts, quality apparel, and even sled-dog puppies. On display is a sled-dog and equipment exhibit. There are also log cabin B&B rentals with traditional sod roofs. This is the place to be for the best breakfast in Tok. In Northway, south of Tok, **Naabia Niign** (⊠ *Mi 1,264, Alaska Hwy.* ☎ *907/778–2234*) is a Native-owned crafts gallery with an excellent selection of authentic, locally made birch baskets, beadwork items, fur moccasins, and gloves. The friendly staff also operate a general store, gas station, bar, and RV park.

WHERE TO PLAY ON THE WAY

If you're headed to Fortymile Country from Fairbanks, you'll drive along the historic Richardson Highway, once a pack-train (think mules with bags) trail and dogsled route for mail carriers and gold miners in the Interior. As quirky places to turn off a highway go, North Pole and Delta Junction are up there with the best of them.

NORTH POLE

It may be a featureless suburb of Fairbanks, but you'd have to be a Scrooge not to admit that this town's year-round acknowledgement of the December holiday season is at least a little bit fun to take in. If you stop in North Pole, don't skip the **Santa Claus House Gift Shop** (⊠ 101 St. Nicholas Dr. ☎ 907/488–2200 or 800/588–4078 ⊕ www.santaclaushouse.com). Look for the giant Santa statue and the Christmas mural on the side of the building. You'll find toys, gifts, and Alaskan handicrafts; Santa is often on duty to talk to children.

The **Knotty Shop** (⊠ Mi 332, 6565 Richardson Hwy., 32 mi south of Fairbanks ☎ 907/488–3014) has a large selection of Alaskan handicrafts as well as a mounted wildlife display and a yard full of spruce-burl sculptures, including a 6-foot mosquito and other wooden animals that photographers find hard to resist. Get served soft drinks, coffee, and ice cream over a spruce-burl counter.

DELTA JUNCTION

A good 100 mi southeast of Fairbanks, Delta is not only a handy stop on the Richardson Highway but is also the official western terminus of the Alaska Highway. It's no surprise,

then, that in summer Delta becomes a bustling rest stop for road-weary travelers. On top of this, it's the largest agricultural center in Alaska, boasting a local farmers' market, meat-and-sausage company, and dairy. Delta is also known for its access to good fishing and its proximity to the Delta Bison Range. Don't expect to see the elusive 500-strong bison herd, though, as they roam free and generally avoid people.

At the actual junction of the Alaska and Richardson highways, stop in the **Delta Chamber of Commerce** (⊕ Box 987, Delta Junction 99737 ☎ 907/895–5068 or 877/895–5068 ⊕ www.deltachamber.org) for more information on the area. Across the street are the **Sullivan Roadhouse Historical Museum** and the **Highway's End Farmer's Market**, open on Wednesday and Saturday mid-May to early September 10 am–3 pm. If you'd like to try local dairy and meat, check out the **Buffalo Center Drive-In** (☎ 907/895–4055 ⊙ May–late Aug., daily 11–10) just south of the Sullivan Roadhouse. Historic landmark **Rika's Roadhouse** (⊠ Mi 275, Richardson Hwy. 99737 ☎ 907/895–4201 ⊕ www.rikas.com), part of Big Delta State Historical Park, is a good detour for the free tours of the beautifully restored and meticulously maintained grounds, gardens, and historic buildings. Don't forget to try the delicious baked goods for lunch or breakfast.

8

CHICKEN

78 mi north of Tok, 109 mi west of Dawson City.

BORDER CROSSING

Crossing into Interior Alaska from the Lower 48 or from the ferry terminals in the Southeast requires border crossings into Canada and then into Alaska. Be very certain of all the requirements for crossing an international border before you travel, including restrictions on pets and firearms and the need for adequate personal identification for every member of the party. Know that even citizens of Canada and the United States traveling between Alaska and Canada are now required to have a passport.

Chicken was, and still is, the heart of the southern Fortymile Mining District, and many of these works are visible along the highway. Chicken (the story goes: they wanted to name the town "Ptarmigan," but nobody new how to spell that), the second town in Alaska to be incorporated, has only a handful of permanent residents, mostly miners and trappers, creating an authentic frontier atmosphere. Do not encroach on private property, as miners rarely have a sense of humor about trespassing. Overland travel to Dawson City winds along a gravel road. Some drivers love it, some white-knuckle it. The road still closes for the entire winter, but in February and March snow-machiners hold a "poker run" on the road from Tok to Dawson City (⊕ *www.alaskatrailblazers.com*). Chicken only has three businesses in town, but what it lacks in infrastructure, it makes up for in atmosphere.

Get a feel for the past on a gold-mining adventure, where finder's keepers is the name of the game (in 2008 one participant walked away with a 1.4-ounce nugget), or tour the historic Pedro Dredge at 9 am and 1 pm daily at the Chicken Gold Camp & Outpost. The Gold Camp also provides meals, drinks, cabins, a campground–RV park, showers, free Wi-Fi, firewood, and espresso, as well as kayaking and other activities. Bluegrass lovers will appreciate the Chickenstock Music Festival on the second weekend in June.

Downtown Chicken, the longest running business in town, has classic wooden porches and provides multiple services: the Chicken Creek Cafe; a saloon; liquor store; emporium with gifts and odds and ends; free Wi-Fi; and overnight parking, rental cabins, and wall tents, along with gas and diesel service. Wild Alaskan baked salmon is available for lunch and dinner.

All in one establishment, you'll find Chicken Creek RV Park & Cabins, the Historic Town of Chicken, and the Goldpanner Gift Shop, which offers free Wi-Fi and an ATM. The RV park has gas and diesel, cabins, hostel rooms, and camping sites. Activities include gold panning and daily tours of Tisha's Schoolhouse at 9 am and 2 pm.

SPORTS, THE OUTDOORS, AND GUIDED TOURS

CANOEING The beautiful **Fortymile River** offers everything from a 38-mi run to a lengthy journey to the Yukon and then down to Eagle. Its waters range from easy Class I to serious Class IV (possibly Class V) stretches. Only experienced canoeists should attempt boating on this river, and rapids should be scouted beforehand. Several access points can be found off the Taylor Highway.

Since 1980 **Canoe Alaska** (☎ *907/883–2628* ⊕ *www.canoealaska.net*) has conducted guided canoe and raft trips on Interior Alaska rivers. Trips (mid-May–Labor Day) range from two to eight days on rivers that vary in difficulty and remoteness. Evening interpretive tours in the *Arctic Voyageur,* a replica of a 34-foot voyageur canoe, are offered on a lake. Multiday *Voyageur* trips, canoe instruction, and rentals to qualified paddlers are also available.

EAGLE

95 mi north of Chicken, 144 mi northwest of Dawson City. Road closed in winter.

Eagle was once a seat of government and commerce for the Interior. An Army post, Ft. Egbert, operated here until 1911, and territorial judge and noted Alaska historian James Wickersham had his headquarters in Eagle until Fairbanks began to grow from its gold strike. The population peaked at 1,700 in 1898. Today there are fewer than 200 residents. Although the majority of the population is gone, the town still retains its frontier and gold-rush character.

The Yukon River has shaped Eagle in more ways than just geographically. In earlier times it provided a vital mode of transportation. Today vacationers use Eagle as a jumping-off point for self-planned journeys through the Yukon–Charley Rivers National Preserve. Eagle was devastated by a flood in 2009, fortunately most historical structures were left undamaged.

The **Eagle Historical Society** (✉ *1st and Berry St.* ☎ *907/547–2325* ⊕ *www. eagleak.org*) has a two- to three-hour walking tour ($7) that visits six museum buildings while regaling participants with tales of the famous people (including Arctic explorer Roald Amundsen and aviation pioneer Billy Mitchell) who have passed through this historic Yukon River border town. One daily tour begins at the courthouse at 9 am from Memorial Day to Labor Day; special tours are available with advance notice. For the extra-curious traveler, there is an extensive archive and photo collection with staff available to help dig into the late 1800s at the office on 3rd and Chamberlain streets. In addition, the Museum Store offers locally made items and locally oriented books.

The **National Park Service and BLM Visitor Center** (✉ *100 Front St.* ☎ *907/547–2233* ⊕ *www.nps.gov/yuch*) is the headquarters for the 2.5-million-acre Yukon–Charley Rivers National Preserve. Informal interpretive programs, talks, and videos are available. Peruse the reference library, maps, and books for sale. It's located off 1st Avenue by the airstrip and the Yukon River, and is open Memorial Day to Labor Day.

8

YUKON TERRITORY

Gold! The happy, shining promise of gold is what called Canada's Yukon Territory to the world's attention with the Klondike Gold Rush of 1897–98. Maybe as many as 100,000 people set off for the confluence of the Yukon and Klondike Rivers, on the promise of gold nuggets the size of poodles just waiting to be picked up. In the end, roughly a dozen of them went home rich, but they all went home rich in memories and stories that are still being told.

Though the international border divides Alaska from Yukon Territory, the Yukon River tends to unify the region. Early prospectors, miners, traders, and camp followers moved readily up and down the river with little regard to national boundaries. An earlier Alaska strike preceded the Klondike find by years, yet Circle was all but abandoned in the stampede to the creeks around Dawson City. Later gold discoveries in the Alaskan Fortymile Country, Nome, and Fairbanks reversed that flow across the border into Alaska.

DAWSON CITY

109 mi east of Chicken.

Dawson City, one of the most beautiful, coolest towns in the north, is the prime specimen of a Yukon gold-rush town. Since the first swell of hopeful migrants more than 100 years ago, many of the original buildings have disappeared, victims of fire, flood, and weathering. But plenty remain, and it's easy to step back in time, going to a performance at the Palace Theatre, originally built in 1899, or stepping into a shop whose building originally went up to serve stampeders. In modern Dawson City street paving seems erratic at best, and the place maintains a serious frontier vibe. But it's also a center for the arts—the Dawson City Music Festival, held each summer, is one of the biggest in Canada, as the whole town turns into one big party and all kinds of music echoes under the midnight sun—and as the last touch of civilization before the deep wild, hikers share tables with hardcore miners at the local restaurants.

In the years leading up to the turn of the 20th century Dawson was transformed from a First Nations camp into the largest, most refined city north of Seattle and west of Winnipeg. It had grand buildings with running water, telephones, and electricity. In 1899 the city's population numbered almost 30,000—a jump of about 29,900 over the previous few years—which all but overwhelmed the Tr'ondëk Hwëch'in, the First Nations Hän-speaking people that inhabited the area. Their chief, a man named Isaac, who is still revered as the savior of the culture, packed his people up and moved them from the confluence, where they had hunted and fished for thousands of years, to the village of Moosehide a few miles downstream. The town he left behind grew into a place where a fresh egg could cost the equivalent of a day's salary down south, and where one of the most profitable jobs was panning gold dust out of the sawdust scattered on saloon floors.

ALASKA HIGHWAY HISTORY

It's hard to overestimate the importance of the Alaska Highway in the state's history. Before World War II there was no road connection between the Alaskan Interior and the rest of North America. Alaska's population center was in the coastal towns of the Southeast panhandle region, and most of the state's commerce was conducted along its waterways. Access to the Interior was via riverboat until 1923, when the railroad connection from Seward through Anchorage and into Fairbanks was completed.

The onset of World War II changed everything. An overland route to the state was deemed a matter vital to national security, to supply war material to the campaign in the Aleutians, and to fend off a potential invasion by Japan. In a feat of amazing engineering and construction prowess, the 1,500-mi-long route was carved out of the wilderness in eight months in 1942. The original road was crude but effective (the first truck to travel it made a blazing average speed of 15 mph), and has been undergoing constant maintenance and upgrading ever since. Today the highway is easily traversed by every form of highway vehicle imaginable, from bicycles and motorcycles to the biggest, lumbering RVs, known not so affectionately by locals as "road barns."

Today Dawson City is home to about 1,800 people, 400 of whom are of First Nation descent. The city itself is now a National Historic Site of Canada. Besides being one of the coolest, funkiest towns in the north, Dawson also serves as a base from which to explore the Tombstone Territorial Park located on the Dempster Highway, a region sometimes referred to as the "Patagonia of the northern hemisphere": a natural wonderland, with plants and animals found nowhere else, living in the spaces between high, steep mountain ranges.

8

GETTING HERE AND AROUND

The Alaska Highway starts in Dawson Creek, British Columbia, and goes almost 1,500 mi to Fairbanks. Drivers traveling north and southbound on the Alaska Highway can make a loop with the Taylor Highway route. This adds 100 mi to the trip, but is worth it. Part with the Alaska Highway at Tetlin Junction and wind through the Fortymile Country past the little communities of Chicken and Jack Wade Camp into Canada. The border is open 8 am to 8 pm in summer. The Canadian section of the Taylor Highway is called Top of the World Highway, and with most of it on a ridgeline between two huge valleys, it really does feel like the top of the world, opening broad views of range after range of tundra-covered mountains stretching in every direction. Join back with the Alaska Highway at Whitehorse.

Numerous bus companies offer package tours or simple shuttle services (⇨ *see Whitehorse Essentials, below*). Regular air service to Dawson flies from Fairbanks in summer. **Air North, Yukon's Airline,** based in Whitehorse, offers direct air service from Whitehorse to Dawson City in summer.

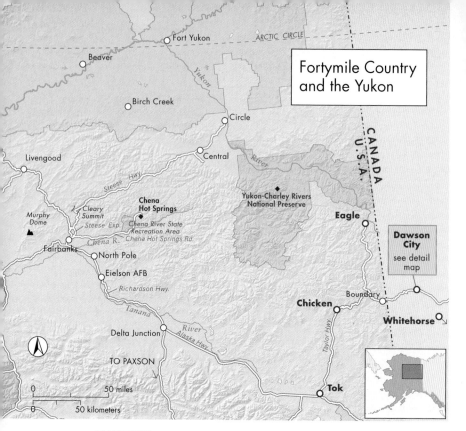

Fortymile Country and the Yukon

ESSENTIALS

Airline Information Air North, Yukon's Airline (☎ 800/661–0407 ⊕ www.flyairnorth.com).

Emergency Assistance Royal Canadian Mounted Police (☎ 867/993–2677, 867/993–5555 for emergencies ⊕ www.rcmp.ca).

Internet Tasty Byte Internet Cafe (✉ 1076 Front St. ☎ 867/993–6100).

Medical Assistance Dawson Health Center (✉ 530 Church St. ☎ 867/993–4444).

Visitor and Tour Information Klondike Visitors Association (✉ 1102 Front St. ☎ 867/993–5575 ⊕ www.dawsoncity.ca ⊙ Year-round). **Visitor Information Centre** (✉ 1102 Front St. ☎ 867/993–5566 ⊙ Early May–late Sept.).

EXPLORING

Dänojà Zho Cultural Centre creates an inviting atmosphere in which to explore the Tr'ondëk Hwëch'in heritage. For countless generations this group of Hän-speaking people lived in the Yukon River drainage of western Yukon and eastern Alaska. This specific language group settled around the mouth of the Klondike River. Through seasonal displays, tours, cultural activities, films, and performances, learn about the traditional and contemporary life of "the people of the river." The gift shop celebrates fine First Nations art, offering unique clothing, beaded footwear, music, and books. The displays are kind of sparse, but it's good to stop in and see what the gold rush was like for the people who were here first and saw there was more value to a good caribou hunt than a bunch of shiny stuff in the ground. ⊠ *1131 Front St., across from Visitor Information Centre* ☎ *867/993–6768* ⊕ *www. trondekheritage.com* ⊠ *$5* ☺ *May–Sept., Mon.–Sat. 10–6.*

The **Dawson City Museum**, housing the Yukon's largest collection, presents exhibits focusing on the gold rush, but also includes the geology and prehistory of the Klondike, as well as of the First Nations. Downstairs offers excellent displays of gold rush material; it might surprise you just how luxurious Dawson managed to be for the lucky few.

A GOOD WALK

Dawson City is small enough that you can walk end to end in about twenty minutes—if you stop and spend five of those watching the river flow by. The Visitor Information Centre has an excellent walking map of town, and following it is one of the best things you can do while here. A lot of the old buildings have displays in the windows showing what they once were—bank, blacksmith, etc. A couple of older buildings have also been filled with historic photos and information Follow the map, or just wander around; it's all worth checking out. Walking tours—in English, French, and Dutch—leave regularly from the VIC.

Upstairs are more household goods, which most people skim through, but don't miss the piece of mammoth meat on the stairway landing. Not many places where you'll see that. Four restored locomotives and other railway cars and gear from the Klondike Mines Railway are housed in an adjacent building, which tends to open at odd hours. The museum also features a library and archives. Daily programs and costumed interpreters are featured during the summer season. ⊠ *Territorial Administration Bldg., 5th Ave.* ☎ *867/993–5291* ⊕ *www.dawsonmuseum.ca* ⊠ *C$9* ☺ *Mid-May–Labor Day, daily 10–6; call ahead for winter visits.*

Diamond Tooth Gerties Gambling Hall (⊠ *Queen and 4th Sts.* ☎ *867/993–5575* ⊕ *www.dawsoncity.ca*), for adults 19 and over only, presents nightly live entertainment and high-energy performances, including cancan, seven days a week from May until late September. It is the only authentic, legal gambling establishment operating in all of the North and the oldest in Canada, although it's mostly just slots and a few table games. Yes, there really was a Diamond Tooth Gertie—Gertie Lovejoy, a prominent dance-hall queen who had a diamond between her two front teeth.

Parks Canada leads tours of **Gold Dredge Number 4**, a wooden-hull gold dredge along Bonanza Creek, about 20 minutes outside town. The one-hour walking tour takes you into what's billed as "the largest wooden hulled, bucket line gold dredge in North America." When it was in operation the dredge ate rivers whole, spitting out gravel and keeping gold for itself. (To get an idea of how much area the dredge affected, think of the economics of this: hauling this enormous piece of machinery this far into the middle of nowhere, at a time when gold was worth less than

8

$20 per ounce, and still making money.) Tours also include a short film about the site and the relocation of the dredge. Nearby you can visit working gold mines or pan for gold yourself in Bonanza Creek, where the Klondike Visitors Association offers a free claim for visitors. Be sure to bring your own supplies (almost every gift shop in town sells gold pans). Exit the Klondike Highway at Km Marker 74. ⊠ *Mi 8, Bonanza Creek Rd.* ☏ *867/993–7200* ⊕ *www.pc.gc.ca* ☜ *C$6.30* ☉ *End May–mid-Sept., daily 10–4; restoration work continues on dredge, so please confirm ahead.*

Jack London Museum (⊠ *8th Ave. and Firth St.* ☏ *867/993–5575* ☜ *C$2* ☉ *May–Sept., daily interpretation presentations*) is literally a stone's throw from Robert Service's cabin. This reproduction of London's home from 1897 to 1898 is constructed with half of the wood from his original wilderness home that was found south of Dawson in the 1930s. The other half was sent to Oakland, California, where a similar structure sits at Jack London Square. The small museum contains photos, documents, and letters from London's life and the gold-rush era. Half-hour talks are given twice daily during peak season.

Scholars still argue the precise details of the lives of writers Robert Service (1874–1958) and Jack London (1876–1916) in Dawson City, but no one disputes that between Service's poems and London's short stories the two did more than anyone else to popularize and romanticize the Yukon. Service lived in his Dawson cabin from 1909 to 1912. The **Robert Service Cabin** (⊠ *8th Ave. and Hanson St.* ☏ *867/993–7237* ☜ *C$6*) is open for visitors June through mid-September, and holds multiple daily readings, including an evening program.

SPORTS, THE OUTDOORS, AND GUIDED TOURS

BOATING The **Klondike River Float Trip** (☏ *867/993–5599 or 800/544–2206* ⊕ *www.graylineyukon.com*) offers a chance to relax on a Class I river. You can put in at the Dempster Highway Bridge or Rock Creek. The journey ends when the Klondike spits you into the Yukon River at Dawson. Don't forget to take advantage of photo ops along the way. Other options include a guided 3½-hour float trip for $75 or a 3½-hour jeep tour for $95. Pick-up is at Westmark Dawson City.

HIKING **Tombstone Territorial Park** (⊠ *Box 600, Dawson City* ☏ *867/993–6850 in Dawson City, 867/667–5648 in Whitehorse, 866/617–2757 toll-free* ⊕ *www.yukonparks.ca* ☉ *Interpretation center open late May–mid-Sept.*), located 1½ hours north of Dawson City and bisected by the Dempster Highway, is a 2,200-square-km (850-square-mi) area dubbed the "Patagonia of the northern hemisphere." Here you'll find some of the best hiking and views of granite peaks in the Yukon. The unique geology and geography of this wilderness supports a vast array of wildlife and vegetation. The park maintains four day-use trails at Km markers 58, 72, 75, and 78, along with one campground and a new interpretation center at Km Marker 71.4, with good displays and great views of the mountains. It's worth stopping in to see how animals make it through the winter here. Throughout the park, backcountry mountaineering and wildlife-viewing options are endless. You can book flightseeing trips over the jagged Tombstones from Dawson City.

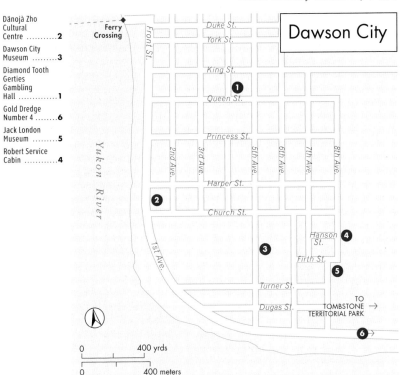

WHERE TO STAY

For expanded hotel reviews, visit Fodors.com.

$$$ ⊞ **Bombay Peggy's.** Named and fashioned after one of the last of Daw-
★ son's legal madams, Peggy's is done in elaborate Victorian gold-rush
style, with heavy, plush draperies and rich color schemes. **Pros:** little
imagination is needed to step back in time thanks to elaborate refurbish-
ing; nice touches like fresh croissants and the "Sherry Hour." **Cons:** no
elevator; not all rooms have air-conditioning. ⊠ *2nd Ave. and Princess
St.* ☎ *867/993–6969* ⊕ *www.bombaypeggys.com* ⊸ *3 rooms, 6 suites*
⚑ *In-room: a/c (some), Wi-Fi* ⊺⊙⊩ *Breakfast.*

$$ ⊞ **Downtown Hotel.** A large collection of local artwork, including mushing scenes and antiques, adds to the hotel's early-1900s decorations.
Pros: courtyard of the annex building has a hot tub; in the heart of
downtown. **Cons:** not all rooms have air-conditioning. ⊠ *2nd Ave.
and Queen St.* ☎ *867/993–5346, 800/661–0514 reservations* ⊕ *www.
downtownhotel.ca* ⊸ *59 rooms, 5 suites* ⚑ *In-room: a/c (some), kitchen
(some), Wi-Fi. In-hotel: restaurant, bar, laundry facilities.*

$$ ⊞ **Eldorado Hotel.** The pioneer-style front to this hotel may be mislead-
ing, as the modern rooms, some with kitchenettes, are outfitted with
decidedly non-1898 amenities such as cable TV. **Pros:** in-hotel bar and
restaurant; top off the evening with a drink at the Sluice Box Lounge.

Cons: no elevator. ⊠ *3rd Ave. and Princess St.* ☎ *867/993–5451, 800/764–3536 from Alaska and Canada* ⊕ *www.eldoradohotel.ca* ⤴ *46 rooms, 16 suites* ⌂ *In-room: a/c (some), kitchen (some), Wi-Fi. In-hotel: restaurant, bar, laundry facilities.*

$$ ⊤ **Triple J Hotel.** Log cabins with kitchenettes, a central hotel, and a detached annex make up this clean, quiet compound next to Diamond Tooth Gerties. **Pros:** coffeemakers and coffee in every room; coin-operated laundry facilities. **Cons:** some rooms could use a face-lift; no DVD or VCR. ⊠ *5th Ave. and Queen St.* ☎ *867/993–5323 or 800/764–3555* ⊕ *www.triplejhotel.com* ⤴ *27 rooms, 22 cabins* ⌂ *In-room: kitchen (some), Wi-Fi. In-hotel: restaurant, bar, laundry facilities.*

$$ ⊤ **Westmark Dawson City.** This downtown two-story hotel is built around a central courtyard and is convenient to the sights. **Pros:** good location; laundry facilities; gold-rush ambience. **Cons:** no elevator; not all rooms have air-conditioning. ⊠ *5th Ave. and Harper St.* ☎ *867/993–5542, 800/544–0970 reservations* ⊕ *www.westmarkhotels.com* ⤴ *177 rooms* ⌂ *In-room: a/c (some), Wi-Fi. In-hotel: restaurant, bar, laundry facilities, business center, some pets allowed* ⊗ *Closed mid-Sept.–mid-May.*

DAWSON CITY MUSIC FESTIVAL

The Dawson City Music Festival, held every July, is the town's biggest party: at venues across town, from a big tent near the museum to inside the beautiful Palace Theatre, musicians from around Canada and around the world get together to jam. The entire town turns out, every hotel room is full, every camping spot taken, and there is no better time to be in Dawson. ⊕ *www.dcmf.com*

WHITEHORSE

337 mi southeast of Dawson City, 600 mi southeast of Fairbanks.

Near the White Horse Rapids of the Yukon River, Whitehorse began as an encampment in the late 1890s, a logical layover for gold rushers heading north along the Chilkoot Trail toward Dawson. The next great population boom came during World War II with the building of the Alcan—the Alaska-Canada Highway. Today this city of more than 22,000 residents is Yukon's center of commerce (only Walmart and Tim Horton's for hundreds of miles), communication, and transportation and the seat of the territorial government.

Besides being a great starting point for explorations of other areas of the Yukon, the town has plenty of diversions and recreational opportunities. You can spend a day exploring its museums and cultural displays—research the Yukon's mining and development history, look into the backgrounds of the town's founders, learn about its indigenous First Nations people, and gain an appreciation of the Yukon Territory from prehistoric times up to the present.

GETTING HERE AND AROUND

Air Canada flies in summer from Anchorage through Vancouver to Whitehorse. **Air North Yukon's Airline** (yes, that's really the name), based in Whitehorse, offers direct, seasonal air service between Alaska and

Canada, flying regular runs from Fairbanks (summer only), Dawson City, and Whitehorse.

To take in all the scenery along the way, you can drive yourself up the Alcan Highway, or let someone else do the driving on a bus tour. Alaska Direct Bus travels to Anchorage and Fairbanks year-round. Alaska/Yukon Trails provides tours from Whitehorse to Dawson City to Fairbanks. MGM Bus Services offers service from Inuvik to Whitehorse year-round when weather permits; charter trips are available. There are multiple rental-car companies, buses, and taxis in Whitehorse; Whitehorse Transit has a city bus circuit that will get you where you need to go.

ESSENTIALS

Airline Contacts Air Canada (☎ 888/247–2262 ⊕ www.aircanada.com). **Air North Yukon's Airline** (☎ 800/661–0407 or 876-668-228 ⊕ www.flyairnorth. com).

Bus Contacts Alaska Direct Bus (⊠ 501 Ogilvie St. ☎ 800/770–6652 in Alaska, 867/668–4833 in Canada ⊕ www.alaskadirectbusline.com). **Alaska/ Yukon Trails** (☎ 800/770–7275 ⊕ www.alaskashuttle.com). **Atlin Express** (☎ 867/668–4444). **Gray Line** (☎ 867/668–3225 or 800/544–2206 ⊕ www. graylineyukon.com). **MGM Bus Services** (☎ 867/777–4295 or 867/678–0129).

City Bus Whitehorse Transit (⊠ 139 Tlingit St. ☎ 867/668–8394 ⊕ www. whitehorse.ca ☜ C$2.50).

Currency Exchange Bank of Montreal (⊠ 111 Main St. ☎ 867/393–8160). **Scotiabank** (⊠ 212 Main St. ☎ 867/667–6231).

Emergency Assistance Royal Canadian Mounted Police (☎ 867/667–5555).

Internet Whitehorse Public Library (⊠ 2071 2nd Ave., Downtown ☎ 867/667–5239 ⊕ www.ypl.gov.yk.ca) has free 60-minute Internet use.

Medical Assistance Medicine Chest Pharmacy (⊠ 406 Lambert St. ☎ 867/668–7000). **Second Avenue Walk-In Clinic** (⊠ 2131 2nd Ave, Suite 102 ☎ 867/667–6119). **Whitehorse General Hospital** (⊠ 5 Hospital Rd. ☎ 867/393–8700).

Post Office Canada Post (⊠ 300 Range Rd. ☎ 867/668-2195).

Rental Cars Budget Rent-A-Car (☎ 867/667–6200 or 800/268–8900 ⊕ www. budget.com). **National Car Rental** (☎ 867/456–2277 or 800/661–0445 ⊕ www.nationalcar.com). **Whitehorse Subaru** (☎ 867/393–6550 ⊕ www. whitehorsesubaru.com).

Taxis 5th Avenue Taxi, Yellow Cab, and Whitehorse Taxi (☎ 867/667–4111). **Yukon Taxi Service** (☎ 867/667–6677).

Visitor and Tour Information At City Hall (⊠ 2121 2nd Ave., Yukon Territory, Canada ☎ 867/668–8687 ⊕ www.visitwhitehorse.com). The **Yukon Visitor Information Centre** (⊠ 100 Hanson St., Yukon Territory, Canada ☎ 867/667–3084 or 800/661–0494 ⊕ www.travelyukon.com ☉ Mid-May–mid-Sept., daily 8-8; mid-Sept.–mid-May, weekdays 8:30–5, Sat. 10–2).

8

EXPLORING

The **Canyon City Archaeological Dig** provides a glimpse into the past of the local First Nations people. Long before the area was developed by Western civilizations, the First Nations people used the Miles Canyon area as a seasonal fish camp. The Yukon Conservation Society conducts free tours of the area twice a day on weekdays in summer; it also leads two-hour hikes Tuesday through Saturday in July and August. All the hikes are free and provide a great way to see the surrounding countryside with local naturalists. The society office houses a bookstore on Yukon history and wilderness and sells souvenirs, maps, and posters. ✉ *302 Hawkins St.* ☎ *867/668–5678* ⊕ *www.yukonconservation.org* ✉ *Free* ⊙ *Tours July–late Aug., weekdays at 10 and 2.*

From gold-rush fever to the birth of Whitehorse, the **MacBride Museum of Yukon History** offers a comprehensive view of the colorful characters and groundbreaking events that shaped the territory. Follow the Yukon River through the history of Whitehorse in the Gold to Government exhibition. The museum also boasts a unique collection of wildlife, geology, historic artifacts, and photographs, alongside fine First Nations beadwork. The gold-rush displays are particularly telling of just what people went through to find a little glint of color. Outdoor artifacts include the cabin of Sam McGee, who was immortalized in Robert Service's famous poem "The Cremation of Sam McGee." MacBride also offers guided tours and a chance to try your hand at one of the Yukon's oldest professions—gold panning. ✉ *1124 1st Ave. and Wood St.* ☎ *867/667–2709* ⊕ *www.macbridemuseum.com* ✉ *C$7* ⊙ *Mid-May–Aug., daily 9:30–5:30; Sept.–mid-May, Tues.–Sat. noon–4.*

Miles Canyon, a 10-minute drive south of Whitehorse, is both scenic and historic. Although the dam below it makes the canyon seem relatively tame, it was this perilous stretch of the Yukon River that determined the location of Whitehorse as the starting point for river travel north. In 1897 Jack London won the admiration—and cash—of fellow stampeders headed north to the Klondike goldfields because of his steady hand as pilot of hand-hewn wooden boats here. You can hike on trails along the canyon or take a two-hour cruise aboard the MV *Schwatka* and experience the canyon from the waters of Lake Schwatka. This lake was created by the dam built in 1958, putting an end to the infamous White Horse Rapids. ✉ *68 Miles Canyon Rd., 1 mi from Whitehorse city center* ☎ *867/668–4716* ⊕ *www.yukonrivercruises.com* ⊙ *Cruises depart daily early June–mid-Sept.*

★ The **SS Klondike**, a national historic site, is dry-docked on the bank of the Yukon River in central Whitehorse's Rotary Park. The 210-foot stern-wheeler was built in 1929, sank in 1936, and was rebuilt in 1937. In the days when the Yukon River was the transportation link between Whitehorse and Dawson City, the *Klondike* was the largest boat plying the river. Riverboats were as much a way of life here as on the Mississippi of Mark Twain, and the tour of the Klondike is a fascinating way to see how the boats were adapted to the north; as an added bonus, in the old days they were also one of the few places where First Nations men could get paying jobs, so there's a rich Native history to the riverboats as well. ✉ *Robert Service Way and 2nd Ave.* ☎ *867/667–4511* *mid-May–mid-Sept., 867/667–3910 rest of year* ⊕ *www.pc.gc.ca/lhn-nhs/yt/ssklondike/index.aspx* ✉ *C$6* ⊙ *Mid-May–mid-Sept., daily 9–6.*

At **Takhini Hot Springs**, off the Klondike Highway, there is swimming in the hot spring–warmed water (suits and towels are for rent), horseback riding, areas for camping with tent and RV sites, picnicking, an outdoor climbing wall, and a licensed (beer and wine) restaurant. ✉ *Km 10, Takhini Hot Springs Rd., 17 mi north of Whitehorse* ☎ *867/456–8000* ⊕ *www.takhinihotsprings.com* ✉ *C$10* ⊙ *May–Sept., daily 8 am–10 pm; call for winter hrs.*

The **Waterfront Walkway** along the Yukon River will take you past a few points of interest. Your walk starts on the path along the river just east of the MacBride Museum entrance on 1st Avenue. Traveling upstream (south), you'll go by the old White Pass and Yukon Route Building on Main Street.

If you're in Whitehorse in late summer, it's possible to see Chinook (king) salmon. They hold one of nature's great endurance records: the longest fish migration in the world, which is more than 2,000 mi from the Bering Sea to Whitehorse. The **Whitehorse Rapids Dam and Fish Ladder** (founded 1958–59) has interpretive exhibits, talks by local First Nations elders, display tanks of freshwater fish and salmon fry, and a platform for viewing the fish ladder. The best time to visit is August, when between 150 and 2,100 salmon (average count is 800) use the ladder to bypass the dam. ✉ *End of Nisutlin Dr.* ☎ *867/633–5965* ⊕ *www.yukonenergy.ca* ✉ *$3 suggested donation* ⊙ *June–Aug., daily; hrs vary, so call ahead.*

Near the Whitehorse Airport is the **Yukon Beringia Interpretive Centre,** which presents the story of the Yukon during the last Ice Age. Beringia is the name given to the large subcontinental landmass of eastern Siberia and Interior Alaska and the Yukon, which stayed ice-free and were linked by the Bering Land Bridge during the latest Ice Age (although Whitehorse wasn't actually part of this; it was glaciated). Large dioramas depict the lives of animals in Ice Age Beringia, and there are replicas of skeletons and a 26,000-year-old horsehide; horses weren't as big back then. ✉ *Mi 886, Alaska Hwy.* ☎ *867/667–8855* ⊕ *www.beringia.com* ✉ *C$6* ⊙ *May–Sept., daily 9–6; Sept.–May, Sat. 1–5.*

The lobby of the Yukon Government Building displays the **Yukon Permanent Art Collection,** featuring traditional and contemporary works by Yukon artists, including a 24-panel mural by artist David MacLagan depicting the historical evolution of the Yukon. In addition to the collection on the premises, the brochure *Art Adventures on Yukon Time,* available at visitor reception centers throughout the Yukon, guides you to artists' studios as well as galleries, festivals, and public art locations. ✉ *2071 2nd Ave.* ☎ *867/667–5811* ✉ *Free* ⊙ *Weekdays 8:30–5.*

The **Yukon Transportation Museum,** next door to the Yukon Beringia Interpretive Centre, takes a great look at the planes, trains, trucks, and snowmachines that opened the North. ✉ *Mi 886, Alaska Hwy.* ☎ *867/668–4792* ⊕ *www.goytm.ca.*

The **Yukon Wildlife Preserve** provides a fail-safe way of photographing rarely spotted animals in a natural setting. Animals roaming freely

8

here include elk, caribou, mountain goats, musk oxen, bison, mule deer, and Dall and Stone sheep. Gray Line Yukon runs two-hour tours with an hour in the preserve. ⊠ *Gray Line Yukon, 2nd Ave. at Steele St.* ☎ *867/668–3225 or 800/544–2206* ⊕ *www.graylineyukon.com* ⊠ *C$30* ⊘ *Tours mid-May–mid-Sept., daily.*

OUTDOOR ACTIVITIES

HIKING   The **Kluane National Park and Reserve** (⊠ *Visitor Center, 119 Logan St., Haines Junction* ☎ *867/634–7207*), about 170 km (100 mi) west of Whitehorse, has millions of acres for hiking. The **Yukon Conservation Society** (☎ *867/668–5678*) leads natural and historical hikes from July through August of varying lengths and difficulty.

SLED-DOG   Whitehorse and Fairbanks organize the **Yukon Quest International Sled-**
RACING   **Dog Race** (☎ *867/668–4711* ⊕ *www.yukonquest.com*) in February. The race's starting line alternates yearly between the two cities. This is one of the longest and toughest races in the north.

WHERE TO EAT

$$$$ ✕ **The Cellar Steakhouse and Wine Bar.** In the Edgewater Hotel in down-
CONTINENTAL   town Whitehorse, this intimate two-room spot—down some stairs, as the name implies—is touted by the locals as the place to go for special occasions. The front room is less formal, with a bar and TV, while the back room, separated by an etched-glass partition, is quieter. The menu offers seafood and meat dishes, complemented by a decent wine list. ⊠ *101 Main St.* ☎ *867/667–2572.*

¢   ✕ **Chocolate Claim.** Choose from fresh-baked breads and pastries, home-
CAFÉ   made soups and sandwiches, salads, and quiches at this charming café
★   and deli. Artwork—ranging from paintings and pottery to rugs and quilts by local artists—displays change monthly, and it's all for sale. On sunny days you can sit outside. Friday happy hour is from 5:15 to 6:45 pm, with live music. ⊠ *305 Strickland St.* ☎ *867/667–2202* ⊕ *www. chocolateclaim.com* ⊘ *Closed Sun.*

$$$–$$$$ ✕ **Klondike Rib & Salmon BBQ.** If you're in the mood for something
SOUTHERN   completely different, this is the place. It's known not just for its wild-game dishes such as musk ox, caribou, and bison, but also for its halibut, salmon, Arctic char, and killer ribs. It's open for lunch, but the famous rib dishes are served only at dinner. Due to its popularity, there's almost always a line, but it's worth the wait—for the best food in town, yes, but also for the chance to dine in the oldest operating building in Whitehorse. ⊠ *2116 2nd Ave.* ☎ *867/667–7554* ⊘ *Closed mid-Sept.–mid-May.*

WHERE TO STAY

For expanded hotel reviews, visit Fodors.com.

$$$ ⊞ **Edgewater Hotel.** On a quiet end of Main Street, this corner hotel, first built during the 1898 gold rush, is in its third incarnation (the first two burned down). **Pros:** rich history; borders the Yukon River. **Cons:** small lobby and hallways to rooms; no continental breakfast. ⊠ *101 Main St.* ☎ *867/667–2572 or 877/484–3334* ⊕ *www.edgewateryukon. com* ⇆ *32 rooms, 4 suites* ♿ *In-room: a/c (some), kitchen (some), Wi-Fi. In-hotel: 2 restaurants, bar.*

$$$–$$$$ 🏨 **High Country Inn**. At this downtown inn you'll find tastefully appointed modern rooms. **Pros:** stay connected with Wi-Fi; try locally brewed beers at the saloon. **Cons:** not all rooms have air-conditioning; standard rooms are minimally decorated, and some of them are really small. ⌂ *4051 Fourth Ave.* ☎ *867/667–4471 or 800/554–4471* ⊕ *www. highcountryinn.yk.ca* ⤳ *82 rooms, 24 suites* ♿ *In-room: a/c (some), kitchen (some), Wi-Fi. In-hotel: restaurant, bar, gym, laundry facilities, some pets allowed.*

$$ 🏨 **Westmark Whitehorse Hotel and Conference Center**. You can catch a nightly Klondike vaudeville show, the *Frantic Follies*, in summer at this full-service hotel in the heart of downtown, the largest hotel in the Yukon. **Pros:** laundry facilities; some pets allowed; breakfast buffet available in the summer season. **Cons:** not the place to go to escape the action; not all rooms have air-conditioning. ⌂ *201 Wood St.* ☎ *867/393–9700, 800/544–0970 reservations* ⊕ *www.westmarkhotels. com* ⤳ *180 rooms, 8 suites* ♿ *In-room: a/c (some), Wi-Fi. In-hotel: restaurant, bar, gym, laundry facilities, some pets allowed.*

8

The Bush

INCLUDING NOME, BARROW, PRUDHOE BAY, AND THE ALEUTIAN ISLANDS

WORD OF MOUTH

"Hop a flight to a native community up in the north—Kotzebue is my fave, or Barrow, or even Nome—just so you can see what Alaska is like off the road system. By around the first of May [. . .] the ice will still be in, so a visit to Kotzebue (above the Arctic circle, on the Arctic Ocean) will allow you to walk a bit on the ocean. Very, very interesting places."

—Gardyloo

WELCOME TO THE BUSH

TOP REASONS TO GO

★ **Spend time in the company of bears:** The Alaska Peninsula has the world's largest concentrations of brown bears, which congregate near salmon runs each year.

★ **Learn about native culture:** Native communities celebrate and support their cultural traditions. Come to the Bush for everything from blanket tossing to arts-and-crafts exhibits.

★ **Go fishing:** You'll see 100-pound salmon, 8-pound trout, and be the only one on your block to know what sheefish tastes like.

★ **Experience the Land of the Midnight Sun:** Only north of the Arctic Circle is the sun above the horizon 24 hours a day; in Barrow the sun doesn't set from mid-May to August.

★ **Get outside like never before:** Want the world to yourself? Bush Alaska includes millions of acres of remote parklands and wildlife refuges, including the least-visited national park in the United States.

1 Southwest. This broad area ranges from the northern shores of the Shelikof Strait to the Yukon-Kuskokwim Delta. It's Alaska's least-developed region; small Native villages are scattered across a wilderness rich in fish and wildlife.

2 Northwest and the Arctic. This region runs from the Seward Peninsula to Alaska's northernmost mountain chain, the Brooks Range, and the vast plain of the North Slope. Home to the Porcupine caribou herd and the Alaska National Wildlife Refuge, the Arctic is a balancing act of pristine wilderness, oil development, and villages where whale meat is still a vital part of the daily diet.

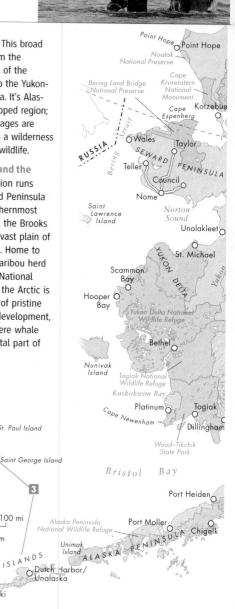

GETTING ORIENTED

As much a lifestyle as a place, "the Bush" generally refers to all of mainland Alaska that lies beyond the road system, plus the western islands. And that really means about 90% of the state. Geographically, though, the Bush encompasses all of western Alaska, from the North Pacific to the Beaufort Sea; that part of Alaska's mainland lying north of the Arctic Circle; and a good chunk of the Interior. Figure it this way: if your cell phone works, you're probably not really in the Bush.

3 Alaska Peninsula, Pribilof Islands, and Aleutian Island Chain. Considered part of the Southwest, the Aleutians are closer to Japan than to San Francisco. Even more remote are the Pribilof Islands; they're the northern edge of Aleut settlement and the seasonal home of hundreds of thousands of seals and breeding birds, some seen nowhere else in North America. It's a birder's paradise.

Updated
by Edward
Readicker-
Henderson

Often when an Alaskan talks about going out to the Bush, they mean anywhere off the grid, which is most of Alaska. However, there's another area that Alaskans call the Bush, which refers to those wild and lonely expanses of territory beyond cities, towns, highways, and railroad corridors, stretching from the Kodiak Archipelago, Alaska Peninsula, and Aleutian Islands in the south through the Yukon-Kuskokwim Delta and Seward Peninsula and into the northern High Arctic. It's just a matter of understanding context.

For the sake of this book, the Bush refers to this territory. The Bush extends over two-thirds of Alaska, where caribou outnumber people and where the summer sun really does shine at midnight; in fact at the state's northern edge it remains in the sky for several weeks in June and July, disappearing altogether for weeks in winter. The Bush is a land that knows the soft footsteps of the Eskimos and the Aleuts, the scratchings of those who searched (and still search) for oil and gold, and the ghosts of almost-forgotten battlefields of World War II.

If you visit the Arctic plains in summer, you'll see an array of bright wildflowers growing from a sponge of rich green tundra dotted with pools of melting snow. Willow trees barely an inch tall might be a hundred years old, and sometimes berry bushes have berries bigger than the bush they grow on. In the long, dark Arctic winter a painter's-blue kind of twilight rises from the ice and snowscapes at midday, but the moon can be bright enough to read by, and on a clear night you will have a new appreciation for the depth of the heavens. Spring and fall are fleeting moments when the tundra awakens from its winter slumber or turns briefly brilliant with autumn colors.

The Brooks Range, which stretches east–west across the state from nearly the sea to the Canadian border, separates the Arctic from the rest of the state. The Brooks are actually a superchain, including several mountain systems, from pale, softly rounded limestone mountains in the east and west to the towering granite spires of the Arrigetch Peaks in the heart of the range. Large portions of the Brooks Range's middle and western sections are protected within Gates of the Arctic National Park and the neighboring Noatak National Preserve; its eastern reaches lie within the Arctic National Wildlife Refuge.

North of the Brooks Range a great apron of land called the North Slope tilts gently toward the Beaufort Sea and the Arctic Ocean. The vast sweep of this frozen tundra brightens each summer with yellow Arctic poppies, bright red bearberry, and dozens of other wildflower species that pepper endless stretches of landscape. Beneath the surface, permanently frozen ground known as permafrost has shifted and shaped

STOMPING GROUNDS

Great herds of caribou—including the western herd with more than a half million animals, and the Porcupine herd with around a hundred thousand—move slowly across the tundra, feeding and fattening for the next winter and attempting to stay clear of wolves and grizzlies. In the Arctic Ocean's Beaufort Sea, polar bears, stained a light gold from the oil of seals they have killed, pose like monarchs on ice floes. One of Alaska's premier wildlands, the Arctic National Wildlife Refuge protects mountain and tundra landscape important to caribou, polar bears, grizzlies, wolves, and musk ox.

this land for centuries, fragmenting it into giant polygons that make a fascinating pattern when viewed from the sky. This same permafrost, due to global climate change, is melting rapidly, radically changing not only the lives of humans, but also the annual migrations of numerous different animals, as well as the very composition of the atmosphere.

At the very edge of this wilderness, where land meets sea, Prudhoe Bay, America's largest oil field, was discovered in 1968. At its peak, more than 2 million barrels a day of North Slope crude from Prudhoe and neighboring basins flowed south via the 800-mi pipeline to the port of Valdez, on Prince William Sound in South Central Alaska. Today the flow has diminished to around 600,000 barrels per day, a number that decreases slightly every year.

The rivers that drain the Brooks Range include the Kongakut, Kobuk, and Sheenjek, names that reflect the native peoples who have lived here for thousands of years, ever since their ancestors crossed the Bering Land Bridge. The great Noatak River defies the Arctic's north–south drainage pattern and runs east–west, making a right-angle turn before emptying into Kotzebue (*kots*-eh-bew) Sound. Perched on this sound is the colorful Eskimo (technically, Inupiaq; the term "Eskimo" is falling out of favor, being replaced by local and more specific terms) town of Kotzebue, the largest Native settlement in the state and the jumping-off point for much of the surrounding area. Native ceremonial dances are demonstrated at Kotzebue's Living Museum of the Arctic, as is the Eskimo blanket toss, a traditional activity dating to prehistoric times, when hunters were bounced high in the air so they could scan the horizon for seals.

BEST BETS FOR DIFFERENT TRAVELERS

For an easy adventure in the wild:

■ Take a tour with Nome Discovery Tours. See left-over artifacts from from the gold rush, explore the tundra, and maybe even see some musk ox.

■ Ride the Alaska Marine Highway to Dutch Harbor. Bring your birding scope. This will get you talking with locals better than any cruise can.

For serious animal watching:

■ Head to Brooks Camp or Halo Bay to see bears.

■ Make your way to the Pribilof Islands for birds and Northern fur seals.

To get deep into the middle of nowhere:

■ Take a guided trip into the Brooks Range and Gates of the Arctic National Park.

■ Travel with Arctic Treks deep into the Alaska National Wildlife Refuge.

If you want major bragging rights:

■ Visit Barrow, the northernmost city on the continent, and probably the only town where you can find whale spears in the hardware store.

Another coastal community, this one first settled by prospectors, is the former gold-rush boomtown of Nome, where you can still pan for riches. In early spring Nome celebrates the appearance of the sun with a golf tournament where the "greens" are painted on the ice of the Bering Sea coast. Nome also serves as the end of the Iditarod Trail Sled Dog Race, which begins in Anchorage the first Saturday in March and finishes about 10 days later, when the fastest dog teams make their way up Front Street to the cheers of locals and visitors alike.

Southwest Alaska includes the biologically productive wetlands of the Yukon-Kuskokwim Delta, where the state's greatest river meets the wild ocean. Sloughs, ponds, marshes, mud, streams, and puddles in these flat regions near sea level can slow water travel to a standstill. The delta is one of the most important migratory flyways for birds in North America, and the waters teem with life. Farther south, Bristol Bay is the site of some of the largest salmon runs in the world. Nearby Wood-Tikchik State Park (the nation's largest, at more than 1.6 million acres) encompasses huge lake systems and vast stretches of untouched wilderness where moose with antlers the size of end tables browse their way through the glaciated landscape. And on the upper reaches of the Alaska Peninsula the brown bears of Katmai rule a vast national park dominated by dramatic volcanic scenery. Also in the Southwest, the lower Alaska Peninsula and the Aleutian (pronounced ah-*loo*-shun) Islands reach well into the Pacific Ocean toward Japan. This chain beckoned Russian explorers to Alaska in the 18th century, as they tried to turn the islands' sea otter population into furs to trade with China for tea. Along the islands, weathered onion-dome Russian Orthodox churches in Aleut villages brace against fierce Pacific winds.

Dutch Harbor, the largest town in the Aleutians and a former U.S. Navy base pounded by Japanese bombs in 1942, is one of America's busiest commercial fishing ports. Deep-sea trawlers and factory ships venture from here into the stormy North Pacific Ocean and the Bering Sea for harvests of bottom fish, crab, and other catches. Unalaska, an ancient Aleut village, is Dutch Harbor's neighbor and home to one of the oldest and most beautiful Russian Orthodox churches in Alaska. North of the Aleutian chain, in the Bering Sea, the remote volcanic islands of the Pribilofs support immense populations of birds and sea mammals, as well as two small Aleut communities, St. George and St. Paul.

Alaskans who live in towns use the Bush as an escape valve, a place to get away. And those who've made the Bush their home are practically heroes to the rest of the state; they're the people who are bold enough to do what the majority of urban Alaskans wish they could do. Bush Alaskans have a deep affection for their raw land that is difficult to explain to strangers. They talk of living with complete independence, "close to nature." A cliché, perhaps, until you realize that these Alaskans reside in the Bush all year long, adapting to brutal winter weather and isolation, preferring to live off the road system. They know a store-bought hamburger will never taste as good as fresh moose meat, and whatever they're missing by not having a TV can't possibly be as interesting as the view out the cabin window. They have accepted the Bush for what it is: dramatic, unforgiving, and glorious.

EXPLORING THE BUSH

Philosophically speaking, the Bush is more of a lifestyle than a location. It brings a new definition to "roughing it"; after you experience the Bush, you come to understand that the term "rural" only applies in the Lower 48, where there's always an urban hub nearby to bail you out. But if a village or town store in the Bush runs out of something, it won't be in stock again until the next delivery—whether it be by boat or by plane—which can take anywhere from a week to a month, maybe even not until the next spring after the ice thaws; hopefully the store didn't just run out of toilet paper! People who live in the boonies know transportation schedules like the backs of their hands, and they know that if they don't show up at the store within hours of the supply boat or plane's arrival, the odds of getting any fresh milk or vegetables are about zero.

Technically, the Bush is more or less any place in mainland Alaska that can't be reached by road. To outsiders the Bush represents three distinct destinations. The southwestern part of the Bush, the Yukon Delta region and Bethel down to the Shelikof Strait, is the preferred territory for sportsmen and those looking to spot big animals. The Aleutian and Pribilof islands and the Alaska Peninsula attract birders and history buffs. And the northern part of the Bush, from Nome to Point Barrow, is for those who see north as a direction to go. A lot of people may say they're traveling to the far north for the Native culture, for a chance to see the beauty of tundra, but really, most of them are doing it for bragging rights.

Of course, just going to Alaska is cause enough to boast, and each region has its own distinct draw. Kodiak and Katmai are great for

9

grizzly viewing and birding, Nome is not only the best place for gold-rush history, but is also known for its large and small wildlife as well as bird-watching in summer. No matter where you go, that distinct Alaskan culture—created by the simple fact that the only people who live here are people who genuinely want to live here—is abundant, distinct, and welcoming.

A tour of the Bush's southwestern region can begin in Bethel, an important outpost on the Yukon-Kuskokwim Delta and surrounded by the Yukon Delta National Wildlife Refuge; off the mainland coast is the undeveloped wilderness of Nunivak Island.

The Alaska Peninsula juts out between the Pacific Ocean and the Bering Sea; here are the Becharof and Alaska Peninsula National Wildlife refuges, as well as the prime bear-viewing area of Katmai National Park and Preserve. To the northeast of the Alaska Peninsula is the Kodiak Archipelago, where you'll find Kodiak National Wildlife Refuge and Shuyak Island State Park.

The Aleutian Islands start where the peninsula ends, and sweep southwest toward Japan. The Pribilof Islands—windswept, grassy, whale bones scattered on the beaches—lie north of the Aleutians, 200 mi off Alaska's west coast. Head north along the Bering Sea coast and you come to Nome, just below the Arctic Circle and the Bering Land Bridge National Preserve. Kotzebue, just above the circle, is a coastal Inupiaq town surrounded by sea and tundra and a jumping-off place for several parklands: Kobuk Valley, Noatak, Cape Krusenstern, and Gates of the Arctic (though the last is more easily reached from the inland village of Bettles). Barrow, another Inupiaq community, sits at the very top of the state, and is the northernmost town in the United States. Follow the Arctic coastline eastward and you reach Deadhorse, on Prudhoe Bay, the custodian to the region's important oil and gas reserves. East of Prudhoe Bay is the embattled Arctic National Wildlife Refuge, the nation's last great chance to truly show that wilderness matters.

PLANNING

WHEN TO GO

The best time to visit is June through August, when the weather is mildest (though you should still anticipate cool, wet, and sometimes stormy weather), daylight hours are longest, and the wildlife is most abundant. Because summer is so short, though, things happen fast, and seasonal activities may need to be crammed into just a couple of weeks.

Go birding in May and August, when migrants come through. The peak wildflower season is usually short, particularly in the Arctic, when most flowers may not blossom until mid-June and then go to seed by late July.

Salmon runs vary from region to region, so it's best to do your homework before choosing dates. For the most part, though, you're looking at July and August, which is also when the tundra starts turning from its summer hues to autumnal colors. The best times for bear-viewing coincide with salmon runs.

GETTING HERE AND AROUND

It's nearly impossible to travel to or around the Bush without taking an air taxi. Still, a few areas are accessible by car or boat. The Dalton Highway connects with the state's highway system and traverses the Arctic, but it only leads to the oil fields of Prudhoe Bay. In the Aleutians, the Alaska Marine Highway, the state's amazing ferry system, makes one trip a month between Kodiak and Dutch Harbor/Unalaska from April through October.

Alaska Airlines flies within the state to most major communities. Peninsula Airways serves the communities on the Alaskan Peninsula, the Aleutian and Pribilof islands, and parts of the Interior and northwest.

Bush-based carriers such as Bering Air also offer flightseeing tours and, weather and politics permitting, specially arranged charter flights to the Providentiya Airport in the Chukotka Region, on the Siberian coast across the Bering Strait. Currently, it is mandatory for Americans to obtain a visa, invitation, and permission to go to Russia (although at this writing both governments are negotiating changes to the situation, so check for the latest information). Frontier Flying Service serves the Interior and the Bering and Arctic coasts. Wright Air Service flies throughout the Interior and Arctic Alaska.

Information about certified air-taxi operations is available from the Federal Aviation Administration. Individual parks and Alaska Public Lands Information centers can also supply lists of reputable air-taxi services. Make your reservations in advance, and always plan for the unexpected; weather can delay a scheduled pickup for days.

Information Alaska Airlines (☎ 800/426–0333 ⊕ www.alaskaair.com). **Alaska Public Lands Information Center** (☎ 907/644–3661 or 866/869–6887 ⊕ www.alaskacenters.gov). **Alaska State Ferry** (☎ 800/642–0066 ⊕ www.ferryalaska.com). **Bering Air** (☎ 907/443–5464, 800/478–5422 in Alaska; 907/443–8988 Russian desk ⊕ www.beringair.com). **Federal Aviation Administration** (☎ 907/271–2000 ⊕ www.faa.gov). **Frontier Flying Service** (☎ 907/450–7250, 800/866–8394 for reservations ⊕ www.flyera. com). **Peninsula Airways** (☎ 907/243–2323 or 800/448–4226 ⊕ www.penair. com). **Wright Air Service** (☎ 907/474–0502, 800/478–0502 in Alaska ⊕ www. wrightairservice.com).

9

HEALTH AND SAFETY

When traveling in the Bush, you should never head out without a decent first-aid kit; you can be a very long way from help out here. The main concern, though, is hypothermia. Watch out for each other. The only other prevalent hazard is bugs—until you've experienced it, it's hard to understand just how thick the mosquitoes and other things that bite can get. Bring plenty of DEET.

MONEY MATTERS

Many small villages don't have bank offices, so visitors should bring cash. Most places within the larger Bush communities accept major credit cards, but don't take that for granted. Always be sure to confirm in advance what sort of payment tour companies, hotels, and restaurants accept. Hub communities that do have bank services are Nome, Bethel, Kotzebue, and Barrow.

RESTAURANTS

The dining options are few when traveling around Alaska's Bush; smaller communities may have one or two eateries, if any at all. On the bright side, you won't need to worry about reservations. If they're open, they'll let you in, and you'll likely be surprised at the variety available: in addition to Alaskan seafood, game, and locally grown vegetables, Mexican and Asian fare are standard, even in the state's remotest corners. All food prices, including at grocery shops, will reflect large transportation charges, so be prepared to pay.

HOTELS

Lodging choices in the Bush are also limited. Some communities have a single hotel; the smallest have none. Others have a mix of hotels and bed-and-breakfasts. As a rule, rooms are simply furnished. You may have to share bathroom or kitchen facilities. Rooms go fast during the summer season, so book as far ahead as possible. And it never hurts to carry a tent as backup so you'll never be without a place to stay.

DINING AND LODGING PRICE CATEGORIES				
	¢	$	$$	$$$	$$$$
Restaurants	under $10	$10–$15	$15–$20	$20–$25	over $25
Hotels	under $75	$75–$125	$125–$175	$175–$225	over $225

Restaurant prices are per person for a main course at dinner. Hotel prices are for two people in a standard double room in high season.

VISITOR INFORMATION

GETTING OUTSIDE

The Bush presents some of the world's best opportunities to participate in backcountry adventures, from canoeing to wildlife-viewing. The following organizations can help you get in touch with your inner explorer.

Contacts Alaska Department of Fish and Game (✉ 1255 W. 8th St., Juneau ☎ 907/465–4100 general information about fish and wildlife, 907/465–4180 sportfishing seasons and regulations; 907/465–2376 licenses ⊕ www.adfg. alaska.gov). **Alaska State Parks Information** (✉ 550 W. 7th Ave., Suite 1260, Anchorage ☎ 907/269–8400 ⊕ www.dnr.alaska.gov). **Anchorage Alaska Public Lands Information Center** (✉ 605 W. 4th Ave., Suite 105, Anchorage ☎ 907/644–3661 or 866/869–6887 ⊕ www.alaskacenters.govc). **Fairbanks**

OVERWHELMED? TAKE A TOUR

Package tours are the most common way of traveling to Bush communities, where making your flight connections and having a room to sleep in at the end of the line are no small feats. During peak season—late May through Labor Day—planes, state ferries, hotels, and sportfishing lodges are often crowded with travelers on organized tours; to create a trip on your own can sometimes mean making reservations a year in advance for the really popular destinations. But the Bush is also large enough that there's always somewhere to go, and wherever you end up the odds are it will be amazing and like nothing you've ever seen before.

The type of tour you choose will determine how you get there. On air tours—the only way to get to most Bush communities—you will fly to and from your destination, getting there relatively quickly and enjoying an aerial perspective of the Arctic en route. Tours to Arctic towns and villages are usually short—one, two, or three days—so it's easy to combine these with visits to other regions.

Bus tours to Deadhorse and Prudhoe Bay go at a more leisurely pace and provide a ground-level view of sweeping tundra vistas, along with the chance of spotting caribou or musk ox. The route crosses the rugged Brooks Range, the Arctic Circle, and the Yukon River, and also brushes the edges of Gates of the Arctic National Park and the Arctic National Wildlife Refuge. Holland America Tours/Gray Line of Alaska operates package tours that travel the Dalton Highway to Deadhorse. Princess Tours runs similar trips.

The Bush is home to many Alaska Native groups, quite a few of which are active in tourism. Often, local Native corporations act as your hosts—running the tours, hotels, and attractions. Nome Tour and Marketing in Nome (book through Alaska Airlines Vacations) provides ground transportation, accommodations, and other services for visitors. The NANA Regional Corporation provides ground transportation and accommodations in Kotzebue as well as at Prudhoe Bay, in conjunction with bus tours. If you visit Barrow and stay at the Top of the World Hotel, Tundra Tours (book through Alaska Airlines Vacations), another Native operation, will be your host.

The Northern Alaska Tour Company conducts highly regarded ecotours to the Arctic Circle, the Brooks Range, and Prudhoe Bay that emphasize natural and cultural history, wildlife, and geology. Groups are limited to 25 people on Arctic day tours and to 10 people on Prudhoe Bay overnight trips. Some tours are completely ground-based; others include a mix of ground and air travel.

Contacts **Alaska Airlines Vacations** (☎ 800/468–2248 ⊕ www. alaskaair.com). **Holland American Tours/Gray Line of Alaska** (☎ 907/479–9660, 800/887–7741 in Alaska, 800/544–2206 for reservations ⊕ www.graylinealaska.com). **NANA Regional Corporation** (☎ 907/442–3301 ⊕ www.nana.com). **Northern Alaska Tour Company** (☎ 907/474–8600 or 800/474–1986 ⊕ www.northernalaska.com). **Princess Tours** (☎ 206/336–6000 in Seattle, 907/479–9660 in Fairbanks; 800/426–0442 reservations ⊕ www.princess.com). **Tundra Tours** (☎ 907/852–3900 ⊕ www. tundratoursinc.com).

9

Alaska Public Lands Information Center (⊠ *Morris Thompson Visitor Center, 101 Dunkel St., Suite 110, Fairbanks* ☎ *907/459-3730 or 866/869-6887* ⊕ *www.nps.gov/aplic).* **U.S. Fish and Wildlife Service** (⊠ *1011 E. Tudor Rd., Anchorage* ☎ *907/786-3309* ⊕ *www.alaska.fws.gov)*

SOUTHWEST

The Southwest region, below the Arctic Circle, encompasses some of Alaska's most remote, inaccessible, and rugged land- and seascapes. Reaching from the Kodiak Archipelago to the Yukon-Kuskokwim Delta, this area contains the world's densest brown bear population and the world's greatest salmon runs. Given all this richness, it's no surprise to learn that Southwest Alaska has some of Alaska's premier parklands and refuges, from Katmai National Park to Aniakchak National Monument and the Kodiak National Wildlife Refuge. Here, too, are dozens of rural communities, most of them small Native villages whose residents continue to engage in a subsistence lifestyle augmented by modern conveniences and, frequently, satellite- and computer-delivered schools.

> **TAKE TO THE SKIES**
>
> Roads in the Bush are few, so airplanes—from jetliners to small bush planes—are the lifelines. Throughout Alaska you'll hear about the legendary pilots of the far north—Noel and Sig Wien, Bob Reeve, Ben Eielson, Harold Gillam, Joe Crosson, Jack Jefford, and others—who won their wings in the early years. They are Alaska's counterparts to the cowboy heroes of the Wild West. And just as in the Wild West, the adventure came with risk: the Bush is where America's favorite humorist, Will Rogers, died in a crash with famed aviator Wiley Post in 1935.

BETHEL

400 mi west of Anchorage.

Spread out on the tundra along the Kuskokwim River, Bethel is a frontier town of about 5,800 residents, originally established by Moravian missionaries in the late 1800s. One of rural Alaska's most important trading centers, it's a hub for 56 native villages in a region roughly the size of the state of Oregon. The Yup'ik Eskimo language and culture are still predominant in this regional center.

The surrounding lowland tundra is a rich green in summer and turns fiery shades of red, orange, and yellow in autumn, when plants burst with blueberries, cranberries, blackberries, and salmonberries. Salmon, arctic grayling, and Dolly Varden (a species of seagoing trout that some biologists continually try to promote to salmon) fill the area's many lakes, ponds, and streams, providing excellent fishing just a few miles outside town. Pretty much everyone in Bethel has smoked, dried, and frozen fish aplenty. The wetlands are also important breeding grounds for more than 60 species of birds, from shrikes to warblers.

The town is also the northernmost freshwater port for oceangoing vessels. Among its businesses are radio and television stations, a theater, credit union, auto repair shop, car-rental agency, beauty/barber shop,

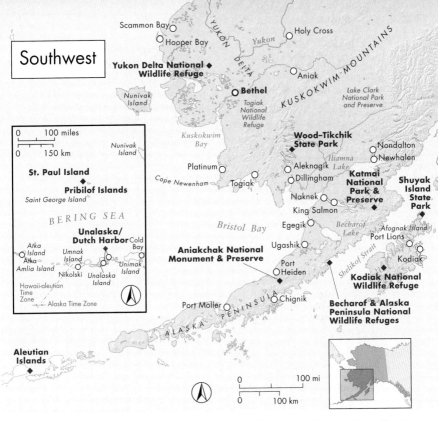

DVD rental store, newspaper, two colleges (including a tribal college), and the largest Alaska Native Health Service field hospital in the state, which is contracted to the tribally owned Yukon-Kuskokwim Health Corporation.

Each year on the last weekend in March Bethel hosts a regional celebration called the Cama-i Dance Festival (in Yup'ik, *cama-i* means "hello"), a great time to experience Native culture. Held in the local high school's gym, which is filled to capacity for the three-day event, this festival of food, dance, music, and crafts draws dance groups from dozens of outlying villages.

GETTING HERE AND AROUND

To get to Bethel, take a flight on Alaska Airlines, Frontier, or Era. Once you're there, the town itself is walkable.

ESSENTIALS

Banking Alaska USA Federal Credit Union (✉ Bethel Native Corporation Bldg., 135 Ridgecrest Dr. ☎ 907/543–2619 ⊕ www.alaskausa.org). **First National Bank Alaska** (✉ 700 Front St. ☎ 907/543–7650 ⊕ www.fnbalaska. com). **Wells Fargo** (✉ 460 Ridgecrest Dr. ☎ 907/543–3875 ✉ 830 River St. ☎ 800/869–3557 ⊕ www.wellsfargo.com).

Emergencies Police (☎ 907/543–3781 in Bethel). **State troopers** (☎ 907/543–2294).

Mail USPS (✉ 1484 Chief Eddie Hoffman Hwy. ☎ 907/543–2525).

Visitor Information Cama-i Dance Festival (⊕ www.bethelarts.com).

EXPLORING

★ The **Yupiit Piciryarait (the people's way of living) Museum** emphasizes cultural education through Native elders, while also showcasing artifacts and artwork of three Native cultures: Dene Athabascan, Cup'ik, and Yup'ik. In its galleries you'll find historic and prehistoric treasures: masks, statues, and carvings in ivory, baleen, and whalebone. The permanent collection features past and present clothing styles plus numerous implements and tools used in traditional subsistence lifestyles of the people inhabiting the Yukon-Kuskokwim region. ✉ 420 Chief Eddie Hoffman Hwy. ☎ 907/543–1819 or 800/478–3521 ⊕ www.ypmuseum.org ⚑ Free ☉ Tues.–Sat. noon–4.

> ### TOUR-SHY?
>
> So you've heard that organized tours are the best way to go but still cringe at the thought of not doing it yourself. What's a traveler to do? Fear not: these resources can help you troubleshoot your own Bush itinerary.
>
> **Alaska Travel Industry Association** (✉ 2600 Cordova St., Suite 201, Anchorage ☎ 907/929–2200, 800/862–5275 for vacation planner ⊕ www.alaskatia.org). **Southwest Alaska Municipal Conference** (✉ 3300 Arctic Blvd., Suite 203, Anchorage ☎ 907/562–7380 ⊕ www.swamc.org).

WHERE TO EAT AND STAY

For expanded hotel reviews, visit Fodors.com.

$$–$$$ ✕**Shogun.** This rural café-style restaurant specializes in Chinese food ECLECTIC and authentic Mexican cuisine, with daily lunch and dinner specials. It also serves Japanese and Italian dishes, plus American-style steaks and seafood. ✉ 320 Tundra St. ☎ 907/543–2272.

$–$$ 🏨**Allanivik Hotel.** Three detached buildings make up this inn, which provides a quiet stay and insightful tips from the Bush-savvy owners. **Pros:** great, knowledgeable staff. **Cons:** many rooms share baths. ✉ 1220 Hoffman Hwy. ☎ 907/543–4305 ⊕ www.allanivik.com ⤶ 30 rooms, 14 with bath ⚒ In-hotel: restaurant.

$$ 🏨**Bentley's Porter House B&B.** Hospitality is never in short supply at this two-story B&B in downtown Bethel. **Pros:** river views; very safe and quiet. **Cons:** not for those who want to stay up late making noise; not all rooms have baths. ✉ 624 1st Ave. ☎ 907/543–3552 ⤶ 35 rooms, 10 with bath ⚒ In-hotel: some pets allowed ⏹Breakfast.

SHOPPING

OFF THE
BEATEN
PATH

Nunivak Island. Due west of Bethel, and separated from the Yukon-Kuskokwim Delta by the Etolin Strait, Nunivak Island is an important wildlife refuge. Part of the **Yukon Delta National Wildlife Refuge,** this site is noted for its large herd of reindeer, a transplanted herd of musk ox, and the Eskimo settlement of Mekoryuk.

For information on the island, contact the U.S. Fish and Wildlife Service (☏ 907/543–3151 ⊕ *yukondelta.fws.gov*) in Bethel. Visitors should check with **Bethel Chamber of Commerce** (☏ *907/543–2911* ⊕ *www.bethelakchamber.org*) about transport and accommodations, which are limited and far from deluxe.

TAKE NOTE

Many Bush communities have voted to be dry areas in order to fight alcohol-abuse problems affecting Alaska's Native peoples. Sale and possession of alcohol is prohibited in dry communities. Enforcement is strict, and bootlegging is a felony. Nome remains wet, with numerous lively saloons, and usually a line at the liquor store.

YUKON DELTA NATIONAL WILDLIFE REFUGE

Surrounds Bethel.

GETTING HERE AND AROUND

There are no roads to or in the refuge. The best way to enter the area is to take a commercial flight to Bethel and then fly into the refuge by air taxi. If you only want to see the smallest edge of the refuge, or are a very strong hiker, it is also possible to walk in by driving 2 mi down Chief Eddie Hoffman State Highway, the only paved road in town, to the Refuge Office and Visitors Center at the end of the road.

ESSENTIALS

Visitor Information Refuge Manager (✉ *Box 346, Bethel 99559* ☏ *907/543–3151* ⊕ *yukondelta.fws.gov*).

EXPLORING

Yukon Delta National Wildlife Refuge, at 20 million acres, is the nation's largest wildlife refuge; nearly one-third of the area is water in the form of lakes, sloughs, bogs, creeks, and rivers—including the **Yukon** and **Kuskokwim** rivers, Alaska's largest. Both are broad and slow by the time they get this close to the sea, and they carry huge amounts of sediment; over the millennia the sediments have formed an immense delta that serves as critical breeding and rearing grounds for an estimated 100 million shorebirds and waterfowl.

Of course, not all of the refuge is wetlands. North of the Yukon River are the Nulato Hills, site of the 1.3-million-acre **Andreafsky Wilderness area,** which includes both forks of the Andreafsky River, one of Alaska's specially designated Wild and Scenic Rivers. Rainbow trout, arctic char, and grayling flourish in upland rivers and creeks; pike, sheefish, and burbot thrive in lowland waters. These abundant waters are also spawning grounds for five species of Pacific salmon. Black and grizzly bears, moose, beavers, mink, and Arctic foxes also call this refuge home. Occasionally, wolves venture into the delta's flats from neighboring uplands.

Given the abundance of fish and wildlife, it's not surprising that the delta holds special importance to surrounding residents. The Yup'ik have lived here for thousands of years; despite modern encroachment, they continue to practice many features of their centuries-old subsistence lifestyle. Access is by boat or aircraft only, and, as in most of

9

Alaska's other remote wildlands, visitor facilities are minimal. Refuge staff can provide tips on recreational opportunities and guides and outfitters who operate in the refuge.

THE OUTDOORS AND GUIDED TOURS

Opportunities for wildlife-watching abound at the Yukon Delta refuge. With so many lakes, ponds, streams, and wetlands, the big thing to do is get in a boat, or hang out on the shore, and watch all the waterfowl. The refuge is also a great place for sportfishing, especially for rainbow trout, salmon, char, pike, grayling, and sheefish. Flat-water paddlers will never run out of water to try, although camping can be a bit marshy and DEET-dependent. Or try hiking and river-floating in the uplands of the Andreafsky Wilderness area. You are a long way from help when you're in the refuge; know what you're doing.

Kuskokwim Wilderness Adventures (☎ 907/543–3900 ⊕ www.kuskofish. com) offers camping, fishing, birding, photo trips, and more, led by local expert Jim McDonald.

> ### NESTING GROUNDS
>
> More than 100 species of birds nest here in the Yukon Delta NWR, traveling from nearly every state and province in North America and from every continent that borders the Pacific Ocean. Many of North America's cackling Canada geese and more than half the continent's population of black brant (Pacific brant goose) are born here. Other birds making the annual pilgrimage to the Yukon Delta refuge include emperor geese, huge tundra swans, gulls, jaegers, cranes, loons, snipe, sandpipers, and the rare bristle-thigh curlew.

WOOD-TIKCHIK STATE PARK

150 mi southeast of Bethel, 300 mi southwest of Anchorage.

GETTING HERE AND AROUND

Like most of the Bush, there is no road access into Wood-Tikchik State Park. The only way in is either by air taxi or by boat. In the summer months it is not uncommon to see kayakers navigating their way through the river systems, their point of origin in the town of Dillingham or farther away via the waters of Bristol Bay. Kayaking the river system is suggested only for experienced kayakers who have very good navigational skills, as it is quite easy to get lost in the labyrinth of mosquito-infested waters.

ESSENTIALS

Visitor Information Walrus Island State Game Sanctuary (⊡ *Division of Wildlife Conservation, 333 Raspberry Rd., Anchorage 99518-1599* ☎ *907/267-2257* ⊕ *www.wildlife.alaska.gov*). **Wood-Tikchik State Park** (⊡ *Box 1822, Dillingham 99576 send correspondence here mid-May–Sept.* ☎ *907/842–2641* ⊡ *550 W. 7th Ave., Suite 1380, Anchorage 99501* ☎ *907/269–8400* ⊕ *www. alaskastateparks.org*).

EXPLORING

In the Bristol Bay region, **Wood-Tikchik State Park** —the nation's largest state park—is a water-based wildland despite its inland setting. Two separate groups of large, idyllic, interconnected lakes, some up to 45 mi long, dominate the park. Grizzlies, caribou, porcupines (people who live in the Bush will tell you they taste like squirrels), eagles, and loons abound in the park's forests and tundra, but Wood-Tikchik is best known for its fish. The park's lakes and streams are critical spawning habitat for five species of Pacific salmon; they also support healthy populations of rainbow trout, arctic char, arctic grayling, and northern pike. And where there are fish, there are fishermen: Wood-Tikchik is kind of a Holy Grail locale for serious anglers; all that water is perfect for canoes and kayaks, too.

EMERGENCY CARE

Anchorage's Alaska Regional Hospital has been operating **Alaska Regional Lifeflight** (☎ 800/478-9111 ⊕ www.alaskaregional.com) medevac services since 1985; it might seem far to go if you get hurt in, say, Kotzebue, but the crew begins emergency care as soon as a passenger is picked up, and planes can taxi right up to the hospital's entrance like regular ambulances.

Managed as a wild area, Wood-Tikchik has no maintained trails and few visitor amenities. ■ TIP➔ Most of its campsites are primitive, and anyone planning to explore the park should be experienced in backcountry travel and camping.

Besides the many large lakes and streams that fill its 1.6 million acres, the park's landscape includes rugged mountains, glaciers, and vast expanses of tundra. Think of it as a kind of CliffsNotes to the best of Alaskan scenery.

THE OUTDOORS AND GUIDED TOURS

Because it is largely a water-based region, it's easiest to explore Wood-Tikchik by boat, whether that's canoe, kayak, or raft. The most popular fly-in float trip is the 90-mi journey from Lake Kulik to Aleknagik, a Yup'ik Eskimo village. Most people doing this trip arrange for drop-off and pick-up services with local guides in Dillingham. The lakes are large enough to behave like small inland seas in stormy weather, so boaters need to be cautious when winds are high; always be prepared for bad weather, know proper emergency procedures, and don't ever go out unless somebody knows where you're headed. The water systems also present some of the world's best sportfishing opportunities for salmon and rainbow trout; anglers come from around the world to stay at wilderness fishing lodges here. Hiking is difficult because of dense brush, except for the uppermost part of the park, where tundra makes on-land travel easier.

FISHING LODGES **Tikchik Narrows Lodge** (☎ 907/243–8450 ⊕ www.tikchiklodge.com) is owned and managed by Bud Hodson, who has been a guide in the region for more than 25 years. The lodge caters primarily to sportfishing enthusiasts who are also looking for comfortable housing and scrumptious gourmet-style meals at night—and who can afford $7,400 for a week's stay, which includes guided fishing trips throughout the region via the lodge's floatplane fleet. The lodge rents kayaks and rafts and provides an air-taxi service into the park's most remote corners. If you're looking to reel one in, **Reel Wilderness Adventures** (☎ *800/726–8323* ⊕ *www.reelwild.com*) offers an alternative to lodges, while emphasizing small groups, gourmet meals, and fully guided fly-fishing for rainbow trout and other species. The $4,000/person 6-day package includes the round-trip flight from Dillingham into the park, all meals, and camp accommodation with hot showers and flush toilets.

KATMAI NATIONAL PARK AND PRESERVE

100 mi southeast of Wood-Tikchik, 290 mi southwest of Anchorage.

★ Katmai is the most famous of Alaska's remote parks for two simple reasons: bears and volcanoes. Although Katmai sees only a fraction of the number of visitors to Denali National Park, its name echoes with just as much mythical force. Remote and expensive (even by Alaska travel standards) to get to, Katmai is true wilderness Alaska, with limited visitor facilities (except for a few nice wilderness lodges)—but that's reason enough to go and have Alaska to yourself. These 4 million acres offer up plenty of opportunities for wildlife-viewing and an extraordinary perspective on the awesome power of volcanoes—still active throughout the park, echoes of the 1912 eruption sequence that was one of the most powerful ever recorded, covering more than 46,000 square mi with ash. Today in this wild, remote area at the northern end of the Alaska Peninsula, moose and almost 30 other species of mammals, including foxes, lynx, and wolves, share the landscape with bears fishing for salmon from stream banks and rivers and along the coast. At the immensely popular **Brooks Falls and Camp** you can see brown bears when the salmon are running in July and September. No special permits are required, though there is a $10 day-use fee at Brooks. Bears are common along the park's outer coast, where they graze on sedge flats, dig clams and sculpin on the beach at low tide (quite a sight!), and fish for salmon. But even on slow bear days it's a beautiful place to be. Ducks fill the park's rivers, lakes, and outer coast, arguing over nesting space with huge whistling swans, loons, grebes, gulls, and shorebirds. Bald eagles perch on rocky pinnacles by the sea. More than 40 species of songbirds call the region home during the short spring and summer, and if you fall back into big mammal mood, Steller sea lions and a couple of species of seals hang out on rock outcroppings.

From Brooks Lodge a daily tour bus with a naturalist aboard makes the 23-mi trip through the park to the **Valley Overlook**. Hikers can walk the 1.5-mi trail for a closer look at the pumice-covered valley floor. (Some consider the return climb strenuous.)

The Katmai area is one of Alaska's premier sportfishing regions. You can fish for rainbow trout and salmon at the **Brooks River**, though seasonal closures have been put in place to prevent conflicts with bears, and only fly-fishing is permitted; check locally for the latest information. For those who would like to venture farther into the park, seek out the two other backcountry lodges, **Grosvenor** and **Kulik**, or contact

When the salmon is moving upstream in Katmai N.P.'s Brooks River, dozens of brown bears with their cubs gather to feast. This one ran up a nearby tree to escape with his catch." —Jose Vigano, Fodors.com photo contest winner

fishing-guide services based in King Salmon. A short walk up the Brooks River brings you to Brooks Falls. Viewing platforms here overlook a 6-foot-high cascade where salmon leap to try and make it upstream, past the bears, to spawn. One platform is right at the falls; the other is a short way below it (an access trail and boardwalk are separated from the river to avoid confrontations with bears). ⌂ *National Park Service, Box 7, King Salmon 99613* ☎ *907/246-3305* ⊕ *www.nps.gov/katm.*

No roads lead to Katmai National Park. To get to it, at the base of the Alaska Peninsula, it's easiest to arrange a flight from Anchorage, where you can take in the amazing scenery along Cook Inlet, rimmed by the lofty, snowy peaks of the Alaska Range (check out ⊕ *www.alaskaair. com* for fares and schedules). They land at **King Salmon,** near fish-famous Bristol Bay, where passengers transfer to smaller floatplanes for the 20-minute hop to **Naknek Lake** and Brooks Camp. Travel to Brooks from King Salmon is also possible by boat. You are required to check in at the park ranger station, next to Brooks Lodge (⇨ *see below*), for a mandatory bear safety talk (for the safety of both you and the bears).

Fodor's Choice
★

At the northern end of the Alaska Peninsula, 200 mi southwest of Anchorage, **McNeil River State Game Sanctuary** was established in 1967 to protect the world's largest gathering of brown bears. Since then, it has earned a reputation as the finest bear-viewing locale in North America, and likely the world—the standard by which all others are measured. The main focus is **McNeil Falls,** where bears come to feed on chum salmon returning to spawn. All those *National Geographic* films you've seen of bears fishing? Odds are this is the spot. During the peak of the chum run (July to mid-August) dozens of brown bears congregate at the falls playing who can slap the most fish out of the water. When the salmon are running thickest, the bears only eat the fattiest parts of the fish—brains, roe, and skin—which means the leftovers are a smorgasbord for other animals; even the plant life depends on nutrients from bear leftovers. As many as 70 bears, including cubs, have been observed along the river in a single day. More than 100 bears have been identified within a single season. Not just the sheer number of bears makes McNeil special; over the years several bears have become highly accustomed to human presence. They will play, eat, nap, and nurse cubs within 15 to 20 feet of the falls viewing pad, sometimes closer—which will let you learn firsthand that bears smell like very wet dogs. Do not think the bears are tame; they are still wild animals and the sanctuary staff makes sure that visitors behave in a nonthreatening, nonintrusive way.

To that end, no more than 10 people a day, always accompanied by one or two state biologists, are allowed to visit bear-viewing sites from June 7 through August 25. Because demand is so high, an annual drawing is held in mid-March to determine permit winners. ■TIP→ Applications must be received by March 1 to be eligible. Nearly all visitors fly into McNeil Sanctuary on floatplanes. Most arrange for air-taxi flights out of Homer, on the Kenai Peninsula. Once you are in the sanctuary, all travel is on foot. ⊠ *Alaska Department of Fish and Game, Division of Wildlife Conservation, 333 Raspberry Rd., Anchorage* ☎ *907/267–2257* ⊕ *www.adfg.state.ak.us.*

SPORTS, THE OUTDOORS, AND GUIDED TOURS

The Katmai region offers an abundance of recreational opportunities, including sportfishing, bear viewing, hiking through the Valley of Ten Thousand Smokes, running the wild and scenic Alagnak River and other clearwater streams, flightseeing, exploring the outer coast, and backpacking through remote and seldom-visited backcountry wilderness.

FLIGHTSEEING AND WILDLIFE VIEWING
Katmai Air Services (☎ *907/246–3079 in King Salmon, summer only; 800/544–0551 in Anchorage* ⊕ *www.katmailand.com*) can arrange flightseeing tours of the park and also does charter flights to Brooks Camp. **Katmailand** (⊠ *4125 Aircraft Dr., Anchorage* ☎ *907/243–5448 or 800/544–0551* ⊕ *www.katmailand.com*) puts together bear-viewing and fishing packages to Katmai National Park, and also arranges trips to Katmai's Valley of Ten Thousand Smokes. **Lifetime Adventures** (☎ *800/952–8624* ⊕ *www.lifetimeadventures.net*) organizes a variety of customized trips for small groups (eight people or fewer), including bear-watching, river kayaking, mountain biking, and hiking in the Valley of Ten Thousand Smokes. **Northwind Aviation** (☐ *Box 646, Homer 99603* ⊠ *1170 Lakeshore Dr., Homer 99603* ☎ *907/235–7482* ⊕ *www.northwindak.com*), in Homer, offers charter flights to Katmai's outer coast and McNeil River.

RIVER RUNNING AND SPORTFISHING
Ouzel Expeditions (☎ *907/783–2216 or 800/825–8196* ⊕ *www.ouzel.com*) guides fishing and river-running trips down the Wild and Scenic Alagnak River and American Creek, which flows through Katmai National Park and is widely known as a rainbow-trout heaven.

WHERE TO STAY

All of the four lodges listed here are on inholdings (publicly owned land inside a protected area) within Katmai National Park. Three are inland, and Katmai Wilderness Lodge is on the remote outer coast.

For expanded hotel reviews, visit Fodors.com.

¢ △ **Brooks Campground.** This National Park Service campground is a short walk from Brooks Lodge, where campers can pay to eat and shower. Designated cooking and eating shelters, latrines, well water, and a storage cache to protect food from the ever-present brown bears are available. Reservations are required. **Pros:** beautiful and outdoor rugged experience; bears aplenty. **Cons:** can be cold and wet; lots of bugs. *Katmai National Park, Box 7, King Salmon 99613 ☎ 907/246–3305 information, 877/444–6777 reservations ⊕ www.nps.gov/katm △ Portable toilets, drinking water, bear boxes, picnic tables, ranger station ⛺ 60 sites ☉ Park is open year-round, but lodge and park services are closed mid-Sept.–June.*

$$$$ 🛏 **Brooks Lodge.** Initially a fishing camp, this lodge has been in operation since 1950. **Pros:** private facilities; bear-viewing at Brooks Falls. **Cons:** fly-fishing only in Brooks River, unless you're a bear. **TripAdvisor:** "comfortable and clean," "lodging is spartan," "here for the bears not luxury." *Katmailand, Inc., 4125 Aircraft Dr., Anchorage 99502 ☎ 907/243–5448 or 800/544–0551 ⊕ www.katmailand.com/lodging/brooks.html ⛺ 16 cabins △ In-room: no TV. In-hotel: restaurant, bar ☉ Closed Sept.–May.*

Fodor's Choice
★

$$$$ 🛏 **Grosvenor Lodge.** Once you've arrived at this remote Katmai National Park lodge, reachable only by floatplane, you have access by motorboat to numerous rivers and streams filled with sport fish. **Pros:** great fishing; accessible to two spawning streams. **Cons:** bathhouse is outside the cabin; absolute seclusion—but isn't that why you picked the place? *Katmailand, Inc., 4125 Aircraft Dr., Anchorage 99502 ☎ 907/243–5448 or 800/544–0551 ⊕ www.katmailand.com/lodging/grosvenor.html ⛺ 3 cabins with shared baths △ In-room: no TV. In-hotel: restaurant, bar ☉ Closed Sept.–May ♨ All meals.*

$$$$ 🛏 **Katmai Wilderness Lodge.** Built on land owned by the Russian Orthodox Church, this rustic lodge straddles the rugged outer coast of Katmai National Park, along the shores of Kukak Bay. **Pros:** private rooms; hot showers; flush toilets. **Cons:** no place to do your shopping. *Box 2749, Kodiak 99615 ☎ 800/488–8767 ⊕ www.katmai-wilderness.com ⛺ 7 rooms △ In-room: no TV, Wi-Fi. In-hotel: restaurant ☉ Closed Oct.–mid-May ♨ All meals.*
★

$$$$ 🛏 **Kulik Lodge.** Positioned along the gin-clear Kulik River, between Nonvianuk and Kulik lakes, this remote wilderness lodge is reachable only by floatplane. **Pros:** great rainbow-trout fishing; modern facilities. **Cons:** BYOT—bring your own tackle. **TripAdvisor:** "very helpful and friendly staff," "comfortable and super clean accommodations," "meals are incredible." *Katmailand, Inc., 4125 Aircraft Dr., Anchorage 99502 ☎ 907/243–5448 or 800/544–0551 ⊕ www.katmailand.com/lodging/kulik.html ⛺ 12 cabins △ In-room: no TV. In-hotel: restaurant, bar ☉ Closed Sept.–May ♨ All meals.*

9

SHUYAK ISLAND STATE PARK

54 mi north of Kodiak Island.

GETTING HERE AND AROUND

On Shuyak Island there are no amenities, groceries, or roads. It is accessible by air or water only. Because it's not as popular a destination as some of the other islands, it's recommended for those who wish to arrive by air to book a flight well in advance (as there are fewer flights out to choose from). It is a popular destination for kayakers. For guided kayaking trips or other expeditions to the island, the best place to start is on Kodiak Island (⇨ *see Kodiak Island in Chapter 6).*

ESSENTIALS

Visitor Information Alaska State Parks, Kodiak District Office (✉ *1400 Abercrombie Dr., Kodiak* ☎ *907/486–6339* ⊕ *www.alaskastateparks.org).*

EXPLORING

Shuyak Island State Park. The 46,000-acre Shuyak Island State Park is one of the most remote and overlooked units in the state parks system. Located at the northern end of the Kodiak Archipelago, it is accessible only by plane or boat. Its rugged outer coastline is balanced by a more protected system of interconnected bays, channels, and passages that make the park a favorite with sea kayakers. It also has excellent wildlife-viewing, especially of seabirds and sea mammals, and top-notch sportfishing for salmon. Wildlife ranges from Sitka black-tailed deer and brown bears to sea otters, sea lions, bald eagles, puffins, and whales. The park has four public-use cabins but no developed campgrounds; limited hiking trails pass through old-growth coastal rain forest.

SPORTS, THE OUTDOORS, AND GUIDED TOURS

For those new to the region or the sport of kayaking, companies based in Kodiak lead trips to local coastal areas, including Shuyak Island. Besides exploring the coastal land- and seascape, paddlers will have a chance to see a variety of birds and marine mammals, possibly including whales. The world holds few thrills quite as great as seeing a whale from kayak height, and hearing them exhale on a still morning. For more experienced kayakers, a limited number of sea-kayaks may be reserved in advance from Sea Hawk Air charter company in Kodiak. The kayaks are located in front of the Big Bay Ranger Station on Shuyak Island and can be picked up when you fly in.

Sea Hawk Air offers floatplane charters, scenic flights and bear-viewing, custom hunting and fishing trips, and Shuyak kayak rentals ✉ *506 Trident Way, Kodiak* ☎ *907/486–8282* ⊕ *www.seahawkair.com.*

WHERE TO STAY

For expanded hotel reviews, visit Fodors.com.

¢ ⛺ **Alaska State Parks Cabins.** Alaska State Parks maintains four public-use cabins on Shuyak Island. **Pros:** scenery that can't be beat; bucket showers available. **Cons:** during the off-season inclement weather can pose potential problems for seaplane pick-ups at the end of your stay. ✉ *Alaska State Parks, Kodiak District Office, 1400 Abercrombie Dr., Kodiak* ☎ *907/486–6339, 907/269–8400 DNR* 🖷 *907/486–3320* ⓓ *DNR Public Information Center, 550 W. 7th Ave., Suite 1260,*

Continued on page 445

WELCOME TO BEAR COUNTRY

(top) Grizzly bears fishing in Katmai National Park (bottom) Polar bear

An 800–pound brown bear plows through the shallows of Pack Creek on Southeast Alaska's Admiralty Island, adroitly flipping a 20-pound salmon out of the current like an NFL lineman snapping a football. This bear, which stands over 8 feet tall when perched on his hind legs, can devour 50 pounds of food every day. And, when sprinting, he can reach speeds of 35 miles per hour. Governmentally speaking, Alaska is a democracy. But in the wilderness, the state is a monarchy—and the bear the undisputed king.

KING OF THE WILDERNESS

A GOOD HOME

Thanks to its vast stretches of wilderness, Alaska is the only state that is home to healthy populations of all three North American ursine species. Polar bears (*Ursus maritimus*) don't venture south of the state's chilly Arctic coastline, while black bears (*Ursus americanus*) and brown bears (*Ursus arctos*; also known as grizzlies) live throughout the state's many refuges and parks. Bear populations are plentiful here: the Alaska Department of Fish and Game estimates that Alaska is home to roughly 100,000 to 200,000 black bears and 25,000 to 38,000 brown bears.

Watching a bear gorge on salmon from a chilly creek or seeing a mother bear wandering the shoreline in the early morning, her two cubs trailing behind her is an unforgettable sight. Sure it's a matter of luck and timing. But sightings like this are a gift from the Alaskan landscape. However, as illustrated by *Grizzly Man*—a 2005 documentary by Werner Herzog about the troubled life and tragic death of Alaska bear activist Timothy Treadwell—Alaska's bears are wild, unpredictable creatures that should *never* be underestimated.

SAFE PLACES TO VIEW BEARS

Bear-viewing in Alaska has become an increasingly popular tourist activity—and one that is safely enjoyed by thousands of visitors using expert outdoor tour guides every year at such locations as Denali National Park & Preserve (⇨ Ch. 7), Kodiak Island (⇨ Ch. 6), Katmai National Park's McNeil River State Game Sanctuary (⇨ Ch. 9), Admiralty Island's Pack Creek (⇨ Ch. 4), Anan Creek Wildlife Observatory (⇨ Ch. 4), and Fish Creek Wildlife Observation Site (⇨ Ch. 4).

Keep in mind that your best bet is to hire an experienced guide and always to check in with rangers at the refuges or parks you plan to visit. It's never certain that you'll see a bear, though your chances increase dramatically if you're visiting one of the aforementioned premier viewing areas during

Strolling black bear

Polar Bear

BEAR OF THE NORTHERN REACHES

Along Alaska's icy northern coast roams the most majestic of all ursine species: the polar bear. Massive in stature (males can reach 1,700 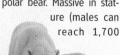 pounds and 11 feet in height), polar bears are also cunning predators that prey chiefly on seals. With relatively short average life spans (15 to 20 years) and one of the slowest reproductive rates of any mammal on earth— females give birth to two cubs every two to five years—polar bear populations are especially vulnerable to human intrusion and, most recently, the continuing retreat of polar sea ice. These bears are worthy of the utmost respect: exercise special caution when traveling along the coastline, as they are known to be aggressive toward humans.

A Kodiak mama bear is followed by two young cubs.

summer salmon runs on a guided tour or if you're traveling in Alaska's more remote backcountry regions. If it's the latter, the chances of an aggressive bear encounter are real but remote.

You should be very well prepared and well versed in safe travel and camping techniques, which include using bear-resistant food containers; never traveling alone; steering clear of forested areas, berry patches, and salmon runs; checking in with park rangers to find out about potential bear zones; and making noise to warn bears that humans are present.

BLACK VERSUS BROWN

Despite their given names, black and brown bears range in color from pure black to nearly blond. Size is the defining characteristic: male brown bears on Kodiak Island—home to the largest brown bear subspecies on Earth—can reach 1,700 pounds and stand 10 feet tall. Male black bears, by comparison, rarely exceed 500 pounds or stand taller than 6 feet. Brown bears have longer claws, longer faces, and a distinct shoulder hump. Brown bears are also more protective of their territory and less intimidated by human intrusion.

Black and brown bears feed on a diverse diet, the staples being salmon, berries, roots, carrion, and the occasional deer, moose, or caribou. Both species hibernate in winter, although bears in the southern coastal regions spend less time hibernating. In the wild, brown and black bears live for 20 to 30 years. Mature female brown and black bears produce a litter of one to four cubs every two years. And thanks to state and federal protections, Alaska's bear populations are holding steady.

THE SOFT SIDE OF TEDDY

Question: How did the bear—one of nature's largest, most fearsome creatures—become such a popular stuffed animal?

Answer: Because Theodore "Teddy" Roosevelt, former U.S. president, avid hunter, and all-around tough guy, refused to shoot a bear while hunting in Mississippi in 1902. Hence "Teddy's bear" was born. If Roosevelt were alive today, there's only one place he'd surely want to visit to see his beloved bears: Alaska.

A playful brown bear

THE BEAR FACTS: TIPS FOR STAYING SAFE

AVOID SURPRISE

Whenever possible, travel in open country, during daylight hours, and in groups. Make constant noise—talking or singing is preferable to carrying "bear bells"—and leave your dog at home. Most attacks occur when a bear is surprised at close quarters or feels threatened.

CAMP WITH CARE

Pitch your tent away from trails, streams with spawning salmon, berry patches, and other food sources. Avoid areas that have a rotten smell or where scavengers have gathered; these may indicate the presence of a nearby food cache, which a bear will aggressively defend.

BE BEAR AWARE

Keep your eyes open for signs of bears: fresh tracks, scat, matted vegetation, or partially consumed salmon.

ISOLATE YOUR FOOD SUPPLIES

Since bears are practically walking noses, it's imperative that you cook meals at least 100 yards from your tents and that you store food and other odorous items away from campsites (*never* in your tent). Hang food between trees or store it in bear-resistant food containers. Thoroughly clean your cooking area and utensils after each use. Store garbage in airtight containers—or burn it—and pack up the remains.

IF YOU ENCOUNTER A BEAR IN THE WILD

1 IDENTIFY YOURSELF. Talk to the bear in a steady, monotone voice. Don't yell. As for running: don't do it. Running has been known to trigger a bear's predatory instincts, and a bear can easily outrun you (remember, brown bears can run as fast as 35 mph). Back away slowly, and give the bear an escape route. Don't ever get between a mother and her cubs.

A grizzly bear strolls Katmai National Park's tidal flats.

2 BIGGER IS BETTER. To increase your apparent size, raise your arms above your head wave them slowly. With two or more people, it helps to stand side by side. In a forested area it may be appropriate to climb a tree, but remember that black bears and young grizzlies are agile tree climbers.

In 2005, fewer than 12 bear maulings occurred in Alaska; two were fatal.

3 AS A LAST RESORT, PLAY DEAD. If a bear charges and makes contact with you, fall to the ground, curl into a ball with your hands behind your neck, and remain passive. If you are wearing a pack, leave it on. Once a bear no longer feels threatened, it will usually end its attack. Wait for the bear to leave before you move. If such an attack persists for more than a few minutes—in other words, if the bear seems intent on actually harming you further—there's only one option: fight back with all of your might. Keep in mind that such worst-case scenarios are exceedingly rare.

Anchorage 99501 ⊕ *dnr.alaska.gov/parks/units/kodiak/shuyak.htm*
⤴ *4 cabins.*

ALEUTIAN ISLANDS, ALASKA PENINSULA, AND PRIBILOF ISLANDS

From the Alaska Peninsula down through the Aleutian chain, this area also includes many islands within the Bering Sea, among them the Pribilof Islands, as well as the Bristol Bay watershed. Altogether, this is a place of enormous biological richness. It harbors many of North America's largest breeding populations of seabirds and waterfowl and a vast fur-seal population. This whole region offers wildlife so diverse and rarefied that is often compared to its counterpart in the southern hemisphere: the Galapagos Islands.

ANIAKCHAK NATIONAL MONUMENT AND PRESERVE

100 mi southwest of Katmai National Park.

GETTING HERE AND AROUND

Aniakchak National Monument and Preserve is expensive to reach, even by remote Alaska standards. The only easy access is by air, usually from the town of King Salmon. Thus, few people visit this spectacular place—and those who do are likely to have the caldera all to themselves. Needless to say, come here and you get permanent bragging rights about what you did on your Alaska vacation.

ESSENTIALS

Visitor Information **Aniakchak National Monument and Preserve** (⌘ *Box 245, King Salmon, 99613* ☎ *907/246–3305* ⊕ *www.nps.gov/ania*).

EXPLORING

Aniakchak National Monument and Preserve, 586,000 acres of protected land, was established by Congress in 1980 to mark the significance of Aniakchak, an extraordinary living volcano that rises to the south of Katmai. Towering more than 4,400 feet above the landscape, the volcano also has one of the largest calderas in the world, with a diameter averaging 6 mi across and 2,500 feet deep; **Surprise Lake** lies within it. Although Aniakchak last erupted in 1931, the explosion that formed the enormous crater occurred before history was written. Because the area is not glaciated, geologists place the blowup after the last Ice Age. It was literally a world-shaking event. The Park Service calls it "one of the least visited units of the National Park system"—maybe a handful of people a year make it out here.

Aniakchak is wild and forbidding country, with a climate that brews mist, clouds, and serious winds much of the year; the caldera is so big that it can entirely create its own local weather patterns, and it really seems to like the bad stuff. Although the **Aniakchak River** (which drains Surprise Lake) is floatable, it has stretches of Class III and IV white water navigable only by expert river runners, and you must travel through open ocean waters to reach the nearest community, Chignik

Bay (or get picked up by plane, along the coast). In other words, this is not something for the unprepared to try, unless you're seriously into hypothermia and have an up-to-date will. An alternate way to enjoy Aniakchak is to wait for a clear day and fly to it in a small plane that will land you on the caldera floor or on Surprise Lake. But be aware that there are no trails, campgrounds, ranger stations, or other visitor facilities here, and it is bear country; you must be prepared to be self-sufficient. Aniakchak is the world in the raw.

SPORTS, THE OUTDOORS, AND GUIDED TOURS

FLIGHTSEEING **Branch River Air** (☎ 907/246–3437 June–Sept., 907/248–3539 Oct.–May ⊕ www.branchriverair.com/), in King Salmon, offers charter flights and flightseeing, and will also arrange fishing and bear-viewing trips.

RIVER RUNNING **Ouzel Expeditions** (☎ 907/783–2216 or 800/825–8196 ⊕ www.ouzel.com) guides river-running trips down the Aniakchak River. Trips begin at Surprise Lake, within the caldera, and end at the coast, and feature white-water rafting and fishing for salmon, char, and rainbow trout.

> **HALLO BAY**
>
> Located at the northern end of the bay, **Hallo Bay Bear Lodge** is an ecofriendly camp that has been running bear-viewing trips for 22 years. Guests stay in rustic yet comfortable heated platform tents or heated cabins and enjoy gourmet meals in an enclosed kitchen. This is true wild bear-viewing: no platforms, just the scenery and the bears, who are very much at home. The price tag, $2,400 for two nights, double occupancy, includes meals, lodging, and naturalist guide services. ☎ 888/535–2237 ⊕ www.hallobay.com ⊘ Closed Oct.–mid-May.

BECHAROF AND ALASKA PENINSULA NATIONAL WILDLIFE REFUGES

★ *Adjacent to Aniakchak National Monument and Preserve, 250 mi to 450 mi southwest of Anchorage.*

GETTING HERE AND AROUND

No visitor facilities are available here, and access is only by boat or plane. Most visitors begin their trips in King Salmon and use guides or outfitters.

ESSENTIALS

Visitor Information **Becharof National Wildlife Refuge** (✉ *Box 277, King Salmon 99613* ☎ *907/246–4250 or 907/246–3339* ⊕ *becharof.fws.gov*).

EXPLORING

The Becharof and Alaska Peninsula National Wildlife Refuges stretch along the southern edge of the Alaska Peninsula. These two refuges encompass nearly 6 million acres of towering mountains, glacial lakes, broad tundra valleys, and coastal fjords. Volcanoes dominate the landscape; there are 14 in all, of which 9 are considered active. **Mt. Veniaminov**—named after Alaska's greatest Russian Orthodox bishop—last erupted in 1993. Other evidence of volcanic activity includes **Gas Rocks**, where gases

BELCHING GIANTS

Some evidence suggests that Alaskans inhabited Katmai's eastern edge for at least 9,000 years up to 1912. But on the morning of June 1 of that year everything changed. After five days of violent earthquakes, the 2,700-foot **Novarupta** blew its top, erupting steadily for the next 60 hours. Rivers of white-hot ash poured into the valley. A foot of ash fell on Kodiak Island, 100 mi away, and in all more than 46,000 square mi of territory ended up under at least an inch of ash, winds carrying yet more ash to eastern Canada and as far as Texas. While Novarupta was belching away, another explosion occurred 6 mi east. The mountaintop peak of **Mt. Katmai** collapsed, creating a chasm almost 3 mi long and 2 mi wide. The molten andesite that held up Mt. Katmai rushed through newly created fissures to Novarupta and was spewed out. Over 2½ days, more than 7 cubic mi of volcanic material were ejected, and the green valley lay under 700 feet of ash. Miraculously, the people who called this remote region home made it out safely; no one was killed.

By 1916 things had cooled off sufficiently to allow scientists to explore the area. A National Geographic expedition led by Dr. Robert F. Griggs reached the valley and found it full of steaming fumaroles (holes in the volcanic terrain that fume smoke), creating a moonlike landscape. The report on what Griggs dubbed the **Valley of Ten Thousand Smokes** inspired Congress in 1918 to declare the valley and the surrounding wilderness a national monument. Steam spouted in thousands of fountains from the smothered streams and springs beneath the ash and gave the valley its name. Although the steam has virtually stopped, an eerie sense of earth forces at work remains, and several nearby volcanoes still smolder, or even threaten to blow every couple of years. Anchorage's airport will sometimes get shut down by smoke or ash from the peninsula's active volcanoes.

The Native peoples never returned to their traditional village sites, though many now live in nearby communities. They are joined by sightseers, anglers, hikers, and other outdoors enthusiasts who migrate to the Katmai region each summer. Fish and wildlife are plentiful, and a few "smokes" still drift through the volcano-sculpted valley.

9

continually seep through cracks in granitic rocks, and **Ukrinek Marrs,** a crater that bears the marks of a violent eruption in 1977.

Aside from the rugged volcanic landscapes, which are reason enough to come, the two refuges are best known for Garden of Eden–quality wildlife. More than 220 species of resident and migratory wildlife use the refuges, including 30 land mammals such as moose and otter; 11 marine mammals, including several kinds of whales; and nearly three-dozen species of fish, with the five main types of salmon. Look up for nearly 150 species of birds, from the bald eagle doing its perfect impersonation of life after taxidermy high in the tree, to Alaska's trickster, the raven, as well as enough waterbirds to keep a hard-core twitcher at the binoculars for a week. Just put the binocs down from time to time to keep an eye out for the brown bears that live in every corner of the refuges.

Becharof Lake, at 35 mi long and up to 15 mi wide, is the second-largest lake in Alaska (behind Lake Iliamna). Fed by two rivers and 14 major creeks, it serves as a nursery to the world's second-biggest run of sockeye salmon. **Ugashik Lakes** are known for their salmon and trophy grayling. The world-record grayling, nearly 5 pounds (most grayling weigh a pound or less), was caught at Ugashik Narrows in 1981.

Remote and rugged, with the peninsula's usual unpredictable weather, the Becharof and Alaska Peninsula refuges draw mostly anglers and hunters; however, backpackers, river runners, and mountain climbers also occasionally visit.

> **TAKE THE HIGHWAY**
>
> The Alaska Marine Highway System, that is. This much-loved form of Alaskan transport is best known for its routes along the Inside Passage. In summer these ferries also depart from Homer, in South Central, and pass by Kodiak on the three-plus-day trip to Dutch Harbor. It's an unforgettable way to see the Southwest's dramatic landscape (☎ 800/642-0066 ⊕ www.ferryalaska.com).

ALEUTIAN ISLANDS

The Aleutians begin 540 mi southwest of Anchorage and stretch more than 1,400 mi.

It is easier to get to the Aleutian Islands than the Pribilof Islands or Alaska Peninsula, because there's a regular ferry service that runs out that way.

Separating the North Pacific Ocean from the Bering Sea, the Aleutian Islands are not a single sequence of islands. Actually, they're a superchain, made of up eight smaller island groups—the Andreanof, Delarof, Fox, Four Mountain, Near, Rat, Shumagin, and Sanak islands. In all, this adds up to more than 275 islands, stretching from the Alaska Peninsula in a southwesterly arc toward Japan. The islands are volcanic in origin, treeless, and alternate between towering (and frequently smoking) volcanic cones, and high tablelands. Separating the islands is some of the wildest, deepest water anywhere: on the Pacific side of the chains the water can be more than 25,000 feet deep, and the north side's Bering Canyon is twice as long as the Grand Canyon, as well as twice as deep, bottoming out at 10,600 feet below the water's surface. The Aleutian Islands and surrounding coastal waters make up one of the most biologically rich areas in Alaska, harboring abundant seabird, marine mammal, and fish populations—and the fish feed the ships of one of the world's busiest fishing fleets.

Before the Russians arrived in the mid-1700s, the islands were dotted with Aleut villages, a total population of perhaps 3,000 people; within a hundred years, that number had dropped to maybe 200 through disease and war. Today's native communities include **Nikolski**, on Umnak Island; **Atka**, on Atka Island; and **Cold Bay**, at the peninsula's tip. Like everybody in the Aleutians, the descendants of the original inhabitants mostly work at commercial fishing or in canneries and as expert guides for those who hunt and fish. The settlements are quite small, and accommodations are scarce.

Visitors aren't allowed on Shemya Island, which has a remote U.S. Air Force base, without special permission. Because of downsizing, the military has closed its Adak operation, and the base's infrastructure provides the core infrastructure for what now is a small coastal community and commercial fishing port.

Unalaska/Dutch Harbor, twin towns midway out the chain, are by far the most populous destinations in the Aleutian Islands. Although they're sometimes called "the Crossroads of the Aleutians," even by Alaska standards people who live here are living remote. Usually referred to simply as "Dutch" (or, by people who spend winter there, "the gulag"), the towns are connected by a bridge that spans a narrow channel between Unalaska and Amaknak islands. (Locals playfully call the span the "Bridge to the Other Side.") Despite the often-harsh weather—this region is known as the "Cradle of Storms" for good reason—the Aleut people and their ancestors have occupied these islands and others in the Aleutians for thousands of years. Today Dutch is the region's tourism center, as well as one of the busiest fishing ports in the world. Scattered around both islands are reminders of history: the Japanese bombed Dutch Harbor during World War II (unexploded ordnance may still be out there, so don't handle any odd metal objects you see while hiking), and you can still explore concrete bunkers, gun batteries, and a partially sunken ship left over from the war.

It's worth the trip out to Dutch on the ferry just for the scenery along the way, but when travelers finally reach the islands they discover a surprisingly gentle landscape of tawny, rolling hills sheltering a town that is built for work, not beauty. Which is not to say the town lacks pretty things. The most dramatic attraction in Dutch is the Holy Ascension Russian Orthodox Church, a perfect blue, onion-dome chapel right on the edge of the water, the best Russian church left in Alaska. The extant buildings date to the 1890s, although there has been a church on the site since 1808. Inside is a collection of Russian icons and artworks that is not to be missed, certainly the most impressive in the Americas. These are not museum pieces; they have been used, regularly, and it shows.

Next to the church is the Bishop's House, which is undergoing continuing restoration. A walk in the graveyard between the two buildings shows the full history of the area: Aleuts, sailors, and, always oriented to face the church, the graves of the Orthodox parishioners.

Easy walking distance from the ferry terminal is the Aleutian World War II National Historic Area Visitor Center, on the edge of the airport. The Aleutians saw heavy fighting through much of the war—some of the outer islands were occupied by Japanese forces for years—and the museum does a nice job of presenting the history of the conflict. At the peak of the war, more than 60,000 servicemen were stationed out here.

The Aleut take on the islands is offered at the Museum of the Aleutians, behind the grocery store, about a 15-minute walk from the ferry. Small, but quite remarkable, displays include original drawings from

Captain Cook's third voyage, a traditional gut parka, and more. A don't-miss stop.

Don't worry about opening hours: if the ferry is in, the town's attractions will be open.

For facilities, the towns have hotels and restaurants that rival those on Alaska's mainland, plus guided adventure tours, many geared toward birders. If you're feeling particularly planning oriented, contact the **Unalaska–Dutch Harbor Convention and Visitors Bureau** (✉ *Box 545, Unalaska 99685* ☎ *907/581–2612 or 877/581–2612* ⊕ *www.unalaska. info*) for a little extra guidance during your visit.

SPORTS, THE OUTDOORS, AND GUIDED TOURS

OUTDOOR ADVENTURING   **Aleutian Adventure Sports.** Since 1994 AAS owner Jeff Hancock has offered an Aleutian resident's outdoor experience, and is the only year-round outfitter operating in the chain. Services include guided hiking, camping, sea kayaking and mountaineering, as well as marine charters for sightseeing and water-taxi. For the intrepid adventurer, gear rentals for mountain bikes, camping gear, and sea kayaks are also available. ✉ *Box 921181, Dutch Harbor* ☎ *907/581–4489* ⊕ *www. aleutianadventure.com.*

WHERE TO STAY

For expanded hotel reviews, visit Fodors.com.

$$$ 🏨 **Grand Aleutian Hotel.** An airy three-story atrium lobby with a large
★   stone fireplace conjures images of a Swiss chalet. **Pros:** bay-view rooms; masseuse on call. **Cons:** a bit generic; once you're inside, you could be almost anywhere. ✉ *498 Salmon Way, Box 921169, Dutch Harbor* ☎ *866/581–3844* ⊕ *www.grandaleutian.com* 🛏 *112 rooms, 2 suites* ⚒ *In-room: Wi-Fi, In-hotel: 2 restaurants, bar, some pets allowed.*

$ 🏨 **Unisea Inn of the Grand Aleutian Hotel.** This inn is the little sister of the Grand Aleutian Hotel, built to accommodate travelers on a budget. **Pros:** what passes for budget prices in the Aleutians; cozy. **Cons:** not as grand as the Grand Aleutian; views not as great either. ✉ *185 Gilman Rd., Box 921169, Dutch Harbor* ☎ *866/581–3844 reservations* 🛏 *25 rooms* ⚒ *In-room: Wi-Fi, In-hotel: restaurant, bar.*

PRIBILOF ISLANDS

200 mi north of the Aleutian Islands, 800 mi southwest of Anchorage.

GETTING HERE AND AROUND

For most travelers it is much easier and more efficient to sign up for package tours that arrange air travel from Anchorage, lodging, ground transportation on the islands, and guided activities. It can be nearly, if not completely, impossible to arrange such things after you arrive. Guest accommodations in the Pribilofs are very limited, with lodgings only on St. George and St. Paul. The best way to hop between islands is by air on Peninsula Airways, but both islands are notorious fog magnets; you should never plan on getting out quite as scheduled.

ESSENTIALS

Airline Contacts Peninsula Airways (☎ *907/771–2510* ⊕ *www.penair.com*).

Emergency Contacts St. George Traditional Clinic (☎ 907/859–2254). St. Paul Health Clinic/APIA (✉ 1990 Polovina Tpke., St. Paul Island ☎ 907/546–2310 or 911).

Mail U.S. Post Office (✉ 2000 Polovina Tpke., St. Paul Island ☎ 907/546–2270).

EXPLORING

The **Pribilof Islands** are a misty, fog-bound breeding ground of seabirds and northern fur seals. Rising out of the surging waters of the Bering Sea, the Pribilofs consist of five islets, a tiny, green, treeless oasis with rippling belts of lush grass contrasting with volcanic rocks. In early summer seals come home from far Pacific waters to mate, and the larger islands, St. Paul and St. George, are overwhelmed with frenzied activity. The seals' barks and growls can roll out several miles to sea.

Although St. Paul and St. George are less than 50 mi apart, the island group itself is a 1,600-mi round-trip from Anchorage, over the massive snowy peaks of the Alaska Peninsula and north of the rocky islands of the Aleutian chain.

About the only visitors to the Pribilofs are commercial fishermen—this is where many of the "Deadliest Catch" boats call their home port—or those who've come to see wildlife. Together, St. Paul and St. George islands are seasonal homes to hundreds of thousands of fur seals (about 80% of them on St. Paul) and nearly 250 species of birds. Some birds migrate here from as far away as Argentina, whereas others are year-round residents. Most spectacular of all is the islands' seabird population: each summer more than 2 million seabirds gather at traditional Pribilof nesting grounds; about 90% of them breed on St. George.

Fodor's Choice ★ At **St. Paul Island** nature lovers can watch members of the largest northern fur-seal herd in the world and more than 180 varieties of birds. In town you can visit with local residents; about 500 descendants of Aleut-Russians live here now, in the shadow of the old but beautifully-cared-for Russian Orthodox church and amid the vestiges of Aleut culture; the local museum shows how the island was once essentially a factory, as the U.S. government controlled sealing, and so the only jobs on the island.

St. George Island is home to nearly 2 million nesting seabirds, but it is much less frequently visited because no organized tours visit here, and accommodations are limited. Even people who live on St. Paul try to avoid going to St. George because it's so easy to get weathered in there.

SPORTS, THE OUTDOORS, AND GUIDED TOURS

The Pribilofs are considered a birders' paradise for good reason: species that are seldom, if ever, seen elsewhere in North America frequently show up here, including an array of "Asian vagrants" blown here by westerly winds. Birders can expect to find all manner of shorebirds, waterfowl, and seabirds, including puffins, murres, red- and

> **DID YOU KNOW?**
>
> Of special interest to birders are the rare vagrant birds of native Asian species, such as the Siberian rubythroat and Eurasian skylark, sometimes blown here by strong winds. But just for day-to-day birding, come here, see a red-legged kittiwake, and make birders back home scream in envy.

9

black-legged kittiwakes, plovers—the list goes on and on. Tour guides are usually hired for their birding skills, but will also show visitors the best places to view seals (well, the seals are kind of hard to miss, since a lot of the adolescent males hang out near the roads) and maybe the occasional whale.

BIRDING
AND SEAL
WATCHING

Contact **Tanadgusix Village Corporation of St. Paul Island** (⊠ *615 E. 82nd Ave., Anchorage* ☎ *907/278–2312 or 877/424–5637* ⊕ *www. alaskabirding.com*) for St. Paul Island tour information. The owners of **Wilderness Birding Adventures** (☎ *907/694–7442* ⊕ *www. wildernessbirding.com*) run regular trips in the Pribilofs; elsewhere in the state, they combine birding, hiking, and river rafting in their wilderness adventures.

WHERE TO STAY

For expanded hotel reviews, visit Fodors.com.

$$$$ 🍽 **King Eider Hotel.** The original King Eider, once a landmark among serious Alaskan travelers, is now just a shuttered building that doesn't look like it will stand much longer. **Pros:** clean, very well cared for, and the only game in town. **Cons:** pretty bare-bones rooms for the price; a lot of rooms share just a couple of baths. ⊠ *523 Tolstoi St., St. Paul* ☎ *907/546–2477 or 907/278–2312, 877/424–5637 to make tour reservations* ⊕ *www.alaskabirding.com* 🛏 *20 rooms, 2 shared baths* ♨ *In-room: no TV.*

$$$$ 🍽 **St. George Tanaq Hotel.** A national historic landmark, St. George Island's only hotel is a small, rustic building with a dark-wood interior and a mix of modern and vintage furniture. **Pros:** National Historic Landmark flavor; can hear the seals from your room. **Cons:** come ready for every weather condition possible, all at once; seals keep light sleepers awake. ⊠ *Downtown St. George* ☎ *907/859–2255* ⊕ *www. stgeorgetanaq.com* 🛏 *10 rooms share 5 baths* ♨ *In-hotel: restaurant.*

NORTHWEST AND THE ARCTIC

This is a largely roadless region of long, dark, sunless winters and short, bright summers, when the sun provides nearly three months of perpetual daylight in places like Barrow. The round-the-clock sunshine lasts for only a few days farther south, but the extended twilight hours turn the midnights bright. The Northwest and Arctic are the land of Eskimos and huge caribou herds and polar bears, a place where people still lead subsistence lifestyles and where the Native cultural traditions live on. This region is also a place of gold rushes past and America's largest oil field, as well as a region with many of Alaska's most remote parklands—not to mention one of the country's grandest refuges, the Arctic National Wildlife Refuge.

NOME

540 mi northwest of Anchorage.

More than a century has passed since a great stampede for gold put a speck of wilderness now called Nome on the Alaska map, but gold

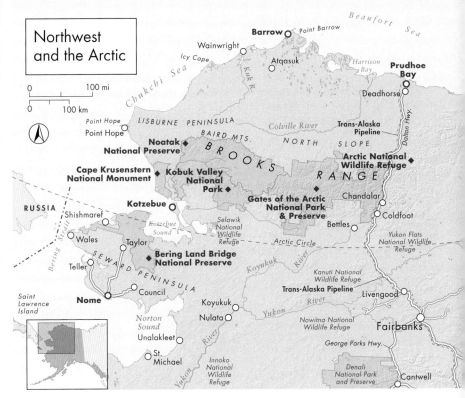

mining and noisy saloons are still mainstays here. This frontier community on the icy Bering Sea once boasted 20,000 people during the gold stampede in the 1890s, but now has only 3,500 year-round residents. At first glance the town may come off as a collection of ramshackle houses and low-slung commercial buildings—like a vintage gold-mining camp or, because of the spooky abandoned monolithic microwave towers from World War II that sit atop Anvil Mountain, the set for an Arctic horror movie—but only a couple of streets back you'll find tidy, modern homes and charming, hospitable shopkeepers. In fact Nome is one of Alaska's greatest places, very much itself, the kind of town where the grocery store sells ATVs next to the meat counter.

Just 165 mi from the coast of Siberia, Nome is considerably closer to Russia than to either Anchorage or Fairbanks. And though you'll find 300 mi of local road system well worth exploring, to get to Nome you must either fly or mush a team of sled dogs.

For centuries before Nome gained fame as a gold-rush town, nomadic Inupiaq Eskimos seasonally inhabited the area in hunting and fishing camps; an archaeological site south of town has the remains of some round pit houses that prove the locals didn't much like corners. The gold stampede—far, far richer than the more famous Klondike strike—

occurred in the 1890s and was over relatively soon, even though gold is still mined by both prospectors and open-pit mining productions.

What Nome is best known for, however, is the Iditarod Trail. Even though parts of the historic trail from Nome to Anchorage were long used as routes for the Native Eskimos and Athabascans, the full trail gained fame in 1925, when Nome was hit with an outbreak of diphtheria. There was no remedy in town, so the serum was ferried by the Alaska Railroad to Nenana, 250 mi from Anchorage, and then a 20-dog sled team ran it the remaining 674 mi in -50 degrees Fahrenheit temperatures over five days and seven hours; Nome was saved. In 1973, in honor of the original Iditarod (a word derived from the Athabascan word haiditarod, meaning "a far, distant place"), an annual race for dog mushers was started. The race begins in Anchorage and traverses snow and tundra for 1,049 mi, to commemorate Alaska's being the 49th state (the actual distance is give or take a few miles, of course; dog sleds don't come with odometers). Thousands of people converge in Nome to watch the dogs and mushers come over the finish line in March. Still more visitors come to Nome in the summer months to take advantage of the beautiful effulgent colors of wildflowers and green grass, its wildlife viewing and birding, and its marvelous end-of-the-world vibe.

Though at first there doesn't seem to be much to this town on the edge of the Bering Sea, there are many relics of the past in and around the area. There are 44 abandoned gold dredges, enormous constructions of steel that are scattered from the outskirts of town to the surrounding miles of tundra beyond. Just east of town on the road out to Council, a quiet summer fishing village inhabited by many locals during the summer, you'll stumble across not only fantastic marshlands for birding, but also the Last Train to Nowhere—a railway built to haul gold that was never finished—quietly rusting away. In the opposite direction, northeast of Nome on the road to Taylor, you'll come to the Pilgrim Hot Springs, the site of an old settlement including the former Our Lady of Lourdes chapel and orphanage for Eskimo children during the 1918 influenza epidemic. And directly north of Nome is the beautiful Native village of Teller, a subsistence village in Grantley Harbor, which may have one of the most perfect locations in the world, set on a buttonhook spit in a sheltered bay. Teller made the world news in 1926, when Roald Amundsen landed his zeppelin Norge here after the first successful flight over the north pole.

The roads to these destinations are unpaved but traversable, and mostly in good shape. From the road you might see herds of reindeer (they like to use the road themselves, since it's easier than running in tundra), musk oxen, grizzly bears, and moose, and a slew of different birds like the long-tailed jaegers, yellow wagtails, and the bristle-thighed curlew, rarely seen in North America.

GETTING HERE AND AROUND

Alaska Airlines Vacations packages air tours to Barrow and Nome. Local arrangements are taken care of by ground operators. The Alaska Travel Industry Association can give tips on air travel and flightseeing opportunities throughout the Bush. From Nome visitors can access Serpentine Hot Springs, in the Bering Land Bridge National Preserve, by charter plane. These hot springs are well maintained despite their location.

If you're set on doing your own driving, head to Alaska Cab Garage or Stampede Ventures, which rent cars and vans of various types. ■TIP➔ Be sure to fill up with gas in Nome, as there are no services once you leave town, and even if the gauge says the tank is full when you rent it, be sure to fill 'er up anyway—sometimes the gauges lie.

ESSENTIALS

Airline and Visitor Contacts Alaska Airlines Vacations (✆ Box 68900, Seattle, WA 98168 ☎ 800/468–2248 ⊕ www.alaskaair.com). **Alaska Travel Industry Association** (✉ 2600 Cordova St., Suite 201, Anchorage 99503 ☎ 907/929–2200, 800/862–5275 for vacation planner ⊕ www.travelalaska.com). **Nome Convention and Visitors Bureau** (✉ 301 Front St. Nome 99672 ☎ 907/443–6555, 800/478–1901 in Alaska ⊕ www.visitnomealaska.com).

Banking Credit Union 1 (✉ 110 Front St. ☎ 800/478–2222 ⊕ www.cu1.org). **Wells Fargo** (✉ 109A Front St. ☎ 907/443–2223 or 800/869–3557 ⊕ www.wellsfargo.com).

Emergency Police (☎ 907/443–5262). **Norton Sound Regional Hospital** (✉ Nome ☎ 907/443–3311 ⊕ www.nortonsoundhealth.org). **State troopers** (☎ 907/443–5525).

Internet City Library (✉ 223 Front St. ☎ 907/443–6628 ⊕ www.nomealaska.org/library/index.html).

Mail USPS (✉ 113 E. Front St. ☎ 907/443–2401).

Vehicle Rental Alaska Cab Garage (☎ 907/443–2939). **Stampede Vehicle Rentals** (☎ 907/443–3838 or 800/354–4606 ⊕ www.aurorainnome.com).

EXPLORING

Since the sun stays up late in the summer months, it's the perfect season for an evening drive to the top of **Anvil Mountain**, near Nome, for a panoramic view of the old gold town and the Bering Sea. Be sure to carry mosquito repellent.

Nome's **Carrie M. McClain Memorial Museum** showcases the history of the Nome gold rush, from the "Lucky Swedes'" discovery in 1898 to Wyatt Earp's arrival in 1899 and the stampede of thousands of people into Nome in 1900. The museum also has exhibits about the Bering Strait Inupiaq Eskimos, plus displays on the Nome Kennel Club and its All-Alaska Sweepstakes. However, the highlight of the museum is the historical photo collection: thousands of pictures from the early days make it a perfect place to lose yourself on a rainy day. ✉ 223 Front St. ☎ 907/443–6630 🆓 Free ⏱ June–early Sept., daily 10–5:30; early Sept.–May, Tues.–Fri. 1–5.

For exploring downtown, stop at the **Nome Convention and Visitors Bureau** (✉ 301 Front St. ☎ 907/443–6555 ⊕ www.nomealaska.org/vc) for a historic walking-tour map, a city map, and information on local activities from flightseeing to bird-watching.

SPORTS, THE OUTDOORS, AND GUIDED TOURS

LOCAL TOURS **Alaska Airlines Vacations** (☎ 800/468–2248 ⊕ www.alaskaair.com) arranges trips to Nome (such as the "Day in Nome" and "Adventure in Nome" packages), including air travel, hotels, and local tours. Visitors seeking to learn more about Nome and the surrounding region can join former Broadway showman Richard Beneville, flat-out one of Alaska's most entertaining guides, who emphasizes Nome's gold-rush and Inupiaq history of the region in his **Nome Discovery Tours** (✉ Box 2024, Nome 99762 ☎ 907/443–2814). If you only have one day in town, spend it with Richard. **Northern Alaska Tour Company** (✉ Box 82991-W, Fairbanks 99708 ☎ 800/474–1986 or 907/474–8600 ⊕ www.northernalaska.com) arranges one-day cultural tours to Nome via Fairbanks or Anchorage.

SLED-DOG RACING The famed **Iditarod Trail Sled Dog Race**—the Olympics of sled-dog racing—reaches its culmination in Nome in mid-March. Racers start in Anchorage for a trip of nine days to two weeks (the record, set in 2011, is an astounding eight days, 18 hours, 46 minutes, 39 seconds). The arrival of the mushers heralds a winter carnival. For dates, starting times, and other information, contact the **Iditarod Trail Committee** (✉ Box 870800, Wasilla 99687 ☎ 907/376–5155 ⊕ www.iditarod.com).

WHERE TO EAT

$$–$$$
STEAK
☁
Fodor's Choice
★
✕**Airport Pizza**. This family-friendly pizza joint isn't like any other. Not only does it make some of the best food in town, with a menu boasting great pizza and toppings, but it also features Tex-Mex, sandwiches, and a full breakfast menu. What's given this restaurant national attention is its delivery service: not only in town, but also to the surrounding Bush villages. Call up, order a pizza, and it'll be put on the next plane out, no extra charge. There are 11 beers on tap (many of which are microbrews), an extensive wine selection, and live music on the weekends. It also has a drive-thru coffee shop. ✉ 406 Bering St. ☎ 907/443–7992 or 877/Pizza70 ⊕ www.airportpizza.com.

$$–$$$
PIZZA
✕**Milano's Pizzeria**. This Front Street restaurant has a casual atmosphere and offers dine-in service as well as takeout. Besides pizzas with a wide assortment of toppings, there's Japanese and Italian food. One side of the restaurant has Italian decor and the other has Japanese. Sit on the side that suits your palate. ✉ 110 W. Front St. ☎ 907/443–2924.

¢–$
AMERICAN
✕**Subway**. Nome's only fast-food restaurant has probably the nicest view you'll ever see from a fast-food chain. Overlooking the Bering Sea through large vista windows, this eatery adjoins the only movie theater in town. When the foreign surroundings and harsh weather start to get you down, a little bit of familiarity can go a long way. Nothing surprising on this menu. ✉ 135 E. Front St. ☎ 907/443–8100.

WHERE TO STAY

For expanded hotel reviews, visit Fodors.com.

$$–$$$
Fodor's Choice
★
🛏**Aurora Inn & Suites**. Located right in the historic district and in walking distance of shops, eateries, and watering holes, the inn offers clean, modern rooms. **Pros:** refreshingly clean; friendly service; sauna. **Cons:** proximity to the bars means it can get a little rowdy outside; most rooms don't have a view. **TripAdvisor:** "quiet and clean," "room was

RICHES OF THE PAST

The region's golden years began in 1898, when three prospectors—known as the Lucky Swedes—struck rich deposits on Anvil Creek, about 4 mi from what became Nome. Their discovery was followed by the formation of the Cape Nome Mining District. The following summer even more gold was found on the beaches of Nome, a place where no one ever would have expected to find gold—placer gold is usually lying on bedrock, but here thousands of winter melts had washed it down to the sea.

Word spread quickly to the south, right about the same time everybody was discovering all the good spots for gold in the Klondike were staked. When the Bering Sea ice parted the next spring, ships from Puget Sound (in the Seattle area) arrived in Nome with eager stampeders, and miners who struck out in the Klondike arrived via the Yukon River to try again in Nome. An estimated 15,000 people landed in Nome between June and October 1900, bringing the area's population to more than 20,000. Dozens of gold dredges were hauled into the region to extract the metal from Seward Peninsula sands and gravels; more than 40 are still standing, though no longer operating (if you explore them, be sure to call out regularly, as warning to any bears that might have taken shelter inside). Among the gold-rush luminaries were Wyatt Earp, the old gunfighter from the O.K. Corral, who mined the gold of Nome the easy way: by opening a posh saloon and serving drinks to thirsty diggers. Also in Nome were Tex Rickard, the boxing promoter, who operated another Nome saloon (money made there later helped him build the

third incarnation of Madison Square Garden, and helped him found the New York Rangers hockey team); and Rex Beach, whose first novel, The Spoilers, was based on the true story of government officials stealing gold from the hardworking miners (it was a best-seller, letting even people warm and cozy down south experience the stampede).

The city of Nome was incorporated in 1901, which means it is now Alaska's oldest first-class city, with the oldest continuously operating school district. But the community's heyday lasted less than a decade; by the early 1920s the bulk of the region's gold had been mined, and only 820 or so people continued to live in Nome.

Although the city's boom times ended long ago, gold mining has continued to the present; depending on the economy, the size of the mines (and the number of offshore minidredges) fluctuates. Visitors are welcome to try their own luck; you can pick up a gold pan at one of Nome's stores and sift through the beach sands along a 2-mi stretch of shoreline east of Nome. Visitors can also contact the **Nome Convention and Visitors Bureau** for information on tours that feature gold panning.

9

CAMPING IN NOME

⚠ **Bureau of Land Management Campground.** The BLM manages a non-fee campground at Mile 40 of the Nome-Taylor Highway. The campground, just off the highway, has six tent sites, and fishing is close by. The maximum length of stay is 14 days. There are a pit toilet and fire rings for cooking, but the only water is in nearby Salmon Lake and Pilgrim River; it must be boiled or otherwise treated. Pros: great fishing and birding; an excellent way to experience the tundra. **Cons:** being out on the tundra means the ever-present risk of high winds; watch out for hungry grizzly bears. ☏ *Bureau of Land Management, Nome Field Office, Box 925, 99762* ☎ *907/443–2177 in Nome, 907/474–2231 in Fairbanks, 907/267–1246 in Anchorage, 800/478–1263 Alaska only* ⊕ *www. ak.blm.gov* ⤴ *6 tent sites* ⚘ *Portable toilets, fire pits, swimming* ⚊ *Reservations not accepted* ☰ *No credit cards* ☉ *Closed Oct.–May.*

spacious," "comfortable and friendly." ⊠ *302 E. Front St.* ☎ *907/443–3838 or 800/354–4606* ⊕ *www.aurorainnome.com* ⤴ *54 rooms* ⚘ *In-room: kitchen (some), Wi-Fi. In-hotel: laundry facilities.*

$ 🏨 **Nome Nugget Inn.** The architecture and decor of the Nugget Inn combine every cliché of the Victorian gold-rush era. **Pros:** cool atmosphere in the public areas; great location. **Cons:** a little less cool in the rooms. ⊠ *315 Front St.* ☎ *907/443–4189 or 877/443–2323* ⊕ *www. nomenuggetinnhotel.com* ⤴ *47 rooms* ⚘ *In-room: Wi-Fi.*

SHOPPING

Nome is one of the best places to buy ivory, because many of the Eskimo carvers from outlying villages come to Nome first to sell their wares to dealers. The **Arctic Trading Post** (⊠ *Bering and Front Sts., across from the Nugget Inn* ☎ *907/443–2686*) has an extensive stock of authentic Eskimo ivory carvings and other Alaskan artwork, jewelry, and books. It's also the place where most of the locals stop for their morning coffee. **Chukotka–Alaska** (⊠ *514 Lomen* ☎ *907/443–4128*) sells both Native Alaskan and Russian artwork and handicrafts as well as books, beads, and furs. The **Maruskiyas of Nome** (⊠ *895 Front St.* ☎ *907/443–2955* ⊕ *www.maruskiyas.com*) specializes in authentic Native Alaskan artwork and handicrafts, including ivory, baleen, and jade sculptures, jewelry, dolls, and masks.

BERING LAND BRIDGE NATIONAL PRESERVE

100 mi north of Nome.

GETTING HERE AND AROUND

The Bering Land Bridge National Preserve is pretty much exactly like it was when people first came to this continent from Asia: it has no trails, campgrounds, or other visitor facilities. Access is largely by air taxi, although there is a road leading from Nome that passes within possible hiking distance.

ESSENTIALS

Air Taxi Contacts **Bering Air** (☎ 907/443–5464 ⊕ www.beringair.com). **North-western Aviation, Inc.** (☎ 907/442–3525 ⊕ www.alaskaonyourown.com).

Visitor Information **National Park Service** (✉ Box 220, Nome 99762 ☎ 907/443–2522 or 907/442–3890 ⊕ www.nps.gov/bela).

EXPLORING

The frozen ash and lava of the 2.8-million-acre **Bering Land Bridge National Preserve** lie between Nome and Kotzebue, immediately south of the Arctic Circle, one of the most remote parks in the world. The Lost Jim lava flow is the northernmost flow of major size in the United States, and the paired *maars* (clear volcanic lakes) are a geological rarity.

Of equal interest are the paleontological features of this preserve. Sealed into the permafrost are flora and fauna—bits of twigs and leaves, tiny insects, small mammals, even the fossilized remains of woolly mammoths—that flourished here when the Bering Land Bridge linked North America to what is now Russia. "Bridge" is something of a misnomer; essentially, the Bering Sea was dry at the time, and the intercontinental connection was as much as 600 mi wide at places. Early peoples wandered through this treeless landscape, perhaps following the musk ox, whose descendants still occupy this terrain, or the mammoths and steppe bison, who are both long gone. Flowering plants thrive in this seemingly barren region, about 250 species in all, and tens of thousands of migrating birds can be seen in season. More than 100 species, including ducks, geese, swans, sandhill cranes, and various shorebirds and songbirds, come here from around the world each spring.

KOTZEBUE

170 mi northeast of Nome.

Kotzebue is Alaska's largest Eskimo community, home to more than 3,000 people. Most of the residents of this coastal village are Inupiaq, whose ancestors have had ties to the region for thousands of years. For most of that time the Inupiaq lived in seasonal camps, following caribou, moose, and other wildlife across the landscape. They also depended on whales, seals, fish, and the wide variety of berries and other plants the rich tundra landscape offers. Besides being talented hunters, the Inupiaq were—and still are—skilled craftsmen and artists, known for their rugged gear, ceremonial parkas, dolls, caribou-skin masks, birch-bark baskets, and whalebone and walrus-ivory carvings.

Built on a 3-mi-long spit of land that juts into Kotzebue Sound, this village lies 33 mi above the Arctic Circle, on Alaska's northwest coast. Before Europeans arrived in the region, the Inupiaq name for this locale was Kikiktagruk; that was changed to Kotzebue after German explorer Otto von Kotzebue passed through in 1818 while sailing for Russia. Kotzebue is the region's economic and political hub and headquarters for both the Northwest Arctic Borough and the NANA Regional Corporation, one of the 13 regional Native corporations formed when Congress settled the Alaskan Natives' aboriginal land claims in 1971.

9

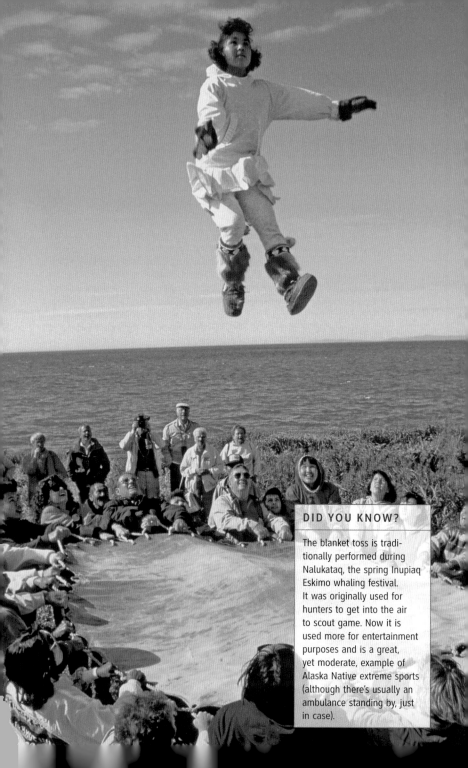

DID YOU KNOW?

The blanket toss is traditionally performed during Nalukataq, the spring Inupiaq Eskimo whaling festival. It was originally used for hunters to get into the air to scout game. Now it is used more for entertainment purposes and is a great, yet moderate, example of Alaska Native extreme sports (although there's usually an ambulance standing by, just in case).

The region's other Eskimo villages have populations of anywhere from 90 to 700 residents.

Just as their ancestors did, modern Inupiaq depend heavily on subsistence hunting and fishing. Some residents also fish commercially. This region of the state has few employment opportunities outside of the government and the Native corporation, but in Kotzebue, the biggest private employer is the Red Dog Mine. Located on NANA land, Red Dog has the world's largest deposit of zinc, and is expected to produce ore for at least 50 years. Local government here, as in many Bush villages, is a blend of tribal government and a more modern borough system. Other facilities and programs include the Maniilaq Health Center and the Northwest Arctic District Correspondence Program.

> **WELCOME TO KOTZEBUE**
>
> Comprising clusters of weather-bleached little houses and a few public buildings on the gravelly shore of Kotzebue Sound, this village provides a glimpse of how Alaska's Eskimos live today. It was an ancient Eskimo trading center; now it is an example of the modern spirit nudging Alaska Natives into the state's mainstream culture without leaving their traditions behind.

Kotzebue has long, cold winters and short, cool summers. The average low temperature in January is –12°F, and midsummer highs rarely reach the 70s. "We have four seasons—June, July, August, and winter," a tour guide jests. But don't worry about the sometimes chilly weather—the local sightseeing company has snug, bright loaner parkas for visitors on package tours. And there's plenty of light in which to take in the village and surrounding landscape: the sun doesn't set for 36 days from June into July. One of summer's highlights is the annual Northwest Native Trade Fair; held each year after the July 4 celebration, it features traditional Native games, seal-hook-throwing contests, and an Eskimo buggy race.

GETTING HERE AND AROUND

As with pretty much everywhere else in the Bush, your main mode of transportation into Kotzebue will be via airplane. **Alaska Airlines** offers regular flights between Anchorage and Kotzebue. Check the Web site for more details. The main air-taxi services serve Kotzebue, and there's a daily flight from Anchorage. Cabs will take you anywhere in town for $5 flat, plus $5 per stop.

ESSENTIALS

Airline Information **Alaska Airlines** (⊕ www.alaskaair.com)

Banking **Wells Fargo** (✉ 360 Lagoon St. ☎ 907/442-3258 or 800/869-3557 ⊕ www.wellsfargo.com).

Emergency **Maniilaq Health Center** (✉ Kotzebue ☎ 800/478/3221 or 907/442-3321 ⊕ www.maniilaq.org). **Police** (☎ 907/442-3351 ⊕ www.kotzebuepolice.com). **State troopers** (☎ 907/442-3222 in Kotzebue).

Internet Access **Chukchi Consortium Library** (✉ 604 3rd St. ☎ 907/442-2410).

Mail **USPS** (✉ *333 Shore Ave.* ☎ *907/442–3291*).

Visitor Information NANA Regional Corporation (*Northwest Alaska Native Association* ☎ *907/442–3301 or 800/478–3301* ⊕ *www.nana.com*). **Northwest Arctic Borough** (✉ *Box 1110, Kotzebue 99752* ☎ *907/442–2500 or 800/478–1110*).

EXPLORING

If you're hiking the wildflower-carpeted tundra around Kotzebue, you are entering a living museum dedicated to **permafrost**, the permanently frozen ground that lies just a few inches below the spongy tundra. Even Kotzebue's 6,000-foot airport runway is built on permafrost—with a 6-inch insulating layer between the frozen ground and the airfield surface to ensure that landings are smooth.

Although most people come to Kotzebue on day trips or overnight package tours, for those with time to linger, the town also serves as a gateway for three exceptional national **wilderness areas**: Cape Krusenstern National Monument, Kobuk Valley National Park, and Noatak National Preserve.

North and east of Kotzebue is the **Brooks Range**, one of Alaska's great mountain ranges. Stretching across the state, much of the range is protected by Gates of the Arctic National Park and Preserve and the Arctic National Wildlife Refuge.

WHERE TO EAT AND STAY

For expanded hotel reviews, visit Fodors.com.

$$$$
PIZZA

✕ **Bayside Restaurant.** One of the few restaurants in Kotzebue, the Bayside is the best place in town for breakfast, and it features a selection of American, Italian, and Chinese food for lunch and dinner. ✉ *303 Shore Ave.* ☎ *907/442–3600.*

$$$

🛏 **Nullagvik Hotel.** This hotel overlooking Kotzebue Sound is built on pilings driven into the ground because the heat of the building would melt the underlying permafrost and cause the hotel to sink. **Pros:** great views; comfortable rooms. **Cons:** no in-house restaurant; flat exterior. ✉ *308 Shore Ave.* ☎ *907/442–3331* ⊕ *www.nullagvik.com* ⤹ *75 rooms.*

CAPE KRUSENSTERN NATIONAL MONUMENT

10 mi north of Kotzebue.

Cape Krusenstern National Monument. Just north of Kotzebue, the 560,000-acre Cape Krusenstern National Monument has important cultural and archaeological value. This is coastal parkland, with an extraordinary series of beach ridges built up by storms over a period of at least 5,000 years. Almost every ridge—more than 100 in all—contains artifacts of different human occupants, representing every known Arctic Eskimo culture in North America. The present Eskimo occupants, whose culture dates back some 1,400 years, use the fish, seals, caribou, and birds of this region for food and raw materials much as their ancestors did. They are also closely involved in the archaeological digs in the park that are unearthing part of their own history.

Cape Krusenstern is a starkly beautiful Arctic land shaped by ice, wind, and sea. Its low, rolling, gray-white hills covered by light-green tundra attract hikers and backpackers, and kayakers sometimes paddle its coastline. The monument is a marvelous living museum. ■ TIP→ It's possible to camp in the park, but be mindful, as are the Native people when they pitch their white canvas tents for summer fishing, that the shoreline is subject to fierce winds. Both grizzlies and polar bears patrol the beaches in search of food, so clean camping is a must.

Check with the National Park Service in Kotzebue about hiring a local guide to the monument, which has no visitor facilities; it's accessible by air taxi and by boat from Kotzebue. ⌂ *National Park Service, Box 1029, Kotzebue 99752* ☎ *907/442–3890* ⊕ *www.nps.gov/cakr.*

KOBUK VALLEY NATIONAL PARK

65 mi east of Kotzebue.

Kobuk Valley National Park lies entirely north of the Arctic Circle, along the southern edge of the Brooks Range. Its 1.14 million acres contain remarkable inland deserts and the **Great Kobuk Sand Dunes** that stand up to 100 feet high and cover 25 square mi. These are home to interesting relict (remnants of otherwise extinct) flora. The park is bisected by the west-flowing **Kobuk River,** a 347-mi-long stream born in the foothills of the western Brooks Range. The Kobuk, whose native name means "big river," has been a major transportation and trade route for centuries. Besides the Kobuk, this park contains two smaller streams that provide delightful river running: the Ambler and the Salmon. These brilliantly clear rivers are accessible by wheeled plane, and each provides a good week's worth of pleasure (if the weather cooperates).

Another place of special interest is the **Onion Portage.** Human occupation here dates back 12,500 years, back to a time when Asia and North America were still connected by the Bering Land Bridge, and the region is rich in archaeological history; herds of caribou that fed the Woodland Eskimo centuries ago are still hunted at Onion Portage by present-day Eskimo residents of the region.

Like most other remote Alaska parks, Kobuk Valley National Park is undeveloped wilderness with no visitor facilities. If you come prepared, it can be a good place for backpacking and river trips. In nearby Kotzebue the National Park Service has a visitor center where staff can provide tips for travel into the park. The villages of Kobuk and Kiana both provide immediate take-off points and have air service. ⌂ *National Park Service, Box 1029, Kotzebue 99752* ☎ *907/442–3890 or 907/442–3760* ⊕ *www.nps.gov/kova.*

NOATAK NATIONAL PRESERVE

20 mi northeast of Kotzebue.

Adjacent to Gates of the Arctic National Park and Preserve, the 6.5-million-acre Noatak National Preserve encompasses much of the basin of the **Noatak River.** This is the largest mountain-ringed river basin in the United States; part of it is designated by the National Park Service as a Wild and Scenic River. Along its 425-mi course this river carves out the "Grand Canyon of the Noatak," and serves as a migration route between arctic and subarctic ecosystems. Its importance to wildlife and plants has resulted in this parkland's designation as an International Biosphere Reserve.

The Noatak River also serves as a natural highway for humans, and offers particular pleasures to river runners, with inviting tundra to camp on and the Poktovik Mountains and the Igichuk Hills nearby for good hiking. Birding can be exceptional: horned grebes, gyrfalcons, golden eagles, parasitic jaegers, owls, terns, and loons are among the species you may see. You may also spot grizzly bears, Dall sheep, wolves, caribou, or lynx, as well as the occasional musk ox. The most frequently run part of the river, ending at Lake Machurak, is mostly an easy Class I–III paddle, worth the trip just for the chance to hunt freshwater snail shells as delicate as origami along the shores of the take-out lake (where the river trip ends). The mountains around the river make for excellent hiking, and along the way the geology goes wild a couple of times, including with a massive pingo—kind of a glacial bubble. As with other parks and preserves in this northwest corner of Alaska, no visitor facilities are available and you are expected to be self-sufficient. Do not neglect the bear precautions. Most trips on the Noatak use the inland town of Bettles as a gateway. ⊕ *National Park Service, Box 1029, Kotzebue 99752* ☎ *907/442–3890 or 907/442–3760* ⊕ *www.nps.gov/noat.*

GATES OF THE ARCTIC NATIONAL PARK AND PRESERVE

180 mi east of Kotzebue.

★ **Gates of the Arctic National Park and Preserve** is entirely north of the Arctic Circle, in the center of the Brooks Range; at 8.2 million acres, it's the size of four Yellowstones. This is parkland on a scale suitable to the country. It includes the **Endicott Mountains** to the east and the **Schwatka Mountains** to the southwest, with the staggeringly sharp and dramatic **Arrigetch Peaks** in between. To the north lies a sampling of the Arctic foothills, with their colorful tilted sediments and pale green tundra. Lovely lakes are cupped in the mountains and in the tundra.

This landscape, the ultimate wilderness, captured the heart of Arctic explorer and conservationist Robert Marshall in the 1930s. Accompanied by local residents, Marshall explored much of the region now included within Gates and named many of its features, including Frigid Crag and Boreal Mountain, two peaks on either side of the North Fork Koyukuk River. These were the original "gates" for which the park is named.

Wildlife known to inhabit the park includes barren-ground caribou, grizzlies, wolves, musk oxen, moose, Dall sheep, wolverines, and smaller mammals and birds. The communities of Bettles and Anaktuvuk Pass are access points for Gates of the Arctic, which has no developed trails, campgrounds, or other visitor facilities (though there is a wilderness lodge on private land within the park). You can fly into Bettles commercially and charter an air taxi into the park or hike directly out of Anaktuvuk Pass. The Park Service has rangers stationed in both Bettles and Anaktuvuk Pass; they can provide information for those entering the wilderness, including the mandatory orientation films and bearproof canisters for food storage. *National Park Service, Box 30, Bettles 99726* ☎ *907/692–5494 in Bettles, 907/661–3520 in Anaktuvuk Pass (this station is sometimes unmanned)* ⊕ *www.nps.gov/gaar.*

> ### DID YOU KNOW?
>
> *Arrigetch* is an Eskimo word meaning "fingers of a hand outstretched," which aptly describes the immensely steep and smooth granite peaks here.

SPORTS, THE OUTDOORS, AND GUIDED TOURS

OUTDOOR ADVENTURING **Arctic Treks** (*Box 73452, Fairbanks 99707* ☎ *907/455–6502* ⊕ *www.arctictreksadventures.com*) guides wilderness hikes and backpacking expeditions, sometimes combined with river trips, in both Gates of the Arctic and the Arctic National Wildlife Refuge, with new trips into the farthest west reaches of the Brooks Range and the North Slope. **Spirit Lights Lodge** (*Box 90, Bettles 99726* ☎ *907/692–5252* ⊕ *www.spiritlightslodge.com*) guides wilderness hikes and backpacking expeditions, sometimes combined with river trips, in Gates of the Arctic.

WHERE TO STAY

For expanded hotel reviews, visit Fodors.com.

$$$$ ★ **Peace of Selby Wilderness.** On Selby and Narvak lakes within Gates of the Arctic National Park, Peace of Selby is perfectly situated for wilderness adventures. **Pros:** endless activity options. **Cons:** small, so reservations and planning are a must. *Box 86, Manley Hot Springs 99756* ☎ *907/672–3206* ⊕ *www.alaskawilderness.net* *1 room in lodge, 4 cabins* ☺ *In-room: no TV. In-hotel: restaurant* ▤ *No credit cards* ☉ *Closed end-Sept.–mid-June, except for specially arranged expeditions Mar. and Apr.*

9

BARROW

330 mi northeast of Kotzebue.

The northernmost community in the United States, Barrow sits 1,300 mi south of the North Pole. The village is 10 mi south of the Beaufort Sea and Point Barrow, from which it takes its name. Point Barrow, in turn, was named in 1825 by British captain Frederick William Beechey, who'd been ordered by the British Navy to map the continent's northern coastline. Beechey wished to honor Sir John Barrow, a member of the British Admiralty and a major force in arctic exploration. The region's Inupiaq Eskimos knew the site as Ukpeagvik, or "place where owls are hunted." Even today, many snowy owls nest in the tundra outside Barrow each summer, though they're not hunted as they once were: they are now protected by federal law.

About 4,000 people inhabit Barrow today, making it easily the largest community on the North Slope. Nearly two-thirds of the residents are Inupiaq Eskimos. Though they remain deeply rooted in their Inupiaq heritage, Barrow's residents have adopted a modern lifestyle. Homes are heated by natural gas taken from nearby gas fields, and the community is served by most modern conveniences, including a public radio station and cable TV and Internet access. The community recreation center has a gymnasium, racquetball courts, weight room, and sauna, and hosts a variety of social events, from dances to basketball tournaments. In Barrow, as in much of Bush Alaska, basketball is the favored sport, played year-round by people of all ages.

Barrow is the economic and administrative center of the **North Slope Borough,** which encompasses more than 88,000 square mi, making it the world's largest municipal government (in terms of area). The village is also headquarters of the **Arctic Slope Regional Corporation,** formed in 1971 through the Alaska Native Claims Settlement Act (ANCSA), as well as the Ukpeagvik Inupiat Corporation, which economically and politically represents the community of Barrow. Several village councils are also headquartered in the town.

GETTING HERE AND AROUND

Alaska Airlines Vacations packages air tours to Barrow and Nome. Local arrangements are taken care of by Native ground operators. The Alaska Travel Industry Association can give tips on air travel and flight-seeing opportunities throughout the Bush.

ESSENTIALS

Contacts **Alaska Airlines Vacations** (✉ *Box 68900, Seattle, WA 98168* ☎ *800/468–2248* ⊕ *www.alaskaair.com*). **Alaska Travel Industry Associa-tion** (✉ *2600 Cordova St., Suite 201, Anchorage 99503* ☎ *907/929–2200, 800/862–5275 for vacation planner* 🖷 *907/561–5727* ⊕ *www.travelalaska.com*). **Bethel Chamber of Commerce** (✉ *Box 329, Bethel 99559* ☎ *907/543–2911* 🖷 *907/543–2255* ⊕ *www.bethelakchamber.org*). **City of Barrow** (✉ *Box 629, Barrow 99723* ☎ *907/852–5871* ⊕ *www.cityofbarrow.org*).

Banking **Wells Fargo** (✉ *1078 Kiogak St., Barrow* ☎ *907/852–6200 or 800/869–3557* ⊕ *www.wellsfargo.com*).

Emergency **Police** (☎ *907/852–6111*). **Samuel Simmonds Memorial Hospi-tal** (✉ *1296 Agvik St., Barrow* ☎ *907/852–4611* ⊕ *www.arcticslope.org/*). **State troopers** (☎ *907/852–3783* ⊕ *www.dps.state.ak.us/ast*).

Internet **Tuzzy Library** (✉ *5421 N. Star St., Barrow* ☎ *800/478-6916* 🖷 *907/852–4050* ⊕ *www.tuzzy.org*).

Mail **USPS** (✉ *3080 Eben Hobson St.* ☎ *907/852–6800*).

Non-natives established a presence at Barrow in the early 1880s, when the U.S. Army built a research station here. Drawn to the area by the Beaufort Sea's abundant whales, commercial whalers established the **Cape Smythe Whaling and Trading Station** in 1893; a cabin from that opera-tion still stands, and is the oldest frame building in Alaska's Arctic. The station is now listed on the National Register of Historic Places (as are the Birnirk dwelling mounds).

By the early 1900s both a Presbyterian church and U.S. post office had been established. Recalling those days, an Inupiat elder named Alfred Hopson once recounted that the famed Norwegian explorer Vilhjal-mur Stefansson used the church as a base for studies of local residents, including measurements of their head sizes. From then on, Stefansson

BARROW'S RICHNESS

Barrow is truly the land of the midnight sun. From mid-May until August the sun doesn't set for more than 80 days. (Conversely, the sun disappears during the dead of winter from November through January—this is called the polar winter.) Despite the season's unending daylight, summertime temperatures can be brisk—you should even be prepared for snow flurries. Nevertheless, midsummer temperatures can occasionally reach the 60s and low 70s. Despite the region's abundant wetlands, Barrow—and the North Slope in general—has a desert climate, with annual precipitation averaging less than 10 inches.

Archaeological evidence from more than a dozen nearby ancient "dwelling mounds" suggests that people have inhabited this area for at least the past 1,500 years. A highlight of those mounds is **Mound 44**, where the 500-year-old frozen body of an Eskimo was discovered. Scientists have been studying her remains to learn more about Eskimo life and culture before encounters with outsiders. Described as members of the **Birnirk culture**, these early residents depended heavily on marine mammals, a tradition that continues to this day. Combining modern technology with traditional knowledge, Barrow's whaling crews annually hunt for the bowhead whales that migrate through Arctic waters each spring and fall. If the whalers are successful in their springtime hunts, they share muktuk—whale meat (to the uninitiated, it tastes kind of like really greasy tuna mixed with steak)—with other members of the village and celebrate their good fortune with a festival called **Nalukataq**. Besides whales, residents depend on harvests of seals, walrus, caribou, waterfowl, grayling, and whitefish.

was known locally as the "head measurer." Oil and gas exploration later brought more whites from the Lower 48 to the area; even more came as schools and other government agencies took root in the region. Hopson, too, played a role in the area's development, as he funneled millions of dollars in tax revenues into road building, sanitation and water services, and heath-care services.

Barrow has opened its annual springtime whale festival to outsiders, and there are several historic sites, including a military installation, points of native cultural importance, and a famous crash site. The Barrow airport is where you'll find the **Will Rogers and Wiley Post Monument,** marking the 1935 crash of the American humorist and his pilot 15 mi south of town.

Drawn by both cultural and natural attractions, visitors to Barrow usually arrive on a one- or two-day tour with Alaska Airlines, the only national carrier serving the area. Packages include a bus tour of the town's dusty roads and major sights. ■ TIP→ Though Barrow's residents invite visitors to attend their annual whale festival in spring, summer is the ideal time to survey the town and its historic sites.

VISITING IN WINTER

Although many people think visiting Alaska in winter is insane, there are plenty of good reasons for doing so. It just takes a bit of an adventurous spirit and proper clothing.

The northern lights (aurora borealis) are active all year long, but it has to get dark before you can enjoy them. On a clear night these shimmering curtains of color in the sky are absolutely breathtaking: rippling reds and greens and blues that seem to make the entire sky come alive. Weather and solar activity have to cooperate in order to make the aurora performances happen, but when they do, the results are astounding. ■TIP➜ To check out aurora borealis activity, look up the forecast at ⊕ www.gedds.alaska.edu/ AuroraForecast.

There are almost no insects in the winter months; if you've visited in summer and been subjected to the mosquitoes, no-see-ums, and white socks, this alone might entice you.

For a real Alaska winter experience, dog mushing is the ultimate. Spectators can watch sprint and long-distance races all over the state, capped off by the Yukon Quest and Iditarod races in February and March. There are numerous outfits in the Interior and South Central that will train you to mush your own team. Fodor's discusses dog mushing and surrounding competitions with the expectation and hope that all the animals are treated with care and respect. And if you hang out with serious mushers, you'll see that their animals are more pampered than the average Park Avenue poodle.

SPORTS, THE OUTDOORS, AND GUIDED TOURS

CULTURAL TOURS From mid-May through September you can take an **Alaska Airlines Vacations** (☎ 800/468–2248 ⊕ vacations.alaskaair.com) package from Anchorage or Fairbanks to "the top of the world" and get a chance to learn about the natural and cultural history of the area. Year-round tours are organized through **Tundra Tours** (☎ 907/852–3900 ⊕ www. tundratoursinc.com). Offered from mid-September through mid-May, the winter tours feature visits to a traditional hunting camp, the whaling station, the DEWS site, and opportunities to visit Point Barrow and watch northern lights. The summer program is highlighted by visits to local historic sites and opportunities to witness traditional cultural activities such as Eskimo dances, sewing demonstrations, and the blanket toss. In both winter and summer, visitors can purchase locally made Inupiaq arts and crafts.

WHERE TO EAT AND STAY

For expanded hotel reviews, visit Fodors.com.

$$–$$$
MEXICAN
★
✕ **Pepe's North of the Border.** The warmth of Pepe's will make you forget that you're in the middle of the Arctic tundra in the most famous restaurant north of Fairbanks. Murals depicting Mexican village scenes highlight the Mission-style decor, and an extensive selection of Mexican dishes, from soft tacos to burritos and flautas, makes this restaurant a favorite of locals and visitors alike. The restaurant's menu is also spiced up with dishes that feature Alaskan seafood and, at the high end of things, steak and lobster. Dinner at Pepe's is surprisingly refined for

being on the very fringe of civilization. ⊠ *1204 Agvik St., next to Top of the World Hotel* ☎ *907/852–8200.*

$ 🛏 **Barrow Airport Inn.** As the name suggests, this modern and well-appointed property is convenient to the airport (it's only two blocks away). **Pros:** convenient; clean; in walking distance of eateries. **Cons:** must like the odd bit of airplane noise; no restaurant on premises. **Trip-Advisor:** "so very nice and friendly," "clean and quiet room," "very clean and newly remodeled." ⊠ *1815 Momeganna St.* ☎ *907/852–2525, 800/375–2527 in Alaska* ⇆ *16 rooms* ⌂ *In-room: kitchen (some)* ⏉ *Breakfast.*

$$$ 🛏 **Top of the World Hotel.** Built in 1974, this refurbished hotel on the
★ shore of the Arctic Ocean has just about every imaginable modern convenience, including cable TV and Internet access. **Pros:** every modern convenience, next door to restaurant, quick walk to the beach. **Cons:** no elevators (which means you're taking the stairs to the top of the world), a little worn in some places. **TripAdvisor:** "clean and comfortable," "great view of the frozen ocean," "amazing in the Arctic." ⊠ *1200 Agviq St.* ☎ *907/852–3900 or 800/882–8478, 800/478–8520 in Alaska* ⊕ *www.tundratoursinc.com* ⇆ *44 rooms* ⌂ *In-room: no a/c, Internet. In-hotel: restaurant, room service.*

SHOPPING

The AC Value Center, or, as it's known locally, **Stuaqpak** (*"Big Store"* ⊠ *4725 Ahkovak St.* ☎ *907/852–6711* ⊕ *www.alaskacommercial.com*), is the largest store in town. Though it mainly sells groceries, the store also stocks Eskimo crafts made by locals, including furs, parkas, mukluks, and ceremonial masks.

PRUDHOE BAY

250 mi southeast of Barrow.

Most towns have museums that chronicle local history and achievements. Deadhorse is the town anchoring life along Prudhoe Bay, but it could also serve as a museum dedicated to humankind's hunt for energy and its ability to adapt to harsh conditions to capture that energy.

The costly, much-publicized Arctic oil and gas project is complex and varied. One-day tours with the Arctic Caribou Inn explore the tundra terrain from oil pipes to sandpipers. Along with chances to spot caribou, wildflowers, and an unusual stand of willow trees at the edge of the Arctic Ocean (for the most part the tree line ends well south of here, but since willows can take almost any weather conditions, these outliers have stuck), the field tour surveys oil wells, stations, and oil-company residential complexes—small cities themselves. Your guide will discuss the multimillion-dollar research programs aimed at preserving the region's ecology and point out special tundra vehicles known as Rolligons, whose great weight is distributed to diminish their impact on delicate terrain.

GETTING HERE AND AROUND

In the past, individual travelers rarely turned up in Deadhorse and Prudhoe Bay. But now that the Dalton Highway has been opened as far north as Deadhorse, adventurous independent travelers are finding their way north. Still, rather than solo-driving a couple hundred miles of gravel road filled with semis going faster than you knew semis could go, most people traveling to Deadhorse come on a tour with one of Alaska's airlines or bus-tour operators. And even those who travel as far as Deadhorse on their own must join a guided tour (arranged through the Arctic Caribou Inn) if they wish to cross the oil fields to get to the Arctic Ocean. You'll find no restaurants around the oil fields, though meals can sometimes be arranged through the Prudhoe Bay Hotel; unless you have official business, though, you're not likely to be invited to linger.

ESSENTIALS

Contacts **Alaska Airline Vacations** (☎ *800/468–2248* ⊕ *www.alaskaairalaska. com*).

WHERE TO STAY

For expanded hotel reviews, visit Fodors.com.

$ ☂ **Arctic Caribou Inn.** Located near the end of the Haul Road, this simple hotel is open only from May through September. **Pros:** it runs good tours; on-site dining. **Cons:** basic accommodations; only during the summer do some of the rooms have clocks and television. ⌖ *Pouch 340111, Prudhoe Bay 99734* ☎ *866/659–2368* ⊕ *www.arcticcaribouinn.com* ⤳ *200 rooms in summer, 44 rooms in winter* ☖ *In-hotel: restaurant, gym.*

$$$ ☂ **Prudhoe Bay Hotel.** Located near the end of the road at Deadhorse, this hotel is primarily intended for the workers employed in the Prudhoe Bay oil-field complex, but tourists are also welcome. **Pros:** convenient; a great view of icy flats and the occasional polar bear. **Cons:** sharing a bathroom with someone who just got off a 24-hour oil-rig shift; has bare necessities only. ⌖ *Pouch 340004, Prudhoe Bay 99734* ☎ *907/659–2449* ⊕ *www.prudhoebayhotel.com* ⤳ *270 rooms, shared bath* ☖ *In-room: no TV (some). In-hotel: restaurant.*

ARCTIC NATIONAL WILDLIFE REFUGE

70 mi southeast of Prudhoe Bay.

Arctic National Wildlife Refuge. The 19-million-acre Arctic National Wildlife Refuge, lying wholly above the Arctic Circle, is administered by the U.S. Fish and Wildlife Service and contains one of the few protected Arctic coastal lands in the United States, as well as millions of acres of mountains and alpine tundra in the easternmost portion of the Brooks Range. This protected region is an area of much dispute, as it is believed to harbor billions of barrels of oil (statistically, hardly a drop in what the country uses). It is sure to be a hot topic for years to come.

★   ANWR is the home of one of the greatest remaining groups of caribou in the world, the **Porcupine Caribou Herd.** The herd, its numbers exceeding 150,000, is unmindful of international boundaries and migrates back and forth across Arctic lands into Canada's adjacent

Arctic National Wildlife Refuge. A hiker stands atop a rocky summit.

Vuntut and Ivvavik National Parks, flowing like a wide river across the expansive coastal plain, through U-shape valleys and alpine meadows, and over high mountain passes.

The refuge's coastal areas also serve as critical denning grounds for polar bears, which spend much of their year on the Arctic Ocean's pack ice. Other residents here are grizzly bears, Dall sheep, wolves, musk ox, and dozens of varieties of birds, from snowy owls to geese and tiny songbirds. The refuge's northern areas host legions of breeding waterfowl and shorebirds each summer. As in many of Alaska's more remote parks and refuges, there are no roads here, and no developed trails, campgrounds, or other visitor facilities. This is a place to experience true wilderness—and to walk with care, for the plants are fragile and the ground can be soft and wet in summer. Footprints in tundra can last a hundred years. You can expect snow to sift over the land in almost any season, and should anticipate subfreezing temperatures even in summer, particularly in the mountains. Many of the refuge's clear-flowing rivers are runnable, and tundra lakes are suitable for base camps (a Kaktovik or Fort Yukon air taxi can drop you off and pick you up). The hiking is worth it; upon scrambling up a ridge, you'll look out on wilderness that seems to stretch forever. ⊠ *Refuge Manager, Arctic National Wildlife Refuge, 101 12th Ave., Room 236, Fairbanks* ☏ *907/456–0250 or 800/362–4546* ⊕ *arctic.fws.gov.*

SPORTS, THE OUTDOORS, AND GUIDED TOURS

EXPERT **Arctic Treks** (☏ *907/455–6522* ⊕ *www.arctictreksadventures.com*) guides
GUIDES wilderness hikes and backpacking expeditions in both Gates of the Arctic and the Arctic National Wildlife Refuge. The owners of **Wilderness**

Birding Adventures (☎ 907/694–7442 ⊕ *www.wildernessbirding.com*) are both experienced river runners and expert birders.

BROOKS RANGE

For those who love vast wilderness landscapes, few places can match the Brooks Range, the "backbone of the Arctic Wilderness"; Alaska's most northerly mountain chain, it stretches east–west across the state above the Arctic Circle. Fortunately, most of this ultimate wilderness is protected by national parklands and the Arctic National Wildlife Refuge. However, it is also a place of great controversy between environmentalists and proponents of oil drilling.

As it stands, you can still go days, and even weeks, without seeing another person. The Brooks are the homeland of grizzlies, wolves, Dall sheep, caribou, moose, musk oxen, and golden eagles. They are also the homeland of Athabascan Indians and Inupiaq and Nunamiut Eskimos, who have lived here for centuries, traveling the mountain pathways and paddling the great rivers like the Noatak.

Arctic Treks (✉ Box 73452, Fairbanks 99707 ☎ 907/455–6522 ⊕ *www. arctictreksadventures.com*) guides wilderness hikes and backpacking expeditions, sometimes combined with river trips, in both Gates of the Arctic and the Arctic National Wildlife Refuge.

Travel Smart
Alaska

WORD OF MOUTH

"The trouble with just 'showing up' in summer is that Alaska is very busy with cruise ship people and other tourists. You might get shut out of some of the best opportunities. . . . There are lots of adventurous and unique experiences to be found. But you need to do research and figure them out."

—enzian

GETTING HERE AND AROUND

■ AIR TRAVEL

Alaska Airlines is the state's flagship carrier, with year-round service from its Seattle hub to Anchorage, Fairbanks, Juneau, Ketchikan, and Sitka. The airline and its subsidiary, Horizon Air, also fly to many other North American cities from Seattle. In addition, Alaska Airlines offers year-round flights between Anchorage and Hawaii.

Other airlines that fly to and from the Lower 48 include American, Continental, Delta, Frontier, United, and US Airways. Note, however, that few offer nonstop flights and many of those that do offer such flights do so only seasonally (primarily in the summer months).

The average travel time (nonstop flights only) from Seattle to Anchorage is 3½ hours. Travel times from other destinations depend on your connection, because you'll probably need to route through other cities. Many of the low-fare flights out of Anchorage depart around 1 am, so be sure you're at the airport on the correct day when flying just after midnight.

Major Airlines Alaska Airlines (🖃 800/252–7522 ⊕ www.alaskaair.com). **American Airlines** (🖃 800/433–7300 ⊕ www.aa.com). **Continental Airlines** (🖃 800/523–3273 ⊕ www.continental.com). **Delta Airlines** (🖃 800/221–1212 ⊕ www.delta.com). **Frontier Airlines** (🖃 800/432–1359 ⊕ www.frontierairlines.com). **United Airlines** (🖃 800/864–8331 for U.S. reservations, 800/538–2929 for international reservations ⊕ www.united.com). **US Airways** (🖃 800/428–4322 ⊕ www.usairways.com).

AIRPORTS

Anchorage's Ted Stevens International Airport is Alaska's main hub. There are also major airports ("major" meaning that they serve jets as well as bush planes) in Fairbanks, Juneau, and Ketchikan. The Fairbanks airport is the largest of the three; Juneau and Ketchikan have few facilities and gates. Sixteen other airports throughout the state also serve jet planes.

Unless you're flying from the West Coast or manage to get a nonstop flight, chances are you'll spend some time in Seattle's international airport, Seattle-Tacoma (known locally as Sea-Tac), waiting for a connection. And Vancouver, Canada, is often the starting point for Alaskan cruises that make their first stop in Ketchikan, Alaska's southernmost town.

You won't find much in terms of entertainment in Ted Stevens, Sea-Tac, or Vancouver's airport, so if you have really long layovers at any of the three, consider taking a taxi into the city. Ted Stevens is only 6 mi from downtown Anchorage; Seattle's downtown area is 14 mi from the airport, and if you don't get stuck in the city's notorious rush-hour traffic you can get there in 20 minutes. It can take 30 to 45 minutes to get to downtown Vancouver from the airport.

There are no departure taxes for travel within the United States. Vancouver's airport does have a departure tax of C$5 for flights within British Columbia and the Yukon or C$10 to U.S. destinations, payable at automatic ticket machines or staffed booths before you board.

Airlines and Airports Airline and Airport Links.com (⊕ www.airlineandairportlinks.com).

Airline Security Issues Transportation Security Administration (⊕ www.tsa.gov).

Airport Information Fairbanks International Airport (*FAI* ⊕ www.dot.state.ak.us/faiiap). **Juneau International Airport** (*JNU* ⊕ www.juneau.org/airport). **Ketchikan Airport** (*KTN* ⊕ www.borough.ketchikan.ak.us/airport/airport.htm). **Seattle-Tacoma International Airport** (*SEA* ⊕ www.portseattle.org/seatac/). **Ted Stevens Anchorage International Airport** (*ANC* ⊕ www.dot.alaska.gov/anc). **Vancouver International Airport** (*YVR* ⊕ www.yvr.ca).

WITHIN ALASKA

Air travel within Alaska is quite expensive, particularly to Bush destinations where flying is the only option. A round-trip flight between Anchorage and Dutch Harbor typically costs more than $900. Flights from Anchorage to Fairbanks or Juneau are a little more forgiving; at this writing, one-way flights run about $120 and $170, respectively.

AIR TAXIS

The workhorse planes of the north are the Beavers, most of which were built in the 1950s and are still flying. The cost of an air-taxi flight between towns or backcountry locations depends on distance and the type of plane used, whether the plane is on floats, the number of people in your group, the length of the flight in each direction (including the time the pilot flies back after dropping you off), and the destination. Typical hourly rates are approximately $600–$800 for a Beaver, with room for up to six people and gear; or $400–$600 for a Cessna 185, with room for three people and gear. Expect to pay more the farther you are from Anchorage.

SMALL PLANES

Many scheduled flights to Bush communities are on small planes that seat 6 to 15 passengers. These planes have played a legendary part in the state's history: bush pilots helped explore Alaska and have been responsible for many dramatic rescue missions. That said, small craft have their inconveniences. They can only transport a limited amount of gear, so plan to leave your large, hard-sided suitcases behind. Small, soft duffels make more sense, and are easier for the pilot to stash in cramped cargo spaces.

Small planes also can't fly in poor weather, which could mean delays counted in days, not hours. And even on good days turbulence might leave you white-knuckled and green in the face. Fortunately, most flights are uneventful, with the scenery below—rather than a rough ride—making them memorable.

Contact Bering Air for flights from Nome or Kotzebue to smaller communities of the Far North; Era Alaska for flights from Anchorage to Cordova, Homer, Iliamna, Kenai, Kodiak, Valdez, and 17 western Alaska villages; and Frontier Flying Service, Inc. (a part of Era Alaska) for flights from Anchorage to Fairbanks, Bethel, and many Bush villages.

Try Warbelow's Air Ventures and Larry's Flying Service for flights out of Fairbanks to Interior destinations. Peninsula Airways (PenAir), based in Anchorage, covers southwestern Alaska, including Aniak, Dillingham, Dutch Harbor, McGrath, King Salmon, Sand Point, St. George, and St. Paul. Wings of Alaska serves several Southeast Alaska towns, including Gustavus, Haines, Juneau, and Skagway. Grant Aviation flies from Anchorage to Homer and Kenai as well as Bethel, Dillingham, Emmonak, and St. Mary's.

Carriers Bering Air (☎ *907/443–5464, 800/478–5422 Nome and Unalakleet reservations; 907/442–3943, 800/478–3943 Kotzebue reservations* ⊕ *www.beringair. com*). **Era Alaska** (☎ *907/266–8394 or 800/866–8394* ⊕ *www.flyera.com*). **Frontier Flying Service** (☎ *907/450–7200 Fairbanks, 907/266-8934 Anchorage, or 800/866–8394* ⊕ *www.frontierflying.com*). **Grant Aviation** (☎ *888/359–4726* ⊕ *www.flygrant.com*). **Larry's Flying Service** (☎ *907/474–9169* ⊕ *www.larrysflying.com*). **PenAir** (☎ *907/771–2640 or 800/448–4226* ⊕ *www.penair.com*). **Warbelow's Air Ventures** (☎ *907/474–0518 or 800/478–0812* ⊕ *www.warbelows.com*). **Wings of Alaska** (☎ *907/789–0790* ⊕ *www. wingsofalaska.com*).

▌ BOAT TRAVEL

If you're looking for a casual alternative to a luxury cruise, travel as Alaskans do, aboard the ferries of the Alaska Marine Highway System. These vessels may not have the same facilities as the big cruise ships, but they do meander through some beautiful regions. In summer you won't be completely without entertainment. Forest

Service naturalists ride larger ferries, providing a running commentary on sights, and select routes also have an Arts-on-Board Program, which presents educators and entertainers.

Most long-haul ferries have cabins with private bathrooms. You'll need to reserve these accommodations in advance or settle for a reclining seat on the aft deck. Most ships also have cheap or free showers as well as spaces where you can roll out sleeping bags or even pitch tents. All long-haul ferries have cafeterias with hot meal service (not included in the fare), along with concession stands and vending machines. Some larger boats even have cocktail lounges.

RESERVATIONS AND FARES

You can make reservations by phone or online and have tickets mailed to you or arrange to pick them up from the ferry office at your starting point. Book as far in advance as possible for summertime travel, especially if you have a vehicle. You should also book ahead for the Bellingham–Ketchikan journey.

You can pay for ferry travel with cash, credit card (American Express, Discover, MasterCard, or Visa), cashier's check, money order, certified check, or personal check from an Alaskan bank.

The Bellingham–Ketchikan route costs roughly $240 one way in summer. Shorter trips cost anywhere from $30 to $190 one way. Note that there are surcharges for vehicles (including motorcycles), bicycles, and kayaks. Renting cabins will also increase the fare significantly.

ALASKAPASS

The AlaskaPass offers rental-car usage and unlimited travel on ferry and rail lines in Alaska, along with rental-car usage and ferry travel in British Columbia and the Yukon. Passes are available for 15 consecutive days of travel ($929), as well as for eight days of travel in a 12-day period ($799) or 12 days of travel in a 21-day period ($979). There's an $85 booking fee. Most travelers book their entire itinerary in advance; if you don't have a car, there's usually room on ferries for those without prebookings.

Information Alaska Marine Highway (☎ 907/465–3941 or 800/642–0066 ⊕ www.ferryalaska.com). **AlaskaPass** (☎ 800/248–7598 ⊕ www.alaskapass.com). **BC Ferries** (☎ 888/223–3779 ⊕ www.bcferries.com). **Inter-Island Ferry Authority** (☎ 907/755–4848 ⊕ www.interislandferry.com).

ROUTES

The Inside Passage route, which stretches from Bellingham, Washington (or Prince Rupert, British Columbia), all the way up to Skagway and Haines, is the most popular route, mimicking that of most major cruise lines. The Bellingham–Ketchikan trip, the longest leg, takes roughly 37 hours. (The trip from Prince Rupert to Ketchikan takes six hours; BC Ferries provide service from Vancouver to Prince Rupert.) Other trips along the Inside Passage take from three to eight hours.

Sporadic summer service across the Gulf of Alaska from either Prince Rupert, Ketchikan, or Juneau links the Southeast with South Central Alaska destinations (trips usually end in Whittier, about 60 mi south of Anchorage). There's further service to limited ports in South Central Alaska as well as connecting service to the Southwest from Whittier and Homer to Kodiak and Port Lions, respectively. Southwest ferries can take you all the way to Dutch Harbor.

Two high-speed catamarans can cut travel time in half. The MV *Fairweather* is based in Juneau and serves Petersburg and Sitka. In summer the MV *Chenega*, based in Cordova, serves Prince William Sound, with stops in Valdez and Whittier. In fall and winter its route changes, serving either the same route as the *Fairweather* or Ketchikan to Juneau via Wrangell and Petersburg.

The Inter-Island Ferry Authority connects Southeast Alaska's Prince of Wales Island with the towns of Ketchikan, Wrangell, and Petersburg.

Note that although major ports like Juneau and Ketchikan will likely have daily departures, service to smaller towns is much more sporadic—one departure per week in some cases.

▌ BUS TRAVEL

Traveling by bus in Alaska can be more economical than traveling by train or by air, but don't count on it being your main mode of travel. Always confirm your trip via phone, as schedules often change at the last minute.

Greyhound Lines of Canada serves Vancouver, with service as far north as Whitehorse in the Canadian Yukon. Two companies provide onward bus service into South Central and Interior Alaska from Whitehorse. Alaska Direct Bus Lines operates year-round van service connecting Anchorage and Fairbanks with Glennallen, Delta Junction, Skagway, and Tok in Alaska, along with Whitehorse in the Yukon. Alaska/Yukon Trails provides year-round bus service between Anchorage and Fairbanks, plus seasonal service connecting Fairbanks with Dawson City in the Yukon.

Denali Overland Transportation has frequent van service in summer between Anchorage, Talkeetna, and Denali National Park and Preserve. The Alaska Park Connection has summertime bus service between Seward and Anchorage, continuing north to Denali. Homer Stage Line provides year-round service between Anchorage and Homer, plus summertime service connecting Seward with Anchorage and Homer.

Quick Shuttle buses run between Vancouver and Seattle. Green Tortoise provides a casual alternative way to travel north, with funky classic buses that are popular with backpackers.

Many bus lines—particularly those heading to Denali—either require or strongly recommend reservations. Accepted forms of payment vary among bus companies, but all accept MasterCard, Visa, and traveler's checks. The AlaskaPass allows unlimited travel on ferry, rail lines, and Holland America buses (Whitehorse to Fairbanks only) in Alaska and the Yukon. *(For more information, see By Boat, above).*

Bus Information Alaska Direct Bus Lines (☎ 800/770-6652 ⊕ www.alaskadirectbusline. com). **Alaska Park Connection** (☎ 800/266-8625 ⊕ www.alaskacoach.com). **Alaska/Yukon Trails** (☎ 800/770-7275 ⊕ www. alaskashuttle.com). **Denali Overland Transportation** (☎ 907/733-2384 or 800/651-5221 ⊕ www.denalioverland.com). **Green Tortoise** (☎ 415/956-7500 or 800/867-8647 ⊕ www. greentortoise.com). **Greyhound Lines of Canada** (☎ 800/661-8747 ⊕ www.greyhound. ca). **Homer Stage Line** (☎ 907/235-2252 Homer, 907/301-8923 Anchorage ⊕ www. stagelineinhomer.com). **Quick Shuttle** (☎ 604/940-4428 or 800/665-2122 ⊕ www. quickcoach.com).

FROM ANCHORAGE			
To	Time by Air	Road Miles	Time by Road
Denali	N/A	264 mi	5–6 hrs
Fairbanks	50 mins	364 mi	7–9 hrs
Homer	50 mins	223 mi	5–6 hrs
Talkeetna	20 mins	113 mi	2–3 hrs
Valdez	40 mins	302 mi	6–8 hrs

▌ CAR TRAVEL

Though journeying through Canada on the Alaska Highway can be exciting, the trek from the Lower 48 states is long. It's a seven-day trip from Seattle to Anchorage or Fairbanks, covering close to 2,500 mi. From Bellingham, Washington, and the Canadian ports of Prince Rupert and Stewart you can link up with ferry service along the Marine Highway to reach Southeast Alaska.

The Alaska Highway begins at Dawson Creek, British Columbia, and stretches 1,442 mi through Canada's Yukon to Delta Junction; it enters Alaska east of

Tok. The two-lane highway is paved for its entire length and is open year-round. Highway services are available about every 50 to 100 mi (sometimes at shorter intervals).

The rest of the state's roads are found almost exclusively in the South Central and Interior regions. They lie mainly between Anchorage, Fairbanks, and the Canadian border. Only one highway extends north of Fairbanks, and one runs south of Anchorage to the Kenai Peninsula. These roads vary from four-lane freeways (rare) to nameless two-lane gravel roads.

If you plan extensive driving in Alaska, join an automobile club such as AAA that offers towing and other benefits. Because of the long distances involved, you should seriously consider a plan (such as AAA Plus) that extends towing benefits to 100 mi in any direction. *The Milepost,* available in bookstores or from Morris Communications, is a mile-by-mile guide to sights and services along Alaska's highways. It's indispensable.

The Alaska Department of Transportation is a great resource for road reports, animal alerts, and other advisories.

Contacts Alaska Department of Transportation (☎ 511 in Alaska, 866/282–7577 outside Alaska ⊕ 511.alaska.gov or www.dot. state.ak.us). **American Automobile Association** (☎ 800/222–4357 ⊕ www.aaa.com). **The Milepost** (☎ 907/272–6070 or 800/726–4707 ⊕ www.themilepost.com). **National Automobile Club** (☎ 800/622–2136 ⊕ www. nationalautoclub.com); membership is open to California residents only.

GASOLINE

Gas prices in the Anchorage area are usually higher than those in the Lower 48, and you can expect to pay even more in Juneau and Ketchikan, and far more in remote villages off the road network, where fuel must be flown in. Fuel prices in Canada along the Alaska Highway are also very high. Most stations are self-serve and take Visa and MasterCard; many also accept other credit cards and debit cards.

Many stations remain open until 10 pm, and in the larger towns and cities some stay open 24 hours a day. Most are also open on weekends, particularly along the main highways. In the smallest villages gas may be available only on weekdays, but these settlements typically have only a few miles of roads.

ROAD CONDITIONS

Driving in Alaska is much less rigorous than it used to be, although it still presents some unusual obstacles. Road construction sometimes creates long delays on the Canadian side of the border, so come armed with patience and a flexible schedule. Also, frost damage creates dips in the road that require slower driving.

Moose often wander onto roads and highways. If you encounter one, pull off to the side and wait for the moose to cross. Be especially vigilant when driving at dusk or at night, and keep your eyes open for other moose in the area, since a mother will often cross followed by one or two calves.

Flying gravel is a hazard along the Alaska and Dalton highways, especially in summer. A bug screen will help keep gravel and kamikaze insects off the windshield, but few travelers use them. Some travelers use clear, hard plastic guards to cover their headlights. (These are inexpensive and are available from garage or service stations along the major access routes.) Don't cover headlights with cardboard or plywood, because you'll need your lights often, even in daytime, as dust is thrown up by traffic in both directions.

Unless you plan to undertake remote highways (especially the Dalton Highway to Prudhoe Bay), you won't need any special equipment. But be sure that the equipment you do have is in working condition, from tires and spare to brakes and engine. Carrying spare fuses, spark plugs, jumper cables, a flashlight with extra batteries, a tool kit, and an extra fan belt is recommended.

If you get stuck on any kind of road, be careful about pulling off; the shoulder can be soft. In summer it stays light late, and though traffic is also light, one of Alaska's many good Samaritans is likely to stop to help and send for aid (which may be many miles away). In winter, pack emergency equipment—a shovel, tire chains, high-energy food, and extra clothing and blankets. Never head out onto unplowed roads unless you're prepared to walk back.

Cell phones are an excellent idea for travel in Alaska, particularly on the main roads. There's no ban on using cell phones in cars in Alaska, and you aren't required to use a hands-free set while driving. Check with your provider about service, though, as gaps in service, even on the road system, are the rule rather than the exception.

RULES OF THE ROAD
Alaska honors valid driver's licenses from any state or country. The speed limit on most highways is 55 mph, but much of the Parks Highway (between Wasilla and Fairbanks) and the Seward Highway (between Anchorage and Seward) is 65 mph. State troopers rigorously enforce these limits.

Unless otherwise posted, you may make a right turn on a red light *after* coming to a complete stop. Seat belts are required on all passengers, and children under age 5 must be in child safety seats.

State law requires that slow-moving vehicles pull off the road at the first opportunity if leading more than five cars. This is particularly true on the highway between Anchorage and Seward, where RV drivers have a bad reputation for not pulling over. Alaskans don't take kindly to being held up en route to their favorite Kenai River fishing spot.

RVS
The secret to a successful RV trip to Alaska is preparation. Expect to drive on more gravel and rougher roads than you're accustomed to. Batten down everything; tighten every nut and bolt in and out of sight, and don't leave anything to bounce around inside. Travel light, and your tires and suspension system will take less of a beating. Protect your headlights and the grille area in front of the radiator. Make sure you carry adequate insurance to cover the replacement of your windshield.

Most of Alaska's public campgrounds accommodate trailers, but hookups are available only in private RV parks. Water can be found at most stopping points, but it may be limited for trailer use. Think twice before deciding to drive an RV or pull a trailer during the spring thaw. The rough roadbed can be a trial.

RV Rentals and Tours ABC Motorhome Rentals (☎ 907/279-2000 or 800/421-7456 ⊕ www.abcmotorhome.com). **Alaska Travel Adventures** (☎ 800/323-5757 or 907/789-0052 ⊕ www.alaskarv.com). **Clippership Motorhome Rentals** (☎ 907/562-7051 or 800/421-3456 ⊕ www.clippershiprv.com). **Fantasy RV Tours** (☎ 800/952-8496 ⊕ www.fantasyrvtours.com). **GoNorth RV Camper Rental** (☎ 907/479-7271 or 866/236-7271 ⊕ www.gonorth-alaska.com). **Great Alaskan Holidays** (☎ 907/248-7777 or 888/225-2752 ⊕ www.greatalaskanholidays.com).

RENTAL CARS
Rental cars are available in most Alaska towns. In Anchorage and other major destinations, expect to pay at least $55–$75 a day or $300 (and up) a week for an economy or compact car with automatic transmission and unlimited mileage. Some locally owned companies offer lower rates for older cars. Also, be sure to ask in advance about discounts if you have an AAA or Costco card, or are over age 50.

Rates can be substantially higher for larger vehicles, four-wheel drives, SUVs, and vans. (Although the extra space for gear and luggage might be nice, note that you don't need four-wheel drive or an SUV to navigate Alaska highways.) Rates are also higher in small towns, particularly those off the road system in Southeast Alaska or the Bush. In addition, vehicles in these remote towns are typically several years old, and some would rate as "beaters."

You must be 21 to rent a car, and rates may be higher if you're under 25. When picking up a car, non-U.S. residents will need a reservation voucher, a passport, a driver's license (written in English), and a travel policy that covers each driver. Reserve well ahead for the summer season, particularly for the popular minivans, SUVs, and motor homes. A 10% state tax is tacked on to all car rentals, and there are also local taxes.

Be advised that most rental outfits don't allow you to drive on some of the unpaved roads such as the Denali Highway, the Haul Road to Prudhoe Bay, and the McCarthy Road. If your plans include any sketchy routes, make sure your rental agreement covers those areas.

Local Agencies Arctic Rent-A-Car
(☎ 888/714–4960 or 907/561–2990 Anchorage, 800/478-8696 or 907/479–8044 Fairbanks ⊕ www.arcticrentacar.com). **Denali Car Rental** (☎ 907/276–1230, 800/757–1230 in Anchorage ⊕ www.denalicarrentalak.com).

Major Agencies Alamo (☎ 800/222–9075 ⊕ www.alamo.com). **Avis** (☎ 800/331–1212 ⊕ www.avis.com). **Budget** (☎ 800/527–0700 ⊕ www.budget.com). **Hertz** (☎ 800/654–3131 ⊕ www.hertz.com). **National Car Rental** (☎ 800/222–9058 ⊕ www.nationalcar.com).

CAR-RENTAL INSURANCE

If you own a car and carry comprehensive car insurance for both collision and liability, your personal auto insurance will probably cover a rental, but read your policy's fine print to be sure. If you don't have auto insurance, then you should probably buy the collision- or loss-damage waiver (CDW or LDW) from the rental company. This eliminates your liability for damage to the car.

Some credit cards offer CDW coverage, but it's usually supplemental to your own insurance and rarely covers SUVs, minivans, luxury models, and the like. If your coverage is secondary, you may still be liable for loss-of-use costs from the car-rental company (again, read the fine print). But no credit-card insurance is valid unless you use that card for *all* transactions, from reserving to paying the final bill.

You may also be offered supplemental liability coverage; the car-rental company is required to carry a minimal level of liability coverage insuring all renters, but it's rarely enough to cover claims in a really serious accident if you're at fault.

U.S. rental companies sell CDWs and LDWs for about $15–$25 a day; supplemental liability is usually more than $10 a day. The car-rental company may offer you all sorts of other policies, but they're rarely worth the cost. Personal accident insurance, which is basic hospitalization coverage, is an especially egregious rip-off if you already have health insurance.

■ CRUISE SHIP TRAVEL

Flip to Chapter 3: Cruising in Alaska for information about cruises and our favorite voyages.

■ TRAIN TRAVEL

The state-owned Alaska Railroad has service connecting Seward, Anchorage, Denali National Park, and Fairbanks, as well as additional service connecting Anchorage and Whittier. The Alaska Railroad also offers a variety of package tours that range from one-day Denali excursions to 10-day tours, which include many excursions along the way between Anchorage and Fairbanks.

Traveling by train isn't as economical as traveling by bus, but it is a wonderful way to go; the scenery along the way is spectacular. Some cars have narration, and food is available on board in the dining car and at the café. Certain private tour companies that offer glitzy trips between Anchorage and Fairbanks hook their luxury railcars to the train. Or sign up for the railroad's Gold Star service on its regular routes—you get confirmed seating in the dome car, priority check-in, and other first-class perks, all for an additional fee, of course.

RESERVATIONS

Reservations are highly recommended for midsummer train travel. You can buy tickets over the phone using a credit card. If your reservation is a month or more ahead of time, the company will mail you the tickets; otherwise you can pick them up at the departure station.

Trains usually leave on time, so be sure to arrive at the station at least 15 minutes prior to departure to ensure that you make it aboard.

The AlaskaPass allows unlimited travel on ferry and rail lines in Alaska. *(See By Boat, above.)*

Information **Alaska Railroad** (☎ *907/265–2494 in Anchorage, 800/544–0552 ⊕ www.alaskarailroad.com).* **Gray Line Alaska** (☎ *907/277–5581 in Anchorage, 907/451–6835 in Fairbanks, 888/452–1737 ⊕ www.graylinealaska.com).* **White Pass and Yukon Route** (☎ *800/343–7373 ⊕ www.wpyr.com).*

ROUTES

Travel aboard the Alaska Railroad is leisurely: Anchorage to Seward ($75 one way) takes four hours, Anchorage to Denali ($117–$146) takes a little more than seven hours, and Anchorage to Fairbanks ($167–$210) takes about 12 hours. The trip to Whittier takes a little more than two hours and costs $65 one-way (but only $80 round-trip).

For a less expensive alternative, ride one of the public dome cars, owned and operated by the railroad. Seating in the public cars is unassigned, and passengers take turns under the observation dome. The railroad's public cars are a great place to meet residents.

Except for the Seward–Anchorage leg, all service operates year-round. Trains run daily in summer; service is reduced from September to late May. Dining cars are available on all trains.

Gray Line of Alaska offers three-day packages that include luxury train travel from Anchorage to Fairbanks or vice versa. You can opt for one-way or round-trip travel. All packages include at least a day of exploring in Denali National Park.

For a scenic and historic five-hour trip between Skagway and Fraser, British Columbia, take the White Pass and Yukon Route, which follows the treacherous path taken by prospectors during the Klondike gold rush of 1897–98. (As this trip is popular with cruise-passenger excursions, advance reservations are strongly recommended.)

ESSENTIALS

■ ACCOMMODATIONS

Off-season hotel rates are often much lower, but most travelers prefer to visit Alaska in summer, when days are long and temperatures are mild. During shoulder season (May and September) travelers may find slightly lower rates, but some businesses and attractions may be closed. Camping is always an option, and, if you're willing to sleep in bunks you can check out the state's many hostels, some of which have family rooms.

BED-AND-BREAKFASTS

Nearly every Alaskan town (with the exception of most Bush villages) has at least one B&B, and dozens of choices are available in the larger cities. At last count, Anchorage had more than 175 B&Bs, including modest suburban apartments, elaborate showcase homes with dramatic vistas, and everything in between.

Reservation Services Alaska Private Lodgings/Stay with a Friend (☎ 907/235-2148 ⊕ www.alaskabandb.com). **Alaska's Mat-Su Bed & Breakfast Association** (⊕ www.alaskabnbhosts.com). **Anchorage Alaska Bed & Breakfast Association** (☎ 907/272-5909 or 888/584-5147 ⊕ www.anchorage-bnb.com). **Bed & Breakfast Association of Alaska** (⊕ www.alaskabba.com). **Bed & Breakfast Association of Alaska, INNside Passage Chapter** (⊕ www.accommodations-alaska.com). **Fairbanks Association of Bed & Breakfasts** (⊕ www.ptialaska.net/~fabb). **Kenai Peninsula Bed & Breakfast Association** (☎ 907/776-8883 or 866/436-2266 ⊕ www.kenaipeninsulabba.com).

HOSTELS

Hostels offer bare-bones lodging at low, low prices—often in shared dorm rooms with shared baths—to people of all ages, though the primary market is young travelers, especially students. Most hostels serve breakfast; dinner and/or shared cooking facilities may also be available. In some hostels you aren't allowed to be in

your room during the day, and there may be a curfew at night. Nevertheless, hostels provide a sense of community, with public rooms where travelers often gather to share stories. Many hostels are affiliated with Hostelling International (HI), an umbrella group of hostel associations with some 4,500 member properties in more than 70 countries. Other hostels are completely independent and may be nothing more than a really cheap hotel.

Membership in any HI association, open to travelers of all ages, allows you to stay in HI-affiliated hostels at member rates. One-year membership is about $28 for adults; hostels charge about $10–$30 per night. Members have priority if the hostel is full; they're also eligible for discounts around the world, even on rail and bus travel in some countries.

There are HI hostels in Ketchikan and Sitka. Many other Alaskan hostels are not affiliated with HI, including options in Anchorage, Denali, Fairbanks, Girdwood, Haines, Homer, Juneau, McCarthy, Petersburg, Seward, Skagway, Slana, Sterling, Talkeetna, Tok, and Wrangell. Most of these are only open seasonally, but hostels in Anchorage, Fairbanks, Girdwood, Homer, Juneau, Skagway, and Talkeetna provide year-round lodging. Hostels.com has contact information for all Alaskan hostels.

Information **Hostels.com** (⊕ *www.hostels.com*). **Hostelling International—USA** (☏ *301/495–1240* ⊕ *www.hiusa.org*).

HOTELS

Alaskan motels and hotels are similar in quality to those in the Lower 48 states. Most motels are independent, but you'll find the familiar chains (Best Western, Comfort Inn, Days Inn, Hampton Inn, Hilton, Holiday Inn, Marriott, Motel 6, Super 8, and Sheraton, among others) in Anchorage.

Westmark Hotels is a regional chain, owned by cruise-tour operator Holland America Westours, with hotels in Anchorage, Fairbanks, Juneau, Sitka, Skagway, Tok, and Valdez in Alaska, plus Beaver Creek, Dawson City, and Whitehorse in Canada's Yukon Territory.

Princess Tours owns a luxury hotel in Fairbanks and lodges outside Denali National Park, near Denali State Park, near Wrangell–St. Elias National Park, and on the Kenai Peninsula. All hotels listed have private bath unless otherwise noted.

WILDERNESS LODGES

To get away from it all, book a lodge with rustic accommodations in the middle of breathtaking Alaskan wilderness. Some of the most popular are in the river drainages of Bristol Bay, throughout the rugged islands of Southeast Alaska, and along the Susitna River north of Anchorage.

Some lodge stays include daily guided fishing trips as well as all meals. They can be astronomically expensive (daily rates of $250–$1,000 per person and up, plus airfare), so if you're not interested in fishing, avoid these.

Lodges in and near Denali National Park emphasize the great outdoors, and some even include wintertime dogsledding. Activities focus on hiking, rafting, flightseeing, horseback riding, and natural-history walks. For getting deep into the wilderness, these lodges are an excel-

lent alternative to the hotels and cabins outside the park entrance.

▌ EATING OUT

Alaska is best known for its seafood, particularly king salmon, halibut, king crab, and shrimp, and you'll find fine seafood on the menu in virtually any coastal Alaskan town. At the open-air, often all-you-can-eat salmon bakes in Juneau, Tok, Denali National Park and Preserve, and Fairbanks expect excellent grilled salmon and halibut.

Anchorage has the greatest diversity of restaurants, including classy steak houses, noisy brewpubs, authentic Thai and Mexican eateries, and a wide variety of other ethnic places.

PAYING

Credit cards are widely accepted in resort restaurants and in many restaurants in major towns like Anchorage. Many small towns have only one or two eateries; some establishments may not take credit cards. *For guidelines on tipping, see Tipping, below.*

RESERVATIONS AND DRESS

During summer high season make reservations as soon as and wherever possible, especially in the Southeast. We specifically mention reservations only when they are essential or when they are not accepted. For popular restaurants, book as far ahead as you can (often 30 days), and reconfirm as soon as you arrive.

Alaska is a casual place. Cruise ships are probably the only places you'll encounter formal wear, though some of the pricier lodges may have dress codes for dinner. We mention dress only when men are required to wear a jacket or a jacket and tie.

WINES, BEER, AND SPIRITS

Alcohol is sold at liquor stores in most towns and cities along the road system, as well as in settlements along the Inside Passage. Alcoholism is a devastating problem in Native villages, and because of this many of these Bush communities are "dry" (no alcohol allowed) or "damp" (limited amounts allowed for personal use, but alcohol cannot be sold). Check the rules before flying into a Bush community with alcohol, or you might find yourself charged with illegally importing it.

Alaska's many excellent microbrews include Glacier BrewHouse, Silver Gulch, Sleeping Lady, Kodiak Brewery, and Moose's Tooth. The state's best-known beer, Alaskan Amber, is made by Alaskan Brewing Company in Juneau.

Anchorage is home to several popular brewpubs, and their beers are sold in local liquor stores. Homer Brewing Company in the town of Homer sells its beers in local bars or in take-away bottles. You'll also find brewpubs in Fairbanks, Haines, Skagway, and Wasilla.

▌ HOLIDAYS

In addition to the standard nationwide holidays, Alaska celebrates two statewide holidays: Alaska Day (October 18), celebrating the transfer of the state's ownership from Russia to the United States; and Seward's Day (last Monday in March), which marks the signing of the treaty that authorized the transfer. Although these are not major holidays, some businesses may be closed, particularly in Sitka.

▌ MONEY

Because of its off-the-beaten-path location, Alaska has always been an expensive travel destination. Major roads link Anchorage with Fairbanks and other cities and towns in South Central and Interior Alaska, but most other parts of the state are accessible only by air or water. This is even true of Alaska's state capital, Juneau. Costs in Anchorage and Fairbanks are only slightly higher than for Lower 48 cities, and you will find discount chain stores, but as you head to more remote parts of the state, prices escalate. In Bush communities food, lodging, and transportation costs can be far higher than in Anchorage, since nearly everything must be brought in by air.

▌ PACKING

Befitting the frontier image, dress is mostly casual day and night. Unless you're on a cruise, pack just one outfit that's appropriate for "dress-up," though even this one set of nice togs probably won't be necessary.

FOR WINTER

Not all of Alaska has the fierce winters usually associated with the state. Winter in the Southeast and South Central coastal regions is relatively mild—Chicago and Minneapolis experience harsher weather than Juneau. But it's a different story in the Interior, where temperatures in the subzero range and biting winds keep most visitors indoors.

The best way to keep warm is to wear layers of clothing, starting with thermal underwear and socks. The outermost layer should be lightweight, windproof, rainproof, and hooded. Down jackets (and sleeping bags) and cotton clothing have the disadvantage of becoming soggy when wet; the newer synthetics (particularly wind-blocking fabrics) are the materials of choice. Footgear needs to be sturdy, and if you're going into the backcountry, be sure it's waterproof. Rubber boots are often a necessity in coastal areas, where rain is a year-round reality. When wearing snow boots, be certain they are not too tight. Restricting your circulation will only make you colder.

FOR SUMMER

Summer travelers should pack plenty of layers, too. Although Alaskan summers are mild, temperatures can vary greatly through the course of a day.

The summer months are infamous for the sometimes dense clouds of mosquitoes and other biting insects. These pests are generally the worst in Interior Alaska but can be an annoyance throughout the state. Bring mosquito repellent with DEET! Also occasionally used (but less effective) is the Avon product Skin So Soft. Mosquito coils may be of some help if you are camping or staying in remote cabins. Head nets are sold in local sporting-goods stores and are a wise purchase if you plan to spend extended time outdoors, particularly in the Interior or on Kodiak Island.

OTHER CONSIDERATIONS

Wherever you go in Alaska (and especially in the Southeast), be prepared for rain. To keep yourself dry, pack a collapsible umbrella or bring a rain slicker, as sudden storms are common.

Always bring good UVA/UVB sunscreen with you on outings, even if the temperature is cool. Sunglasses are also essential, especially for visits to glaciers. A pair of binoculars will help you track any wildlife you encounter.

∎ PASSPORTS

U.S. citizens of all ages traveling between the United States and other countries by air need to present a valid U.S. passport.

All American citizens now need either a passport (for all modes of travel and for anywhere in the world) or a passport card

(for land or sea travel only between the United States and Canada, Mexico, Bermuda, and the Caribbean).

Note that parents traveling with small children should bring photocopies of their children's birth certificates to avoid any problems.

U.S. Passport Information U.S. Department of State (☎ *877/487–2778* ⊕ *travel.state.gov/ passport*).

∎ SAFETY

Alaska does have a high crime rate, but that doesn't mean it's unsafe for tourists.

Women are generally safe in Alaska, but sexual assaults do occur at an alarming rate, so a little extra caution is in order when traveling alone. Common sense is enough of a safeguard in most cases: don't hike in secluded areas alone, be sure to keep your hotel room door locked, don't accept drinks from strangers, and take cabs if you're returning to your hotel late at night. Some of the out-in-the-middle-of-nowhere work towns can resemble frontier towns a little *too* much, and women may experience unwanted attention (catcalls and the like).

In addition to following the bear-safety rules *listed below*, women who are camping during their menstrual cycle should take extra care in how they dispose of feminine hygiene products—seal them tightly in plastic bags and store them in bear-proof containers.

OUTDOOR SAFETY

Alaska is big, wild, and not particularly forgiving, so travelers lacking outdoor experience need to take precautions when venturing away from the beaten path. If you lack backcountry skills or feel uncomfortable handling yourself if a bear should approach, hire a guide, go on guided group tours, or join a class at the National Outdoor Leadership School, which is based in Palmer (one hour north of Anchorage).

Education **National Outdoor Leadership School** (☎ 907/745–4047 or 800/710–6657 ⊕ www.nols.edu).

BEARS

The sight of one of these magnificent creatures in the wild can be a highlight of your visit. By respecting bears and exercising care in bear country, neither you nor the bear will suffer from the experience. Remember that bears don't like surprises. Make your presence known by talking, singing, clapping, rattling a can full of gravel, or tying a bell to your pack, especially when terrain or vegetation obscures views. Travel with a group, which is noisier and easier for bears to detect. If possible, walk with the wind at your back so your scent will warn bears of your presence. And avoid bushy, low-visibility areas whenever possible.

Give bears the right-of-way—lots of it—especially sows with cubs. Don't camp on animal trails; they're likely to be used by bears. If you come across a carcass of an animal or detect its odor, avoid the area entirely; it's likely a bear's food cache. Store all food and garbage away from your campsite in specially designed bear-proof containers (not just airtight ones not designed with bears in mind—there's a chance bears will be able to detect and open them). The Park Service supplies these for hikers in Denali and Glacier Bay national parks and requires that backcountry travelers use them. If a bear approaches you while you are fishing, stop. If you have a fish on your line, cut your line.

If you do encounter a bear at close range, don't panic, and, above all, don't run. You can't outrun a bear, and by fleeing you could trigger a chase response from the bear. Talk in a normal voice to help identify yourself as a human. If traveling with others, stand close together to "increase your size." If the bear charges, it could be a bluff; as terrifying as this may sound, the experts advise standing your ground. If a brown bear actually touches you, then drop to the ground and play dead, flat on your stomach with your legs spread and your hands clasped behind your head. If you don't move, a brown bear will typically break off its attack once it feels the threat is gone. If you are attacked by a black bear, you are better off fighting back with rocks, sticks, or anything else you find, since black bears are more likely to attack a person as prey. Polar bears can be in remote parts of the Arctic, but tourists are highly unlikely to encounter them in summer.

For more information on bears, ask for the brochure "Bear Facts: The Essentials for Traveling in Bear Country" from any of the Alaska Public Lands offices. Bear-safety information is also available on the Internet at ⊕ *www.state.ak.us/adfg.*

▮ TAXES

Alaska does not impose a state sales tax, but individual cities and boroughs have their own taxes. (Anchorage has no sales tax.)

In addition to local taxes, a hotel tax is often applied to your hotel bill. Rates are variable, generally ranging 2%–6%.

You won't have to pay any departure taxes if you're flying within the United States. Vancouver's airport has a departure tax of C$5 for flights within British Columbia and the Yukon or C$10 to U.S. destinations, payable at automatic ticket machines or staffed booths before you board your flight.

▮ TIME

Nearly all of Alaska lies within the Alaska time zone, 20 hours behind Sydney, nine hours behind London, four hours behind New York City, three hours behind Chicago, and one hour behind Los Angeles and western Canada. The nearly unpopulated Aleutian Islands are in the same time zone as Hawaii, five hours behind the East Coast. Alaska observes Daylight Saving Time and changes its clocks along with the Lower 48.

TIPPING

In addition to tipping waiters and waitresses, taxi drivers, and baggage handlers, tipping others who provide personalized services is common in Alaska. Tour-bus drivers who offer a particularly informative trip generally receive a tip from passengers at the end of the tour. Fishing guides are commonly tipped around 10% by their clients, particularly if the guide helped them land a big one. In addition, gratuities may also be given to pilots following a particularly good flightseeing or bear-viewing trip; use your discretion.

TOURS

For certain types of travelers, package tours in Alaska can eliminate some of the guesswork and logistics-induced headaches that often accompany a self-planned tour. For others, the grandeur of the 49th state begs to be explored without such a fixed itinerary. The choice, dear Alaska traveler, is yours.

Several cruise lines—including Holland America and Princess Cruises and Tours—offer "cruisetours" that combine the comforts of cruise-ship travel with inland forays to luxury lodges. A host of smaller tour companies offer package tours as well. Standouts include **Alaska Tours**, which offers tours in almost every corner of the state; and **Alaska Railroad Scenic Rail Tours**, which operates a variety of train-based tours between the state's iconic destinations, including Seward, Denali, and Kenai Fjords. In addition, chances are good that there's a tour operation with itineraries to match your needs and interests—whatever those may be.

Organization United States Tour Operators Association (*USTOA* ☎ 212/599–6599 ⊕ www.ustoa.com).

Recommended Companies Alaska Airlines Vacations (☎ 866/500–5511 ⊕ www.alaskaair.com). Alaska Bound (☎ 231/439–3000 or 888/252–7527 ⊕ www.alaskabound.com). Alaska Railroad Scenic Rail Tours

TIPPING GUIDELINES FOR ALASKA	
Bartender	$1–$5 per round of drinks, depending on the number of drinks
Bellhop	$1–$5 per bag, depending on the level of the hotel
Coat Check	$1–$2 per item checked unless there is a fee, then nothing
Hotel Concierge	$5 or more, if he or she performs a service for you
Hotel Doorman	$1–$2 if he helps you get a cab
Hotel Maid	$1–$3 a day (either daily or at the end of your stay, in cash)
Hotel Room-Service Waiter	$1–$2 per delivery, even if a service charge has been added
Porter at Airport or Train Station	$1 per bag
Restroom Attendants	Small change or $1 in more-expensive restaurants
Skycap at Airport	$1–$3 per bag checked
Taxi Driver	15%–20%, but round up the fare to the next dollar amount
Tour Guide	10% of the cost of the tour
Valet Parking Attendant	$1–$2, but only when you get your car
Waiter	15%–20%, with 20% being the norm at high-end restaurants; nothing additional if a service charge is added to the bill

(☎ 907/265–2494 or 800/544–0552 ⊕ www.alaskarailroad.com). **Alaska Tour & Travel** (☎ 907/245–0200 or 800/208–0200 ⊕ www.alaskatravel.com). **Alaska Tours** (☎ 907/277–3000 or 866/317–3325 ⊕ www.alaskatours.com). **Alaska Wildland Adventures** (☎ 907/783–2928 or 800/334–8730 ⊕ www.alaskawildland.com). **Gray Line of Alaska** (☎ 907/277–5581 or 888/452–1737

⊕ www.graylinealaska.com). **Holland America Line** (☎ 877/932–4259 ⊕ www.hollandamerica.com). **Homer Travel & Tours** (☎ 907/235–7751 or 800/478–7751 ⊕ www.alaskahomertravel.com). **Knightly Tours** (☎ 206/938–8567 or 800/426–2123 ⊕ www.knightlytours.com). **Princess Cruises** (☎ 800/774–6237 ⊕ www.princess.com). **Viking Travel, Inc.** (☎ 907/772–3818 or 800/327–2571 ⊕ www.alaskaferry.com).

SPECIAL-INTEREST TOURS
ECOTOURS
Contact Alaska Wildland Adventures (☎ 907/783–2928 or 800/334–8730 ⊕ www.alaskawildland.com).

LEARNING VACATIONS
Contacts Earthwatch Institute (☎ 978/461–0081 or 800/776–0188 ⊕ www.earthwatch.org). **National Audubon Society** (☎ 212/979–3000 or 800/274-4201 ⊕ www.audubon.org). **Natural Habitat Adventures** (☎ 303/449–3711 or 800/543–8917 ⊕ www.nathab.com). **Nature Expeditions International** (☎ 954/693–8852 or 800/869–0639 ⊕ www.naturexp.com). **Naturequest** (☎ 800/369-3033 ⊕ www.naturequesttours.com). **Oceanic Society Expeditions** (☎ 415/441–1106 or 800/326–7491 ⊕ www.oceanicsociety.org). **Sierra Club** (☎ 415/977–5500 ⊕ www.sierraclub.org). **Smithsonian Journeys** (☎ 877/338–8687 ⊕ www.smithsonianjourneys.org).

NATIVE TOURS
Contacts Alexander's River Adventure (☎ 907/474–3924 ⊕ fairbanks-alaska.com/alexander.htm). **Cape Fox Tours** (☎ 907/225–4846 ⊕ www.capefoxtours.com). **Goldbelt Tours** (☎ 888/820–2628 ⊕ www.goldbelttours.com). **Northern Alaska Tour Company** (☎ 907/474–8600 or 800/474–1986 ⊕ www.northernalaska.com). **Sitka Tours** (☎ 907/747–7290 or 888/270–8687 ⊕ www.sitkatours.com).

NATURAL HISTORY TOURS
Contacts Camp Denali (☎ 907/683–2290 ⊕ www.campdenali.com). **Great Alaska Adventure Lodge** (☎ 907/262–4515 or 800/544–2261 ⊕ www.greatalaska.com). **Hallo Bay Wilderness Camp** (☎ 907/235–2237 or 888/535–2237 ⊕ www.hallobay.com).

PHOTOGRAPHY TOURS
Contacts Alaska Photography Tours (⊕ www.alaskaphotographytours.com). **Joseph Van Os Photo Safaris** (☎ 206/463–5383 ⊕ www.photosafaris.com). **Naturally Wild Photo Adventures** (☎ 740/774–6243 ⊕ www.naturallywild.net).

▌TRIP INSURANCE

Comprehensive trip insurance is valuable if you're booking a very expensive or complicated trip (particularly to an isolated region) or if you're booking far in advance. Comprehensive policies typically cover trip cancellation and interruption, letting you cancel or cut your trip short because of a personal emergency, illness, or, in some cases, acts of terrorism in your destination. Such policies also cover evacuation and medical care. Some also cover you for trip delays because of bad weather or mechanical problems as well as for lost or delayed baggage.

Another type of coverage to look for is financial default—that is, when your trip is disrupted because a tour operator, airline, or cruise line goes out of business. Generally you must buy this when you book your trip or shortly thereafter, and it's only available to you if your operator isn't on a list of excluded companies.

Always read the fine print of your policy to make sure that you are covered for the risks that are of most concern to you. Compare several policies to make sure you're getting the best price and range of coverage available.

Comprehensive Travel Insurers Access America (☎ 800/284–8300 ⊕ www.accessamerica.com). **AIG Travel Guard** (☎ 800/826–4919 ⊕ www.travelguard.com). **CSA Travel Protection** (☎ 800/771–1197 ⊕ www.csatravelprotection.com). **HTH Worldwide** (☎ 610/254–8700 ⊕ www.hthworldwide.com). **Travelex Insurance** (☎ 800/228–9792 ⊕ www.travelex-insurance.com). **Travel**

Insured International (☎ 800/243–3174 ⊕ www.travelinsured.com).

Insurance Comparison Sites **Insure My Trip. com** (☎ 800/487–4722 ⊕ www.insuremytrip. com). **Square Mouth.com** (☎ 800/240–0369 or 727/564-9203 ⊕ www.squaremouth.com).

MEDICAL INSURANCE AND ASSISTANCE

Consider buying trip insurance with medical-only coverage. Neither Medicare nor some private insurers cover medical expenses anywhere outside the United States. Medical-only policies typically reimburse you for medical care (excluding that related to preexisting conditions) and hospitalization abroad, and provide for evacuation. You still have to pay the bills and await reimbursement from the insurer, though.

Another option is to sign up with a medical-evacuation assistance company. Membership gets you doctor referrals, emergency evacuation or repatriation, 24-hour hotlines for medical consultation, and other assistance. International SOS Assistance Emergency and AirMed International provide evacuation services and medical referrals. MedjetAssist offers medical evacuation.

Medical Assistance Companies **AirMed International** (☎ 800/356–2161 ⊕ www. airmed.com). **International SOS** (⊕ www. internationalsos.com) **MedjetAssist** (☎ 800/527–7478 ⊕ www.medjetassist.com).

Medical-Only Insurers **International Medical Group** (☎ 800/628–4664 ⊕ www.imglobal. com). **Wallach & Company** (☎ 800/237–6615 or 540/687–3166 ⊕ www.wallach.com).

▌VISITOR INFORMATION

The Alaska Travel Industry Association (a partnership between the state and private businesses) publishes the *Alaska Vacation Planner,* a free, comprehensive information source for statewide travel year-round. Alaska's regional tourism

councils distribute vacation planners highlighting their local attractions.

Get details on Alaska's vast public lands from Alaska Public Lands Information centers in Ketchikan, Tok, Anchorage, and Fairbanks.

British Columbia and Yukon **Tourism British Columbia** (☎ 800/435–5622 ⊕ www.hellobc. com). **Tourism Yukon** (☎ 800/661–0494 ⊕ www.travelyukon.com).

Regional Information **Kenai Convention & Visitors Bureau** (☎ 907/283–1991 ⊕ www. visitkenai.com). **Kenai Peninsula Tourism Marketing Council** (☎ 907/262–5229 or 800/535–3624 ⊕ www.kenaipeninsula. org). **Southeast Alaska Discovery Center** (☎ 907/228–6220 ⊕ www.fs.fed.us/r10/ tongass/districts/discoverycenter). **Southwest Alaska Municipal Conference** (☎ 907/562– 7380 ⊕ www.southwestalaska.com).

Statewide Information **Alaska Department of Fish and Game** (☎ 907/267–2510 Anchorage, 907/262–2737 Soldotna, 907/235–6930 Homer, 907/465–4116 Juneau, 907/459–7385 Fairbanks sportfishing seasons and regulations, 907/465–2376 license information ⊕ www. state.ak.us/adfg). **Alaska Division of Parks** (☎ 907/269–8400 Anchorage, 907/451–2705 Fairbanks ⊕ www.alaskastateparks.org). **Alaska Public Lands Information Center** (☎ 866/869–6887, 907/644–3611 in Anchorage, 907/459–3730 in Fairbanks, 907/228– 6220 in Ketchikan, 907/883–5667 in Tok ⊕ www.nps.gov/aplic). **Alaska Travel Industry Association** (☎ 907/929–2200, 800/862– 5275 to order Alaska Vacation Planner ⊕ www. travelalaska.com).

ONLINE TRAVEL TOOLS

Alaska.com is a subsidiary of the *Anchorage Daily News* and has travel features, photo galleries, and a service that allows you to order a variety of brochures and e-newsletters. **Alaska Department of Fish and Game** has tips on wildlife viewing, news on conservation issues, and information about fishing and hunting licenses and regulations. **Alaska Geographic** has links to sites with information on the state's public lands, national parks, forests, and wildlife refuges, as well as an online bookstore where you can find maps and books about the Alaskan experience. **Alaska Magazine** posts some of its feature stories online, and maintains an extensive statewide events calendar. **Alaska Native Heritage Center** has information on Alaska's Native tribes, as well as links to other cultural and tourism Web sites.

Contact Alaska.com (⊕ *www.alaska.com*). **Alaska Department of Fish and Game** (⊕ *www.adfg.gov*). **Alaska Geographic** (⊕ *www.alaskageographic.org*). **Alaska Magazine** (⊕ *www.alaskamagazine.com*). **Alaska Native Heritage Center** (⊕ *www.alaskanative.net*).

INDEX

PHOTO CREDITS